MATH IN CONTEXT 8

AUTHORS

Frank Ebos, Senior Author
Faculty of Education
University of Toronto

David W. McKillop
Nova Scotia Teacher's College
Truro, Nova Scotia

Elizabeth Milne
Cowichan Secondary School
Duncan, British Columbia

Barbara J. Morrison
Calgary Separate School Board
Calgary, Alberta

Bob Robinson
Hamilton Board of Education
Hamilton, Ontario

Kay Whelan
Labrador City Collegiate
Labrador City, Newfoundland

CONTRIBUTING WRITER

Jack Thomson
Northumberland Newcastle Board of Education
Brighton, Ontario

REVIEWERS/CONSULTANTS

Karen Allan
Whitby, Ontario

Ruth Beaman
St. Catharines, Ontario

Jean Crawford
Calgary, Alberta

Julie Esteban
Winnipeg, Manitoba

Gus Hawko
Avondale, Newfoundland

James P. Hulsman
Peterborough, Ontario

Ernest Leenheer
Duncan, British Columbia

Margaret Martin
Saskatoon, Saskatchewan

Steve Martin
Scarborough, Ontario

Katie Pallos-Haden
Stony Plain, Alberta

Barrie Street
Vancouver, British Columbia

David M. Upton
Grand Bay, New Brunswick

Ron Woo
Coquitlam, British Columbia

Nelson Canada

I$\textcircled{T}$P ™

International Thomson Publishing
The trademark ITP is used under license

© Nelson Canada
A Division of Thomson Canada Limited, 1994

Published in 1994 by
Nelson Canada,
A Division of Thomson Canada Limited
1120 Birchmount Road
Scarborough, Ontario
M1K 5G4

ISBN 0-17-604710-7

Canadian Cataloguing in Publication Data

Ebos, Frank, 1939–
  Math in context 8

Rev. ed.
Includes index.
ISBN 0-17-604710-7

1. Mathematics – Juvenile literature. I. Title.
QA107.E26 1994   510   C94–930364–X

The symbol for year is a. For the sake of clarity, the word year has been used, in full, in place of a.

Printed and bound in Canada

4567890 / FP / 321098

Project Manager
Colin Garnham

Editorial Consultant
Joe Banel

Supervising Editor
Cecilia Chan

Art Director and Designer
Rob McPhail

Cover Design
Art Direction: Bruce Bond
Design: Liz Nyman

The authors wish to express their thanks to Rose Mary Ebos, Andrew Clowes, Sandra Mark, Stephen Cowie, Lesley Ebos, Lori Ebos, Michael Ebos, Bill Allan, Ruta Demery, Sue Gauthier, Lorraine Tuson, Sharon Kerr, Dolores Pritchard, Ann Ludbrook, and Bonnie DiMalta.

Illustration

Creative Art
62, 185, 284, 285, 350–351 Kathryn Adams; **340–341, 352** Jamie Au; **14 bottom** David Bathurst; **387** Tad Biernot; **86–87, 148–149, 312–313** Bill Boyko/Mixed Nuts; **131** Gary Clement; **328 top** Sharon Foster; **198** Victor Gad; **81, 105, 126, 134, 158, 245, 375** Don Gauthier; **296–297** Kevin Ghiglione; **36, 60** Heather Graham; **80, 178, 206, 252–253, 290–291** Scott Gwilliams; **314** Margaret Hathaway; **14 bottom, 30–31, 40, 73, 83, 96, 108, 267, 382, 383 right, 385, 443** Michael Herman; **14 middle, 176, 197, 208, 211, 242** Ron Job; **319, 323, 326, 331, 432–433** Bo Kim Louie; **90, 320–321** Chris Middleton; **161 top right, 342, 343, 347, 386** Odile Ouellet; **334–335, 420–421** Pierre-Paul Pariseau; **46–47** Andrew Plewes; **362–363** Steve **Redman**; **102, 103** Adam Rogers; **54, 56, 57, 128–129, 222–223, 240** Margo Stahl; **328 bottom** Tracy Walker; **299** Peter Yundt; **322** Paul Zwolak.

Technical Art
12, 13, 110, 111 bottom left, 131, 333, 374 Irma Ikonen; **310** Catherine Jordan.

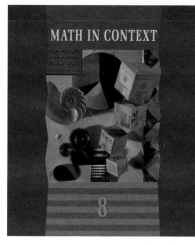

MATH IN CONTEXT

8

TABLE OF CONTENTS

CHAPTER 1 COMMUNICATING WITH NUMBERS

CHAPTER 2 INTEGERS

CHAPTER 3   EXPLORING PATTERNS AND RELATIONSHIPS

CHAPTER 4   THE NATURE OF MATH

CHAPTER 5   COMMUNICATING WITH MEASUREMENT

CHAPTER 6   MAKING CONNECTIONS: MEASUREMENT

CHAPTER 7   WORKING WITH FRACTIONS

CHAPTER 8   BUILDING MATHEMATICS: RATIONAL NUMBERS

CHAPTER 9   INTERPRETING DATA

CHAPTER 10   RATIO AND RATE

CHAPTER 11   PERCENT

Here are some features you will find in your book.

Math in a Real Context
Your book helps you to see how math relates to everyday situations both inside and outside the classroom.

Problem Solving
There are many opportunities for you to learn and apply problem solving skills. Some are seen on the following pages.
- Activities in all chapters help you develop your problem solving skills.
- Skills and strategies for working with mathematics are organized using your *Problem Solving Plan*.

Manipulatives
Many activities involve materials to help you explore new concepts and develop new skills.

Working Together
Activities throughout the book give you the chance to learn mathematics with a partner or in small groups.

Making Connections
Your book continually helps you to apply the skills you have learned, involves you in research to extend your learning, and introduces you to some of the famous people involved in developing mathematics.

Math Journal
Keeping a journal helps you to record your feelings about mathematics. It also encourages you to summarize all you learn using examples of your own.

Technology

"Technology Insight" pages extend your understanding of the impact of technology, including calculators and computers.

Calculators

Look for calculator key sequences suggested throughout. These sequences show you how to use a calculator more efficiently.

Explorations

Exploration activities help you to develop mathematical concepts for yourself.

Across the Curriculum

Look for thematic pages that extend and apply mathematics to other subject areas and other real situations.

Calculation Sense

These activities extend your ability to select appropriate calculation strategies.

Self Evaluation

Your book provides many opportunities to check your knowledge and to think about the strategies you use in working with mathematics.

Review

Chapter Reviews and Cumulative Reviews offer a chance to look back at the mathematics you have learned and the problem solving skills you have used.

Thematic Indexes and Glossary

These features at the end of the book can help you work more efficiently.

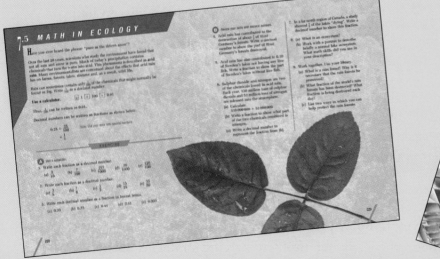

PROBLEM SOLVING

One of the main reasons you study mathematics is to develop your ability to solve problems, not only in mathematics but in everyday situations.

Problems fall into two main categories.

    I   The path to the solution is immediately clear.

    II The path to the solution is not immediately clear.

For a problem of the second type, a plan can help you find a solution. On the next page is a four-stage *Problem Solving Plan*. As you learn to solve problems, you will want to add your own ideas. Use this plan as an outline and personalize it as the year progresses. Modify and add to it to meet your own needs as you develop new strategies and skills.

Each of the activities below provides suggestions that can help you learn mathematics. Complete each one and use your answers to help you learn and plan your study of mathematics.

Activity 1

    Copy the *Problem Solving Plan* into your Math Journal. Leave space at each stage to record additional strategies, skills, and key questions as you develop your own *Problem Solving Plan*. Be sure to refer to your plan throughout the year to help you solve problems.

Activity 2

    In your earlier work with mathematics, you solved a variety of problems and recorded your strategies in your journal.

    (a) Make sure you have your journal with you as you begin the year.

    (b) Make sure there is an example for each strategy used.

Activity 3

    Your book will introduce you to other problem solving strategies.

    (a) Look through your book and list some problem solving strategies used.

    (b) Compare your list with the strategies you have in your journal from last year. Which strategies do you recognize?

Your Problem Solving Plan

1. Think About the Problem.

As you start any problem, ask yourself these two questions:
- What am I asked to find?
- What am I given?

When you think about the problem, ask yourself:
- Do I understand the given information?
- Which words are most important in this problem?
- Can I identify information that is not needed?
- Is there any information missing?

Record other strategies that can help you think about the problem.

2. Think About a Strategy.

Look for a skill or strategy that will help you solve the problem.
For example, can you
- see a pattern?
- act out the problem?
- draw a diagram?
- solve a simpler problem?
- work backwards?
- use manipulatives?

Record other strategies that you can use to solve problems.

Remember to ask yourself, "What do I *already* know that can help me solve the problem?"

3. Work It Out.

In this stage, you will actually solve the problem. While solving it, ask yourself questions like the following:
- Will the strategy lead to the solution easily?
- Are my assumptions valid?
- Are there other strategies that might make the solution easier?
- Do I understand each step of the solution?

Record other strategies for monitoring the progress of your solution.

4. Think About Your Solution.

Look back at your solution and ask yourself questions like the following:
- Does the solution make sense?
- Can I explain the solution to my partner?
- Can I verify the solution?
- Did I answer the question that was originally asked?
- What have I discovered that can help me solve other problems?

Record other strategies that can help you think about your solution.

Here are some problems for you to try.
- List the strategies that could be used to solve the problem.
- Have you tried the strategies before?

PROBLEM 1

Someone has estimated that there are about 105 flashes of lightning each second on the earth.

(a) Estimate the number of flashes in one year.

(b) Calculate how many there are. How reasonable was your estimate?

PROBLEM 2

The diagram shows the solution to a problem.

(a) What might the problem be?

(b) Explain how you would arrive at the solution.

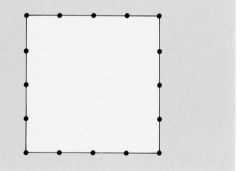

PROBLEM 3

The diagram shows some information.

(a) What problem can be solved using the diagram?

(b) Is there any information missing in (a)?

PROBLEM 4

The height of each step is shown. There are 30 steps between each floor. You walk up five floors.

(a) How many metres have you moved vertically?

(b) How many metres have you moved horizontally?

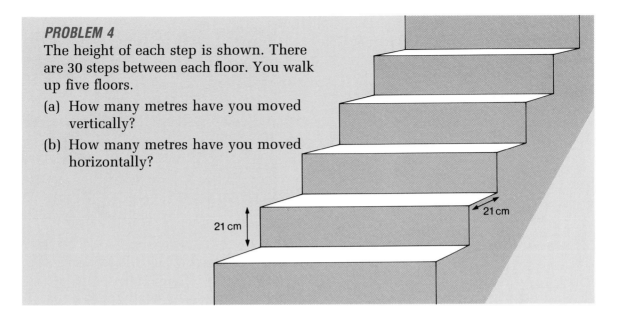

21 cm

21 cm

PROBLEM 5

(a) Copy and complete the following chart using the diagrams.

Number of Points	Number of Line Segments
2	1
3	3
4	6
5	?
6	?
7	?

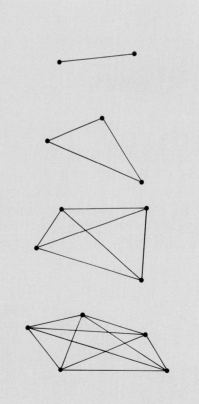

(b) What pattern do you see in the number of line segments joining points?

(c) Use the pattern to predict the number of line segments joining 9 points. Check your prediction by drawing a diagram.

(d) Use the pattern. How many line segments can be drawn for 25 points?

PROBLEM 6

Jim and Sanjay run around a circular track. Jim, running in the opposite direction, meets Sanjay every 15 s. Sanjay runs around the track in 40 s. How long does it take Jim to run around the track?

PROBLEM 7

Arlene wants to cut a cube of wood into 27 identical cubes. Find the least number of cuts needed to complete the task.

PROBLEM 8

A farmer decided to build a fence along one side of a pen. Her plan was to place posts 8 m apart. However, she bought five posts too few. She decided to build the fence with the posts 10 m apart. How many posts did she purchase?

CALCULATION SENSE

When you add, subtract, multiply, and divide, there are many ways to arrive at an answer. You can

- use a calculator.
- do the calculation mentally.
- use paper and a pencil.

You have to decide which method is best in the particular situation. Remember to estimate when appropriate and check to see whether your answer is reasonable.

The following inventories can help you develop speed and accuracy. Try various methods to arrive at the answers.

- Make a list of skills you learned.
- Create questions that can be answered using these skills.

Skills Inventory Number	Date Tried	Number Correct	Time Taken

SKILLS INVENTORY 1

(a) Create expressions involving addition and subtraction.

(b) Find each answer for (a).

SKILLS INVENTORY 2

(a) Create expressions involving multiplication and division.

(b) Find each answer for (a).

SKILLS INVENTORY 3

(a) Create expressions involving a topic of your own.

(b) Find each answer for (a).

EXPLORING WITH MANIPULATIVES

There are many ways to explore ideas in mathematics. Manipulatives can help you solve problems by letting you "see" the problems more clearly. Try these explorations using manipulative materials.

EXPLORATION 1

Use the toothpick pattern shown.

(a) Remove two toothpicks so that exactly two squares remain.

(b) Using the same toothpick pattern, create a similar problem. Compare your problem with others in your class.

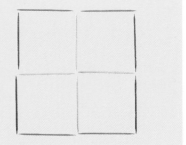

EXPLORATION 2

A square is cut out of paper and folded along its diagonals as shown to the right. The square has a side length of 10 cm.

(a) How many triangles are created by the sides of the square and the folds?

(b) Find the area of each triangle.

(c) Find the perimeter of each triangle.

The first four triangular numbers are shown using the counters below.

(a) What are the next three triangular numbers?

(b) Create and solve a similar problem.

For the following, choose the manipulative you think will best help you solve the problem.

A hexomino is a shape made of six squares each connected with another along a common side.

(a) How many hexominos are there?

(b) Which of the hexominos can be used to form a cube?

1. Which of the manipulatives on these pages have you used before?

2. Look through the book for other uses of manipulatives. How do you think they will help you?

During the year, you will work with partners and in small groups to develop mathematical concepts. Here are some ideas that can help you work cooperatively with others.

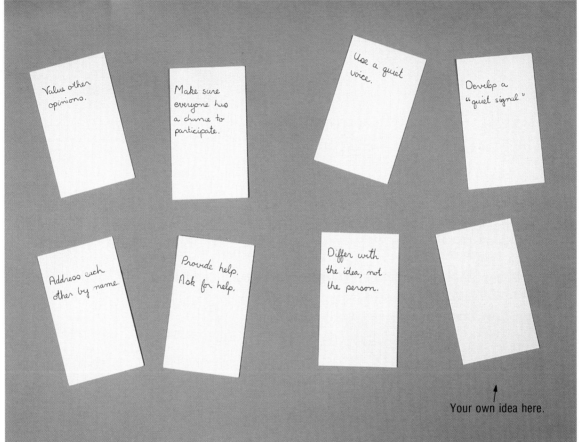

Value other opinions.

Make sure everyone has a chance to participate.

Use a quiet voice.

Develop a "quiet signal."

Address each other by name.

Provide help. Ask for help.

Differ with the idea, not the person.

Your own idea here.

LOOKING AHEAD

Look through your book for activities that involve working in pairs or groups.

(a) How do you think working with others will help you learn mathematics? Write your answers in your journal.

(b) Create a class bulletin board like the one shown. Add any ideas you have to help you work cooperatively with others.

TECHNOLOGY AND MATHEMATICS

Technology and mathematics are strongly linked. Technology can help you solve mathematical problems. At the same time, a knowledge of mathematics is often needed in the development of new technology. Technology and mathematics support and serve each other.

LOOKING AHEAD 1

Look through the book for "Technology Insight" pages.

(a) What kinds of technology do you see?

(b) What careers that involve technology can you list?

(c) How do you think working with technology can help you learn mathematics?

LOOKING AHEAD 2

Look through the book for calculator key sequences.

(a) Which sequences can help you check your work on the previous pages?

(b) Refer to the manual for your calculator. How else can your calculator be used to check your work?

(c) Refer to the manual for your calculator. Make a list of the keys on your calculator. Describe what each key is used for. Try the examples provided to practise using each key.

MAKING CONNECTIONS

Links to Real Life

Mathematics is constantly used by people in many careers. Can you think of people you know whose job involves mathematics? Arrange an interview with one of them to find out what mathematics is used. Some possible people to interview are:

- a local pharmacist
- a variety store owner
- a plumber or carpenter
- a farmer

- a coach
- a taxi driver
- a designer
- a social worker

LOOKING AHEAD

Develop a questionnaire similar to the one below to help organize your questions. Then write a short report on the math skills the person uses. Are there any mathematics skills used that you did not think of?

"I always scale an illustration. I work large and then reduce to make the illustration look crisp."
— Janet Long, graphic artist

"I need to calculate quickly, when training, to figure out whether I'm still on schedule."
— Ann Peel, race walker

"You have to approach a lot of farm problems by breaking them down step-by-step and solving them slowly, one at a time.
— Dana Patterson, dairy farmer

"When planning a stage set, I measure the room and furniture and then make paper models. It is easier to move cutouts around than to try to visualize the room."
— Trevor Briggs, stage hand

Questionnaire — Pharmacist

1. What types of medicine are dispensed by the person?

2. What is the ratio of tablets dispensed to liquids dispensed?

3. How does the pharmacist measure the exact dosage?

4. How else does a pharmacist use mathematics?

Links to Other Subjects

Did you know that mathematics is involved in some way with every other school subject?

LOOKING AHEAD 1

(a) Look through the book for sections that have the words "Math in" as part of their title.

(b) How do they relate to other subjects you study in school?

(c) Give an example of your own of how mathematics can help you in other subjects.

Links Within Mathematics

Knowing how one area of mathematics affects another can help you solve problems.

LOOKING AHEAD 2

(a) List some of the skills you have used in geometry.

(b) Describe how your skills with geometry can help you when you build something.

(c) In what other parts of mathematics can your skills also help?

(d) Pick your own math topic. Repeat parts (a), (b), and (c) for your topic.

MATHEMATICS AS COMMUNICATION

Listening, speaking, reading, and writing about mathematics regularly will help your understanding grow. Working together with other people in your class, either in pairs or in groups, gives you a good opportunity to discuss mathematical ideas.

LOOKING AHEAD 1

As you work in groups on problems throughout the year, keep a list of the kinds of questions you ask and statements you make in your journal. Use them whenever you work with a partner or in a group.

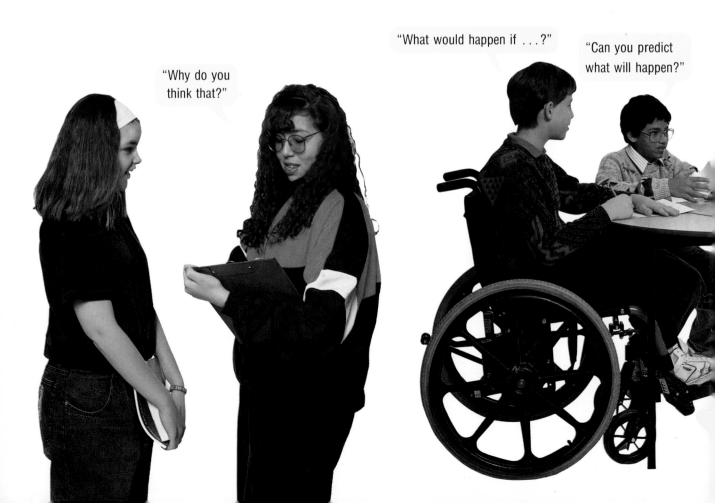

"Why do you think that?"

"What would happen if . . .?"

"Can you predict what will happen?"

The following words have occurred in your earlier work in mathematics. Use an example to illustrate the meaning of each word. These words will help you in the future.

(a) addend
(b) angle
(c) bisect
(d) decimal point
(e) distance
(f) quotient
(g) estimate
(h) intersect
(i) line segment
(j) odd number
(k) right angle
(l) perpendicular

Locate the glossary and indexes at the back of this book. How can you use these pages to help you learn and use mathematics?

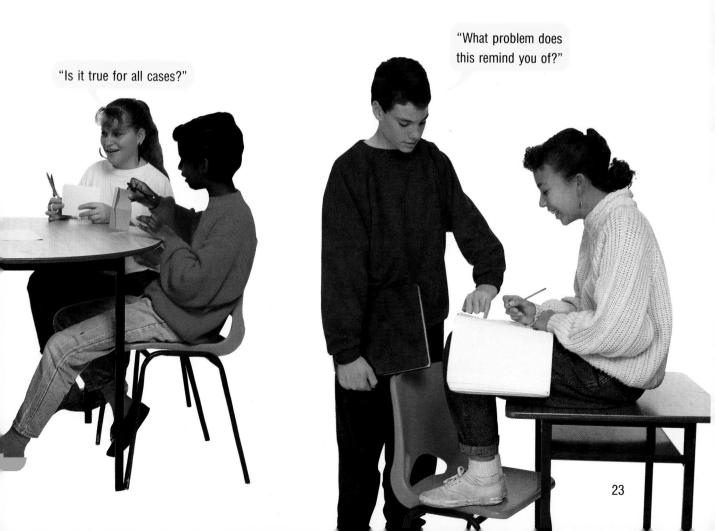

"Is it true for all cases?"

"What problem does this remind you of?"

USING A MATH JOURNAL

Keeping a math journal will help you become a better communicator in mathematics. Here are some ways you can use your journal.

- Record your personal *Problem Solving Plan* and strategies.
- Try out ideas. Experimenting can help you shape an idea or solve a problem.
- Express your feelings about mathematics. Noting your feelings can help provide solutions when you least expect them.
- Keep a list of tips for self improvement in mathematics. What do you do well? Where do you need more help?
- List new mathematical terms. Defining them in your own words with examples will help you understand them better.

Remember to date your entries. You will find it interesting to look back at a later date to see how your feelings about, and understanding of, mathematics have changed.

Using a Portfolio

Here is another idea to help you record your work and see your progress. Start a portfolio and include items like the following:

- drafts or "tryouts" for future reference
- finished projects (a place to showcase your work)
- articles from newspapers and magazines that help you illustrate your work
- math puzzles that you enjoyed

You can make a portfolio by stapling together file folders or poster board. List the contents on the outside for quick reference.

SELF EVALUATION

Your book offers many opportunities to check your progress in mathematics. A page at the end of each chapter is devoted to just this.

As you solve problems during the year, ask yourself questions like the following to help evaluate your own progress.

- Do I apply the strategies I have learned?
- Can I reword the problem in a simpler form?
- Can I summarize my observations verbally and in writing?
- Are my answers reasonable? How do I know?
- Have I made any assumptions? What are they?

Add to this list throughout the year. Keep a copy of your questions in your journal.

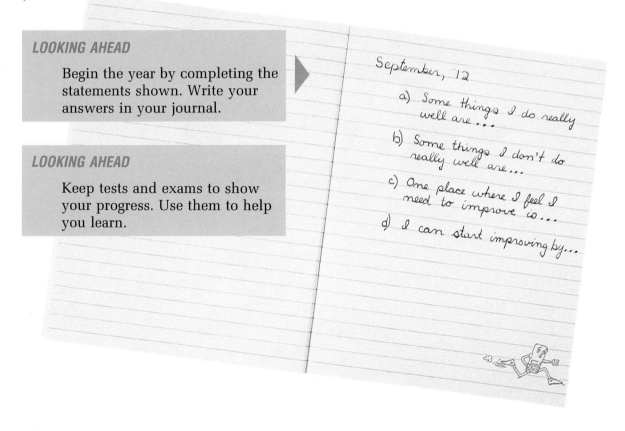

LOOKING AHEAD

Begin the year by completing the statements shown. Write your answers in your journal.

LOOKING AHEAD

Keep tests and exams to show your progress. Use them to help you learn.

September, 12

a) Some things I do really well are...

b) Some things I don't do really well are...

c) One place where I feel I need to improve is...

d) I can start improving by...

1 COMMUNICATING WITH NUMBERS

What patterns do you see in each picture?

In your journal, describe each pattern in your own words. Try to use numbers to help your description.

In what way can a panda be described as "symmetrical"?

This drop of water has been "frozen" by an electronic flash with a duration of 0.001 s.

The World Trade Centre has about 43 000 windows! What pattern would you use to wash all the windows as quickly as possible?

Here is a chance to explore some of the patterns in numbers. In your journal, summarize any patterns you see.

EXPLORATION ① *Work with a Partner*

1. Choose pictures from this book.

   (a) What patterns do you see in your pictures?

   (b) In your own words, describe each pattern. How can you use numbers to help your description?

   (c) How else is mathematics involved in each picture?

EXPLORATION ② *Work in Groups*

2. (a) Use counters to represent each shape shown below. How many counters of each colour are there?

   A   B   C   D

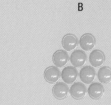  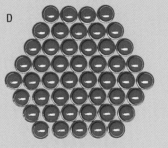

   (b) Suggest a pattern to find the number of counters in each ring.

   (c) Continue the shapes above making more rings. Repeat parts (a) and (b) using your shapes.

   (d) Predict how many counters there would be in the outside ring of the next shape. Place the ring. Is your prediction correct?

   (e) Predict how many counters there would be in the tenth ring. Place the rings. Is your prediction correct?

3. Use the shapes shown in Question 2.

   (a) Suggest a relationship to find the total number of counters used in each shape.

   (b) How many counters will there be in the next shape? Verify your answer.

   (c) Suppose you continued the pattern for ten more shapes. How many counters would be used?

Work Together

4. Select any month from any calendar.

    (a) Choose 9 numbers in a square array.

    (b) Find the sum of the numbers in the middle row, the middle column, and a diagonal of your square.

    (c) Multiply the middle number in your array by 3. What do you notice?

    (d) Use your results in (a), (b), and (c). What relationship(s) do you see?

    (e) Test your relationship(s) in (d) on other groups of 9 numbers from your calendar. Why do you think the relationship(s) works?

5. (a) Use another month from your calendar. Put squares and rectangles around groups of numbers.

    (b) Suggest patterns and relationships you see in the groups of your numbers. Justify why you think your relationships work.

EXPLORATION ④ *Work with a Partner*

6. (a) Use your calendar from Exploration 3 and follow these steps.

       A Have your partner put a square around a square array of 16 numbers.

       B Mentally add the numbers in each corner. Write the sum on a piece of paper and put it in your pocket.

       C Have your partner circle one number in the calendar and cross out the numbers that are in the column and row of the circled number.

       D Have your partner circle a number that has not been circled or crossed out. Cross out all remaining numbers in the column and row.

       E Repeat Step D until all numbers are circled or crossed out. Then, have your partner find the sum of all circled numbers.

    (b) What do you notice about your sum in Step E?

    (c) Repeat the steps in (a) for other calendars. In your journal, explain how to predict your partner's sum before the numbers are selected.

1.2 COMMUNICATING WITH NUMBERS

Astronomers often create standard measures to communicate easily with other astronomers around the world. For example, one **astronomical unit** is the average distance from the earth to the sun: namely, 149 600 000 km.

Each digit of the astronomical unit has a certain face value. A place value chart can help you represent the number effectively.

Read as "One hundred forty-nine million six hundred thousand."

Read as "three hundred twenty-six point four five."

10^8 Hundred Millions	10^7 Ten Millions	10^6 One Millions	10^5 Hundred Thousands	10^4 Ten Thousands	10^3 One Thousands	10^2 Hundreds	10^1 Tens	10^0 Ones		$\frac{1}{10^1}$ Tenths	$\frac{1}{10^2}$ Hundredths	$\frac{1}{10^3}$ Thousandths
1	4	9	6	0	0	0	0	0				
						3	2	6	•	4	5	

The number 326.45 is written in **standard form**. It can be written in **expanded form** as shown below.

$$3 \times 100 + 2 \times 10 + 6 \times 1 + 4 \times 0.1 + 5 \times 0.01$$

or

$$3 \times 10^2 + 2 \times 10 + 6 \times 1 + 4 \times \frac{1}{10} + 5 \times \frac{1}{10^2}$$

EXERCISE

A Make a copy of the place value chart shown above.

1. Write each number in standard form.
   (a) 10^5 (b) 10^3 (c) 10^2 (d) 10^6 (e) 10^8

2. For each number, what is the place value of the digit 3?
   (a) 379   (b) 3892   (c) 4093   (d) 57.831

3. Write each number in expanded form and in words.
   (a) 489.36   (b) 7809   (c) 1008.256   (d) 301.105

4. Write the following in standard form.
   (a) $5 \times 1000 + 4 \times 100 + 2 \times 10 + 1 \times 0.1$

   (b) $9 \times 10^3 + 7 \times 10^2 + 3 \times 10 + 3 \times \frac{1}{10^3}$

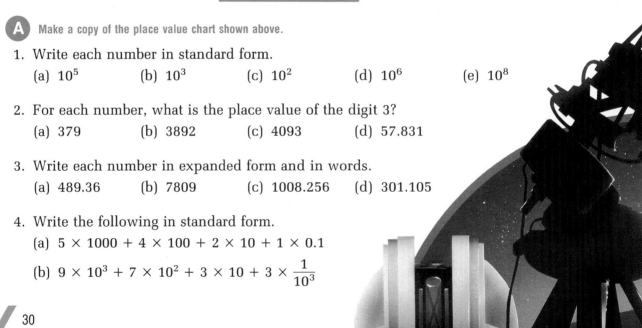

30

Review how to read and write numbers.

5. Write the numbers in standard form.

   (a) Skylab fell on its thirty-four thousand nine hundred eighty-first orbit of the earth.

   (b) Lake Superior is about six hundred thirteen kilometres long.

   (c) The distance from Halifax to Vancouver is six thousand fifteen kilometres.

6. Write the numbers in expanded form.

   (a) The diameter of the sun is one million three hundred ninety-two thousand kilometres.

   (b) Jupiter is seven hundred seventy-seven million nine hundred fifty thousand kilometres from earth.

   (c) The distance across the rings of Saturn is two hundred seventy-three thousand five hundred kilometres.

7. (a) Estimate how many students are in your school. Write your estimate in expanded form and in words.

   (b) Estimate how many people are in a city in your province. Write your estimate in expanded form and in words.

8. Did you know that the first colour photograph was taken in 1862?

   (a) Write all the numbers possible using the digits of the date.

   (b) Write each number from (a) in expanded form and in words.

9. There are 1000 chairs in an auditorium. They are to be arranged so that there are the same number of chairs along two walls.

   (a) How many chairs are along each wall?

   (b) Write your answer from (a) in expanded form and in words.

MAKING CONNECTIONS

Because distances in space are so vast, astronomers have devised a more convenient measure than the kilometre, the **light year**. One light year is the distance light travels in one year: namely, 9 460 528 405 000 km.

A **parsec** is another measure used by astronomers. One parsec is 3.2 light years. Use your library.

(a) Find the distance between the planets of the solar system in kilometres and astronomical units.

(b) Find information about stars. Write the distance between some stars in light years and parsecs.

(c) Write a paragraph describing the solar system. Use the words "light years" and "parsec" and use numbers written in expanded form, standard form, and words.

1.3 ESTIMATE AND COMPARE

Lance's class went on a trip to the animal fair. Lance **estimated** the price of his bus ticket to be about $11.00. The **exact** cost of his bus ticket was $10.87. Gina's class went on a camping trip. Her bus ticket cost $10.45. Which student paid less?

To compare numbers, you compare digits with the same place value as shown below.

10.45		10.87	Think:
↑		↑	< is read as "less than".
4 tenths	<	8 tenths	> is read as "greater than".

Since 10.45 < 10.87, Gina's ticket cost less.

EXERCISE

A Review your work with place value.

1. Which is greater?
   (a) 5.3, 2.7   (b) 6.8, 7.4   (c) 2.5, 2.8   (d) 3.9, 3.5

2. Replace ■ with < or >.
   (a) 2.09 ■ 2.9   (b) 0.87 ■ 0.88   (c) 6.7 ■ 6.8   (d) 0.05 ■ 0.009

3. Which number has the greatest value?
   (a) 0.3, 0.09, 0.10   (b) 0.006, 0.66, 0.06   (c) 1.4, 1.5, 0.9, 0.756

4. Write the numbers in order from least to greatest. Then, write the next three numbers in the pattern.

   (a) 2.2, 4.2, 5.2, 1.2, 3.2

   (b) 1.5, 4.5, 6.0, 3.0, 7.5

5. Write two numbers between each pair.

   (a) 503 and 505   (b) 3634 and 3643

   (c) 50.2 and 50.5 (d) 1.8 and 1.9

   (e) 3.17 and 3.16 (f) 2.27 and 2.25

6. The DBS Tower, in Montreal, is 97.54 m tall. The Place Bell Canada Tower is 94.49 m tall. Which tower is taller?

7. On a school trip, Sanjay paid $17.28 for his bus ride. On a different trip, Samir paid $17.44 for a bus ticket. Which student paid more?

8. Brown's photography charges $22.28 to develop a roll of film. Red's photography charges $21.44 to develop the same roll of film. To which place would you take your film to be developed? Why?

9. (a) Estimate how far you travel to school each day.

   (b) Did you know that if the oceans were to flood the earth, the average depth of water would be 2.5 km? Is this depth greater than your distance in (a)?

10. Use the coins shown below.

    (a) How many different amounts can you make using the coins? Write the amounts in order from least to greatest.

    (b) Create a similar problem of your own. Compare your problem with others in your class.

MAKING CONNECTIONS

Have you ever heard the slogan "Over five billion served"? Work together.

(a) What fast food chain uses this slogan in their advertising?

(b) Is the number used an estimate or an exact number?

(c) Create a fast food chain of your own. Write a slogan to advertise the company. Use a number in the slogan.

(d) Is your number in (c) an estimate or a rounded number?

(e) Test your slogan on others in the class. Modify it if you wish.

1.4 ROUNDING NUMBERS

A laser was used to measure the height of Della Falls in British Columbia. The laser measured the height to be 440.746 m.

Often, rounded numbers are used to report numbers. Here is how to describe the height of Della Falls, in rounded numbers.

When rounding a number, look at the digit to the right of the one being rounded.
• If it is 5 or greater than 5, you round up.
• If it is less than 5, you round down.

Round To Two Decimal Places

440.74 6   Think: 6 is greater than 5. Round up
↓   to the next value, 5.
440.75

Round To One Decimal Place

440.7 4 6   Think: 4 is less than 5. Keep the digit 7
↓   when rounding.
440.7

EXERCISE

 A   Review all your skills for rounding.

1. How is the answer found in each?
   (a) 417 is 420 to the nearest ten.
   (b) 6.23 is 6.2 to the nearest tenth.

2. To what place has each number been rounded?
   (a) $465 \doteq 470$ (b) $12.78 \doteq 12.8$

3. Round each number as indicated.
   (a) 5.83, one decimal place
   (b) 4.631, two decimal places

Work together.

4. Round each number as indicated.

(a) 79 g to the nearest ten grams

(b) 4.96 g to the nearest gram

(c) 496.3 mL to the nearest mL

(d) 34.55 m to the nearest metre

(e) 4.501 kg to the nearest kilogram

5. The number of days needed for each planet to orbit the sun is shown. Write the number of days
   • to the nearest day.
   • to the nearest tenth of a day.

(a) Mercury, 87.969 d

(b) Venus, 224.701 d

(c) Mars, 686.980 d

(d) Saturn, 10 759.203 d

(e) Earth, 365.256 d

6. Refer to the chart.

Ocean	Greatest Depth (km)
Pacific	10.915
Atlantic	8.648
Arctic	5.122
Indian	7.125

(a) Round the depth of each ocean to the nearest tenth of a kilometre.

(b) Arrange the oceans in order from least depth to greatest depth.

7. Round each of the measures to one decimal place.

(a) The length of a ribbon worm was measured to be 54.86 m.

(b) A white shark was found to be 18.52 m long.

(c) A giant squid was found to be 17.37 m in length.

8. Write the length of the coastline of each province to the first decimal place.

Province	Length of Coastline (km)
(a) British Columbia	7024.43
(b) Manitoba	917.71
(c) New Brunswick	1524.67
(d) Newfoundland	17 792.11
(e) Nova Scotia	5828.23
(f) Ontario	1210.72
(g) Prince Edward Island	1107.68
(h) Quebec	10 843.35
(i) Northwest Territories	25 111.17
(j) Yukon	342.93

9. Use the information in the previous question. Arrange the provinces in order from shortest to longest coastline.

10. Refer to the collage of ads below.

(a) For which ads can you calculate an exact cost?

(b) For which ads will you need to round to find the cost?

| On Thursday, there were 785 people watching the track meet. On Friday, there were 861 people, and on Saturday, there were 2694 people. How many people watched the track meet in all? | During the triple jump, Aaron made two attempts. His total distance was 48.96 m. His first attempt was a distance of 23.85 m. How far did Aaron jump on his second attempt? |

To solve each problem above, Aaron arranged the expressions in columns.

```
  785        Think: Estimate.
  861        800 + 900 + 2700 = 4400
+2694
 4340
```

Thus, 4340 people watched in all.

```
 48.96       Think: Estimate.
-23.85       49 − 24 = 25
 25.11
```

Thus, the second attempt was 25.11 m.

Aaron could have also used the following calculator key sequences.

| c | 785 | + | 861 | + | 2694 | = | 4340 |

| c | 48.96 | − | 23.85 | = | 25.11 |

Aaron also realized that the same calculations can be used to solve other problems. Two problems are shown below.

| "On Tuesday, I scored 785 points playing a video game. On Wednesday, I scored 861 points. On Thursday, I scored 2694 points. What was my total score?" | "I earned $48.96 on my paper route. I spent $23.85 on a video game. How much money do I have left?" |

Activity   Before you begin the exercise, work with a partner to
(a) create other problems using the calculations above.
(b) compare your problems with others in your class.

A Use a calculator to help you.

1. Simplify. (a) $15.3 + 14.7$ (b) $8.36 + 1.6$ (c) $7.63 + 1.27$ (d) $4.36 + 2.8$

2. Add. (a) $\begin{array}{r} 789 \\ +\ 65 \end{array}$ (b) $\begin{array}{r} 78.9 \\ +\ 6.5 \end{array}$ (c) $\begin{array}{r} 7.89 \\ +0.65 \end{array}$ (d) $\begin{array}{r} 0.789 \\ +0.065 \end{array}$

   (e) In your journal, describe any patterns you see in (a) to (d).

3. Simplify. (a) $4.3 - 0.7$ (b) $2.45 - 0.38$ (c) $9.18 - 8.23$ (d) $2.66 - 1.7$

4. Subtract. (a) $\begin{array}{r} 963 \\ -386 \end{array}$ (b) $\begin{array}{r} 96.3 \\ -38.6 \end{array}$ (c) $\begin{array}{r} 9.63 \\ -3.86 \end{array}$ (d) $\begin{array}{r} 0.963 \\ -0.386 \end{array}$

   (e) In your journal, describe any patterns you see in (a) to (d).

B Make a final statement for each problem you create.

5. Estimate each answer. Then calculate.

   (a) $\begin{array}{r} 23.69 \\ 4.81 \\ +\ 1.96 \end{array}$ (b) $\begin{array}{r} 2906 \\ 1243 \\ +1008 \end{array}$ (c) $\begin{array}{r} 123.45 \\ 321.54 \\ +213.45 \end{array}$

   (d) $\begin{array}{r} 4969 \\ -2306 \end{array}$ (e) $\begin{array}{r} 130.00 \\ -129.54 \end{array}$ (f) $\begin{array}{r} 269.41 \\ -139.41 \end{array}$

6. (a) Chris travels 83 km. Raul travels 79.6 km. Who travels further? By how much?

   (b) Write a problem of your own that has the same numerical solution as (a). Compare your problem with others in your class.

7. Evaluate each. Then, create a problem that uses each as a solution.

   (a) $1964.3 + 1415.8 - 2134.9$

   (b) $2691.35 + 4432.41 + 1829.96$

   (c) $123 - 0.38 + 0.75$

   (d) $23.69 - 9 - 6.54 + 22.1$

8. (a) Play this game with a partner.

   A Roll one die six times. After each roll place the number on one of the cards shown.

   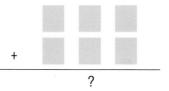

   B Once a number has been put on a card, it cannot be changed.

   C Find the sum. If your sum is a 4 digit number, you score two points. If it is a 3 digit number, you score one point. The first player to score 10 points wins.

   (b) Create a similar game using subtraction as suggested below. Play the game with your partner.

   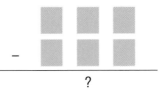

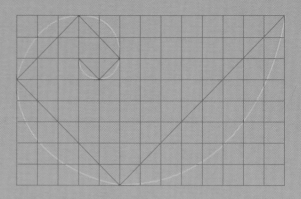

Did you know that you can see spiral patterns in many plants and animals? Here is a chance to explore spiral patterns. Work with a partner. In your journal, write any patterns and relationships you see in each exploration.

EXPLORATION ① *Work with a Partner*

1. (a) Follow these steps to construct a spiral. Use grid paper like that shown or a geoboard with elastics.

   Step 1 In the middle of the grid paper, draw a diagonal across a 1×1 square from the top left corner to the bottom right corner.

   Step 2 Use the 1×1 square to the right of the square in Step 1. Draw a diagonal so that the two diagonals form a V shape.

   Step 3 Use the 2×2 square above the diagonals. Draw a diagonal. The diagonal goes from the bottom right corner to the top left corner.

   Step 4 Refer to the diagram. How would you describe this step?

   (b) Continue the steps above until a spiral is suggested.

2. Use your spiral from Question 1.

   (a) For each square you drew, write the length of the side.

   (b) Look for a pattern in your numbers in (a). Based on your pattern, predict the length of the side in the tenth square you would use. Then, place curved lines to show the spiral.

   (c) Extend the pattern in (a) to include 15 consecutive numbers.

   (d) Suggest other patterns and relationships in the numbers you have written in (c). Compare your patterns to others in the class.
   • How are they alike?   • How are they different?

NUMBERS

Work with a Partner

The numbers shown below are called **Fibonacci Numbers**.
   1, 1, 2, 3, 5, 8, 13, 21, 34, 55, . . .
You used these numbers in Exploration 1.

3. (a) Describe a pattern to obtain Fibonacci Numbers.

   (b) Write the next four numbers in the pattern.
      A Multiply the greatest and the least of the four numbers.
      B Multiply the two middle numbers.
      C By how much do your numbers in A and B differ?

   (c) Repeat the steps of part (b) for other consecutive Fibonacci numbers.
      What pattern do you notice?

4. Look for other patterns when multiplying the Fibonacci Numbers.

   (a) Write an example of each pattern.

   (b) Compare your patterns with others in the class. How are they alike?
      How are they different?

Work Together

5. Use the Fibonacci Numbers from Exploration 1.

   (a) Write any four consecutive Fibonacci Numbers.

   (b) Divide the largest number by the smallest number and round to one
      decimal place.

   (c) Repeat part (b) using four other consecutive Fibonacci Numbers.
      What do you notice?

   (d) Where have you seen the number in (c) previously?

6. Look for other patterns when dividing the Fibonacci Numbers.

   (a) Write an example of each pattern.

   (b) Compare your patterns with others in your class. How are they alike?
      How are they different?

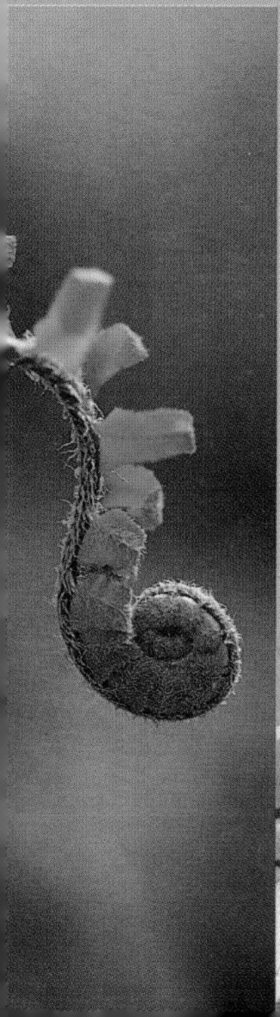

Renate is a lifeguard. She earns $8.75 each hour. How much will she earn in 3.25 h?

Pat earned $58.10 in 3.5 h as the supervising lifeguard. How much did she earn each hour?

Jasper solved the problems above. He arranged the expressions as follows.

```
    8.75        Think: 8.75 is about 9.
  × 3.25               3.25 is about 3.
  ------               9 × 3 = 27
   43 75
   17 500
  262 500
  -------
  28.4375     Think: Round to the nearest cent.
                    An estimated answer can help
                    you place the decimal point correctly.
```

$$3.5\overline{)58.10} \Rightarrow 35\overline{)581.0}$$

```
              16.6
       35 ) 581.0
              35
             ---
             231
             210
             ---
             210
             210
             ---
               0
```

Thus, Renate will earn $28.44.

Thus, Pat earned $16.60 each hour.

Jasper could have also used the following calculator key sequences.

| c | 8.75 | × | 3.25 | = | 28.4375

| c | 58.10 | ÷ | 3.5 | = | 16.6

Jasper also realized that the same calculations can be used to solve other problems. Two of the problems are shown below.

Renate jogged 8.75 km each hour for 3.25 h. How far did she jog in all?

Pat used 58.10 g of salt in 3.5 L of solution. How much salt is in each litre?

Activity   Before you begin the exercise, work with a partner to
(a) create other problems using the calculations above.
(b) compare your problems with others in your class.

A Check whether your answers are reasonable.

1. The digits for each answer are shown. Estimate to place the decimal point.
   (a) 3.6 × 4; 144
   (b) 47.5 × 3.7; 17575
   (c) 8.7 × 3.5; 3045

2. Find the product.
   (a) 0.7 × 0.5
   (b) 2.37 × 14
   (c) 15 × 0.14
   (d) 0.41 × 0.21
   (e) 0.23 × 1.4
   (f) 15 × 3.2
   (g) 1.7 × 3.23
   (h) 14.8 × 12.39

3. The digits for each answer are shown. Estimate to place the decimal point.
   (a) 1.25 ÷ 5; 25
   (b) 26.88 ÷ 2.5; 10752
   (c) 46.08 ÷ 0.28; 16457

4. Divide.
   (a) $3\overline{)270}$
   (b) $40\overline{)1600}$
   (c) $5\overline{)555}$
   (d) $56\overline{)4984}$
   (e) $3\overline{)2.7}$
   (f) $4\overline{)1.6}$
   (g) $5\overline{)3.5}$
   (h) $6\overline{)0.48}$

B Remember: Look for clue words.

5. (a) Lana jumped over 12 barrels on her skates for a total length of 6.2 m. What is the distance across each barrel?

   (b) Create a problem that has the same numerical solution as (a).

6. Tickets for rides at a fair cost 80¢ each. A book of 6 tickets costs $4. Samir buys 24 tickets. How much would he save by purchasing 4 books instead of individual tickets?

7. Twenty students in a class gave $17.50 each for trip expenses. The total amount collected was $34.50 more than needed. How much did the trip actually cost for each student?

8. Two fishing records were set in Canada.
   • Ken Fraser caught a tuna with a mass of 678.6 kg at Auld Cove.
   • Larry Daunis caught a lake trout with a mass of 29.5 kg in Great Bear Lake.

   (a) Estimate which has the greater mass.
       A: 100 lake trout   B: 4 tuna

   (b) Calculate the masses in (a). How reasonable was your estimate?

9. (a) Use the information below. Create a problem based on the information.

   (b) Solve your problem. Compare your problem with others in your class.

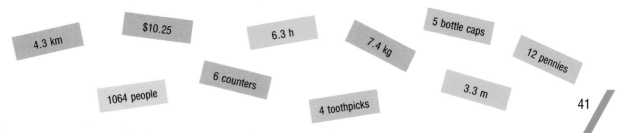

4.3 km $10.25   6.3 h   5 bottle caps   7.4 kg   12 pennies   6 counters   1064 people   4 toothpicks   3.3 m

1.8 CALCULATION SENSE: PATTERNS

Think of situations where you may need to do mental calculations to find an answer. The pictures will give you some ideas.

Now, work with a partner to complete the activities. In your journal, write the patterns that you see.

Multiply

by 10	by 100	by 1000
10 × 38 = ?	100 × 465 = ?	1000 × 369 = ?
10 × 3.8 = ?	100 × 46.5 = ?	1000 × 36.9 = ?
10 × 0.38 = ?	100 × 4.65 = ?	1000 × 3.69 = ?
10 × 0.038 = ?	100 × 0.465 = ?	1000 × 0.369 = ?

Divide

by 10	by 100	by 1000
865 ÷ 10 = ?	874.3 ÷ 100 = ?	4693 ÷ 1000 = ?
86.5 ÷ 10 = ?	87.43 ÷ 100 = ?	469.3 ÷ 1000 = ?
8.65 ÷ 10 = ?	8.743 ÷ 100 = ?	46.93 ÷ 1000 = ?
0.865 ÷ 10 = ?	0.874 3 ÷ 100 = ?	4.693 ÷ 1000 = ?

Use your calculator to verify each pattern using numbers of your own.

EXERCISE

A Find each answer mentally.

1. Multiply each by 10, 100 and 1000.
   (a) 468   (b) 371   (c) 0.125   (d) 1.57

2. Divide each by 10, 100 and 1000.
   (a) 468   (b) 36.9   (c) 0.129   (d) 1.48

3. Copy and complete each chart.

×	10	100	1000
3.82	?	?	?
1.012	?	?	?
17.54	?	?	?

÷	10	100	1000
48.6	?	?	?
74.3	?	?	?
3.892	?	?	?

Review the patterns you have learned.

4. (a) Find the missing values.

A	B
$6243 \div 10 = ?$	$6243 \times 0.1 = ?$
$941.3 \div 10 = ?$	$941.3 \times 0.1 = ?$
$54.68 \div 10 = ?$	$54.68 \times 0.1 = ?$

(b) What do you notice about your answers in columns A and B?

(c) Suggest a rule for multiplying a number by 0.1.

5. (a) Find the missing values.

C	D
$6243 \div 100 = ?$	$6243 \times 0.01 = ?$
$941.3 \div 100 = ?$	$941.3 \times 0.01 = ?$
$54.68 \div 100 = ?$	$54.68 \times 0.01 = ?$

(b) What do you notice about your answers in columns C and D?

(c) Suggest a rule for multiplying a number by 0.01.

MAKING CONNECTIONS

The pictures in this section show various occupations where mental calculations may be needed.

(a) List the occupations shown and the mental math skills that may be needed in each occupation.

(b) List other occupations that may require mental math skills. List the mental math skills.

(c) Write a story involving one of the occupations you have listed. Include in the story some calculations that may be needed to be done mentally by the reader.

---

6. (a) Find the missing values.

E	F
$6243 \div 1000 = ?$	$6243 \times 0.001 = ?$
$941.3 \div 1000 = ?$	$941.3 \times 0.001 = ?$
$54.68 \div 1000 = ?$	$54.68 \times 0.001 = ?$

(b) What do you notice about your answers in columns E and F?

(c) Suggest a rule for multiplying a number by 0.001.

7. Use your own examples. Suggest a rule for dividing by 0.1, 0.01, and 0.001.

8. Calculate.

(a) 200×3.4 (b) 0.1×50

(c) $350 \div 0.01$ (d) 35×0.1

(e) 950×100 (f) $0.311 \div 100$

(g) 0.08×0.01 (h) $2.35 \div 0.1$

9. Simplify.

(a) $325 \div 0.001$ (b) 0.01×12

(c) 750×0.1 (d) $4.2 \div 10$

(e) $2.1 \div 0.001$ (f) 3.2×0.1

(g) $0.311 \div 100$ (h) $1.005 \div 1000$

10. (a) Copy the design shown below onto grid paper.

(b) Make four straight cuts to divide the design into five parts that form a square.

Sara saw chocolate bars advertised at 4 for $2.25. How much would she pay for one chocolate bar?

To calculate the cost, divide.

225¢ ÷ 4 = 56.25¢

A store owner will often round the price up to the nearest cent. Thus, Sara would pay 57¢ for one chocolate bar.

Work with a partner to complete the exercises. One of you can pretend to be the owner and the other the customer. In your journal, write whether you think the price has been rounded fairly.

B Review your skills for rounding numbers.

1. What would you expect to pay for one item? Give reasons for your answer.
   (a) 2 apples sell for 51¢
   (b) 3 limes sell for 91¢
   (c) 5 pens sell for $2.99
   (d) 3 pieces of gum sell for 10¢

2. Binders are on sale. You can buy 4 binders for $6.22.
   (a) How much will you pay for one binder?
   (b) Have the skills for rounding been used fairly to calculate the cost of one binder?

3. Three shirts can be bought for $35.00. You only want one shirt.
   (a) How much would you expect to pay for one shirt?
   (b) You have $11.75. Do you have enough money to buy the shirt?

4. Joe's market is selling bottles of pop at 2 for 99¢. Gina's store is selling cases of 6 bottles at $2.99. For a party, you need to buy 5 bottles of pop. At which store will you spend the least amount of money? Give reasons for your answer.

5. (a) Tins of lunch meat are on sale. You can buy 3 tins for $2.00. How much will you pay for one tin?
   (b) Refer to the ads shown. Create a problem using the ads. Compare your problem with others.

1.10 ORDER OF OPERATIONS

Bruce works at the Pizza Castle. He earns $5.60 for each hour worked between 12:00 and 20:00. After that, he earns $8.40 each hour. Yesterday, he worked 4 h between 12:00 and 20:00 and 4 h after 20:00. How much did he earn in all?

To find his earnings, Bruce calculated the following expression.

$4 \times \$5.60 + 4 \times \$8.40$

$= \$22.40 + \$33.60$
$= \$56.00$

ORDER OF OPERATIONS
• Do the calculations in brackets first.   • Then do multiplication and division in the order they appear.   • Then do addition and subtraction in the order they appear.

The order of operations was used to solve the problem above. Write the order of operations in your journal and use it when needed.

EXERCISE

A Use the order of operations.

1. Calculate.
   - (a) $1.5 - 1.3 + 2.7$
   - (b) $15.6 + 5.4 + 7.2$
   - (c) $1.5 \div 0.5 - 2.3$
   - (d) $9.4 + 11.6 \times 5.1$
   - (e) $6.4 \times 1.3 - 3.7$
   - (f) $3.6 - 5.4 \div 1.8$

2. Calculate. Which has the least value? Which has the greatest value?
   - (a) $64.48 \div 5.2 - 8.94$
   - (b) $2.958 \div 3.4 + 0.13$
   - (c) $3.5 + 1.5$
   - (d) $6.38 - 3.5 \times 1.8$
   - (e) $1.6(3.8 + 4.9)$
   - (f) $4.8(9.6 - 3.8)$

3. Replace ■ with < or >.
   - (a) $2.1 + 5.6 \times 3.8 \ ■ \ 2.4 \times 2$
   - (b) $33.28 - 6.40 - 0.50 \ ■ \ 3.4 \times 6.4 - 5.2$
   - (c) $3.6 \div 1.2 \ ■ \ 2.7 \times 3.3 - 4.8$
   - (d) $5.4 + 1.1 \times 3.0 \ ■ \ 5.2(12.4 - 9.8)$

B Review your *Problem Solving Plan*.

4. Brad also works at Pizza Castle. He earns $7.20 for each hour worked between 12:00 and 20:00. He earns $10.80 for each hour after 20:00. How much will he earn for working from 14:00 to 22:00?

5. At the beginning of an experiment, the temperature of a solution was 22°C. After 1 h, the temperature was 18°C and after 2 h, the temperature was 13°C. Find the average temperature of the solution during this time.

From movie classics to modern TV shows and channels like MTV, films and television have entertained audiences for years.

In this section, you will solve problems that deal with movies and TV shows. For example:

The greatest number of "takes" for a television commercial is given by the expression 12.7 + 5.1 × 3.0. Find the greatest number of takes.

$$12.7 + 5.1 \times 3.0 = 12.7 + 15.3$$
$$= 28.0$$

The greatest number of takes was 28.

To evaluate the expression, the order of operations was used. A calculator can also be used to help you evaluate expressions.

| c | 5.1 | × | 3.0 | = | + | 12.7 | = | 28

Have fun with the problems below, and remember, *that's entertainment!*

A Review the Order of Operations.

1. Al, Bill, Carol, Dan, and Eric are going to the movies.
   (a) In how many ways can they stand in line together?
   (b) In how many different ways can they sit together?

2. The number of TV shows produced by Aaron Spelling is given by the expression $125 \times 5 + 229 \times 5$.

   (a) Evaluate $125 \times 5 + 229 \times 5$.

   (b) How many TV shows has he produced?

3. The number of kilometres of film Aaron Spelling has produced is given by the expression $2517.75 + 155 \times 7.5$. How many kilometres of film has Aaron Spelling produced?

4. The TV show that attracted the most viewers was the final episode of M*A*S*H. The show attracted 125 000 000 people in the United States and Canada. If 0.87 of the people were from the United States, how many were from Canada?

5. Use your journal.

   (a) Pick your favourite TV show. Give reasons why it is your favourite.

   (b) Create a math problem using your favourite show. Have others solve it.

6. The country with the largest number of movie houses per person is San Marino. It has one screen for every 3190 people. There are 22 330 people in San Marino. How many screens are there in all?

C

7. From a Bryan Adams special, $10 251 was collected from ticket sales. Of this, $6250 was collected from adult ticket sales. Student tickets cost $4.45 and adult tickets cost $6.50.

   (a) How many people were at the concert?

   (b) Create a similar problem of your own. Solve the problem.

WORKING TOGETHER
Looking Up Data

Have you ever wondered how much money a movie star makes for one picture or one television series?

(a) Predict which actor or actress you think makes the most money and how much. Now find the actor and the character portrayed. Are you surprised at the amount made?

(b) Use the Guinness Book of World Records. Find the movies that cost the most to make. Did the movies make any money?

(c) Create a problem of your own about actors and movies. Solve your problem and compare your problem with others in your class.

1.12 PROBLEM SOLVING: MORE THAN ONE ANSWER

Often, you will be faced with a problem that has more than one answer.

For example, to buy cookies from a vending machine, you will need 70¢. Rhonda puts a "loonie" coin into the machine. How can she receive her change?

She could receive
- 1 quarter and 1 nickel.
- 3 dimes.
- 6 nickels.
- 2 dimes and 2 nickels.

How else can she receive her change?

EXERCISE

 B Look for more than one answer to each problem.

1. (a) Julius has bought an 80¢ orange juice with a "loonie" coin. In how many ways can he receive the change?
   (b) Create a similar problem of your own. Have others in the class solve your problem.

2. Carlene parks her car on the second floor of an underground parking lot. She takes the elevator up 20 floors.
   (a) At what floor will she arrive? Give reasons for your answer.
   (b) Compare your answer with others in your class. How are they alike? How are they different?
   (c) What assumptions have you made in your solution?

3. Write the number 1000 as the sum of two or more consecutive numbers.

4. Choose five different digits and arrange them in the boxes so that you have the difference shown. Compare your answer with others in your class.

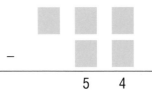

5. (a) Move two toothpicks so that the figure shows two squares.
   (b) Use toothpicks to create a similar problem of your own. Compare your problem with others in your class.

Videotapes and video cassette recorders are relatively new inventions. However, they have become very popular in a short space of time and many people now have them in their homes. Working in pairs or groups, answer the questions below to find out more about the world of video. Use your library.

Video History

1. In 1956, the AMPEX Corporation produced a system for recording pictures on magnetic tape.

   (a) How was the system first used?

   (b) Why was it never used in the home?

   (c) Could you use the tapes needed in this system in today's VCRs? Give reasons for your answer.

2. In 1972, the first video cassette recorders came on the market.

   (a) How many different types were there?

   (b) What was the problem with having this many different types?

Video Today

3. (a) About how many movies do you think are currently available on video? Compare your estimate with others in your class.

   (b) About how many new movies do you think come out on video each year? Compare your estimate with others in your class.

4. (a) Shown above are a number of "stills" from a videotape of a tennis player in action. How do you think the tennis player can use these frames? List other uses of a VCR.

   (b) Predict the most common use of a VCR in your school. Survey your class or school. What is the most common use of a VCR? How accurate was your prediction?

CHAPTER REVIEW

1. What is the place value of 7 in each?

    (a) 4576   (b) 22.07   (c) 35.709   (d) 67 908

2. Calculate.

    (a)   4783   (b)   38.76   (c)   4741
         +3128   +15.94   −1358

    (d)   736   (e)   407.27   (f) 15) 64 590
         × 58   × 11.63

3. Round each number.

    (a) 753, to nearest ten
    (b) 26.983, to nearest tenth
    (c) 1 657 984.32, to nearest thousand
    (d) 12.345 98, to nearest thousandth
    (e) 12 946.345, to nearest hundred

4. Calculate.

    (a) $5 + 7 + (12 + 10) \times 2$
    (b) $3.2 + 2.8 + 4.36 \times 5.13$
    (c) $3.5 + 10 \times 0.36 - 435 \div 100$
    (d) $2.7 \div 100 \times 10 \times 10 - 2.7$
    (e) $3.6 \times (100 - 50) \times 2$

5. The smallest book has a width of 0.14 cm. What distance would the books stretch if the 200 copies sold were laid down side by side?

6. A case of oranges has about 95 oranges. A train has 4950 cases.

    (a) How many oranges are there in all?
    (b) How many dozens of oranges are there in all?
    (c) If each half dozen oranges sells for $0.99, what is the value of the entire shipment?

THINKING ABOUT

Have you updated your Problem Solving Plan with skills like the following?
- using manipulatives
- using patterns

Are the solutions in your notebook clearly organized? If not, how can they be improved?

Write two examples of how you might, in your daily life, need the skills in this chapter.

MAKING CONNECTIONS

Refer to the opening pages of the chapter.

(a) Create a problem of your own using the pictures. Solve your problem.

(b) Compare your problem with others in your class. Solve the other problems.

How do you rate your skills with computation when
- using a calculator?
- using paper and pencil?

What can you do to improve your computation skills?

Choose a question on this page. Describe to your partner how you can solve it. Have your partner suggest how your description can be improved.

MATH JOURNAL

In this chapter, you have used many math symbols and skills to help you communicate mathematics.

(a) List all symbols and skills you have learned.

(b) Write an example to show how to communicate with each.

SELF EVALUATION

1. Replace ■ by < or >.
   (a) 0.375 ■ 0.357
   (b) 1.013 ■ 1.301
   (c) 812.38 ■ 81 238
   (d) 7.14 ■ 7.135

2. Calculate.

   (a)   5718
            3176
        +   814

   (b)   10.418
          51.414
        + 3.198

   (c)   50 000
        −13 476

   (d) 57 896 × 5671
   (e) 19.142 × 22.07

   (f) 289.44 ÷ 6.7
   (g) 365.23 ÷ 108.4

3. The average person blinks 25 times each minute. How many times will you blink while you are at school today?

4. Evaluate.
   (a) 2.3 + 5.4 − 3.6
   (d) 12.5 ÷ 0.5 ÷ 0.5 × 100
   (b) 39 × 34 − 60
   (e) 9.73 + 100 × 2.36 − 25.5
   (c) 415 − 8.3 ÷ 4.6
   (f) 12.3(1.2 − 0.7) − 3.3

5. The total of the registration fees for a convention was $47 310. There were 380 people. How much did each delegate pay to register?

6. The largest bird is the North African Ostrich. The mass of one has been recorded at 156.4 kg. A tortoise in the Indian Ocean has been recorded with a mass of 148.7 kg. Which has a greater mass? By how much?

7. Cherrapunji, India holds the record for the greatest annual rainfall. They had 26 443 mm in one year. How much rain, on average, fell each day?

8. The average height of five students is 158.5 cm. Six students who have an average height of 163.5 cm are added. What is the new average height?

2 INTEGERS

These pictures suggest opposite ideas.
List what you think they might be.

- Have you ever thought about how many people are
  needed to operate a train? Make a list of the people
  involved and what they do.
- What math is suggested by a travelling train? Make a list.
- What math is suggested by the gondolas? Make a list.

Integers can help you express opposite ideas.

$5 gained	3 km North
$5 lost	3 km South

Refer to the previous pages. How are opposite ideas suggested?

For example, suppose you go 2 km up in a gondola and then 2 km back down in a gondola. You can use integers to write this as follows:
- +2 represents 2 km up. This is read as "positive two".
- −2 represents 2 km back down. This is read as "negative two".

The explorations help you understand integers.

EXPLORATION ①   Discuss

1. (a) On the previous pages, the pictures suggested opposite ideas. List the opposite ideas.
   (b) Use the pictures on this page. List the opposite ideas shown.
   (c) Use newspapers and magazines to find other scenes that illustrate opposite ideas. Suggest what integers might be used to represent the opposite ideas.

2. Write an integer suggested by each. Write its opposite.
   (a) a profit of 8 dollars   (b) a loss of 6 points   (c) 500 m down
   (d) 5 steps up   (e) 9 steps North   (f) a gain of 10 kg

3. Suggest pictures that could be used to describe each integer. Write the opposite of each integer.
   (a) −3   (b) +7   (c) +11   (d) −13   (e) −8   (f) +1

Did you know that some oil wells go down as much as 500 m? Write this as an integer.

NUMBERS

EXPLORATION ② Work with a Partner

You can use black and red disks to represent integers.

represents +1 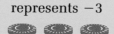 represents −1

represents +3

represents −3

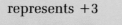

4. (a) Write the integer represented by each group of disks.
   (b) Describe a scene using each integer.
   (c) Describe a scene using the opposite of each integer.

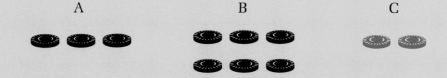

A   B   C

EXPLORATION ③ Work in Pairs

Suppose you rode your bike 4 km east of your home and then 2 km back towards your home. Use disks to represent your distance from home.

4 km east   Think: 1 black disk together with 1 red disk gives a net result of zero.

2 km west   Thus, 2 black disks together with 2 red disks represent a net result of zero.

2 black disks left over represent +2. Thus, you are 2 km east of your home.

5. (a) Write the net result of the integers represented by each group below.
   (b) Describe a scene that involves the integers, including the net result.

A   B   C

6. (a) Set up disks to show integers, and find the net result.
   (b) Describe a scene that involves the integers, including the net result.

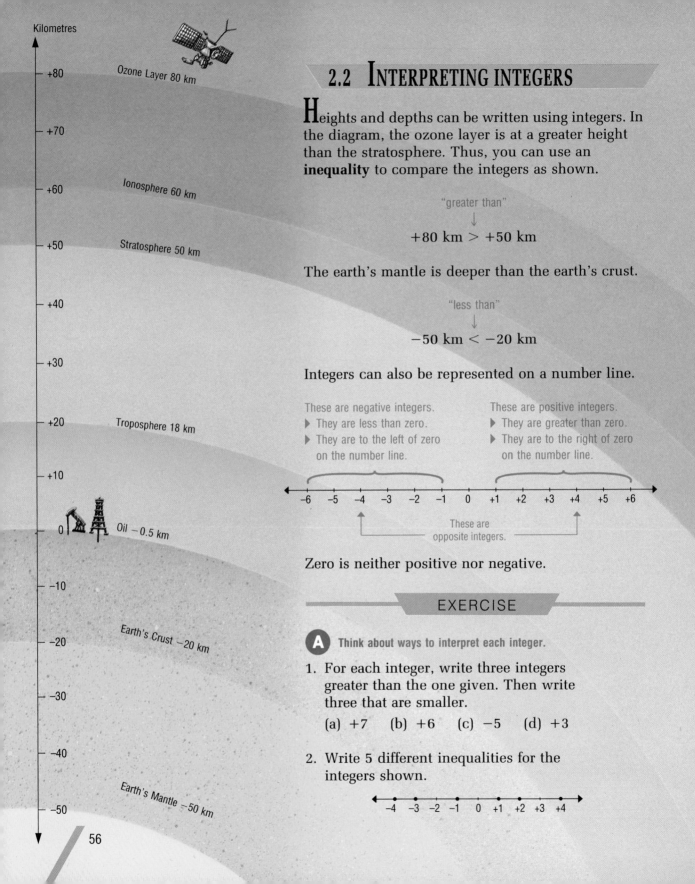

Kilometres

+80 — Ozone Layer 80 km

+70 —

+60 — Ionosphere 60 km

+50 — Stratosphere 50 km

+40 —

+30 —

+20 — Troposphere 18 km

+10 —

0 — Oil −0.5 km

−10 —

−20 — Earth's Crust −20 km

−30 —

−40 —

−50 — Earth's Mantle −50 km

56

2.2 INTERPRETING INTEGERS

Heights and depths can be written using integers. In the diagram, the ozone layer is at a greater height than the stratosphere. Thus, you can use an **inequality** to compare the integers as shown.

"greater than"
↓

$$+80 \text{ km} > +50 \text{ km}$$

The earth's mantle is deeper than the earth's crust.

"less than"
↓

$$-50 \text{ km} < -20 \text{ km}$$

Integers can also be represented on a number line.

These are negative integers.
▶ They are less than zero.
▶ They are to the left of zero on the number line.

These are positive integers.
▶ They are greater than zero.
▶ They are to the right of zero on the number line.

←——┼———┼———┼———┼———┼———┼———┼———┼———┼———┼———┼———┼———┼——→
   −6 −5 −4 −3 −2 −1   0 +1 +2 +3 +4 +5 +6

These are opposite integers.

Zero is neither positive nor negative.

EXERCISE

A Think about ways to interpret each integer.

1. For each integer, write three integers greater than the one given. Then write three that are smaller.

   (a) +7   (b) +6   (c) −5   (d) +3

2. Write 5 different inequalities for the integers shown.

   ←——•———•———•———•———•———•———•———•———•——→
     −4 −3 −2 −1   0 +1 +2 +3 +4

B Work with a partner.

3. Write an inequality for each pair of integers.
   (a) $+4, -3$ (b) $-1, -3$ (c) $+1, +5$

4. Use the information shown.

   Regional Forecast

Noon Temperature	(°C)
Bonnyville	-10
Brandon	$+3$
Cold Lake	-8
Dauphin	-2

   (a) Choose any two cities. Write an inequality using the temperatures.
   (b) What place had the highest temperature? the lowest?
   (c) Write the temperatures in order from highest to lowest.
   (d) Create a problem of your own using the temperatures. Solve it.

5. Use the earth diagram on the previous page. Write an inequality to compare
   (a) the height of the ozone layer and the height of the troposphere.
   (b) the depth of the earth's crust and the depth for finding oil.

6. (a) Write an integer for a temperature suitable for each activity.
     • skating on a river
     • swimming in a river
     • raking leaves
   (b) Choose any two activities. Write an inequality for the integers.
   (c) Write your integers from (a) in order from least to greatest.
   (d) Add activities of your own to the list. Complete parts (a), (b), and (c) for your activities.

7. Place red disks and black disks into a box or a bag. Remove a handful of disks.
   (a) What integer is represented by the red disks? by the black disks?
   (b) Write an inequality using your integers in (a).
   (c) Repeat parts (a) and (b) for other handfuls of disks.

MAKING CONNECTIONS

The integer $+1984$ represents the year Marc Garneau became the first Canadian to travel into space. Part of a date line is shown below.

Atlas D.
Rocket 1963

(a) Copy the date line and the figures on it.
(b) Draw figures of your own to represent the following dates. Use your library to help you find the dates.
   • Columbus' birthday.
   • The year the Great Pyramid was completed.
   • Your birthday.
(c) Choose a date past the year 3000. In your journal, describe an event that could take place in that year. Use integers in your description.

BC	−3000	−2500	−2000	−1500	−1000	−500	0	500	1000	1500	2000

Sphinx 2250 BC

Columbus 1492

You have used red and black disks to help you interpret integers. These same disks can be used to help you add and subtract integers. As you complete each exploration, use your journal to summarize all patterns that can help you add and subtract integers.

EXPLORATION ① *Work Together*

1. The expression (+4) + (+2) is represented by disks.

   (a) What is the net result of adding 4 black disks and 2 black disks?
   (b) Use your work in (a). What is the answer for (+4) + (+2)?

2. (a) Use disks to represent (−4) + (−2). What is the net result?
   (b) Use your work in (a). What is the answer for (−4) + (−2)?

3. The expression (−4) + (+2) is represented by disks.

   Remember:
   1 black disk together with
   1 red disk gives a net result
   of zero.

   (a) What is the net result of adding 4 red disks and 2 black disks?
   (b) Use your work in (a). What is the answer for (−4) + (+2)?

4. (a) Use disks to represent (+4) + (−2). What is the net result?
   (b) Use your work in (a). What is the answer for (+4) + (−2)?

5. (a) Write an addition expression using the disks below. What is the net result?
   (b) Set up red and black disks of your own. Write an addition expression using your disks. Find the answer.

   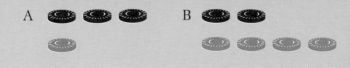

Work in a Group

6. The integer +4 is shown by disks.

    (a) What is the net result of taking 2 black disks from 4 black disks?

    (b) Use your work in (a). What is the answer for $(+4) - (+2)$?

7. (a) Use disks to show −4. Take away 2 red disks.

    (b) Use your work in (a). What is the answer for $(-4) - (-2)$?

8. Use disks to represent each expression. Then, write the answer.

    (a) $(+5) - (+2)$ (b) $(-3) - (-2)$ (c) $(-7) - (-4)$ (d) $(+6) - (+4)$

9. (a) Write subtraction expressions similar to those in Question 8.

    (b) Use disks to represent each expression in (a). Find the answer.

10. Jacques wants to find the answer to $(+2) - (-3)$. He uses disks and the following steps.

Step 1	*Step 2*	*Step 3*
Think: Jacques realizes he cannot subtract red disks from black disks.	Jacques decides to represent +2 in another way.	Jacques then removes 3 red disks. What is the net result?

(a) Interpret each step above. Describe, in your journal, what Jacques is doing in each step.

(b) What is the answer for $(+2) - (-3)$?

11. (a) Describe how you would use disks to find $(-2) - (+3)$.

    (b) What is the answer for $(-2) - (+3)$?

12. (a) Use disks to answer each of the following.
    A: $(-3) - (+2)$ B: $(+5) - (-4)$ C: $(+7) - (-3)$

    (b) Use disks to represent your own expressions involving integers. What are the answers?

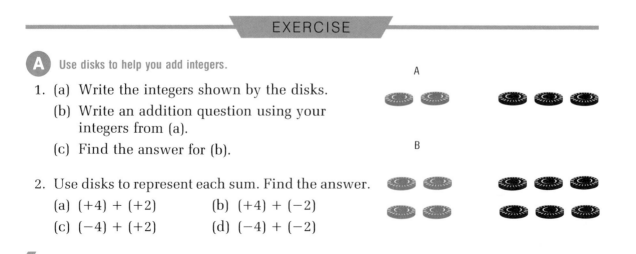

Kelly and Yvonne were competing for
the Canada Fitness Award in an
Endurance Race.
• In the first interval, Kelly went 3 m less than Yvonne.
• During the next interval, Kelly went 5 m more than Yvonne.
At the end of the second interval, who was leading?

Think: Interpret what is given.
• 3 m less can be represented by −3.   • 5 m more can be represented by +5.

To solve the problem, calculate (−3) + (+5) using disks as shown.

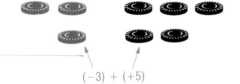

Think:

(−3) + (+5)

Think: Interpret your result. The net result is 2 black disks or +2. Thus, (−3) + (+5) = +2.

Thus, Kelly is +2 m ahead of Yvonne after the second interval.

EXERCISE

A Use disks to help you add integers.

1. (a) Write the integers shown by the disks.
   (b) Write an addition question using your
       integers from (a).
   (c) Find the answer for (b).

2. Use disks to represent each sum. Find the answer.
   (a) (+4) + (+2)   (b) (+4) + (−2)
   (c) (−4) + (+2)   (d) (−4) + (−2)

A

B

Check that your answers are reasonable.

3. Complete each pattern. Use manipulatives to help you. Continue the pattern for two more steps.

   (a) $(+4) + (-1) = ?$
       $(+4) + 0 \quad = ?$
       $(+4) + (+1) = ?$
       $(+4) + (+2) = ?$

   (b) $(-5) + (-2) = ?$
       $(-5) + (-1) = ?$
       $(-5) + 0 \quad = ?$
       $(-5) + (+1) = ?$

4. (a) Use disks to show each.
     • climbing up 5 steps and then down 3 steps
     • a rise in temperature of 2°C followed by a drop of 6°C

   (b) Choose an example of your own. Use disks to show a scene involving integers.

5. Calculate.

   (a) $(+5) + (-3)$ (b) $(-12) + (-8)$
   (c) $(-6) + (+12)$ (d) $(+15) + (-19)$
   (e) $(-7) + (-13)$ (f) $(+22) + (-43)$
   (g) $(-8) + (+12)$ (h) $(+12) + (-7)$

6. Which expression has the greatest value? the least value?

   (a) $(+2) + (-5)$ (b) $(-7) + (+11)$
   (c) $(-5) + (-8)$ (d) $(-4) + (-4)$
   (e) $(-9) + (+7)$ (f) $(+8) + (-5)$
   (g) $(+3) + (+5)$ (h) $(-4) + (+7)$

7. Which pair of integers has the greatest sum? the least sum?

   (a) $(-11), (+6)$ (b) $(-10), (-3)$
   (c) $(+4), (-2)$ (d) $(-7), (+8)$
   (e) $(+2), (+3)$ (f) $(-4), (+9)$

8. Ron and Al were in a marathon. After 1 h, Al ran 5 m less than Ron. During the next hour, Al ran 9 m more than Ron.

   (a) Represent the distances using disks.

   (b) Find the sum. $(-5) + (+9)$

   (c) Interpret your result.

9. The tallest mountain in the world is Mauno Koa mountain in Hawaii. Its base is 5486 m below sea level. Its peak is 9687 m higher than its base. How far above sea level is the peak?

10. Lake Bakal in Moscow is the world's deepest lake. Its surface is 446 m above sea level. The lake is 1931 m deep. How far below sea level is Lake Bakal's deepest point?

11. Construct two dice, A and B, numbered with the integers shown.
    A: +1 +2 +3 +4 +5 +6
    B: −1 −2 −3 −4 −5 −6

   (a) Roll the dice 10 times and add the integers at each roll.

   (b) Have your partner roll the dice 10 times and add the integers.

   (c) The player closest to −3 is the winner of the game.

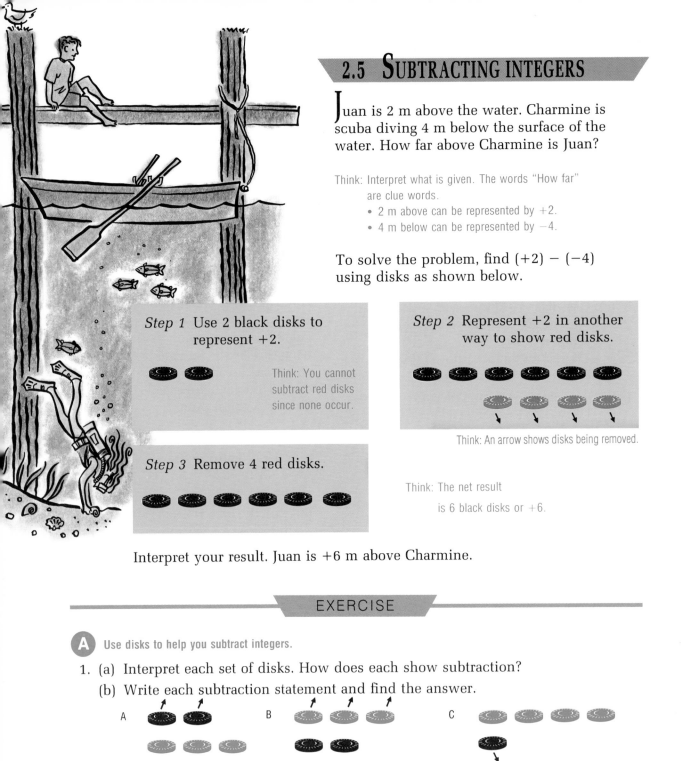

2.5 SUBTRACTING INTEGERS

Juan is 2 m above the water. Charmine is scuba diving 4 m below the surface of the water. How far above Charmine is Juan?

Think: Interpret what is given. The words "How far" are clue words.
- 2 m above can be represented by +2.
- 4 m below can be represented by −4.

To solve the problem, find (+2) − (−4) using disks as shown below.

Step 1 Use 2 black disks to represent +2.

Think: You cannot subtract red disks since none occur.

Step 2 Represent +2 in another way to show red disks.

Think: An arrow shows disks being removed.

Think: The net result is 6 black disks or +6.

Step 3 Remove 4 red disks.

Interpret your result. Juan is +6 m above Charmine.

EXERCISE

A Use disks to help you subtract integers.

1. (a) Interpret each set of disks. How does each show subtraction?
   (b) Write each subtraction statement and find the answer.

   A   B   C

2. Use disks to represent each difference. What is the answer?
   (a) (+5) − (−3)   (b) (+5) − (+4)   (c) (−8) − (+4)   (d) (−9) − (−5)

Review your skills with integers.

3. Complete each pattern. Use disks to help you. Continue the pattern for two more steps.

   (a) $(+5) - (+2) = ?$
   $(+5) - (+1) = ?$
   $(+5) - 0 \quad = ?$
   $(+5) - (-1) = ?$

   (b) $(-3) - (-2) = ?$
   $(-3) - (-1) = ?$
   $(-3) - 0 \quad = ?$
   $(-3) - (+1) = ?$

4. Calculate.

   (a) $(+4) - (-3)$ (b) $(+8) - (-8)$

   (c) $(-3) - (+6)$ (d) $(-12) - (+8)$

   (e) $(-7) - (-9)$ (f) $(-6) - (+4)$

   (g) $(+3) - (-5)$ (h) $(+4) - (+6)$

5. Which expression has the least value?

   (a) $(+6) - (-4)$ (b) $(-11) - (-6)$

   (c) $(-5) - (+12)$ (d) $(+14) - (-9)$

   (e) $(-6) - (-13)$ (f) $(+8) - (-5)$

6. Which pair of integers has the least difference?

   (a) $(-10), (+5)$ (b) $(-9), (-2)$

   (c) $(+3), (-1)$ (d) $(-7), (-8)$

7. Pam is 4 m above the water. Jenny is scuba diving 2 m below the surface of the water.

   (a) Represent the distances using integers.

   (b) Find the difference. $(+4) - (-2)$

   (c) Interpret your result. How far is Jenny from Pam?

8. Use disks to help you interpret each. What is the net result?

   (a) diving 4 m below the surface and then rising 2 m

   (b) standing on a diving board 3 m above water and diving 3 m below water

9. The melting point of krypton is $-157°C$. The melting point of platinum is $+1773°C$. How much greater is the melting point of platinum?

10. The coldest temperature recorded in Canada last year was $-45°C$ in Midale, Saskatchewan. The coldest ever recorded in Canada was $-63°C$ in Snag, North West Territories. Find the difference in temperatures.

11. The air temperature is $-15°C$. With a wind of 16 km/h, the temperature feels like $-26°C$. By how much does the temperature seem to change?

12. Work with a partner. Use the dice made in Question 11, Section 2.4.

    (a) Roll the dice.

    (b) Use the operation of addition or subtraction to find the greatest value.

    (c) A correct answer in (b) is worth one point. Alternate turns with a partner. Ten points wins the game.

2.6 SUBTRACTING INTEGERS: PATTERNS

You have used manipulatives to help you understand how to add and subtract integers. You can also use a pattern to help you subtract integers.

To subtract $(-5) - (+4)$, think as follows.

$(-5) - (+4) = ?$ Think of the subtraction another way.
$(-5) = ? + (+4)$ The answer is -9.
Thus, $(-5) - (+4) = -9$.

You can use a related addition as shown below to explore patterns.

Subtract	Compare with	Related Addition
$(-5) - (-4) = -1$	$\longrightarrow$	$(-5) + (+4) = -1$
$(-5) - (+4) = -9$	$\longrightarrow$	$(-5) + (-4) = -9$
$(+5) - (-4) = +9$	$\longrightarrow$	$(+5) + (+4) = +9$
$(+5) - (+4) = +1$	$\longrightarrow$	$(+5) + (-4) = +1$

By comparing a subtraction with a related addition, a pattern occurs:
to subtract an integer, you add its opposite.

EXERCISE

A Review your skills with integers.

1. For each subtraction, write a related addition. Then find the answer.
   (a) $(+6) - (+8)$ (b) $(+9) - (+8)$ (c) $(+9) - (+9)$ (d) $(-7) - (+3)$
   (e) $(-4) - (-3)$ (f) $(+6) - (-8)$ (g) $(+3) - (-2)$ (h) $(-4) - (-8)$

2. Calculate. (Think of a related addition.)
   (a) $(+5) - (-3)$ (b) $(+5) - (+4)$ (c) $(-8) - (+4)$ (d) $(-3) - (+6)$
   (e) $(-9) - (-5)$ (f) $(+9) - (-4)$ (g) $(-5) - (+3)$ (h) $(-2) - (-4)$

B Remember: To subtract an integer, add its opposite.

3. Subtract.
   (a) $(+6) - (+8)$ (b) $(-7) - (+3)$
   (c) $(+4) - (-3)$ (d) $(+8) - (-8)$
   (e) $(-3) - (+6)$ (f) $(-12) - (+8)$
   (g) $(-7) - (-9)$ (h) $(-6) - (+4)$

4. Calculate.
   (a) $(-3) + (-4) - (+2)$
   (b) $(-6) - (-8) - (+9)$
   (c) $(-12) - (-4) + (-3)$
   (d) $(-7) + (-3) + (-2)$

2.7 PROBLEM SOLVING: ANOTHER WAY

You have seen how to use manipulatives to add and subtract integers. You can represent integers on a number line.

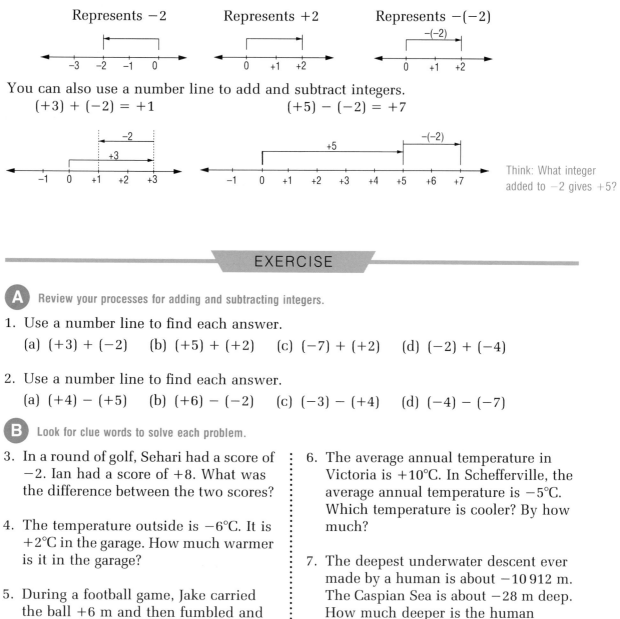

Represents −2   Represents +2   Represents −(−2)

You can also use a number line to add and subtract integers.

$$(+3) + (−2) = +1 \qquad\qquad (+5) − (−2) = +7$$

Think: What integer added to −2 gives +5?

EXERCISE

A Review your processes for adding and subtracting integers.

1. Use a number line to find each answer.
   (a) $(+3) + (−2)$ (b) $(+5) + (+2)$ (c) $(−7) + (+2)$ (d) $(−2) + (−4)$

2. Use a number line to find each answer.
   (a) $(+4) − (+5)$ (b) $(+6) − (−2)$ (c) $(−3) − (+4)$ (d) $(−4) − (−7)$

B Look for clue words to solve each problem.

3. In a round of golf, Sehari had a score of −2. Ian had a score of +8. What was the difference between the two scores?

4. The temperature outside is −6°C. It is +2°C in the garage. How much warmer is it in the garage?

5. During a football game, Jake carried the ball +6 m and then fumbled and lost +2 m. What was Jake's actual gain on the play?

6. The average annual temperature in Victoria is +10°C. In Schefferville, the average annual temperature is −5°C. Which temperature is cooler? By how much?

7. The deepest underwater descent ever made by a human is about −10 912 m. The Caspian Sea is about −28 m deep. How much deeper is the human descent than the depth of the Caspian Sea?

65

2.8 ORDERED PAIRS

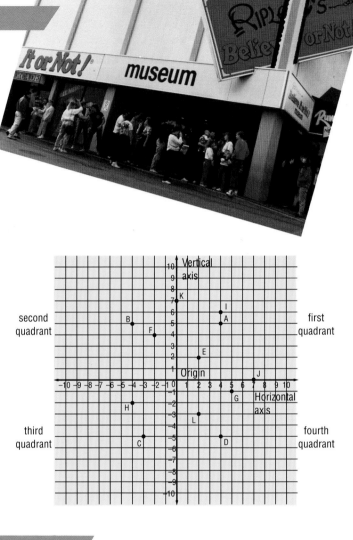

You can use integers to describe a position on the earth's surface. Two pieces of information are needed. For example, to locate the *Ripley's Believe It or Not Museum* in Niagara Falls, you would use the following number and street name: 4960 Clifton Hill.

To describe an exact position on a grid, you use two number lines called a **vertical axis** and a **horizontal axis**.

You use an ordered pair to show the position of a point. The numbers are called the **coordinates** of the point. To plot the ordered pair, you find its exact location on a coordinate grid.

B(−4, +5)

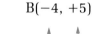

This number tells you how far, and in which direction, to move along the horizontal axis.

This number tells you how far, and in which direction, to move along the vertical axis.

EXERCISE

 List all new words you have learned.

1. Refer to the grid. Write the name of the point shown by each ordered pair.

   (a) (+2, +2)   (b) (−2, +4)   (c) (+5, −1)   (d) (−4, −2)   (e) (+4, +6)

2. Refer to the grid. Copy and complete using the labelled points.

   (a) (■, −5)   (b) (■, −3)   (c) (+2, ■)   (d) (■, +5)   (e) (−4, ■)
   (f) (−3, ■)   (g) (+7, ■)   (h) (0, ■)   (i) (■, 0)   (j) (+4, ■)

3. In which quadrant does each ordered pair in Question 2 lie?

4. Draw a coordinate grid.

   (a) Plot these points.
       A(-1, -1)   B(-1, 5)   C(6, -1)

   (b) Use a straight line to connect A to B, A to C, and B to C.

   (c) What geometric figure have you drawn in (b)?

5. Draw a coordinate grid.

   (a) Plot these points.
       A(4, -4)   B(-4, -4)   C(0, 8)

   (b) Use a straight line to connect A to B, A to C, and B to C.

   (c) What geometric figure have you drawn in (b)?

6. These ordered pairs represent a geometric figure.
   A(-3, 3) B(6, 3) C(1, -2) D(-8, -2)

   (a) Predict the figure.

   (b) Join the points in order.

   (c) What geometric figure is drawn?

   (d) Create a similar shape of your own on a grid. Write the directions needed to form your shape. Give your directions to others in the class to find the shape.

7. Plot the following ordered pairs.
   $(-4, 5)$ $(-2, 3)$ $(2, 3)$ $(4, 5)$ $(0, 7)$

   (a) Draw a line to join each point to each of the other points.

   (b) How many different lines have you drawn?

8. The coordinates of three vertices of rectangle PQRS are
   P(7, 3)   Q(7, -5)   R(-5, -5).

   (a) In what quadrant is vertex S?

   (b) Plot the ordered pairs. What are the coordinates of S?

   (c) Write the coordinates of a point on side PQ.

   (d) Write the coordinates of the point of intersection of diagonals PR and QS.

9. Work together. Four counters are arranged as shown below. Move two counters, each one at a time, so that the pattern to the right is formed.

MAKING CONNECTIONS

You can describe any location in the world using longitude lines and latitude lines. Use your library and answer the following in your journal.

(a) Find out what longitude and latitude lines are. How are they used?

(b) Describe the place where you live using longitude and latitude lines.

(c) Similarly, describe where Oak Island, Nova Scotia, is located. For what is Oak Island noted? Write a brief description of Oak Island.

(d) Pick a place of your own. Describe its position using longitude and latitude lines. Write a short story about the place you pick.

2.9 PATTERNS ON A GRID

Amanda wanted to know what time the surprise party was to start. To keep the time secret, Hugh answered, "Use a straight line to join the ordered pairs in the given order."

$(2, -1), (-2, -1), (-2, 3),$
$(2, 3), (2, -4), (-2, -4)$

 Think: +3 can be written as 3.

Amanda then plotted and joined the points as shown on the grid. The surprise party was to start at 9:00.

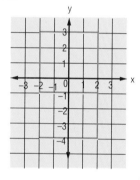

EXERCISE

A Use a grid of your own for Questions 1 and 2.

1. Line AB has end points with coordinates A(−5, −2) and B(−2, 3).
   (a) Draw the line on a grid.
   (b) Write the ordered pairs for two other points on the line.
   (c) Suppose the line was extended in both directions. Predict the coordinates of two other points on the line. Then, extend the line. Was your prediction correct?

2. One side of a square has coordinates A(−2, −2) and B(−2, 2).
   (a) Draw line AB on a grid.
   (b) Write ordered pairs that describe the other three sides.
   (c) Choose a point on each side of the square. Write its coordinates.
   (d) Join the ordered pairs in (c). What shape have you formed?

B Review your skills with ordered pairs.

3. (a) Square ABCD has vertices A(1, 3),
       B(1, −2), and C(6, −2).
       Write the missing coordinates of D.

   (b) Suppose AB is made twice as long
       by moving B. Predict the
       coordinates of the vertices of the
       new square ABCD. Draw the
       square. Was your prediction
       correct?

4. (a) A code shown by ordered pairs is
       used to make a word. To decode it,
       draw a grid and plot the points.
       Find each letter of the word.

   > Join (−7, 1) to (−7, 3) to (−6, 2).
   > Join (−6, 2) to (−5, 3) to (−5, 1).
   > Join (−4, 1) to (−2, 3) to (0, 1).
   > Join (−3, 2) to (−1, 2).
   > Join (0, 3) to (2, 3) and (1, 1) to (1, 3).

   (b) Use the method in (a) to create a
       word of your own.

5. (a) A coded message is sent using
       ordered pairs. Follow these
       instructions and plot the points to
       decode the message.

   > Join (−6, 7) to (−4, 7) to (−4, 3).
   > Join (−4, 3) to (−6, 3) to (−6, 7).
   > Join (8, 3) to (9, −1) to (9.5, 1).
   > Join (9.5, 1) to (10, −1) to (11, 3).
   > Join (6, 0) to (4, 0) to (4, 4).
   > Join (4, 4) to (6, 4) to (6, 0).
   > Join (13, −2) to (13, 2) to (15, −2).
   > Join (15, −2) to (15, 2).
   > Join (0, 5) to (1, 5) to (2, 4) to (2, 2).
   > Join (2, 2) to (1, 1) to (0, 1) to (0, 5).
   > Join (−8, 8) to (−10, 8) to (−10, 4).
   > Join (−10, 4) to (−8, 4) to (−8, 6).
   > Join (−8, 6) to (−9, 6).

   (b) Use the method in (a) to create a
       message of your own.

6. (a) Suppose an ant is to crawl around
       the square. What directions would
       you give the ant to complete the
       trip?

   (b) Create a similar
       problem of your
       own using
       another shape.
       Give your
       directions to
       someone else
       in the class to
       find the shape.

7. Play this game with a partner.

   (a) Construct two cubes with the
       integers −3, −2, −1, 0, +1, and +2
       on them.

   (b) Draw a coordinate grid with labels
       −3, −2, −1, 0, +1, and +2.

   (c) Place disks on the coordinate grid
       so that each point is covered by a
       disk.

   (d) Each player takes turns rolling the
       dice constructed. Create an
       ordered pair using the dice and
       remove the disk covering that
       ordered pair. If there is no
       disk, the turn is lost.

   (e) Keep playing the game
       until five disks are
       removed in a row,
       column, or diagonal.

2.10 PROBLEM SOLVING: SOLVE A SIMPLER PROBLEM

Find the sum of the first 50 even integers shown below.

$2 + 4 + 6 + 8 + \ldots + 94 + 96 + 98 + 100$

1. Think About the Problem.

(a) Think of what you must find.
  - The sum of the integers above.
(b) Think of what you are given.
  - The expression shown.

2. Think About a Strategy.

(a) Think of a strategy you could use.
  - You could use a calculator. But this could be time consuming.
  - Solve a simpler problem to find a pattern in the sum.
(b) Think of a reason for the strategy.
  - A pattern can be used when you solve a similar problem.

3. Work It Out.

Find the sum of simpler sums. Look for a pattern.

First Sum	**Second Sum**	**Third Sum**	**Fourth Sum**
$2 + 4 = 6$	$2 + 4 + 6 = 12$	$2 + 4 + 6 + 8 = 20$	$2 + 4 + 6 + 8 + 10 = 30$
Think: $2 \times 3 = 6$	Think: $3 \times 4 = 12$	Think: $4 \times 5 = 20$	Think: $5 \times 6 = 30$

Interpret the pattern shown above. What do you notice?

Thus, the sum of the first 50 even integers is given by $50 \times 51 = 2550$.

4. Think About Your Solution.

The sum of the expression is 2550.
- Can you solve the problem another way?
- Is your answer reasonable?

Extend the Problem.
How can you use the method above to find the sum of the following? Work together to find a method.

$$1 + 3 + 5 + 7 + \ldots + 93 + 95 + 97 + 99$$

B Use your *Problem Solving Plan*.

For each problem, think of a simpler problem.

1. Find each sum.
   (a) $2 + 4 + 6 + 8 + \ldots + 48 + 50$
   (b) $2 + 4 + 6 + 8 + \ldots + 998 + 1000$

2. Find each sum.
   (a) $1 + 3 + 5 + 7 + \ldots + 49$
   (b) $1 + 3 + 5 + 7 + \ldots + 997 + 999$

3. Find the sum of the following.
   (a) $(+1) + (-2) + (+3) + \ldots + (+9)$
   (b) $21 + 22 + 23 + \ldots + 69 + 70$

4. Find the sum of the first 50 positive integers.

5. Find the sum of each expression.
   (a) $1 + 2 - 3 + 4 - \ldots - 49 + 50$
   (b) $-1 - 2 - 3 - \ldots - 22 - 23 - 24$

Use all your Problem Solving Skills.

6. A bus route has 14 stops. At the first stop, it picks up one passenger, at the next stop two, and so on.
   (a) How many passengers were picked up over the entire route?
   (b) What assumptions have you made in part (a)?

7. Over a 12 h period, how many times will a minute hand and an hour hand form a right angle?

8. Choose six different digits and place them on the cards so that the following expression is true.

$$+ \quad \frac{\boxed{}\ \boxed{}\ \boxed{}}{1 \quad 0 \quad 0 \quad 0}$$

CALCULATION SENSE

To help you add integers quickly, look for opposites.
$(+4) + (+3) + (-4) = +3$ Think: $(+4) + (-4) = 0$

1. Calculate.
   (a) $(+5) + (-5) + (+2)$
   (b) $(+5) + (-7) + (+7)$
   (c) $(+3) + (-2) + (-3)$

2. Calculate.
   (a) $(+2) + (-4) + (-5) + (-2)$
   (b) $(+6) + (-5) + (-6) + (+2)$
   (c) $(+6) + (-3) + (+3) + (-6)$

Have you ever heard people say "To solve a problem, you need to gather as much information as possible."?

To win the game on this page, you will have to gather as much information as possible and think one step ahead of your competitor.

Marking Off Your Territory

On the following boards, a series of dots are shown. Follow these rules to play a game of *Marking Off Your Territory.*

1. Each player takes turns drawing a horizontal, vertical, or diagonal line on the board. The line can only go from one dot to another and cannot pass through other dots.
2. A player marks off territory by completing 3-sided or 4-sided figures using the lines drawn. Each territory marked off earns a score of +1. The territory marked off must be shown clearly by each player and marked accordingly.
3. Territory that is marked off cannot be within someone else's territory, or overlap other marked off territory. If this happens, the player earns a score of −1.
4. The first player to earn 10 points wins.

Game 1

Game 2

Game 3
Make a board of your own.
Use your board to play
your partner.

Many discoveries are made because people dare to go "one step beyond".

For example, by going beyond the 8000 m point on a mountain, explorers found plants could exist at a level of 8199 m.

Stepping Stone
Make a copy of this game.
In this game, you must scale to the top of the mountain from the starting point indicated, moving from one "stepping stone" to the next that is adjacent to it. To go to the next "stepping stone", you must first evaluate the next expression. If the value is less than or equal to 2, you can move. The player who gets to the top of the mountain first wins.

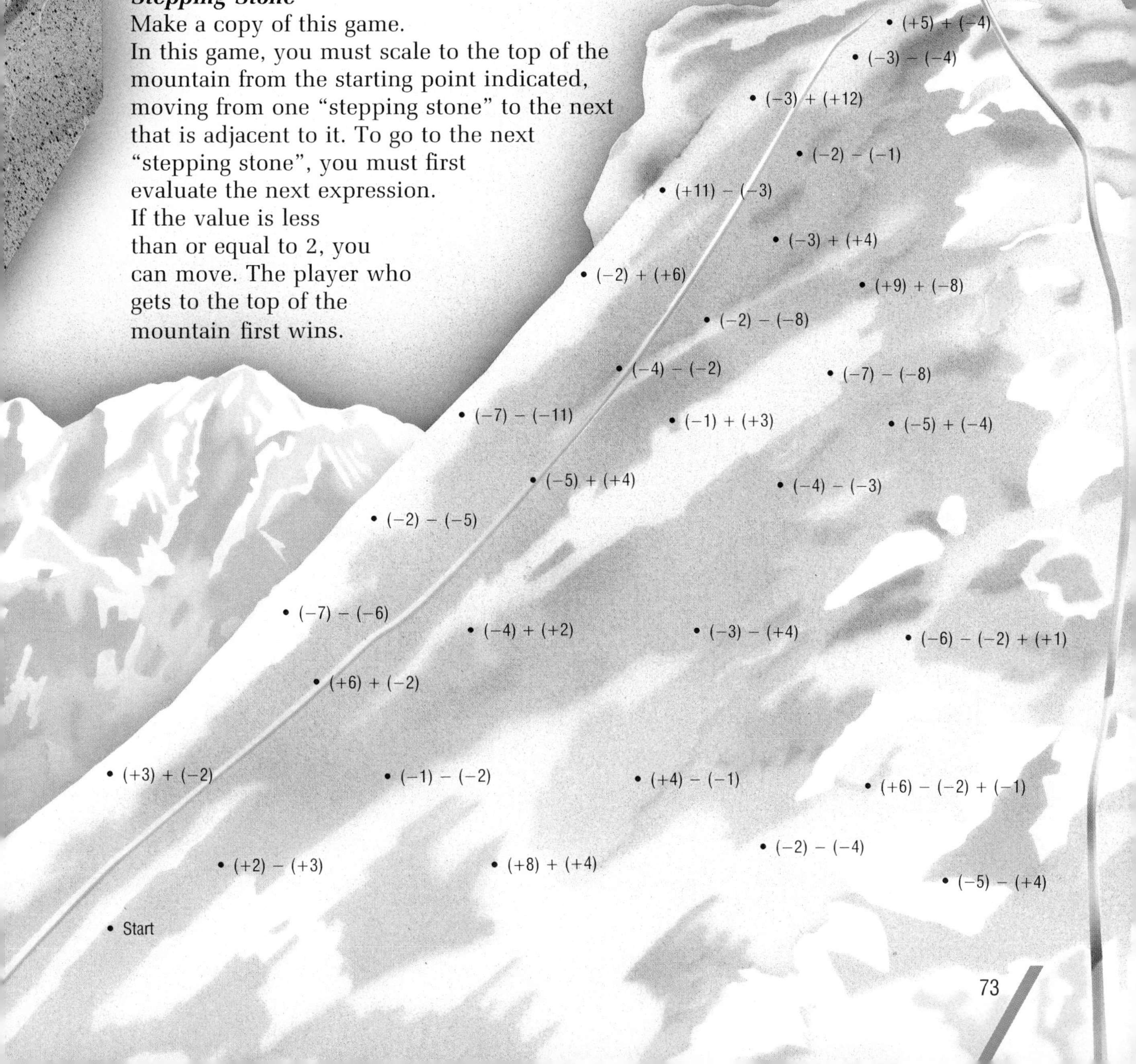

- (+5) + (−4)
- (−3) − (−4)
- (−3) + (+12)
- (−2) − (−1)
- (+11) − (−3)
- (−3) + (+4)
- (−2) + (+6)
- (+9) + (−8)
- (−2) − (−8)
- (−4) − (−2)
- (−7) − (−8)
- (−7) − (−11)
- (−1) + (+3)
- (−5) + (−4)
- (−5) + (+4)
- (−4) − (−3)
- (−2) − (−5)
- (−7) − (−6)
- (−4) + (+2)
- (−3) − (+4)
- (−6) − (−2) + (+1)
- (+6) + (−2)
- (+3) + (−2)
- (−1) − (−2)
- (+4) − (−1)
- (+6) − (−2) + (−1)
- (+2) − (+3)
- (+8) + (+4)
- (−2) − (−4)
- (−5) − (+4)
- Start

73

You have seen how to use disks to add and subtract integers. Disks can also help you multiply integers. Work together to complete this exploration. In your journal, summarize the patterns and relationships you find.

EXPLORATION *Work Together*

1. Nine black disks are shown.
   (a) How would you use these disks to give meaning to $(+3) \times (+3)$?
   (b) What is the answer for $(+3) \times (+3)$?

2. Nine red disks are shown.
   (a) How would you use these disks to give meaning to $(+3) \times (-3)$?
   (b) What is the answer for $(+3) \times (-3)$?

3. (a) Write a product for each group of disks shown.
   (b) Write the answer for each product from (a).

4. (a) Use disks to represent each product.
   A $(+5) \times (-3)$ B $(+4) \times (-2)$
   C $(+3) \times (-4)$ D $(+4) \times (-4)$
   (b) Interpret your disks in (a). Find the answer for each product.

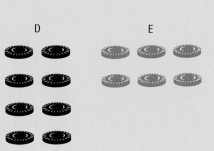

5. (a) Set up red and black disks in groups in your own way.
   (b) Write a product using your disks.
   (c) Write the answer for your product.

2.14 MULTIPLYING INTEGERS

In the previous section, you explored how to multiply integers using disks. A pattern can help you multiply integers.

Integers stay the same.

Integers decrease.

Think: What pattern do you see? Write your answer in your journal.

Think: What pattern do you see? Write your answer in your journal.

$$(+4) \times (+3) = +12$$
$$(+4) \times (+2) = +8$$
$$(+4) \times (+1) = +4$$
$$(+4) \times 0 = 0$$
$$(+4) \times (-1) = -4$$
$$(+4) \times (-2) = -8$$
$$(+4) \times (-3) = -12$$

Think: Summarize the patterns in the products.

EXERCISE

A Remember: $(-3) \times (+6) = (+6) \times (-3)$

1. (a) Find the sum. $(-3) + (-3) + (-3) + (-3) + (-3)$

   (b) Use your result in (a). Find the answer for $(+5) \times (-3)$.

2. Find the missing values of ■. Continue the pattern for two more steps.

   (a) $(+2)(+2) = +4$
   $(+2)(+1) = ■$
   $(+2)(0) = ■$
   $(+2)(-1) = ■$

   (b) $(+1)(+3) = +3$
   $(0)(+3) = ■$
   $(-1)(+3) = ■$
   $(-2)(+3) = ■$

   (c) $(-2)(+2) = -4$
   $(-2)(+1) = ■$
   $(-2)(0) = ■$
   $(-2)(-1) = ■$

B Work together. Use manipulatives or a pattern to help you.

3. Use a pattern to find each product.

   (a) $(+5) \times (+2)$ (b) $(-3) \times (+6)$

4. Find each product.

   (a) $(+6)(-3)$ (b) $(+4)(-2)$
   (c) $(-6)(+3)$ (d) $(-4)(+2)$
   (e) $(-6)(-3)$ (f) $(+7)(-2)$

5. Which product has the greatest value?

   (a) $(+3)(+4)$ (b) $(+4)(+3)$
   (c) $(-3)(+6)$ (d) $(-2)(+4)$
   (e) $(+3)(-3)$ (f) $(+3)(-6)$

6. What do you notice about each product?

   (a) $(-3) \times (+12)$ (b) $(+9) \times (-4)$
   (c) $(-6) \times (+6)$ (d) $(-18) \times (+2)$

7. Write in your journal.

   (a) The product of a positive integer and a positive integer is a ■■■■■ integer.

   (b) The product of a negative integer and a positive integer is a ■■■■■ integer.

75

2.15 MULTIPLYING TWO NEGATIVE INTEGERS

What you learn in one part of mathematics can often be used in another part of mathematics. For example, you have seen the following products.

$(+4) \times (+2) = +8$

positive positive positive
integer integer product

$(+4) \times (-2) = -8$

positive negative negative
integer integer product

$(-4) \times (+2) = -8$

negative positive negative
integer integer product

A pattern can be used to find the product of two negative integers.

The integers decrease.

The integers stay the same.

Think: What pattern do you see? Write your answer in your journal.

Think: What pattern do you see? Write your answer in your journal.

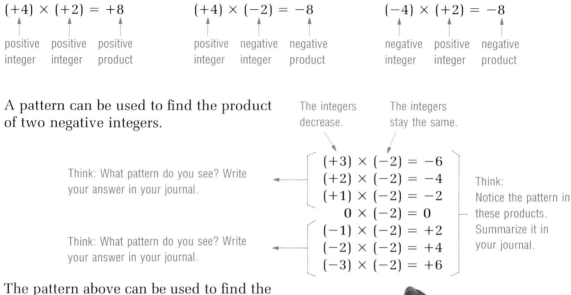

$(+3) \times (-2) = -6$
$(+2) \times (-2) = -4$
$(+1) \times (-2) = -2$
$0 \times (-2) = 0$
$(-1) \times (-2) = +2$
$(-2) \times (-2) = +4$
$(-3) \times (-2) = +6$

Think:
Notice the pattern in these products. Summarize it in your journal.

The pattern above can be used to find the product of two negative integers as shown below.

Think:

$(-3) \times (-2) = ?$

$(-3) \times (+2) = -6$
$(-3) \times (+1) = -3$
$(-3) \times 0 = 0$
$(-3) \times (-1) = +3$
$(-3) \times (-2) = +6$

Thus, $(-3) \times (-2) = +6$.

A calculator can be used to multiply two negative numbers. Use the following calculator key sequence to find the product of $(-3) \times (-2)$.

[c] 3 [+/−] [×] 2 [+/−] [=] 6

A Remember: $(-3) \times (+1)$ can be written as $(-3)(+1)$.

1. Find the missing values.

(a) $(-3)(+1) = ?$
$(-3)(0) \quad = ?$
$(-3)(-1) = ?$
$(-3)(-2) = ?$

(b) $(-5)(+1) = ?$
$(-5)(0) \quad = ?$
$(-5)(-1) = ?$
$(-5)(-2) = ?$

(c) $(-4)(+2) = ?$
$(-4)(+1) = ?$
$(-4)(0) \quad = ?$
$(-4)(-1) = ?$

2. Decide on a pattern to help you find each product. What is the answer?

(a) $(-3)(-4)$
(b) $(-6)(-5)$
(c) $(-8)(-9)$
(d) $(-5)(-2)$
(e) $(-11)(-3)$
(f) $(-6)(-10)$
(g) $(-7)(-3)$
(h) $(-8)(-2)$

B Review your patterns for multiplying integers.

3. Calculate. (Think of a pattern.)

(a) $(-9)(-4)$
(b) $(-8)(-5)$
(c) $(-7)(-5)$
(d) $(-6)(-3)$
(e) $(-6)(-5)$
(f) $(-8)(-3)$
(g) $(-5)(-11)$
(h) $(-12)(-9)$

4. Multiply.

(a) $(-6)(-4)$
(b) $(-12)(0)$
(c) $(+14)(0)$
(d) $(-11)(-12)$
(e) $(0)(-13)$
(f) $(+8)(-7)$
(g) $(-2)(-8)$
(h) $(-4)(+5)$

5. Find the products. Write your answers in order from least to greatest.

(a) $(+8)(+2)$
(b) $(-3)(-6)$
(c) $(-4)(+4)$
(d) $(-11)(-12)$

6. Write in your journal.

(a) The product of a negative integer and a positive integer is a ▬▬▬ integer.

(b) The product of a negative integer and a negative integer is a ▬▬▬ integer.

7. Tracey has 14 red disks and 4 black disks. Sue has three times as many red disks and twice as many black.

(a) How many black disks and red disks does Sue have?

(b) Find the net result of Sue's disks.

8. Work with a partner. Reach into a box and remove a handful of disks.

(a) Create an expression that has the least value using the disks.

(b) Have your partner also create an expression with the least value.

(c) Compare your expressions. The person with the least value scores +1. The first player to obtain +10 wins.

The skills you learned for multiplying integers can help you divide integers. Look at the following patterns.

Multiply $(+2)(+4) = +8$ $(+2)(-4) = -8$ $(-2)(+4) = -8$ $(-2)(-4) = +8$

suggests   suggests   suggests   suggests

Divide $(+8) \div (+4) = +2$ $(-8) \div (-4) = +2$ $(-8) \div (+4) = -2$ $(+8) \div (-4) = -2$

The pattern suggests that to divide integers, think of a related product. For example,

$$(-15) \div (+3) = (?) \leftarrow \text{suggests} \rightarrow (?) \times (+3) = -15.$$

Think: What multiplied by $+3$ gives you -15?
Since $(-5) \times (+3) = -15$, $? = -5$.
Thus, $(-5) \times (+3) = -15$.

The pattern for dividing integers can be used to solve problems. For example, on a video game, Andrea scored -21 points in $+3$ seconds. On average, how many points did she score each second?

To solve the problem, you need to find the quotient. $(-21) \div (+3)$

Think: $(-21) \div (+3) = ?$ suggests $? \times (+3) = -21$
Since $(-7) \times (+3) = -21$, $? = -7$.
Thus, $(-21) \div (+3) = -7$.

Thus, Andrea averaged -7 points each second.

You can use a calculator to divide integers. Use the following key sequence to divide.

C 21 +/− ÷ 3 = −7

A Review how to multiply integers.

1. Copy and complete the chart. Find the missing values.

Division	Related Multiplication	Think:
(a) $(-18) \div (-3) = ?$	$? \times (-3) = -18$	$? = \blacksquare$
(b) $(-18) \div (+3) = ?$	▬▬▬▬▬▬	$? = \blacksquare$
(c) $(+18) \div (-3) = ?$	▬▬▬▬▬▬	$? = \blacksquare$
(d) $(+18) \div (+3) = ?$	▬▬▬▬▬▬	$? = \blacksquare$

Think: Ask yourself, "By what number do I multiply to get the answer?"

2. For each,
   - first decide whether the answer is positive or negative.
   - then find the quotient.

   (a) $(+25) \div (-5)$ (b) $(-36) \div (+12)$ (c) $(-66) \div (-11)$ (d) $(+54) \div (+9)$

3. Use your journal. Illustrate each answer with an example of your own.
   (a) When is the quotient of integers positive?
   (b) When is the quotient of integers negative?

B Check that your answers are reasonable.

4. Find the following quotients.
   (a) $(+10) \div (-2)$ (b) $(-15) \div (+5)$
   (c) $(-36) \div (-12)$ (d) $(+15) \div (-3)$
   (e) $0 \div (+10)$ (f) $(-49) \div (+7)$

5. Divide.
   (a) $(+90) \div (-10)$ (b) $0 \div (-2)$
   (c) $(+50) \div (-25)$ (d) $(-121) \div (-11)$
   (e) $(-150) \div (-15)$ (f) $(+144) \div (-12)$

6. Divide. Write your answers from least to greatest.
   (a) $(+10) \div (-5)$ (b) $(-18) \div (+3)$
   (c) $(-33) \div (+11)$ (d) $(+25) \div (-5)$
   (e) $(-24) \div (-8)$ (f) $(+16) \div (+4)$

7. Find three possible pairs of integers that can be used to give each quotient.
   (a) -4 (b) $+6$ (c) -9 (d) $+12$

8. The temperature dropped 10°C over 5 d. On average, by how much did the temperature change each day?

9. (a) Work together. Construct the cards shown below. Put the cards into a box. Reach in and select one card.

   (b) Write three pairs of integers whose quotient gives the value on the card.

   (c) Score +1 for each correct pair, −1 for each incorrect pair. The first player to score +10 wins the game.

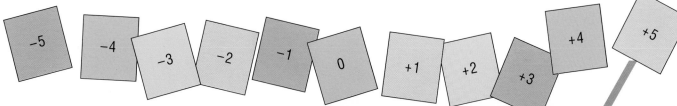

2.17 ORDER OF OPERATIONS

Often, in math, what you learn for one type of number applies to other types. What you learn for whole numbers and decimal numbers applies to integers. Thus, the order of operations also applies to integers.

$$(-3) \times [(+15) + (-3)]$$
$$= (-3) \times [+12]$$
$$= -36$$

Think:
Brackets first.
Then multiply.

The order of operations is used in solving problems like the following.

In Anne's experiment, the temperature in a container was checked every 3 min. Initially, the temperature was +10°C. After 3 min, the temperature was −16°C. After 6 min, the temperature was −24°C. Find the average temperature.

Think: To find the average, add the three temperatures and divide by three.

$$[(+10) + (-16) + (-24)] \div (+3)$$
$$= [-30] \div (+3)$$
$$= -10$$

The average temperature is −10°C.

EXERCISE

A Review the order of operations.

1. Calculate. Why are your answers different?
   A $(-32) \div (+16) + (-8)$
   B $(-32) + (+16) \div (-8)$

2. Calculate. Why are your answers different?
   A $(-36) \div [(-6) \div (-6)]$
   B $[(-36) \div (-6)] \div (-6)$

3. Calculate.

   (a) $(-4) + (+16) \div (-4)$

   (b) $[(-4) + (+16)] \div (-4)$

   (c) $(-8) \times (-9) + (+5)$

4. Evaluate.

   (a) $(-8) \div (-4) + (+2)$

   (b) $(-8) \div [(-4) + (+2)]$

   (c) $(-8) - [(-4) \div (+2)]$

   (d) $[(-8) - (-4)] \div (+2)$

5. Calculate. Arrange your answers in order from least to greatest.

   (a) $(-6) \times (+3) - (-2)$

   (b) $(-4) - (+2) \times (+2)$

   (c) $(-6) + (-12) \div (-2)$

   (d) $(-6) \times (-3) \div (+9)$

6. The following calculator key sequence calculates $(-10) + (-4) \div (-2)$.

   $\boxed{c}\ 4\ \boxed{+/-}\ \boxed{\div}\ 2\ \boxed{+/-}\ \boxed{+}\ 10\ \boxed{+/-}\ \boxed{=}\ -8$

   Use a calculator to find each answer.

   (a) $(-3) + (-2) \times (+5)$

   (b) $(-4) \times (+7) - (-12) \div (-4)$

   (c) $(-5) - (-3) \times (+12) - (-6)$

7. Mineral deposits are found at the following depths.
   -232 m, -321 m, -225 m, -154 m.

   (a) Find the average of the depths.

   (b) Interpret your answer. At what average depth will mineral deposits be found?

8. In an experiment, the temperature in a container dropped every 5 min. Initially, the temperature was 8°C. After 5 min, the temperature was -4°C. After 10 min, the temperature was -7°C. Find the average temperature.

9. (a) Place a number of black and red disks into a box. Reach into the box and pull out a handful of disks.

   (b) Use the disks to write an expression that contains two operations. Calculate your expression.

WORKING TOGETHER

Work with a partner and write a short paragraph to answer each.

A What do you think is meant by a computer getting sick?

B What do you think a *virus* is? What do you think a *computer virus* is?

C What do you think is meant by a *computer worm*? Use your library to find out. Why is it called a *computer worm*?

By learning how to create problems, you can become a better problem solver. When creating a problem, be sure that the following two questions can be answered.

- What are you asked to find?
- What are you given?

Using the same information, different people can create different problems. After you have completed the exercise, compare your problems with others in the class. Discuss how the problems are alike and how the problems are different.

EXERCISE

For each, add information to create a problem. Solve your problem.

1. (a) A freight train pulled 200 box cars. It took 2.5 h to arrive at its destination.

   (b) A computer with a keyboard, a monitor, and a printer sells for $1395. The screen sells for $395.

   (c) There were originally 24 cans in the case. There are now only 16 cans.

   (d) The temperature in Ioco was −3°C. The temperature in Truro was −5°C. The temperature in Victoria was 10°C.

   (e) The top of Mount Logan is about 2350 m above sea level. The top of the CN Tower is about 650 m above sea level.

   (f) The melting point of mercury is −38.9°C. The boiling point of mercury is 356°C.

For each, solve the problem and create a similar problem of your own.

2. (a) The sum of three different positive integers is +99. The smallest of the numbers is +32. Find the largest of the three numbers.

   (b) Four integers are placed in the magic square shown. The magic sum is +88. Copy and complete the magic square.

3. Use the cards shown below.

   (a) How many pairs of integers have a sum of +7?

   (b) How many groups of three cards have a sum of −10?

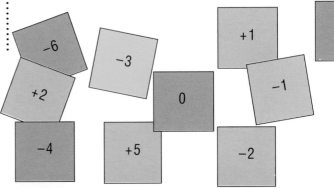

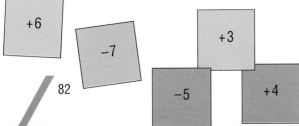

TECHNOLOGY INSIGHT: HOME OF THE FUTURE

Could the home of the future be in a tower more than 2 km above the ground? Could people travel between buildings on high speed computer-controlled rail systems?

This type of dwelling may be necessary because of the rapidly increasing world population. Estimates have put the world population at approximately 10 billion people by the year 2250.

Work together on the following questions. Use your imagination to think of how your world would change by the year 2250. Your library may help.

1. (a) What type of materials could be used to build towers as high as those described above?
   (b) Do you think solar panels would be used to help save energy? What other alternatives might there be?

2. It has been suggested that every home would one day have a computer.
   (a) Do you think there would be mail delivery or would every home receive mail by computer?
   (b) How can you ensure that mail is not read by someone else if it is delivered by computer?

3. It has been suggested that television screens would cover an entire wall.
   (a) What is a hologram?
   (b) Would you like to see a hologram image on a television screen that covers an entire wall? Give reasons for your answer.

4. In your journal, describe what you think a typical day would be like in the year 2250. Include, in your description, a job you would like, how you would travel to your job, and how technology would affect your job.

CHAPTER REVIEW

1. Write an integer to represent each.
   (a) scoring 10 points in a game
   (b) a walk of 2 km west   (c) a profit of $120

2. Replace ■ by < or > to make each true.
   (a) +6 ■ +2   (b) −2 ■ +3   (c) 0 ■ −4

3. Show the opposite of each integer on a number line.
   (a) +2   (b) −3   (c) +6

4. Write the next three integers in each pattern.
   (a) −2, −1, 0, +1, +2, . . .
   (b) +3, −2, +1, 0, +1, −2, . . .

5. Calculate.
   (a) (−9) + (+12)   (b) (−5) − (−14)   (c) (+8) − (+17)

6. Decide if the answer is positive or negative. Then calculate.
   (a) (+4) × (+7)   (b) (−18) ÷ (−3)   (c) (−27) ÷ (+3)
   (d) (+2) × (−9)   (e) (−11) ÷ (+11)   (f) (+8) × (−8)

7. Calculate.
   (a) (−5) + (−12) ÷ (−3)   (b) [(+8) − (−7)] ÷ (−5)
   (c) (+8)(−3) ÷ (−6)   (d) (−8) − (−4)(−2)

8. When a hockey player is on the ice and her team scores, she receives a +1. If the opposing team scores, she receives a −1. Find her score for each game using the chart below.

Team Scores	Opposition Scores
2 goals	1 goal
1 goal	3 goals
2 goals	0 goals
3 goals	1 goal

THINKING ABOUT

List any new problem solving strategies you learned in your Problem Solving Plan.

Summarize all relationships and patterns from this chapter in your journal.

Discuss with a partner how the skills with integers are like the skills with decimal numbers and how they are different.

MATH JOURNAL

Refer to a dictionary.
(a) Write the meaning of "positive" and "negative" using a dictionary.
(b) How are the words used in this chapter?
(c) How are your answers in (a) and (b) alike? How are they different?
(d) How confident are you with your skills with integers? What can you do if you need more help?

THE CHAPTER

Make a list of all skills and strategies you learned in this chapter. Write an example of each.

One memory aid for deciding on the sign of a product is shown. Can you make another?

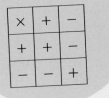

×	+	−
+	+	−
−	−	+

MAKING CONNECTIONS

Refer to the opening pages of the chapter.
(a) Create a problem using the pictures and the skills in this chapter.
(b) Solve your problem.
(c) Compare your problem with others in the class. Solve any new problems you see.

SELF EVALUATION

1. Write an integer to represent each.
   (a) a drop in temperature of 4°C
   (b) a jog of 2 km north

2. Write two other integers between each pair.
   (a) −1, +3   (b) −9, −4   (c) +2, −4

3. Use < or > to make each true.
   (a) (−4) ■ (+6)   (b) (+8) ■ (−5)   (c) (−5) ■ (−1)

4. Show the opposite of each integer on a number line.
   (a) −5   (b) +6   (c) −4   (d) −7

5. Write the integers in order from least to greatest.
   (a) −3, −5, +6, −6, +9   (b) +11, −7, +8, −11, −15

6. Calculate.
   (a) (+7) + (−3)   (b) (−5) + (−2)
   (c) (−10) + (+7)   (d) (−4) − (−3)
   (e) (−11) − (+8)   (f) (+12) − (−9)

7. Decide whether the answer is positive or negative. Then calculate.
   (a) (+30) ÷ (−6)   (b) (−4)(+7)
   (c) (−24) ÷ (−12)   (d) (−23) × 0
   (e) (−30)(−6)   (f) (−16) ÷ (−4)

8. A golf match was played. The scores were as follows.
   Frank +8   Lori −3   Rose +2
   Mike −1   Lesley +1
   The lowest score wins the tournament. Who won?

9. The temperature at 06:00 was −4°C. The temperature rose 2°C each hour until 11:00. What was the temperature at 11:00?

85

MATH IN THE CALGARY

Did you know that the motto of the Olympic games is "Citius-Altius-Fortius" which means "Faster-Stronger-Higher"? Athletes will spend a large part of their lives to become faster, stronger, and higher. Their reward is to compete in the Olympic games and, for the best of those athletes, a medal for winning a competition.

The Olympic games are held in different countries around the world. Both the summer and the winter Olympic games have been held in Canada. In 1976, the summer games were held in Montreal and in 1988, the winter games were held in Calgary. In the following problems, you will learn more about some of the individual achievements at the winter Olympic games in Calgary.

EXERCISE

A Use a calculator.

1. Matti Nykanen, nicknamed the "Flying Finn", won the most gold medals. The number of gold medals won is given by $[(-5) + (-4)] \div (-3)$.
   How many gold medals did the "Flying Finn" win?

2. On the 70 m ski jump, Eddie "the Eagle" jumped a distance of 55 m. He finished in last place 34.5 m behind the winner, Matti Nykanen.

   (a) Write an expression, using integers, to find how far Matti Nykanen jumped.

   (b) Evaluate your expression. How far was the winning jump?

3. The Olympic torch was carried by volunteers. Each carried the torch for 1 km. The number of volunteers is shown by the expression $(+700) - (-150) \times (+2)$.

   (a) How many volunteers carried the torch?

   (b) How many kilometres was the Olympic torch carried?

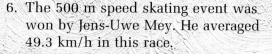
 B Review your skills with whole numbers and decimal numbers.

4. (a) Estimate how many medals can be won at an Olympic games.

   (b) The number of medals won is given by $(-355) \div (-5) + (+73)$. Evaluate the expression. How reasonable was your estimate?

5. Use your result from Question 4. Divide it by 28.8 to show the number of medals won by Canadians. How many medals did Canadians win?

6. The 500 m speed skating event was won by Jens-Uwe Mey. He averaged 49.3 km/h in this race.

   (a) What was his winning time?

   (b) The top Canadian was Guy Thibault. He was 0.5 s behind the winner.
   - What was his time?
   - What was his average speed?

7. In the women's combined skiing event, the winner earns the lowest score. Four Canadian women placed in the top 13. Their scores were:

   Nancy Gee $207.72 \div 12.00 + 86.55$
   Karen Percy $6.41 \times 6.00 + 12.28$
   M. McKendry $49.56 + 88.2 \div 6.30$
   Kerin Lee $22.38 + 45.97 - 3.09$

   The top Canadian finished fourth overall. Who was she?

8. The men's downhill ski race was won by Pirmin Zubriggen of Switzerland. His winning time was 1 min 59.63 s. His average speed down the course was 120 km/h. Find the length of the course.

Activity
List records established at the most recent Olympics. Create and solve problems based on those records.

3 EXPLORING PATTERNS AND

D id you know that mathematics can help explain card tricks? Look for a pattern in this card trick to find the secret in the trick.

Step 1 Using numbered cards, tiles, or a deck of playing cards, have a partner shuffle the cards and lay them out in a Q shape as shown. Any number of cards can be put in the tail of the Q.

Step 2 Tell your partner that you can predict the card at which he or she will finally stop in the next step. Write it on a piece of paper and put it in the middle of the Q.

Step 3 Have your partner count the cards clockwise, starting at the bottom of the tail of the Q. Have your partner stop anywhere and count the same number counterclockwise, but this time skipping the cards in the tail.

Step 4 Have your partner check the paper to see that the card recorded on it is indeed the card he or she finally stops at in step 3.

In your journal, describe how you think this trick is done.

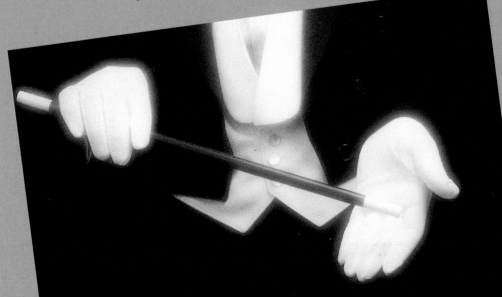

RELATIONSHIPS

Starting to the right of the tail, count to the right the same number of cards as contained in the tail. This will be the card at which your partner always stops.

3.1 EXPLORING NUMBER

Do you know the story *A Christmas Carol* by Charles Dickens? Bob Cratchit worked for Ebenezer Scrooge adding long columns of numbers.

Unfortunately, Bob Cratchit was never able to explore the patterns and relationships that existed in the numbers with which he worked. The following will help you explore patterns Bob Cratchit could not.

EXPLORATION ①   *Work with a Partner*

1. (a) Use square tiles to form the shapes shown below. How many tiles are there in all? How many tiles are in the length and width of each shape?

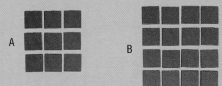

   (b) Suggest a relationship to find the number of tiles in each shape.

2. (a) Create other squares using tiles.
   (b) Repeat the steps of Question 1 for your squares.

EXPLORATION ②   *Work in a Group*

3. (a) Use square tiles to form the shapes shown below. How many tiles are there in all? How many tiles are in the length and width of each shape?

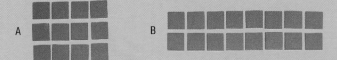

   (b) Suggest a relationship to find the number of tiles in each shape.

4. (a) Create other shapes using tiles.
   (b) Repeat the parts of Question 3 using your shapes.

EXPLORATION ③ *Work with a Partner*

5. (a) Place square tiles into a box.
    Step 1 Remove a handful of tiles and record the number.
    Step 2 Use the tiles to construct as many different rectangles as you can. Record the length and width of each rectangle.

   (b) Repeat the steps in (a) for other handfuls of tiles.

   (c) Use your results from (a) and (b). For which numbers can you construct only one rectangle? more than one rectangle?

6. Refer to all the rectangles constructed in the previous question.

   (a) Which rectangles have the same number of tiles for their length?

   (b) Which rectangles have different numbers of tiles for their length?

   (c) In your journal, suggest how the rectangles might be related.

EXPLORATION ④ *Work Together*

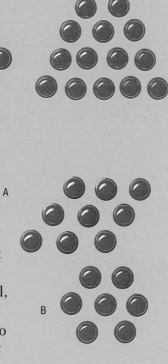

7. (a) Use counters to form the shapes shown. How many counters are there in each?

   (b) Suggest a pattern to find the number of counters in each shape.

8. (a) Create other triangles like those shown in Question 7.

   (b) Repeat the parts of Question 7 for your shapes.

EXPLORATION ⑤ *Work with a Partner*

9. Place counters into a box.

   (a) Remove a handful of counters and construct different shapes using the counters. Some shapes are shown.

   (b) Give each shape you construct a name. In your journal, explain why you named it as such.

   (c) Summarize any relationships you see. Use counters to show an example of your relationship. Compare your relationships with others in your class.

3.2 FACTOR SENSE

You see many different colours in this book. However, the printer used only four different ink colours: red, yellow, blue, and black. By mixing these **primary colours**, all other colours are created.

Similarly, in mathematics, there are **prime numbers**. Prime numbers are numbers for which tiles can be arranged to form only one rectangle. When tiles can be arranged to form more than one rectangle, the number is a **composite number**.

5 is a prime number

Think: Only one possible arrangement.

6 is a composite number

Think: More than one possible arrangement.

The length and width of each rectangle above show the **factors** of each number. The rectangles above suggest the following.

- A prime number has factors of 1 and itself. The factors of 5 are 1 and 5.

- A composite number has factors other than 1 and itself. The factors of 6 are 1, 2, 3, and 6.

To find the prime factors of a number, you can use your tiles. You can also use the following methods.

Use a Factor Tree

60
12 X 5
4 X 3 X 5
2 X 2 X 3 X 5

Think: Ask yourself whether each number is prime. If not, find its factors.

Thus, 60 = 2 × 2 × 3 × 5.

Use Division

```
2 | 60
2 | 30
3 | 15
    5
```

The prime factors of 60 are 2, 2, 3, and 5.

A Use tiles to help you.

1. (a) Form all possible rectangles for the numbers 3, 6, 11, 15, and 21.

   (b) Which numbers are prime? Which are composite?

2. (a) Form all possible rectangles for the numbers 4, 10, 20, and 25.

   (b) What are the factors of each number? the prime factors of each?

3. Write all the factors for each number.

   (a) 20   (b) 84   (c) 99   (d) 100   (e) 71   (f) 83

   (g) List all the prime numbers from 1 to 100.

B Review prime and composite numbers.

4. (a) Write all the prime factors of 30.

   (b) How can you use the prime factors to find the original number?

5. All the prime factors of a number are shown. What is the number?

   (a) 2, 3, 5   (b) 2, 2, 3, 3   (c) 3, 5, 7

MAKING CONNECTIONS

List some words that are based on the root word "prime". For example, primate. Write their meanings.

(a) How are the meanings of your words alike? How are they different?

(b) Why do you think prime numbers are named as such?

(c) Describe how large prime numbers are found. Then, use the method to find a large prime number.

6. Write the prime factors for each number.

   (a) The first female pilot flew in 1909.

   (b) The first motorcycle race took place from Paris to Nantes in 1896.

   (c) The first commercial radio broadcast took place in 1922.

7. Tanya practises swimming each day. She swims 750 m.

   (a) Find all factors of 750.

   (b) What is the most likely length of the pool? Give reasons for your answer.

8. Use the cards shown below.

   (a) How many three digit numbers can you create using the cards?

   (b) How many of the numbers you can create have 3 as a factor?

To practise for a tournament, Rob bought 12 tennis balls and Angela bought 9. The tennis balls come in packages; each package has the same number. Find the greatest possible number of tennis balls in each package.

Think: Construct the different rectangles for each number of tiles. The length and width of the rectangles are the factors of the number.

Factors of 12   **Factors of 9**

The factors of 12 are 1, 2, 3, 4, 6, 12.
The factors of 9 are   1, 3, 9.

Think: The length and width show the factors of 9 and 12.

You can interpret your factors to mean that there are at most 3 tennis balls in each package.

The **greatest common factor** of 9 and 12 is 3.

Tiles can also help you solve problems with multiples.

Rob and Angela play soccer. Rob's team plays every 3 d. Angela's team plays every 4 d. When will the teams play on the same day?

Think: You can use tiles to help you. A red tile means no game is played that day. A green tile means a game is played that day. When do green and red tiles line up?

Rob's Team   (multiples of 3)

Angela's Team (multiples of 4)

The multiples of 3 are 3, 6, 9, 12, 15, 18, 21, 24, . . .
The multiples of 4 are 4, 8, 12, 16, 20, 24, . . .

Think: Use a pattern.

The common multiples of 3 and 4 are 12, 24, 36, . . .
Thus, Rob and Angela will play on days 12, 24, 36, . . .

The **least common multiple** of 3 and 4 is 12.

A Use your tiles.

1. (a) Form as many rectangles as possible with 8 tiles; 12 tiles.
   (b) Use your results from (a). What are the factors of 8 and 12?
   (c) What is the greatest common factor of 8 and 12?

2. (a) Form as many rectangles as possible with 15 tiles; 25 tiles.
   (b) Use your results from (a). What are the factors of 15 and 25?
   (c) What is the greatest common factor of 15 and 25?

3. (a) List multiples of 3 and multiples of 5.
   (b) What is the least common multiple of 3 and 5?

4. (a) Find the greatest common factor of each pair.
       (i) 8, 4   (ii) 16, 24   (iii) 15, 18   (iv) 12, 18
   (b) Find the least common multiple of each pair.
       (i) 12, 18   (ii) 27, 45   (iii) 40, 50   (iv) 36, 27

B Review least common multiple and greatest common factor.

5. Laura and Paul bought packages of hockey cards. Laura has 24 cards. Paul has 20 cards.
   (a) Find the greatest common factor of 20 and 24.
   (b) Interpret your answer. How many cards do you think are in each package?

6. Short track speed skating was first introduced at the 1988 Winter Olympics. While warming up, Sylvie skated 444 m. Mario skated 777 m. How far around might the oval be? Give reasons for your answer.

7. Tom paid $3.00 for cartons of milk. Jan paid $3.75. How many cartons did each buy? Justify your answer.

8. In a marathon, Knud stops at every four water stops. Monique stops at every five water stops. At what point will they both stop for water if they run together? What assumptions have you made?

9. Work together. The toothpicks form three squares that are the same size.
   (a) Use these toothpicks to form six squares the same size and shape.
   (b) Create a similar problem using toothpicks. Compare your problem with others in your class.

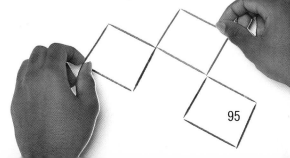

95

3.4 SQUARES AND SQUARE ROOTS

A square stamp has an area of 9 cm². Find the length of each side of the stamp.

The area of the stamp can be written as follows.

3 cm × 3 cm = 9 cm².

Think: What number, multiplied by itself, gives you 9? In this case, 3.

Thus, the length of the stamp is 3 cm.
- Since 3 × 3 = 9, 9 is called a **perfect square**.
- The numeral 3 is the **principal** or **positive square root** of 9.

You can use tiles to help you find square roots as shown below. Represent the number, using tiles, as a square. Then, find the length of one side of the square.

Think: The square root of 9 is 3.   Think: The square root of 16 is 4.

You can use square roots to help you solve problems.

The flag shown is square and has an area of 529 cm². Find the length of the flag.

Think: Interpret what you are given.
- The flag is square. It covers an area of 529 cm².
- Use guess and check to solve.

Estimate	Product	Equal to 529?
21	21 × 21 = 441	Too Low.
25	25 × 25 = 625	Too High.
23	23 × 23 = 529	Correct.

Thus, the flag has a length of 23 cm.

You can use the $\boxed{\sqrt{}}$ key on your calculator to solve the problem as shown.

$\boxed{\text{c}}$ 529 $\boxed{\sqrt{}}$ 23

Think: The symbol $\sqrt{}$ is used to show the principal square root.

A Use your tiles to help you.

1. Find the principal square root of each number.
   (a) 9   (b) 16   (c) 49   (d) 81

2. (a) Write each number as a product of its prime factors.
       (i) 25   (ii) 49   (iii) 121   (iv) 169
   (b) What do you notice about your answers?
   (c) Use your answers from (a) to help you calculate each.
       (i) $\sqrt{25}$ (ii) $\sqrt{49}$ (iii) $\sqrt{121}$ (iv) $\sqrt{169}$

3. Use your calculator to find each of the following.
   (a) $\sqrt{125}$ (b) $\sqrt{215}$ (c) $\sqrt{4.41}$ (d) $\sqrt{1.69}$

4. Find the length of each side of the square mat.
   (a)   (b)   (c)

   25 m²   16 m²   1.44 m²

B Use a calculator.

5. Wrestling is usually performed on a square mat with area 144 m². What are the dimensions of the mat?

6. The area of a square stamp is 2.89 cm². What are its dimensions?

7. A warehouse has an area of 2940 m². It is divided into 15 equal square sections. Find the dimensions of each section.

8. Surinam, in South America, is roughly shaped like a square. It covers an area of about 100 489 km². Find the length of each side of Surinam.

9. The earliest carpet found is a square Seythian woollen carpet made about 4 BC. It covers an area of 3.24 m². What is the length of each side?

10. You can use manipulatives to help you solve a problem. Read and solve this problem. *You have a piece of paper 8 cm by 18 cm. You need to form a square with an area of 144 cm². Find the least number of cuts needed.*

3.5 EXPLORING FACTORS

You have learned how to find the prime factors of a number. In this section, you will explore ways to determine if a number is a factor of a given number. As you complete each exploration, use your journal to
- summarize any relationships.
- write an example to describe the relationship.

EXPLORATION ①   *Factors of 2*

1. (a) For which numbers can you use tiles to form a rectangle with a length of 2?

    9   24   25   38   50   16   46

   (b) Interpret your answers from (a). Which numbers have a factor of 2?

   (c) What characteristic suggests a number has a factor of 2?

EXPLORATION ②   *Factors of 5*

2. (a) For which numbers can you use tiles to form a rectangle with a length of 5?

    10   40   15   55   70   75   25   88

   (b) Interpret your answers from (a). Which numbers have a factor of 5?

   (c) What characteristic suggests a number has a factor of 5?

EXPLORATION ③   *Factors of 3 and 9*

3. (a) A number that has a factor of 3 is divisible by 3. Which numbers have a factor of 3?

    3618   4842   8684   4202   2691   2463

   (b) For each number in (a), find the sum of the digits. Which sums have a factor of 3?

   (c) Write a test for deciding whether a number is divisible by 3.

4. (a) A number that has a factor of 9 is divisible by 9. Which numbers have a factor of 9?

    441   8639   48 213   96 322

   (b) For each number in (a), find the sum of the digits. Which sums have a factor of 9?

   (c) Write a test for deciding whether a number is divisible by 9.

Factors of 4 and 8

5. (a) A number that has a factor of 4 is divisible by 4. Which numbers have a factor of 4?

   6324   4862   9632   38 964   29 443

   (b) Use the last 2 digits of each number. Which of these numbers are divisible by 4?

   (c) Compare your answers from (a) and (b). What relationship helps you decide whether a number is divisible by 4?

   (d) Write a test for deciding whether a number is divisible by 4.

6. (a) A number that has a factor of 8 is divisible by 8. Which numbers have a factor of 8?

   8112   49 244   89 156   38 108   96 126

   (b) Use the last 3 digits of each number. Which of these numbers are divisible by 8?

   (c) Compare your answers from (a) and (b). What relationship helps you decide whether a number is divisible by 8?

   (d) Write a test for deciding whether a number is divisible by 8.

Factors of 6

7. (a) Which numbers have 2 as a factor and 3 as a factor?

   40   42   55   72   75   66   84

   (b) Which number(s) in (a) have 6 as a factor?

   (c) What relationship would you use to decide if a number has a factor of 6?

Your Own Exploration

When is a number divisible by 25?

8. (a) Choose numbers that are multiples of 25. Use a calculator to verify that they have 25 as a factor. Then choose numbers that are not multiples of 25.

   (b) Use your results from (a). Construct a divisibility test to determine if a number has 25 as a factor.

   (c) Check your test using the following numbers. Does it work?

   75   160   225   5275   6430   8525   9650   12 348

3.6 PROBLEM SOLVING: COMBINING SKILLS

Sometimes, you need to combine your problem solving skills to solve problems.

 For example, divide the square shown into four equal parts in different ways.

Look for a Pattern

Work Backwards

Solve a Simpler Problem

Solve a Similar Problem

Guess and Check

Use Manipulatives

Draw a Diagram

1. Think About the Problem.

(a) Think of what you must find.
  • How to divide a square into four equal parts.

(b) Think of what you are given.
  • The square above.

2. Think About a Strategy.

(a) Think of a strategy you could use.
  • Cut a square from a piece of paper.
  • Try various cuts to see if they work.

(b) Think of a reason for your strategy.
  • Guessing a solution and using manipulatives to check if it will lead to possible solutions.

3. Work It Out.

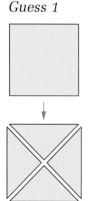

Guess 1

Four equal pieces.

Guess 2

Four equal pieces.

Guess 3

Four equal pieces.

4. Think About Your Solution.

Three solutions are shown above. Find any others.

B Use your *Problem Solving Plan.*

1. (a) List different ways to find the square root of a number.

   (b) Find the square root of each number.
   (i) 75   (ii) 144   (iii) 729
   (iv) 22.09 (v) 12.96 (vi) 282.24

2. A triangle with all sides the same length is shown.

   (a) Make a larger copy of the triangle.

   (b) Cut it into 2 equal pieces in 3 different ways.

3. (a) Copy the letter shown onto grid paper.

   (b) Use 3 straight cuts to cut the letter so that the pieces form a square.

4. Draw a circle.

   (a) Find the greatest number of parts you can divide the circle into using
   • 1 line segment.
   • 2 line segments.

   (b) Predict the greatest number of parts you can divide the circle into using 10 line segments.

5. Use the toothpick pattern shown.

   (a) Move exactly 4 toothpicks to form exactly 6 squares.

   (b) Move exactly 4 toothpicks to form exactly 5 squares.

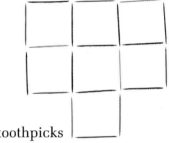

6. Place four pennies into a pattern so that each penny is the same distance from all other pennies.

WORKING TOGETHER

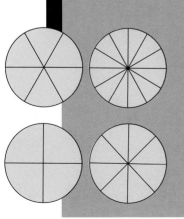

Try this game with two other players.
1. Cut four large circles into parts as shown to the left.
2. Put the pieces into a box. Each player takes ten pieces.
3. The players take turns to put down one piece at a time to complete a circle.
4. If a player does not have a piece that fits the circle, the player passes. The player who puts the last piece of the circle in place wins.

Have you ever heard the expression "a picture is worth a thousand words"? A picture is also worth a thousand clues when it helps you solve problems.

For example, Lori takes the bus to school. As she entered the school on one particularly windy day, she saw the people in this picture. How many of those people do you think walked to school?

On a windy day, the people who walk to school would likely have their hair blown about. There are three people with wind blown hair. Thus, it appears that three people walked to school.

A number of pictures are shown. A question accompanies each picture.

- Answer the question related to each picture. Give reasons for your answers.
- Compare your answers with others.
    How are the answers alike?
    How are they different?

1. Rollo's class was assigned a project on one of the following topics: the African elephant, oil fields, parachutes, the Sahara Desert. Which topic do you think Rollo chose?

2. This shows a scene on a day in February. Do you think it is safe to skate on the river?

3. What time of day was the picture taken?

4. Look at the photograph. Which building is the tallest?

5. In your journal, describe when you would use a picture to help you solve a problem.

6. Often, pictures are shown so that they imply information to the viewer. Use a picture of your own.

   (a) Create a question based on the information in the picture.

   (b) Compare your question with others in the class. Answer the other questions.

   (c) Create a class bulletin board of your pictures and the problems created.

To work with geometry, you need to know the relationships between figures and angles. Some of these relationships are shown below. As you complete each exploration, record in your journal any relationships you think about.

To look for relationships, you need to measure angles using a protractor as shown.

Place the centre of the protractor on B. Align the arm marked 0° along one ray. Read the angle as shown below.

∠ABF = 45°   ∠ABE = 90°
∠ABD = 150°   ∠ABC = 180°

What is the measure of ∠FBE? of any other angles?

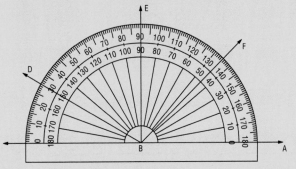

Think: ∠ABC is a **straight angle**.

EXPLORATION ① *Work Together*

1. (a) Measure ∠PQS and ∠ABC. Find the sum.
   (b) Trace the angles using tracing paper. Cut them out. Place arm QS along arm BA. What is the measure of the total angle?
   (c) What do you notice about your sum in (a) and your measure in (b)?

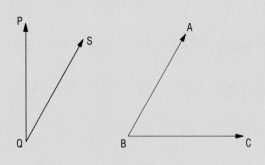

2. The two angles shown in Question 1 are **complementary angles**.
   (a) Suggest a relationship that determines if two angles are complementary.
   (b) Draw pairs of complementary angles, placing them at random on your paper. Have a partner match the pairs.
   (c) Collect pictures that suggest complementary angles. Start a collage using the pictures and identify the pairs of complementary angles.

EXPLORATION ② *Work in Groups*

3. (a) Measure ∠PQS and ∠ABC. Find the sum.
   (b) Trace the angles using tracing paper. Cut them out. Place arm PQ along arm AB. What is the measure of ∠SQC?
   (c) What do you notice about your sum in (a) and your measure in (b)?

4. The two angles shown in Question 3 are **supplementary angles**.
   (a) Suggest a relationship that determines if two angles are supplementary.
   (b) Draw pairs of supplementary angles, placing them at random on your paper. Have a partner match the pairs.
   (c) Collect pictures that suggest supplementary angles. Start a collage using the pictures and identify the pairs of supplementary angles.

EXPLORATION ③ *Work in Groups*

5. (a) Trace the intersecting lines shown.
   (b) Name two pairs of opposite angles.
   (c) Fold ∠AED onto ∠BEC. What do you notice?
   (d) Fold ∠DEC onto ∠AEB. What do you notice?

6. **Opposite angles** are formed by two intersecting lines. They share a vertex.
   (a) Suggest a relationship for the measures of opposite angles.
   (b) Draw intersecting lines of your own. Identify the opposite angles on your diagram and write their measures.
   (c) Compare your diagram with others in the class. What do you notice?
   (d) What relationships do you notice for opposite angles?

EXPLORATION ④ *Work with a Partner*

7. **Adjacent angles** share a common vertex and ray, and their interiors do not intersect.
   (a) Name four pairs of adjacent angles in the picture.
   (b) What other types of angles do you see?

Previously, you explored the relationship between complementary angles and between supplementary angles.

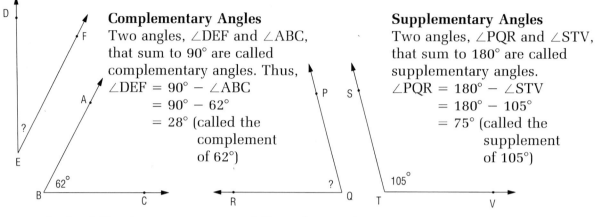

Complementary Angles
Two angles, ∠DEF and ∠ABC, that sum to 90° are called complementary angles. Thus,
∠DEF = 90° − ∠ABC
= 90° − 62°
= 28° (called the
complement
of 62°)

Supplementary Angles
Two angles, ∠PQR and ∠STV, that sum to 180° are called supplementary angles.
∠PQR = 180° − ∠STV
= 180° − 105°
= 75° (called the
supplement
of 105°)

In the following activity, your skills with complementary angles and supplementary angles are used to create an object. In your journal, summarize how complementary and supplementary angles are used.

Activity
Seven pieces of paper are shaped as shown.
1. Copy and cut out each piece.
2. Put the pieces of paper together so that the angles formed by the edges are either complementary or supplementary angles.
3. What shape have you created?

EXERCISE

A Use the object formed in the activity.

1. Measure the angles formed by the adjoining pieces. Identify all complementary angles and supplementary angles.

2. (a) Use any strip of paper. Cut it into 2 parts.
   (b) Measure the angles formed by the cut.
   (c) Do your angles form complementary or supplementary angles?

3. Find the missing measure in each.

(a)

(b)

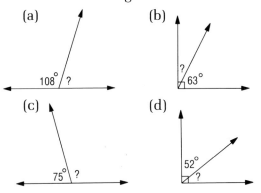

(c)

(d)

4. Find the complement of each angle.

(a) 20°   (b) 50°   (c) 15°

5. Find the supplement of each angle.

(a) 23°   (b) 150°   (c) 115°

6. A piece of wood is shown. At what angle would you cut another piece to

(a) form complementary angles?

(b) form supplementary angles?

7. Find the missing measure in each.

(a)

(b)

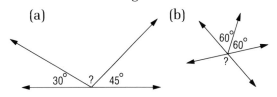

8. Two strips of paper are shown.

(a) At what angle would you cut one strip so that both complementary angles and supplementary angles can be formed with the other strip?

(b) Copy and cut the strips. Show how you would form the angles.

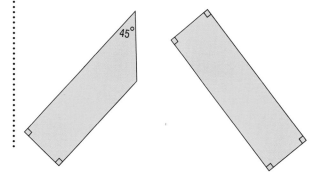

MAKING CONNECTIONS

Elizabeth Berry was born in 1965 and has worked for both Michael Jackson and George Michael as a lighting engineer. Thanks to her, the entertainers' concerts were spectacular visually as well as musically.

(a) What do you think a lighting engineer does? What other careers might make use of these skills?

(b) List and discuss with others the math skills that might be used by a lighting engineer.

(c) In your journal, describe how lighting is used to make a more effective concert.

The drawing of the evergreen tree shows a triangle. What type of triangle is it? In the following explorations, you will explore relationships for classifying triangles. Write your observations and classifications in your journal.

EXPLORATION ① Work with a Partner

An **equilateral triangle** is a triangle with three sides equal in length.

1. Use tracing paper to copy and cut out equilateral △ABC.

   (a) Put your copy on top of △ABC to the right. Place ∠A over ∠B, ∠B over ∠C, and ∠C over ∠A.

   (b) What do you notice about the angle measures?

2. Repeat Question 1 for other equilateral triangles of your own.

EXPLORATION ② Work Together

An **isosceles triangle** is a triangle with two sides equal in length.

3. Draw any isosceles triangle PQR so that PQ is the same length as PR.

   (a) Fold your triangle so that side PR lies on side PQ.

   (b) What do you notice about ∠R and ∠Q?

4. Repeat Question 3 for isosceles triangles of your own. Suggest a relationship between the angle measures of an isosceles triangle.

EXPLORATION ③ *Work in a Group*

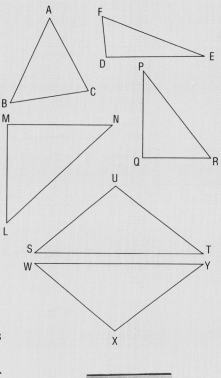

5. The triangles shown are **scalene**.

   (a) Measure the side lengths of each triangle. What do you notice?

   (b) Measure the angles in each triangle. What do you notice?

   (c) Use your results. How would you classify a scalene triangle?

6. Use the triangles shown.

   (a) How are the triangles alike? How are they different?

   (b) How else can you classify these triangles?

EXPLORATION ④ *Work in Pairs*

7. Draw and cut out any triangle. Label the angles as shown.

   (a) Tear off the three angles and fit them together as shown. Find the sum of the angles.

   (b) Use your results from (a). Predict the sum of the angles in a triangle.

   (c) Repeat parts (a) and (b) for other triangles.

8. Draw any equilateral triangle. Label the angles as shown below and fold the triangle.

   (a) Fold ∠1 down to touch its "opposite" side.

   (b) Fold ∠2 and ∠3 to touch ∠1. What type of angle have you formed? What is its measure?

   (c) Suggest a relationship for the sum of the angles in a triangle.

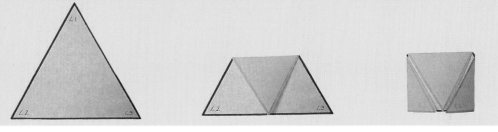

B

?

40°

A

25°

C

3.11 SOLVING PROBLEMS

Angles help strengthen a crane. Did you know that the angles are adjusted automatically as the crane moves to keep its mass distributed evenly?

Two such angles are shown on the crane. Find the missing measure of the third angle.

In the previous exploration, you found that the sum of the angles in any triangle is 180°. To find the missing measure, you can use this fact.

From the diagram, $\angle A + \angle C = 65°$.
Thus, $\angle B = 180° - 65°$
$= 115°$

The missing measure is 115°.

EXERCISE

A Review the sum of the angles in a triangle.

1. (a) How are $\angle A$, $\angle B$, and $\angle C$ related?

   (b) Find the measure of $\angle B$.

2. Find the measures of the missing angles.

   (a)   (b)

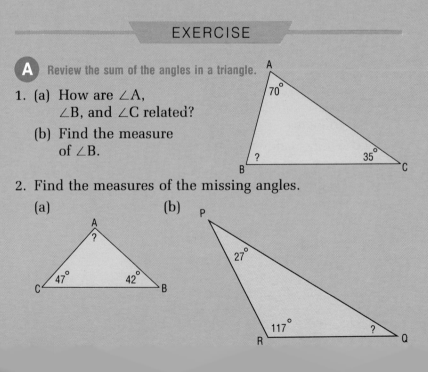

3. Measure the sides of each triangle. Classify each triangle.

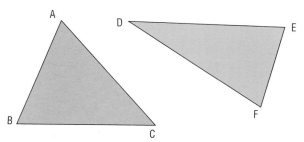

4. Measure the angles of each triangle. Classify each triangle.

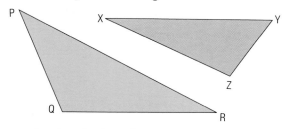

5. A triangle has these properties.
   $\angle H = 35°$ $\angle J = 45°$ $HJ = 5$ cm

   (a) Draw a sketch of the triangle.

   (b) Find the missing angle measure.

6. (a) Construct $\triangle ABC$ so that AB = BC = 12 cm and AC = 6 cm.

   (b) Classify the triangle.

   (c) Measure only one angle. Find the measures of the other two angles.

7. For strength, a bridge is constructed using beams that form triangles. Find all missing angle measures. (Hint: Look for a pattern.)

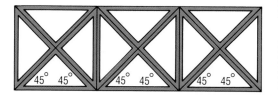

8. The following figures can each be made using isosceles triangles. Work with a partner.

   (a) Copy and cut out each shape.

   (b) Find the least number of triangles needed to construct each figure.

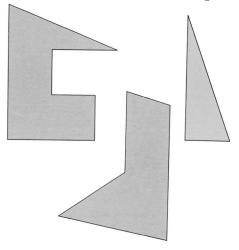

9. Shown below are straws that represent the sides of triangles.

   (a) Construct as many triangles as you can.

   (b) Name each triangle. Explain why you named it as such.

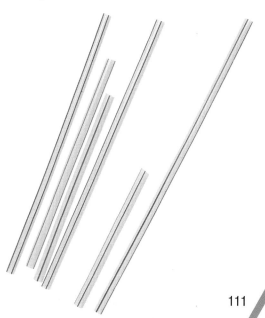

111

Previously, you explored the relationships in a triangle. In this section, you will explore the relationships between two triangles. Use tracing paper to complete each exploration.

EXPLORATION ① *Slides*

1. A triangle is placed at position S and slid to position F.
   (a) Describe different ways the triangle can go from S to F.
   (b) How are the triangles alike? How are they different?

2. (a) List pairs of angles in S and F that correspond. Compare their measures. What do you notice?
   (b) List pairs of segments in S and F that correspond. Compare their measures. What do you notice?

EXPLORATION ② *Flips*

3. A triangle is placed at S and flipped over line ℓ to F.
   (a) Describe how the triangle can go from S to F.
   (b) How are the triangles alike? How are they different?

4. (a) List pairs of angles in S and F that correspond. Compare their measures. What do you notice?
   (b) List pairs of segments in S and F that correspond. Compare their measures. What do you notice?

5. (a) Draw a triangle of your own on tracing paper and label it S. Move your triangle to a new position, F.
   (b) Repeat Questions 1, 2, 3, and 4 for your triangles.

EXPLORATION ③ Turns

6. A triangle is placed at S and turned around O to F.

   (a) Describe how the triangle can go from S to F.

   (b) How are the triangles alike? How are they different?

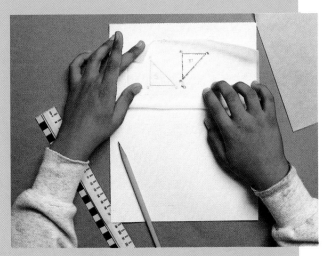

7. (a) List pairs of angles in S and F that correspond. Compare their measures. What do you notice?

   (b) List pairs of segments in S and F that correspond. Compare their measures. What do you notice?

8. (a) Draw a triangle of your own on tracing paper and label it S. Turn your triangle around any point, O, to a new position, F.

   (b) Repeat Questions 6 and 7 for your triangles.

EXPLORATION ④ Discuss with a Partner

9. (a) Pick a triangle below and trace it onto tracing paper.

   (b) Use your triangle from (a). Find other triangles shown below to which your triangle can be "moved".

   (c) Describe different ways that (b) can be done.

   (d) Repeat the above, starting with a different triangle from below.

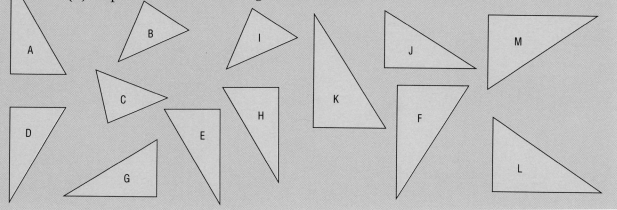

Did you know that artists and designers often use mathematics in their work? Work with a partner to complete the activities and summarize your observations in your journal.

ACTIVITY ① Poster Paint

Have you ever looked for designs and patterns in "ink blots"?

1. Some blots are shown in the pictures below.
   (a) What shapes do you see in each?
   (b) Trace one shape that you think can be used to create the complete picture. Label it S.
   (c) Describe different ways that S can move to create the complete picture.

2. (a) Follow the steps shown to the left to create blots of your own. Complete the parts of Question 1 for your blots.
   (b) Compare your blots with others in the class. How are they alike? How are they different?

ACTIVITY ② *Using a Stencil*

3. Use a piece of cardboard.
   (a) Cut out any shape.
   (b) On a large sheet of paper, trace your shape a number of times to create a design.
   (c) In your journal, describe the transformation techniques you used to create your design.
   (d) Repeat parts (a) to (c) to create other designs.

ACTIVITY ③ *Creating a Design*

4. The covers on books, tapes, and compact discs are designed to catch your eye. In the covers shown below, transformation techniques have been used in their design.
   (a) In your journal, describe the transformation techniques used.
   (b) Do you find the covers catchy? Why?
   (c) Design a similar cover of your own. Ask others in the class to offer suggestions for improvement and modify it as needed.

115

3.14 PROBLEM SOLVING: EXTRA INFORMATION

To solve some problems, you need to decide what information is relevant. Sometimes, extra information is given that is not really needed.

In the exercise, you will find some information is extra. Write it under the heading **Irrelevant Information**. Then solve the problem. In your journal, describe how you determined that this information is irrelevant.

EXERCISE

 B Use your *Problem Solving Plan*.

For each problem below,
- decide which information is extra.
- solve the problem.

1. Dave practises swimming each day. He swims 650 m. He also practises his start off the blocks.
   (a) Find all factors of 650.
   (b) What is the most likely length of the pool?

2. Raji and Genette each have $1.00. Raji spent 48¢ on gum. Genette spent 80¢ on gum. Each package of gum costs the same. How much does each package cost?

3. Fran and Carla practise karate 4 h each day. The karate mat is square and has an area of 64 m². Find the dimensions of the mat.

4. Carlene has these toothpicks left in a box. She scatters them on her desk. How can she use the toothpicks to form exactly five squares?

For each problem below,
- solve the problem.
- rewrite the problem with extra information.

5. Jeremy travels 48 km to practice each day. Of this, he travels 16 km on the highway. He has 220 practice days each year. How many kilometres does he travel to practice each year?

6. Marlene opened her piggy bank to buy a case of juice for $5.40. She had $3.60 in nickels and dimes. If the dimes had been nickels and the nickels dimes, she would have had enough money. How many nickels did Marlene have?

7. Use your library to find the length and width of each place.
   - Soho Square, London
   - Plaza de Mayo, Buenos Aries
   (a) Are the places squares? If so, find the dimensions.
   (b) If not, then how could you redesign the place so that it is square?

Your world is changing rapidly because of new developments in technology, particularly computer technology. Computers are involved in a surprising number of products. For example, even though VCRs and microwave ovens are not called computers, they are operated using computer chips.

But is there a limit to what computers can do? The activities help you explore this question.

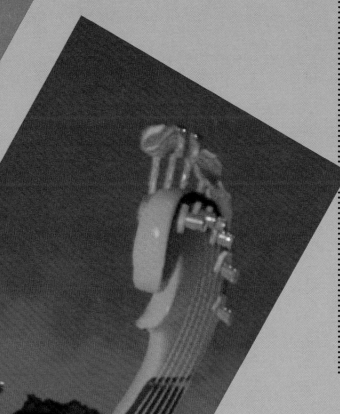

1. Computers are used in industrial design.
   (a) Describe how you think computers can help an industrial designer.
   (b) List some of the advantages and disadvantages of designing machines on a computer.

2. Pilots can practise handling certain situations on a flight simulator.
   (a) What is a flight simulator?
   (b) List some of the advantages and disadvantages of using a flight simulator instead of a real airplane.

3. A computer graphic is shown.
   (a) Describe how you think the picture was created on a computer screen.
   (b) Suppose you are an artist. Would you prefer to work on a computer or on a canvas? Give reasons for your answer.

4. Use your library to find another use for the computer. In your journal,
   (a) describe the computer's function.
   (b) write a paragraph telling how you feel about its function. Do you agree with the function of the computer? Can you see any way to improve its function?

CHAPTER REVIEW

1. Which of the following are prime numbers?

    (a) 10   (b) 11   (c) 21   (d) 24

2. Find the greatest common factor of each pair.

    (a) 10, 14   (b) 15, 30   (c) 18, 24

3. Find the least common multiple of each pair.

    (a) 6, 8   (b) 17, 34   (c) 15, 20

4. Which numbers have a factor of 3?

    (a) 6395   (b) 3538   (c) 9486   (d) 4617

5. A race is run on an oval track with two turns. A race car is built so that the steering wheel will last 150 full turns. The race is 500 km. What is the most likely distance around the track? Give reasons for your answer.

6. Find the missing measures in the diagram below.

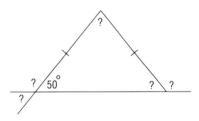

7. Find each of the following numbers.

    (a) The number has the digits 1, 2, 3, and 5, and has 8 and 2 as factors.

    (b) The number has the digits 1, 3, 6, and 8, and has 9 and 3 as factors.

8. A field has an area of 9720 m². To make more money, a farmer divides the field into 30 equal square plots and rents them. Find the dimensions of each plot.

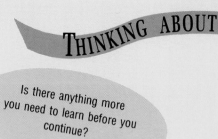

Is there anything more you need to learn before you continue?

What else would you like to know about prime numbers? Share your ideas with a partner.

How can you work with a small group to review the skills in this chapter?

MAKING CONNECTIONS

Refer to the opening pages of the chapter.

(a) Create a problem of your own using the pictures. Solve the problem using the skills in this chapter.

(b) Compare your problem with others in your class. Solve the other problems.

What kinds of problems are still difficult for you? How can you get help?

What do you do when you come to a "dead end" and think you can go no further?

How would you rate your knowledge of geometry? What part of it can you improve?

MATH JOURNAL

In this chapter, you have explored many patterns and relationships.
- List all patterns and relationships.
- Write an example to illustrate each.

SELF EVALUATION

1. Which of the following are composite numbers?

   (a) 31   (b) 27   (c) 49   (d) 51

2. Find the greatest common factor of each pair of numbers.

   (a) 12, 24   (b) 8, 12   (c) 36, 80

3. Write each as a product of prime factors.

   (a) 12   (b) 35   (c) 36   (d) 54

4. At the hockey game, every eighteenth person receives a puck and every twelfth person receives a team poster.

   (a) Which person(s) receive both a puck and a poster?

   (b) Suppose 22 people received both a puck and a poster. What is the most likely number of people at the game? Give reasons for your answer.

5. There are 398 people waiting at the airport. Each taxi holds 3 people.

   (a) Is 398 divisible by 3?

   (b) Interpret your result. Will any taxi leave the airport without 3 people?

6. What transformation is used so that $\triangle$XYZ is moved to each image in colour?

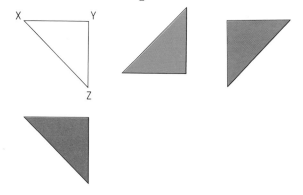

PRACTICE: CUMULATIVE REVIEW

1. Write the decimal numbers in order from least to greatest.
   (a) 0.125, 1.25, 1.025, 1.52   (b) 30.9, 33.09, 3.3339, 3.039
   (c) Round the greatest number in (a) and (b) to one decimal place.

2. Calculate.
   (a) 3.8 − 2.47 + 3.32 + 0.25   (b) 45.3 × 0.86 × 10 × 1000
   (c) 5.21 + 9.3 ÷ 3 − 1.7 × 4.1   (d) 9.18 ÷ (3.75 − 2.84) ÷ 7.2

3. Evaluate.
   (a) −8 + 5   (b) −24 − 27   (c) 36 × (−7)
   (d) −50 ÷ −10   (e) −6 × 3 + 4 ÷ 2   (f) (18 − 8 × 2) ÷ (−2)

4. The population of Halifax was once listed as 490 000. To what place value does the population appear to have been rounded? Give reasons for your answer.

5. Nora earned $98.19. She saved $24 and spent the rest equally on a book, a pair of shoes, and a sweater. How much did the sweater cost?

6. The temperature in a room dropped from 20°C to −4°C. When a heater was turned on, it raised the temperature 3°C every 20 min. How long did it take the temperature of the room to reach 20°C again?

7. Each day, Bill and Peter collected bottles to recycle. Each person collected the same number of bottles as he did the day before. Eventually, Peter had collected 221 bottles and Bill had collected 306 bottles.
   (a) What is the most likely number of bottles collected by each person each day? Give reasons for your answer.
   (b) What is the most likely number of days they took to collect all the bottles? Give reasons for your answer.

CALCULATION SENSE

Copy and complete the following.

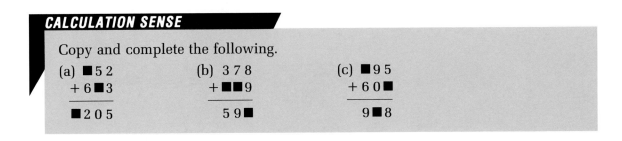

(a) ■5 2
   + 6 ■3
   ―――――
    ■2 0 5

(b) 3 7 8
   + ■■9
   ―――――
     5 9■

(c) ■9 5
   + 6 0■
   ―――――
    9■8

120

1. Brian and Sanda were to run for 1 h. After 20 min, Brian was leading by 6 m. During the next 40 min, Sanda ran 4 m farther than Brian. Who ran further in one hour?

2. (a) How many triangles are there in the figure to the right?

   (b) Create a similar problem. Compare your problem with others in your class.

3. Jana's horse is in a field 106.5 m long and 49.7 m wide. A fence is built around the field with posts placed 7.1 m apart. How many posts are needed to complete the fence?

4. Work with a partner.

   (a) How many metres can you walk in one second?

   (b) How long do you think you would take to walk around the equator?

5. A glass of soda is shown to the right.

   (a) Decide how you can share exactly half of the glass without measuring it.

   (b) Use your steps in (a) for a cylinder full of water. Was your plan successful?

6. (a) Find the greatest common factor of 14 and 63. Then divide 63 − 14 by your answer. What do you notice?

   (b) Find the greatest common factor of 24 and 72. Divide 72 − 24 by your answer. What do you notice?

   (c) Find the greatest common factor of 126 and 108. Divide 126 − 108 by your answer. What do you notice?

   (d) Based on your answers from (a) to (c), what result appears to be true?

4 The Nature of Math

Scientists need quick and easy ways of expressing very large and very small numbers. Think of some objects that are very large or very small. List them in your journal and estimate the size of each.

Then, refer to the pictures on these pages. They are pictures of everyday objects. Predict what object each picture represents and estimate the actual size of each.

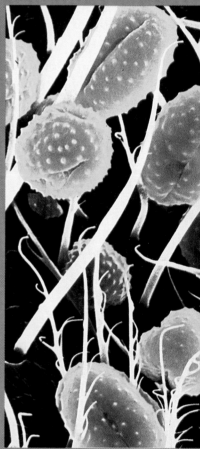

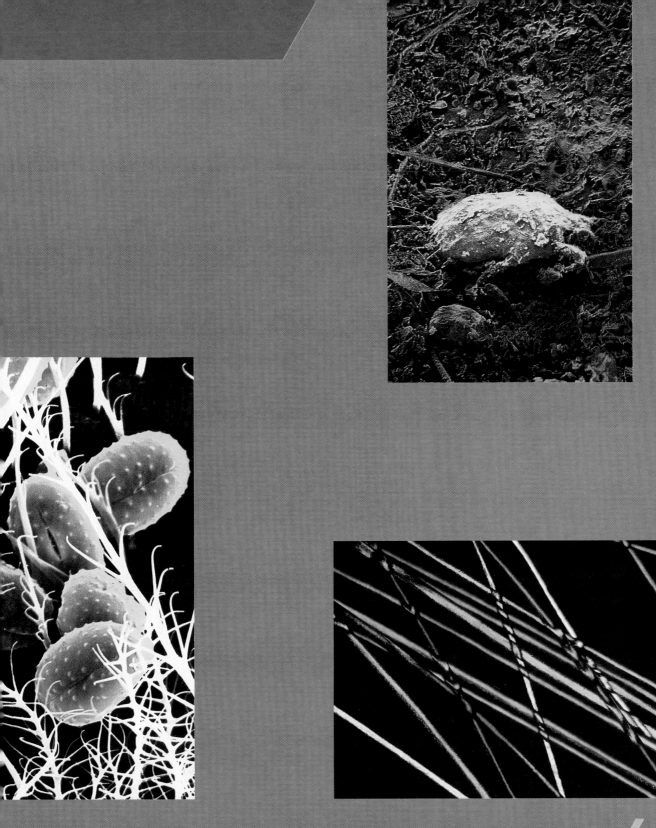

In mathematics, you can often discover relationships by organizing information and looking for patterns. In the explorations below, decide on the best way to organize your work. In your journal, describe any relationships you notice.

EXPLORATION ① Work with a Partner

1. Use a rectangular piece of paper. Fold the piece of paper in half and then open it.

   (a) How many times have you folded the paper?

   (b) Into how many equal parts is the paper divided?

2. Use another rectangular piece of paper. Fold the paper in half once, then in half again, and open it.

   (a) How many times have you folded the paper?

   (b) Into how many equal parts is the paper divided?

3. (a) Repeat the parts of Question 2 by folding another piece of paper in half three times and then another piece of paper in half four times.

   (b) Into how many equal parts is each paper divided?

4. (a) Fold a piece of paper in half as many times as you like.

   (b) Have your partner predict the number of equal parts into which the paper will be divided. Open up the paper to check the prediction.

EXPLORATION ② Work in a Group

5. (a) Start with one penny. Use one penny to double its height.

   (b) Use enough pennies to double the height in (a). How many pennies do you have?

6. (a) How many times will you need to double the height of one penny to have at least $10? to have at least $20?

   (b) How many times will you need to double the height of one penny to match your own height? How many pennies are there?

4.2 EXPONENTS

When you fold a single piece of paper in half, you obtain two equal parts. When you fold the two equal parts in half, you obtain four equal parts. If this process is continued three more times, the number of equal parts is found as follows.

$$2 \times 2 \times 2 \times 2 \times 2 = 32$$

Expressions like the one above can be written in a more compact form. Look for patterns in the chart.

Factor Form	Exponent Form
$2 \times 2 \times 2 \times 2 \times 2$	2^5 ←
$(+4) \times (+4) \times (+4)$	$(+4)^3$
$(-6) \times (-6)$	$(-6)^2$

Think: 5 is the number of times 2 is repeated. It is read as "two to the exponent five".

Before starting the exercise, refer to the explorations on the previous page. Write in exponent form the numerals used in each exploration.

EXERCISE

A Use your journal to summarize all relationships.

1. Write each in exponent form. Then evaluate.
   (a) 3×3 (b) $(-4) \times (-4)$ (c) $2 \times 2 \times 2$ (d) $(-6) \times (-6) \times (-6)$

2. Write each as a repeated multiplication. Then evaluate.
   (a) 3^4 (b) $(-4)^3$ (c) 6^2 (d) 8^3 (e) 10^2 (f) $(-5)^4$

B Work together.

3. Find the value of each number written in exponent form.
   (a) In 16 min 52.66 s, Reg Morris ate 3^3 kippers.
   (b) The most complex Scottish dance ever held involved 4^4 people.

4. Find the number of small squares on a checkerboard. Write it in exponent form.

5. When a single cell divides, you obtain two new cells. When the two new cells divide, you obtain four new cells. How many new cells will you have if the process is continued eight more times?

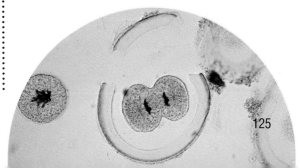

In mathematics, words are often used to describe relationships. When a number is written in exponent form, each part has a special name as shown to the right.

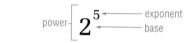

power $\rightarrow 2^5 \leftarrow$ exponent, base

When communicating with exponents, you can use special words.

You can read 4^2 as "four squared".

Think: You can visually think of 4^2 using this square. Remember. $4^2 = 16$

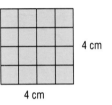

4 cm

4 cm

You can read 4^3 as "four cubed".

Think: You can visually think of 4^3 using this cube. Remember. $4^3 = 64$

4 cm

4 cm   4 cm

Your skills with exponents can be used to solve problems like the following.

Fred has one pet gremlin and Jan has one pet gremlin. The gremlins double when fed after midnight. Fred fed his gremlins 6 times after midnight. Jan fed her gremlins 8 times after midnight. How many gremlins will there be in all?

$2^6 + 2^8 = 64 + 256$ Think: Evaluate each power first.
$ = 320$

There are now 320 gremlins in all.

Think: You can also use a calculator.

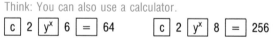

In the problem above, the powers were evaluated before adding. Thus, the order of operations is modified as follows. Write this order of operations in your journal.

- Brackets first.
- Then evaluate powers.
- Then multiply and divide in order.
- Then add and subtract in order.

A Review the order of operations.

1. Find the missing exponent.
   (a) $10^{\blacksquare} = 100$ (b) $5^{\blacksquare} = 125$ (c) $2^{\blacksquare} = 64$ (d) $4^{\blacksquare} = 64$

2. Evaluate.
   (a) $3^2 + 3$ (b) $3^2 \div 3$ (c) $3^2 - 3$ (d) $3^2 \times 3$

3. Find the value of each expression.
   (a) $5^2 + 2^3$ (b) $4^4 - 3^5$ (c) $7^2 + 3^2$ (d) $5^4 - 4^5$

4. Calculate.
   (a) $3^4 - 2^5$ (b) $3^4 - 4^3$ (c) $4^2 + 3^2$ (d) $2^4 - 3^2$

5. Calculate.
   (a) $3^4 \times 3$ (b) $4^2 - 6 \times 3$ (c) $3^5 \div (5^2 - 2^3)$ (d) $10^3 - 5^3$

B Use a calculator.

6. Which is greater?
   A The sum of three squared and five cubed.
   B The difference of four cubed and two squared.
   C The sum of three cubed and three cubed.

7. Which expression has the greater value?
   (a) $3^2 + 2$ or $2^2 + 3$
   (b) $4^2 \div 2^4$ or $4^2 - 2^4$
   (c) $10 + 1^5$ or $10^2 - 1^{100}$
   (d) $2^4 + 5$ or $5^2 - 2$

8. A solution has a paramecium cell and an amoeba cell. Over time, the amoeba doubled 5 times and the paramecium doubled 9 times. How many cells are now in the solution?

9. Work with a partner.
   (a) Write an expression, using exponents, to show the total number of squares on a checker board.
   (b) Evaluate your expression from (a).

10. Copy and complete the magic square.

2^2		
$1^2 + 2^2 + 3^2$		
$6^2 - 6 \times 4$		2^4

C

11. In an experiment, Lana has three red blood cells and four glucose cells. Over time, the red blood cells divide five times and the glucose cells seven times. How many cells are there?

127

There are many relationships to explore and discover in mathematics.

Activity 1 Copy and complete the chart. What patterns do you notice?

Expression	Expanded Form	Exponent Form
$3^2 \times 3^3$	$(3 \times 3) \times (3 \times 3 \times 3)$	$3^5 = 3^{2+3}$
$5^3 \times 5^4$	$(5 \times 5 \times 5) \times (\blacksquare \times \blacksquare \times \blacksquare \times \blacksquare)$	$5^7 = 5^{3+4}$
$18^2 \times 18^3$	$(18 \times 18) \times (18 \times 18 \times 18)$	$18^5 = 18^{\blacksquare + \blacksquare}$
▬▬▬	▬▬▬	▬▬▬
▬▬▬	▬▬▬	▬▬▬

Activity 2 Copy and complete the chart. What patterns do you notice?

Expression	Expanded Form	Value	Exponent Form
$3^4 \div 3^2$	$(3 \times 3 \times 3 \times 3) \div (3 \times 3)$	9	$9 = 3^2 = 3^{4-2}$
$7^5 \div 7^1$	$(7 \times 7 \times 7 \times 7 \times 7) \div 7$	2401	$2401 = 7^4 = 7^{5-\blacksquare}$
$15^3 \div 15^2$	$(15 \times 15 \times 15) \div (\blacksquare \times \blacksquare)$	15	$15 = 15^1 = 15^{\blacksquare - \blacksquare}$
▬▬▬	▬▬▬	▬▬▬	▬▬▬
▬▬▬	▬▬▬	▬▬▬	▬▬▬

The patterns shown in the activities above suggest the following.

Multiplying Powers	
$3^2 \times 3^4 = 3^{2+4}$	Think: Use the same base
$\qquad = 3^6$	and add the exponents.

Dividing Powers	
$5^5 \div 5^3 = 5^{5-3}$	Think: Use the same base
$\qquad = 5^2$	and subtract the exponents.

These relationships can be used to solve problems.

The circumference of the earth is about 10^4 km. The circumference of the sun is about 10^6 km. About how many times greater is the circumference of the sun?

$$\frac{\text{The circumference of the sun}}{\text{The circumference of the earth}} = \frac{10^6}{10^4}.$$

$$10^6 \div 10^4 = 10^{6-4}$$
$$= 10^2$$
$$= 100$$

The circumference of the sun is about 100 times the circumference of the earth.

A Review how to evaluate powers.

1. Write each as a single power. Then evaluate.

   (a) $2^3 \times 2^2$ (b) $3^4 \times 3^2$ (c) $2^5 \times 2^3$ (d) $2^4 \div 2^2$

2. Evaluate.

   (a) $2^3 \times 2^4$ (b) $3^4 \times 3$ (c) $2^4 \times 2^4$ (d) $3^2 \times 3^4$

   (e) $5^3 \div 5$ (f) $10^4 \div 10^2$ (g) $4^5 \div 4^3$ (h) $5^3 \div 5^2$

3. Calculate.

   (a) $2^2 \times 4^4 \div 2^5$ (b) $2^3 + 2^4 \times 3^3$ (c) $4^2 - 2^3 \times 2^2$ (d) $5^3 + 2^5 - 3^2$

B Review the order of operations.

4. Mars is about 7^{10} km from the sun. Saturn is about 7^{11} km from the sun. About how many times the distance from the sun to Mars is the distance from the sun to Saturn?

5. A midge's wing can beat 10^3 times each second.

   (a) How many times can you blink your eyes in 1 s?

   (b) How many times faster can a midge's wing beat than your eyes can blink?

6. A kangaroo can hop at about 6^2 km/h. A bear can run at about 2^5 km/h. Which is faster? How many times faster?

7. There was one lily pad in a pond. Each year, the number of lily pads doubled. After eight years, the pond is half covered. After how many years will the pond be completely covered?

8. (a) In how many ways can you fold a page to show these creases?

   (b) Repeat (a) for your own pattern.

MAKING CONNECTIONS

Johann Elbert Bode used a relationship to find the actual distance from the sun to Mercury, Venus, Earth, Mars, Jupiter, and Saturn. Use your library and record your findings in your journal.

(a) Summarize the relationship that Bode used.

(b) Write the distance from the sun to each planet as a power.

4.5 PROBLEM SOLVING: LOOK FOR A PATTERN

A chart can often help you organize your work and find a pattern in the solution. For example, find the last digit when you evaluate 2^{48}.

1. Think About the Problem.

(a) Think of what you must find.
   • The last digit in the power 2^{48}.

(b) Think of what you are given.
   • The power 2^{48}.

2. Think About a Strategy.

(a) Think of a strategy you could use.
   • Evaluate 2^1, 2^2, 2^3, ... until you observe a pattern for the last digit.

(b) Think of a reason for your strategy.
   • By evaluating simple powers, a pattern may be seen.

3. Work It Out.

Use a chart to organize your solution.

Exponent	Power	Value
1	2^1	2
2	2^2	4
3	2^3	8
4	2^4	16
5	2^5	32
6	2^6	64
7	2^7	128
8	2^8	256
9	2^9	512
10	2^{10}	1024
11	2^{11}	2048
12	2^{12}	4096
.	.	.
.	.	.
.	.	.

Think:
The value of 2^4 ends in 6.
The value of 2^8 ends in 6.
The value of 2^{12} ends in 6.

.

.

2^{48} ends in 6.
Summarize the pattern.

4. Think About Your Solution.

Use the pattern. You see that 2^{48} has a last digit of 6.
   • Why can you not simply evaluate 2^{48} using a calculator?
   • What other patterns do you see in the solution?
   • Create and solve a similar problem.

B Use your *Problem Solving Plan*.

1. Use the example.
   (a) What is the last digit of 2^{39}?
   (b) What is the last digit of 2^{49}?
   (c) What pattern helped you answer (a) and (b)?

2. (a) Use a chart and evaluate the following.
   $$3^1, \ 3^2, \ 3^3, \ \ldots, \ 3^{12}$$
   (b) Predict the last digit when you evaluate 3^{44}.
   (c) Create a similar problem of your own. Compare your problem to others in the class.

3. Use a calculator.
   (a) Evaluate the following $33^2, \ 333^2, \ 3333^2$.
   (b) Predict the value of $333\,333\,333^2$.
   (c) Create a similar problem of your own. Compare your problem to others in the class.

4. (a) Find the sum of the first two odd numbers.
   (b) Find the sum of the first three odd numbers.
   (c) Use your results from (a) and (b). Find the sum of the first 100 odd numbers.

5. Find the least number, greater than one, that can be written as a power with an exponent of two, an exponent of three, and an exponent of four.

6. The switch on a fan is shown to the right. Suppose the switch is turned 3474 times from the setting shown. At what speed setting will the fan be operating?

7. The needle on Al's compass is pointing at east. Suppose he turns 90° clockwise 6417 times. At what direction will the needle point? Refer to the picture below. Create and solve a similar problem.

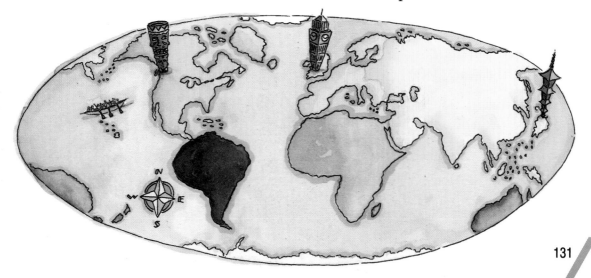

Did you know that pollen has a mass of about 10^{-6} g? To interpret this mass, you need to understand negative exponents. Negative exponents and zero exponents are explored below.

EXPLORATION ① Work with a Partner

1. (a) Copy and complete. Use the pattern for multiplying powers.
   (i) $2^4 \times 2^0 = 2^?$ (ii) $3^5 \times 3^0 = 3^?$ (iii) $5^0 \times 5^4 = 5^?$ (iv) $3^0 \times 3^7 = 3^?$

   (b) Copy and complete. Use the pattern for dividing powers.
   (i) $2^4 \div 2^0 = 2^?$ (ii) $3^5 \div 3^0 = 3^?$ (iii) $5^4 \div 5^0 = 5^?$ (iv) $3^7 \div 3^0 = 3^?$

   (c) Use your results from (a) and (b). Suggest a value for any base with an exponent of zero. Justify your answer.

2. Use your results from Question 1.
   (a) Suggest a value for any base with an exponent of zero.
   (b) Give an example of your value in (a).

3. (a) Copy and complete each of the following.
   (i) $2^4 \times 2^{-1} = 2^?$ (ii) $3^5 \times 3^{-1} = 3^?$ (iii) $5^4 \times 5^{-1} = 5^?$ (iv) $3^3 \times 3^{-1} = 3^?$

   (b) Use your results from (a). Suggest a value for any base with a negative exponent. Justify your answer.

4. (a) What is the value of 10^0?
   (b) Write a decimal number to represent 10^{-1}.
   (c) Use the pattern suggested in (a) and (b). Write a decimal number for 10^{-2}.

EXPLORATION ② Work in Groups

5. (a) Fold a scrap piece of paper in half 3 times.
   Step 1 Write a power to represent the number of parts shown by the folds.
   Step 2 Cut the page in half along a crease. Write a power to represent the number of parts shown by the folds on one half of the page.
   Step 3 Repeat Steps 1 and 2 until you have only one square remaining.

   (b) Use your results from (a). Answer the following.
   (i) $2^3 \div 2$ (ii) $2^2 \div 2$ (iii) $2^1 \div 2$

4.7 MAKING CONNECTIONS

After you complete an exploration in mathematics you should summarize it. The following is a summary of the relationships from the previous section.

Zero Exponents
$8^0 = 1, 2^0 = 1, 4^0 = 1$

Negative Exponents
$7^{-3} = \dfrac{1}{7^3}, 2^{-1} = \dfrac{1}{2}, 4^{-2} = \dfrac{1}{4^2}$

You will use these relationships to complete the following exercise.

EXERCISE

 A Review your relationships for powers.

1. Write each as a power with a positive exponent.
   (a) 2^{-4} (b) 4^{-1} (c) 3^{-5} (d) 6^{-3} (e) 5^{-2} (f) 10^{-7}

2. Write each as a power with a negative exponent.
   (a) $\dfrac{1}{3^3}$ (b) $\dfrac{1}{6^3}$ (c) $\dfrac{1}{4^2}$ (d) $\dfrac{1}{2^5}$ (e) $\dfrac{1}{10^4}$ (f) $\dfrac{1}{7^3}$

B Interpret your answers.

3. Evaluate.
   (a) $4^{-3} \times 3^0$ (b) $5^0 + 5^3$
   (c) $3^0 \times 3^{-1}$ (d) $4^{-2} + 2^0$

4. Calculate.
   (a) $3^0 \times 3^{-2} \div 3^0$ (b) $5^{-2} \times 3^0 \times 5^3$
   (c) $3^2 \div 3^{-3} + 3^0$ (d) $3^{-3} \times 7^0 \times 3^3$

5. Copy and complete. Then write the next three rows.

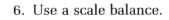

(a)	$\dfrac{1}{10}$	0.1	10^{-1}
(b)	$\dfrac{1}{100}$	0.01	10^{-2}
(c)	?	0.001	?

6. Use a scale balance.
   (a) Find the mass of three different coins, in kilograms. Write the masses as powers.
   (b) Write an expression that gives the mass of each coin in (a). Have others in your class evaluate your expression.

7. Use a scale balance. Find a 1 g mass.
   (a) Find objects that have a mass less than 1 g. Some are shown below.
   (b) Start a collage of items that have a mass less than 1 g. Estimate the mass of each as a power.

4.8 SOLVING PROBLEMS

In this chapter, you have studied many relationships involving powers. A summary is shown. Use the relationships to solve the problems that follow.

Dividing Powers
$5^5 \div 5^3 = 5^{5-3}$ Think: Keep the base the
$\qquad = 5^2$ same and subtract exponents.

Multiplying Powers
$4^4 \times 4^2 = 4^{4+2}$ Think: Keep the base the
$\qquad = 4^6$ same and add exponents.

Negative Exponents
$7^{-3} = \frac{1}{7^3}, 2^{-1} = \frac{1}{2}, 4^{-2} = \frac{1}{4^2}$

ORDER OF OPERATIONS

- Simplify brackets first.
- Then simplify exponents.
- Then multiply and divide in order.
- Then add and subtract in order.

Zero Exponents
$8^0 = 1, 2^0 = 1, 4^0 = 1$

EXERCISE

B Remember the order of operations.

1. Write a power for each.
   (a) $3^5 \times 3^2 \div 3^4$ (b) $2^7 \div 2^3 \times 2^4$
   (c) $7^2 \div 7^0 \times 7^2$ (d) $3^6 \times 3^2 \times 3^{-1}$
   (e) $2^3 \times 2^5 \div 4^0$ (f) $3^{-1} \times 3^3 \times 3^{-2}$
   (g) $4^3 \div 4^5 \times 5^0$ (h) $3^0 + 2^0 \times 4^0$

2. Evaluate.
   (a) $5^{-3} \times 3^0$ (b) $5^{-2} \times 5^4 + 6^0$
   (c) $3^2 + 3^3 \div 3^{-1}$ (d) $7^2 + 16^0$
   (e) $200 \div (3^3 - 7)$ (f) $15^3 \times 3^4$
   (g) $3^3 - 2^2 + 3^0$ (h) $7^2 \times 4^3 - 3^5$

3. The mass of a dime is about 2 g. The mass of a hairy-winged beetle egg is about 10^{-6} g. Which mass is greater? By how many times?

4. Did you know that the shortest recorded centipede is 2^{-1} cm long?
   (a) Measure the length of your thumb.
   (b) How many times the length of the centipede is the length of your thumb?

5. Look at the science fiction characters below. Use the characters and the powers 3^2, 5^3, and 10^{10} to write a math story of your own. Give each character a name.

Here is a game that you can play with a partner in your class. Before you begin the game, construct a red die and a brown die using the patterns shown.

The numbers on the red die are −1, 0, 1, 2, 3, and 4, and they represent the exponents.

The numbers on the brown die are 1, 2, 3, 4, 5, and 6, and they represent the bases.

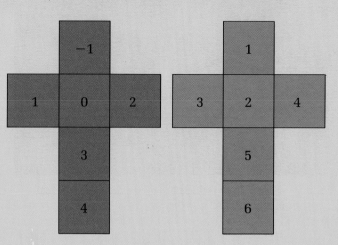

Rules
1. Each player takes turns rolling the dice.
2. Each player makes a power using the numbers on the dice and marks the square containing the value of the power.
3. If a player creates a power, and the value of it has already been marked on the board, the turn is lost.
4. The winner is the first to mark six squares in a row, column, or diagonal.

5	7776	3	625	1296	8
$\frac{1}{6}$	4	16	$\frac{1}{2}$	6	216
6	3	125	$\frac{1}{5}$	9	81
4	$\frac{1}{3}$	16	1	25	1
27	$\frac{1}{4}$	256	64	5	25
1	36	2	4	$\frac{1}{3}$	16

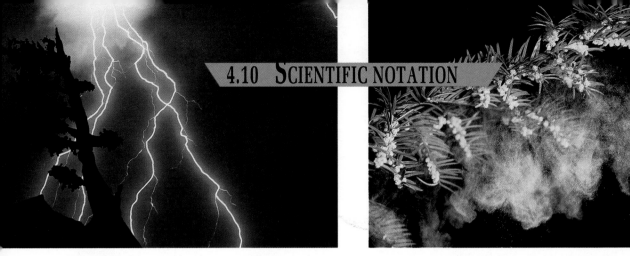

4.10 SCIENTIFIC NOTATION

Did you know that a lightning bolt can strike in 0.000 007 14 s?

Did you know that about 2 000 000 grains of pollen can be released by one flower?

The numbers in each caption above are written in standard form. These numbers can be written in a more compact form as shown below.

$$0.000\,007\,14 = 7.14 \times 0.000\,001$$
$$= 7.14 \times \frac{1}{1\,000\,000}$$
$$= 7.14 \times 10^{-6}$$

$$2\,000\,000 = 2 \times 1\,000\,000$$
$$= 2 \times 10 \times 10 \times 10 \times 10 \times 10 \times 10$$
$$= 2 \times 10^6$$

Think:
Powers of 10 are used.
The number is between 1 and 10.

The numbers above have been written in **scientific notation**.

Very large and very small numbers can be shown in scientific notation on a calculator.

Calculator Key Sequence

$\boxed{\text{c}}$ 10 $\boxed{\times}$ $\boxed{=}$ $\boxed{\times}$ $\boxed{=}$ $\boxed{\times}$ $\boxed{=}$

Screen

$\boxed{1 \quad 08}$ Think: $\boxed{1 \quad 08}$ means 1×10^8

EXERCISE

A Review your skills with exponents.

1. Write each number in standard form.
   (a) 10^1 (b) 10^2 (c) 10^3 (d) 10^4 (e) 10^5 (f) 10^6
   (g) 10^{-1} (h) 10^{-2} (i) 10^{-3} (j) 10^{-4} (k) 10^{-5} (l) 10^{-6}

2. Use your results from Question 1. Write each number in standard form.
   (a) 3.7×10^5 (b) 4.8×10^7 (c) 6.8×10^{10} (d) 2.8×10^{-8} (e) 7.7×10^{-6}

3. Write each in scientific notation.

(a) 125 000

(b) 823 000 000

(c) 927 000 000

(d) 0.000 073

(e) 0.000 000 148

(f) 0.000 000 3

B Review the meaning of negative exponents.

4. Write each number in standard form.

(a) The farthest distance between the earth and the sun is about 1.52×10^8 km.

(b) The closest distance between the earth and the sun is about 1.47×10^8 km.

(c) Light can travel 1 m in 3.0×10^{-9} s.

5. Write each number in scientific notation.

(a) Lightning can travel 8 400 000 km each hour.

(b) One of the smallest insects, the parasitic wasp, has a mass of 0.000 005 g.

(c) The population of the world in 2025 is expected to be 8 180 000 000.

6. Use your library to find large and small numbers of your own.

(a) Write the numbers in standard form and in scientific notation.

(b) Start a class collage using the numbers. Use pictures to show what the numbers represent.

7. Refer to your calculator manual.

(a) Find out how numbers can be represented in scientific notation.

(b) Show numbers in this section on your calculator.

8. Write each calculator display in scientific notation.

(a) | 3.89   15 |

(b) | 1.26   −11 |

9. Use the manual for your calculator.

(a) In your journal, describe how numbers in scientific notation can be multiplied.

(b) Use your calculator to find each product.

(i) $3.6 \times 10^8 \times 4.2 \times 10^{-3}$

(ii) $7.9 \times 10^{-4} \times 8.9 \times 10^{-2}$

(iii) $4.6 \times 10^{11} \times 3.2 \times 10^{15}$

(c) In your journal, describe how the order of operations can help you find the products in (b).

10. Use a calculator to solve each.

(a) The heaviest satellite is 0.025 17 times the mass of the moon. The moon has a mass of 7.3×10^{19} kg. Find the mass of the satellite.

(b) The White Dwarf Star has a diameter 4×10^{-3} times that of the sun. The diameter of the sun is 1.39×10^9 m. Find the diameter of the White Dwarf Star.

11. Put pennies side by side as shown.

(a) Estimate the number of pennies in 1 m.

(b) Estimate the number of pennies that go around your school; around Earth. Write your estimate in scientific notation.

Patterns in mathematics occur in many different ways. For example, the Braille system uses a pattern of raised dots to represent letters and numbers.

ACTIVITY ①

The Braille letters of the alphabet are shown.

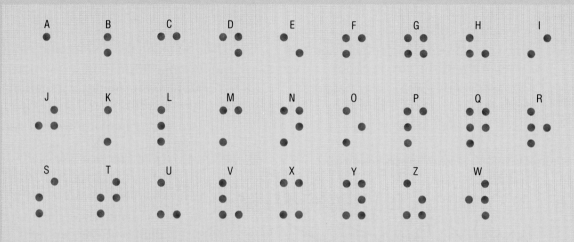

(a) Use disks of your own to create each letter.

(b) Some letters appear to be related to others. How are the letters D, F, H, and J related?

(c) Find other relationships among the letters. How are the letters alike? How are they different?

(d) How will your answers in (b) and (c) help you remember letters?

ACTIVITY ②

What word is represented by each of the following?

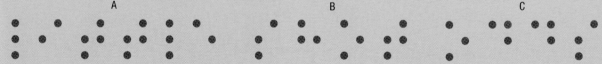

Use your disks to represent math words shown in Braille. Use math words learned so far. Compare your words to those of others in your class. Translate the other words.

ACTIVITY ③

(a) Translate the following question shown in Braille. Answer the question.

(b) Choose a question of your own and represent it using Braille.

How do you think Braille could be incorporated into computer software and hardware?

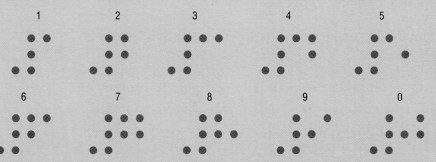

ACTIVITY ④

(a) The Braille Numbers 0, 1, 2, . . . , 9 are shown below. Use disks of your own to represent each number.

1	2	3	4	5

6	7	8	9	0

(b) How are letters and numbers alike? How are they different? How can you determine if a pattern of dots is a letter or a number?

(c) What patterns can help you remember numbers?

(d) Pick some expressions from this book. Represent them in Braille using disks. Evaluate the expressions.

4.12 USING VARIABLES

Mark delivers newspapers each morning before school. He earns $0.14 for each newspaper he sells, as shown in the chart.

Newspapers Sold	Amount Earned
1	$0.14
2	$0.28
3	$0.42

A symbol, n, can be used to represent the number of newspapers sold. You can use it to show the total amount, written in dollars, as the following **variable expression**.

$$0.14 \times n \quad \text{or} \quad 0.14n$$

— a variable —

Suppose Mark delivered 62 newspapers.
The amount he earned is found as follows.

Use $n = 62$.
$$0.14n = 0.14(62)$$
$$= 8.68$$

Think: Replace n by 62, the number of newspapers sold.

Thus, Mark earned $8.68 this morning.

Your skills with variable expressions can help you solve problems.

Claudio sells hot dogs and hamburgers at a stand. Each hot dog sells for $1.65 and each hamburger for $2.25. He sold 16 hot dogs and 22 hamburgers.

(a) Write a variable expression to show how much Claudio collected.

(b) Find how much Claudio collected.

(a) Let h represent the number of hamburgers sold.
Let d represent the number of hot dogs sold.
The expression, in dollars, for the amount Claudio collected is given by $1.65d + 2.25h$.

(b) Use $d = 16$ and $h = 22$.
$$1.65d + 2.25h$$
$$= 1.65(16) + 2.25(22)$$
$$= 26.40 + 49.50$$
$$= 75.90$$

Thus, Claudio collected $75.90 yesterday.

EXERCISE

A Review how to evaluate a variable expression.

1. (a) Replace g by 5 in $g + 12$.
   (b) Replace h by 3 in $7 - h$.
   (c) Replace a by 7 in $3a - 4$.
   (d) Replace k by 6 in $\frac{1}{2}k$.

2. Use p to represent the number of team points. Interpret each answer.
   (a) Replace p by 6 in $2p + 6$.
   (b) Replace p by 36 in $3p + 7$.

3. Find the value of each for $m = 2$.
   (a) $m + \frac{1}{2}$ (b) $m - \frac{1}{2}$ (c) $\frac{m}{2}$ (d) $\frac{1}{2}m$ (e) $3m$ (f) $2.5m$

4. Use $k = 2$ and $d = 3$ to evaluate each of the following.
   (a) $3.6k + 2d$ (b) $4.2d - 1.3k$ (c) $2.7k + 0.4d$ (d) $0.9d - 0.7k$

B Make sure your calculations are reasonable.

5. Find the value of each for $x = 3$.
   (a) x^2 (b) x^3 (c) 5^x
   (d) 2^x (e) $x^2 + x$ (f) $5x + x$

6. Use $a = 3.3$ and $b = -2.7$. Which has the greatest value?
   (a) $4a + 2b$ (b) $5b - 3a$ (c) $3a - 2b$

7. Ned earns $0.34 for one magazine sold.
   (a) Write a variable expression to show how much he earns.
   (b) Last week he sold 132 magazines. How much did he earn?

8. Claudio also sells French fries and onion rings. Each order of fries costs $1.25 and onion rings cost $1.40. Yesterday, he sold 25 orders of fries and 30 orders of onion rings.
   (a) Write an expression for the total amount Claudio collected.
   (b) Find the total amount collected.

9. The distance in kilometres, d, a roadrunner runs is given by $d = 25t$, where t is number of hours. How far can a roadrunner run in 1.5 h?

10. Lori works in a shoe store. She earns $2.32 for each pair of shoes sold and $3.15 for each pair of boots. She sold 8 pairs of shoes and 11 pairs of boots.
    (a) Write an expression for the amount Lori earned.
    (b) Find how much she earned.

11. (a) Find the thickness of a dime and a penny.
    (b) Stack 10 pennies and 10 dimes. Write an expression for the height of the stack. Find the height.
    (c) Find the height of a stack of 40 dimes and 60 pennies.
    (d) Find the height of a stack of your own.

$3h + 7$

People who can read Braille translate raised dots into words. Similarly, in mathematics, you translate English words into mathematical symbols. Use the chart below to help you.

English Expression	Symbol
sum, more, increase	+
difference, less, decrease	−
product, times, of	×
divided by, quotient	÷
the number tripled	$3n$
one quarter of the number	$\frac{1}{4}n$

$5d - 3$

An expression is translated below.

You can use your skills with translation to help you solve problems.

The height of the sail on this sailboard is the product of 3 and 6 cm less than the length of the board. The board is 140 cm long. Find the height of the sail.

Let h represent the length of the board.

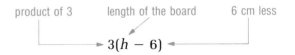

Use $h = 140$.
$$3(h - 6) = 3(140 - 6)$$
$$= 3(134)$$
$$= 402$$

$3(h - 6)$

The height of the sail is 402 cm.

A Review your skills with substitution.

1. Use the variable *t* for Trina's age to write each variable expression.

   (a) 3 years older than Trina   (b) 3 years younger than Trina

   (c) $\frac{1}{2}$ of Trina's age   (d) 3 times as old as Trina

2. Use an appropriate symbol to translate each of the following.

   (a) 3 times a number increased by 5

   (b) the product of 5 and 3 more than a number

   (c) one third of a number increased by twice the number

3. (a) The variable, *m*, represents money earned. Write a problem for each.

   (i) $m + 6$ (ii) $m - 7$ (iii) $m + 3$ (iv) $2m$ (v) $5m - 3$

   (b) Suppose $m = 7$. Evaluate each expression in (a).

B Use your *Problem Solving Plan.*

4. The largest curtain ever made had a height 19 m longer than 7 times its width.

   (a) Write a variable expression for the height of the curtain.

   (b) The width of the curtain is 56 m. Find the height of the curtain.

5. Anita sells magazine subscriptions. Each hour she earns $3.65 plus $1.50 for each subscription sold.

   (a) Write an expression for the amount she earns each hour.

   (b) How much did she earn if she sold 15 subscriptions in 1 h?

   (c) Solve the problem using numbers of your own.

6. Use the pictures on the previous page. Write a problem for each expression. Solve the problems.

7. The largest inhabited castle is Windsor Castle. It is rectangular with a length 3 times its width plus 22 m.

   (a) Write an expression for the length of the castle.

   (b) The width of the castle is 164 m. Find the length of the castle.

8. Let one penny represent 1 kg.

   (a) What mass would 5 pennies represent? 8 pennies represent?

   (b) Create 4 masses that can be used to represent each whole number mass from 1 kg to 40 kg.

4.14 USING PROBLEM SOLVING SKILLS

A printing company charges 12¢ for each ticket printed plus a standard set-up charge of $8.00. Write an expression for the cost of tickets printed and find how many tickets can be printed for $30.20.

Let n represent the number of tickets printed.

| 12 | number of tickets printed | plus | 800¢ | is | 3020¢ |
| $12n$ | + | 800 | = | 3020 |

Think: Write all totals using cents.

The sentence $12n + 800 = 3020$ is called an **equation**. When you find the value of n that makes both sides of the equation equal, you have **solved** the equation. To solve the equation, you can use your problem solving skill *guess and check*.

Think: Organize your solution using a chart.

Estimate n	$12n + 800$	Equal to 3020?
100	2000	Too low.
200	3200	Too high.
175	2900	Closer. But low.
190	3080	Closer. But high.
185	3020	Correct.

Thus, 185 tickets can be printed for $30.20.

Now work with a partner. Create a similar problem of your own. Solve the problem and have another pair of students check your solution. If your solution is incorrect, have them tell you why.

A Review your skills with integers.

1. Three values of the variable are shown. Which one makes the equation true?

   (a) $n + 7 = 12$ 3, 4, 5   (b) $2r - 3 = 9$ 5, 6, 7

   (c) $3x + 2 = 2$ $-1, 0, 1$ (d) $5 + 2n = 15$ 4, 5, 6

2. Solve each equation. List all the values you tried to make the equation true.

   (a) $k + 5 = 9$ (b) $12 - q = 3$ (c) $3x + 7 = 19$

3. Solve each equation.

   (a) $a + 1 = 5$ (b) $2y = 8$ (c) $m - 3 = 6$ (d) $\frac{x}{2} = 5$

B Review your skills of translating English into mathematics.

4. Choose an appropriate variable. Write and solve an equation for each statement.

   (a) A number doubled is equal to 20.

   (b) A number, decreased by 7, is 17.

   (c) A number times 7, plus 4, is 60.

5. Did you know that some mammals, like the platypus, lay eggs? Its average life span is n in the equation $3n + 18 = 168$. Find the average life span of a platypus.

6. Use the problem on the previous page.

   (a) How many tickets can be printed for $56.72?

   (b) How many tickets can be printed for $93.44?

7. The commission, C, earned for selling magazines is shown by $C = 5 + 4n$; n is the number of magazines sold.

   (a) Solve. $49 = 5 + 4n$

   (b) Interpret your answer from (a).

8. The amount, A, earned selling ice cream bars is shown by $A = 1700 + 25n$, where n is the number of ice cream bars sold.

   (a) Solve. $3750 = 1700 + 25n$

   (b) Interpret your answer from (a).

9. Refer to the collage of ads below.

   (a) Sam has $10 to spend on groceries. Make a list of the groceries he can buy.

   (b) Write an equation using your list from (a). Solve it.

4.15 ASKING USEFUL QUESTIONS

A scientist often finds the solution to a problem by inspecting its various parts and asking useful questions.

In mathematics, you solve problems in a similar way. Where possible, you should **inspect** an equation and decide whether you can obtain the solution by asking useful questions. List the useful questions asked to solve the equation below.

Activity

For each invention shown above,
- what questions might have been asked by a scientist to help create the invention?
- write a short paragraph about how the person might have felt when they invented each of the above. Look up each invention to help.

For example, you can solve the equation $2p + 3 = 15$ as follows.

Solve. $2p + 3 = 15$

Think: ■ + 3 = 15
■ = 12

Ask yourself:
What number added to 3 equals 15?
In this case, 12 + 3 = 15. Thus, $2p = 12$.

Solve. $2p = 12$

Think: 2 × ■ = 12

Ask yourself:
What number multiplied by 2 equals 12?

Solve.

2■ = 12
■ = 6

Thus, the solution to $2p + 3 = 15$ is $p = 6$.

You can check your solution to the problem.

Think: Left Side = $2p + 3$ Right Side = 15
= 2(6) + 3
= 15 ∖ Solution is
correct.

EXERCISE

A Remember: Ask useful questions to solve the equation.

1. Find a value of ■ that makes each equation true.

   (a) $■ + 4 = 9$ (b) $■ - 12 = 8$ (c) $2(■) = 16$ (d) $\dfrac{■}{3} = 9$

2. (a) To solve $2x + 3 = 13$, what simpler equation might you solve?
   (b) Solve the equation from (a).

3. Find the value of n.
   (a) $2n + 8 = 12$ (b) $n - 6 = 2$ (c) $6 - n = 4$ (d) $2n = 20$

B Remember to check your solutions.

4. Solve.
   (a) $6y - 3 = 15$ (b) $3 + 4k = 23$
   (c) $\dfrac{1}{3}y - 1 = 9$ (d) $\dfrac{1}{2}h + 6 = 16$

5. For each problem,
   • write an equation.
   • think of a simpler equation to solve.
   • solve the problem.

   (a) Seven times a number minus 22 is 30. Find the number.
   (b) Two thirds of a number, decreased by 5, is 1. What is the number?
   (c) One third of a number, increased by 16, is 23. What is the number?

6. Phoebe is 10 years old. Doug is 2 times Phoebe's age plus 3 years. Find Doug's age.

7. (a) Copy and cut out the figure.
   (b) Use two cuts to form three parts that fit together to form a square. Find the area of the square.

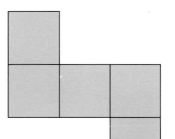

Agriscience is a term that describes any job relating to plants, animals, and renewable resources. Agriscience supplies products like silk, wool, fresh fruits and vegetables and it accounts for about one out of every five jobs in Canada in some form.

Agriscience helps Canadians to maintain a good standard of living. Other countries in the world are trying to implement agriscience techniques to help improve their standard of living. Most countries hope to have it in place by the year 2000.

Before you begin the exercise, complete the following activities in your journal.

Activity 1
Write a short paragraph describing how your standard of living is affected by the occupations shown in these pictures.

Activity 2
Some agriscience professionals claim that we are a "water planet". Do you agree with the statement? Why?

B There are many people involved in agriscience careers.

1. Farmers form a large part of the agriscience work force.

   (a) Estimate the number of farmers you think are in Canada.

   (b) The average farm produces enough food and fibre to feed n Canadians in $5n - 33 = 547$. How many Canadians does the average farm feed?

2. Canadian farmers are able to supply goods so efficiently that, on average, only 14¢ of each dollar you earn is spent on food. Suppose you earn $375 each week.

   (a) Write an expression for the amount you spend on food each week.

   (b) How much will you spend in (a)?

3. The agriscience industry in North America has assets of about 1×10^{12} dollars (one trillion dollars). An estimate has been made on the length of time you need to count to one trillion by ones. The estimate will have you counting continually for 31 710 a.

   (a) How many days are in 31 710 a? Write your answer in scientific notation.

   (b) On average, how many numbers would you be able to say each day?

   (c) How can you determine the accuracy of the estimate above?

4. A sand particle has a diameter of 5×10^{-2} mm.

   (a) The diameter of a gravel particle is 40 times that of sand. Find the diameter of a gravel particle.

   (b) The diameter of a clay particle is 25^{-1} times that of sand. Find the diameter of a clay particle.

MAKING CONNECTIONS

In North America, about 400 000 people are hired each year in the agriscience field.

(a) What is the main agriscience field in your province?

(b) Make a list of the various occupations that are involved in the agriscience industry. List the math skills you think are needed by each occupation.

(c) In your journal, describe whether you are surprised at some of the occupations you listed in (b). Which of these occupations might you enjoy?

4.17 PROBLEM SOLVING

Sometimes, when you work on a problem,
- you might get an answer that is unreasonable.
- you might find the problem is impossible to solve.

For example, you might get an area described by a negative number or a person's age of more than 200 years.

For each problem in this section,
- if the problem is impossible, rewrite it so it is possible.
- if the problem is unreasonable, rewrite it so it is reasonable.

EXERCISE

 Use your *Problem Solving Plan.*

1. Harley is 14 years younger than Neil. Lisa is 26 years older than Neil. Lisa is 37 years of age. How old is Harley?

2. Bill needs to get over the hill in 1 min. The hill is 1 km up and 1 km back down again. Bill can average a speed of 60 km/h going up the hill. How long will it take Bill to get down the other side of the hill?

3. Use a geoboard.
   (a) How many different squares can you form on your geoboard?
   (b) Find the area of each square that you form.

4. Of the 23 students in a class, 4 play either hockey or baseball. There are 16 hockey players and 6 of them play both sports. How many students play only baseball?

5. How can you make a total of 50¢ using exactly nine coins?

6. A number, when divided by 4, 5, or 6 gives a remainder of 2. The number is divisible by 7. Find the least possible value of the number.

7. There are an even number of students in a classroom. There are five more girls than boys. How many boys and girls can be in the classroom?

8. The following 4 × 4 × 4 cube has been made from centicubes. How many centicubes have 3 faces showing? have 2 faces showing? have 1 face showing? have no faces showing?

TECHNOLOGY INSIGHT: A PROJECT

Computers have high-frequency oscillating circuits which can unintentionally pick up radio frequencies. These **radio frequency waves** can "leak" out of the computer and interfere with other appliances. For example:

- A television close to a computer can show interference on the screen.
- A computer disc might get erased if it gets too close to a telephone.

For the following project, you will need
- a computer.
- a battery operated radio.
- a pencil and a piece of paper.
- a ruler.
- a tape measure.

EXPLORATION   *Work with a Partner*

Step 1
Place a computer in the middle of a room. Use squared paper to draw a diagram of the room. Let the centre square represent the computer.

Step 2
Turn on a radio and take one step back from the front of the computer. Walk around the computer. Indicate, on your grid, when you hear interference on the radio by shading the square you are in. Shade the square dark if the interference is strong and light if the interference is not strong. You may need to walk around the computer more than once.

Step 3
1. (a) Are there any areas where a strong signal suddenly becomes weak?

   (b) Are there any areas where a weak signal suddenly becomes strong?

   (c) Does the interference you hear form a pattern? If so, describe the pattern in your journal.

2. How far from your computer do you need to stand so that there is no interference as you walk around the computer?

3. Create a similar experiment of your own that will allow you to get more accurate results. Compare your experiment with others in your class. Complete the experiment you think is most reasonable.

CHAPTER REVIEW

1. Evaluate.
   (a) $4^3 - 5^2$ (b) $2^5 + 3^2$ (c) $5^4 + 3^4$
   (d) $5^3 + 3^2 - 9^2$ (e) $3^5 - 2^4 - 8^0$ (f) $7^2 - 16 - 3^2$

2. Calculate.
   (a) $7^2 \times 7^3$ (b) $4^4 \times 4^2$
   (c) $3^{-4} \times 3^2$ (d) $3^3 - (2^2 \times 4^0)$
   (e) $100 \div (2^2 \times 5)$ (f) $3^5 \times 3^2 \div 3^4$

3. Write each English phrase in mathematical form.
   (a) two years older than Bob
   (b) Raul's age divided by three
   (c) 7 kg more than Brian's mass

4. Solve.
   (a) $m + 6 = 12$ (b) $3k - 8 = 22$
   (c) $2c + 3 = 11$ (d) $4x - 8 = 24$
   (e) $3y + 9 = 9$ (f) $3 - 5k = 18$

5. Al picks grapes. Each day he earns $8.35 plus $0.95 for each bushel he picks.
   (a) How much did Al earn if he picked 12 bushels?
   (b) How many bushels did he pick if he earned $20.70?

6. Lesley works part-time in a supermarket. She earns $65.00 for the first 10 h she works in a week, and $10.25 for each hour over 10.
   (a) Write an expression to show how much Lesley earns each week.
   (b) How much will she earn if she works 12 h? if she works 15.5 h?

7. The amount of snow that fell is the quotient of 30 and 1 cm less than the height of a daffodil. The daffodil has a height of 11 cm. How much snow fell?

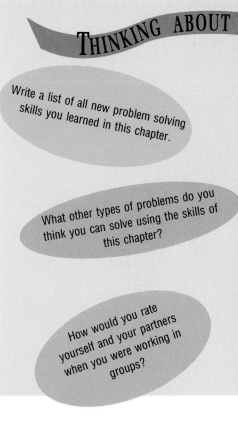

THINKING ABOUT

Write a list of all new problem solving skills you learned in this chapter.

What other types of problems do you think you can solve using the skills of this chapter?

How would you rate yourself and your partners when you were working in groups?

MAKING CONNECTIONS

Refer to the opening pages of the chapter.

(a) Create a problem of your own using the pictures. Solve your problem using the skills in this chapter.

(b) Compare your problem with others in your class. Solve the other problems.

Which problems on this page are best solved mentally? Give reasons for your choice.

Find an interesting fact of your own that involves a very small number. Create a problem using the fact.

Which problems in the chapter did you find difficult to solve? What did you do to try and solve them?

MATH JOURNAL

Throughout the chapter, you have worked with relations and expressions. In your journal,
- write how you can evaluate an expression so that others can follow your directions.
- write an example, from your own life, where evaluating an expression was useful.
- cut out an example from a newspaper where evaluating an expression is needed.

1. Write each as a single power. Then evaluate.
   (a) $3^5 \div 3^3$ (b) $2^2 \times (-2)^3$ (c) $(-5)^3 + 2^2$

2. Calculate.
   (a) $3^4 - 2^5$
   (b) $3^4 - 4^3$
   (c) $8^2 \div 4 - 2^4$
   (d) $2^8 \times 2^4 \div 2^2$
   (e) $20 \div [3^3 - (2^4 + 6)]$
   (f) $3^5 \times 4^2$

3. Write each number in standard form.
   (a) The van can hold about 1.6×10^6 beans.
   (b) The Cray 2 computer can complete 1 calculation every 4.0×10^{-9} s.

4. Write each number in scientific notation.
   (a) The longest golf course is 7300 m long.
   (b) The shortest earthworm is 0.000 047 5 m long.

5. An expression is given by $3p + 2q$. Find the value of the expression for each.
   (a) $p = 2, q = 0$ (b) $p = 0, q = 3$ (c) $p = 4, q = 1$

6. Solve.
   (a) $m - 31 = 40$
   (b) $2x + 11 = 25$
   (c) $3x - 4 = 5$
   (d) $4x - 7 = 21$
   (e) $3a + 6 = 12$
   (f) $6p - 8 = 16$

7. Ken sells computer programs. He earns $300 for each computer program he sells.
   (a) Write an expression for the amount of money he earns.
   (b) How much will he earn if he sells 10 programs? 15 programs?

8. Dahlia earned $10 more than twice the amount earned by Sally. Dahlia earned $24. How much did Sally earn?

5 COMMUNICATING ABOUT MEASURE

How would your life be different if measurements were not accurate? Think of two examples for your journal.

Referring to these photographs, communicate to a partner why accurate measurements are important.

EXPLORATION ① Work with a Partner

1. Use a piece of string and a ruler to measure your hand span, your arm span, your height, and the length of your hand (distance from the tip of your finger to your wrist).

   (a) Then do the following calculations.
      • Hand Span ÷ Arm Span
      • Arm Span ÷ Height

   (b) Prepare a class chart for the results from (a). Do you see any patterns?

2. Which of these statements are reasonable? What information would you collect to justify your answer?

   (a) "Your hand span is about the length of your hand."

   (b) "Your arm span is about your height."

3. Refer to Question 2. Create other statements about your body. Make measurements to support your statement.

EXPLORATION ② Work in a Group

4. Use circular objects like those suggested in the chart.

   (a) Copy and complete the chart.

   (b) For each, calculate *distance around ÷ distance across*. Do you see any patterns?

   (c) Find the average of your results from (b). What do you notice? Communicate your observations to your group.

   (d) Find the average of the class results. What do you notice?

5. (a) Based on your results above, what relationships or patterns do you see?

   (b) Choose other circular objects of your own. Collect data for your objects to test your relationships from (a).

Object	Distance Around	Distance Across
Glass		
Wheel		
Can		
?		

EXPLORATION ③ *Work with a Partner*

6. Copy and complete this chart using the figures on the grid.

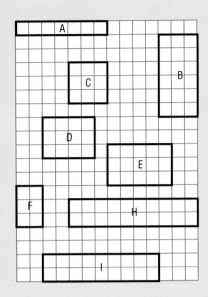

Length	Width	Distance Around	Number of Squares Covered

7. Use your chart. Communicate your answers to the following to your partner.

   (a) What relationships do you see between the length and width of a figure and the distance around the figure?

   (b) What relationships do you see between the length and width of a figure and the number of squares covered by the figure?

8. (a) Use grid paper to draw other rectangles. Use the length and width to predict the distance around and the number of squares covered.

   (b) Based on your results, make a summary of your findings in this exploration.

EXPLORATION ④ *Communicating Together*

9. Accurate measurements are needed to make things work properly. Look at the picture.

   (a) What measurement skills were needed?

   (b) How were the measurement skills used?

   (c) Why is accuracy important?

10. (a) Choose a picture from the chapter introduction. Repeat Question 9 for this picture.

    (b) Choose any picture of your own. Repeat Question 9 for your picture.

5.2 PATTERNS AND PERIMETER

Suppose you are sewing tablecloths to sell at an arts and crafts show. To place trim around each tablecloth costs $2.50 per metre. How much does the trim for each tablecloth below cost?

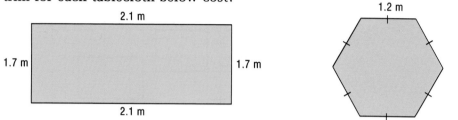

To calculate the cost, you first find the distance around each tablecloth. The distance around is called the **perimeter**.

Perimeter
= 2.1 m + 2.1 m + 1.7 m + 1.7 m
= 2 × 2.1 m + 2 × 1.7 m
= 7.6 m

Perimeter
= 1.2 m + 1.2 m + 1.2 m + 1.2 m + 1.2 m + 1.2 m
= 6 × 1.2 m
= 7.2 m

Cost = 7.6 × $2.50
     = $19.00

Cost = 7.2 × $2.50
     = $18.00

The above calculations suggest the following relationships for finding perimeter.

Rectangle
Perimeter = 2 × length + 2 × width
$$P = 2l + 2w$$

Hexagon
Perimeter = 6 × side length
$$P = 6s$$

As you do the exercises, look for patterns to help you find the perimeter. Write the patterns in your journal and communicate them to others in the class.

EXERCISE

A Look for patterns to help you find the perimeter.

1. Find the perimeter of each.

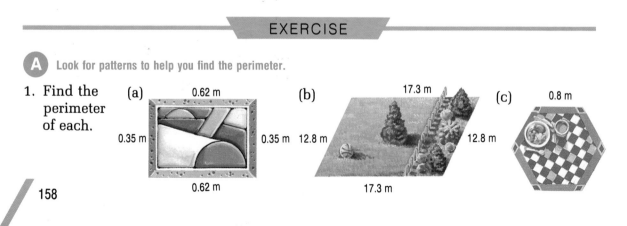

(a) 0.62 m, 0.35 m, 0.62 m

(b) 17.3 m, 12.8 m, 17.3 m

(c) 0.8 m, 12.8 m

2. (a) Some items are suggested. Find these or similar items and make measurements.

   (b) Find the perimeter of each.

B Use a calculator.

3. One side of a square tablecloth is 1.8 m long. Trim costs $0.80/m.

   (a) Find the perimeter.

   (b) Find the cost of trim around the tablecloth.

4. Find the cost of putting insulation around all sides of a window measuring 80 cm by 35 cm. The cost of insulation is 6.5¢/cm.

5. A stained glass window is in the shape of a regular octagon. All sides measure 31.5 cm. The cost to frame the window is $0.30 for each centimetre. Find the cost of the frame around the window.

6. One of the largest omelettes ever made was prepared in Kitchener, Ontario. The rectangular pan used measured 9.1 m by 3.1 m.

   (a) Find the perimeter of the pan.

   (b) How many people can stand around the pan if each person needs 45 cm of room?

7. Fencing costs $18.65 for each metre. Find the cost to fence the parking lot.

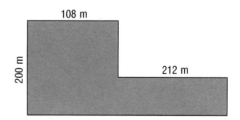

WORKING TOGETHER

(a) Measure the distance around any bicycle wheel.

(b) Estimate the distance around your school yard.

(c) Ride the bicycle around the school yard once. How many times does the wheel of the bicycle turn?

(d) Calculate the perimeter of your school yard. Compare it with (b).

(e) Find other places where you can use the same strategy to find the perimeter. Find the perimeter. What assumptions have you made?

Steve and Marge measured a variety of circular objects and recorded their observations in the chart shown. They measured the distance around each object, called the **circumference**, and the distance across, called the **diameter**. They calculated *circumference ÷ diameter* and the results are shown in the chart.

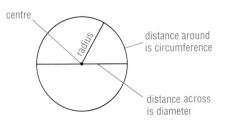

centre

radius

distance around is circumference

distance across is diameter

From the chart, you can see that the circumference, C, divided by the diameter, d, has about the same value. The symbol π is used to represent this value as shown below.

Circumference (C)	Diameter (d)	C ÷ d
18.5 cm	5.9 cm	3.14
14.1 cm	4.5 cm	3.13
41 cm	13 cm	3.15
15.5 cm	4.9 cm	3.16
16.2 cm	5.1 cm	3.17
22.8 cm	7.3 cm	3.12
31.4 cm	10.0 cm	3.14

$$\frac{C}{d} = \pi \qquad \text{or} \qquad C = \pi \times d$$

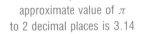

circumference   diameter

approximate value of π
to 2 decimal places is 3.14

Knowing this relationship will help you solve problems like the following.

Suppose you are riding a Ferris wheel. It has a diameter of 80.0 m. What distance have you travelled after one turn of the wheel? Round your answer to the nearest metre.

Use $C = \pi \times d$.
$C \doteq 3.14 \times 80.0$
$= 251.2$

Think:

| c | 3.14 | × | 80 | = | 251.2 |

In one turn, you will travel about 251 m.

Did you know that one of the world's largest Ferris wheels is in Niagara Falls? It is so large that it once started to sink into the ground.

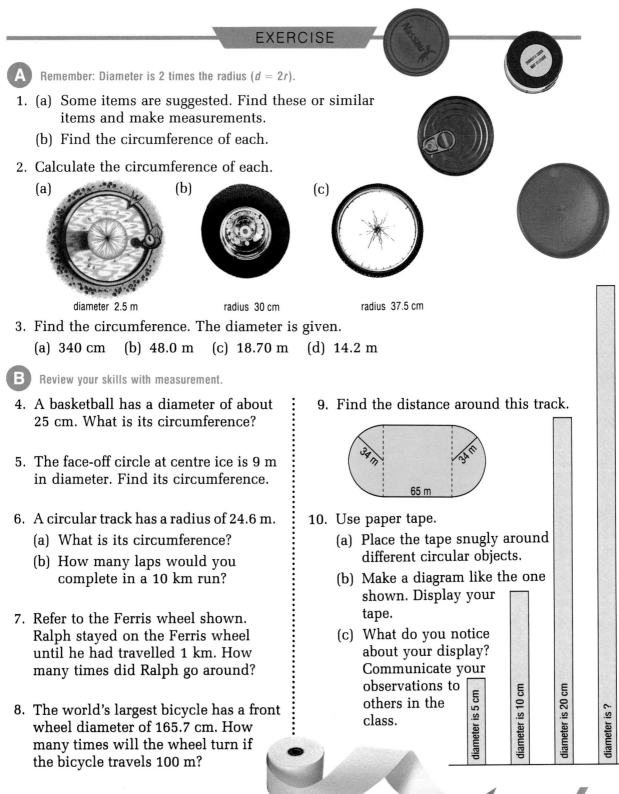

A Remember: Diameter is 2 times the radius ($d = 2r$).

1. (a) Some items are suggested. Find these or similar items and make measurements.

   (b) Find the circumference of each.

2. Calculate the circumference of each.

   (a)   (b)   (c)

   diameter 2.5 m   radius 30 cm   radius 37.5 cm

3. Find the circumference. The diameter is given.

   (a) 340 cm   (b) 48.0 m   (c) 18.70 m   (d) 14.2 m

B Review your skills with measurement.

4. A basketball has a diameter of about 25 cm. What is its circumference?

5. The face-off circle at centre ice is 9 m in diameter. Find its circumference.

6. A circular track has a radius of 24.6 m.

   (a) What is its circumference?

   (b) How many laps would you complete in a 10 km run?

7. Refer to the Ferris wheel shown. Ralph stayed on the Ferris wheel until he had travelled 1 km. How many times did Ralph go around?

8. The world's largest bicycle has a front wheel diameter of 165.7 cm. How many times will the wheel turn if the bicycle travels 100 m?

9. Find the distance around this track.

   34 m   34 m

   65 m

10. Use paper tape.

    (a) Place the tape snugly around different circular objects.

    (b) Make a diagram like the one shown. Display your tape.

    (c) What do you notice about your display? Communicate your observations to others in the class.

    diameter is 5 cm   diameter is 10 cm   diameter is 20 cm   diameter is ?

5.4 CIRCLES AND DESIGNS

The following parts of a circle can be used to construct designs.

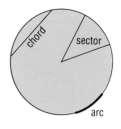

- A **chord** is any line that joins two points on a circle.
- An **arc** is any part of the circumference of the circle.
- A **sector** is a cut, or slice, of a circle formed by two radii and an arc.

EXERCISE

 B Make a sketch before you construct each design.

1. Refer to the diagrams at the top of the page.
   (a) How are arcs, chords, and sectors used to construct each design?
   (b) Construct and shade each design.
   (c) Construct a design of your own that uses one of the parts of a circle. Shade your design.

2. Use dot paper to construct an exact copy of each. Decide how arcs are used to construct the design.
   (a)   (b)

3. (a) What parts of the circle are used to construct the design shown?
   (b) Construct and colour the design.

4. Construct a design of your own that uses
   (a) only arcs.
   (b) only chords.
   (c) chords and arcs.
   (d) chords and sectors.

5. Many companies use logos to communicate information about their products. One example is shown below.
   (a) Use the Yellow Pages to find other logos. Decide how the parts of a circle are used to construct each design.
   (b) Suppose you are a designer. Choose a product and design a logo to communicate your product.

Tennis Canada

Have you ever wondered how a telephone works?

Activity 1   *Work with a Partner*
Step 1 Choose a circular object and trace it.
Step 2 Fold the circle in half. Mark the fold.
Step 3 Fold the circle in half a different way. Mark
the fold.
Step 4 Decide where the centre of the circle is
located. Communicate your decision to others.

Activity 2   *Work with a Partner*
1. Use two cans without tops. Follow steps A, B, C, and D.
   A Trace the bottom of each can onto paper. Find the centre of the bottom.
   B Use a nail to make a hole in the centre of the bottom in each can.
   C Put the ends of a long piece of string in the holes you made and then tie
   a knot in each end of the string.
   D Wax the string and pull the cans apart so that the string is tight. Write a
   message and read it into the can. Have your partner record the
   message. Did you communicate your message clearly?

2. (a) Repeat the steps of Question 1 with a longer string.
   (b) What is the longest string you can use and still have an effective
   telephone? Communicate your reasons to your partner.

Activity 3   *Work in a Group*
3. (a) Use a circular lid and trace it onto paper. Find its centre.
   (b) Place the lid on a piece of Styrofoam as shown. Hammer a nail
   through the centre of the lid to make a spinning top. The point
   of the nail must stick out about 2 cm.
   (c) Spin your top. What is the longest time your top can spin?

4. Repeat the steps of Question 3 for other lids. Which top will spin
   the longest?

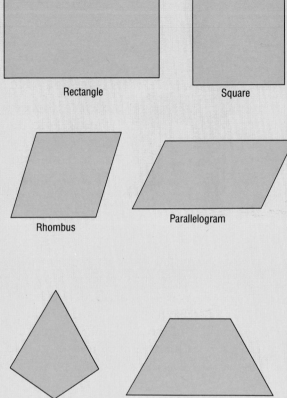

Often, you explore relationships among geometric figures and apply the relationships to solve problems. Work with a partner to complete the following explorations. In your journal, write any relationships you discover.

EXPLORATION ① Work Together

A **quadrilateral** is a figure with four sides. Some quadrilaterals have special properties and are given special names.

1. (a) Measure the sides and angles of each quadrilateral shown.
   (b) What relationships do you see for the side lengths of each quadrilateral?
   (c) What relationships do you see for the angle measures of each quadrilateral?

2. Use your relationships in Question 1.
   (a) What relationships would uniquely describe each quadrilateral?
   (b) Test your relationships from (a) on quadrilaterals of your own.

EXPLORATION ② Work in Groups

3. (a) Copy the quadrilaterals above onto tracing paper. Draw both diagonals for each.
   (b) Use the chart to record information about each quadrilateral. What relationships do you see?
   (c) Draw quadrilaterals of your own. Test your relationships on your quadrilaterals.
   (d) Decide how you can describe each quadrilateral uniquely using your relationships from (c).

Name of Quadrilateral	Are the Diagonals Equal in Length?	Do the Diagonals Bisect Each Other?	Do the Diagonals Form 90° Angles?

EXPLORATION ③ *Work with a Partner*

4. Use the quadrilaterals shown on the previous page.
   (a) Measure the angles in each quadrilateral.
   (b) Find the sum of the measures from (a) to the nearest 10°.
   (c) Draw three quadrilaterals of your own. Measure the angles in each quadrilateral.
   (d) Find the sum of the measures from (c) to the nearest 10°. What do you notice? Communicate your observations to your partner.
   (e) Based on your results, what conclusions can you make?

EXPLORATION ④ *Work in Small Groups*

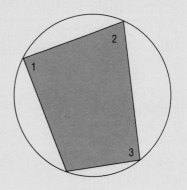

5. Draw a quadrilateral in a circle like the one shown. Angles 1 and 3 are called **opposite angles**.
   (a) Measure the opposite angles. Find the sum of the opposite angles to the nearest 10°.
   (b) Draw another circle and a quadrilateral in the circle. Find the sum of the opposite angles to the nearest 10°. What do you notice? Communicate your observations to your group.
   (c) Repeat part (b) for other quadrilaterals that you draw inside a circle.
   (d) Based on your results, what relationships do you see in quadrilaterals drawn in a circle? Test your relationships with other quadrilaterals.

EXPLORATION ⑤ *Summarize Your Results*

6. (a) Make a summary of all the relationships you have found in each exploration with quadrilaterals.
   (b) Provide an example of your own to show each relationship.

5.7 COMMUNICATING ABOUT QUADRILATERALS

In the previous section, you explored various relationships in quadrilaterals. You summarized your relationships in Exploration 5.

The following two relationships are used to solve problems in the exercise.

The sum of the angles in a quadrilateral is 360°.
$\angle A + \angle B + \angle C + \angle D = 360°$

When a quadrilateral is drawn in a circle, the sum of the opposite angles is 180°.

$\angle 1 + \angle 3 = 180°$
$\angle 2 + \angle 4 = 180°$

EXERCISE

A Review the relationships in quadrilaterals.

1. List the special properties of each quadrilateral.
   • rectangle   • square   • rhombus   • parallelogram   • kite   • trapezoid

2. (a) "I am a quadrilateral whose diagonals are equal. Which quadrilateral am I?"
   (b) "I am a quadrilateral whose diagonals form 90° angles. Which quadrilateral am I?"

3. Find the missing measure of the fourth angle in each quadrilateral.

(a)

(b)

(c)

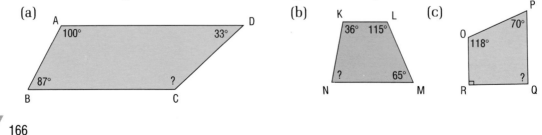

4. Find the missing measures of the angles in each quadrilateral drawn in a circle.

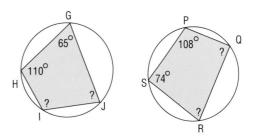

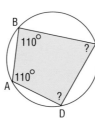

B Work with a partner to solve each problem.

5. (a) "I am a quadrilateral whose diagonals bisect each other. My opposite sides are equal in length. Which quadrilateral am I?"

(b) "I am a quadrilateral whose diagonals are perpendicular bisectors. My diagonals are also equal in length. Which quadrilateral am I?"

(c) "I am a quadrilateral whose diagonals are perpendicular bisectors. My opposite sides are equal in length. Which quadrilateral am I?"

6. (a) "We have the property that our opposite angles are equal. Which quadrilaterals can we be?"

(b) "We have the property that our diagonals meet at 90°. Which quadrilaterals can we be?"

7. (a) "In our club, all the diagonals bisect each other. Which quadrilaterals are in our club?"

(b) "In our club, the opposite sides of each quadrilateral are equal and parallel. Which quadrilaterals are in our club?"

(c) "In our club, all quadrilaterals have opposite angles that are equal. Which quadrilaterals are in our club?

8. Quadrilateral PQRS is constructed inside a circle so that ∠P = 74° and ∠Q = 103°. Find ∠R and ∠S.

9. Quadrilateral ABCD is constructed inside a circle so that ∠A = 56° and ∠B = 116°. Find ∠C and ∠D.

10. Work with a partner. Put an elastic on a geoboard to form the quadrilateral shown below.

(a) Communicate all the properties of the quadrilateral to your partner.

(b) Now, make one change to the elastic so that a different quadrilateral is formed. Have your partner communicate all the properties of this quadrilateral.

(c) Repeat (a) and (b) using other quadrilaterals.

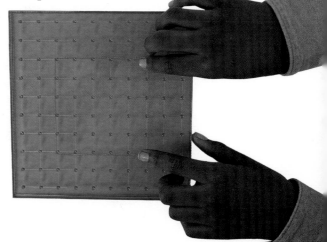

There are many games that you can play with your friends to help you use mathematics. One of those games is a form of Tic Tac Toe.

Rules
1. Decide which player goes first.
2. The player selects a square and is allowed one minute to think of an expression that will give the value in the square. The expression must contain at least one multiplication and one other operation. For example, $3 \times 5 + 2 = 17$.
3. The other player checks the expression. If it is correct, the square is won. If not, the turn is lost.
4. To win the game, a player must
   • use each operation at least once.
   • be the first to take a row, column, or diagonal.

Board 1

17	22	54
38	64	13
51	40	52

Board 2

35	67	59
44	38	61
57	19	26

Board 3

12.2	17.3	44.7
18.3	11.9	23.1
14.6	33.3	7.5

Activity
Create a board of your own. Use the rules to play the game with others in the class.

The following game is based on checkers. Review how to play a game of checkers and add the following rules. Play one game using the white squares and one game using the coloured squares. Then create a game board of your own and play the game with a partner.

1. To move a checker from one square to the next diagonally, each player must first mentally evaluate the expression in the square you want to move to.
2. Each player has only one minute to evaluate the expression. The second player checks the answer.
3. If the answer is correct, the player moves to that square. If not, the turn is lost.
4. You can jump a checker if it is diagonally in a square touching yours.
5. The winner is the player with checkers left on the board.

$2^3 + 3^2$	$(-12) - (-3)$	22×15	17×2.99	$12.65 + 18.27$	$125 + 75$	64×11	$74.8 \div 0.5$
$156 \div 3$	28×60	0.25×24	300×23	$0 \times 1 \times 2 \times 3 \times 4 \times 5 \times \ldots \times 50$	$\sqrt{28 \times 8}$	$\sqrt{100} \div \sqrt{25}$	$76.23 + 12.65$
28×5	$\frac{1}{10} \times 4.9$	24×1.98	$\frac{3^2 + 4^2}{5^2}$	$1860 \div 12$	0.3×10^2	3^5	$\frac{56}{8} + 12$
$\frac{4005}{45}$	$4250 \quad 30 + 600$	$0.1 \div 1000$	$20 - 11.98$	4×721	40×36	$\frac{1800}{200}$	$18 \times 2 \times 5$
28×25	$69.3 + 23.7$	$168 \div 8$	0.9×4.3	12×150	10×19.76	$27 + 3 - 7$	$45 + 48$
$6 \times 9 \times 50$	$7 \times 2 \times 5$	$83 - 28$	$149.6 \div 100$	$\frac{19 - 3 \div 3}{9 \times 2}$	$3 \times 7 \times 2$	$45 \div 9 - 5$	21×7
212.5×4	$3^2 + 4^2$	5×499	$357 - 135$	$\frac{9^2 + 1}{26 + 5}$	3×252	$15 \times 10 \times 5 \times 2$	$\frac{19 - 3 \times 5}{8 \div 4 \times 2}$
801×6	$900 \div 10^2$	$\frac{333}{33}$	$(13 - 1) \div 3$	40×28	$\sqrt{16 \times 9}$	81×9	$202 \quad 163 + 412$

5.10 AREA OF A RECTANGLE

To find the areas of rectangles, Joaquin used the tiles shown to the right. From the tiles, he noticed a relationship for finding the area of a rectangle.

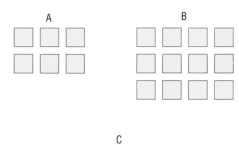

A

B

C

	Length	Width	Area	Length × Width
A	3 cm	2 cm	6 cm^2	6 cm^2
B	4 cm	3 cm	12 cm^2	12 cm^2
C	6 cm	3 cm	18 cm^2	18 cm^2

Based on his work, Joaquin identified the following relationship for finding the area of a rectangle.

Area = length × width

A = l × w

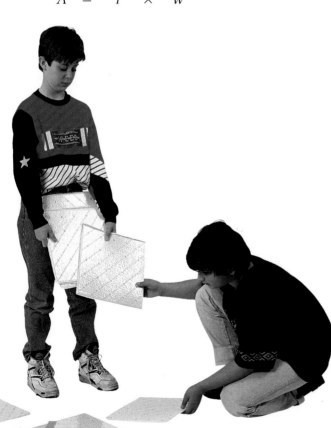

This relationship is used to solve problems like the following.

Kim needs to cover the floor of a gym with tiles. The floor is 17.6 m long and 22.5 m wide. A box of tiles covers an area of 5.0 m^2. How many boxes of tiles does Kim need to cover the floor?

Think: Find the area of the floor.
   Use $A = l \times w$.
      $A = 17.6 \times 22.5$
        $= 396$

Number of boxes needed

$$= \frac{\text{area of floor}}{\text{area covered by one box of tiles}}$$

$$= \frac{396}{5.0}$$

$$= 79.2$$ Remember: Round up to the number of boxes needed, namely, 80.

Kim will need 80 boxes of tiles.

A Check that your answers are reasonable.

1. (a) Some items are suggested to the right. Find these or similar items and measure to find each area.

   (b) Find other items of your own. Find each area.

2. Find the area of each rectangle.

   (a)

   1.4 cm

   2.3 cm

   (b)

   5.8 m

   3.2 m

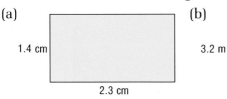

3. The length of a rectangle is 11.3 cm. Its width is 22.5 cm.

   (a) Sketch a diagram to show the information.

   (b) Find the area.

B Read all problems carefully.

4. The dimensions of a rectangular field are 102.3 m and 96.2 m. Find the area of the field.

5. A large display area is to be covered by tiles. The display area is 34.0 m long and 27.4 m wide. One box of tiles covers 5.3 m². How many boxes of tiles are needed?

6. The largest iceberg ever seen was an Antarctic iceberg. Its top was rectangular with a length of 335 km and a width of 97 km.

   (a) Find the area of the top.

   (b) Compare it with the area of Nova Scotia. Are you surprised?

7. The largest indoor ice rink measures 75.2 m by 107.3 m. Each person needs about 20 m² on which to practise. How many people can be on the ice at once?

8. Work with a partner. Use six tiles.

   (a) Make a shape from your tiles so that all tiles are connected along at least one edge as shown.

   (b) Trace the shape. Can the shape be folded into a box?

   (c) Keep using six tiles and see which shapes can be folded into a box.

   (d) Create a problem of your own using tiles. Compare your problem with others in the class.

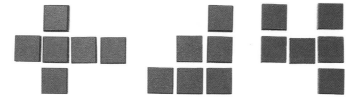

To solve problems, you will often use the problem solving skill of *looking for a pattern*. For example, earlier you explored patterns to help you find the relationship between the length, width, and area of a rectangle.

In the following explorations, you will explore area patterns in parallelograms, triangles, trapezoids, and circles. These patterns will lead you to relationships for the area covered by each shape. As you find each relationship, summarize it in your journal and explain it to your partner.

EXPLORATION ① *Area of a Parallelogram*

1. (a) Draw a parallelogram of your own on grid paper.

   (b) Cut the shaded right triangle from your parallelogram as shown in Step 1. Place it on the other side as shown in Step 2. What is the shape?

   (c) Measure to find the area of the shape you constructed in (b).

   (d) How does your answer from (c) help you find the area of a parallelogram?

   (e) Repeat the steps above for other parallelograms.

2. Based on your results from Question 1, suggest a relationship to help you find the area of a parallelogram.

Step 1

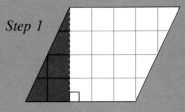

Step 2

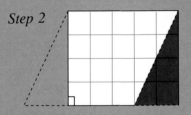

EXPLORATION ② *Area of a Triangle*

3. (a) Draw a parallelogram on grid paper. Measure to find its area.

   (b) Cut your parallelogram into two triangles. Compare their size and shape.

   (c) Find the area of each triangle in (b).

   (d) How do your answers above help you find the area of a triangle?

   (e) Repeat the steps above for other parallelograms.

4. Based on your results from Question 3, suggest a relationship to help you find the area of a triangle.

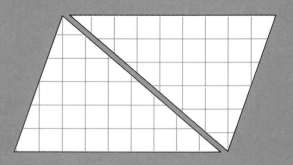

Area of a Trapezoid

5. (a) Draw two trapezoids that are the same size and shape on grid paper.

   (b) Cut out your trapezoids and put them together as shown. What is the new shape?

   (c) Measure to find the area of the shape you have constructed.

   (d) How does your answer from (c) help you find the area of a trapezoid?

   (e) Repeat the steps above for other trapezoids.

6. Based on your results from Question 5, suggest a relationship to help you find the area of a trapezoid.

EXPLORATION ④ *Area of a Circle*

7. (a) On a piece of cardboard, draw a circle with a radius of 10 cm.

   (b) Cut the circle along its diameter to form two semicircles. What is the distance around the circular part of each semicircle?

   (c) Cut each semicircle into equal sectors as shown in Step A below.

   (d) Separate the sectors and fit them together as shown in Step B below. What shape is suggested?

   (e) What is the length of the shape in Step B? What is the height?

   (f) What is the area of the shape in Step B?

   (g) Choose another circle. Repeat Steps A and B to find its area.

8. (a) Based on your results from Question 7, suggest a relationship to help you find the area of a circle.

   (b) Use your relationship to find the area of other circles.

Step A   *Step B*

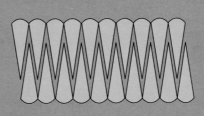

5.12 AREA OF A PARALLELOGRAM

The skills you learn in one part of mathematics can help you solve problems in other parts of mathematics. For example, in the previous section, you explored how to find the area of a rectangle. This skill can be used to help you find the area of a parallelogram as follows.

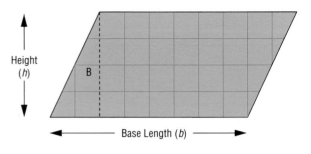

Triangle B is placed as shown to form a rectangle. The area of the rectangle is the same as the area of the parallelogram.

$$\text{Area of parallelogram} = \text{area of rectangle}$$
$$= \text{length} \times \text{width}$$
$$= 8 \text{ cm} \times 4 \text{ cm}$$
$$= 32 \text{ cm}^2$$

Thus, the area of the parallelogram is 32 cm².

In both the rectangle and the parallelogram,
- the base lengths are equal.
- the heights (widths) are equal.

Thus, a relationship to find the area of a parallelogram is shown to the right.

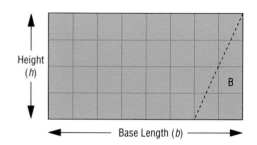

Area of parallelogram = base length × height

$$A = b \times h$$

This relationship can help you solve problems like the following.

A desert island in the South Pacific is roughly shaped like a parallelogram with dimensions as shown. Find the area of the island to one decimal place.

$$\text{Area} = \text{base length} \times \text{height}$$
$$= 0.75 \text{ km} \times 2.50 \text{ km}$$
$$= 1.875 \text{ km}^2$$

Thus, the area of the island is about 1.9 km².

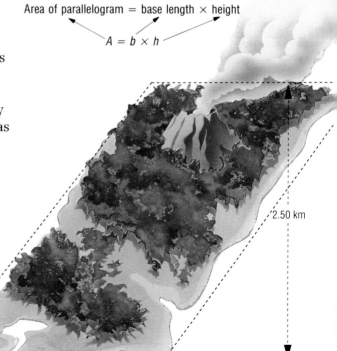

2.50 km

0.75 km

EXERCISE

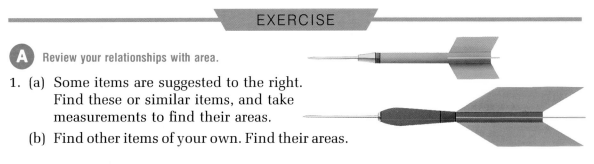

A Review your relationships with area.

1. (a) Some items are suggested to the right.
    Find these or similar items, and take
    measurements to find their areas.

   (b) Find other items of your own. Find their areas.

2. Find the area of each shingle. What do you notice about your answers?

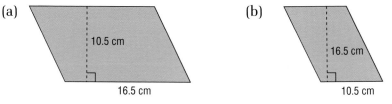

(a) 10.5 cm   16.5 cm

(b) 16.5 cm   10.5 cm

3. The base of a parallelogram measures 14 cm. Its height measures 24 cm.

   (a) Sketch a diagram to show the information.   (b) Find the area.

B Remember: Write a concluding statement for each problem.

4. A field is shaped like a parallelogram.
   It has a base length of 175 m and a
   height of 225 m. Find its area.

5. The base of a parallelogram measures
   11.20 cm. Its height measures 8.54 cm.
   Find its area.

6. The plastic flight on a dart is in the
   shape of a parallelogram. Its base
   length is 3.2 cm and its height is
   1.7 cm. Each dart has 4 flights. Find
   the area of plastic used for the flights
   on each dart.

7. Oak Park is in the shape of a
   parallelogram. Its base measures 205 m
   and its height 75 m. One bag of seed
   costs $8.95 and covers 85 m².

   (a) Find the area of the park.

   (b) Find the cost to seed the park.

8. Use a geoboard and elastics.

   (a) Choose a number for the area of a
       parallelogram (such as 8 cm²).

   (b) Create parallelograms each having
       the chosen area. How many are
       there?

MAKING CONNECTIONS

Research archery in your
library.

(a) How can you win an archery
    tournament?

(b) How are parallelograms
    used to design an arrow?
    What mathematics is used
    in archery?

(c) What special words are
    used (like flight) in archery?

You can use the relationship for the area of a parallelogram to find the area of a triangle.

Step 1 Trace and cut out the parallelogram.

Step 2 Cut the parallelogram along a diagonal to form two triangles.

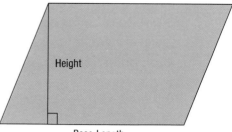

The two triangles shown are the same size and shape. Each triangle has half the area of the parallelogram.

Area of a parallelogram = base length × height

Area of a triangle = $\frac{1}{2}$ × base length × height

$$A = \frac{1}{2} \times b \times h$$

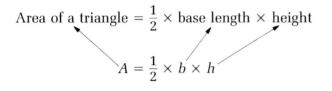

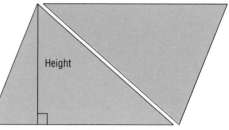

This relationship is needed to solve problems like the following.

A solar panel is shaped like a triangle. It is 1.2 m high and has a base length of 0.8 m. Find the area of each panel to one decimal place.

Use $A = \frac{1}{2} \times b \times h$.

Area $= \frac{1}{2} \times 0.8$ m $\times 1.2$ m

$= 0.48$ m^2

The area of each panel is about 0.5 m^2.

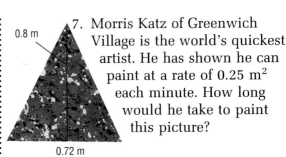

A Look for patterns.

1. (a) Find the items shown or similar ones, and take measurements to find their areas.

   (b) Find other items of your own. Find their areas.

2. Find the area of each medallion.

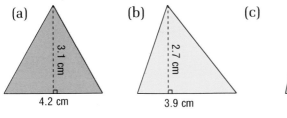

(a) 3.1 cm 4.2 cm

(b) 2.7 cm 3.9 cm

(c) 8.8 cm 14.3 cm

3. A triangle has a base length of 8 cm. It has a height of 5 cm.

   (a) Sketch a diagram to show the information.　(b) Find the area.

B Use a calculator.

4. The dorsal fin of a shark is shaped like a triangle. It is 15.4 cm wide at the base and 22.3 cm high.

   (a) Sketch the dorsal fin.

   (b) Find the area of the dorsal fin.

5. Did you know that the piranha is the most ferocious fresh water fish in the world? Its teeth are triangular. Each is about 0.6 cm high and about 0.5 cm wide at the base.

   (a) Sketch a tooth of a piranha.

   (b) Find the area of each tooth.

6. A protected area of land is in the shape of a triangle with base 3.2 km and height 2.6 km. Calculate its area.

7. Morris Katz of Greenwich Village is the world's quickest artist. He has shown he can paint at a rate of 0.25 m² each minute. How long would he take to paint this picture?

0.8 m

0.72 m

8. (a) Use six toothpicks to form four identical triangles.

   (b) Find the greatest number of triangles you can form with eight toothpicks.

   (c) Create a similar problem of your own using toothpicks. Compare it with others in your class.

Y ou have seen how the relationship for the area of a parallelogram can help you develop a relationship for the area of a triangle. This same relationship can help you develop a relationship for the area of a circle.

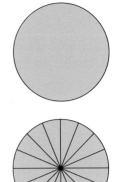

Step 1 Draw a circle and cut it into 16 equal sectors. (Hint: Fold the circle first.)

Step 2 Put your sectors together as shown. The shape suggests a parallelogram.

- The base of the parallelogram is shown by $\pi \times r$. How do you know?
- The height of the parallelogram is shown by r. How do you know?

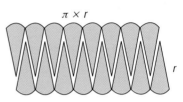

Thus,   area of a circle = area of parallelogram
                              = base length × height

$$A = \pi \times r \times r$$

This relationship is needed to solve problems like the following.

A lawn sprinkler rotates and sprays water 7.5 m from its centre. What area of lawn is watered by the sprinkler to the nearest square metre?

Use $A = \pi \times r \times r$
   $A \doteq 3.14 \times 7.5 \times 7.5$
     $= 176.625$

Thus, the area watered is about 177 m².

Think: You can write the area of a circle in a more compact form as shown.
$A = \pi \times r \times r$
  $= \pi \times r^2$

 A Remember: $\pi \doteq 3.14$.

1. (a) Find the items shown or similar ones, and take measurements to find their areas.

   (b) Find other items of your own. Find their areas.

2. Find the area of each circle.

   (a) radius 2 cm
   (b) radius 3.5 cm
   (c) diameter 2.6 cm

 B Check that your answers are reasonable.

3. (a) A discus used in the Olympics has a radius of 11 cm. Find the area of the discus.

   (b) When throwing a discus, an athlete throws it from a circle. The diameter of the circle is about 2.8 m. Find its area.

4. (a) The smallest functional record has a diameter of 33.3 mm. Find the area of the record.

   (b) Make an accurate drawing of the record in (a).

   (c) Compare its area with the area of a CD. How many times greater is the area of a CD?

5. The largest omelette ever made had a diameter of 9.1 m. It used 54 763 eggs and 240 kg of cheese.

   (a) Find the area of the omelette.

   (b) Estimate how much the omelette cost to prepare.

   (c) Estimate how many people the omelette can feed.

6. (a) Measure the diameter of one of your disks. Find its area.

   (b) Estimate how many disks will fit on this page. Then calculate.

   (c) Now fit as many disks as possible on this page. Compare your result with (b).

7. Lids for paint cans have a diameter of 20 cm. The lids are punched out of a rectangular piece of tin 1.5 m by 1.2 m.

   (a) Find the area of each lid.

   (b) How many lids can you punch out of one sheet? What assumptions have you made?

C

8. Kennedy owns the sprinkler described on the opposite page. His lawn measures 30.5 m by 40.5 m.

   (a) Estimate the least number of times he will need to change the position of the sprinkler so that the entire lawn is watered.

   (b) Create and solve a similar problem.

179

5.15 WORKING BACKWARDS

Alfreda wants to put a fence around her rectangular garden. She knows that her garden covers an area of 187 m² and is 11 m along one side. How many metres of fence will Alfreda need to buy?

Use $A = l \times w$.

$187 = 11 \times w$

$\dfrac{187}{11} = w$

$17 = w$

Think: To solve the problem, work backwards from the area.

Think: $\dfrac{187}{11} = \dfrac{11 \times w}{11}$

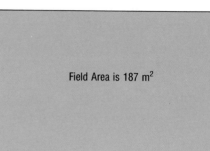

Field Area is 187 m²

11 m

Thus, the width of the garden is 17 m.

Use $P = 2 \times l + 2 \times w$.

$= 2 \times 11 + 2 \times 17$

$= 56$

Think: To find the length of fence Alfreda needs, find the perimeter of the garden.

Thus, Alfreda needs to buy 56 m of fence.

EXERCISE

B Review your skills with perimeter and area.

1. The area of a rectangle is 16 cm². Its length is 8 cm. Find its width.

2. The base length of a parallelogram is 10 cm. Its area is 75 cm². Find its height.

3. The height of a triangle is 13 mm. Its area is 32.5 mm². Find the length of its base.

4. A piece of rectangular panelling covers an area of 3.2 m². The width of each piece is 1.6 m.
   (a) Find the length of each piece.
   (b) How many pieces are needed to panel a wall with an area of 36 m²?

5. Fernandez wants to put a fence around his rectangular garden. He knows the garden covers an area of 33.5 m² and has a length of 7.4 m. How many metres of fence should he buy?

6. Sandy's backyard covers an area of 315 m². It is 21 m long. To fence the yard, posts are placed every 1.5 m. How many posts are needed?
   (a) Record the information on a diagram.
   (b) Think of what manipulatives you can use to solve the problem.
   (c) Solve the problem.

5.16 PERIMETER AND AREA

John said to Susan, "I have 12 tiles. I wonder how I can arrange the tiles to form a rectangle with the greatest perimeter?"

To solve his problem, John manipulated the tiles as shown below. Each tile measures 1 cm by 1 cm.

Perimeter is 14 cm.

Perimeter is 16 cm.

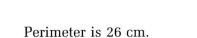
Perimeter is 26 cm.

Thus, the greatest perimeter is 26 cm when the tiles are arranged in one row.

EXERCISE

B Use tiles to help you.

1. How many different rectangles can you construct with a perimeter of 10 cm? of 12 cm?

2. Choose a perimeter of your own.
   (a) How many different rectangles can you make with your perimeter?
   (b) Which shape has the greatest area?

3. A rectangle has an area of 16 cm² and side lengths that are whole numbers.
   (a) Find the length and width of all possible rectangles.
   (b) What are the dimensions of the rectangle with the greatest perimeter for the given area?

4. (a) Choose an area for a rectangle.
   A Find the length and width of all possible rectangles.
   B What are the dimensions of the rectangle with the greatest perimeter for your area?
   (b) Choose other areas and repeat (a). Do you see a pattern?

5. (a) Choose a perimeter that has a whole number of units.
   A Find the length and width of all possible rectangles.
   B What are the dimensions of the rectangle with the greatest area?
   (b) Choose other perimeters and repeat (a). Do you see a pattern?

To solve some problems, you can think of the problem in a simpler way. For example, to find the area of the following parking lot, look for shapes within the parking lot whose areas you know how to find.

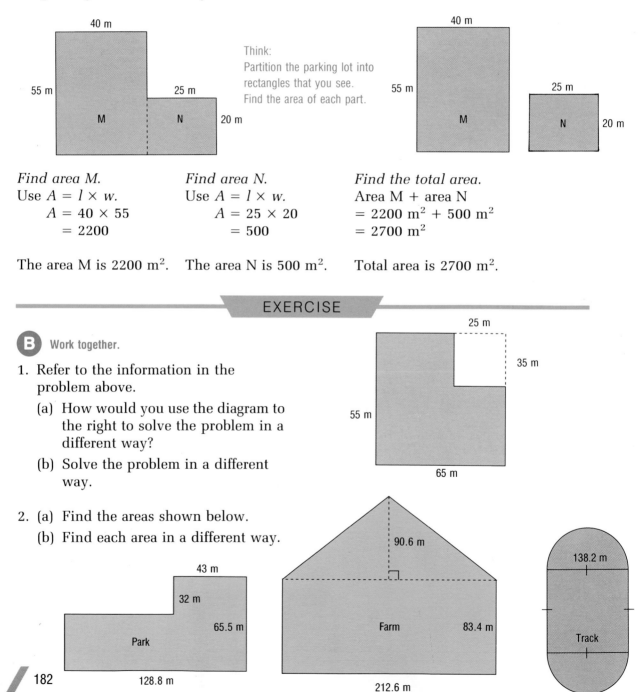

Think:
Partition the parking lot into rectangles that you see.
Find the area of each part.

Find area M.
Use $A = l \times w$.
$\quad A = 40 \times 55$
$\quad\quad = 2200$

The area M is 2200 m².

Find area N.
Use $A = l \times w$.
$\quad A = 25 \times 20$
$\quad\quad = 500$

The area N is 500 m².

Find the total area.
Area M + area N
$= 2200 \text{ m}^2 + 500 \text{ m}^2$
$= 2700 \text{ m}^2$

Total area is 2700 m².

EXERCISE

B Work together.

1. Refer to the information in the problem above.
   (a) How would you use the diagram to the right to solve the problem in a different way?
   (b) Solve the problem in a different way.

2. (a) Find the areas shown below.
   (b) Find each area in a different way.

TECHNOLOGY INSIGHT: AREA OF A POLYGON

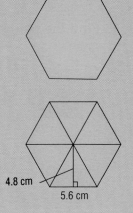

In order to write a computer program, you need to know the mathematics involved.

In the previous section, you solved simpler problems in order to solve a given problem. The same process can be used to find the area of a regular hexagon as shown.

Find the area of each triangle.

Use $A = \frac{1}{2} \times b \times h$.

$A = \frac{1}{2} \times 5.6 \times 4.8$

$= 13.44$

Find the total area.

Total area $= 6 \times 13.44 \text{ cm}^2$

$= 80.64 \text{ cm}^2$

4.8 cm

5.6 cm

Thus, the area of the regular hexagon is about 81 cm².

You now use the math you know to write the following computer program.

```
10 REM     A PROGRAM TO CALCULATE AREA
20 INPUT  ''THE HEIGHT OF EACH TRIANGLE IS''; H
30 INPUT  ''THE BASE LENGTH OF EACH TRIANGLE IS''; B
40 LET    A = 6 * (B * H)/2
50 PRINT  ''THE AREA OF THE HEXAGON IS''; A; ''SQUARE CM''
60 END
```

To test whether a program works, RUN the program using known values. RUN this program using the hexagon above. Is the output reasonable?

EXERCISE

1. Use the program to find the area of each regular hexagon.

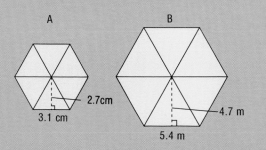

A

B

2.7cm

3.1 cm

4.7 m

5.4 m

2. What changes would you make to the program to find the area of a regular octagon? Use the new program to find the area of each regular octagon.

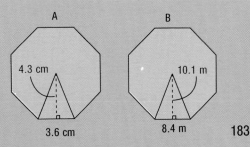

A

B

4.3 cm

3.6 cm

10.1 m

8.4 m

183

1. Find the perimeter and area of each.

(a) 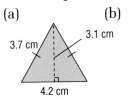 (b)

2. Find the area of the park.

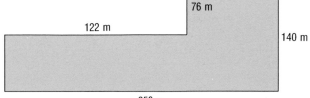

3. Fred's baseball strike zone has a height of 25.3 cm. Home plate is always 30 cm wide. What is the area of Fred's strike zone?

4. Chris planted a hedge around a garden. The rectangular garden measures 16.2 m by 12.6 m.

   (a) Find the perimeter.

   (b) She put a hedge plant every 30 cm. She also put one at each corner. How many plants were used?

5. The world's largest clock face is the floral clock in Tokachigaoka Park, Japan. It is 18 m in diameter.

   (a) Find the area covered by the clock face.

   (b) How far will the tip of the hour hand move in 1 h? What assumptions have you made?

6. The world's smallest bicycle has wheels about 2.5 cm in diameter. How far will a point on the wheel travel in 20 turns?

Have you solved problems in the chapter clearly so that you understand what you did?

Have you recorded in your journal all relationships you investigated?

Keep updating your Problem Solving Plan. What new strategies have you added?

MAKING CONNECTIONS

Refer to the opening pages of the chapter.

(a) Create a problem using one of the pictures.

(b) Solve your problem.

(c) Compare your problem with others in your class.

SELF EVALUATION

1. Find each area.

(a)

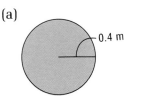

3.2 m

5.7 m

(b)

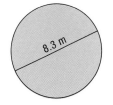

0.9 m

1.3 m

3.9 m

2. Find the circumference and area of each circle.

(a)

0.4 m

(b)

8.3 m

3. During the rainy season, drainage ditches are used to transfer water from one river to another as shown. Calculate the area enclosed by the drainage ditches.

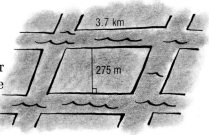

3.7 km

275 m

4. Chairs are to be placed along all walls of a gymnasium. The gym is 45.5 m long and 62.5 m wide. The chairs are placed exactly 1 m apart.

(a) Find the perimeter of the gymnasium.

(b) How many chairs will be needed in all? What assumptions have you made?

5. The smallest commercial building is located in Vancouver. The floor is 1.6 m wide and 30 m long. Find the perimeter and area of the floor.

6. "I am a quadrilateral whose diagonals are perpendicular bisectors of each other. My diagonals are not the same length. Which quadrilateral am I?"

MATH JOURNAL

Throughout the chapter, you have learned and used a number of new symbols, vocabulary, and problem solving skills.
- List them in your journal.
- Write an example of your own to illustrate each.

If you had lived in medieval times, your neighbourhood castle would have been a great place to live!

Though they were usually dark, cold, and damp, castles were huge and had the finest art and furniture. The best parties were always held in castles.

Castles were also good places to hide from enemy raiders who wanted to separate you from all that nice art and furniture.

Here's a chance to work together and design your own castle. You will use your measuring skills, as well as a pair of compasses and a straightedge. Where needed, perform the calculations that will give you the appropriate dimensions of the castle. Remember, this is a "basic" castle. You should add your own design features to make it unique.

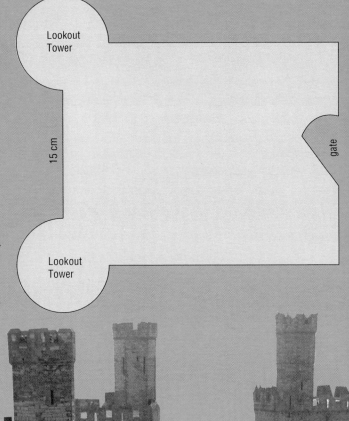

Lookout Tower

15 cm

Lookout Tower

gate

Step 1 Building the floor.

(a) Use a piece of cardboard and draw the floor of the castle shown. How much cardboard will you need?

(b) Each "lookout tower" has an area of 9π cm². What is the circumference of each tower? (Remember how to find the radius.)

(c) The walls are eight times as long as the radius of a lookout tower. What is the length of each wall?

(d) The gate is placed in the centre of the wall and is $\frac{1}{3}$ the length of its wall. Where will it be placed?

Did you know that it took nearly 2000 labourers to build the Caernarfon Castle in Wales? The labourers and servants of the castle lived in little rooms constructed directly into its walls.

Step 2 Building the tower.

(a) The tower is about 10 cm in height. What is the length and width of the piece of cardboard needed for each tower?

(b) Before you fold your cardboard and attach it to the floor, a door must be made in the tower.

Step 3 Building the walls.

(a) The walls are 8 cm high. How much cardboard is needed for each wall?

(b) Cut out each wall. Attach them to your floor plan.

Step 4 Building the walls and gate.
The gate to your castle should not be more than 8 cm tall.

(a) What is the length and width of the gate?

(b) How much cardboard is needed for the gate?

When you cut out the gate, only cut along one side of the gate and across the top. The other side of the gate will stay attached to the wall and will swing open.

Step 5 The Finishing Touches.
Go to your library and find pictures of other castles. Use the pictures to add features to your castle so that it is the way you would like it to be.

Once you have finished your castle, compare your castle with others in your class. If you see any different design features that you would like to include on your castle, do it.

6 MAKING CONNECTIONS: MEASURE

Did you know that the fastest motorcycle in the world can reach a speed of 283 km/h? In your journal, describe what measurement skills you need to design a motorcycle.

Did you know that sand yachting originated in Belgium in 1595? Sand yachts like these can reach speeds of 100 km/h. Estimate the height of a sand yacht.

Manufacturers know that their packages need to catch the shopper's eye. How successful are the packages above?

Each package shown is an example of a polyhedron. A **polyhedron** is a three dimensional figure where all faces are flat. Prisms and pyramids are two types of polyhedra. Some prisms and pyramids are shown below.

Prisms are named according to the shape of the base.

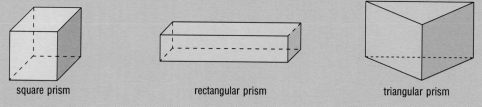

square prism   rectangular prism   triangular prism

Pyramids are also named according to the shape of the base.

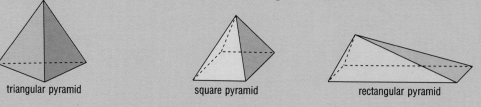

triangular pyramid   square pyramid   rectangular pyramid

In the explorations that follow, work with a partner to explore polyhedra. Use your journal to summarize any patterns you see.

EXPLORATION ① Pyramids and Prisms

1. (a) Refer to the packages on the previous page. Give a name to each package and explain why you gave it that name.

   (b) Use magazines and newspapers to find examples of pyramids and prisms of your own. Give a name to each and explain why you gave it that name.

   (c) Sketch other packages that you know. Give a name to each and explain why you gave it that name. (Hint: You may need to go to a grocery store to find packages.)

   (d) For each package, what did the manufacturer do to catch your eye?

EXPLORATION ② Using Packages

2. (a) Take apart a box like the one shown and flatten it on your desk. This is called a **net**.

   (b) Make measurements to find the area covered by the net.

   (c) Use your results from (b). What is the area covered by the complete surface of the box?

3. Repeat the steps of Question 2 for other boxes of your own. Make measurements and find the area covered by the surface of each box.

EXPLORATION ③ Working with Nets

4. Copy and cut out the nets shown. What polyhedron can be formed by each net?

5. Find prisms and pyramids of your own.

   (a) Trace each face to construct a net on cardboard.

   (b) Cut out the net and fold it to create the prism or pyramid.

6. Draw a pyramid and prism of your own. Make measurements to construct a net. Cut out the net to create your shape. Give a name to the polyhedron.

If you were a manufacturer, you would want to know the cost of each package before actually making it. To find the cost, you need to know how much material will be needed. To find the amount of material used to make the box of Bran Flakes, for example, you need to find the total area of all faces. This is the **surface area**. You can unfold the box to show its net as shown below and find the area of each face.

A
Use $A = l \times w$.
$A = 30 \times 19$
$= 570$

B
Use $A = l \times w$.
$A = 30 \times 8$
$= 240$

C
Use $A = l \times w$.
$A = 19 \times 8$
$= 152$

Think: Each face occurs twice.

Total area = 2 × area of face **A** + 2 × area of face **B** + 2 × area of face **C**
$= 2 \times 570 \text{ cm}^2 + 2 \times 240 \text{ cm}^2 + 2 \times 152 \text{ cm}^2$
$= 1924 \text{ cm}^2$

The box of Bran Flakes has a surface area of 1924 cm².
Thus, 1924 cm² of material are needed to make the Bran Flakes package.

EXERCISE

A Review how to name polyhedra.

1. (a) Use the nets shown. Find the area of each face.
   (b) Find the total surface area.
   (c) Name the figure formed when the net is folded.

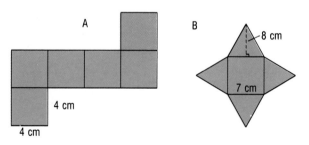

2. Draw a net for each package.

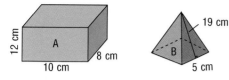

(a) Find the area of each face.

(b) Find the surface area of each package.

3. The dimensions of a box are 18.5 cm by 12.0 cm by 10.0 cm. Find its surface area.

4. A triangular prism has a base with a length of 3.2 cm and a height of 4.5 cm. The height of the prism is 5.2 cm. Find its surface area.

5. A pyramid has a square base with a length of 10.5 cm. Each triangular face has a height of 8.3 cm. Find its surface area.

6. (a) Find the surface area of the cheese box.

(b) To make the package, it costs 0.18¢ for each square centimetre. Find the cost.

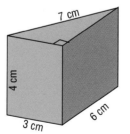

7. A Toblerone box is shown below.

Suppose the material used to make the package costs 0.05¢ for each square centimetre. Find the total cost of the package.

8. Refer to the package of Bran Flakes on the previous page. Packages are cut from large sheets 1.2 m by 1.5 m.

(a) How many packages can be cut from one sheet? What assumptions have you made?

(b) Create a similar problem of your own. Compare your problem with others in your class.

9. Find any package of your own.

(a) Draw the package. Mark all dimensions. Draw the net.

(b) Find the surface area in (a).

10. The figures below have been cut and folded from pieces of paper.

(a) Fold pieces of paper to form the figures below. Find the surface area of each.

(b) Use another piece of paper and fold it to form a figure of your own. Name the figure. Repeat (a).

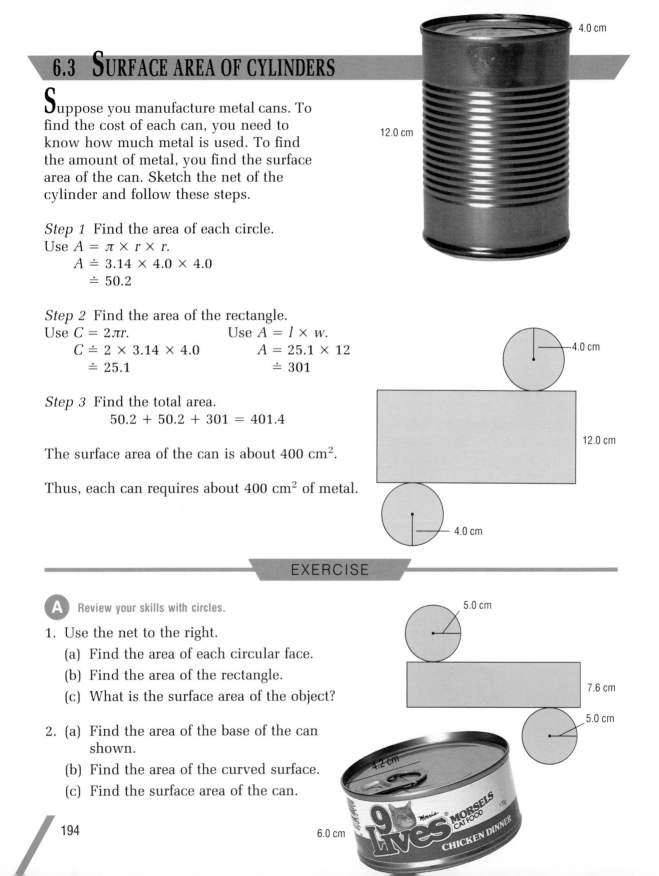

6.3 SURFACE AREA OF CYLINDERS

4.0 cm

Suppose you manufacture metal cans. To find the cost of each can, you need to know how much metal is used. To find the amount of metal, you find the surface area of the can. Sketch the net of the cylinder and follow these steps.

12.0 cm

Step 1 Find the area of each circle.
Use $A = \pi \times r \times r$.
$$A \doteq 3.14 \times 4.0 \times 4.0$$
$$\doteq 50.2$$

Step 2 Find the area of the rectangle.
Use $C = 2\pi r$.   Use $A = l \times w$.
$$C \doteq 2 \times 3.14 \times 4.0 \qquad A = 25.1 \times 12$$
$$\doteq 25.1 \qquad\qquad\qquad \doteq 301$$

4.0 cm

Step 3 Find the total area.
$$50.2 + 50.2 + 301 = 401.4$$

The surface area of the can is about 400 cm².

Thus, each can requires about 400 cm² of metal.

12.0 cm

4.0 cm

EXERCISE

A Review your skills with circles.

5.0 cm

1. Use the net to the right.
   (a) Find the area of each circular face.
   (b) Find the area of the rectangle.
   (c) What is the surface area of the object?

7.6 cm

5.0 cm

2. (a) Find the area of the base of the can shown.
   (b) Find the area of the curved surface.
   (c) Find the surface area of the can.

4.2 cm

6.0 cm

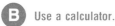

B Use a calculator.

3. Find the surface area of each cylinder.

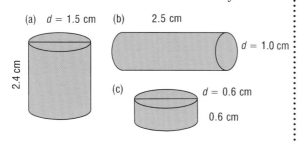

(a) *d* = 1.5 cm   (b)   2.5 cm

2.4 cm

d = 1.0 cm

(c)   *d* = 0.6 cm

0.6 cm

4. (a) Obtain each can shown below.
   (b) Estimate the surface area of each.
   (c) Measure to calculate the surface area. How reasonable was your estimate?

5. The height of a can is 10.0 cm. The diameter of its base is 9.4 cm.
   (a) Find its surface area.
   (b) Metal costs 0.08¢ for each square centimetre. How much will the can cost to make?

6. A display drum is 1.5 m tall. It has a radius of 0.7 m.
   (a) Find the surface area of the drum.
   (b) One can of spray paint covers an area of 5.5 m². How many cans are needed to paint the drum?

7. A rectangular prism, triangular prism, and cylinder have equal base areas and heights.
   (a) Estimate which shape requires the most and the least paint to cover it completely. Then calculate.
   (b) How accurate was your estimate?

8. (a) Cut out a strip made of eight squares like the one shown below.
   (b) Show how you can fold the strip to form a cube where each face is one square. Find its surface area.

C

9. A tennis ball has a diameter of about 7 cm. There are 3 balls in a can. About how much material is needed to make the can?

MAKING CONNECTIONS

Collect as many can labels as possible and measure the length and the width of each label.
- Use your measurements to find the surface area of each can. What assumptions have you made?
- Design a can label of your own to replace one of those you collected. What makes yours unique?

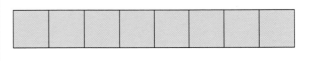

6.4 PROBLEM SOLVING: MANIPULATIVES

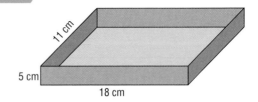

The baking pan shown to the right has the dimensions shown. Work with a partner.

Activity
- Calculate the surface area of the pan.
- Use a piece of paper or cardboard to construct the pan.
- How much paper is wasted?

Step 1
The net of the pan is shown to the right. The surface area is calculated as follows.

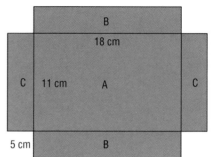

Surface area
$= 2 \times$ area face B $+ 2 \times$ area face C $+ 1 \times$ area face A
$= 2 \times 90 \text{ cm}^2 + 2 \times 55 \text{ cm}^2 + 198 \text{ cm}^2$
$= 488 \text{ cm}^2$

Step 2
Draw the net. Cut out the net, fold it, and keep the paper that is not used.

Step 3
Measure the length and the width of the pieces that have not been used.

The total paper wasted is ■ cm².

EXERCISE

B Work together and use paper from your notebook.

1. Refer to the box shown to the right.
   (a) Calculate the surface area of the box.
   (b) Draw the net of the box on a piece of paper. Cut out and fold the net.
   (c) How much paper is wasted when constructing the box?

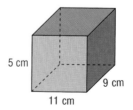

2. Suppose large sheets of cardboard are purchased by a manufacturer to make boxes like that in Question 1. The sheets are 4.75 m long and 3.60 m wide.

   (a) How many boxes can be made from each sheet?

   (b) How much cardboard is wasted with each sheet?

3. Sam has four green socks and six red socks in a drawer. He removes one sock at a time. How many socks will he need to remove to ensure he has a pair?

4. Ashley finds that she can make one new pen from the remains of four old pens. She finds 25 old pens. How many new pens can she make?

5. (a) Draw a rectangle with a length of 10 cm and a width of 25 cm.

   (b) Cut out and fold the rectangle to make a container that holds as much as possible. How much paper did you waste?

6. (a) Predict the figure you will have by cutting out and folding this net.

   (b) Trace, cut out, and fold the net. How accurate was your prediction?

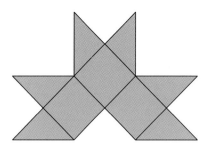

7. Use a label from a can.

   (a) Draw the net of the can using the label.

   (b) Suppose the can is cut from a sheet of metal 1 m long and 2 m wide. How many cans can be cut out of the sheet? How much metal is wasted?

8. (a) Painted cubes are cut as shown below. How many unpainted cubes will there be?

   (b) Create a similar problem of your own. Compare your problem to others in the class.

197

6.5 IRREGULAR AREAS

Suppose you are the captain of the Star Ship *Enterprise*. Your mission is to capture and analyze the cell structure of the Galactica Gorilla. Your chief surgeon has removed one cell from the animal and has placed it on the grid shown below. What is the area covered by the cell?

1. The area is greater than 16 square units. (Count the number of whole units inside as shown.)

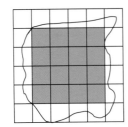

2. The area is less than 34 square units. (Count the number of whole units covered or partially covered by the cell.)

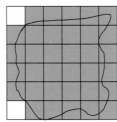

3. Find the average of the two numbers.   Think: $\dfrac{16 + 34}{2} = 25$

The cell has an area of about 25 square units.

EXERCISE

 B   Use the method above.

1. Each of the following cells was collected and stored on the *Enterprise*.
   - Find the area of each cell.
   - Create a name for the life form that is made of each cell.
   - In your journal, write a short story to describe how one of these cells was obtained.

(a)   (b)   (c)   (d)   (e)

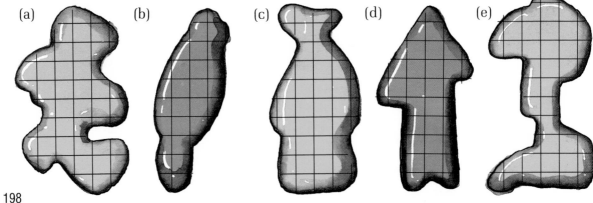

6.6 MAKING CONNECTIONS: USING AREA

Previously, you saw how to find the area covered by irregular shapes. Before you begin the following exercise, review your skills for finding irregular area.

EXERCISE

 Check that your answers are reasonable.

1. Find the number of square units covered by each.

   (a) 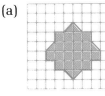   (b) 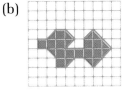   (c)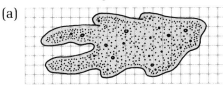

2. An amoeba and a paramecium are drawn on grids below.
   - Find the number of square units covered by each.
   - Which has the greater area? What assumptions have you made?

   (a) 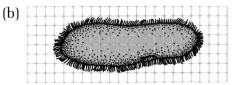   (b)

3. A map of part of Canada is drawn on the grid below. Work together.

   (a) Find the area, in square units, for each province shown. Which has the greatest area? the least area?

   (b) The actual area covered by Manitoba is $652\,000$ km^2. Use this information to estimate the areas of the other provinces shown.

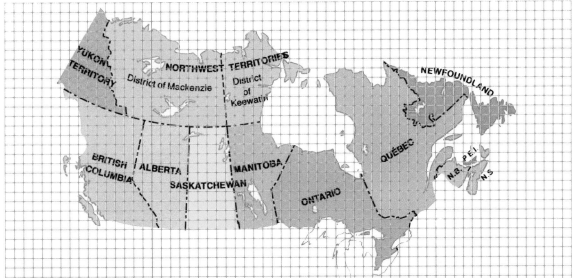

6.7 THINKING VISUALLY

Suppose you are a designer and are hired to design packages to catch the eye of the consumer. To design packages effectively, you will need to visualize them before they are made.

In the investigation,
- copy each net onto cardboard and cut it out.
- fold the net to show your package. Then creatively use colour on your package. In your journal, explain why you feel your design is effective.

INVESTIGATION

1. (a) Copy and cut out the net shown for a toothpaste box. On the net, write the word TOOTHPASTE so that, when the net is folded, two facing sides show the word.

   (b) Fold the net. Did you write the words in the correct position?

2. (a) Copy and cut out the net shown for a can. You are to place the name of the food on the front, back, and top of the can. Where will you place each name?

   (b) Fold the net. Did you write the name in the right place?

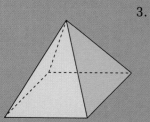

3. Suppose you are hired to design a foil wrap for the piece of chocolate shown.

   (a) Measure the dimensions of the piece of chocolate.

   (b) What is the least amount of material you will need for the package?

   (c) What name will you put on your package to catch the consumer's eye? Give reasons for your choice.

4. (a) Predict the figure you will have by cutting out and folding each net.

   (b) Cut out and fold each net. How accurate was your prediction?

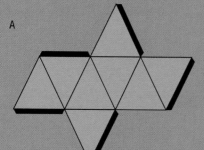

A

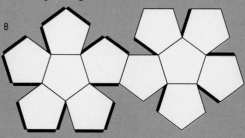

B

Have you ever tried to draw a three-dimensional object on a two-dimensional page? The following steps will help you draw objects **in perspective**. Any object drawn in perspective appears as though it is three-dimensional.

Step 1
Sketch the front face. Select a vanishing point, VP.

Step 2
Draw the receding lines toward the vanishing point, VP.

Step 3
Complete the object. Darken all lines.

VP

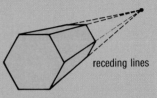

VP

receding lines

Activity
Sketch the following objects in perspective. Draw each object so that it appears as though you are looking at it from the position given.

View from top left

View from bottom left

View from bottom right

View from top right

People package and store items in different ways. Use your journal to describe what you think is stored in each container above. Do you think there is a more effective way of storing the material?

EXPLORATION ① *Work Together*

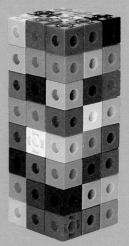

1. Use centicubes to construct the rectangular solid shown.

   (a) What is its length, width, and height?

   (b) What is its volume? (Hint: How many centicubes are there?)

   (c) How are your answers in (a) and (b) related?

   (d) Construct other rectangular solids of your own. Repeat the above parts. How are your answers related?

2. Use your answers to the previous questions.

   (a) Suggest a relationship for finding the volume of a rectangular solid.

   (b) Test your relationship on rectangular solids of your own.

3. Two rectangular solids are shown below.
   • Find the volume of each.
   • Use centicubes and construct one rectangular solid whose volume is equal to the sum of the volumes of the rectangular solids shown.

   (a)   (b)

To find the volume of an irregular solid, you can find the volume of water it displaces. Work together to complete the exploration.

Activity

Step 1
Fill a container as shown with water to the opening of the spout. Then, lower a rock into the container.

Step 2
Catch the water that overflows in a measuring cylinder. The volume of water displaced is equal to the volume of the rock.

4. Use the relationship above. Measure the volume of each.

   (a) a ball   (b) a rock   (c) a pencil   (d) a block of wood   (e) a bottle

   (f) Choose an irregular item of your own. Measure its volume.

EXPLORATION ③   *Work in a Small Group*

5. (a) Construct a cube and a pyramid so that each has the same base length and height.

   (b) Fill your pyramid with some material like Styrofoam chips and pour them into the cube. To fill the cube, how many times will you pour the contents of the pyramid? What do you notice?

6. (a) Construct a cylinder and a cone so that each has the same base diameter and height.

   (b) Fill your cone with some material like Styrofoam chips and pour them into the cylinder. To fill the cylinder, how many times will you pour the contents of the cone? What do you notice?

6.10 VOLUME AND CAPACITY

Use centicubes to construct each solid shown. By counting, you can find the volume of each solid.

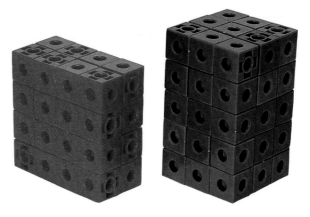

- The red solid has a volume of 32 cm³.
- The green solid has a volume of 45 cm³.

The centicubes can help you see relationships that can be used to find volume.

Volume = number of centicubes $\times$ number of
in bottom layer   layers
= length × width × height
$V = \underbrace{l \times w \times h}_{\text{area of base}}$

= $B \times h$

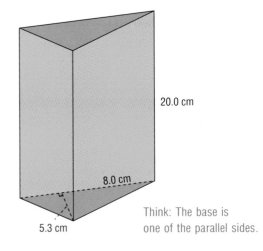

20.0 cm

8.0 cm

5.3 cm

Think: The base is one of the parallel sides.

The pattern can be used to find the volume of the cheese shown to the right.

Find the area of the base.
Use $B = \frac{b \times h}{2}$.
  $B = \frac{8.0 \times 5.3}{2}$
  = 21.2

Find the volume.
Use $V = B \times h$.
  $V = 21.2 \times 20.0$
  = 424.0

Thus, the volume of the cheese is 424 cm³.

> **Activity** When you find the greatest volume of water an aquarium can hold, you are finding its capacity. List other items for which you would find the capacity. Write them in your journal.

A To calculate volume, dimensions need to be in the same units.

1. Find the volume of each.

   (a)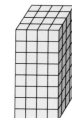

   (b)
   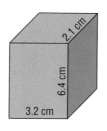
   2.1 cm
   6.4 cm
   3.2 cm

   (c)
   12.7 cm
   3.8 cm
   15.2 cm

2. How much does each box hold?

   (a)

   3.0 cm
   3.5 cm
   21.0 cm

   (b)
   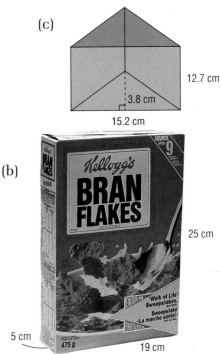
   25 cm
   5 cm
   19 cm
   475 g

B Volume = Area of Base × Height

3. The dimensions of Sara's aquarium are 33.5 cm by 34.5 cm by 33.1 cm. Find its capacity.

4. The dimensions of Michael's closet are 0.9 m by 1.2 m by 2.4 m. How much air is in Michael's empty closet?

5. The base area for a door stop is 2.0 cm². Its height is 4.4 cm. Find the volume of the door stop.

6. The dimensions of Ed's rectangular room are 13.5 m by 13.1 m by 2.7 m.

   (a) How much air can it hold?

   (b) The cost of heating the room is 10.25 ¢/m³ per month. Find the monthly cost of heating the room.

7. The base area for a cheese wedge is 16 cm². Its height is 2 cm. Find the volume of the wedge.

8. Work in groups. Use 24 centicubes.

   (a) Create a rectangular solid whose surface area is 24 square units. Why is this solid "special"?

   (b) Use centicubes of your own to create a "special" solid of your own. What is its surface area? What is its volume?

6.11 VOLUME OF CYLINDERS

2.0 m

27.0 m

How would you find the volume of marble in one column of the building in this picture?

Think: Draw a diagram of one column.

You can find the volume of marble in one column as follows.

Find the area of the base.
Use $B = \pi \times r \times r$.
$$B \doteq 3.14 \times 2.00 \times 2.00$$
$$\doteq 12.56$$
Area of base is about 12.6 m².

Find the volume.
Use $V = B \times h$.
$$V = 12.56 \times 27.0$$
$$= 339.12$$

The volume of marble used in one column is about 339 m³.

Think: How much marble is needed for all the columns?

EXERCISE

A Remember: Use $\pi \doteq 3.14$.

1. The area of the base of each cylinder is shown. Find the volume.

(a)

12 cm

Area is 26 cm²

(b) Area is 16.8 cm²

6.8 cm

(c) Area is 15.3 m²

4.3 m

2. (a) Predict which cylinder has the greatest volume.
   (b) Find each volume. How reasonable was your prediction?

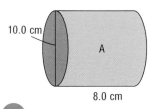

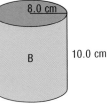

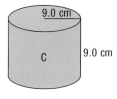

B Check that your answers are reasonable.

3. A drum has a radius of 0.6 m and a height of 1.2 m.
   (a) Draw and label the drum.
   (b) Find its volume.

4. (a) Obtain each can shown below.
   (b) Estimate the volume of each can.
   (c) Measure to calculate the volume. How reasonable was your estimate?

5. A juice can has a height of 8.0 cm. The radius of the base is 5.2 cm. How much juice will the can hold?

6. A well is 12.5 m deep. Its diameter is 175.0 cm. Find the amount of dirt removed to dig the well.

7. An ore sample is shaped like a cylinder and has a length of 0.8 m. It has a radius of 2.5 cm. How much rock is in the sample?

8. A can for tennis balls has a height of 22.5 cm. It has a radius that is $\frac{1}{6}$ of its height. Find the volume of air in the can.

9. A label from a can of beans is shown.
   (a) Work together to decide how to find the volume of the can using the label.
   (b) Find the volume of the can with this label.
   (c) Use labels of your own. Find the volume of the can.

C

10. Wax candles are 25 cm tall and 3 cm in diameter. Blocks of wax with dimensions 13.5 cm by 7.5 cm by 7.5 cm are melted to make the candles. How many candles can be made from 5 blocks of wax?

Previously, you explored the relationship between the volume of a cube and the volume of a pyramid as well as the volume of a cylinder and the volume of a cone. You found the following relationships.

Volume of a Pyramid

Volume of a Cone

Thus, volume of a pyramid is

$$V = \frac{1}{3}(B \times h)$$

Thus, volume of a cone is

$$V = \frac{1}{3}(B \times h)$$

The above relationships can be used to solve problems as shown below.

Suppose you are playing a new video game called *Pyramid Power*. You need to find the volume of the pyramid to gain points.

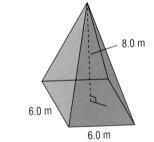

8.0 m

6.0 m

6.0 m

Use $V = \frac{1}{3}(B \times h)$. Think: $B = 6.0 \times 6.0$
$$= 36$$
$$V = \frac{1}{3}(36 \times 8.0)$$
$$= 96$$

The pyramid has a volume of 96 m³.

Suppose you are a magician and can make milk disappear from a cone shaped newspaper. How much milk can you make disappear?

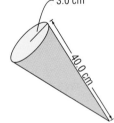

3.0 cm

40.0 cm

Use $V = \frac{1}{3}(B \times h)$. Think: $B = \pi \times r \times r$
$$= 3.14 \times 3.0 \times 3.0$$
$$V = \frac{1}{3}(28.26 \times 40.0) \quad = 28.26$$
$$= 376.8$$

You can make about 380 cm³ of milk disappear.

A Review your volume relationships.

1. Each pair of objects has the same height.
   (a) Find the area of each base. (b) Find the volume of each object.

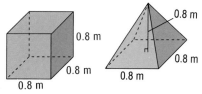

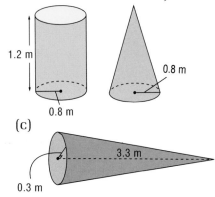

2. Calculate the volume of each.

   (a)

   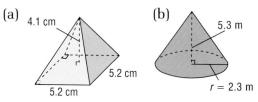

   (b)

   (c)

B Think of which relationship you use to find volume.

3. A pyramid has a height of 95 m and a square base 176 m on each side. Find its volume.

4. If each object is the same height, which holds more?
   • a cone with a base diameter of 5.4 cm
   • a pyramid with a square base 5.4 cm on each side

5. A cone has a height of 12.2 cm and a base diameter of 3.6 cm. Find its volume.

6. An ice cream cone has a height of 14.5 cm and a diameter of 5.0 cm. How much melted ice cream can it hold?

7. In a magic show, Rita rolled up a newspaper into a cone and filled it completely with milk. The cone was 10.7 cm across and 30.4 cm high. What volume of milk disappeared?

8. A community needs about 5000 m³ of salt for its roads this winter. Its storage cone has a base diameter of 19.6 m and is 32.3 m high. Can the community store enough salt for the winter?

9. Work together.
   (a) Attach 28 straws to form the frame of the kite as shown below.
   (b) Find the area of paper used to completely cover the kite below.
   (c) Use paper to design a kite of your own. Find the amount of air that can be in your kite at any one time.

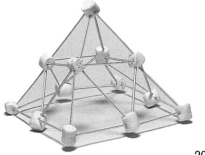

- Did you know that when you sneeze, air is released through your nose at about 160 km each hour?

- Did you know that during your lifetime you will eat about 30 000 kg of food?

Mathematics is often used to help you discover facts about your body. Before you begin the exercise, try the following activity.

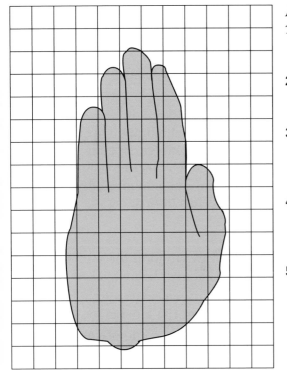

Activity

1. Trace your hand on a 1 cm grid with your fingers closed. Go only to your wrist.

2. Use your skills with irregular areas to find the area covered by your hand.

3. The skin on your hand represents 0.01 of the skin on your body. Multiply your answer from Question 2 by 100 to find the surface area of skin on your body.

4. Did you know that you shed your skin completely at least once each year? How much skin will you shed each week?

5. (a) In your journal, write how you feel now that you have finished the activity. Are you surprised with the result?

   (b) Keep track of all your results about your body in this section. Record which results surprise you and why.

EXERCISE

 A Review your measurement skills.

1. When you digest food, it passes through your small intestine, which has a diameter of about 2.5 cm and a length of about 6.5 m. What is the capacity of the small intestine?

2. The large intestine also helps you to digest food. It is about 7.5 cm in diameter and about 1.8 m long.

   (a) What volume of food can the large intestine hold?

   (b) Which can hold the greater amount of food — the large intestine or the small intestine?

B Use your journal to record all facts about your body.

3. (a) Measure your body mass.

   (b) Multiply your body mass by 0.7.

   (c) About $\frac{7}{10}$ of your body is water. Interpret your answer from (b). How many litres of water are in your body?

4. Use these facts to find the mass of water in your brain.
   - It has a mass of about 1.3 kg.
   - About $\frac{8}{10}$ of your brain is water.

5. The surface area of one lung will cover an entire tennis court.

   (a) Find the area covered by the tennis court.

   (b) Interpret your result from (a). What is the approximate surface area of one lung?

23.8 m

8.2 m

6. A bedroom is 4.0 m long, 3.0 m wide, and 2.5 m high. You breathe enough air each day to fill the bedroom to capacity.

   (a) Find the capacity of the bedroom.

   (b) Interpret your result from (a). How much air do you breathe each day?

   (c) Estimate about how many times you will take a breath in one day.

   (d) On average, what volume of air goes into your lungs on each breath?

7. Did you know that you need your sense of smell in order to taste? Try the following with a partner.

   (a) Cut a piece of apple and potato so that both are about the same size.

   (b) Close your eyes, plug your nose, and have your partner put one of the two pieces into your mouth. Can you taste which you have?

8. Did you know if you put all the blood vessels in your body end-to-end, they would go around the earth $2\frac{1}{2}$ times?

   (a) Find the circumference of the earth. What is the total length of your blood vessels?

   (b) A ball of string is shown below. How many packages of string would you need to represent the total length of your blood vessels?

6.14 PROBLEM SOLVING

The solution you find to a problem will sometimes differ from the solution others find. For example, three people were asked to find the dimensions of a regular field with an area of 2100 m². They answered the problem differently.

Rajib's Answer
12 m × 175 m

Jessie's Answer
20 m × 105 m

Chris's Answer
30 m × 70 m

Each answer is different *and* correct.

For each problem, there is more than one solution. Work with a partner and find more than one solution. Decide whether one answer is more reasonable.

EXERCISE

 B Work with a partner.

1. You need 1500 m of fence for a yard.
   (a) Find the dimensions of the yard.
   (b) Find a different answer.

2. (a) The product of two integers is +18. Find the two integers.
   (b) Find a different answer.

3. A field covers an area of 2500 m².
   (a) Find thè dimensions of the field.
   (b) Find a different answer.

4. Use at most nine toothpicks.
   (a) Show how to make seven equilateral triangles. Find a different answer.
   (b) Create and solve a similar problem.

5. (a) Copy the diagram below. Place a digit into each box to make the multiplication true.
   (b) Find a different answer.

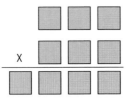

6. Find two different answers for each.
   (a) Use four 2's, and any operations, to make 16.
   (b) Use four 9's, and any operations, to make 100.

TECHNOLOGY INSIGHT: CHANGES IN DIMENSIONS

Y̶ou can use this program to investigate how the volume of a cylinder or a prism changes as its dimensions change.

```
10 INPUT ''DO YOU HAVE A PRISM? Y OR N''; A$
20 INPUT ''WHAT IS THE HEIGHT?''; H
30 IF A$ = ''N'' THEN 70
40 INPUT ''WHAT IS THE LENGTH AND WIDTH?''; L, W
50 LET A = L * W
60 GOTO 90
70 INPUT ''WHAT IS THE RADIUS?''; R
80 LET A = 3.14 * R ∧ 2
90 PRINT ''THE VOLUME IS''; A * H
100 END
```

Did you know that one dimension change entered can help automatically redraw the design?

For exercises 1 to 4, use this chart for a rectangular solid.

l	*w*	*h*	Prediction	Volume
15 cm	10 cm	20 cm	?	?

For exercises 5 to 8, use this chart for a cylinder.

Radius	Height	Prediction	Volume
10 cm	20 cm	?	?

1. (a) Predict the volume when the height is changed to 10 cm.
   (b) Calculate the volume in (a).

2. (a) Predict the volume if the width is changed to 5 cm.
   (b) Calculate the volume in (a).

3. If the length of an aquarium is tripled, how will its volume change?

4. Suggest how a change in one measurement will affect the volume of a prism.

5. (a) Predict the volume when the height is changed to 40 cm.
   (b) Calculate the volume in (a).

6. (a) Predict the volume if the radius is changed to 20 cm.
   (b) Calculate the volume in (a).

7. If the height of a cylinder is tripled, how will its volume change?

8. Suggest how a change in one measurement will affect the volume of a cylinder.

1. (a) Draw the net for each shape.

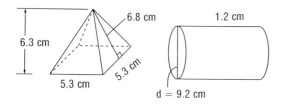

   (b) Find the surface area and volume for each shape in (a).

2. The height of a sealed can is 10 cm. The diameter is 9.4 cm.

   (a) Draw the net of the can.

   (b) If tin costs 0.18¢ for each square centimetre, how much will the can cost to make?

3. A tent is shaped like a pyramid. It has a square base with side lengths of 3.2 m. It is 1.6 m high. How much air is inside the tent?

4. Wind chimes are made of hollow metal cylinders. Each cylinder has its top and bottom removed. One chime is 0.5 m long and 3.2 cm across. What area of metal is used?

5. Did you know that the world's tallest chimney is located in Sudbury, Ontario and is used for the production of nickel? It is 379.6 m tall and has a base diameter of 35.4 m.

   (a) How much smoke will the chimney hold?

   (b) Why do you think they made the chimney so tall?

6. Anna's aquarium has dimensions of 80 cm by 60 cm by 60 cm. What are the possible dimensions of an aquarium that has a quarter of the volume of this aquarium? How do you know?

Describe what you learned from others when working in a group.

Describe a problem solving strategy you used when solving a problem on this page.

Make a list of memory aids you can use to help you distinguish each relationship in the chapter.

MAKING CONNECTIONS

Refer to the opening pages of this chapter.

(a) Create a problem of your own using the pictures. Compare your problem to others in the class.

(b) What kind of objects can be designed, or built, using the skills in this chapter?

MATH JOURNAL

In this chapter, you have solved problems using your skills with surface area and volume.

- Draw all the shapes that you have studied in this chapter. Name each shape. Give reasons why you named each as such.
- Make a list of all the relationships you have looked at.
- Give an example of each relationship to show how it is used.

SELF EVALUATION

1. Find the volume and surface area of each figure.

2. A prism is 10 m high. It has a triangular base with an area of 12.8 m². Find its volume.

3. A juice can has a height of 8.0 cm. The radius of the base is 5.2 cm. How many millilitres of juice will the can hold?

4. A pyramid has a square base, 5.4 m on each side. It is 3.8 m high. Find its volume.

5. A cereal box is 22.2 cm long, 6.4 cm wide, and 26.7 cm tall. Cardboard for the box costs 0.008¢ for each square centimetre.
   (a) Find the cost to make the box.
   (b) What assumptions have you made in (a)?

6. Gravel is stored in a cone-shaped pile. The cone is 18.3 m tall and has a base radius of 21.2 m. Find the amount of gravel the cone holds.

7. How much material is used to make a can for tennis balls 15.3 cm tall with a base radius of 3.2 cm?

8. Use centicubes to construct a shape for which the number of volume units equals the number of surface area units.

1. Calculate.

   (a) $\sqrt{25}$ (b) 16^2 (c) 3.5^3 (d) $\sqrt{144}$ (e) $\sqrt{22.5}$

2. Find the factors of each number.

   (a) 75   (b) 81   (c) 120   (d) 441   (e) 262

3. Construct an exact copy of the gate.

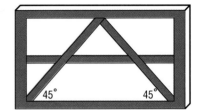

4. Find the missing value in each.

   (a)
   ```
        1 2 ■
      × 5 ■ 7
      ────────
        8 ■ 1
      7 3 8 0
    ■ 1 5 0 0
    ────────
    ■ 9 7 ■ 1
   ```

   (b)
   ```
        5 1 9
      ×   7 ■
      ────────
      ■ 1 1 ■
    3 6 ■ ■ 0
    ────────
    3 9 4 4 4
   ```

5. Calculate.

   (a) $(-3) + (-5)$ (b) $(-5)(-4)(-3)$ (c) $(+7) - (-2)$

   (d) $(-15) \div (+5)$ (e) $(+22) + (+12)$ (f) $(+35) - (+21)$

   (g) $(-9) + (-3) \times (-5)$ (h) $(-6) \times (-3) \div (+2)$ (i) $(+8) - (-8) \times (0)$

6. How many times will you run around the track to the right to complete a 1500 m race?

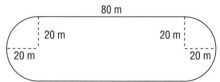

7. To fence a square yard, Brian and Sue used 170.2 m of fence. The fence cost $7.62 for each metre. Find the cost to fence the field.

MAKING CONNECTIONS

There are five polyhedra that are called Platonic solids.
- What are the names of the Platonic solids?
- Why are they so named?
- Draw the net for each Platonic solid.
- Construct the Platonic solids. Find the surface area of each.
- Imagine you are a designer. For what could you use these solids?

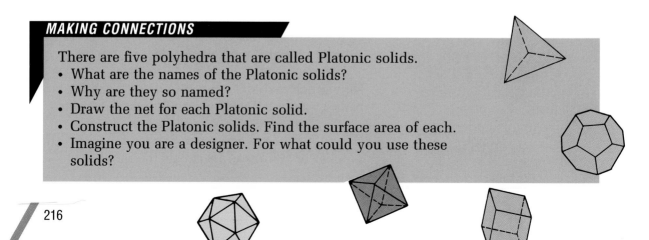

CUMULATIVE REVIEW: PROBLEM SOLVING

1. The first 202 whole numbers are placed in columns as shown.

A	B	C	D	E
5	4	3	2	1
6	7	8	9	10
15	14	13	12	11

   and so on

   (a) Under what letter will the last number appear?

   (b) Write a similar problem. Compare your problem with others in the class.

2. A pie is cut as shown to the right.

   (a) Find the greatest number of pieces into which the pie can be divided by four straight cuts.

   (b) Create a similar problem of your own.

3. Al spent $6.45 on 2 hamburgers, one order of fries, and 2 glasses of milk. Josef spent $4.50 on one hamburger, two orders of fries, and one glass of milk. How much will you spend on one hamburger, one order of fries, and one glass of milk?

4. (a) Trace a dime onto a piece of paper. Cut out the hole represented by the dime.

   (b) Use coins. Which coins can you fit through the hole in (a) without enlarging the hole or ripping the paper?

CALCULATION SENSE

To help you calculate surface area, look for patterns. To help you multiply, you can also look for patterns. Do the calculations below. What pattern can help you multiply by 11 quickly?

1. Calculate.
   (a) 11×121
   (b) 11×230
   (c) 11×422
   (d) 11×314
   (e) 11×203
   (f) 11×141

2. Calculate.
   (a) 193×11
   (b) 815×11
   (c) 605×11
   (d) 304×11
   (e) 158×11
   (f) 270×11

7 WORKING WITH FRACTIONS

Did you know that the red wolf almost became extinct 20 years ago? There are now 50 in captivity, only a tiny fraction of the original population. List two ways you think the red wolf can be released into the wild.

Did you know that a deer grew the largest recorded set of antlers? They measured 4.3 m across. Estimate your arm span as a fraction of 4.3 m.

Did you know that about ten bird species are threatened with extinction? This estimate was only $\frac{1}{5}$ of this amount ten years ago. List any suggestions you can to help protect endangered species.

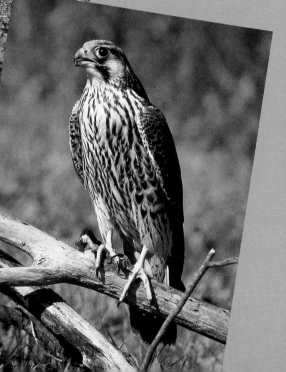

You have probably used sentences like the following:

- I'll see you in *half* an hour.
- One *quarter* of the game has ended.

Think: Half is written as $\frac{1}{2}$.
Quarter is written as $\frac{1}{4}$.

Fractions are used to describe part of a whole. The explorations will use sheets of paper to show you ways to communicate with fractions. You can also use other manipulatives.

EXPLORATION ① *Work with a Partner*

1. Use a sheet of paper.
   (a) Fold the sheet of paper to show two equal parts.
   (b) Unfold the paper. How much of the paper is on one side of the crease? How much is on the other side of the crease?
   (c) Write a fraction to describe each part in (b).

2. Use another sheet of paper.
   (a) Fold the sheet of paper in half and then in half again.
   (b) Unfold the sheet of paper. How many equal parts are there?
   (c) Write a fraction to describe each part in (b).

3. Use another sheet of paper.
   (a) Fold the sheet of paper in half and then into quarters.
   (b) Unfold the sheet of paper. How many equal parts are there?
   (c) Write a fraction to describe each part in (b).

EXPLORATION ② *Work with a Partner*

4. (a) Fold a sheet of paper in half.
   (b) Fold another sheet of paper of the same size in half and then in half again.
   (c) Compare your sheets of paper. How is $\frac{1}{2}$ related to $\frac{2}{4}$?

5. (a) Fold a sheet of paper in half and then in half again.
   (b) Fold another sheet of paper of the same size into eight equal parts.
   (c) Compare your sheets of paper. How is $\frac{2}{4}$ related to $\frac{4}{8}$?
   (d) How is $\frac{1}{2}$ related to $\frac{4}{8}$?

EXPLORATION ③ *Work in a Group*

6. Copy the diagram to the right using tracing paper.

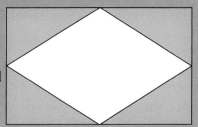

   (a) Cut out your copy of the diagram.

   (b) Cut the shaded parts from the diagram.

   (c) Do the shaded pieces fit exactly over the unshaded piece?

   (d) Interpret your answer from (c). What part of the original diagram is shaded?

7. Create a problem of your own similar to Question 6.

   (a) Solve your problem.

   (b) Compare your problem with others in your class. Solve the other problems.

EXPLORATION ④ *Work in a Group*

8. (a) Copy the shape shown below.

   (b) What fraction of the shape do you think is shaded?

   (c) Trace and cut out the part that is shaded. How many shaded pieces are needed to cover the shape completely?

   (d) Use your results from (c). What fraction of the shape is shaded?

9. Draw a shape of your own. Shade part of the shape.

   (a) Estimate what fraction of your shape is shaded.

   (b) Have others estimate the shaded part of your shape.

7.2 COMMUNICATING WITH FRACTIONS

Ten species of birds are shown. Seven of them are close to extinction. You can write a fraction to show this relationship.

numerator: number of species close to extinction

$\dfrac{7}{10}$

denominator: total number of species shown

Thus, the fraction of the species shown that are close to extinction is $\frac{7}{10}$.

In the fraction $\frac{7}{10}$, the numerator is less than the denominator. The fraction is called a **proper fraction**. In the fraction $\frac{10}{7}$, the numerator is greater than the denominator. The fraction is called an **improper fraction**.

You can use two sheets of paper to help you interpret $1\frac{1}{2}$ as follows.
Fold each sheet in half and colour 3 parts.

Each coloured part is $\frac{1}{2}$ of a sheet of paper.
There are 3 coloured parts; so 3 halves are coloured.
But $1\frac{1}{2}$ sheets of paper are coloured.
Thus, $1\frac{1}{2} = \frac{3}{2}$.

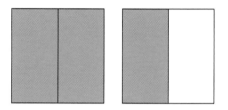

EXERCISE

A Use diagrams to help you.

1. Use the diagram to write

   (a) $2\frac{1}{3}$ as an improper fraction.

   (b) $\frac{7}{4}$ as a mixed number.

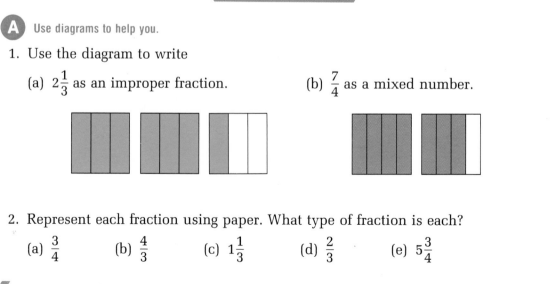

2. Represent each fraction using paper. What type of fraction is each?

   (a) $\frac{3}{4}$ (b) $\frac{4}{3}$ (c) $1\frac{1}{3}$ (d) $\frac{2}{3}$ (e) $5\frac{3}{4}$

3. (a) Use a diagram to show how you can share 5 large cookies equally among 4 friends.

(b) Write a fraction to show the number of cookies each receives.

4. Write each as a mixed number.

(a) $\frac{5}{3}$ (b) $\frac{9}{2}$ (c) $\frac{11}{5}$

5. Write each as an improper fraction.

(a) $2\frac{3}{4}$ (b) $4\frac{1}{5}$ (c) $3\frac{3}{8}$

6. What part of an hour is each?

(a) 30 min (b) 15 min (c) 10 min

7. A bus has 52 seats. Of these, 27 are taken. Write a fraction to show what part of the bus is full.

8. A garden has 22 flowers. Of these, 14 are roses. Write a fraction to show what part of the garden is roses.

9. A chocolate bar has 10 pieces. Jan ate 7. What fraction did Jan eat?

C

10. Nikki bought four boxes of 12 donuts. There are 15 jelly donuts. Write a mixed number to show how many boxes of donuts are not jelly donuts.

11. (a) Estimate the fraction of paper that is shaded in each diagram. Write each fraction.

(b) Draw a design of your own on squared paper. Estimate the fraction of paper your design occupies. Write the fraction.

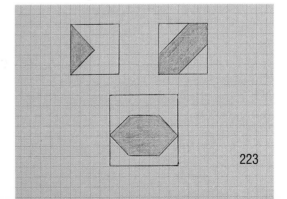

223

7.3 EQUIVALENT FRACTIONS

Two sheets of paper have been folded. One has been folded to form two equal parts. Each part represents $\frac{1}{2}$ of the sheet.

The other has been folded to form four equal parts. Each part represents $\frac{1}{4}$ of the sheet. By placing one sheet on top of the other, you see that $\frac{1}{2}$ of the first sheet covers $\frac{2}{4}$ of the second sheet. Thus, $\frac{1}{2} = \frac{2}{4}$.

The fractions $\frac{1}{2}$ and $\frac{2}{4}$ are different ways of writing the same part of a whole. They are **equivalent fractions**. Equivalent fractions can be found as follows.

$$\frac{1}{2} = \frac{1 \times 2}{2 \times 2} \qquad \text{Think: } \frac{2}{2} = 1 \qquad \frac{1}{3} = \frac{1 \times 3}{3 \times 3} \qquad \text{Think: } \frac{3}{3} = 1 \qquad \frac{5}{15} = \frac{5 \div 5}{15 \div 5} \qquad \text{Think: } \frac{5}{5} = 1$$

$$= \frac{2}{4} \qquad\qquad\qquad = \frac{3}{9} \qquad\qquad\qquad = \frac{1}{3}$$

$\frac{5}{15}$ is written in **lowest terms** as $\frac{1}{3}$.

Equivalent fractions can be used to help you solve problems.

At the Bridlegate checkpoint, $\frac{5}{8}$ of the drivers wore seatbelts.
At the Spruce checkpoint, $\frac{7}{12}$ of the drivers wore seatbelts.
At which checkpoint did the greater fraction of drivers wear seatbelts?

Think: To compare, write each fraction with the lowest common denominator.

Bridlegate: $\dfrac{5}{8} = \dfrac{5 \times 3}{8 \times 3}$ $\qquad\qquad$ Spruce: $\dfrac{7}{12} = \dfrac{7 \times 2}{12 \times 2}$

$\qquad\qquad\qquad = \dfrac{15}{24}$ $\qquad\qquad\qquad\qquad\qquad = \dfrac{14}{24}$

Since $15 > 14$, then $\frac{15}{24} > \frac{14}{24}$.
Thus, the Bridlegate checkpoint has the greater fraction of drivers wearing seatbelts.

A Review your skills with fractions.

1. Draw one diagram for each pair of equivalent fractions.

   (a) $\dfrac{1}{2}, \dfrac{3}{6}$ (b) $\dfrac{2}{3}, \dfrac{4}{6}$ (c) $\dfrac{3}{4}, \dfrac{9}{12}$

2. Use a diagram to help you find the value of ■.

   (a) $\dfrac{3}{4} = \dfrac{■}{8}$ (b) $\dfrac{2}{3} = \dfrac{6}{■}$ (c) $\dfrac{2}{10} = \dfrac{■}{5}$

3. Use the diagram to find the values of ■.

   (a) $\dfrac{1}{3} = \dfrac{1 \times ■}{3 \times ■} = \dfrac{2}{6}$

   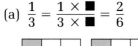

   (b) $\dfrac{4}{8} = \dfrac{4 \div ■}{8 \div ■} = \dfrac{1}{2}$

   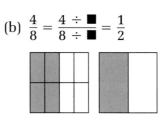

 B Check whether your answers are reasonable.

4. Write two equivalent fractions for each.

   (a) $\dfrac{2}{3}$ (b) $\dfrac{4}{5}$ (c) $\dfrac{2}{9}$

5. Which fraction in each pair is greater?

   (a) $\dfrac{1}{4}, \dfrac{3}{8}$ (b) $\dfrac{1}{3}, \dfrac{1}{4}$ (c) $\dfrac{3}{2}, \dfrac{5}{3}$

6. Write each fraction in lowest terms.

   (a) $\dfrac{4}{10}$ (b) $\dfrac{8}{16}$ (c) $\dfrac{9}{27}$

7. The mass of an elephant's skin is $\dfrac{1}{8}$ of its total mass. The mass of your skin is $\dfrac{4}{25}$ of your total mass. Which has a greater fraction of mass in skin?

8. At the Birchmount checkpoint, $\dfrac{3}{5}$ of the drivers wore seatbelts. At the Warden checkpoint, $\dfrac{4}{7}$ of the drivers wore seatbelts. At which checkpoint did the greater fraction of drivers wear seatbelts?

9. In pre-season games, Mac completed $\dfrac{5}{12}$ of his passes. John completed $\dfrac{8}{17}$ of his passes. Which player would you start in the opening game? Why?

10. (a) Drop ten paper cups. Write a fraction to show the portion of paper cups in each position below.

    (b) Repeat (a) five times. Write the fractions.

225

7.4 PROBLEM SOLVING: USE A SPECIFIC CASE

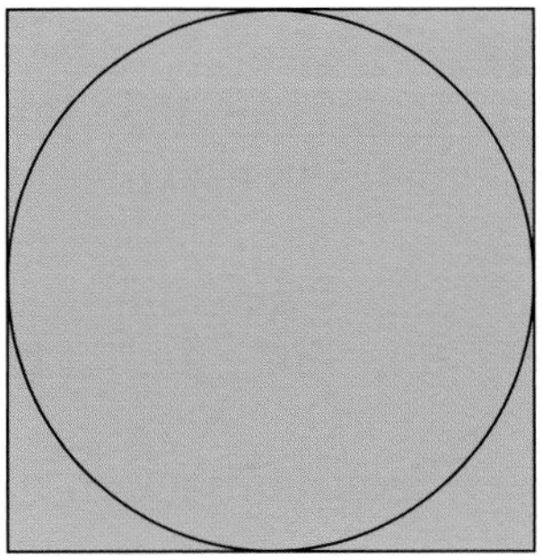

The top of a drum is cut out from a square piece of plastic. Estimate the fraction of the plastic that is not used.

1. Think About the Problem.

(a) Think of what you must find.
   - The fraction of a square not covered by a circle.

(b) Think of what you are given.
   - The information in the diagram.

2. Think About a Strategy.

(a) Think of a strategy you could use.
   - Introduce your own measure and calculate the areas.

(b) Think of a reason for your strategy.
   - You can use your own values to find the fractions.

3. Work It Out.

Use a sheet of paper. Suppose the side length of the square is 4 cm.

Square Sheet
The area of the square sheet can be calculated as follows.

$$\text{Area} = 4 \text{ cm} \times 4 \text{ cm}$$
$$= 16 \text{ cm}^2$$

The area of the square is 16 cm².

Circular Piece
The area of the circle is found as follows.

Use $A = \pi r^2$ Think: $\pi \doteq 3.14$
$$\doteq 3.14 \times 2 \times 2$$
$$\doteq 12.56$$

The area of the circle is 12.56 cm².

The fraction can be written as $\dfrac{\text{area of circle}}{\text{area of square}} = \dfrac{12.56}{16}$.

An estimate for the fraction is $\frac{3}{4}$.

4. Think About Your Solution.

Thus, about $\frac{1}{4}$ of the plastic is not used.

Repeat the calculations above using a square sheet of paper with a side length of 5 cm. Compare your solution with others in your class. What do you notice?

B Use your *Problem Solving Plan.*

1. For the Naval Day Parade, new signs with the logo shown are needed.

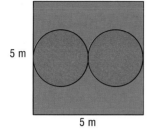

5 m

5 m

   (a) What fraction of the sign is red?

   (b) What fraction of the sign is green?

2. The barn is in the shape of a semi-circle. What fraction of the land is occupied by the barn?

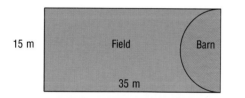

15 m   Field   Barn

35 m

3. A horse is tied with a rope in one corner of a square field. The rope has the same length as one side of the field. On what fraction of the field can the horse graze?

4. Kim and Pat enter a 12 km bicycle race. Kim rode three times as fast as Pat. If they finished the race at the same time, what fraction of the course did Pat complete before Kim started?

5. Colin has a package of paper that he shares with Dave, Jack, and Frank.
   • Frank took $\frac{1}{6}$ of the paper.
   • Dave took $\frac{1}{4}$ of the paper left.
   • Jack took $\frac{1}{3}$ of the paper left.
   Who has the greatest number of sheets of paper?

MAKING CONNECTIONS

Long ago, astronomers believed there were only as many stars as the naked eye could see. Today, astronomers can see many stars through telescopes like the Hubble Telescope.

• Estimate the number of stars you see here.
• When was the Hubble Telescope first used?
• What stars has the telescope shown astronomers?
• What mathematics do you think is needed to construct the telescope?

7.5 MATH IN ECOLOGY

Have you ever heard the phrase: "pure as the driven snow"?

Over the last 20 years, scientists who study the environment have found that not all rain and snow is pure. Much of today's precipitation contains chemicals that turn the water into acid. This phenomenon is described as **acid rain**. Many environmentalists are concerned about the effects that acid rain has on farms, forests, lakes, streams, and, as a result, wildlife.

Rain can sometimes contain only $\frac{1}{100}$ of the chemicals that might normally be found in fog. Write $\frac{1}{100}$ as a decimal number.

Use a calculator.　　　　$\boxed{c}$ 1 $\boxed{\div}$ 100 $\boxed{=}$ 0.01

Thus, $\frac{1}{100}$ can be written as 0.01.

Decimal numbers can be written as fractions as shown below.

$$0.25 = \frac{25}{100}$$

Think: Use your skills with decimal numbers.

$$= \frac{1}{4}$$

EXERCISE

A Use a calculator.

1. Write each fraction as a decimal number.

   (a) $\frac{5}{10}$　　(b) $\frac{7}{100}$　　(c) $\frac{257}{1000}$　　(d) $\frac{36}{1000}$　　(e) $\frac{126}{100}$

2. Write each fraction as a decimal number.

   (a) $\frac{3}{5}$　　(b) $\frac{7}{8}$　　(c) $\frac{1}{2}$　　(d) $\frac{15}{25}$　　(e) $\frac{35}{50}$

3. Write each decimal number as a fraction in lowest terms.

   (a) 0.30　　(b) 0.75　　(c) 0.44　　(d) 0.41　　(e) 0.003

4. Acid rain has contributed to the destruction of about $\frac{1}{2}$ of Germany's forests. Write a decimal number to show the part of Germany's forests destroyed.

5. Acid rain has also contributed to 0.10 of Sweden's lakes not having any live fish. Write a fraction to show the part of Sweden's lakes without live fish.

6. Sulphur dioxide and nitrogen are two of the chemicals found in acid rain. Each year, 130 million tons of sulphur dioxide and 53 million tons of nitrogen are released into the atmosphere.

   (a) Calculate.
   $$130\,000\,000 + 53\,000\,000$$

   (b) Write a fraction to show what part of the two chemicals combined is nitrogen.

   (c) Write a decimal number to represent the fraction from (b).

7. In a far north region of Canada, a study showed $\frac{1}{5}$ of the lakes "dying". Write a decimal number to show this fraction.

8. (a) What is an ecosystem?

   (b) Work with a partner to describe briefly a normal lake ecosystem. What math skills did you use in your description?

9. Work together. Use your library.

   (a) What is a rain forest? Why is it necessary that the rain forests be preserved?

   (b) What fraction of the world's rain forests has been destroyed? What fraction is being destroyed each day?

   (c) List two ways in which you can help protect the rain forests.

When developing skills to solve problems, manipulatives can often help.

EXPLORATION ① **Work in a Group**

1. Use a sheet of paper.
   (a) Fold the paper into four equal parts.
   (b) Shade $\frac{1}{2}$ of the paper. How many parts have been shaded?
   (c) Shade a further $\frac{1}{4}$ of the sheet.
   (d) What fraction of the paper has been shaded in all? What is $\frac{2}{4} + \frac{1}{4}$?
   (e) Interpret your answer from (d). Find the value of $\frac{1}{2} + \frac{1}{4}$.

2. Use another sheet of paper.
   (a) Fold the paper into eight equal parts.
   (b) Shade $\frac{3}{4}$ of the paper. How many parts have been shaded in all?
   (c) Shade a further $\frac{1}{8}$ of the sheet.
   (d) What fraction of the paper has been shaded in all? What is $\frac{6}{8} + \frac{1}{8}$?
   (e) Interpret your answer from (d). Find the value of $\frac{3}{4} + \frac{1}{8}$.

3. Use another sheet of paper.
   (a) Fold the paper into six equal parts.
   (b) Shade $\frac{1}{2}$ of the paper. How many parts have been shaded in all?
   (c) Shade a further $\frac{1}{3}$ of the sheet.
   (d) What fraction of the paper has been shaded in all? What is $\frac{3}{6} + \frac{2}{6}$?
   (e) Interpret your answer from (d). Find the value of $\frac{1}{2} + \frac{1}{3}$.

A Write your answers in lowest terms.

1. Write a subtraction question suggested by each diagram. Write the answer.

(a) 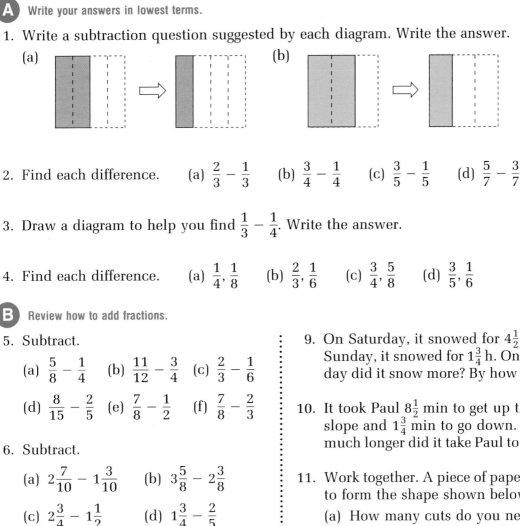 (b)

2. Find each difference. (a) $\frac{2}{3} - \frac{1}{3}$ (b) $\frac{3}{4} - \frac{1}{4}$ (c) $\frac{3}{5} - \frac{1}{5}$ (d) $\frac{5}{7} - \frac{3}{7}$

3. Draw a diagram to help you find $\frac{1}{3} - \frac{1}{4}$. Write the answer.

4. Find each difference. (a) $\frac{1}{4}, \frac{1}{8}$ (b) $\frac{2}{3}, \frac{1}{6}$ (c) $\frac{3}{4}, \frac{5}{8}$ (d) $\frac{3}{5}, \frac{1}{6}$

B Review how to add fractions.

5. Subtract.

(a) $\frac{5}{8} - \frac{1}{4}$ (b) $\frac{11}{12} - \frac{3}{4}$ (c) $\frac{2}{3} - \frac{1}{6}$

(d) $\frac{8}{15} - \frac{2}{5}$ (e) $\frac{7}{8} - \frac{1}{2}$ (f) $\frac{7}{8} - \frac{2}{3}$

6. Subtract.

(a) $2\frac{7}{10} - 1\frac{3}{10}$ (b) $3\frac{5}{8} - 2\frac{3}{8}$

(c) $2\frac{3}{4} - 1\frac{1}{2}$ (d) $1\frac{3}{4} - \frac{2}{5}$

7. Jan packed $\frac{1}{2}$ of a box of granola bars on the first day of counsellor training. She ate $\frac{1}{8}$ of a box. What fraction of a box was left?

8. Francesca's class collected $\frac{1}{3}$ t of bottles. Of these, $\frac{1}{7}$ t were not recycled. What mass of bottles were recycled?

9. On Saturday, it snowed for $4\frac{1}{2}$ h. On Sunday, it snowed for $1\frac{3}{4}$ h. On which day did it snow more? By how much?

10. It took Paul $8\frac{1}{2}$ min to get up the ski slope and $1\frac{3}{4}$ min to go down. How much longer did it take Paul to go up?

11. Work together. A piece of paper is cut to form the shape shown below.

(a) How many cuts do you need so that the cut pieces can be arranged to form a square?

(b) What is the least number of cuts you need?

(c) Create a similar problem using a shape of your own.

Yesterday, $\frac{1}{2}$ of all television shows were sports. Of these sports shows, $\frac{3}{4}$ were broadcasting the Olympics. What fraction of all television shows were broadcasting the Olympics?

Think: • $\frac{1}{2}$ of all television shows were sports.   • Of these, $\frac{3}{4}$ were showing the Olympics.
    • Fold and shade paper to find $\frac{3}{4}$ of $\frac{1}{2}$. Solve the problem.

Find $\frac{1}{2}$.   Find $\frac{3}{4}$ of $\frac{1}{2}$.

Think: Fold the paper in half.

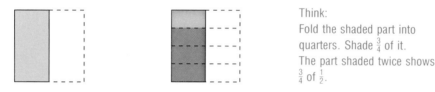

Think:
Fold the shaded part into quarters. Shade $\frac{3}{4}$ of it. The part shaded twice shows $\frac{3}{4}$ of $\frac{1}{2}$.

From the diagram, $\frac{3}{4}$ of $\frac{1}{2} = \frac{3}{8}$. This result suggests the following method for multiplying fractions. Remember: The word "of" indicates multiplication.

$$\frac{3}{4} \times \frac{1}{2} = \frac{3 \times 1}{4 \times 2}$$

Think: Multiply the numerators and denominators.

$$= \frac{3}{8}$$

Thus, $\frac{3}{8}$ of all television shows were broadcasting the Olympics.

EXERCISE

A   Use folded and shaded paper to help you.

1. Write the multiplication expression suggested by each diagram. Find the answer.

(a)   (b)   (c)

2. To find $\frac{1}{3}$ of $\frac{1}{4}$, think of a diagram.

   (a) Draw the diagram.   (b) Find the product.

3. Find each product.   (a) $\frac{1}{4} \times \frac{2}{5}$ (b) $\frac{1}{3} \times \frac{1}{3}$ (c) $\frac{2}{3} \times \frac{4}{7}$ (d) $\frac{1}{2} \times \frac{1}{3}$

B Work with a partner and use manipulatives.

4. Calculate.

(a) $\frac{2}{5} \times \frac{3}{5}$ (b) $\frac{4}{7} \times \frac{3}{5}$ (c) $\frac{3}{4} \times \frac{5}{7}$

(d) $\frac{3}{4} \times \frac{5}{8}$ (e) $\frac{1}{2} \times \frac{5}{8}$ (f) $\frac{7}{8} \times \frac{3}{5}$

5. Multiply.

(a) $\frac{1}{2} \times \frac{1}{3}$ (b) $\frac{3}{5} \times \frac{2}{7}$ (c) $\frac{2}{5} \times \frac{3}{8}$

(d) $\frac{8}{27} \times \frac{15}{17}$ (e) $\frac{3}{10} \times \frac{7}{8}$ (f) $\frac{5}{8} \times \frac{13}{35}$

6. To multiply three fractions, follow the same steps as for multiplying two fractions. Find the products.

(a) $\frac{1}{2} \times \frac{3}{4} \times \frac{1}{5}$ (b) $\frac{2}{3} \times \frac{5}{6} \times \frac{5}{8}$

(c) $\frac{1}{6} \times \frac{1}{5} \times \frac{7}{8}$ (d) $\frac{3}{5} \times \frac{1}{2} \times \frac{1}{5}$

7. The gas tank of a bus is $\frac{3}{4}$ full. A trip uses $\frac{1}{5}$ of the gas in the tank. What fraction of a tank is left after one trip?

8. Roxanne took $\frac{2}{5}$ of her savings with her on a holiday trip. She used $\frac{1}{4}$ of the money she took to buy gifts. What fraction of her savings did she spend on gifts?

9. (a) How many rectangles, with unique areas, can you put on a geoboard?

   (b) What fraction of the rectangles are squares?

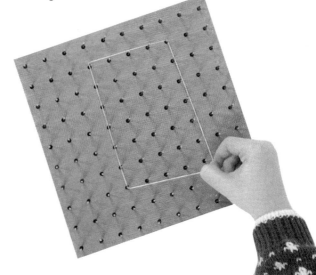

7.10 MULTIPLYING MIXED NUMBERS

The skills you learn for multiplying fractions also extend to multiplying mixed numbers. However, to use those skills, you first need to write each mixed number as an improper fraction.

$$1\frac{3}{4} \times 2\frac{1}{2} = \frac{7}{4} \times \frac{5}{2}$$
$$= \frac{7 \times 5}{4 \times 2}$$
$$= \frac{35}{8} \text{ or } 4\frac{3}{8}$$

In some questions, you can simplify your work before you multiply. For example, $\frac{3}{4} \times \frac{1}{6}$ can be simplified as shown.

$$\frac{3}{4} \times \frac{1}{6} = \frac{\overset{1}{\cancel{3}}}{4} \times \frac{1}{\underset{2}{\cancel{6}}}$$
$$= \frac{1 \times 1}{4 \times 2}$$
$$= \frac{1}{8}$$

EXERCISE

B Review your skills with fractions.

1. Write each product in lowest terms.

   (a) $\frac{1}{2} \times \frac{2}{5}$ (b) $\frac{2}{5} \times \frac{1}{4}$ (c) $\frac{1}{3} \times \frac{3}{4}$

   (d) $\frac{2}{3} \times \frac{3}{5}$ (e) $\frac{4}{5} \times \frac{1}{2}$ (f) $\frac{3}{4} \times \frac{2}{5}$

2. Calculate.

   (a) $\frac{1}{2} \times \frac{2}{3}$ (b) $\frac{3}{5} \times \frac{2}{3}$ (c) $\frac{2}{5} \times \frac{5}{8}$

   (d) $\frac{8}{25} \times \frac{15}{16}$ (e) $\frac{4}{21} \times \frac{7}{8}$ (f) $\frac{5}{8} \times \frac{16}{35}$

3. Find each product.

   (a) $1\frac{2}{3} \times 2\frac{1}{2}$ (b) $1\frac{3}{4} \times 2\frac{3}{5}$

   (c) $2\frac{3}{4} \times 1\frac{1}{2}$ (d) $3\frac{1}{4} \times 2\frac{1}{3}$

4. Calculate.

   (a) $8\frac{1}{2} \times 2\frac{1}{4}$ (b) $\frac{3}{4} \times 1\frac{7}{10}$

   (c) $3\frac{1}{3} \times 2\frac{1}{10}$ (d) $3\frac{2}{3} \times 4\frac{1}{5} \times 1\frac{3}{8}$

   (e) $4\frac{1}{2} \times 3\frac{1}{3} \times 2\frac{1}{4}$ (f) $3\frac{1}{4} \times 2\frac{1}{2} \times 4\frac{1}{6}$

5. Precipitation fell for $4\frac{1}{2}$ h on Sunday. Suppose $\frac{2}{3}$ of this time it snowed. For how many hours did it snow?

6. Crystal swam $5\frac{1}{3}$ lengths of a pool. Brenda swam $1\frac{1}{2}$ times as much. How many lengths did Brenda swim?

7.11 EXTENDING YOUR WORK

Sometimes, to develop your "mental" math skills, you can look for patterns. For example, each of the following products is equal to 1. In your journal, explain why the product is equal to 1.

- $\dfrac{3}{5} \times \dfrac{5}{3} = \dfrac{3 \times 5}{5 \times 3}$

  $\qquad = \dfrac{15}{15}$

  $\qquad = 1$

- $\dfrac{1}{3} \times 3 = \dfrac{1}{3} \times \dfrac{3}{1}$ Think: $3 = \dfrac{3}{1}$

  $\qquad = \dfrac{1 \times 3}{3 \times 1}$

  $\qquad = 1$

Since the product of $\dfrac{3}{5}$ and $\dfrac{5}{3}$ is equal to 1, you can say

- $\dfrac{3}{5}$ is the **reciprocal** of $\dfrac{5}{3}$.
- $\dfrac{5}{3}$ is the **reciprocal** of $\dfrac{3}{5}$.

Skills with reciprocals are needed to divide fractions. Compare any patterns you see in this section with others in your class and record them in your journal.

EXERCISE

 B Review your skills with fractions.

1. Find the products. Which pairs are reciprocals?

   (a) $\dfrac{1}{3} \times 3$ (b) $\dfrac{7}{8} \times \dfrac{1}{8}$ (c) $\dfrac{1}{4} \times 4$

   (d) $1\dfrac{4}{5} \times \dfrac{5}{9}$ (e) $\dfrac{4}{5} \times 1\dfrac{1}{5}$ (f) $2\dfrac{2}{3} \times \dfrac{3}{8}$

2. Calculate.

   (a) $\dfrac{2}{3} \times \dfrac{3}{2}$ (b) $\dfrac{1}{5} \times 5$ (c) $\dfrac{4}{9} \times \dfrac{9}{4}$

   (d) $\dfrac{2}{3} \times \dfrac{3}{5}$ (e) $10 \times \dfrac{3}{10}$ (f) $\dfrac{2}{3} \times \dfrac{3}{2}$

3. Find the values of ■.

   (a) $\dfrac{2}{3} \times ■ = 1$ (b) $■ \times \dfrac{2}{7} = 1$

   (c) $■ \times \dfrac{3}{7} = 1$ (d) $\dfrac{4}{7} \times ■ = 1$

   (e) $\dfrac{1}{3} \times ■ = 1$ (f) $■ \times \dfrac{2}{5} = 1$

4. Write the reciprocal of each product.

   (a) $\dfrac{2}{3} \times \dfrac{3}{5}$ (b) $\dfrac{4}{5} \times \dfrac{4}{5}$ (c) $\dfrac{7}{8} \times \dfrac{1}{2}$

   (d) $1\dfrac{4}{5} \times \dfrac{5}{4}$ (e) $\dfrac{3}{4} \times 1\dfrac{1}{3}$ (f) $\dfrac{4}{5} \times \dfrac{3}{2}$

Cheryl has $\frac{1}{2}$ of a cake. What fraction of the cake will each person receive if she divides her piece of cake among 2 people? among 3 people? To answer these questions, use a diagram.

Divide among 2 people.

Divide among 3 people.

Think: $\frac{1}{2} \div 2 = \frac{1}{4}$

$\frac{1}{2} \times \frac{1}{2} = \frac{1}{4}$

Think: $\frac{1}{2} \div 3 = \frac{1}{6}$

$\frac{1}{2} \times \frac{1}{3} = \frac{1}{6}$

The pattern suggests that *to divide a fraction, you multiply by its reciprocal* as follows.

$$\frac{1}{4} \div \frac{3}{4} = \frac{1}{4} \times \frac{4}{3}$$

$$= \frac{1}{3}$$

$$5\frac{1}{3} \div 1\frac{3}{5} = \frac{16}{3} \div \frac{8}{5}$$

$$= \frac{16}{3} \times \frac{5}{8}$$

$$= \frac{10}{3} \text{ or } 3\frac{1}{3}$$

Think: Write each as an improper fraction.

Use this pattern to solve some problems.

Brad plants trees to help preserve an orchard. Suppose he planted trees for $\frac{3}{4}$ h. Each tree took $\frac{1}{8}$ h to plant. How many trees did he plant?

$$\frac{3}{4} \div \frac{1}{8} = \frac{3}{4} \times \frac{8}{1}$$

$$= \frac{3 \times 2}{1 \times 1}$$

$$= 6$$

Thus, Brad planted 6 trees.

A Review your skills with reciprocals.

1. Write the division question suggested by each diagram. Find the answer.

   (a)   (b)   (c)

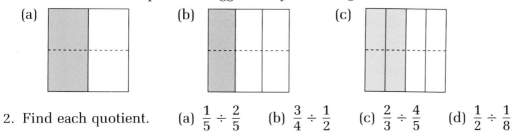

2. Find each quotient. (a) $\frac{1}{5} \div \frac{2}{5}$ (b) $\frac{3}{4} \div \frac{1}{2}$ (c) $\frac{2}{3} \div \frac{4}{5}$ (d) $\frac{1}{2} \div \frac{1}{8}$

3. Draw a diagram to help you find $\frac{1}{3} \div 4$. Write the answer.

B Verify your solution by multiplying.

4. Find each quotient.

   (a) $3 \div \frac{3}{4}$ (b) $6 \div \frac{3}{7}$ (c) $15 \div \frac{5}{7}$

   (d) $\frac{2}{3} \div 2$ (e) $\frac{6}{7} \div 3$ (f) $\frac{3}{5} \div 5$

5. Divide.

   (a) $\frac{3}{4} \div \frac{3}{8}$ (b) $\frac{1}{2} \div \frac{3}{5}$ (c) $\frac{1}{8} \div \frac{3}{11}$

   (d) $\frac{2}{3} \div \frac{3}{4}$ (e) $\frac{1}{5} \div \frac{3}{4}$ (f) $\frac{3}{5} \div \frac{2}{3}$

6. After Greg's party, there was $\frac{1}{2}$ of a pizza left. Greg split the pizza evenly among three people. What fraction of the pizza did each receive?

7. Chan knitted for $\frac{3}{4}$ h. Each row took $\frac{1}{20}$ h to knit. How many rows did she knit?

8. A server takes $\frac{1}{10}$ h to clear a table. How many tables can be cleared in $\frac{1}{2}$ h?

WORKING TOGETHER

Sixteen disks are lined up in rows of two as shown. Your partner secretly selects one of the disks without showing it.

(a) What four questions can you ask to enable you to determine which disk has been selected?

(b) Try your questions on your partner.

7.13 DIVIDING WITH MIXED NUMBERS

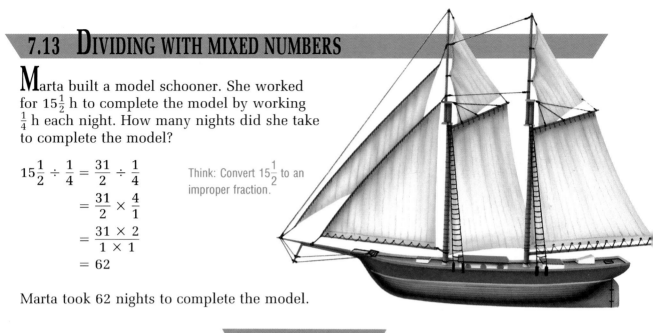

Marta built a model schooner. She worked for $15\frac{1}{2}$ h to complete the model by working $\frac{1}{4}$ h each night. How many nights did she take to complete the model?

$$15\frac{1}{2} \div \frac{1}{4} = \frac{31}{2} \div \frac{1}{4}$$

Think: Convert $15\frac{1}{2}$ to an improper fraction.

$$= \frac{31}{2} \times \frac{4}{1}$$

$$= \frac{31 \times 2}{1 \times 1}$$

$$= 62$$

Marta took 62 nights to complete the model.

EXERCISE

B Check that your answers are reasonable.

1. Find each quotient.

   (a) $1\frac{1}{3} \div \frac{3}{5}$

   (b) $3\frac{1}{2} \div \frac{3}{5}$

   (c) $2\frac{1}{4} \div \frac{5}{7}$

   (d) $1\frac{3}{5} \div \frac{2}{3}$

   (e) $2\frac{2}{5} \div \frac{2}{3}$

   (f) $1\frac{4}{5} \div \frac{3}{4}$

   (g) $2\frac{2}{5} \div \frac{5}{6}$

   (h) $2\frac{1}{3} \div \frac{1}{6}$

2. Divide.

   (a) $1\frac{1}{4} \div \frac{1}{2}$

   (b) $2\frac{2}{3} \div \frac{1}{3}$

   (c) $2\frac{1}{3} \div \frac{1}{6}$

   (d) $1\frac{1}{3} \div 1\frac{2}{3}$

   (e) $3\frac{1}{2} \div 2\frac{1}{2}$

   (f) $5\frac{1}{3} \div 2\frac{1}{4}$

   (g) $5\frac{2}{5} \div 1\frac{1}{2}$

   (h) $8\frac{4}{5} \div 2\frac{1}{2}$

   (i) $4\frac{3}{4} \div 1\frac{9}{10}$

   (j) $5\frac{1}{5} \div 2\frac{1}{3}$

3. Singh takes $2\frac{1}{2}$ min to read a page of his novel. How many pages can he read in $\frac{1}{2}$ h?

4. Charlene ran $2\frac{1}{4}$ laps of a track in $8\frac{3}{4}$ min. Find how long she took to complete each lap.

5. Saftar works part-time in a shirt factory. It takes him $\frac{1}{4}$ h to cut out a pattern. How many patterns can he cut in a $7\frac{1}{2}$ h shift?

6. The answers form a pattern. Find the pattern. Make up two more questions that continue the pattern.

   (a) $\frac{1}{8} \div \frac{1}{4}$

   (b) $\frac{1}{4} \times 2\frac{2}{3}$

   (c) $\frac{1}{2} \times 1\frac{1}{2}$

   (d) $1\frac{1}{5} \div 1\frac{1}{2}$

7.14 ORDER OF OPERATIONS

he order of operations you learned for whole numbers extends to your work with fractions. Record the order of operations in your journal. Then give reasons why each line of the solution below is correct.

$$\left(\frac{1}{5} + \frac{3}{5}\right) \div \frac{4}{15} = \frac{4}{5} \div \frac{4}{15}$$

$$= \frac{4}{5} \times \frac{15}{4}$$

$$= 3$$

EXERCISE

B   Review the order of operations.

1. Calculate. Why are the answers from column A different from those from column B?

A	B
(a) $\left(\frac{1}{5} + \frac{3}{5}\right) \times \frac{5}{8}$	$\frac{1}{5} + \frac{3}{5} \times \frac{5}{8}$
(b) $\left(\frac{2}{3} - \frac{1}{4}\right) \div \frac{1}{4}$	$\frac{2}{3} - \frac{1}{4} \div \frac{1}{4}$
(c) $\left(\frac{2}{5} + \frac{7}{10}\right) \times \frac{1}{2}$	$\frac{2}{5} + \frac{7}{10} \times \frac{1}{2}$

2. Calculate.

(a) $\frac{2}{3} + \frac{1}{4} - \frac{1}{6}$ (b) $\frac{2}{3} - \frac{1}{2} + \frac{5}{6}$

(c) $\frac{3}{8} \times \frac{4}{5} \div \frac{9}{25}$ (d) $\frac{2}{3} \div \frac{4}{9} \times \frac{1}{2}$

(e) $\frac{4}{5} + \frac{3}{10} \div \frac{3}{5}$ (f) $\frac{1}{2} - \frac{3}{5} \times \frac{1}{6}$

3. Use $<$, $>$ or $=$ to make each true.

(a) $1\frac{1}{2} - \left(\frac{1}{3} - \frac{1}{6}\right) \bullet 3\frac{3}{4} + 4\frac{2}{3} \div \frac{1}{4}$

(b) $\left(2\frac{3}{4} + 1\frac{1}{3}\right) \div \frac{1}{4} \bullet \left(3\frac{3}{4} - 2\frac{1}{2}\right) \div \frac{1}{8}$

(c) $\left(\frac{5}{8} + \frac{1}{4}\right) \div \frac{1}{2} \bullet 1\frac{1}{2} \div \frac{9}{10} - \frac{1}{3}$

(d) $\left(\frac{3}{4} + \frac{2}{3}\right) \times 1\frac{1}{4} \bullet \left(\frac{3}{4} - \frac{1}{2}\right) \div \frac{1}{8}$

4. Work with a partner and use coins like those shown below.

(a) In how many ways can you write a fraction to show part of $1.00?

(b) Write the fractions from (a).

You have learned many skills with fractions that can help you solve problems. Make sure you have recorded all the skills in your journal and written your own example for each skill. Then, solve the problems below. Write any clue words you find beside the appropriate skill you have written in your journal.

EXERCISE

 B Review the order of operations.

1. Did you know that on average you spend $\frac{1}{3}$ of your life sleeping? If you live to be 75, how many hours will you have slept?

2. Sandi works at the Stay-Clean Car Wash. A car is washed in $\frac{1}{5}$ h and waxed in 12 min. How many cars can be washed and waxed in $8\frac{1}{2}$ h?

3. Tracy and Jack were mowing lawns of equal size. After one hour, Tracy had completed $\frac{3}{4}$ of her lawn and Jack had completed $\frac{4}{5}$ of his lawn.

   (a) Who had more lawn to finish?

   (b) By how much?

   (c) How long will it take each person to complete the job?

   (d) What assumptions have you made in your solution to (c)?

4. A ride on a roller coaster takes $2\frac{1}{2}$ min. Grant has paid for seven rides. How long is Grant on the roller coaster? What assumptions have you made?

5. An airplane uses 90 L of fuel for a $2\frac{1}{2}$ h flight. How much fuel will be used in a 1 h flight? What assumptions have you made?

6. Ferdinand spends $\frac{1}{3}$ of his day sleeping, $\frac{1}{4}$ of his day on school work, and $\frac{1}{8}$ of his day watching television. Half of his remaining time is spent on his hobby. How many hours does he spend on his hobby?

7. (a) Copy the figure below onto a piece of cardboard.

   (b) Cut along the dotted lines.

   (c) Use your cutouts. What fraction of the large square is covered by the small shaded square?

TECHNOLOGY INSIGHT: LIVING IN SPACE

Writers have often inspired scientists to achieve new discoveries. For example, Arthur Clarke's books have inspired Gerald O'Neill with his work with space colonies.

ACTIVITY ① Work in a Group

Physicist Gerald O'Neill has designed detailed plans for several space stations. Each would be a permanent "apartment building" floating through space and housing thousands of people.

(a) O'Neill called his space stations self-supporting. What did he mean?

(b) What would be the cost of building a space station?

(c) How much was spent on the Apollo rockets? Is this more than the cost of one space station?

(d) Does your group feel that the amount in (c) would be a worthwhile investment? Give reasons for your answer.

(e) What technology do you think will be used on a space station?

ACTIVITY ② Work with a Partner

Use your library to help answer the following.

(a) What are the Salyut stations?

(b) How many such stations are there?

(c) What are the dimensions of each?

(d) How is power supplied to each station?

(e) What special equipment is used in each Salyut station to allow people to eat and sleep?

(f) What math skills do you think are needed to operate a space station?

ACTIVITY ③ Work on your Own

Suppose you are the captain of the star ship *Enterprise*.

(a) Prepare a log for the day. What did you and your crew do?

(b) Describe all math skills and technology you and your crew used today.

1. What fraction of each figure is shaded? Write the fraction in lowest terms.

   (a)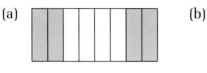

   (b)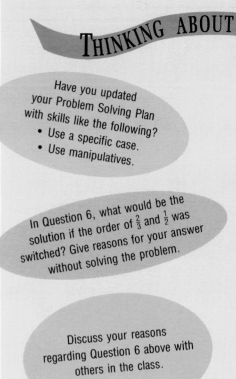

2. Calculate.

   (a) $\dfrac{3}{10} + \dfrac{1}{10}$

   (b) $\dfrac{5}{12} - \dfrac{1}{3}$

   (c) $\dfrac{3}{4} - \dfrac{2}{5}$

   (d) $\dfrac{5}{6} + \dfrac{7}{10}$

3. Calculate.

   (a) $1\dfrac{5}{6} - \dfrac{7}{10}$

   (b) $2\dfrac{1}{3} + 7\dfrac{7}{8}$

   (c) $4\dfrac{2}{3} - 1\dfrac{1}{4}$

   (d) $5\dfrac{3}{7} + 4\dfrac{1}{8}$

4. Multiply or divide.

   (a) $1\dfrac{1}{3} \times \dfrac{7}{5}$

   (b) $4 \div \dfrac{3}{2}$

   (c) $3\dfrac{1}{3} \times 1\dfrac{4}{7}$

   (d) $6\dfrac{1}{4} \div 3\dfrac{1}{3}$

5. Calculate.

   (a) $\dfrac{2}{3} + \dfrac{1}{4} - \dfrac{1}{6}$

   (b) $\dfrac{2}{3} - \dfrac{1}{2} + \dfrac{5}{6}$

   (c) $\dfrac{4}{5} + \dfrac{3}{10} \div \dfrac{3}{5}$

   (d) $\dfrac{1}{2} - \dfrac{3}{5} \times \dfrac{1}{6}$

6. In a book, $\frac{2}{3}$ of the pages have pictures and $\frac{1}{2}$ of the pages have words. What fraction of the book has words and pictures? What assumptions are made?

7. There are four quarters in each basketball game. So far, the junior team has played 39 quarters.

   (a) How many games have they played?

   (b) How many quarters are left in the current game?

THINKING ABOUT

Have you updated your Problem Solving Plan with skills like the following?
- Use a specific case.
- Use manipulatives.

In Question 6, what would be the solution if the order of $\frac{2}{3}$ and $\frac{1}{2}$ was switched? Give reasons for your answer without solving the problem.

Discuss your reasons regarding Question 6 above with others in the class.

MAKING CONNECTIONS

Refer to the opening pages of the chapter.

(a) Create a problem of your own using the pictures. Solve your problem.

(b) Compare your problem with others in your class. Solve the other problems.

How do you rate your skills with fractions? How can you improve them?

How can you use a calculator to improve your skills with fractions?

Choose a question on this page. Describe to your partner how you can solve it. Have your partner suggest how your description can be improved.

MATH JOURNAL

In this chapter, you have used many math symbols and skills to help you communicate mathematics.

(a) List all symbols and skills you have learned.
(b) Write an example to show how to communicate with each symbol and skill.

SELF EVALUATION

1. Write each fraction in lowest terms.

   (a) $\frac{15}{20}$ (b) $\frac{21}{30}$ (c) $\frac{20}{36}$ (d) $\frac{15}{45}$

2. Arrange each group of fractions in order from least to greatest.

   (a) $\frac{2}{7}, \frac{4}{7}, \frac{1}{14}, \frac{5}{14}$ (b) $\frac{3}{5}, 2\frac{1}{2}, \frac{2}{10}, \frac{2}{3}, 1\frac{1}{2}, \frac{4}{5}$

3. For the following fractions, pick those whose decimal values will be greater than 0.50, and write them as decimal numbers.

   (a) $\frac{1}{3}$ (b) $\frac{4}{5}$ (c) $\frac{5}{8}$ (d) $3\frac{1}{2}$

4. Calculate.

   (a) $\frac{3}{5} + \frac{1}{10}$ (b) $\frac{3}{4} - \frac{7}{12}$ (c) $\frac{9}{10} - \frac{3}{5}$

   (d) $\frac{3}{2} + \frac{1}{3}$ (e) $\frac{5}{7} \times \frac{3}{5}$ (f) $\frac{7}{8} \div \frac{5}{8}$

   (g) $\frac{2}{3} \div \frac{1}{3}$ (h) $\frac{3}{8} \times \frac{4}{5}$ (i) $\frac{1}{3} \div \frac{4}{5}$

5. Add or subtract.

   (a) $1\frac{5}{6} + \frac{7}{10}$ (b) $4\frac{1}{8} - 3\frac{1}{2}$ (c) $1\frac{2}{3} + \frac{3}{4}$

   (d) $6\frac{1}{4} - 3\frac{1}{3}$ (e) $3\frac{3}{5} + 2\frac{2}{3}$ (f) $4\frac{4}{9} - 3\frac{2}{3}$

6. Calculate. In your journal, describe the pattern that helps you to calculate quickly.

   (a) $\frac{2}{3} \times \frac{3}{2}$ (b) $\frac{3}{4} \times \frac{4}{3}$ (c) $\frac{7}{11} \div \frac{7}{11}$

   (d) $\frac{1}{8} \times 8$ (e) $\frac{4}{5} \times \frac{5}{4}$ (f) $\frac{2}{3} \div \frac{2}{3}$

7. The gas tank in a bus is $\frac{7}{8}$ full. During each trip around its route, the bus uses $\frac{1}{12}$ of a tank of gas. How many trips around the route can the bus make?

8 BUILDING MATHEMATICS:

Write a brief paragraph explaining how numbers are used in each of the activities shown.
• How are the numbers alike? How are they different?

Did you know that a pitcher's statistics often include rational numbers?

RATIONAL NUMBERS

Did you know that gains and losses with stocks are recorded using rational numbers?

Did you know that an altimeter measures the height of an airplane above ground level?

Earlier, you used integers to express opposite ideas.

4 kg gained (+4)	5 km right (+5)
4 kg lost (−4)	5 km left (−5)

These numbers also show opposite ideas.

- a gain of $4\frac{1}{2}$ kg, use $+4\frac{1}{2}$

- a loss of $3\frac{1}{2}$ kg, use $-3\frac{1}{2}$ kg

You can use red and black squares and part squares to represent rational numbers.

represents +1   represents $+\frac{1}{2}$

represents −1   represents $-\frac{1}{2}$

Thus, $-3\frac{1}{2}$ can be represented as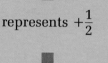

$+3\frac{1}{2}$ can be represented as

When you walk $+3\frac{1}{2}$ km and then $-3\frac{1}{2}$ km, you are back at your starting point.

A black square together with a red square represents a net result of 0.

A $\frac{1}{2}$ black square together with a $\frac{1}{2}$ red square represents a net result of zero.

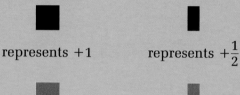

EXPLORATION ① *Work with a Partner*

1. What rational number is represented by the following?

   (a) ■■■■   (b) ▬▬▬■   (c) ▬■

2. Use materials to represent each number.

   (a) $+3$ (b) -4 (c) $-7\frac{1}{2}$ (d) $+6\frac{1}{2}$ (e) $-5\frac{1}{2}$ (f) $-\frac{1}{2}$

3. (a) Suggest how you might use materials to represent the following numbers.

   (i) $-3\frac{7}{8}$ (ii) $+4\frac{3}{4}$ (iii) $-5\frac{3}{4}$ (iv) $+7\frac{1}{8}$ (v) $+2\frac{1}{8}$

   (b) Write numbers of your own. Use materials to represent each number.

EXPLORATION ② *Work with a Partner*

4. Tanya walks $3\frac{1}{2}$ km away from the park and then $2\frac{1}{2}$ km towards the park.

   The squares show her distance
   from the park. What is her
   distance from the park?
   Interpret your answer.

5. For each,
   (a) write the net result of the squares.
   (b) describe a situation that can be illustrated by the squares.

6. Arrange squares of your own.
   (a) Write the net result of the squares.
   (b) Describe a situation that can be illustrated by the squares.

8.2 RATIONAL NUMBERS

Numbers were developed because of a need. For example, the first numbers used were the natural (counting) numbers.

$$N = \{1, 2, 3, 4, 5, 6, \ldots\}$$

Then, the need to represent zero occurred and the whole numbers were used.

$$W = \{0, 1, 2, 3, 4, 5, \ldots\}$$

When the need to represent opposite ideas occurred, the integers were used.

$$I = \{\ldots -3, -2, -1, 0, +1, +2, +3, \ldots\}$$

Rational numbers are used to show numbers between integers. Some examples of rational numbers are:

$$\frac{+2}{+3}, \quad \frac{-7}{+2}, \quad \frac{+3}{-2}, \quad \frac{6}{-3}, \quad \frac{+7}{-4}.$$

The above numbers can be written in other forms:

$$+\frac{2}{3}, \quad -3\frac{1}{2}, \quad -1\frac{1}{2}, \quad -2, \quad -1\frac{3}{4}.$$

You use your previous skills with fractions and integers to work with rational numbers.

$$\frac{-2}{-3} = \frac{2}{3}, \qquad \frac{-3}{5} = \frac{3}{-5} = -\frac{3}{5}$$

Rational numbers can also be written in lowest terms as shown below.

$$\frac{6}{-9} = \frac{6 \div (-3)}{-9 \div (-3)} \qquad\qquad \frac{-3}{-15} = \frac{-3 \div (-3)}{-15 \div (-3)} \qquad\qquad \frac{-9}{6} = \frac{-9 \div (+3)}{6 \div (+3)}$$

$$= \frac{-2}{3} \text{ or } -\frac{2}{3} \qquad\qquad = \frac{+1}{+5} \text{ or } \frac{1}{5} \qquad\qquad = \frac{-3}{2} \text{ or } -1\frac{1}{2}$$

EXERCISE

A Review your skills with integers.

1. Write each rational number with a positive denominator.

   (a) $\dfrac{5}{-8}$ (b) $\dfrac{-3}{-4}$ (c) $\dfrac{7}{-3}$ (d) $\dfrac{-1}{-10}$ (e) $\dfrac{4}{-7}$

2. Write another rational number equivalent to each.

   (a) $\dfrac{-12}{8}$ (b) $\dfrac{14}{-4}$ (c) $\dfrac{-21}{-9}$ (d) $\dfrac{-18}{-8}$ (e) $\dfrac{-35}{-7}$

3. Write each rational number in lowest terms.

   (a) $\dfrac{6}{-8}$ (b) $\dfrac{3}{-6}$ (c) $\dfrac{-8}{-12}$ (d) $\dfrac{-3}{9}$ (e) $\dfrac{-12}{-16}$

4. Which rational numbers are expressed in lowest terms?

   (a) $\dfrac{-1}{2}, \dfrac{2}{-4}, \dfrac{-2}{-4}, \dfrac{1}{-2}$ (b) $\dfrac{-8}{12}, \dfrac{-4}{6}, \dfrac{-2}{3}$ (c) $\dfrac{-10}{-6}, \dfrac{-5}{-3}, \dfrac{5}{3}$

B Remember: These rational numbers are equivalent: $\dfrac{-1}{2} = -\dfrac{1}{2} = \dfrac{1}{-2}$.

5. Write each of the following in lowest terms.

   (a) $\dfrac{-4}{2}$ (b) $\dfrac{-8}{-4}$ (c) $\dfrac{12}{6}$

   (d) $\dfrac{-15}{3}$ (e) $\dfrac{-16}{-4}$ (f) $\dfrac{-25}{-5}$

6. Write two equivalent rational numbers for each.

   (a) $\dfrac{4}{-5}$ (b) $\dfrac{-2}{3}$ (c) $\dfrac{1}{-2}$

   (d) $\dfrac{-13}{5}$ (e) $\dfrac{1}{3}$ (f) $\dfrac{-7}{-4}$

7. Write each of the following in lowest terms with a positive denominator.

   (a) $\dfrac{14}{-10}$ (b) $\dfrac{6}{-30}$ (c) $\dfrac{-8}{12}$

   (d) $\dfrac{-30}{-100}$ (e) $\dfrac{-28}{-8}$ (f) $-\dfrac{-12}{-10}$

8. Rewrite the magic square so that all rational numbers are in lowest terms.

$\dfrac{+2}{24}$	$\dfrac{-6}{12}$	$\dfrac{-2}{24}$
$\dfrac{-2}{6}$	$\dfrac{-6}{36}$	$\dfrac{0}{5}$
$\dfrac{1}{4}$	$\dfrac{+2}{12}$	$\dfrac{-5}{12}$

9. A square number and a triangular number are shown.

   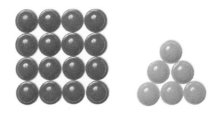

   (a) What square number is also a triangular number?

   (b) Create and solve a similar problem.

8.3 RATIONAL NUMBERS AS DECIMALS

Rational numbers can be expressed in different ways. To find the decimal equivalent of a rational number, you divide the numerator by the denominator.

Fraction Form

$\frac{5}{8}$ of the team is female.

Decimal Form

0.625 of the team is female.

Think: Divide the numerator by the denominator. | c | 5 | ÷ | 8 | = | 0.625

Decimal numbers like 0.625 are called **terminating decimals**. When you try to find the decimal equivalent of $+\frac{2}{3}$, you obtain a **repeating decimal**.

$$+\frac{2}{3} = +0.666\ldots$$

| c | 2 | ÷ | 3 | = | 0.6666666

Decimal numbers like +0.666... are often written in a compact form as follows:

$$+0.666\ldots = +0.\dot{6} \text{ or } +0.\overline{6} \qquad -3.45454545\ldots = -3.\dot{4}\dot{5} \text{ or } -3.\overline{45}$$

Writing in decimal form is useful when comparing rational numbers. For example, you write $\frac{-12}{29}$ and $-\frac{13}{31}$ as decimal numbers to determine which is greater.

$$\frac{-12}{29} = -0.414 \text{ (to 3 decimal places)} \qquad -\frac{13}{31} = -0.419 \text{ (to 3 decimal places)}$$

Since $-0.414 > -0.419$, it follows that $\frac{-12}{29} > -\frac{13}{31}$.

Activity

You can explore mathematics with a calculator.

(a) Calculate the decimal equivalent of $-\frac{1}{11}$, $-\frac{2}{11}$, and $-\frac{3}{11}$.

(b) Use the pattern to predict the decimal equivalent of $-\frac{4}{11}$.

(c) Check your prediction with a calculator.

A Review your skills with fractions.

1. Write each as a decimal number.

   (a) $\frac{3}{8}$ (b) $\frac{2}{5}$ (c) $\frac{3}{4}$ (d) $\frac{1}{8}$ (e) $\frac{5}{8}$

   (f) $\frac{1}{2}$ (g) $\frac{3}{5}$ (h) $\frac{7}{8}$ (i) $\frac{4}{5}$ (j) $\frac{12}{16}$

2. Write each decimal number in a compact form.

   (a) $3.333\ldots$ (b) $3.777\ldots$ (c) $35.252525\ldots$ (d) $21.312312\ldots$

B Use a calculator to help you solve each problem.

3. Write each as a decimal number.

   (a) $+\frac{3}{8}$ (b) $\frac{-2}{11}$ (c) $-\frac{7}{8}$

   (d) $-\frac{7}{11}$ (e) $+\frac{4}{9}$ (f) $\frac{-3}{7}$

   (g) $+\frac{3}{9}$ (h) $+\frac{5}{12}$ (i) $-\frac{1}{15}$

4. Write each rational number as a decimal number. Which number in each pair is greater?

   (a) $+\frac{12}{23}, +\frac{14}{29}$ (b) $-\frac{3}{17}, -\frac{5}{26}$

   (c) $+\frac{2}{28}, +\frac{2}{17}$ (d) $-\frac{4}{25}, \frac{-3}{20}$

5. Solution A has a temperature of $-4°C$. Solution B has a temperature of $-7\frac{1}{2}°C$. Which solution is colder?

6. During the year, Jacques' mass changed by $-18\frac{3}{4}$ kg. Alain's mass changed by $-23\frac{1}{5}$ kg. Whose mass changed more?

7. (a) Calculate decimal numbers for $\frac{1}{2}$, $\frac{1}{20}$, and $\frac{1}{200}$.

   (b) Use the pattern to predict the decimal number for $\frac{1}{2000}$. Check your prediction.

8. (a) Calculate decimal numbers for $-\frac{15}{90}, -\frac{15}{900}$, and $-\frac{15}{9000}$.

   (b) Use the pattern to predict the decimal numbers for $-\frac{15}{90\,000}$ and $-\frac{15}{900\,000}$.

9. Eight Smarties have the same size and shape. Seven of them have the same mass. How can you use a scale balance twice to find the Smartie with a different mass?

8.4 PROBLEM SOLVING: WIND CHILL FACTOR

Actual Temperature:
−20°C
Wind Speed:
32 km/h
Wind Chill Factor:
−44°C

Scientists have recorded data to explore the change in temperature when there is a wind blowing. The table shows the temperature you feel when the actual temperature is combined with the effect of the wind at different speeds.

	Wind Chill Factor Chart											
Speed (km/h)	Actual Thermometer Reading (°C)											
	10	5	0	−5	−10	−15	−20	−25	−30	−35	−40	−45
8	9	3	−3	−8	−13	−18	−23	−28	−33	−38	−44	−50
16	4	−2	−9	−15	−21	−26	−33	−38	−44	−50	−57	−64
24	2	−6	−13	−20	−26	−33	−40	−45	−51	−58	−65	−73
32	0	−8	−16	−22	−30	−37	−44	−49	−55	−63	−71	−79
40	−1	−9	−18	−25	−32	−40	−47	−53	−59	−67	−76	−83
48	−2	−11	−19	−27	−34	−41	−50	−55	−62	−70	−78	−87
56	−3	−12	−20	−28	−36	−42	−52	−57	−64	−72	−81	−89

Suppose the wind speed is 32 km/h. If the actual temperature of the air is −20°C, the chart shows the temperature will feel like −44°C. This apparent temperature of −44°C is called the **wind chill factor**.

You can also estimate the wind chill factor for values between those given in the chart. Suppose the actual temperature is −27.5°C and the speed of the wind is 40 km/h. You estimate the wind chill factor to be about −56°C.

Think:
−27.5°C is half-way between −25°C and −30°C.
−56°C is half-way between −53°C and −59°C.
The wind chill factor is about −56°C.

Use the table on the previous page.

1. Suppose the air temperature is −15°C. What is the wind chill factor when the wind blows at

    (a) 16 km/h?   (b) 32 km/h?   (c) 40 km/h?

2. Suppose the wind is blowing at a speed of 24 km/h. What is the actual temperature if the wind chill factor is

    (a) −10°C?   (b) −15°C?   (c) −40°C?

 Use your *Problem Solving Plan*.

3. Copy and complete the chart.

Location	Temperature	Wind Speed	Wind Chill Factor
(a) Innuik	−10°C	40 km/h	?
(b) Tiksi	−25°C	?	−45°C
(c) Zemlya	?	32 km/h	−71°C
(d) Point Barrow	−15°C	56 km/h	?

4. At Mirny, Antarctica, the air temperature was −25°C.

    (a) Estimate the wind chill factor when the wind started to blow at 12 km/h.

    (b) A wind of 32 km/h would cause the wind chill factor from (a) to drop by how many degrees?

5. At Shackleton, Antarctica, the temperature was −32.5°C with no wind. Melanie drove her snowmobile at 32 km/h. Estimate the wind chill factor.

6. On Ellesmere Island in the Arctic, the wind chill factor was −40°C. The wind speed was 12 km/h. Estimate the actual air temperature.

7. A survey crew used sleds to move from Knox Coast to Kemp Land in the Antarctic. They travelled at a speed of 24 km/h. The actual air temperature was −7.5°C.

    (a) How can you estimate the wind chill factor?

    (b) Use your plan from (a). Estimate the wind chill factor.

8. Scientists have protective clothing made to withstand temperatures as low as −65°C. The air temperature is −42.5°C.

    (a) Estimate the wind chill factor if the wind speed is 24 km/h.

    (b) Should the scientists go outside in their protective clothing? Give reasons for your answer.

9. (a) At Point Barrow, the wind was blowing at a speed of 36 km/h. The air temperature was −43°C. Estimate the wind chill factor.

    (b) Create and solve a problem using the chart. Compare your problem with others in your class.

Many companies offer stocks to the public. A person can buy the stock and thus own a share of the company. Stocks are sold on a stock exchange in places such as Vancouver, Toronto, Montreal, and other places around the world. Stock prices are reported daily in the financial section of most newspapers.

- $+\frac{1}{2}$ indicates a gain of $\$\frac{1}{2}$ or 50¢.

- $-1\frac{1}{4}$ indicates a loss of $\$1\frac{1}{4}$ or $1.25.

Stock Exchange Report   Date: March 4

Stock	Sales	High	Low	Change
A & A Foods	3 300	$6\frac{1}{4}$	$6\frac{1}{8}$	$-2\frac{1}{4}$
Cam Net Comm	2 000	$6\frac{3}{8}$	$6\frac{1}{4}$	$+1\frac{3}{8}$
Clearly Cdn	6 057	$27\frac{3}{8}$	$26\frac{7}{8}$	$+\frac{7}{8}$
Cominco	11 200	$20\frac{3}{8}$	$19\frac{7}{8}$	$-\frac{1}{2}$
Intl Cablecstng	700	$7\frac{1}{4}$	$6\frac{7}{8}$	$+\frac{1}{4}$
MacMillan bf	1 500	$17\frac{3}{8}$	$17\frac{3}{8}$	$+\frac{1}{4}$
Noranda Inc	15 000	$16\frac{7}{8}$	$16\frac{7}{8}$	$+2\frac{1}{2}$
Taseko Mines	14 500	$8\frac{1}{4}$	$7\frac{1}{2}$	$-\frac{1}{8}$

Company name   Shares sold   Highest price per share   Lowest price per share   Change from yesterday's closing price

MARKET

 A Use the stock market report.

1. What is the day's highest price for each stock? the lowest?
   - (a) A & A Foods
   - (b) Cominco
   - (c) Noranda Inc
   - (d) Taseko Mines

2. What change occurred for each stock?
   - (a) A & A Foods
   - (b) Cominco
   - (c) Taseko Mines
   - (d) Clearly Cdn

B Use your *Problem Solving Plan.*

3. Which stock is higher?
   - (a) A & A Foods or Noranda Inc
   - (b) Intl Cablecstng or Cam Net Comm

4. Which stock is lower?
   - (a) Taseko Mines or Cominco
   - (b) MacMillan bf or Noranda Inc

5. (a) Which stocks sold at a price higher than $10\frac{1}{2}$?
   - (b) Which stocks sold at a price lower than $9\frac{1}{8}$?

6. (a) Which stocks had the day's high between $5\frac{1}{4}$ and $11\frac{1}{2}$?
   - (b) Which stocks had the day's low between $10\frac{1}{4}$ and $25\frac{1}{4}$?

7. (a) Which stock costs the least amount to purchase?
   - (b) Which stock costs the greatest amount to purchase?

8. Write the stocks in order from least to greatest according to
   - (a) the low price.
   - (b) the high price.
   - (c) the change from yesterday's closing price.

9. Which company had the most stock sold on the day? the least?

MAKING CONNECTIONS

(a) Use a stock market report from a newspaper or magazine.
   - Create a problem using the report.
   - Solve your problem and compare it with others in your class. Solve the other problems.

(b) In the stock market, gains and losses are recorded as rational numbers. Use the *Guinness Book of World Records*.
   - What was the greatest gain for a stock in one day?
   - What was the greatest loss for a stock in one day?
   - Research why stocks vary in price during a day.

Squares and half squares in black and red can help you add and subtract rational numbers. Complete each exploration with a partner. Summarize any patterns you observe.

EXPLORATION ① Work with a Partner

1. The squares and half squares shown represent the expression $(+3\frac{1}{2}) + (+2\frac{1}{2})$.

Think

(a) What is the result of adding 3 black squares and 2 black squares?

(b) What is the result of adding a black half square and a black half square?

(c) Interpret your results to find the answer to $(+3\frac{1}{2}) + (+2\frac{1}{2})$.

(d) Create similar expressions. Use squares and half squares to find the answers.

2. (a) Use squares and half squares to represent $(-3\frac{1}{2}) + (-2\frac{1}{2})$. What is the net result?

(b) Interpret your work in (a). What is the answer to $(-3\frac{1}{2}) + (-2\frac{1}{2})$?

(c) Create similar expressions. Use squares and half squares to find the answers.

EXPLORATION ② Work Together

3. The squares and half squares shown represent the expression $(+3\frac{1}{2}) + (-2\frac{1}{2})$.

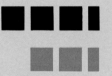

(a) What is the result of adding 3 black squares and 2 red squares?

(b) What is the result of adding a black half square and a red half square?

(c) Interpret your results to find the answer to $(+3\frac{1}{2}) + (-2\frac{1}{2})$.

(d) Create similar expressions. Use squares and half squares to find the answers.

4. (a) Use squares and half squares to show $(-3\frac{1}{2}) + (+2\frac{1}{2})$. What is the net result?

(b) What is the answer to $(-3\frac{1}{2}) + (+2\frac{1}{2})$?

(c) Create similar expressions. Use squares and half squares to find the answers.

5. To subtract rational numbers, you need to refer to your earlier skills with integers. The rational number $+2\frac{1}{2}$ is shown using manipulatives.

    (a) What is the result of taking $2\frac{1}{2}$ black squares from the $2\frac{1}{2}$ black squares?

    (b) Interpret your results to find the answer to $(+2\frac{1}{2}) - (+2\frac{1}{2})$.

6. Jennifer used materials to subtract these rational numbers.

    (a) Interpret her work to find $(+1\frac{1}{2}) - (-2\frac{1}{2})$.

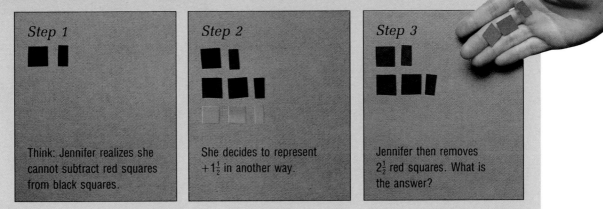

Step 1

Think: Jennifer realizes she cannot subtract red squares from black squares.

Step 2

She decides to represent $+1\frac{1}{2}$ in another way.

Step 3

Jennifer then removes $2\frac{1}{2}$ red squares. What is the answer?

    (b) Interpret each step above. In your journal, describe what Jennifer is doing in each step. Then find the answer to $(+1\frac{1}{2}) - (-2\frac{1}{2})$.

    (c) Write your own similar expressions. Use squares and half squares to find the answers.

7. Compare the skills of adding and subtracting integers and fractions with those of adding and subtracting rational numbers. In your journal, describe how the skills are alike and how they are different.

8.7 ADDING RATIONAL NUMBERS

The skills you use to fly a small airplane extend to flying a large airplane.

The skills you use to add integers and add fractions extend to adding rational numbers. Compare the examples below. How are they alike? How are they different?

$$\frac{1}{2} + \frac{3}{8} = \frac{4}{8} + \frac{3}{8} \qquad \left(+\frac{1}{2}\right) + \left(\frac{-3}{8}\right) = \left(+\frac{4}{8}\right) + \left(\frac{-3}{8}\right)$$
$$= \frac{4+3}{8} \qquad\qquad\qquad = \frac{+4 + (-3)}{8}$$
$$= \frac{7}{8} \qquad\qquad\qquad\quad = +\frac{1}{8}$$

The skills above can be used to add rational numbers like the following.

$$-\frac{17}{5} + \frac{17}{4} = \frac{-68}{20} + \frac{+85}{20}$$
$$= \frac{-68 + 85}{20}$$
$$= \frac{17}{20}$$

Think: $\dfrac{-68}{20} = \dfrac{-17 \times 4}{5 \times 4}$

What skills would pilots of large and small planes have in common?

You can also use rational numbers written in decimal form to add rational numbers as shown below.

$$(-3.4) + (+4.25) = +0.85$$

$\boxed{\text{c}}$ 3.4 $\boxed{+/-}$ $\boxed{+}$ 4.25 $\boxed{=}$ 0.85

EXERCISE

A Review your skills with integers.

1. What is the sum?

   (a) $\left(+\frac{1}{2}\right) + \left(+\frac{1}{2}\right)$ (b) $\left(+\frac{1}{4}\right) + \left(-\frac{3}{4}\right)$ (c) $\left(\frac{-3}{4}\right) + \left(+\frac{1}{4}\right)$ (d) $\left(\frac{-2}{3}\right) + \left(+\frac{1}{3}\right)$

2. What is the sum?

   (a) $\left(+3\frac{1}{2}\right) + \left(+2\frac{1}{2}\right)$ (b) $\left(+4\frac{1}{4}\right) + \left(-2\frac{3}{4}\right)$ (c) $\left(-2\frac{3}{7}\right) + \left(-1\frac{4}{7}\right)$

3. Add.

(a) $\dfrac{-3}{4} + \dfrac{-5}{8}$ (b) $\dfrac{-1}{5} + \dfrac{-4}{10}$

(c) $\dfrac{-2}{5} + \dfrac{-3}{10}$ (d) $+\dfrac{1}{2} + \dfrac{-1}{4}$

4. Add.

(a) $\dfrac{-3}{5} + \dfrac{+1}{3}$ (b) $+\dfrac{1}{2} + \dfrac{-2}{3}$

(c) $\dfrac{-3}{5} + \dfrac{-3}{4}$ (d) $+\dfrac{7}{4} + \dfrac{-3}{5}$

(e) $\dfrac{-2}{3} + \dfrac{-1}{6}$ (f) $\dfrac{-11}{10} + \dfrac{-6}{5}$

5. Add.

(a) $(+6.3) + (+3.4)$

(b) $(+4.2) + (-3.1)$

(c) $(-4.4) + (+3.2)$

(d) $(-3.1) + (-2.2)$

(e) In your journal, describe a way you can decide the greatest sum before adding.

6. Evaluate each expression that has a sum greater than 0. How did you know the sum was greater than 0 before adding?

(a) $(+6.2) + (+3.4)$

(b) $(+3.1) + (-6.3)$

(c) $(-3.8) + (-4.1)$

(d) $(-9.2) + (-6.9)$

(e) $(+8.3) + (-4.7)$

(f) $(+5.8) + (-5.9)$

(g) $(-3.8) + (+4.1)$

(h) $(-4.4) + (-5.6)$

7. Your normal body temperature is 37°C. Suppose you have a fever that increases your body temperature by 1.5°C. What is your body temperature?

8. (a) Comstock started the trading day at $\$+8\frac{3}{4}$. At the end of the day, it showed a gain of $\$-1\frac{1}{2}$. What was the trading price at the end of the day?

   (b) Refer to the stock market report shown in Section 8.5. Create addition problems using numbers from the report. Solve your problems and compare them with others in your class.

9. Construct two cubes numbered with the rational numbers shown.
   A: $+1.1, +2.2, +3.3, +4.4, +5.5, +6.6$
   B: $-1.1, -2.2, -3.3, -4.4, -5.5, -6.6$

   (a) Find all possible sums when these cubes are tossed.

   (b) Which score do you think will occur most often?

8.8 SUBTRACTING RATIONAL NUMBERS

What you learn in selling video games would apply if you were selling computers.

Similarly, what you learn when you add rational numbers extends to help you subtract rational numbers. Compare the following examples. How are they alike? How are they different?

$$\frac{5}{9} - \frac{1}{3} = \frac{5}{9} - \frac{3}{9} \qquad \frac{-5}{9} - \left(+\frac{1}{3}\right) = \frac{-5}{9} - \left(+\frac{3}{9}\right)$$
$$= \frac{5-3}{9} \qquad\qquad = \frac{-5-(+3)}{9}$$
$$= \frac{2}{9} \qquad\qquad = \frac{-8}{9}$$

The skills above can be used to subtract rational numbers like the following.

$$\frac{11}{5} - \frac{-7}{4} = \frac{11 \times 4}{5 \times 4} - \frac{-7 \times 5}{4 \times 5}$$
$$= \frac{44 - (-35)}{20}$$
$$= \frac{79}{20} \text{ or } 3\frac{19}{20}$$

How is selling video games like selling computers? How is it different?

You can also subtract rational numbers written in decimal form.

$$+5.375 - (-2.25) = +7.625$$

| c | 5.375 | − | 2.25 | +/− | = | 7.625 |

EXERCISE

A Review your skills with adding rational numbers.

1. Subtract.

   (a) $\frac{3}{4} - \frac{1}{4}$
   (b) $-\frac{2}{3} - \frac{-1}{3}$
   (c) $\frac{-4}{5} - \frac{-3}{5}$
   (d) $-\frac{3}{5} - \left(+\frac{1}{5}\right)$

2. Subtract.

   (a) $\left(+1\frac{1}{2}\right) - \left(+2\frac{1}{4}\right)$
   (b) $\left(+3\frac{1}{3}\right) - \left(+2\frac{1}{3}\right)$
   (c) $\left(+1\frac{1}{2}\right) - \left(-2\frac{1}{4}\right)$

3. Find each difference.

   (a) $\dfrac{5}{-12} - \dfrac{-3}{4}$ (b) $\dfrac{-1}{4} - \dfrac{-4}{8}$

   (c) $\dfrac{3}{6} - \dfrac{-2}{3}$ (d) $\dfrac{1}{-8} - \dfrac{-3}{4}$

4. Subtract. Which answer is the greatest?

   (a) $(+5.3) - (+2.4)$

   (b) $(+5.2) - (-3.1)$

   (c) $(-4.4) - (5.2)$

   (d) $(-8.7) - (9.6)$

5. Calculate only those with a value greater than 0.

   (a) $(-4.2) - (-4.6)$

   (b) $(-9.7) - (-7.4)$

   (c) $(-8.8) - (-5.2)$

   (d) $(+6.3) - (-6.4)$

   (e) $(-4.3) - (+3.6)$

   (f) $(-4.9) - (+6.1)$

6. Calculate. Which has the greatest value?

   (a) $\dfrac{-3}{4} - \dfrac{1}{-4}$ (b) $\dfrac{1}{2} - \dfrac{-2}{3}$

   (c) $\dfrac{3}{-7} - \dfrac{-5}{8}$ (d) $\dfrac{7}{10} - \dfrac{-4}{5}$

   (e) $\dfrac{-4}{5} - \dfrac{+3}{7}$ (f) $\dfrac{3}{4} - \dfrac{2}{-3}$

7. Kim estimated a painting job to be $3\frac{1}{2}$ d. The job took $5\frac{1}{4}$ d.

   (a) Write an expression to show how many days over Kim went.

   (b) Calculate your expression from (a). By how many days was Kim over?

8. Refer to the stock market report shown in Section 8.5. Create problems using numbers from the report. Solve your problems. Compare them with others in your class.

9. The temperature in Okotoks was $-8°C$. The temperature rose to $+7.5°C$. What is the change in temperature?

10. Find the missing rational numbers in this magic square. In your journal, describe two ways you can find the magic sum.

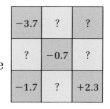

-3.7	?	?
?	-0.7	?
-1.7	?	$+2.3$

11. Work with a partner. Use the cubes you made in Section 8.7.

    (a) Each of you roll the cubes 5 times.

    (b) Use the numbers rolled to create an expression that has the greatest value. The player who has the greater value wins.

8.9 MULTIPLYING RATIONAL NUMBERS

When you study mathematics, you can help yourself by comparing any new work you do with earlier work learned.

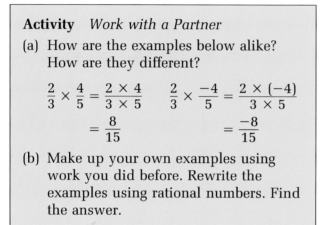

Activity   *Work with a Partner*

(a) How are the examples below alike? How are they different?

$$\frac{2}{3} \times \frac{4}{5} = \frac{2 \times 4}{3 \times 5} \qquad \frac{2}{3} \times \frac{-4}{5} = \frac{2 \times (-4)}{3 \times 5}$$

$$= \frac{8}{15} \qquad\qquad = \frac{-8}{15}$$

(b) Make up your own examples using work you did before. Rewrite the examples using rational numbers. Find the answer.

You can also multiply rational numbers written in decimal form.

$(-0.75) \times (+0.625) = -0.468\,75$ | c | 0.75 | +/− | × | 0.625 | = | −0.46875

In the exercise, you will solve problems involving rational numbers.

EXERCISE

A   Review your skills with multiplying fractions.

1. Calculate.

  (a) $\left(+\frac{1}{2}\right) \times \left(-\frac{1}{4}\right)$ (b) $\left(+\frac{1}{2}\right) \times \left(-\frac{1}{2}\right)$ (c) $\left(-\frac{1}{2}\right) \times \left(-\frac{1}{4}\right)$

  (d) $\left(+\frac{1}{2}\right) \times \frac{1}{-5}$ (e) $\frac{-1}{3} \times \frac{2}{-5}$ (f) $\frac{-2}{3} \times \frac{-3}{2}$

2. Multiply.

  (a) $(-5.5) \times (-3.5)$ (b) $(+6.5) \times (-2.5)$ (c) $(-4.5) \times (+3.5)$

  (d) $(-2.4) \times (-3.5)$ (e) $(+4.3) \times (-2.2)$ (f) $(-4.7) \times (+3.6)$

3. Evaluate. Write each answer with a positive denominator.

(a) $\dfrac{1}{3} \times \dfrac{-3}{5}$

(b) $\dfrac{-2}{3} \times \dfrac{-1}{3}$

(c) $\dfrac{4}{5} \times \dfrac{-3}{7}$

(d) $\dfrac{-2}{3} \times \dfrac{-3}{-4}$

4. Multiply. Write your answer in simplest form.

(a) $\dfrac{4}{5} \times \dfrac{-20}{25}$

(b) $\dfrac{-3}{2} \times \dfrac{-1}{3}$

(c) $\dfrac{0}{-10} \times \dfrac{1}{6}$

(d) $\dfrac{4}{10} \times \dfrac{-5}{8}$

5. Calculate.

(a) $\left(-1\dfrac{1}{2}\right) \times \left(+2\dfrac{1}{2}\right) \times \left(-3\dfrac{1}{4}\right)$

(b) $\left(+\dfrac{3}{4}\right) \times \left(-\dfrac{1}{4}\right) \times \left(+2\dfrac{1}{2}\right)$

(c) $\left(-3\dfrac{2}{5}\right) \times \left(-1\dfrac{2}{3}\right) \times \left(-\dfrac{3}{10}\right)$

6. Multiply.

(a) $\dfrac{5}{11} \times 2\dfrac{1}{3}$

(b) $3\dfrac{4}{7} \times 5\dfrac{7}{12}$

(c) $12\dfrac{3}{13} \times \left(-\dfrac{9}{14}\right)$

(d) $\left(-8\dfrac{2}{5}\right) \times \left(-10\dfrac{1}{2}\right)$

7. Refer to the stock market report in Section 8.5.

(a) Create and solve a multiplication problem using numbers from the report.

(b) Solve the problem.

8. The cost to rent a bus for a team was split evenly among 20 members. At the last minute, 10 fans decide to travel with the team. The cost for each member is reduced by $1\dfrac{1}{2}$. How much did the bus cost?

9. Julia feeds her dog $\dfrac{2}{3}$ of a can of dog food twice a day. If she bought enough dog food to last at least two weeks, how many cans did she buy?

MAKING CONNECTIONS

Have you ever heard of Babe Ruth or Hank Aaron? Both were baseball players who are in the *Hall of Fame*.

(a) Find the number of hits each player had.

(b) Find the number of times each player was up to bat.

(c) The batting average is found by dividing the number of hits by the number of times at bat. What is the batting average of each player?

(d) Which player had the better batting average?

8.10 DIVIDING RATIONAL NUMBERS

To develop a new skill, you can often relate to a similar, but simpler, situation.

Activity
Compare the following. How are they alike? How are they different?

$$\frac{3}{4} \div \frac{2}{5} = \frac{3}{4} \times \frac{5}{2}$$

$$= \frac{3 \times 5}{4 \times 2}$$

$$= \frac{15}{8}$$

$$\frac{-3}{4} \div \frac{2}{-5} = \frac{3}{-4} \times \frac{-5}{2}$$

$$= \frac{3 \times (-5)}{(-4) \times 2}$$

$$= \frac{-15}{-8} \text{ or } \frac{15}{8}$$

Think: $\dfrac{-15}{-8} = \dfrac{15}{8}$

Your skills with dividing rational numbers can be used to solve problems. Remember: You can use a calculator to help you.

The change in air temperature recorded during a plane's takeoff was $-25\frac{1}{5}°C$ in 6 min. What was the average temperature change each minute?

$$\left(-25\frac{1}{5}\right) \div 6 = \frac{-126}{5} \div \frac{6}{1}$$

$$= \frac{-126}{5} \times \frac{1}{6}$$

$$= -\frac{126}{30} \text{ or } -4\frac{1}{5}$$

Thus, the average temperature change was $-4\frac{1}{5}°C$ each minute.

A Review your skills with dividing fractions.

1. Divide.
   (a) $(-7.0) \div (-3.5)$ (b) $(+7.5) \div (-2.5)$ (c) $(-4.5) \div (+1.5)$
   (d) $(+2.5) \div (-0.5)$ (e) $(-15.3) \div (-5.1)$ (f) $(+0.5) \div (+0.5)$

2. Calculate.
   (a) $\left(+\frac{1}{2}\right) \div \left(-\frac{1}{4}\right)$ (b) $\left(+\frac{1}{3}\right) \div \left(-\frac{1}{2}\right)$ (c) $\left(-\frac{1}{2}\right) \div \left(-\frac{1}{4}\right)$
   (d) $\left(+\frac{1}{2}\right) \div \left(+\frac{1}{3}\right)$ (e) $\left(-\frac{2}{5}\right) \div \left(+\frac{1}{4}\right)$ (f) $\left(-\frac{4}{5}\right) \div \left(-\frac{1}{2}\right)$

3. Divide.
   (a) $(+10.5) \div (-2.25)$ (b) $(-12.3) \div (-4.1)$ (c) $(-36.3) \div (+12.1)$
   (d) $(+10.2) \div (-5.1)$ (e) $0 \div (+10)$ (f) $(-49.7) \div (+7.1)$

B Work with a partner. Use a calculator.

4. Divide. Write your answers in order from least to greatest.
   (a) $\frac{9}{10} \div \frac{3}{5}$ (b) $\frac{3}{4} \div \frac{2}{3}$
   (c) $\frac{-1}{3} \div \frac{1}{8}$ (d) $\frac{3}{-2} \div \frac{-1}{3}$
   (e) $\frac{-1}{3} \div \frac{-9}{10}$ (f) $-\frac{4}{9} \div \frac{-3}{4}$

5. Calculate.
   (a) $(+12.5) \div (-2.5) \div (-5.0)$
   (b) $(-30.5) \div (+6.1) \div (-5.0)$
   (c) $(-70.4) \div (+2.2) \div (-32.0)$
   (d) What do you notice?

6. Divide.
   (a) $\left(+\frac{1}{2}\right) \div \left(-4\frac{1}{3}\right)$
   (b) $\left(-20\frac{3}{8}\right) \div (+5)$

7. If Roma can read one page in $1\frac{3}{4}$ min, how long will it take her to read a 210-page novel?

8. The change in water temperature recorded during a submarine's descent was $-15\frac{3}{4}°C$ in $2\frac{1}{2}$ h. Find the average temperature change each hour.

9. The price of Bjorn's tennis stock changed $-\$3\frac{3}{4}$ in $4\frac{1}{2}$ d. On average, how much did the stock price change each day?

10. In how many different ways can four stamps be attached? One way is shown.

8.11 PROBLEM SOLVING: ILLUSIONS

Some artists, such as M.C. Escher, create art that plays tricks on your eyes. They can make you see things that are impossible.

© 1955 M.C. Escher/Cordon Art–Baarn–Holland

Activity 1
(a) Refer to the Escher art shown. What illusions do you see?

(b) Create a similar illusion. Try it on others in your class.

Activity 2
Look at the circles shown.

(a) Which circle appears larger? Why?

(b) Measure the circle. Was your choice in (a) correct?

(c) Create a similar design. Compare your design with others.

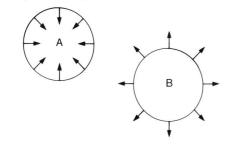

Activity 3
(a) In the diagram, which pair of lines appear to be parallel? Verify your choice.

(b) Sketch a similar diagram. Compare your diagram with others in your class.

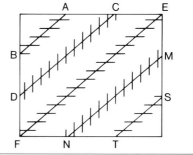

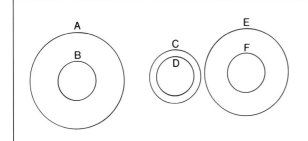

Activity 4
(a) Which of the circles appear to have the same circumference? Verify your choice.

(b) Create a similar design using circles. Compare your design with others in your class.

270

From supermarket check-outs to sophisticated assembly plants, computers are used in many places and in a variety of ways.

Using computers has many advantages. For example, a car designer

- can draw a design more quickly and accurately.

- can store the design in the memory of the computer to work on it at a later date.

- can turn the design on the screen to see it from different angles.

Work with a partner to complete the exercise.
You may need to use the library.

1. Many professional sports teams use computers to analyze data on other teams.
   (a) How are the data gathered? How are they used?
   (b) What advantages does storing information in a computer have? What disadvantages?

2. Computers are used to manage the transportation routes of many bus companies.
   (a) How are computers used to manage the bus routes?
   (b) List three ways in which computers can help buses run more efficiently.

3. In a supermarket, many items are priced using a bar code.
   (a) How does the bar code work?
   (b) How does the bar code help the manager keep track of inventory?
   (c) How does the bar code speed up (or slow down) a check-out line?

9 780176 036836

9 780176 026684

CHAPTER REVIEW

1. Write each of the following in lowest terms.

   (a) $\dfrac{-2}{4}$ (b) $\dfrac{-9}{-12}$ (c) $\dfrac{5}{10}$ (d) $-\dfrac{16}{24}$

2. Use < or > to make each statement true.

   (a) $+5.5 \blacksquare -3.2$ (b) $-4.4 \blacksquare -4.2$ (c) $+2\dfrac{1}{4} \blacksquare -3\dfrac{1}{2}$

3. Write each of the following as a decimal number.

   (a) $\dfrac{12}{21}$ (b) $-\dfrac{17}{25}$ (c) $\dfrac{13}{-20}$ (d) $-\dfrac{15}{45}$

4. Calculate.

   (a) $(+2.5) + (-1.25)$ (b) $(-1.5) + (+0.75)$

   (c) $(-1.25) - (-0.5)$ (d) $(+4.5) - (-2.5)$

   (e) $(-1.5) \times (+0.5)$ (f) $(+2.25) \times (-3.5)$

   (g) $(-3.2) \div (+1.6)$ (h) $(+15.3) \div (-5.1)$

5. Evaluate.

   (a) $\left(-\dfrac{1}{2}\right) + \left(-\dfrac{1}{2}\right)$ (b) $\left(-\dfrac{1}{2}\right) + \left(-\dfrac{1}{4}\right)$

   (c) $\left(-\dfrac{3}{4}\right) - \left(+\dfrac{3}{7}\right)$ (d) $\left(-\dfrac{4}{5}\right) \times \left(-\dfrac{1}{2}\right)$

   (e) $\left(+\dfrac{3}{4}\right) \div \left(-\dfrac{4}{7}\right)$ (f) $\left(-\dfrac{2}{5}\right) \div \left(-\dfrac{1}{3}\right)$

6. The loudest snore recorded was one of $87\dfrac{1}{2}$ decibels by Melvin Switzer. Write the noise level as a rational number.

7. In a video game, Ramon scored a total of -14.5. Vito had a score of -9.5. The greater score wins the game. Who won the game? By how much?

8. (a) Find the decimal numbers represented by $-\dfrac{1}{7}$, $-\dfrac{2}{7}$, and $-\dfrac{3}{7}$.

   (b) Use your results from (a). Predict the decimal numbers for $-\dfrac{4}{7}$ and $-\dfrac{5}{7}$. Check your prediction.

THINKING ABOUT

In your journal, describe how working with rational numbers in fraction form is like working with rational numbers in decimal form.

When working with rational numbers, do you prefer to work with the fraction form or the decimal form? Give reasons for your answer.

In Question 7, what would happen to your answer if Ramon's and Vito's scores were switched?

MAKING CONNECTIONS

Refer to the opening pages of the chapter.

(a) Create and solve a problem using the pictures.

(b) Compare your problem with others in your class. Solve the other problems.

How are working with fractions and working with rational numbers alike? How are they different?

How are working with integers and working with rational numbers alike? How are they different?

MATH JOURNAL

Throughout the chapter, you have learned many new words and skills that can be used to solve problems.
- List all the new words and skills you have learned.
- Write an example of your own to illustrate each word and skill that you listed.

SELF EVALUATION

1. Write each rational number with a positive denominator.

   (a) $\dfrac{3}{-7}$ (b) $\dfrac{-5}{-9}$ (c) $\dfrac{5}{-2}$ (d) $\dfrac{-2}{-7}$

2. Write each rational number in lowest terms.

   (a) $\dfrac{6}{-8}$ (b) $\dfrac{4}{-8}$ (c) $\dfrac{-8}{-12}$ (d) $\dfrac{3}{-15}$

3. (a) Write each rational number you wrote in Question 2 with a positive denominator.

   (b) Write the decimal equivalent for each rational number from (a).

4. Which rational number is greater?

   (a) $-\dfrac{3}{4}$ or $\dfrac{-5}{8}$ (b) $\dfrac{15}{17}$ or $\dfrac{17}{19}$ (c) $-\dfrac{5}{7}$ or $-\dfrac{7}{8}$

5. Calculate.

   (a) $(-0.75) + (+0.5)$ (b) $(-0.5) - (-0.25)$

   (c) $(+3.25) + (-4.5)$ (d) $(-3.3) + (-0.8)$

   (e) $(-4.5) \times (-2.3)$ (f) $(+3.8) \div (-2.4)$

6. Evaluate.

   (a) $\dfrac{-3}{4} + \dfrac{-1}{4}$ (b) $\dfrac{-3}{8} + \dfrac{-7}{8}$ (c) $\left(-2\dfrac{3}{5}\right) + \left(-1\dfrac{7}{10}\right)$

   (d) $\dfrac{-2}{5} - \dfrac{-4}{8}$ (e) $\dfrac{-1}{4} - \dfrac{-3}{7}$ (f) $\left(-1\dfrac{3}{5}\right) - \left(+2\dfrac{1}{4}\right)$

7. Calculate. Write your answers in lowest terms.

   (a) $\dfrac{-1}{2} \times \dfrac{1}{-3}$ (b) $\dfrac{-1}{3} \times \left(-2\dfrac{3}{4}\right)$ (c) $\dfrac{2}{3} \div \dfrac{-4}{9}$

   (d) $-3\dfrac{2}{3} \times \dfrac{-2}{3}$ (e) $2\dfrac{2}{5} \div \dfrac{12}{25}$ (f) $\dfrac{1}{-5} \times \dfrac{3}{-4}$

8. The temperature was $-4°C$. It dropped $5°C$. What was the final temperature?

9 INTERPRETING DATA

Did you know that data collected about fresh snow indicates that it reflects about 85% of the sun's energy? How do you think this data was collected? What do you think will happen if the energy reflected drops to 55%?

Did you know that data collected about the forests of the world indicates that they absorb about 90% of the sun's energy? How do you think this data was collected? What do you think will happen if the energy absorbed drops to 70%?

Suppose you want to publish a new magazine. How can you predict the most popular type of magazine? One way would be to ask all the people who read magazines. This means you would ask the entire **population**. However, this would be very time-consuming and expensive, and probably impossible.

You could **survey** a **sample** of the population. The questions you ask must be clear and precise. Three commonly used types of surveys are shown below.

EXPLORATION ① Work in a Group

1. A **questionnaire** is a list of standard questions that are given to each person. The person usually writes the answers.

   (a) List questions you would ask to find the most popular type of magazine. Choose various people to answer them.

   (b) Based on your results, what is the most popular type of magazine?

2. In a **phone survey**, you ask questions and collect data over the telephone.

   (a) Phone some people and ask them your list of questions.

   (b) Based on your results, what is the most popular type of magazine?

3. In an **interview**, you ask people questions in person and record their responses.

   (a) Ask people to answer your list of questions.

   (b) Based on your results, what is the most popular type of magazine?

Activity
Write the advantages and disadvantages of each type of survey.

For each of the explorations, work in a group and display the data that you collect. Brainstorm ways to display the data and then make a prediction to answer the questions at the end of each exploration. Follow these steps.

Step 1 Collect data to answer the question.
Step 2 Suitably display your data.
Step 3 Draw a conclusion based on your data.

EXPLORATION ② *Work in a Group*

4. (a) Predict the favourite hobby of your class.
   (b) Collect data and record the favourite hobbies. Display your data.
   (c) Based on your data, what hobby is most popular in your class?
   (d) Was your prediction in (a) accurate? Why do you think this is so?

5. (a) Predict the favourite place to study.
   (b) Collect data and display the data of the favourite places to study.
   (c) Based on your data, what type of study room would you design for the students in your class?
   (d) Repeat parts (a), (b), and (c) to test a prediction of your own. Was your prediction reasonable?

EXPLORATION ③ *Work with a Partner*

Sometimes, data can be collected from an experiment. Once the data are collected and displayed, patterns can be seen and predictions made.

6. (a) Toss ten plastic cups and let them land on a flat surface.
   (b) Use a chart or pictures to record the number that landed up, the number that landed down, and the number that landed on the side.
   (c) Repeat (a) and (b) another four times.

7. Use your results from Question 6.
   (a) Predict how many of 100 plastic cups will land on their sides. In your journal, describe how you made the prediction.
   (b) Toss 100 plastic cups and record the results. How accurate was your prediction?

Bradford School had students complete a questionnaire to determine whether they preferred a trip to see the totem poles in Stanley Park, Signal Hill in St. John's, the Calgary Tower, or the Ontario Science Centre.

They recorded the results in the following table.

Type of Field Trip		
	Tally	Frequency
Totem Pole	‖‖ ‖‖ ‖‖ ‖‖	20
Signal Hill	‖‖ ‖‖ ‖‖ ‖	16
Calgary Tower	‖‖ ‖‖ ‖‖ ‖‖ ‖‖ ‖‖ ‖‖ ‖	37
Science Centre	‖‖ ‖‖ ‖	12

Think: Each stroke, or **tally**, shows one vote for the type of trip.

The **frequency** of each result is the number of votes. Eighty-five students returned the survey.

The table above is called a **frequency table**. Based on the results, the students at Bradford School went to the Calgary Tower.

EXERCISE

 A Review how to collect data.

1. Use the frequency table to the right.

   (a) Copy and complete the table.

   (b) What was the most favourite type of music? the least favourite?

   (c) Suppose you own a music store. You are ordering 1550 compact discs (CDs) for your next shipment. How many of each type of CD will you order?

Favourite Type of Music		
Type	Tally	Frequency
Country	‖‖ ‖	
Rock	‖‖ ‖‖ ‖‖ ‖	
Jazz	‖‖‖	
Blues	‖‖ ‖‖ ‖‖	
Classical	‖‖ ‖‖	

2. A music store sold the following types of recorded music last week.

   CDs (C)   Cassette Tapes (T)

C	C	T	T	T	T	C	T	C	C	C	T	T	C
C	C	C	T	T	T	T	T	T	C	T	C	T	C
T	T	C	C	T	C	C	C	T	C	C	T	T

   (a) Construct a frequency table to show the information in a compact way.

   (b) You expect to sell a total of 2500 CDs and cassettes next week. How many of each should you have in stock?

3. The following data were collected on food purchases at the school cafeteria. Soup (H), Sandwich (S), Daily Special (D), and Burger (B)

B	D	B	S	D	H	S	S	H	H	B	B	S	D
H	D	B	D	S	H	S	S	S	B	D	S		
H	S	D	B	H	S	H	D	B	H	S	H	D	B

   (a) Construct a frequency table to show the information in a compact way.

   (b) You expect to sell 3000 items each week. How many of each would you make each week?

4. Work with a partner to find the most popular form of entertainment, such as radio, TV, or books.

   (a) How will you collect the data? What types of questions will you ask?

   (b) Collect and display your data.

   (c) Interpret your data. What is the most popular form of entertainment?

5. A manufacturer of breakfast preserves wanted to determine the favourite type and predicted that 1500 units of the preserves would sell.

   (a) How many units of each should be made based on the following data?

Favourite Preserves		
Preserves	Tally	Frequency
Grape Jam	||||| ||||| ||	12
Strawberry Jam	||||| ||||| ||||| ||||| |||	23
Marmalade	||||| ||||| ||||| |||	18
Honey	||||| ||||| ||||| |||||		21
Peanut Butter	||||| ||||| ||||| ||||| ||||| ||	27

   (b) Survey your class. How many units would you make?

279

A survey was taken to determine the most popular type of television show.

Sitcoms	60
Dramas	30
Miniseries	80
Talk Shows	90
Detective	20
Cartoons	100
Other	40

The data was displayed using the graphs below. The data can be interpreted.

As a Pictograph

Think: You can use these steps.
1. Decide on a suitable title.
2. Choose a suitable symbol.
3. Choose how much each symbol represents.
4. Draw each symbol the same size.

As a Bar Graph

Think: You can use these steps.
1. Choose a suitable title.
2. Choose a suitable scale and labels for each bar.
3. Use the same width for each bar.
4. Use the same distance for the spaces between the bars.

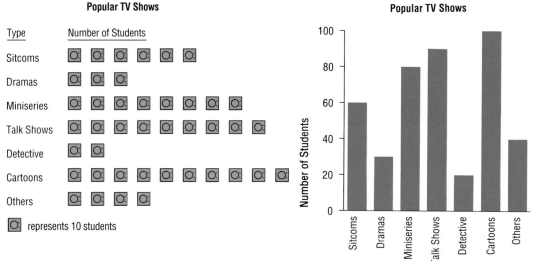

Popular TV Shows

Type	Number of Students
Sitcoms	☉ ☉ ☉ ☉ ☉ ☉
Dramas	☉ ☉ ☉
Miniseries	☉ ☉ ☉ ☉ ☉ ☉ ☉ ☉
Talk Shows	☉ ☉ ☉ ☉ ☉ ☉ ☉ ☉ ☉
Detective	☉ ☉
Cartoons	☉ ☉ ☉ ☉ ☉ ☉ ☉ ☉ ☉ ☉
Others	☉ ☉ ☉ ☉

☉ represents 10 students

Popular TV Shows

Activity
In your journal, write when you think it is more appropriate to display data using a bar graph and when it is more appropriate to use a pictograph.

EXERCISE

A Use the pictograph and bar graph on the previous page.

1. (a) Refer to the pictograph. How many people chose a detective show? a cartoon?
   (b) What was the least popular type of show?
   (c) Create a problem of your own using the data in the graph. Solve it.

2. (a) Refer to the bar graph. How many people chose a talk show? a drama?
   (b) Create a problem of your own using the data in the graph. Solve it.

B Interpret your results.

3. (a) What information is displayed in the bar graph?
   (b) What team do you think will win the Stanley Cup?
   (c) Do you need more information to predict the winner? What kind of information?
   (d) Create a problem of your own based on the data in the graph. Solve it.

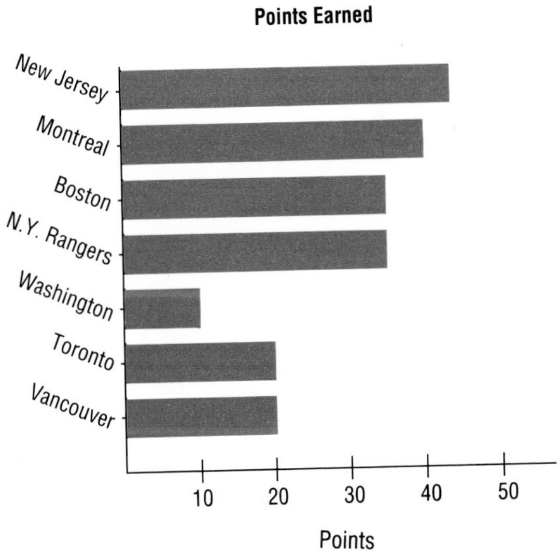
Points Earned
New Jersey
Montreal
Boston
N.Y. Rangers
Washington
Toronto
Vancouver
10
20
30
40
50
Points

4. (a) What information is displayed in the pictograph?
   (b) Create a problem based on the data in the pictograph. Solve it.
   (c) Compare your problem with others in your class.

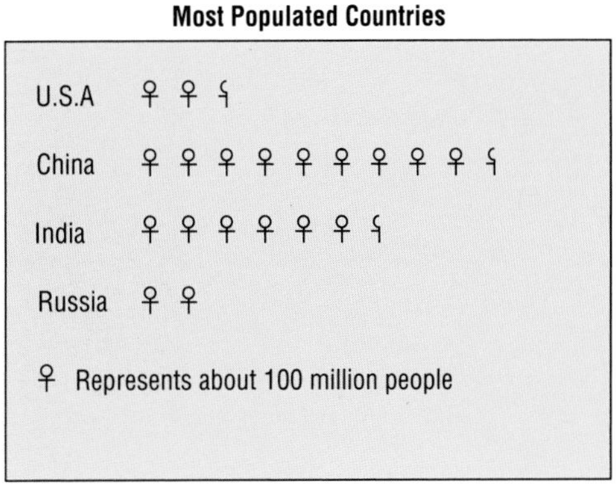
Most Populated Countries
U.S.A
China
India
Russia
Represents about 100 million people

5. Conduct a survey to find the most popular type of TV show in your school.
   (a) Construct a bar graph and a pictograph to display your data.
   (b) Interpret your data. What type of TV show is most popular in your school?
   How is your data like the data on the previous page? How is it different?

9.4 COMPARING DATA

An advertiser will monitor the popularity of television shows with each showing. If a show continues to be popular, the advertiser will continue to buy commercial time. One way to obtain data on television shows is to use the television ratings.

Double Leaf Plot

Samples were taken ten times each month to compare the ratings. The data are shown to the right. The following double leaf plot uses the television ratings to compare the people (in thousands) watching a television show over two consecutive weeks. The show is aired five days a week.

Last Month	This Month
37 000	36 000
38 000	39 000
47 000	42 000
48 000	43 000
52 000	45 000
65 000	54 000
82 000	63 000
83 000	80 000
89 000	82 000
91 000	90 000

Television Ratings (Viewers in Thousands)						
Last Month			This Month			
Ones			Tens	Ones		
	8	7	3	6	9	
	8	7	④	2	3	⑤
		2	5	4		
		5	6	3		
			7			
⑨	3	2	⑧	0	2	
			1	9	0	

For this sample, 45 000 viewers were watching. ← (row with ⑤)

No data were recorded in this part.

For this sample, 89 000 viewers were watching. ← (row with ⑨)

Read from right to left. → (row with 1)

Read from left to right. ← (row with 0)

282

B Work with a partner.

1. Last week, *General Street* had the following number of viewers each day: 31 000, 47 000, 55 000, 63 000, 78 000. This week, the number of viewers are: 33 000, 42 000, 57 000, 68 000, 77 000.

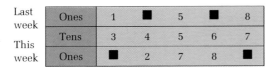

Last week	Ones	1	■	5	■	8
This week	Tens	3	4	5	6	7
	Ones	■	2	7	8	■

(a) Copy and complete a double leaf plot based on the above data.

(b) During which week would you prefer to have advertised? Justify your answer.

2. A cartoon is shown each week. Last month, the number of viewers were 15 000, 22 000, 31 000, and 8000. This month, the number of viewers were 14 000, 26 000, 6000, and 32 000.

(a) Construct a double leaf plot to compare the data.

(b) During which month would you prefer to have advertised? Why?

(c) Would you continue to advertise on this cartoon? Why?

3. Last week, families were surveyed at different times to find the number of hours spent watching television.

Block A				Block B			
53	76	39	31	61	79	36	69
74	51	67	58	58	78	64	20
41	57	68	65	66	24	42	68
68	65	77	54	65	51	65	78
72	22	56	58	23	55	63	43

(a) Construct a double leaf plot to compare the above data.

(b) Create a problem of your own using the data. Solve it.

4. Work together.

(a) What questions would you ask to find the most popular television show in your school?

(b) Collect and display your data.

(c) Interpret your results. What is the most popular show?

(d) Compare your results to the actual ratings. How are they alike? How are they different?

MAKING CONNECTIONS

Did you know that Arthur Charles Nielsen invented a way to determine the popularity of television shows? He initially used a sample of 1170 homes with televisions. You will learn more about the Nielsen rating later in the chapter.

(a) What was Nielsen's occupation before he created the rating?

(b) What is an Audimeter? How is it used to collect data?

(c) How might you display the data collected by an Audimeter?

(d) How might advertisers and producers use the data?

9.5 LINE GRAPHS

The amount of water dripping from all the taps at Northern School was recorded in the following table.

Time Elapsed (h)	Volume of Water (mL)
1	365
2	710
3	1005
4	1290
5	1620

The data can be displayed as shown.

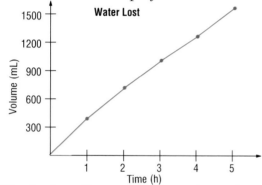

Think: You can use these steps:
1. Draw and label the axes.
2. Plot the appropriate points.
3. Join the points in order.
4. Give your graph a title.

The **broken line graph** above is used to show data which are constantly changing over time. You can answer many different questions using the line graph.

Activity

Use the graph above. Create a problem of your own using the data displayed. Solve your problem.

EXERCISE

A Review your methods for displaying data.

1. Use the line graph to the right.
   (a) How are each of the axes of the graph labelled? What are the units?
   (b) What was the height of the plant after 3 d?
   (c) Extend the graph. What do you think the height will be after 11 d?

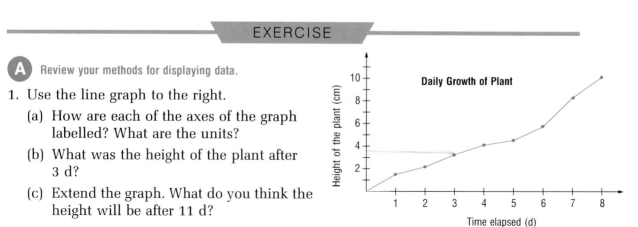

B Check that your interpretation is reasonable.

2. Did you know that a dripping hot water tap can cost thousands of dollars over a lifetime? The volume from a dripping tap is shown in the table.

   (a) Use a broken line graph to display the data.

   (b) Find the volume of water lost after 3 h.

   (c) Estimate the volume lost each day.

   (d) Create and solve a problem using the data.

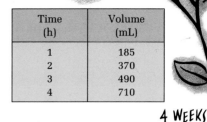

Time (h)	Volume (mL)
1	185
2	370
3	490
4	710

3. The data shows the depth of water in a reservoir at the beginning of each month.

   (a) Use a broken line graph to display the data.

   (b) Use your graph to estimate the depth of water

   (i) at $2\frac{1}{2}$ months.   (ii) at $7\frac{1}{2}$ months.

   (c) Create and solve a problem using the data.

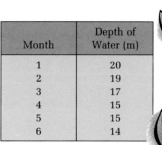

Month	Depth of Water (m)
1	20
2	19
3	17
4	15
5	15
6	14

4. The data shows the amount of money raised by a school for a new pool.

   (a) Use a broken line graph to display the data.

   (b) The goal for the first week was $5000. Based on the data, do you think the goal was achieved?

   (c) The goal for the end of the month is $25 000. Based on the data, do you think the goal was achieved?

Time (d)	Amount ($)
1	400
2	1000
3	1350
4	2200
5	2700
6	3400

5. (a) Work together. Pick a starting point and walk around your school. Count how many paces you take after 10 s, 20 s, and so on.

   (b) Draw a broken line graph to display the data.

   (c) Create a problem of your own using the data. Compare your problem with others in your class.

6. (a) Use the plant growing up the side of the page. Draw a broken line graph to display the data.

   (b) Create and solve a problem of your own using the data.

   (c) Grow a bean plant of your own. Record the height of the plant after each week. Display your data.

   (d) How tall was your plant in the middle of each week? How tall do you think it will grow?

5 WEEKS

4 WEEKS

3 WEEKS

2 WEEKS

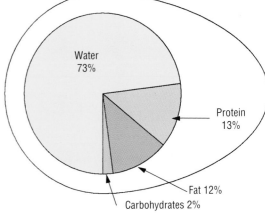

Food Content of an Egg

9.6 CIRCLE GRAPHS: PERCENT

A **circle graph** is often used to show comparisons that involve percents. For example, the circle graph shown to the right compares the food content found in one egg. What information is shown by the graph?

In a circle graph, each piece of data is expressed as a percent. To find the actual percent, you use the following steps. Refer to the circle graph.

Step 1 Measure the central angle.
The central angle for the apple is 144°.

Step 2 What part of the circle is your measure in *Step 1*? $\frac{144}{360}$

Step 3 Find the percent. $\frac{144}{360} \times 100\% = 40\%$

Thus, 40% of the people chose an apple as their favourite fruit.

Favourite Fruits

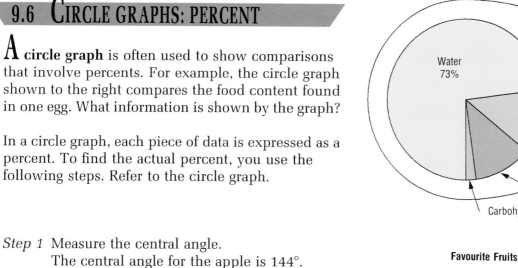

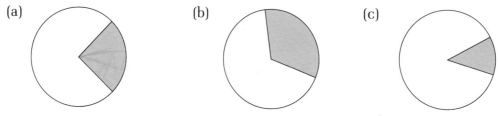

EXERCISE

A Review your skills with measuring angles.

1. Calculate the percent of the circle that has been shaded.

   (a)   (b)   (c)

   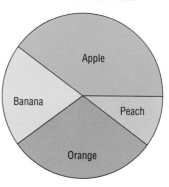

2. Find the actual percent of the people who chose the apple, peach, and orange as their favourite fruit in the circle graph above.

3. The percent of time people spend watching some types of TV shows is given in the circle graph.

Favourite TV Shows

(a) What percent of the time is spent watching dramas?

(b) What other comparisons can you make?

4. The circle graph shows the food components of cheddar cheese.

Food Components of Cheddar Cheese

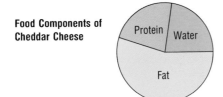

(a) What is the most abundant component in cheddar cheese? the least abundant?

(b) Estimate the mass of each component in a 500 g piece of cheddar cheese.

5. Use the circle graph below.

Distribution of Blood Types

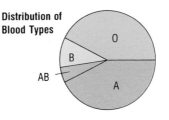

(a) Calculate the percent of people in each blood group.

(b) Which blood type is most common?

6. In a survey, people indicated their favourite radio stations. The results are shown in the circle graph.

Favourite Radio Stations

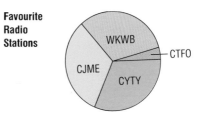

(a) What percent of people prefer to listen to WKWB?

(b) What other comparisons can you make?

WORKING TOGETHER

Different types of fruit are shown.

(a) Find the mineral content of each fruit.

(b) After you have completed the next section, draw a circle graph to display the data you found.

(c) Complete parts (a) and (b) for fruit of your own.

9.7 WORKING WITH CIRCLE GRAPHS

he Canadian exports for one year were the following.

Forest Products 18%	Minerals 20%	Wheat 6%
Motor Vehicles and Parts 18%	Crude Oil 10%	Other 28%

A circle graph is constructed to display the data.

Value of Exports

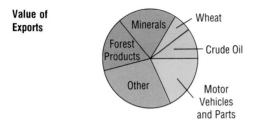

	Percent	Angle
Forest Products	18%	18% of 360° = 64.8°
Minerals	20%	20% of 360° = 72°
Wheat	6%	6% of 360° = 21.6°
Crude Oil	10%	10% of 360° = 36°
Motor Vehicles and Parts	18%	18% of 360° = 64.8°
Other	28%	28% of 360° = 100.8°
	Total 100%	Total 360°

EXERCISE

B Use your skills with percent.

1. The fishing industry is currently one of Canada's greatest money makers.

   Net Value of Fishing in Millions
   B.C. $200   N.S. $150
   Nfld. $90   N.B. $40

   (a) Construct a circle graph to show the percent of the revenue generated in each province.

   (b) Create a problem of your own for the data. Solve it.

2. For the following hockey income
   • construct a circle graph.
   • create and solve a problem of your own.

   Revenue

Sponsors	$ 6 000
Registrations	$25 000
Dances	$ 3 500
Ticket Sales	$ 2 750

3. The data shows Canada's employment structure last year.

Agriculture and Forestry	6%
Mining	3%
Manufacturing	19%
Construction	5%
Trade and Transportation	26%
Insurance and Real Estate	5%
Services	36%

   Construct a circle graph to display the information.

4. Work together. Use the Smarties from one box as shown below.

   (a) Construct a circle graph to show the percent of each colour.

   (b) Use a box of Smarties of your own. Complete part (a).

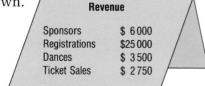

9.8 PROBLEM SOLVING: THINKING VISUALLY

To solve some problems, you need to be able to "picture the situation" in your mind. Then you will be able to solve the problem.

Blocks are stacked in a corner as shown. How many of the blocks are completely invisible from your view?

Think:
- There is 1 block hidden in the second row.
- There are 3 blocks hidden in the third row.
- There are 6 blocks hidden in the fourth row.
  Look at the pattern.
- There will be 10 blocks hidden in the fifth row.

Using the pattern, there are 1 + 3 + 6 + 10 or 20 blocks hidden in all.

EXERCISE

 Use your *Problem Solving Plan*.

1. Copy this figure into your notebook. Add one more line to the figure so you have eight triangles instead of two.

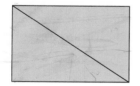

2. (a) One cube is painted white on the outside, then cut into 27 equal parts. How many of the parts have no paint?

   (b) Write a problem of your own similar to (a). Solve the problem and have others in the class solve the problem.

3. (a) Use tracing paper to make four copies of this triangle. The triangle has an area of one square unit.

   (b) Use your triangles to make a
   - trapezoid
   - hexagon
   - rhombus
   - parallelogram

   (c) What is the area of each figure in part (b)?

4. The hexagon shown represents a whole amount. How many whole amounts does each shape represent?

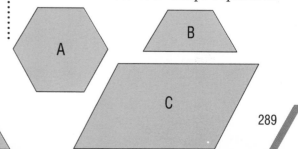

So far, you have learned different ways to collect and display data. You can use these skills to design a theme park.

Follow the activities to write, and present, a proposal that describes your theme park. You and your partners may be able to combine the activities to make the data collecting more efficient. Before you begin the activities, brainstorm what you may need for your proposal. Collect the data and make decisions about all aspects you think are important for your proposal.

PROJECTS

ACTIVITY ① Decide on a Theme

For a theme park to be successful, it needs to attract visitors.

1. Plan and conduct a survey to determine the most popular theme for your area. As you design this survey, decide how many people you should survey and the best way to gather the data.

2. Display your data from Question 1. When you display your data, it is important that potential investors see that the park will be popular.

ACTIVITY ② Where Should You Build the Park?

You need to decide where you would build such a park. As part of your presentation, you need to show the best place to build.

3. Conduct a survey to determine where people feel the best place would be for the park. Your survey should also determine why the particular place was chosen. (For example, a particular spot may be chosen because it is on a bus route, or it is easily accessible by car.)

4. Display your data from Question 3.

ACTIVITY ③ What About Parking?

A park must have parking.

5. As part of your survey, find the percent of people who would use their cars to drive to your park. Use this percent, and the number of people you feel would enter your park at its busiest time, to determine the number of parking spaces needed.

6. Display your data from Question 5.

ACTIVITY ④ Draw a Plan

7. Once you have gathered all your data, draw a plan of your theme park. Include everything that you feel should be in the theme park.

PEANUTS reprinted by permission of UFS, INC.

You do not need to make up statistics as Lucy does with Schroeder. Data are always there for you to find. You only need to collect them. The way you collect the data can often influence the conclusions you get.

Obtaining a sample may appear to be straightforward, but a sample can give misleading results if not carefully prepared. In the following exploration, you will explore cases in which samples have been taken and conclusions drawn. Each of the samples, as well as the conclusions drawn, were actually made.

EXPLORATION ① A Sample

For each case below, work with a partner to discuss potential problems with the conclusion drawn. Present a way that the sample could have been taken to provide a more reasonable conclusion.

1. An orange seller tested the quality of oranges in a shipment by opening one crate and testing a few of the oranges on the top. Since the oranges tested were good, the whole shipment was passed as good.

2. As the spacecraft Mariner 4 flew past Mars in 1965, it photographed about 10% of Mars' surface. Since there was no plant or animal life in these pictures, Mars was declared a dead planet.

3. During its first month of operation, a reflector in the Hubble telescope was found to be defective. Since the telescope cost millions of dollars to construct, the money was said to have been wasted.

When conducting a survey, ensure that you ask your questions of a representative sample of the population. Work with a partner to discuss each of the following.

4. Data were gathered, and conclusions made, using the methods described below. Is each conclusion valid? Give reasons for your answers.

   (a) *Survey*   The people living near railroad tracks were asked if they wanted the tracks moved.

   Conclusion Most people want the tracks moved.

   (b) *Survey*   People in the line-up for a carnival were asked whether they liked to go on rides.

   Conclusion Most people like to go on carnival rides.

   (c) *Survey*   Sales of jeans over a one-year period were examined.

   Conclusion Most people prefer to wear styled jeans.

5. Predict the likely results of a survey of favourite pastimes if the following people were polled. Give reasons for your prediction.

   (a) children at a nursery school   (b) people at a baseball game

   (c) members of a rock band   (d) students in your class

EXPLORATION ③ *Making Connections*

6. When you survey an entire population, you are conducting a **census**.

   (a) How often is a census taken in Canada? When was the last census?

   (b) How are the data gathered?

   (c) Use the data shown. They were taken from a Canadian census. Create a problem using the data. Solve it.

   (d) Now find other data from a census. Create a problem using the data. Solve the problem.

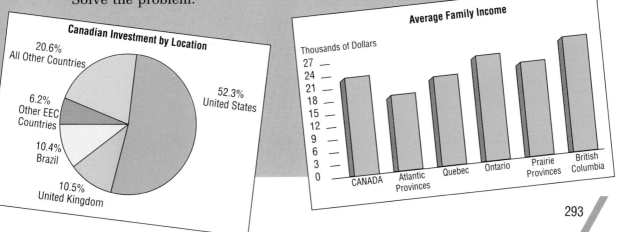

Canadian Investment by Location

20.6% All Other Countries

6.2% Other EEC Countries

10.4% Brazil

10.5% United Kingdom

52.3% United States

Average Family Income

Thousands of Dollars

27, 24, 21, 18, 15, 12, 9, 6, 3, 0

CANADA   Atlantic Provinces   Quebec   Ontario   Prairie Provinces   British Columbia

Murray receives $26.00 each month as his allowance. He surveyed his friends and found they received the following amounts.

- Fred $42.00
- Joaquin $38.00
- Juan $34.00
- Jane $24.00
- Janet $36.00
- Lianne $24.00

Murray remembered that the mean, median, and mode can provide useful information about a set of data. He calculated each as follows.

Mean

$$\text{Mean} = \frac{\text{total amount of allowance}}{\text{number of people}}$$

$$= \frac{\$42.00 + \$34.00 + \$36.00 + \$38.00 + \$24.00 + \$24.00}{6}$$

$$= \$33.00$$

Thus, the mean allowance is $33.00.

Median   Murray arranged the allowances in order.

$42.00, $38.00, $36.00, $34.00, $24.00, $24.00

Thus, the median allowance is $35.00.

Think: The median is the middle allowance. Since there are an even number of values, use the mean of the middle two values.

$$\frac{\$36.00 + \$34.00}{2} = \$35.00$$

Mode   The allowance that occurs most frequently is $24.00. Thus, the mode allowance is $24.00.

Activity

(a) To convince his parents that he needs a raise in his allowance, Murray could report the median allowance as the average allowance his friends receive. In your journal, describe the argument Murray could use.

(b) Conduct a survey to determine how people in your school spend their allowance or money they earn. Display the data you collect.

A Record all definitions in your journal.

1. (a) Find the mean, median, and mode for the following data.

    2, 9, 9, 3, 4, 6, 3, 5, 2, 1, 3

   (b) Which measure, the median, mode, or mean, is the easiest to obtain? Why?

2. Use examples to illustrate each.

   (a) The mean of a set of data is 45. Must 45 be a value in the set?

   (b) The median of a set of data is 62. Must 62 be a value in the set?

B Use a calculator.

3. For artistic impression, Elizabeth earned these scores from seven judges. The greatest and the least scores are always omitted.

   5.4, 5.8, 5.5, 5.4, 5.4, 5.9, 5.8

   (a) Find the mean, median, and mode.

   (b) Which measure do you think should be used to calculate Elizabeth's score? Give reasons for your answer.

4. For technical merit, Jerome earned these scores in a figure skating competition. The greatest and the least scores are always omitted.

   5.8, 5.7, 5.9, 5.8, 5.6, 5.8, 5.9

   (a) Find the mean, median, and mode.

   (b) Which measure do you think should be used to calculate Jerome's score? Give reasons for your answer.

5. Suppose you own a dress shop. To order some dresses, you need to know which dress size sells the most. Do you need to find the mean, median, or mode? Why?

6. The number of emergency cases that occurred over nine consecutive hours at St. Joseph's Hospital was recorded.

   38, 40, 28, 26, 39, 41, 28, 42, 36

   You are a doctor in charge of assigning staff to the emergency ward this weekend. One doctor can handle eight emergency cases each hour. How many doctors will you assign to each shift? Give reasons for your answer.

7. Toss 20 coins, like those shown below, five times and record the results.

   (a) Predict the mean, median, and mode for the number of heads appearing.

   (b) Test your prediction. Was it reasonable? If not, then explain why it is unreasonable.

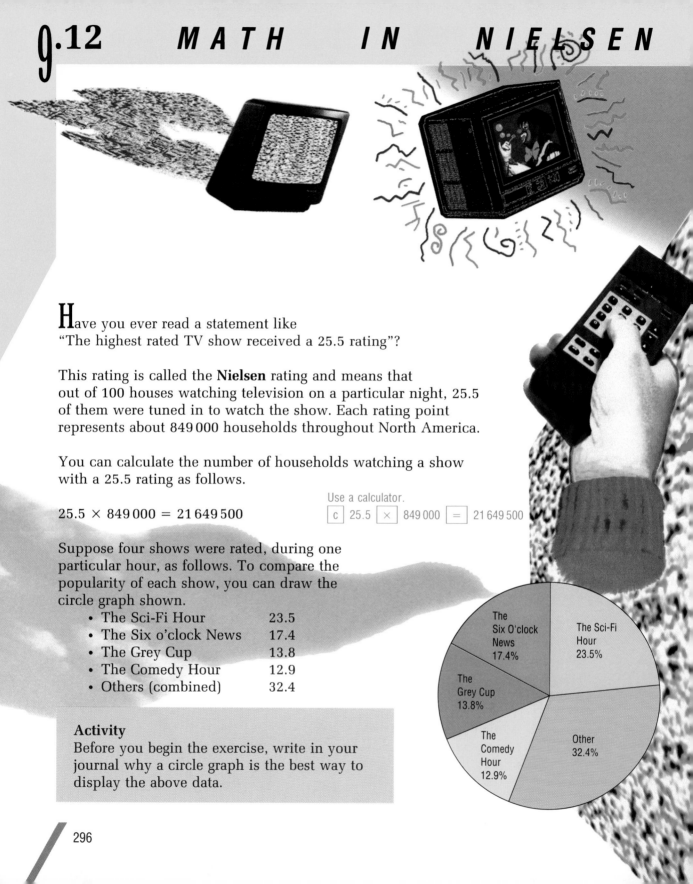

Have you ever read a statement like
"The highest rated TV show received a 25.5 rating"?

This rating is called the **Nielsen** rating and means that
out of 100 houses watching television on a particular night, 25.5
of them were tuned in to watch the show. Each rating point
represents about 849 000 households throughout North America.

You can calculate the number of households watching a show
with a 25.5 rating as follows.

$25.5 \times 849\,000 = 21\,649\,500$

Use a calculator.

| c | 25.5 | × | 849 000 | = | 21 649 500 |

Suppose four shows were rated, during one
particular hour, as follows. To compare the
popularity of each show, you can draw the
circle graph shown.

- The Sci-Fi Hour　　　　23.5
- The Six o'clock News　　17.4
- The Grey Cup　　　　　13.8
- The Comedy Hour　　　12.9
- Others (combined)　　　32.4

Activity
Before you begin the exercise, write in your
journal why a circle graph is the best way to
display the above data.

The Six O'clock News 17.4%

The Sci-Fi Hour 23.5%

The Grey Cup 13.8%

The Comedy Hour 12.9%

Other 32.4%

RATINGS

B Review your skills for analyzing data.

1. Suppose *60 Minutes* had a rating of 17.9 last week.

   (a) How many households were watching *60 Minutes* last week?

   (b) What percent of all households in North America were watching *60 Minutes*?

2. During a Super Bowl game, the ratings reached a high of 27.8.

   (a) How many households were watching the Super Bowl?

   (b) What percent of all households in North America were watching the Super Bowl?

3. The last episode of M*A*S*H received the highest Neilsen rating of any show ever. It received a rating of 77.

   (a) How many households watched the last episode of M*A*S*H?

   (b) What percent of the households in North America were watching?

4. (a) At one time, the ratings for shows playing opposite each other were the following. Display this data.

   The Cosby Show 25.5
   20/20 14.3
   Hockey Playoffs 13.8
   Baseball Game 11.8

   (b) Create a problem of your own using the data. Solve your problem.

5. The Nielsen Ratings are often printed in the entertainment section of a newspaper.

   (a) What was the highest rated show last week?

   (b) How many households were watching the show?

   (c) Write the ratings for shows that are broadcast at the same time.

   (d) Draw a circle graph to display your data from (c). What assumptions have you made?

Graphs are very useful for presenting data in a clear and visual way. However, they can sometimes be used to distort information.

For example, the sporting goods store *Basebat* showed the amount of sales for themselves and for their nearest competitor, *Ballgluv*, as the following:

Basebat $2 000 000
Ballgluv $1 000 000.

Basebat then used the graph to the right to display the information. How does the graph distort the information?

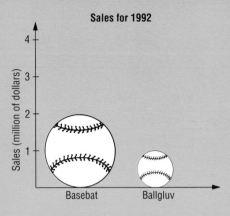

Sales for 1992

Examine the graph. The ball for *Basebat* is twice the diameter of the ball for *Ballgluv*. This increases the area by four times. Thus, it appears that the sales for *Basebat* are four times that of *Ballgluv*.

When displaying data, a graph that is visually appealing can be effective. This graph, used to compare the sales of three toothpastes, is visually appealing but not accurate. What information is displayed inaccurately?

Like the graph above, the tube representing *Toothglo* covers an area about four times that of *Toothshine*. Thus, it creates the effect that *Toothglo* generates about four times as much sales as *Toothshine*.

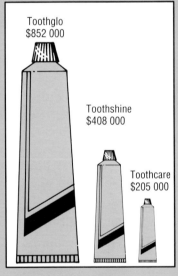

Toothglo
$852 000

Toothshine
$408 000

Toothcare
$205 000

Activity

(a) Decide how you would change the graph above so that it is visually appealing and accurately compares the amount of sales for the sporting goods stores.

(b) Find examples of graphs used to display data in magazines or newspapers. Decide whether the information is displayed accurately.

(c) Create a problem of your own using the data and solve.

B Each graph uses data collected during a survey. Work with a partner.

1. A survey was conducted to determine which magazine is easiest to read.

   (a) Does the graph display information that is not accurate? Why?

   (b) Show the graph you would use to display the information accurately.

   (c) Create and solve a problem of your own using the data.

2. A survey was conducted to determine which magazine carries the most interesting advertisements.

   (a) Does the graph display information that is not accurate? Why?

   (b) Show the graph you would use to display the information accurately.

   (c) Create and solve a problem of your own using the data.

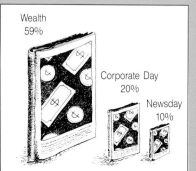

3. A survey was conducted to determine which magazine carries the most interesting stories.

   (a) Does the graph display information that is not accurate? Why?

   (b) Show the graph you would use to display the information accurately.

   (c) Create and solve a problem of your own using the data.

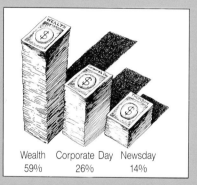

4. A survey was conducted to determine which magazine best keeps its readers up to date.

   (a) Does the graph display information that is not accurate? Why?

   (b) Show the graph you would use to display the information accurately.

   (c) Create and solve a problem of your own using the data.

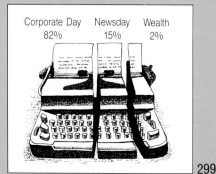

299

9.14 PROBLEM SOLVING: CHOOSE A GRAPH

You have used many different graphs to display and analyze data.

EXERCISE

Review the ways in which you can display data.

1. The number of players on each inter-school team is the following.

Basketball	7
Field Hockey	11
Indoor Soccer	8
Volleyball	9

   (a) Which type of graph best displays the data? Justify your choice.

   (b) Draw the graph.

2. The data show the food content of a 300 g container of yogurt.

Water	228 g	Carbohydrates	54 g
Protein	12 g	Fat	6 g

   (a) Which type of graph best displays the data? Justify your choice.

   (b) Draw the graph.

   (c) Create a problem of your own using your graph. Compare your problem with others in your class.

3. The data below shows the vitamins and minerals in one serving of different cereals.

   (a) Which type of graph best displays the data? Justify your choice.

   (b) Draw the graph.

   (c) Create a problem of your own using the graph. Compare your problem with others in your class.

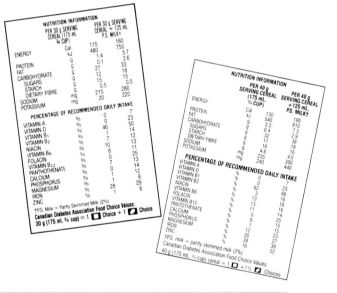

MAKING CONNECTIONS

Go to the supermarket and find various items such as dog food, cat food, tins of meat, and so on.

(a) List the ingredients in each item that you find at the supermarket.

(b) Which type of graph best displays the ingredients? Display the data.

The idea for television came long before the first broadcast. Sending sound and image patterns along airwaves was first experimented with in 1875. It was Scottish engineer, John Logie Baird, who first gave a practical demonstration of television years before the first television broadcast.

On November 2, 1936, the first regular television program was broadcast by the British Broadcasting System (BBC) in London, England. It was broadcast from Alexandra Place in North London and was called *Here's Looking at You*.

Work with a partner to complete the following exercises. You may need to use your library.

1. (a) When was a television show first broadcast in Canada?

   (b) What was the show?

2. (a) When was a television show first broadcast in North America?

   (b) What was the show?

3. On September 1, 1939, all television broadcasts were stopped suddenly.

   (a) Why was this done?

   (b) What was one program that was being broadcast at the time?

   (c) Is the program from (b) still running?

4. (a) How much would it cost you to buy a television today?

   (b) How much did it cost to buy a television in 1939? in 1959?

   (c) How would you display your data from parts (a) and (b)? Why did you make this choice?

5. Sometimes, when you watch a program, the picture appears to be cut off on the top and bottom. Why does this happen?

6. By 1982, video equipment was becoming popular. That year, there were 13 million video recorders sold around the world. By 1986, this number had increased to 128 million.

   (a) How many video recorders were sold this year around the world?

   (b) How many video recorders were sold this year in Canada?

   (c) How would you display the data from parts (a) and (b)?

   (d) Why do you think that video recorders are so popular?

7. (a) Who was Philo T. Farnsworth?

   (b) How did he change the way people watched television in the 1930's?

CHAPTER REVIEW

1. Calculate the mean, median, and mode.
   (a) 10, 12, 12, 14, 24, 12, 22, 22
   (b) 13.2, 8.9, 2.8, 17.4, 3.6, 13.2, 7.7, 13.2

2. The heights of students in a classroom, in centimetres, are shown.

157	173	182	163	159	146	172	179
153	161	159	165	159	154	152	162
159	166	163	168	154	172	159	162

   (a) Display the data.
   (b) Use your results from (a) to find the mean, median, and mode.

3. (a) Construct a frequency table to show the make of jeans worn.

   Levis (L)   Wrangler (W)
   Designer (D)   Other (O)

W	L	L	O	D	O	L	W	L	D	O	L
L	O	L	W	L	D	O	L	L	W	L	O
L	O	D	L	W	O	W	L	W	D	O	L

   (b) Display your data using an appropriate graph.
   (c) Use your graph. Which make of jeans is most popular? Which is least popular?

4. The daily high temperatures for one week at Honey Harbour are shown.

   31°C   28°C   23°C   23°C   28°C   27°C   25°C

   (a) A newscaster reported that the average temperature at Honey Harbour last week was 23°C. Is this statement misleading?
   (b) Calculate the mean and the median for the temperatures.
   (c) Which measure is most representative of the temperatures? Give reasons for your answer.

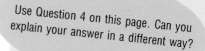

THINKING ABOUT

Use Question 4 on this page. Can you explain your answer in a different way?

Use your methods for displaying data from this chapter. Explain when you feel it is most appropriate to use each method.

Why do you think you should find the mean, median, and mode when finding the 'average' for a set of data?

MAKING CONNECTIONS

Refer to the opening pages of the chapter.
(a) Create a problem of your own using the pictures. Solve your problem.
(b) Compare your problem with others in the class. Solve the other problems.

Look at the problems in this chapter. Have you ever solved problems like these before?

List any assumptions you have made when solving the problems on this page.

In Question 4, what if the temperature was 40°C after 10 min? How would your solution be like the one you have now? How would it be different?

MATH JOURNAL

Throughout the chapter, you have analyzed and interpreted data.

(a) Find some data of your own in newspapers or magazines.

(b) Interpret what you think the data represents.

(c) Compare your interpretation with the one given. How are they alike? How are they different?

SELF EVALUATION

1. A survey on the number of viewers watching a Grey Cup game was taken. Would a telephone survey be useful? Give reasons for your answer.

2. The human body consists of the following.

    Muscle 49.8%   Fat   18.6%
    Bone   17.8%   Other 13.8%

    (a) Construct a circle graph to display the data.

    (b) Interpret your graph. What tissue makes up most of your body?

3. The number of people attending a satellite tennis tournament is shown for each day.

Day	1	2	3	4	5	6	7	8	9
Attendance	965	836	753	921	862	903	1048	2012	6012

A tournament official was overheard saying that "about 2000 people attended the tournament each day".

    (a) How can the official justify this statement?

    (b) Do you agree with the statement? Give reasons for your answer.

4. The table shows the temperature inside an oven after it is turned on.

Time (min)	0	5	10	15	20	25
Temp. (°C)	25	50	125	160	180	180

    (a) Construct a graph of your own to show the data. Give reasons for your choice of graph.

    (b) During which 5 min interval was there the greatest temperature increase?

    (c) At what temperature do you think the oven was set?

    (d) Estimate the temperature inside the oven after 7 min.

10 Ratio and Rate

With a partner, discuss how mathematics is involved in each picture. Then, write a problem that can be solved using information in one of them. Have others in the class solve the problem you created.

Refer to a dictionary. In your journal, write the meanings of the words "ratio" and "rate". After you have completed the chapter, compare your meanings with those found in this chapter. Decide how the meanings are alike and how they are different.

Have you ever noticed that there are more wieners in a package than there are buns? You often need two packages of wieners for every three packages of buns.

A **ratio** can be written to compare the number of packages of wieners to the number of packages of buns.

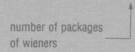

2 : 3

number of packages of wieners — number of packages of buns

This ratio can also be written as 2 to 3 or $\frac{2}{3}$. You read the ratio as "2 is compared to 3" or "2 to 3".

The order in which you write the **terms** is important.

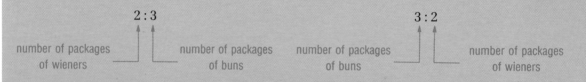

2 : 3

number of packages of wieners — number of packages of buns

3 : 2

number of packages of buns — number of packages of wieners

Work together to complete the explorations. Use your journal to record your observations and results.

EXPLORATION ① *Work in a Group*

Packages of wieners are represented by yellow counters and packages of buns by green counters.

1. Write a ratio to show each comparison.

(a)   (b)   (c)

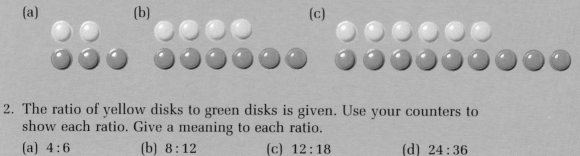

2. The ratio of yellow disks to green disks is given. Use your counters to show each ratio. Give a meaning to each ratio.

(a) 4 : 6   (b) 8 : 12   (c) 12 : 18   (d) 24 : 36

If 10 000 people each ate 2 hot dogs, then how many packages of each are needed?

EXPLORATION ②   *Work with a Partner*

3. (a) Andrew and Bonnie used a different number of disks to show **equivalent** ratios. Write in your journal what you think **equivalent** means.

   (b) How are Andrew's and Bonnie's ratios alike? How are they different?

4. (a) Show the ratio of yellow disks to green disks as 16 : 12.

   (b) Show each ratio using disks.
      • 12 : 9   • 8 : 6   • 4 : 3

   (c) How are your ratios alike? How are they different?

5. (a) Write the ratio of the number of green disks to the number of yellow disks.

   (b) Use fewer disks to show the ratio.

   (c) Use more disks to show the ratio.

   (d) How are your ratios in (a) and (b) alike? How are they different?

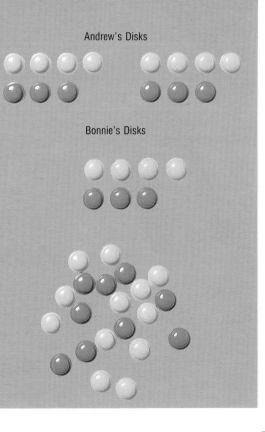

Andrew's Disks

Bonnie's Disks

307

10.2 EQUIVALENT RATIOS

One week, Video Rent-all rented out 500 comedy videos and 300 action videos. You can write a **ratio** to compare the number of comedy videos rented to the number of action videos rented.

Ratio Form: 500 : 300   **Fraction Form:** $\frac{500}{300}$

Each ratio above is a two term ratio and is read as "500 compared to 300". You can find ratios **equivalent** to 500 : 300 by multiplying or dividing each term by the same number.

Divide by 100   **Multiply by 10**
  500 : 300   500 : 300
    5 : 3 ◄—— in lowest terms   5000 : 3000

In lowest terms, the ratio of the number of comedy videos rented to the number of action videos rented is 5 : 3.

Video Rent-all also rented 150 drama videos. A three term ratio can be written as follows. To write the ratio in lowest terms, divide each term by the greatest common factor.

$$\text{500 : 300 : 150}$$

number of   number of   number of
comedy   action   drama

In lowest terms, the ratio is 10 : 6 : 3.

EXERCISE

A Review the meaning of equivalent ratios.

1. (a) Write the ratio represented by the disks.
   (b) Use more disks to represent an equivalent ratio.

   (i)   (ii)   (iii)

308

2. A recipe requires 6 L of flour and 3 L of sugar.

   (a) Use disks to compare the amount of flour to sugar.

   (b) Show other equivalent ratios using disks. Write the ratio.

3. Write 2 equivalent ratios for each.

   (a) $1:4$ (b) $5:6$ (c) $7:4$ (d) $1:2:3$ (e) $5:2:7$

4. Write an equivalent ratio in lowest terms.

   (a) $2:10$ (b) $10:6$ (c) $8:4$ (d) $5:10:15$ (e) $18:9:3$

B   Write all ratios in lowest terms. Use your disks.

5. In the string section of an orchestra, there are 11 violins, 3 violas, and 2 cellos. Interpret what is meant by each.

   (a) $2:3$ (b) $3:2$ (c) $11:2$
   (d) $11:3$ (e) $11:3:2$ (f) $3:2:11$

6. Use the information for each tower.

   CN 533 m   Eiffel 300 m
   Calgary 192 m   Skylon 160 m

   (a) Write a ratio to compare the height of the CN Tower to that of the Calgary Tower.

   (b) Compare the heights of the CN Tower, the Calgary Tower, and the Skylon Tower.

7. Ed's flight to Ottawa took 45 min. The bus ride to the airport took 3 h. Write a ratio to compare the time on the bus to the time on the plane.

8. Work together.

   (a) Decide which measures you need to make for each of the following.
   - hand span : arm span
   - height : arm span
   - arm : leg

   (b) Compare your ratios with others in the class. What patterns do you see? (Round to nearest cm.)

   (c) Decide on other possible ratios. Make appropriate measurements. Compare your measures. What patterns do you see?

C

9. To grow and sell vegetables, Brian bought 64 packages of seed. He bought cucumber seeds, tomato seeds, and bean seeds in the ratio $2:5:1$. How many packages of each did he buy?

WORKING TOGETHER

A Project

- List some of the categories of videos available for rent.
- Visit a local video store. Estimate the number of videos rented daily in your categories. Show ratios to compare.
- Survey your class to find the most popular category. Show ratios to compare the videos listed. Was your above estimate reasonable based on your class results?

In a bottle drive last week, your team collected 16 bottles and was able to recycle 12. This week, your team has just collected 24 bottles. How many does your team expect to recycle?

Think: To solve the problem, use your skills with equivalent ratios.

Let ■ represent the number of bottles recycled. Use a ratio equivalent to $16:12$.

number of bottles collected — number of bottles recycled

The first term is 24. When solving problems, it is often useful to write the ratios in fraction form.

$$\frac{16}{12} = \frac{24}{\blacksquare}$$

Think: Write $\frac{16}{12}$ as an equivalent ratio in lowest terms. $\frac{16}{12} = \frac{4}{3}$

$$\frac{4}{3} = \frac{24}{\blacksquare}$$

Think: Multiply each term by the same number.

$$\frac{4}{3} = \frac{24}{18}$$

Think: Interpret your result.

Out of 24 bottles collected, your team expects to recycle 18.

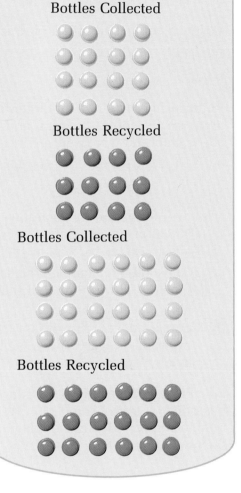

Think: You can use disks to help you solve the problem as shown below.

Bottles Collected

Bottles Recycled

Bottles Collected

Bottles Recycled

When you write two equivalent ratios, you are writing a **proportion** as shown below.

$$\frac{12}{16} = \frac{24}{32}$$

Think: $12 \times 2 = 24$
$16 \times 2 = 32$

$$\frac{12}{16} = \frac{3}{4}$$

Think: $12 \div 4 = 3$
$16 \div 4 = 4$

A Review your skills with equivalent ratios.

1. Find each missing value.

   (a) $\frac{3}{5} = \frac{3 \times 7}{5 \times ?}$ (b) $\frac{5}{7} = \frac{5 \times ?}{7 \times 8}$ (c) $\frac{15}{20} = \frac{15 \div ?}{20 \div 5}$ (d) $\frac{25}{35} = \frac{25 \div 5}{35 \div ?}$

2. Disks are used to suggest a proportion. Write the proportion and the missing number of disks to make the proportion true.

   (a)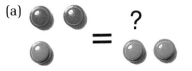

   (b)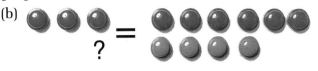

B Work together to solve the following problems.

3. Use disks to find the missing terms.

   (a) $\frac{3}{6} = \frac{\blacksquare}{12}$ (b) $\frac{9}{12} = \frac{3}{\blacksquare}$ (c) $\frac{\blacksquare}{12} = \frac{3}{4}$

4. Solve each proportion. Use disks.

   (a) $2 : 3 = \blacksquare : 15$ (b) $15 : 5 = 45 : \blacksquare$

   (c) $8 : \blacksquare = 4 : 3$ (d) $\blacksquare : 4 = 25 : 100$

5. In Allanville, 1 out of every 6 homes recycles bottles. There are 48 homes in the area. How many homes recycle bottles?

6. Last week, Fatima stopped 25 of 35 shots on goal. So far this week, she has faced 21 shots. How many do you think she has stopped?

7. When the pedal on a bike has turned 3 times in fourth gear, the rear wheel has turned 7 times. When the pedal turns 12 times, how many times does the rear wheel turn?

8. (a) How might a fraction be used to describe each diagram? Interpret your result.

   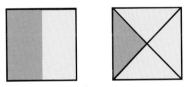

   (b) How might a ratio be used to describe each diagram in (a)?

   (c) Draw a figure of your own. Use a ratio to describe your diagram. Then, use a fraction.

C

9. In Martha's store, the ratio of bags of plain chips sold to onion chips to ketchup chips is $3 : 4 : 5$. Martha usually sells 72 bags of chips in a week.

   (a) How can you use disks to find the number of bags of onion chips sold?

   (b) Solve the problem in (a).

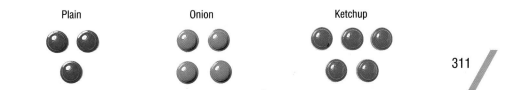

Plain   Onion   Ketchup

To maintain a licence in Canada, AM radio stations must play 3 Canadian songs for every 7 non-Canadian songs. Radio station CJNR played 21 Canadian songs yesterday. How many non-Canadian songs did they play?

1. Think About the Problem.

(a) Think of what you must find.
 • How many non-Canadian songs were played? (Use ■ to represent this.)

(b) Think of what you are given.
 • Number of Canadian songs played to non-Canadian songs played is 3 to 7.
 • Number of Canadian songs played yesterday was 21.

When you hear a DJ, there are lots of other people behind the scenes. How many do you think there are?

2. Think About a Strategy.

(a) Think of a strategy you could use.
 • Write the ratio 3 : 7.

  Canadian songs ⌐   └ non-Canadian songs

 • Write as a proportion. $\dfrac{3}{7} = \dfrac{21}{\blacksquare}$

(b) Think of a reason for the strategy.
 • You need to find the missing term of a proportion.

3. Work It Out.

Solve the proportion.

$\dfrac{3}{7} = \dfrac{21}{\blacksquare}$ Think: $\dfrac{3}{7} = \dfrac{3 \times 7}{7 \times 7} = \dfrac{21}{49}$

$\dfrac{3}{7} = \dfrac{21}{49}$ Interpret your work. ■ = 49

Thus, 49 non-Canadian songs were played.

4. Think About Your Solution.

• Are there other ways to solve the problem?
• Is your answer reasonable?

INDUSTRY

A Review your skills with ratios and proportions.

1. (a) Use disks to show the information: A radio station plays 2 slow songs for every 3 rock songs.

   (b) Write a ratio to show the information.

   (c) Use disks. Find the number of slow songs played if 18 rock songs were played.

   (d) Find the number of rock songs played if 160 slow songs were played.

2. (a) Write a ratio to show the information: A radio station plays 8 commercials for every 5 songs.

   (b) Find the number of commercials played if 125 songs were played.

B Use your *Problem Solving Skills.*

3. Radio station CNJR expects 1 out of every 5 listeners to call during the year. The station estimates there are 100 000 listeners. How many listeners are expected to call?

4. For every 0.5 h spent in a recording studio, a musical group rehearses for 10.0 h. The group plans to spend 2.0 h in a recording studio. How many hours should the group rehearse?

5. In a survey of musical tastes, the ratio of girls to boys interviewed was 15:5. There were 102 boys interviewed. How many girls were interviewed?

6. A band goes on tour to promote a new CD. It is estimated that 1 out of every 8 people attending the concert will buy the CD at the concert. The organizers ordered 2 cases of 144 CDs. How many people are expected?

7. A radio station plays 1 commercial for every 4 songs. A programmer has already selected 36 songs and 5 commercials. How many more commercials need to be selected?

C

8. You and Alex have the same number of tapes. The ratio of female to male vocalists in Alex's collection is 3:4, and 2:5 in yours. There are 36 male vocalists in all. How many of each type of vocalist do you and Alex have?

9. (a) Change the position of three toothpicks to create three squares.

   (b) Create a problem of your own using toothpicks. Solve it.

313

10.5 ESTIMATING WITH RATIOS

Last year, during a live-release fishing derby, 1230 fish were caught and released. Of these, 270 were trout. Estimate a ratio for trout caught and released to total fish caught and released.

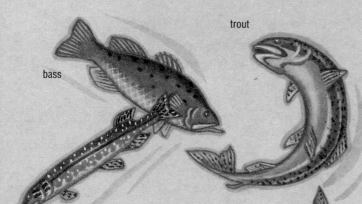

bass

trout

pike

Last year, the ratio was

$$\frac{270}{1230}$$ ← number of trout caught and released
← total fish caught and released

$$\frac{270}{1230} \doteq \frac{250}{1250}$$ Think: Make an estimate for each term.
270 is about 250.
1230 is about 1250.

$$\doteq \frac{1}{5}$$

Thus, an estimate for $\frac{270}{1230}$ is $\frac{1}{5}$.

This year, about 1500 fish are expected to be caught. About how many fish might be trout?

Think: Use your estimate of the given ratio.

Let ■ represent the number of trout.

$$\frac{1}{5} = \frac{\blacksquare}{1500}$$ Think: Write a proportion.

Solve the proportion.
Interpret your answer.

$$\frac{1}{5} = \frac{300}{1500}$$ ■ = 300

Thus, about 300 fish might be trout.

Remember: Try Question 5.

EXERCISE

A Review your estimating skills.

1. Write an estimate for each ratio. Justify your estimate.
   (a) 35 : 72   (b) 310 : 400   (c) 213 : 2000   (d) 250 : 190

2. For each proportion, estimate the missing term.
   (a) $\frac{1}{3} = \frac{\blacksquare}{260}$ (b) $\frac{3}{2} = \frac{\blacksquare}{135}$ (c) $\frac{3}{4} = \frac{50}{\blacksquare}$ (d) $\frac{5}{3} = \frac{125}{\blacksquare}$

3. Last year, 1962 fish were caught in the St. Lawrence River. Of these, 214 were salmon. This year, 2308 fish were caught. About how many do you expect to be salmon?

4. Last year, 22 390 fish were caught in Georgian Bay. Of these, about 1150 were muskie. This year, about 20 100 fish were caught. How many do you expect to be muskie?

5. Use the drawings on the previous page.

   (a) Estimate a simple ratio of pike to bass.

   (b) Create a problem of your own based on this estimate. Compare it with others in the class.

6. (a) Work together to move from A to B by turning right or moving up. In how many different ways can you mark a path from A to B?

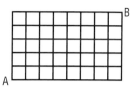

   (b) Use squared paper. Create a problem similar to (a). Compare it with others in the class.

C

7. The ratio of tapes to CDs that Joe has is 1 : 12. Juan has the same total number of tapes and CDs as Joe, but his ratio of tapes to CDs is 12 : 1. Juan has 24 tapes. How many tapes does Joe have?

MAKING CONNECTIONS

You have probably seen gold chains advertised as 10 karat (10 K) and 18 karat (18 K). The term **karat** describes the ratio of the mass of gold to the mass of other metals in the chain. For example, in a 10 K chain, the ratio of the mass of gold to the mass of other metals is 10 : 14. Pure gold is shown by 24 K.

amount of gold ⌐ ⌐ amount of other metals

8. Write a ratio to describe

   (a) a 12 K chain.   (b) an 18 K chain.

9. You own a 10 K chain with a mass of 48 g. What mass of gold is in the chain?

10. Work with a partner. Find jewellery ads in the newspaper. Estimate the mass of gold in each piece advertised.

10.6 PROBLEM SOLVING: CLUE WORDS

Use Clue Words

Trial and Error

Working Backwards

Draw a Diagram

Use Manipulatives

Look for a Pattern

?

Solve a Simpler Problem

Good problem solvers know that certain words are useful to solve problems. The words may suggest the strategies you might use. Look for clues.

You and Karl share the amount won from a lottery ticket. Karl receives $3 for every $5 won. The lottery ticket won $80. How much does Karl receive?

Think: Look for clues. Which words suggest a strategy? ("$3 for every $5" suggests a ratio.)

■ represents the amount Karl receives.

$$\frac{3}{5} = \frac{\blacksquare}{80}$$ Solve the proportion.

$$\frac{3}{5} = \frac{48}{80}$$ Interpret your work. Thus, ■ = 48.

Thus, Karl receives $48.

EXERCISE

B Use your *Problem Solving Plan*.

1. For every 25 phone calls saying *yes* to a new highway, there were 48 saying *no*. If there were 75 phone calls saying *yes*, what number do you expect to say *no*?

2. Kate and Lance agree to share the profits from a yard sale in the ratio 5 : 2. Kate's profits are $150. What is Lance's share of the profit?

3. (a) Find the number of rectangles formed in each diagram.
   (b) Use a pattern. Predict the number of rectangles in the tenth diagram.
   (c) Use tiles of your own and create a pattern. Find the tenth diagram in your pattern.

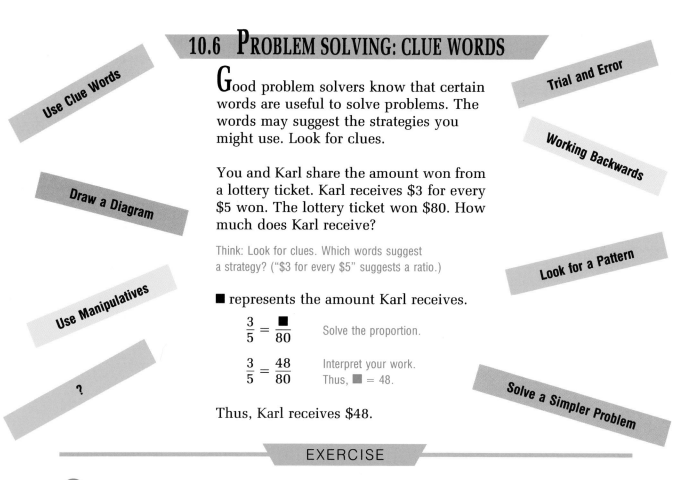

10.7 MAKING CONNECTIONS: GOLDEN RATIO

Designers know that certain ratios are pleasing to the eye.

A

B

C

1. (a) Use the shapes A, B, and C to complete the following table.

	Measure Length	Measure Width	Calculate Length ÷ Width
A			
B			
C			

(b) Refer to the chart. What do you notice about your answers in the last column?

2. In the previous question, the ratio of length to width for the rectangles was about 1.6 : 1. Rectangles that have this ratio for their side lengths are called **golden rectangles**.

	Width	Length
(i)	5 cm	8 cm
(ii)	50 cm	82 cm
(iii)	150 mm	289 mm
(iv)	36 m	75 m

(a) How can you decide if a rectangle is a golden rectangle? In the chart, which rectangles are golden rectangles?

(b) Working in groups, search art books, architecture books, and newspapers to find other examples of golden rectangles.

* Registered trade-mark of Visa International Service Association

317

10.8 RATE

In a ratio, the quantities being compared are expressed in the same units. However, you might need to compare quantities expressed in different units. Such a comparison is called a **rate**.

For example, Monique works for a bicycle manufacturer. The manufacturer can build 48 bicycles in each eight hour shift. How many bicycles are built each hour?

Think: Your skills with ratio and proportion can help
you to solve the problem.

$$\frac{48 \text{ bicycles}}{8 \text{ h}} = \frac{\blacksquare}{1 \text{ h}}$$

Think: Write as a proportion.

$$\frac{48 \text{ bicycles}}{8 \text{ h}} = \frac{6 \text{ bicycles}}{1 \text{ h}}$$

Think: Divide each term by 8. Interpret your result.

Thus, the manufacturer builds 6 bicycles each hour.

The second term in the rate $\frac{6 \text{ bicycles}}{1 \text{ h}}$ is 1. A rate like this is often called a **unit rate** and can be read as "6 bicycles per hour". To solve some problems, or make comparisons, unit rates are often helpful.

A Remember: The terms of rates have different units.

1. Interpret each rate. Remember: Use disks to help you interpret and work with ratios.

   (a) $\dfrac{120 \text{ km}}{10 \text{ h}}$ (b) $\dfrac{\$76}{8 \text{ albums}}$ (c) $\dfrac{\$5}{3 \text{ h}}$ (d) $\dfrac{30 \text{ m}}{1 \text{ s}}$

2. Interpret each rate. In what situation might each occur?

   (a) 25¢/g   (b) 100 km/h   (c) $36/kg   (d) 60 m/s

3. Write a unit rate for each.

   (a) 400 km travelled in 5 h   (b) $399 earned in 3 weeks

   (c) 6 bottles of juice for $2.40   (d) 3 cans of soup for $0.99

B Use your *Problem Solving Plan.*

4. Yesterday, Monique earned $57.75 during an 8 h shift.

   (a) How much did she earn each hour?

   (b) How much will she earn in a 40 h week?

5. Gertrude built nine bicycles in 25 h. At this rate, how many bicycles will she build in a 40 h week?

6. In Wawa, 26 cm of snow fell in an 8 day period. In Dartmouth, 40 cm of snow fell in 12 days. In which city was the rate of snowfall greater? Give reasons for your answer.

7. The fastest recorded rate in canoeing was 9.6 km in 1 h . Find the distance travelled in 50 s at this rate.

MAKING CONNECTIONS

Galileo Galilei was born in Pisa in 1564. According to legend, he climbed to the top of the Leaning Tower of Pisa. He dropped two pieces of metal with masses in the ratio of 10 : 1. To the crowd's surprise, they both hit the ground at the same time. Use your library.
   • From his experiment, what conclusions did Galileo make?
   • For what other discoveries is Galileo famous?

10.9 SOLVING PROBLEMS USING RATE

Suppose you are looking for a part-time job. You are offered the choice of these two jobs.

Day Camp Instructor
$6.75 for each hour

Market Cashier
$50.00 for working
a typical 8 h day

You would be working 15 h per week at either job.
- Which job should you accept?
- How much will you earn each week?

Think: Organize your calculation and interpret your results.

Day Camp Instructor
In 1 h, you will earn $6.75.
In 15 h, you will earn $101.25.

Market Cashier
In 8 h, you will earn $50.00.
In 1 h, you will earn $6.25.
In 15 h, you will earn $93.75.

To make more money, you should take the day camp instructor's job. You will earn $101.25 each week (and probably have more fun).

EXERCISE

A Review your skills using rate.

1. Ray earned $42.30 in a 5 h shift last weekend.
   (a) How much will he earn in 1 h? (b) How much will he earn in 8 h?

2. Toni earned $47.20 in a 9 h shift on Saturday. How much will she earn in
   (a) 1 h?   (b) 10 h?   (c) 3 h?   (d) 6.5 h?

3. A plane travels at 120 km/h. How far will it travel in
   (a) 1 h?   (b) 10 h?   (c) 3 h?   (d) 6.5 h?

4. A car travels 160 km in 2 h.
   (a) Express as a unit rate in km/h. (b) How far will it travel in 4.5 h?
   (c) How long will it take to travel 480 km?

5. Use the items on the conveyor belt.

   (a) Estimate the cost of each item.

   (b) Estimate the total cost of the purchase.

   (c) Which item do you think has the greatest unit cost?

6. The most intense rainfall ever occurred in Barst, Guadeloupe. At the time, 75 mm of rain fell in 2 min. How much rain is expected in

   (a) 8 min?   (b) 1 h?   (c) 3.5 h?

   (d) What assumptions did you make?

7. Maria is offered 2 part-time jobs.
   • Drug Store: $7.15 for each hour
   • Supermarket: $58.80 for 8 h
   She will work 11 h each week. Which job should she accept?

8. (a) Find the speed of each animal in metres per second.

Animal	Distance	Time
Bear	500 m	36.2 s
Cheetah	100 m	3.2 s
Elephant	20 m	1.8 s
Lion	200 m	8.0 s
Rabbit	250 m	16.5 s
Squirrel	400 m	72.7 s
Zebra	500 m	128.5 s

   (b) Which animal would get a ticket for speeding by your school?

9. In your journal, describe what you are looking for when you look for a summer job. You might include rate of pay, outdoor or indoor jobs, etc.

C

10. (a) A nursery claims that 2.5 kg of Green Gro grass seed will plant an area of 1200.0 m^2. How much is needed to plant a square park 0.5 km long?

    (b) Work together. Find seed prices from catalogues or newspapers. Use the ad to find the cost of seeding needed to plant each area in (a).

MAKING CONNECTIONS

You can determine how far away a thunderstorm is. For example, at 20°C, sound travels at a speed of 344 m/s. The speed of sound varies according to the air temperature. Use your library.

• What relationship gives the speed that sound travels according to air temperature?
• Determine the distance from a thunderstorm if thunder is heard (a) 2 s (b) 4.5 s after a flash of lightning.
• Devise a simple method to estimate the distance you are from a thunderstorm.

10.10 SCALE DRAWINGS

What would you need to do to fit the Eiffel Tower on this page? The Eiffel Tower, in Paris, is actually 300 m in height.

Scale drawings are useful when you can't fit the actual object on your page. The measured height of the tower on this page is 20 cm.

A **scale** is used to compare the measure on the drawing to the actual measure on the object.

measure on
drawing

actual measure
on object

Scale: 20 cm   *represents*   300 m

Think: To write the scale in lowest terms, divide each term by 20.

Scale: $\dfrac{20}{20}$ cm   *represents* $\dfrac{300}{20}$ m

1 cm   *represents*   15 m

The scale can be written as a ratio. To write a **scale ratio**, both terms need the same units.

1 cm *represents* 15 m   Think: 1 m = 100 cm
1 cm *represents* 1500 cm   15 m = 15 × 100 cm

The scale ratio is 1 : 1500.

measure
on drawing

actual measure
on object

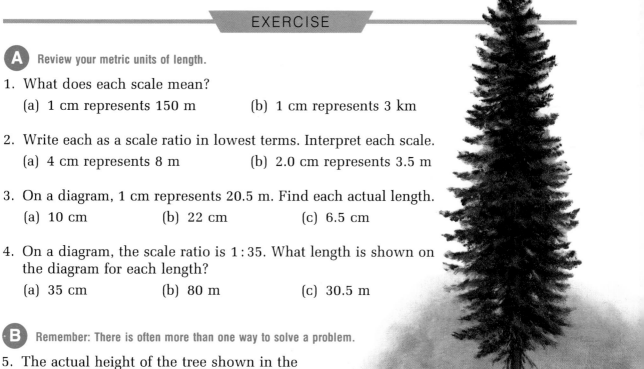

EXERCISE

A Review your metric units of length.

1. What does each scale mean?

   (a) 1 cm represents 150 m

   (b) 1 cm represents 3 km

2. Write each as a scale ratio in lowest terms. Interpret each scale.

   (a) 4 cm represents 8 m

   (b) 2.0 cm represents 3.5 m

3. On a diagram, 1 cm represents 20.5 m. Find each actual length.

   (a) 10 cm   (b) 22 cm   (c) 6.5 cm

4. On a diagram, the scale ratio is 1:35. What length is shown on the diagram for each length?

   (a) 35 cm   (b) 80 m   (c) 30.5 m

B Remember: There is often more than one way to solve a problem.

5. The actual height of the tree shown in the drawing is 35 m. What is the scale of the drawing?

6. A billboard showing a train has a scale of 1.0 m represents 19.0 m. The train in the billboard is 4.5 m long. Find the actual length of the train.

7. The scale ratio in a photo is 1:500. Niagara Falls is 51 m high. Would the height of Niagara Falls fit on a photograph measuring 10 cm by 12 cm?

8. (a) The Gateway to the West Arch has an actual height of about 192 m. On a scale drawing, the height is 38 cm. What scale was used to construct the drawing?

   (b) Use your library to find a tower or monument. What scale would you use to draw on this page the monument you found?

9. Work in small groups.

   (a) A pair of coins is shown. The coin on the left is rolled around the coin on the right. (No slipping is allowed.) Predict the direction the coin will face after it rolls half the circumference. Test your prediction.

   (b) Use other pairs of coins that are alike. Repeat part (a). What do you notice?

   (c) Use pairs of coins that are both different. Repeat part (a) using these coins.

Have you ever been to the capital of Canada? Suppose you want to walk from the Rideau Centre to the Parliament Buildings. About how far do you have to walk? The scale on a map gives you information to find the actual distance. The scale can occur in three forms.

As a statement:
1 cm represents 160 m.

As a scale ratio:
1 : 16 000

As a ruled line:
metres 0   200   400   600

Think: To answer the problem, measure the distance on the map.
This is about 3 cm. Then use the map scale to find the actual distance.

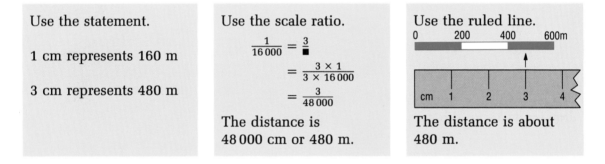

Use the statement.

1 cm represents 160 m

3 cm represents 480 m

Use the scale ratio.

$$\frac{1}{16\,000} = \frac{3}{\blacksquare}$$

$$= \frac{3 \times 1}{3 \times 16\,000}$$

$$= \frac{3}{48\,000}$$

The distance is
48 000 cm or 480 m.

Use the ruled line.

0   200   400   600m

cm   1   2   3   4

The distance is about
480 m.

The actual distance walked from the Rideau Centre to the Parliament Buildings is about 480 m.

EXERCISE

A Review how to read a scale. Work together.

1. The scale on a map shows 1 cm represents 10 km. What is the distance of each measure on the map?
   (a) 1 cm   (b) 5 cm   (c) 3.5 cm   (d) 11.2 cm   (e) 6.76 cm

2. The scale on a map is 1 : 100 000. What is the measure on the map for each actual distance?
   (a) 10 km   (b) 100 km   (c) 125 km   (d) 24.7 km   (e) 3.25 km

3. Which of the following represent the same scale?
   A 1 cm represents 5 km   B 1 : 1 000 000   C 1000 : 1

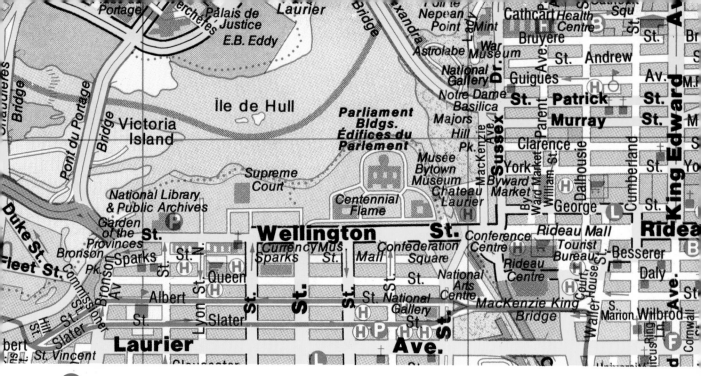

4. Use the map above. About how far will you walk from the Parliament Buildings to the Supreme Court?

5. (a) Work together. Choose other places on the map. Estimate the distances between them.

(b) Calculate each distance in (a). How accurate was your estimate?

6. The distance you have walked, according to the map, is 3 cm. You start at the National Gallery. Locate 2 places at which you could finish.

7. The scale on a map of British Columbia shows 1 cm represents 100 km. The actual distance from Golden to Salmon Arm is 225 km. What is the measured distance on the map between these two places?

8. (a) Work together and use an atlas. Estimate the ratio of the length of the Great Lakes waterway system to the distance across Canada.

(b) Use actual lengths to write a ratio for the length of the Great Lakes waterway system to the distance across Canada. How reasonable was your estimate in (a)?

(c) Create similar problems of your own. Solve the problems.

9. Work with a partner. Use the method shown below to find distances on the map above.

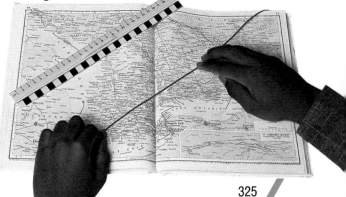

325

10.12 MAGNIFICATION

You can use your skills with scale drawings to help you draw very small objects. Lady bugs are a lot smaller than the one shown. What do you think is the scale ratio of this drawing?

The actual length of this lady bug is 4 mm. To find the scale ratio, measure the length of the lady bug shown.

The scale ratio is found as follows.

measure on   actual measure
drawing   on object

12 cm   represents 4 mm
 3 cm   represents 1 mm
30 mm represents 1 mm

Thus, the scale ratio is 30 : 1.

EXERCISE

A   Review what scale ratio means.

1. The scale ratio on a diagram is 100 : 1. What are the lengths of the actual objects?

    (a) 25 cm   (b) 2.7 cm   (c) 13.23 cm   (d) 8.75 cm

2. Write each as a scale ratio in lowest terms.

    (a) 20 cm represents 4 mm   (b) 4 m represents 20 cm

    (c) 15.5 cm represents 3.1 mm   (d) 12 cm represents 2.4 mm

3. A scale is 5 cm represents 1 mm. Find the actual length of each measure in the diagram.

    (a) 15 cm   (b) 25 cm   (c) 50.5 cm   (d) 22.37 cm

B Remember: To write a scale ratio, use the same units.

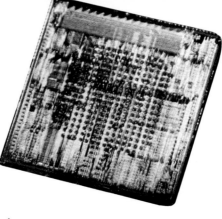

4. The microchip shown is enlarged. The scale is 1 cm represents 0.2 cm.

   (a) Write the scale as a scale ratio.

   (b) Measure all sides. Find the length and width of the actual microchip.

5. The scale on a drawing of a flea shows 5 cm represents 2 mm. Lily measured the drawing of the flea to be 7 cm. Find the actual length of the flea.

6. To draw the smallest water flea, a scale of 100 : 1 is used. The length of the flea on a drawing is 2.5 cm. Find the length of the actual flea.

7. Make measurements to find each actual measure on the lady bug.

   (a) One dot on its back.

   (b) The width of the body.

8. The shortest known snake is the worm snake. It measures 119 mm. Which scale would you use to draw the length in your notebook? Be prepared to justify your answer.

   (a) 2 : 1   (b) 100 : 1   (c) 1000 : 1

9. (a) Work in a group. Refer to the Guinness Book of World Records. Make a list of interesting facts about the largest and the smallest.

   (b) Create a problem of your own using your facts. Compare your problem with other groups.

10. The scale shown is 20 : 1. What is the actual width of the insect's head?

MAKING CONNECTIONS

The following are close-up photos of some everyday items. With a partner, discuss what these everyday items are. Once you have identified the items, estimate what scale ratio was used.

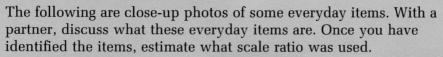

10.13 PROBLEM SOLVING

In his book *Paddle to the Amazon*, Don Starkell tells how he and his son, Dana, canoed from Winnipeg to South America.

> Dana and his father set out to explore a river. For 1.5 h, they paddled at a speed of 5 km/h. Suddenly, they came upon rapids and turned around. It took them another 2.5 h to return to camp. What was their average speed that day?

Distance travelled one way = speed × time
$$= 5 \text{ km/h} \times 1.5 \text{ h}$$
$$= 7.5 \text{ km}$$

Average speed = $\dfrac{\text{total distance travelled}}{\text{total time taken}}$

$$= \frac{7.5 \text{ km} + 7.5 \text{ km}}{1.5 \text{ h} + 2.5 \text{ h}}$$

Think: Use a calculator.

$$= 3.75 \text{ km/h}$$

The average speed was about 3.8 km/h.

EXERCISE

 Use your *Problem Solving Plan*.

1. The next day, Dana and his father paddled at a speed of 3.5 km/h. After 2.5 h, they decided to paddle back to camp. It took 3.0 h to paddle back. What was their average speed?

   (a) How far did the boat travel?

   (b) What was the average speed for the entire trip?

2. (a) Use the map shown. Work together and make measurements to find the scale ratio of the map.

   (b) Get a copy of *Paddle to the Amazon* (or a similar book). Create problems of your own using the book.

   (c) In your journal, describe how you would prepare to travel down the Amazon for one day.

Imagine how many books there are in print today. How do you think publishers and librarians keep track of all the books?

Computer systems are used by publishers and librarians to keep track of the growing number of books. The central processing unit of a computer will hold in its memory a detailed record of every book in print. In order that the book can be placed in memory, a piece of software from a disk must be used. The disk is programmed so that the user can type in the book title, along with other relevant information, and have it stored in the computer's memory.

Other kinds of software allow many people in many occupations to perform tasks quickly and easily. In the activities that follow, work together to describe briefly the type of software that these occupations use.

1. Suppose you want to order a book from a publisher.
   (a) What information do you think is most often given to the publisher?
   (b) Describe how the publisher's software would work.

2. Computer systems are necessary for the smooth operation of an airline. As a customer, you will pass your ticket to a receptionist who will then tell you what your seat will be. Describe how the software that is used by the receptionist would work.

3. When you go to a bank and deposit money, your bank book is often updated by having it inserted into a computer. Describe how the software that is used by the bank teller would work.

4. Choose an occupation of your own.
   (a) Describe the occupation.
   (b) Describe how the software that is used by a person in your occupation would work.

1. Write each ratio in lowest terms. Use disks to help you.

   (a) $12:36$ (b) $15:5$ (c) $28:7$ (d) $20:10$

2. Write each ratio in lowest terms.

   (a) It took 2 h to row upstream. It took 0.5 h to row back again.

   (b) A pool was filled in 18.0 h. It was emptied in 4.5 h.

   (c) Jorge jogged for 2.5 km. He walked 250 m to "warm down".

3. Find the unit cost of each item.

   (a) 25 hockey sticks for $400

   (b) 25 m of tape for 95¢

   (c) 3.5 m of material for $32.50

4. Find the missing terms.

   (a) $\dfrac{3}{6} = \dfrac{\blacksquare}{12}$ (b) $\dfrac{\blacksquare}{12} = \dfrac{3}{4}$ (c) $15:5 = 45:\blacksquare$

5. Asham can type 96 words in 2 min. How many words can Asham type in

   (a) 1 min?   (b) 3 min?   (c) 12.5 min?

6. Last week, Pat stopped 20 out of 30 shots taken. This week, Pat faced 36 shots. How many shots do you think Pat stopped?

7. For each, the actual measurement is given. What scale would you choose to draw each to fit on a page of your notebook?

   (a) The smallest bird in the world is the male hummingbird. It has a wing span of 3.8 cm.

   (b) The longest river in Canada is the South Saskatchewan River measuring about 1900 km.

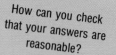

How can you check that your answers are reasonable?

How can you work with a partner to review the skills in the chapter?

What new problem solving skills can you add to your Problem Solving Plan?

MAKING CONNECTIONS

Refer to the opening pages of this chapter and review the definitions of the words "ratio" and "rate" that you wrote.

(a) Based on what you have learned in this chapter, how accurate were your definitions?

(b) How would you modify your definitions now?

SELF EVALUATION

1. Write a ratio in lowest terms for each. Use disks to help you.
   (a) For every 20 g of sugar, Charlene uses 30 g of flour.
   (b) For every tonne of paper collected on Earth Day, Jan collected 100 kg of bottles.

2. A grasshopper is drawn with a scale ratio 3 : 1.
   (a) Calculate the actual length of the body.
   (b) How long are the antennae?
   (c) A grasshopper can jump 76 times its actual length. How far can this grasshopper jump?

3. Find each missing term.
   (a) $\dfrac{9}{12} = \dfrac{\blacksquare}{3}$ (b) $\dfrac{2}{3} = \dfrac{14}{\blacksquare}$ (c) $\blacksquare : 7 = 25 : 35$

4. Find each missing value.
   (a) $\dfrac{60 \text{ km}}{2 \text{ h}} = \dfrac{\blacksquare \text{ km}}{4 \text{ h}}$ (b) $\dfrac{25 \text{ g}}{10 \text{ mL}} = \dfrac{40 \text{ g}}{\blacksquare \text{ mL}}$

   (c) $\dfrac{75 \text{ m}}{8 \text{ s}} = \dfrac{100 \text{ m}}{\blacksquare \text{ s}}$

MATH JOURNAL

What types of problems are still difficult for you to solve?

Compare what you have written today with previous entries in your mathematics journal to see if there is a pattern. What can you do to overcome the problems you are having?

5. Use the chart. For each player, compare the number of

	Wayne	Mario	Steve
Games	75	69	80
Goals	34	58	72

   (a) goals scored to games played.
   (b) games played to goals scored.
   (c) games played by Wayne to Mario to Steve.
   (d) goals scored by Wayne to Mario to Steve.

6. The actual distance between two cities is 245 km. Rolland drives his car at 70 km/h. How long will it take to drive between the two cities?

1. Write each decimal number as an equivalent fraction.

   (a) 0.175   (b) 0.064   (c) $0.0\overline{18}$ (d) 8.08888...   (e) $1.\overline{705}$

2. Calculate.

   (a) $3\frac{1}{2} - 2\frac{2}{3} + 1\frac{1}{4}$ (b) $1\frac{4}{9} \times \frac{3}{13}$ (c) $5\frac{3}{5} \div 1\frac{3}{4}$ (d) $\frac{3}{4} \times \frac{2}{3} \div 1\frac{1}{2}$

3. Calculate.

   (a) $(-1)(+3)$ (b) $(-3)(+22)$ (c) $(-9) - (-8)$ (d) $(-7) + (-2)$
   (e) $(+15) \div (-5)$ (f) $(+8) + (-2)$ (g) $(-5)(-3)$ (h) $(-12) \div (+4)$

4. Write the number in each sentence in scientific notation.

   (a) The farthest distance the earth is from the sun is about 152 000 000 km.

   (b) The world's oldest cake has a diameter of 0.11 m.

5. A pie has a diameter of 40 cm. How many identical pie crusts can be cut from a piece of dough 2.5 m long and 1.5 m wide?

6. Find the least number of lines needed to cut the figure into five equal parts.

7. A can of tomatoes is 12.4 cm in height and has a base radius of 4.1 cm. Find the area of the label used on the can.

CALCULATION SENSE

Sometimes, you can group factors to multiply expressions quickly.

$5 \times 3 \times 2 \times 7 \times 2 \times 5 = 10 \times 10 \times 21$
$= 100 \times 21$
$= 2100$

$5 \times 2 = 10$

Calculate. Look for groups.

(a) $5 \times 3 \times 2 \times 6$ (b) $2 \times 4 \times 5 \times 7$ (c) $6 \times 2 \times 4 \times 5$

(d) $4 \times 2 \times 7 \times 5 \times 2 \times 5$ (e) $2 \times 5 \times 6 \times 2 \times 6 \times 5$ (f) $2 \times 3 \times 2 \times 5 \times 5$

PROBLEM SOLVING: CUMULATIVE REVIEW

1. Refer to the materials shown. How many different shapes can you make from the figures?

2. What is the last digit when you multiply the first 16 prime numbers? Give reasons for your answer.

3. A coast guard patrol plane was at a height of 50 m when it detected an object 30 m below sea level.

   (a) Write an integer to describe each number.

   (b) Interpret your integers. How far is the plane from the object?

4. A number added to 25 gives a perfect square. The same number subtracted from 196 also gives a perfect square. What is the number?

5. (a) Replace ■ with the correct operations to make each statement true.
   (i) 8 ■ 2 ■ 6 = 10   (ii) 5 ■ 9 ■ 3 = 2   (iii) 7 ■ 4 ■ 14 = 2

   (b) Working with a partner, create a problem of your own similar to those in (a). Exchange your expression with those of others in your class.

6. One of the world's deepest caves is found in France. It has a depth of 1170 m. It took Jean's group 10 min to descend the first 40 m. How long do you think it will take Jean's group to completely descend to the bottom of the cave? How did you arrive at your conclusion?

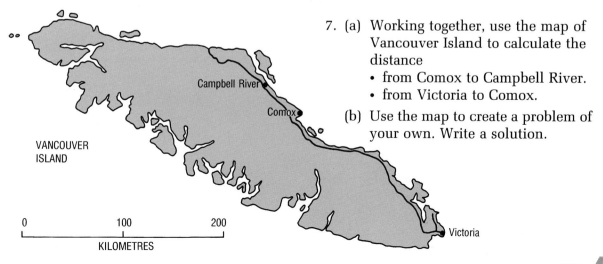

7. (a) Working together, use the map of Vancouver Island to calculate the distance
   • from Comox to Campbell River.
   • from Victoria to Comox.

   (b) Use the map to create a problem of your own. Write a solution.

333

11 PERCENT

In your journal, suggest an answer to each question. Then, suggest a math problem that can be solved using the information in the pictures.

Once you have finished the chapter, review your answers to the questions and the problems you have written.

What do you think is meant by a 10% discount?

10% off

What do you think is meant by 2% milk?

335

Sandra cuts a piece of cardboard into 100 pieces. The cardboard is blue on one side and yellow on the other. She puts the pieces into a box and shakes them.

Of the 100 pieces showing, 29 of them are yellow. You write this as "29% (read as '29 percent') of the pieces are yellow".

EXPLORATION ① Work in a Group

1. Use cardboard pieces like those shown above.
   Step A Put the pieces in the box and shake them.
   Step B Write the number of yellow pieces as a percent.
   Step C Write the number of blue pieces as a percent.
   Step D Repeat the steps above two more times.

EXPLORATION ② Work in a Group

2. Work together and place 100 pennies in a box.
   Step A Shake the box thoroughly.
   Step B Record the percent of pennies that show heads and the percent that show tails.
   Step C Repeat the steps above two more times.

3. Use your results from Question 2. Which statement below seems most likely? Discuss with others and give reasons for your choice.
   A When 100 pennies are shaken, about 30% of them will show heads.
   B When 100 pennies are shaken, about 50% of them will show heads.
   C When 100 pennies are shaken, about 70% of them will show heads.

EXPLORATION ③ Work Together

4. (a) Find examples of percent used in newspapers and magazines. Suggest examples that would be suitable for a bulletin board. Make the bulletin board.

   (b) Start a percent journal of your own and continue to collect examples of percent.

11.2 MEANING OF PERCENT

Kate assists at the library every Friday afternoon. Of the 100 books in the return cart one day, 25 were fiction. She can say that "25% of the books are fiction". The percent symbol, %, is a concise way of writing "out of 100". She can write the percent as a fraction and a decimal number as shown below.

As a Percent

25%

As a Fraction

$25\% = \dfrac{25}{100} = \dfrac{1}{4}$

As a Decimal Number

$25\% = \dfrac{25}{100} = 0.25$

EXERCISE

 A Use your tiles from the previous page.

1. What percent is shaded in the diagram? Write your answer as a percent, fraction, and decimal number.

2. Write each as a fraction and a percent.
   (a) 0.73   (b) 0.68   (c) 0.03
   (d) 0.54   (e) 0.32   (f) 0.98

3. Write as a percent and a decimal number.
   (a) $\dfrac{17}{100}$ (b) $\dfrac{23}{100}$ (c) $\dfrac{11}{100}$

 B Write all fractions in lowest terms.

4. At the zoo, Jessica learned that 2% of the animals are lions. Use manipulatives to suggest the meaning of 2% of the animals are lions.

5. Write each as a percent.
   (a) 20 out of 100 people surveyed
   (b) 45 ha from a 100 ha farm

6. In Switzerland, 90 L of every 100 L of milk is used to make cheese. What percent is used to make cheese?

7. (a) Work together. Write the percent of thumbtacks below that point up.
   (b) Shake 100 thumbtacks in a box. Record the number that point up. Repeat ten times.
   (c) Based on your results, what percent of thumbtacks in the box will point up?

11.3 PERCENT STRATEGIES

Tony's class was invited backstage at a concert. Of the 25 students in the class, 20 were able to go. What percent of Tony's class went backstage?

Think: You can answer this question using different strategies.

Use an Equivalent Fraction

Write an equivalent fraction for $\frac{20}{25}$ with 100 as the denominator.

$$\frac{20}{25} = \frac{\blacksquare}{100}$$
$$= \frac{20 \times 4}{25 \times 4}$$
$$= \frac{80}{100} \text{ or } 80\%$$

Multiply by 100%

Multiply $\frac{20}{25}$ by 100% to obtain the percent.

$$\frac{20}{25} \times 100\% = 80\%$$

Thus, 80% of the students went backstage.

The following skills with percent are needed to solve problems. In your journal, write any patterns you see.

• Write 0.625 as a percent.	• Write $12\frac{1}{2}\%$ as a decimal.	• Write 87.5% as a fraction.
$0.625 \times 100\% = 62.5\%$	$12\frac{1}{2}\% = 12.5\%$ *Think:* $\frac{12.5}{100}$ $= 0.125$	$87.5\% = \frac{87.5}{100}$ *Think:* $\frac{875}{1000}$ $= \frac{7}{8}$
0.625 is written as 62.5%.	$12\frac{1}{2}\%$ is written as 0.125.	87.5% is written as $\frac{7}{8}$.

You can write repeating decimal numbers as percents as shown below.

$$\frac{1}{3} = 0.33\dot{3}$$
$$= \frac{33.\dot{3}}{100}$$
$$= 33.3\% \text{ (to one decimal place)}$$

A Make a list of percent skills used.

1. Write each as a decimal number.

   (a) 62.5%   (b) 12.8%   (c) 19.4%   (d) 75.3%   (e) 88.9%

2. Write each as a percent.

   (a) 0.73   (b) 0.48   (c) $\frac{3}{5}$ (d) $\frac{4}{5}$ (e) $\frac{2}{3}$

3. Write each percent as a decimal number and as a fraction.

   (a) $8\frac{1}{2}\%$ (b) $9\frac{1}{4}\%$ (c) $75\frac{1}{10}\%$ (d) $87\frac{5}{8}\%$ (e) $4\frac{2}{3}\%$

4. Find the missing values.

   (a) $\frac{1}{2} = \frac{\blacksquare}{100}$ (b) $\frac{1}{10} = \frac{\blacksquare}{100}$ (c) $5\% = \frac{\blacksquare}{100}$ (d) $0.96 = \frac{\blacksquare}{100}$

B Review how to multiply and divide by 100 mentally.

5. Of 20 students at a concert, 16 sat in the balcony. Find the percent that sat in the balcony.

6. Of all the water on the earth, 0.96 of it is salt water. What percent of the earth's water is salt water?

7. Free oxygen makes up about 20% of the atmosphere. What fraction of the atmosphere is free oxygen?

8. A farmer planted $\frac{2}{3}$ of a farm. What percent of the farm was planted?

WORKING TOGETHER

Working with a partner, place an unknown number of white beans and brown beans into a box or bag.

(a) Reach in and pull out a handful of beans.

(b) Write the percent of the beans that are brown.

(c) Repeat parts (a) and (b) ten times.

(d) Based on your results, predict what percent of the beans are brown beans. Give reasons for your prediction. How can you verify your prediction?

11.4 PERCENT OF A NUMBER

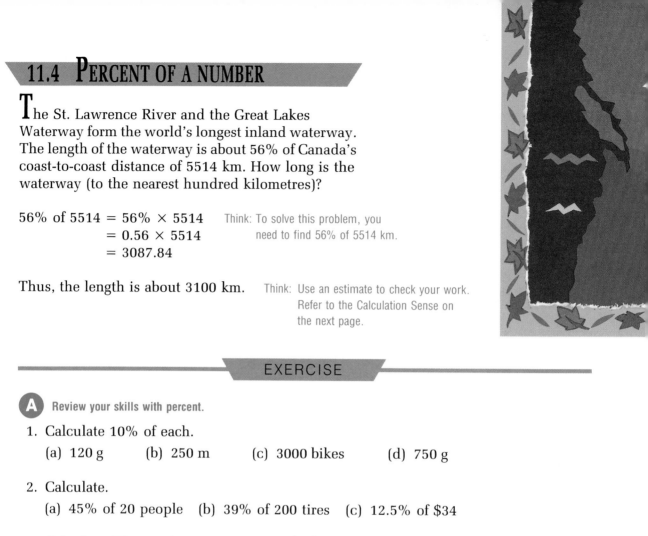

The St. Lawrence River and the Great Lakes Waterway form the world's longest inland waterway. The length of the waterway is about 56% of Canada's coast-to-coast distance of 5514 km. How long is the waterway (to the nearest hundred kilometres)?

$$56\% \text{ of } 5514 = 56\% \times 5514$$
$$= 0.56 \times 5514$$
$$= 3087.84$$

Think: To solve this problem, you need to find 56% of 5514 km.

Thus, the length is about 3100 km.

Think: Use an estimate to check your work. Refer to the Calculation Sense on the next page.

EXERCISE

A Review your skills with percent.

1. Calculate 10% of each.
   (a) 120 g   (b) 250 m   (c) 3000 bikes   (d) 750 g

2. Calculate.
   (a) 45% of 20 people   (b) 39% of 200 tires   (c) 12.5% of $34

3. Calculate. Then estimate. Was your calculation reasonable?
   (a) Of the 2190 words in a report, about 5% were spelled incorrectly.
   (b) Of the 316 kg of tomatoes harvested, 15% were still green.

B Check that your answers are reasonable.

4. Rick owns 255 stamps. About 20% are worth more than $100. How many of his stamps are worth more than $100?

5. Did you know that 90% of the mass of an orange is water? An orange has a mass of 122.3 g. What mass of water is in the orange?

6. About 33.3% of the movies shown on TV are Canadian. If 4820 movies are shown, how many are Canadian?

7. Of the students surveyed, 72.4% chose "We are the Champions" as the new school song. There were 384 students surveyed. About how many chose "We are the Champions"?

8. Refer to the example on the previous page. The Ottawa River is about 41% as long as the entire inland waterway. How long is the Ottawa River?

9. (a) Rajib sailed from one end of Lake Ontario to the other. About what percent of the Great Lakes Waterway did he travel?

   (b) Create a problem using the map above. Compare your problem with others in your class.

10. Jane plants this farm. She will plant 30% lettuce, 10% peas, and the rest beans. Copy the farm and show how she can plant the vegetables.

CALCULATION SENSE

Your skills with percent can help you estimate answers.

$$28\% \text{ of } 323 \doteq \frac{1}{4} \times 320$$
$$= 80$$

$$56\% \text{ of } 5514 \doteq 60\% \text{ of } 6000$$
$$= 3600$$

1. Estimate each.
   (a) 32% of 60 (b) 17% of 77
   (c) 43% of 175 (d) 22% of 448

2. Estimate each.
   (a) 28% of 3443 (b) 53% of 1808
   (c) 37% of 3884 (d) 56% of 5486

11.5 ESTIMATING PERCENT

Did you know that printed photographs are made up of different coloured dots? For example, in a green background, about 180 of 480 dots are blue and the rest are yellow. About what percent of the dots are blue?

Think: Estimate.
180 → is about → 200
480 → is about → 500
$\frac{200}{500} = \frac{2}{5} \times 100\%$
    $= 40\%$

About 40% of the dots are blue.

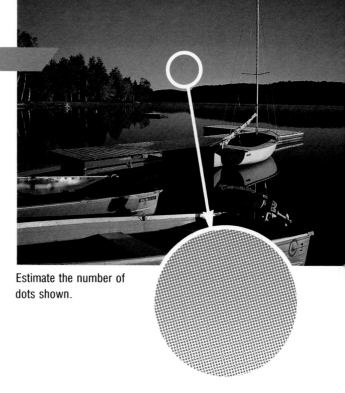

Estimate the number of dots shown.

Your skills with estimation can be used to solve problems.

About what percent of the dock is stained?

The stained part is less than $\frac{1}{2}$ the entire dock. About 4 stained parts would cover the entire dock. Thus, about $\frac{1}{4}$ of the dock is stained.

Think: $\frac{1}{4} = \frac{1}{4} \times 100\%$ or 25%

About 25% of the dock is stained.

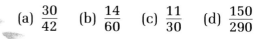

EXERCISE

A Work with a partner to find reasonable estimates.

1. Estimate a percent for each.

(a) $\frac{30}{42}$ (b) $\frac{14}{60}$ (c) $\frac{11}{30}$ (d) $\frac{150}{290}$

2. Estimate the percent of each dock that has been stained.

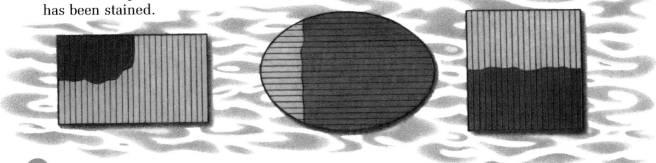

3. Of the 128 people on the *Maid of the Mist*, 43 wore glasses. Estimate the percent of people wearing glasses.

4. Pine trees under 2 m tall cannot be cut. Of the 300 trees on a farm, 48 are less than 2 m tall. Estimate the percent of trees that cannot be cut.

5. Of the 318 students in a school, 212 brought their lunch. Estimate the percent of students who brought lunch.

6. A sample of 193 computers was tested, and 18 had defects. Estimate the percent of computers that had defects.

7. There were 282 people at a log rolling contest. Of these, 63 rolled the log for more than 2 min. Estimate the percent of people who rolled the log for more than 2 min.

8. The amount of money Anna earned and saved each month is shown.

Month	Earned ($)	Saved ($)
June	227	66
July	315	93
Aug.	420	88

(a) Estimate the percent of her earnings that Anna saved each month.

(b) In which month did Anna save the greatest percent?

9. Of the 218 runners registered for a marathon, 184 finished.

(a) Estimate the percent of runners who finished.

(b) Use your results from (a). How many of the runners shown below do you think will finish the marathon? Give reasons.

(c) Create a problem of your own using the picture.

11.6 OTHER PERCENTS

A tub of popcorn can be described in the following three ways.

- Less than 100% full
- 100% full
- More than 100% full

You can solve problems involving percents *greater than* 100%.

The Famous Actors Cinema had 110 customers on Friday. On Saturday, the attendance increased to 220% of Friday's attendance. Find the attendance on Saturday.

Think: Use your skills with percent and a calculator.

220% of 110 people = 2.20 × 110 people   Think: 220% = 2.20
                   = 242 people

Thus, the attendance on Saturday was 242 people.

Your percent skills can be used to write percents *greater than* 100%.

• Write 1.5 as a percent.	• Write $3\frac{3}{4}$ as a percent.	• Write 180% as a decimal number.
$1.5 = 1.5 \times 100\%$ $\quad = 150\%$	$3\frac{3}{4} \times 100\% = 3.75 \times 100\%$ $\quad\quad\quad\quad = 375\%$	$180\% = \frac{180}{100}$ $\quad\quad = 1.8$

You can use the same skills to write percents *less than* 1%.

Write 0.001 as a percent.

$0.001 \times 100\% = 0.1\%$

Write 0.5% as a decimal number.

$0.5\% = \frac{0.5}{100}$
$\quad\quad = 0.005$

A Review your skills with percent.

1. Write each as a decimal number.

    (a) 130%   (b) 250%   (c) 375%   (d) 0.65%   (e) 0.53%   (f) 0.55%

2. Write each as a percent.

    (a) 1.5   (b) 2.6   (c) 0.008   (d) $\dfrac{7}{1000}$ (e) $5\dfrac{1}{4}$ (f) $4\dfrac{3}{8}$

3. Calculate.

    (a) 150% of 200 cm   (b) 175% of 100 mg   (c) 275% of 20 kg

4. Calculate.

    (a) 0.75% of 500 kg   (b) 0.85% of $212 000   (c) 0.88% of 5500 km

5. (a) The shape to the right represents 100%. Draw this shape as often as needed to represent 275%.

    (b) Repeat part (a) using a shape of your own.

B Check whether your answers are reasonable.

6. Yesterday, 235 customers were at a movie. Today, the attendance increased to 305% of yesterday's. Find today's attendance.

7. Did you know that the vocabulary of a two-year-old is about 29 words? By age four, the vocabulary will increase by 213%. How many words are in the vocabulary of a four-year-old?

8. (a) In your journal, sketch diagrams to show
    • greater than 100%.
    • less than 1%.

    (b) Refer to the popcorn on the previous page. Describe other ways you can show such comparisons.

9. (a) Work with a partner. Each of you blow up a balloon as much as you can in one breath. Measure its diameter.

    (b) Now each of you add one more breath to the balloon. Measure its diameter.

    (c) By what percent has the diameter increased?

345

11.7 PROBLEM SOLVING: COMBINING SKILLS

Riverview School is planning a walk-a-thon. Students can walk either 10 km or 20 km. There are 370 students signed for the 10 km walk and 140 for the 20 km walk.

Based on previous years' experience, it is expected that 10% of students in the 10 km walk and 45% of students in the 20 km walk will not finish. What percent of students are not expected to finish the walk?

1. Think About the Problem.

(a) Think of what you must find.
  • The percent of students who will not finish the walk.

(b) Think of what you are given.
  • 370 students signed up for a 10 km walk.   10% will not finish.
  • 140 students signed up for a 20 km walk.   45% will not finish.

2. Think About a Strategy.

(a) Think of a strategy you could use.
  • Find the total number of students who will not finish the walk.
  • Find the total number who will not finish the walk as a percent.

(b) Think of a reason for the strategy.
  • The percent that will not finish in each distance is given.

3. Work It Out.

Step 1 Find the number of 10 km walkers who will not finish.

10% of 370 = 0.10 × 370 = 37

Step 2 Find the number of 20 km walkers who will not finish.

45% of 140 = 0.45 × 140 = 63

Step 3 Find the total number of walkers who will not finish as a percent. Do the calculation.

$$\frac{\text{Total number who won't finish}}{\text{Total number of students}} = \frac{37 + 63}{370 + 140}$$

$$= \frac{100}{510} \text{ or } 0.196 \quad \text{Think: } 0.196 = 19.6\%$$

4. Think About Your Solution.

Thus, about 20% of the students are not expected to finish the walk.
Check whether your answer is reasonable.

B Use your *Problem Solving Plan.*

1. On Friday 20 girls and 80 boys went to the zoo. 100% of the girls and 10% of the boys saw the elephants.

   (a) How many boys saw the elephants?

   (b) What percent of students saw the elephants?

2. As a fundraiser, students collected 370 kg of cans and 140 kg of bottles. The recycling plant found that 15% of the cans and 35% of the bottles could not be recycled. What percent of the total mass collected could not be recycled?

3. A baker has made 30 pies. They are either blueberry or pecan. There are 50% more blueberry pies than pecan. How many of each are there?

4. What percent of the area covered by the swimming pool and the sidewalk is covered by the pool? the sidewalk?

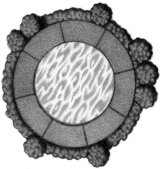

5. Arrange 19 counters in eight rows with five counters in each row.

C

6. In one week, the recycling plant collected 8000 cans and 6500 bottles. However, only 35% of the bottles and 55% of the cans could be recycled. How many cans and bottles were left over?

MAKING CONNECTIONS

Constance Reid's interest in mathematics dates from 1952 when she learned how one of the first computers had been used to discover several new, very large "perfect" numbers — numbers, like 6 and 28, that are the sum of all their divisors except themselves.

Use your library and work with a partner.
- Write a short paragraph to describe the impact computers have made on solving problems since 1952. Suggest the types of problems that can be solved on the computer.
- Start a bulletin board to show the impact computers have had on society. Use pictures and articles found in newspapers and magazines.
- Find out more about Constance Reid's contribution to mathematics.

Sometimes, to check your solution or prediction, you can set up an experiment to collect and analyze data. Work in groups to complete each investigation.

For each of the following investigations,
- predict an answer to the question you want to solve.
- set up the investigation and collect the data.
- use your results to find the answer. Was your prediction reasonable?

INVESTIGATION ① Work with a Partner

Have you ever wondered what will happen if you shorten or lengthen the rope on a swing?

Experiment 1
1. Cut three different lengths of string, each longer than 15 cm. Attach an eraser, each with the same mass, to the end of each length of string.

2. Attach the free end of each string to your desk.

3. Gently pull each eraser back and let go. Time one complete swing.

4. Compare the length of time for one complete swing. What do you notice?

Experiment 2
Collect data for a swing.
1. Have people of different masses sit on the swings.

2. Have them swing until they reach the same height.

3. Time one complete swing for each person. Compare the length of time for each complete swing. What do you notice?

INVESTIGATION ② Work in a Group

In the picture, a basketball and a soccer ball have been dropped from different heights. Work with a partner to complete the following.

1. Predict what percent of the original height each ball bounces.

2. Drop each ball. Measure the height each ball reaches after one bounce.

3. Use your results from Question 2. What percent of the original height does each ball bounce?

INVESTIGATION ③ Work with a Partner

Have you ever been in a revolving restaurant? These restaurants are at the top of a tower and revolve so that you can see the whole city.

1. Two tables are shown in the revolving restaurant below.
   (a) After the restaurant turns once, how far has table A travelled? table B?
   (b) Suppose the restaurant turns twice each hour. Which table will travel faster?
   (c) Where would you choose a table if you wanted to travel the slowest in the restaurant? Give reasons for your answer.

2. Put a streamer in between the spokes of a bicycle wheel.
   (a) Predict how many times faster a spot on the tire will travel than a spot on the streamer.
   (b) Suppose the wheel takes 5 s to turn once. Determine the distance travelled by each spot. Find how fast each spot is moving.

3. Create a similar problem of your own using a carnival ride that you design. Solve your problem and compare your solution with others in your class.

17.5 m

A   B

11.9 SALES TAX

Suppose you work in a store in Newfoundland and have just sold a tape player for $34. To calculate the total cost, you must add the Provincial Sales Tax.

The Provincial Sales Tax (PST) is 12% in Newfoundland.

To calculate the total cost, you must also add the Goods and Services Tax (GST) of 7%.

Price of tape player:	$34.00	Think
PST:	4.08	0.12×34
GST:	2.38	0.07×34
Total:	$40.46	

Thus, the total cost of the tape player is $40.46.

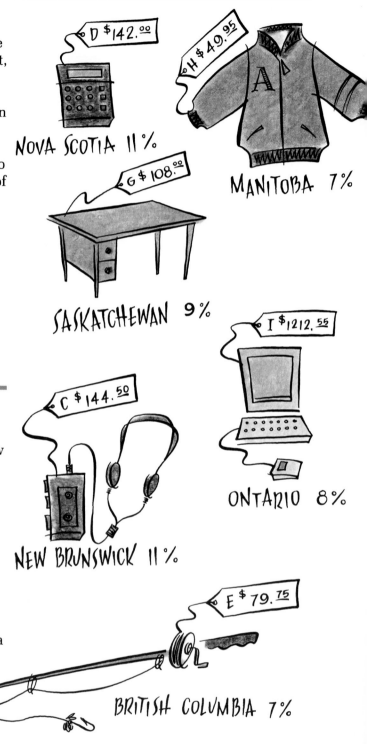

NOVA SCOTIA 11%

MANITOBA 7%

SASKATCHEWAN 9%

NEW BRUNSWICK 11%

ONTARIO 8%

BRITISH COLUMBIA 7%

D $142.⁰⁰

H $49.95

G $108.⁰⁰

I $1212.⁵⁵

C $144.⁵⁰

E $79.⁷⁵

EXERCISE

A Review how to find the percent of a number.

1. In your journal, make a chart to show the sales tax for each province.

2. Calculate the sales tax, at the rate shown, for each purchase in each province.

3. Calculate the sales tax in Manitoba for a pair of jeans costing $31.70. What is the total cost?

4. Calculate the sales tax in Nova Scotia for a watch costing $33.50. Find the total cost.

A $862.⁰⁰

NEWFOUNDLAND 12%

F 399.⁹⁹

ALBERTA 0%

B $352.⁹⁹

PRINCE EDWARD ISLAND 10%

J $412.⁰⁰

QUEBEC 6½%

B Remember: Calculate the GST and necessary PST.

5. A tape costs $7.75.
   (a) Estimate the total cost in Ontario.
   (b) Calculate the total cost.

6. A pair of jeans costs $39.78.
   (a) Estimate the total cost in P.E.I.
   (b) Calculate the total cost.

7. During a shopping spree in New Brunswick, Lori purchased the following items:
   • a jacket for $49.95.
   • shoes for $62.50.
   • a video for $39.95.
   How much did she pay in all?

8. Refer to the items shown on these pages.
   (a) Find the total cost of each item in the province shown.
   (b) Calculate the total cost of the items in your province.

9. Suppose you have $330 and you want to buy the following items:
   • stereo speakers for $215.
   • 4 blank tapes for $3.95 each.
   • 4 new CDs for $13.95 each.
   In which province(s) could you make your purchase?

10. On a summer trip to a neighbouring province, Sheryl purchased the following items:
    • a provincial emblem for $11.90.
    • three postcards for $8.60.
    She paid a total of $23.99.
    (a) In which province(s) might she have made the purchases?
    (b) In which province(s) might she be going to school?

11. Samir has $1425 to purchase the following items:
    • monitor and keyboard, $625
    • hard drive, $515
    • mouse, $75
    • software, $85
    In which province(s) could he make the purchases?

12. Five nickels and five dimes are arranged as shown. You can
    • move only one coin at a time.
    • move a coin into an adjacent empty space.
    • jump over exactly one coin.
    Find the minimum number of "moves" needed to reverse the pattern.

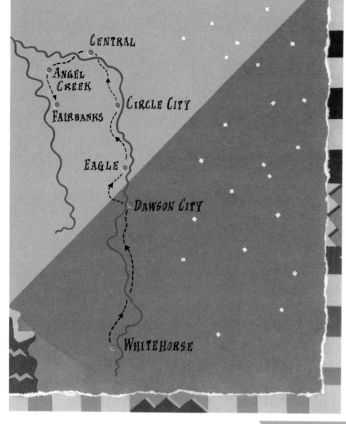

CENTRAL
ANGEL CREEK
CIRCLE CITY
FAIRBANKS
EAGLE
DAWSON CITY
WHITEHORSE

11.10 FINDING THE NUMBER

The *Yukon Quest International Sled Dog Race* traces the historic route of the Yukon pioneers. The greatest distance between any two of the six resupply points is 464 km. This is 29% of the route's total distance. How long is the route?

29% of the route is 464 km.

1% of the route is $\frac{464}{29}$ km or 16 km.

100% of the route is
100×16 km = 1600 km.

Thus, the route is 1600 km long.

Think: Check that your answer is reasonable.
30% of 1600 = 480. √ yes

EXERCISE

A In your journal, record any new skills you have learned.

1. Find the missing value.
   (a) 1% of a number is 3.
       100% of the number is ■.
   (b) 1% of a price is $5.
       100% of the price is ■.
   (c) 1% of a number is 17.2.
       100% of the number is ■.

2. Find 100% of each.
   (a) 1% of a number is 8.
   (b) 1% of a number is 15.6.
   (c) 5% of a number is 6.

3. (a) Part of a strip is shown in blue. Measure it. This strip represents 10% of the full length.
   (b) How many strips are needed to represent the whole length? What is the whole length?
   (c) Complete this sentence: 10% of ■ is 4 cm.
   (d) For each partial strip below, make up and solve a problem of your own.

4. Find the value of each.
   (a) 6% of ■ is 24 cm.
   (b) 9% of ■ is $45.
   (c) 10% of ■ is 20 L.
   (d) 25% of ■ is 50 kg.

5. In a shipment of Walkmans, 1% are broken. There are 6 broken Walkmans. How many Walkmans are there in all?

6. Of Gina's hockey cards, 1% are rare. She has 5 rare cards. How many cards does she have in all?

7. Akim has a team of 8 dogs. This is 5% of the number of dogs in the race. How many dogs are in the race?

8. Of the people surveyed, 8% did not reply. There were 42 people who did not reply. How many people in all were surveyed?

9. The mass of a table tennis ball is 2.5 g. Its mass is 10% of the mass of a golf ball. Find the mass of a golf ball.

10. In the Dog Race, D. Sawatzky won $2250. This was 3% of the prize money. How much prize money was there in all?

11. Suppose you need to find 5 more volunteers for the recycling drive. This number is 20% of the total volunteers you need. How many volunteers do you need?

12. In Ed's school, 210 students helped during Earth Day. This is 35% of all the students in the school. How many students are in Ed's school?

13. Belinda and Armand left a 15% tip of $7.50. What was the total bill? (Did you know that TIP means To Improve Performance?)

C

14. Greg grew 10% taller and then grew another 20% taller. He grew 33 cm in all. Find Greg's original height.

15. (a) To find the distance of her total trip, Jan gave this clue. "I know that 25% of 10% of the distance is 6 km." Use strips to help you find the length of the trip.
    (b) Create a similar problem that can be solved using strips. Solve your problem and compare it with others in the class.

11.11 READING CAREFULLY

To solve problems, you have to read them carefully. For example, Beavertown School is putting on the play, *A Silent Journey*.

Ticket Sales   Brent sold 50 of the 250 tickets. What percent of the total sales was Brent's?

> Think: You must find what percent one number is of another.

$$\frac{50}{250} \times 100\% = 20\%$$

Brent's sales were 20% of the total sales.

Staging   The cost of staging the play was $500. Of this, 55% was spent on costumes. What amount was spent on costumes?

> Think: You must find the percent of a number.

$$55\% \text{ of } \$500 = 0.55 \times \$500$$
$$= \$275$$

Thus, $275 was spent on costumes.

Donations   The school donated $125 for the play. This represents 25% of all donations. What was the total amount of donations?

> Think: You must find the whole amount.

25% of donations is $125.

1% is $\$\frac{125}{25}$.

100% of donations is $100 \times \$\frac{125}{25} = 100 \times \$5$
$$= \$500.$$

Thus, the total amount of donations was $500.

A Remember: To solve a problem ask yourself:

• What am I given?   • What am I asked to find?

1. Calculate. Is your answer reasonable?
   (a) What percent is 45 of 255?   (b) Find 5% of 600 students.
   (c) 15% of what number is 66?   (d) 50% of what amount is $37?

2. Calculate. Check your answers.
   (a) 75% of $335 is what amount?   (b) What percent is 10 L of 45 L?
   (c) 125 g is 35% of what mass?   (d) 75% of $325 is what amount?

B Use a calculator.

3. Tom wants to raise money for charity. He collects $75. This is 20% of his goal. What is Tom's goal?

4. At Olympic Stadium, 85% of the seats were full. There were 37 500 people. What is the seating capacity of Olympic Stadium?

5. Lesley was at bat 120 times last season. She got 35 hits. What percent of the time did she get a hit?

6. Did you know that air is 78% nitrogen? Calculate the amount of nitrogen in 6.5 m³ of air. Round your answer to one decimal place.

7. At the opening of the play, Brent sold 77 raffle tickets. This represents 22% of all the raffle tickets. Find the total number of raffle tickets.

8. Bob wanted to lose 8 kg. He had lost 3 kg. What percent had he lost?

9. During intermission, 55% of all the soft drinks available were sold. There were 480 soft drinks. How many were sold?

10. Of the 365 people at a play, about 35% were students. How many were students?

11. Ted has 15 coins worth a total of $1. What percent of the coins are pennies?

12. Refer to the items at the bottom of this page. Work with a partner to create a problem using a skill with percent for each item. Compare your problem with others in your class.

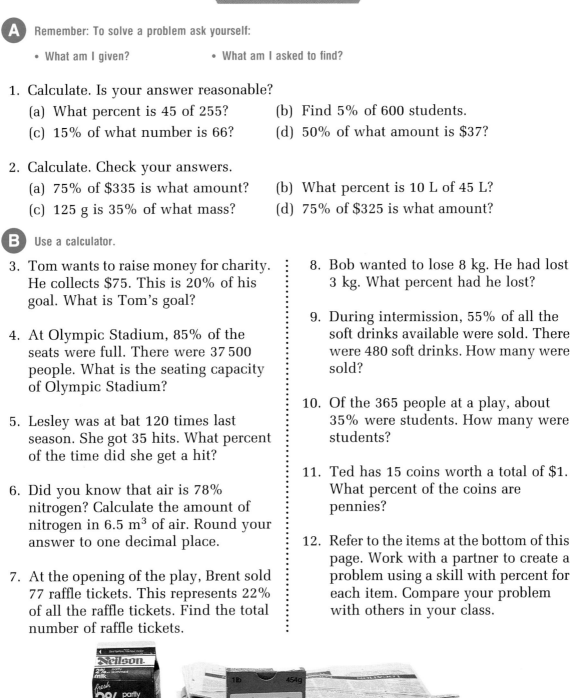

11.12 SIMPLE INTEREST

When you buy a Canada Savings Bond, you are in fact lending the government money. The government then pays you for borrowing your money.

- The amount you invested is the **principal**.
- The money paid to you is the **interest**.
- The interest paid to you is a percent of the principal called the **rate of interest**.

If you buy a $1000 Canada Savings Bond and it pays you 10% simple interest per year, how much interest will you receive at the end of 1 year?

Principal (amount invested)	$1000	Think: 10% of $1000
Rate of interest	10%	$= 0.10 \times \$1000$
Amount of time	1 year	$= \$100$

After 1 year, you will receive $100 in interest.

After 3 years, interest paid will be $300.   Think: 3 years × $100 = $300

After 6 months, interest paid will be $50.   Think: 0.5 years × $100 = $50

The calculations suggest the following pattern to calculate simple interest.

Interest = principal × rate of interest × length of time (in years)

$I = P \times r \times t$ (in years)

You can use the pattern to calculate interest on money borrowed.

Ivor needed $1150.00 to buy a computer. He borrowed this money at a simple interest rate of 11.5% for 6 months. At the end of 6 months, what was the total cost of his loan?

$$I = Prt$$
$$= (1150.00)(0.115)(0.5)$$
$$= 66.125$$
$$\doteq 66.13$$

Total cost = Principal + Interest
$$= \$1150 + \$66.13$$
$$= \$1216.13$$

Thus, the total cost of Ivor's loan was $1216.13.

CANADA SAVINGS BONDS

A wonderful place for your savings to grow.

Canada

Buy yours from Oct. 17 to N

LES OBLIGATIONS D'EPARGNE DU CANADA

Un moyen par excellence pour faire fructifier vos épargnes.

1 1er nov.

A Review how to calculate simple interest.

1. Calculate the simple interest paid on each deposit.

	Amount of Deposit	Rate of Interest	Time
(a)	$250	6.0%	1 year
(b)	$520	8.5%	0.5 year
(c)	$700	$7\frac{1}{2}$%	$2\frac{1}{2}$ years

2. Calculate the simple interest paid on each loan.

	Amount of Loan	Rate of Interest	Time
(a)	$960	12%	2 years
(b)	$580	10.5%	4 years
(c)	$450	$11\frac{1}{2}$%	6 months

B Estimate first. Then calculate.

3. Find the simple interest payable on each of these loans.

  (a) $45 at 10% per year for 1 year

  (b) $125 at 12% per year for 6 months

4. Basia cashed $150 worth of savings bonds. She had them for one year. The bonds paid simple interest at 7% per year. How much money did she receive?

5. Mark cashed a $500 savings bond. He had the bond for 1.5 years. The bond paid simple interest at 7% per year. How much money did he receive?

6. Research the interest rates paid on Canada Savings Bonds. Create, and solve, a problem of your own using the interest rates.

7. Suppose you borrow $3325 to buy a computer and printer. You plan to pay the money back in 8 months. The interest rate is 6.25% per year. What is the total cost of the computer?

8. Al borrowed $2575 for a business. He plans to pay the money back in 18 months. The interest rate is 12.25% per year. What is the total cost of the loan?

9. Work in groups. Twelve pieces of a puzzle are shown. Nine of them can be used to make a circle. Copy the pieces. Which nine will you need?

11.13 PROBLEM SOLVING: MAKING A PROFIT

Glena bought a 1949 Canadian Silver dollar in mint condition for $20. Years later, she sold it for $175. Express the profit she made as a percent.

The profit she made is found as follows.

Original purchase price: $20
Amount of profit: $155
Profit as a percent: $\frac{\$155}{\$20} \times 100\% = 775\%$
Glena earned a profit of 775%.

This coin commemorates Newfoundland becoming part of Canada.

EXERCISE

 Remember: Profit is the increase in value of an item.

1. Calculate the profit as a percent.
   (a) Original cost of coin: $12   (b) Original cost of stamp: $600
       Increase in price: $3   Increase in price: $450

2. Suppose you bought a 1948 dime for $15. Later, you sold it for $750. Express the profit as a percent.

3. Bob bought a commemoration stamp for $105. He later sold it for $468. Express the profit Bob made as a percent.

4. (a) Find a picture of the most valuable Canadian coin. What is its value?
   (b) Suppose you originally purchased the coin for $50. Express the profit you would make as a percent.

5. (a) Work with a partner. Research some special Canadian coins and stamps. Find out why each was issued.
   (b) Find the current value of each special coin and stamp. Create a problem using the values and compare your problem with others in your class.

Businesses often use computers. For example, they use computers to calculate prices for a sale and wages for employees.

- A manufacturer suggests a **list price** of $400 for a stereo.
- The store decides to sell the stereo at less than the list price. For example, you could be offered a **rate of discount** of 10%. Thus, the **selling price** is found as follows.

Discount = rate of discount × list price   Selling price = list price − discount
    = 10% of $400   = $400 − $40
    = 0.10 × $400   = $360
    = $40

- The sales clerk may be paid a **commission**.
  The commission paid is a percent of the selling price.

This program calculates the selling price and commission paid on any item.

```
10 INPUT ''THE LIST PRICE IS''; L
20 INPUT ''THE RATE OF DISCOUNT AS A DECIMAL IS''; R
30 INPUT ''THE RATE OF COMMISSION AS A DECIMAL IS''; C
40 LET D = L * R
50 LET DR = L - D
60 LET CO = DR * C
70 PRINT ''THE SELLING PRICE IS $''; DR
80 PRINT ''THE COMMISSION EARNED IS $''; CO
90 END
```

1. To test a program, you can RUN it using known data. Use the program to
   (a) calculate the selling price of the stereo above.
   (b) calculate the commission paid if Josie earns 5% commission.
   (c) Is the computer's output reasonable?

2. Videos sell regularly for $23.95. At a sale, a 25% discount is given. Wendy earns 4.5% commission on all sales. Use the program to calculate the selling price and commission.

3. Find data of your own and create problems using the data. Use the computer program above to solve your problems.

CHAPTER REVIEW

1. Write each of the following as a fraction and a decimal number.
   (a) 30% (b) 75% (c) 80% (d) 45%

2. Write each as a percent.
   (a) $\frac{4}{5}$ (b) $\frac{9}{10}$ (c) $4\frac{3}{4}$ (d) $\frac{13}{20}$

3. Estimate the percent of each farm that is plowed.
   (a)
   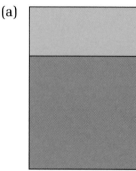
   (b)
   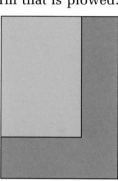

4. Recently, 75% of the kettles made were recalled. If 120 kettles were made, how many were recalled?

5. Amanda and Claire received the following marks:
   Amanda: 43 out of 50   Claire: 34 out of 40
   Who has the greater percent?

6. A $1000 savings bond paid 6.25% simple interest per year. It was cashed 6 months after purchase.
   (a) How much interest was earned?
   (b) How much cash was received in all?

7. Terri used 80% of a tape to record a k.d. lang concert. The concert lasted 2.5 h. How many hours are available on the tape?

8. Last week, 62 players tried out for the hockey team. Only 22 players will be selected. What percent of the players will make the team?

THINKING ABOUT

Select a question. How would you explain the process you used to a Grade 7 student?

Describe two ways you can determine whether your answer is correct?

Throughout the chapter, you worked with others to solve problems. In your journal, describe how well you learned working with others.

MAKING CONNECTIONS

Refer to the opening pages of the chapter and review what you felt was meant by 2% milk and a 10% discount.

(a) How accurate was your understanding?

(b) How can you improve what you wrote?

(c) Create a problem based on the opening pages. Compare your problem with others in your class.

In your journal, describe the types of problems you still find difficult.

Can you explain in your own words how you got each solution?

Write all the clue words you used to help you solve the problems.

MATH JOURNAL

Have you ever had an "Aha!" experience, or felt the mental "click" that occurs when the reasons for a process fall neatly into place? In your journal, write a short paragraph about any such "clicks" you have had this year. Describe how you felt at the time.

SELF EVALUATION

1. Write each as a decimal number and a fraction.

   (a) 15%   (b) 35%   (c) 105%   (d) 245%

2. Write each of the following as a percent.

   (a) $\dfrac{4}{25}$ (b) $\dfrac{3}{30}$ (c) $\dfrac{45}{75}$ (d) $\dfrac{24}{64}$

3. In a class of 32 students, 4 are left-handed. What percent of the students are left-handed?

4. Calculate.

   (a) 55% of 8 cm   (b) 32% of 50 L

5. Calculate.

   (a) 60% of what amount is $20?

   (b) Find 12.5% of a 4 L jug.

   (c) What percent of a $600 loan does $150 repay?

6. Carla sold 16% of the tickets to the dance. There were 175 tickets printed. How many tickets did Carla sell?

7. The square shown to the right represents 100%. Draw diagrams to represent 50% and 140%.

8. A painting was originally purchased for $18 000. Its value increased to 850% of its original value. What is the current value of the painting?

9. Nancy purchased the following items in Saskatchewan:
   • a television for $295.
   • a VCR for $375.
   • a bicycle for $175.
   What will she pay in all for her purchases including PST and GST?

12 EXPLORING GEOMETRY

Each picture illustrates an important development in the field of geometry. In your journal, write a short paragraph to explain why you think each is important.

Did you know that this device can help you measure distance and direction?

Did you know the Aztecs were one of the first people to try to create a calendar?

Did you know that Archimedes often drew figures in the sand?

Did you know that Pythagoras used a rope with knots to explore a relationship?

363

EXPLORATION ①   *Work in a Group*

1. (a) Use any three objects shown above. Trace the objects to create a design with circles, similar to the ones shown. Shade your design.

   (b) In your journal, record the instructions for making your design.

   (c) What patterns are created by the circles?

   (d) For what type of company would your design make an appropriate logo? Create a name for the company.

2. (a) Create another design using three circular objects. Shade your design.

   (b) Repeat parts (b), (c), and (d) of Question 1 for your design from (a).

3. The design to the right is created using circular objects and straight lines.

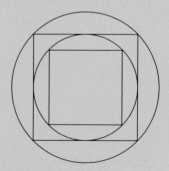

   (a) Make a copy of this design in your journal.

   (b) What patterns do you notice in your designs?

   (c) Add straight lines to each of your designs from Questions 1 and 2. What patterns do you notice?

   (d) How are your new designs alike?
       How are they different?

EXPLORATION ② *Work in a Group*

4. (a) Use pipe cleaners and straws to construct the triangle shown to the right. Measure the angles. What do you notice about the angles?

   (b) Measure the sides. What do you notice?

   (c) Make a smaller triangle than the one shown. Repeat parts (a) and (b) for your triangle.

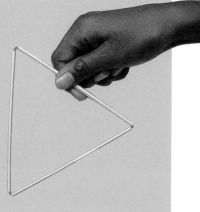

5. Use your triangle from Question 4. Make one change in the triangle. Measure the angles and side lengths. What do you notice?

6. Use your triangle from Question 4. Make two changes in the triangle. Measure the angles and side lengths. What do you notice?

EXPLORATION ③ *Work in a Group*

7. (a) Cut out two strips of cardboard and attach the ends using paper fasteners as shown. Open and close the strips to create different angles.

   (b) Use your angle-maker to help you copy angles in the classroom. Which angles have the same measure?

   (c) Use your angle-maker to make exact copies of the angles shown below. (Angles with the same measure are called **congruent angles**.)

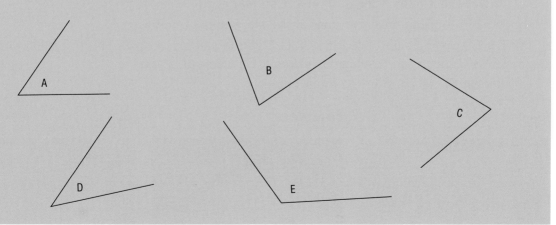

Step 1   *Step 2*   *Step 3*

INVESTIGATION ① *Work in a Group*

1. (a) The photographs at the top of the page show the steps to **bisect a line segment**. What does it mean to bisect a line segment?

   (b) In your journal, describe each of the steps shown above.

   (c) Draw any line and label it AB. Bisect AB. Check your work.

   (d) The photographs above also show the steps to construct a **perpendicular bisector**. What does it mean to construct a perpendicular bisector?

   (e) Describe the steps needed to construct a perpendicular bisector.

   (f) Draw any line and label it AB. Construct a perpendicular bisector to AB. Label the perpendicular bisector PQ. Check your work.

INVESTIGATION ② *Work with a Partner*

2. (a) The photographs at the bottom of the page show the steps to **bisect an angle**. What does it mean to bisect an angle?

   (b) In your journal, describe each of the steps shown below.

   (c) Draw any angle and label it ∠ABC. Use the steps you described to bisect ∠ABC. Name the new angles formed. Check your work.

   (d) Repeat the steps to bisect other angles.

Step 1   *Step 2*   *Step 3*

Step 1	Step 2	Step 3

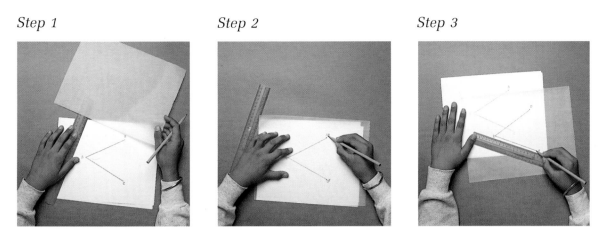

INVESTIGATION ③ *Work in Small Groups*

3. The pictures above show the steps used to **copy** an angle. In your journal, describe each of the steps.

4. (a) Draw any angle and label it ∠ABC.
   (b) Use the steps to make an exact copy of ∠ABC. Label the copy ∠DEF.
   (c) Check your work. Is ∠ABC = ∠DEF?
   (d) Repeat the steps above for other angles.

INVESTIGATION ④ *Work Together*

5. Find examples of angles and straight lines in newspapers and magazines.
   (a) Copy and bisect each angle.
   (b) Draw the perpendicular bisector for each line.

Did you know that Curtis Hibbert is one of Canada's foremost gymnasts? One of the events in which he competes is the parallel bars. In your journal, describe how you can determine if the bars are parallel.

EXPLORATION ① **Work with a Partner**

1. The two lines shown to the right are **parallel**. Two lines are parallel if they can be extended forever and never meet.

   (a) How can you use tracing paper to make a copy of the parallel lines?

   (b) Make a copy of the parallel lines.

2. (a) Describe how you might use a straight edge to construct
      • two parallel lines. • three parallel lines.

   (b) Construct the lines in (a).

3. (a) Make a copy of the logo shown.

   (b) Use a straight edge to construct a logo that includes parallel lines.

   (c) Describe a company that could use your design as their advertising logo.

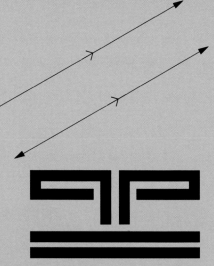

4. Use the Yellow Pages to find logos that appear to use parallel lines.

   (a) Make a copy of one of the logos. Shade it.

   (b) In your journal, describe how you can use a straight edge to determine whether the lines are parallel.

   (c) Make an exact copy of another logo. What skills with parallel lines did you use?

EXPLORATION ②   *Work Together*

5. A line intersecting parallel lines is called a **transversal**. Two parallel lines, a transversal, and the angles formed are shown.

   (a) Which angles appear to be equal to angle ①?

   (b) Construct an exact copy of angle ①. Put your copy on top of your choices in (a). Were your choices correct?

   (c) Find other angles equal to angle ①. Measure to check.

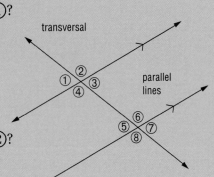

6. (a) Which angles appear to be equal to angle ②?

   (b) Construct an exact copy of angle ②. Put your copy on top of your choices in (a). Were your choices correct?

   (c) Find other angles equal to angle ②.

7. Draw your own parallel lines and transversal.

   (a) Identify all angles that are equal on your diagram.

   (b) Do you see any other relationships? Compare your relationships with others in your class. How are they alike? How are they different?

EXPLORATION ③   *Work with a Partner*

8. (a) Do the red lines shown below appear to be parallel? How can you check?

   (b) Create a diagram with a similar effect. Compare it with others in your class. How can you check if the others use parallel lines?

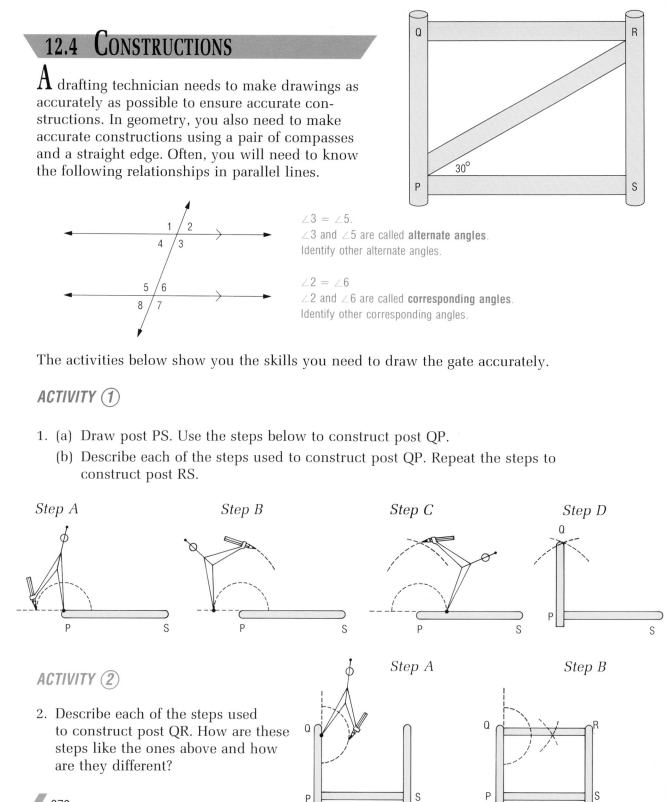

12.4 CONSTRUCTIONS

A drafting technician needs to make drawings as accurately as possible to ensure accurate constructions. In geometry, you also need to make accurate constructions using a pair of compasses and a straight edge. Often, you will need to know the following relationships in parallel lines.

∠3 = ∠5.
∠3 and ∠5 are called **alternate angles**.
Identify other alternate angles.

∠2 = ∠6
∠2 and ∠6 are called **corresponding angles**.
Identify other corresponding angles.

The activities below show you the skills you need to draw the gate accurately.

ACTIVITY ①

1. (a) Draw post PS. Use the steps below to construct post QP.
   (b) Describe each of the steps used to construct post QP. Repeat the steps to construct post RS.

Step A   *Step B*   *Step C*   *Step D*

ACTIVITY ②

Step A   *Step B*

2. Describe each of the steps used to construct post QR. How are these steps like the ones above and how are they different?

A Review your skills with a pair of compasses and a straight edge.

1. In each diagram, a construction has been performed.

   (a) In your journal, write the steps used in each construction.

   (b) Complete each construction.

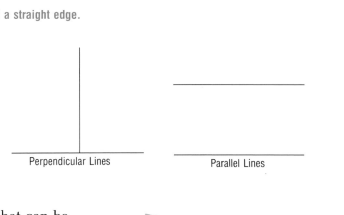

Perpendicular Lines   Parallel Lines

 B Use your construction skills.

2. (a) Choose three strips of cardboard that can be used to create a triangle.

   (b) In your journal, write the steps you would use to construct a triangle with these sides.

   (c) Use your steps from (b) to construct the triangle.

   (d) Have your partner follow your instructions to create the triangle. How are the triangles alike? How are they different?

3. (a) Choose four strips of cardboard that can be used to create a rectangle.

   (b) In your journal, write the steps you would use to construct a rectangle with these sides.

   (c) Use your steps from (b) to construct the rectangle.

   (d) Have your partner follow your instructions to create the rectangle. How are the rectangles alike? How are they different?

4. For each of the following, make an exact copy.

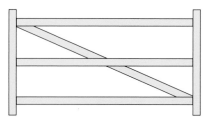

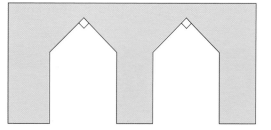

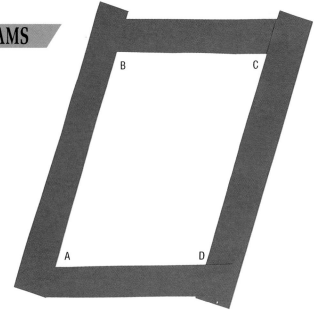

Strips of paper are used to create the parallelogram shown. A **parallelogram** is so named because the opposite sides are parallel. In the activities below, you will explore other properties of a parallelogram.

ACTIVITY ① *Work in a Group*

1. Use the parallelogram shown.
   (a) Measure ∠A and ∠C; ∠B and ∠D. What do you notice?
   (b) Measure AD and BC; AB and DC. What do you notice?

2. (a) Trace and cut out the parallelogram shown.
   (b) Fold the parallelogram along each diagonal. Label the point of intersection of the diagonals as E.
   (c) Measure AE and CE; DE and BE. What do you notice?

3. Use strips of cardboard to create a parallelogram of your own.
   (a) Repeat Questions 1 and 2 for your parallelogram.
   (b) Summarize all your observations about the properties of a parallelogram.

ACTIVITY ② *Work in a Group*

4. (a) Use the steps below to create a parallelogram with a special property.
   (b) Measure each side length of your parallelogram. What do you notice?
   (c) Draw its diagonals. Label the point of intersection as E. Measure ∠AED, ∠AEB, ∠BEC, and ∠CED. What do you notice?
   (d) Measure AE, BE, CE, and DE. What do you notice?
   (e) Repeat parts (a) to (d) for other special parallelograms.

Step 1

Step 2

Step 3

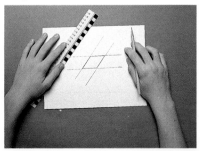

12.6 PROBLEM SOLVING: USING A DIAGRAM

To solve some problems, it helps to sketch a diagram and record the information on it. For example, to find the area covered by a picture frame, the diagram to the right can be drawn.

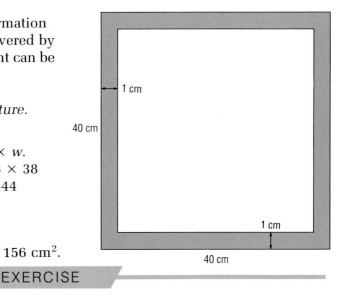

Area of frame and picture.

Use $A = l \times w$.
$= 40 \times 40$
$= 1600$

Area of picture.

Use $A = l \times w$.
$= 38 \times 38$
$= 1444$

Think: Subtract. $1600 \text{ cm}^2 - 1444 \text{ cm}^2 = 156 \text{ cm}^2$

Thus, the area of the picture frame is 156 cm².

EXERCISE

B   Use your *Problem Solving Plan*.

1. (a) What is the area covered by this picture frame?

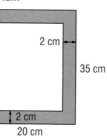

(b) Find the area of picture frames that you find at home or at school.

2. How many parallelograms are on the following grid? (Hint: Trace the figure and the various parallelograms.)

3. Five stamps are connected in different ways as shown below.

(a) In how many ways can you connect five stamps?

(b) Repeat part (a) using tiles.

(c) How are your answers in (a) and (b) alike? How are they different? Give reasons for any differences.

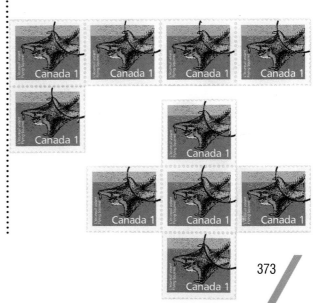

373

Try the following activities to determine how observant you are. Work with a partner to complete each activity.

ACTIVITY ① *Remembering Visually*

Step 1 Look at the shape to the right for 5 s.

Step 2 Turn the page and describe the shape.

Step 3 Compare your description with that of your partner. Decide who gave the more accurate description.

Step 4 Repeat the steps above for the other two shapes. Allow 1 min to look at all the shapes simultaneously.

Step 5 Repeat Steps 1 to 4 for shapes of your own.

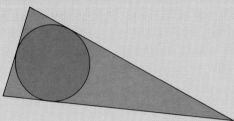
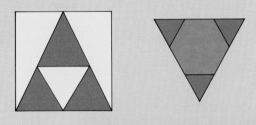

ACTIVITY ② *Describing Visually*

Step 1 Look at the picture below to the left for 30 s.

Step 2 Turn the page. Write a description in your journal.

Step 3 Compare your description with that of your partner. Decide who gave the more accurate description.

Step 4 Repeat the steps above using the picture to the right.

Step 5 Repeat Steps 1 to 3 using pictures of your own.

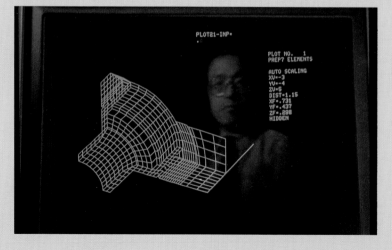

ACTIVITY ③ *What's My Line?*

Shown below are two cartoons with words missing. In your journal, write words to complete the cartoons. Compare your version with others in your class. Then, create a cartoon of your own. Compare it with others in your class.

1.

2.

In the following, you will explore triangles that have the same size and shape and triangles that have the same shape but not the same size. Record in your journal any relationships you see.

EXPLORATION ① *Work with a Partner*

1. (a) Use tracing paper to copy triangle A.
   (b) Which other triangles have the same size and shape as triangle A?
   (c) What do you notice about the measure of the sides and angles of the triangles from part (b)?
   (d) Repeat the above for triangle B.

2. Use your copy of triangle A.
   (a) Which triangles have the same shape but are not the same size as triangle A?
   (b) What do you notice about the measure of the angles of each triangle from part (a)?
   (c) Repeat parts (a) and (b) for triangle B.

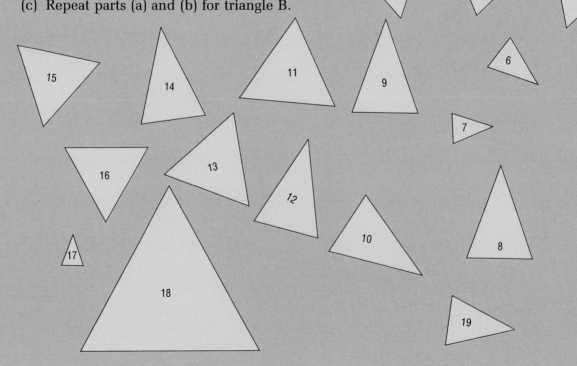

Work with a Partner

3. (a) Use pipe cleaners and straws to construct △ABC with the measurements shown.

   (b) Compare your △ABC with others in your class. What do you notice?

   (c) Can you construct a different triangle with the same measures? Give reasons for your answer.

   A, 13.0 cm, 12.5 cm, B, 13.5 cm, C

4. (a) Use pipe cleaners and straws to create a triangle with your own measures of sides.

   (b) Switch triangles with your partner, and copy your partner's triangle.

   (c) Can you construct a different triangle with the same measures? Explain.

5. (a) Use pipe cleaners and straws to construct △XYZ with the measurements shown.

   (b) Compare your △XYZ with others in your class. What do you notice?

   (c) Can you construct a different triangle with the same measures? Why?

   X, 9.5 cm, 55°, Z, 13.5 cm, Y

6. (a) Use pipe cleaners and straws to create a triangle with your own measures of two sides and an angle. Refer to Question 5.

   (b) Switch triangles with your partner, and copy your partner's triangle.

   (c) Can you construct a different triangle with the same measures? Why?

7. (a) Use pipe cleaners and straws to construct △DEF with the measurements shown.

   (b) Compare your △DEF with others in your class. What do you notice?

   (c) Can you construct a different triangle with the same measures? Why?

   D, 106°, 32°, F, 8.5 cm, E

8. (a) Use pipe cleaners and straws to create a triangle with your own measures of two angles and a side. Refer to Question 7.

   (b) Switch triangles with your partner, and copy your partner's triangle.

   (c) Can you construct a different triangle with the same measures? Why?

12.9 CONGRUENT TRIANGLES

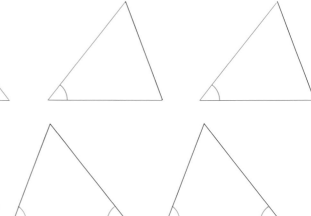

Every triangle has six parts — three sides and three angles. To construct a given triangle, you do not need to know the measures of all six parts. Knowing the measures of three certain parts will enable you to construct a unique triangle. All triangles drawn with the same measures are **congruent**.

The three parts you need were explored in the previous section and are summarized below.

Conclusion 1 *Side-Side-Side*
If three sides of a triangle are known, you can construct congruent triangles.

Conclusion 2 *Side-Angle-Side*
If two sides and the contained angle of a triangle are known, you can construct congruent triangles.

Conclusion 3 *Angle-Side-Angle*
If two angles and a contained side of a triangle are known, you can construct congruent triangles.

EXERCISE

 Review your skills with constructions.

1. Refer to the triangles in the previous section. Measure to decide which triangles are congruent to triangles A and B.

2. Measure to decide which triangle(s) is congruent to triangle B.

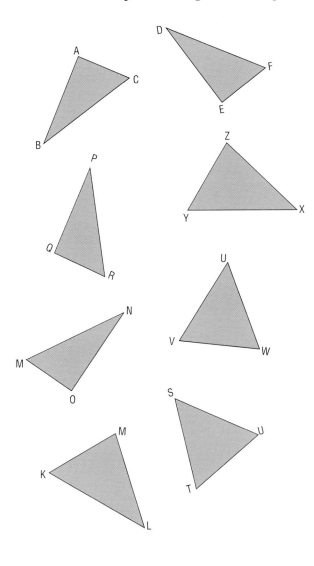

B Before you construct a triangle, make a sketch.

3. Find each pair of congruent triangles.

4. A triangle has these measures:
   ∠H = 35°, ∠J = 45°, HJ = 5 cm.
   (a) Draw a sketch of the triangle.
   (b) Construct the triangle.
   (c) Measure the remaining parts.
   (d) Why is HJ called a contained side?

5. A triangle has these measures:
   JK = 5 cm, ∠K = 90°, KL = 6 cm.
   (a) Draw a sketch of the triangle.
   (b) Construct the triangle.
   (c) Measure the remaining parts.
   (d) Why is ∠K called a contained angle?

6. (a) Cut a strip of paper 40 cm long and 5 cm wide.
   (b) Cut off part of one end so that it is not square.
   (c) Bisect the angle formed by side B and the cut edge by folding.
   (d) Now bisect the angle formed by side A and the fold in (c).
   (e) Repeat the steps above until the creases become the same length.
   (f) Measure the angles formed by the sides and the creases. What angle have you approximated?

Did you know that this building is gold plated? Estimate the surface area of the building. Estimate the cost to gold plate the building.

Look at the picture. How many square corners do you see? A square corner is an example of a **right angle**. A right angle is an angle whose measure is 90°.

Any triangle that contains a right angle is called a **right triangle**. A right triangle is shown below.

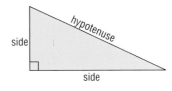

Pythagoras studied the properties of right triangles. In the explorations that follow, you will also study some of the properties of right triangles.

INVESTIGATION ① *Work Together*

1. (a) Cut straws with these lengths:
      3 cm, 4 cm, 5 cm, 8 cm, 7 cm,
      12 cm, 13 cm, 15 cm, and 17 cm.

   (b) Make as many triangles as you can using the straws.

   (c) Identify those triangles that have right angles. Trace a copy of each triangle.

2. Use a copy of a right triangle from Question 1.

   (a) Draw a square on each side of the triangle. Find the area of each square.

   (b) Do you notice any relationship among the areas? What is it?

3. Pythagoras drew a square on each side and the hypotenuse of a right triangle as shown.

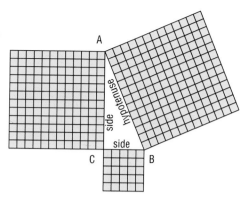

(a) Calculate the area of the square drawn on each side.

(b) Calculate the area of the square drawn on the hypotenuse.

(c) How does the area of the square drawn on the hypotenuse seem to relate to the areas of the squares drawn on the sides?

4. The side lengths of various right triangles are shown in the chart.

(a) Draw each right triangle using the side lengths given. Measure the hypotenuse.

(b) Draw a square on each side of the right triangle. Find the area of each square.

(c) How does the area of the square drawn on the hypotenuse seem to relate to the areas of the squares drawn on the sides?

Side 1	Side 2	Hypotenuse
4.0 cm	3.0 cm	?
8.0 cm	6.0 cm	?
6.0 cm	3.0 cm	?
3.5 cm	2.6 cm	?
4.8 cm	5.6 cm	?

INVESTIGATION ③ *Write Together*

5. Review all the results you found in Investigations ① and ②.

(a) Make a summary of all observations and relationships you found.

(b) Use an example to help you show any relationships.

WORKING TOGETHER

Did you know that quilts often have squares in their designs? The squares can be cut along the diagonal to form right triangles. A quilt design called the *cactus basket* is shown to the left.

(a) Measure to find the length of each side in each right triangle.

(b) Find the length of the hypotenuse in each right triangle.

(c) What relationships do you see in the quilt?

(d) Why do you think the quilt is named cactus basket?

(e) Design a quilt of your own and name it. Have others in your class answer parts (a) to (d) for your quilt design.

12.11 THE PYTHAGOREAN RELATION

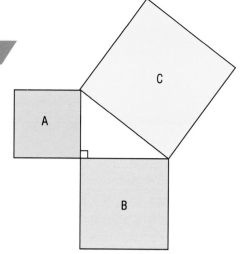

Throughout your work, you have repeated the following steps many times.

Step 1 You learn a concept.
Step 2 You practise the concept.
Step 3 You use the concept to solve problems.

In your work on properties of right triangles, you found this relationship:

$$\text{area of square A} + \text{area of square B} = \text{area of square C}$$

$$a^2 + b^2 = c^2$$

Think: Use symbols to represent each area.
Area of Square A can be written as a^2.
Area of Square B can be written as b^2.
Area of Square C can be written as c^2.

The relationship above is called the **Pythagorean Relation**. It can be stated as follows: "In any right triangle, the square of the hypotenuse is equal to the sum of the squares of the other two sides."

The Pythagorean Relation can be used to help you solve problems.

Jon sailed a boat from the marina 30 km north and then 40 km east. How far was he from the marina?

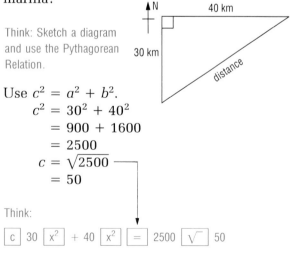

Think: Sketch a diagram and use the Pythagorean Relation.

Use $c^2 = a^2 + b^2$.
$$c^2 = 30^2 + 40^2$$
$$= 900 + 1600$$
$$= 2500$$
$$c = \sqrt{2500}$$
$$= 50$$

Think:

| c | 30 | x^2 | + 40 | x^2 | = | 2500 | $\sqrt{\ }$ | 50 |

Thus, Jon was 50 km from the marina.

A Use a calculator.

1. The sides of a right triangle are shown. Use the Pythagorean relation to find ■.

   (a) $3^2 + 4^2 = ■^2$ (b) $5^2 + 12^2 = ■^2$ (c) $15^2 + 8^2 = ■^2$

2. Calculate the length of the hypotenuse in each.

   (a)   (b)   (c)

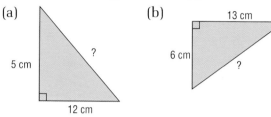

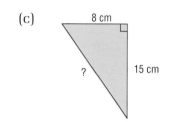

B Draw a diagram to help you.

3. (a) Jean measured the sides of a right triangle to be 6 cm and 8 cm. Find the length of the hypotenuse.

   (b) Tanya measured the sides of a right triangle to be 24 cm and 26 cm. What is the measure of the hypotenuse?

4. Jocelyn sailed her boat from the marina 12 km north and 16 km east. How far is she from the marina?

5. A gate is shown below with the support beam sketched. Find the length of the support beam.

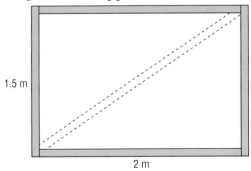

6. (a) Find the length of the throw from home plate to second base.

   (b) Brad plays shortstop. He is exactly halfway between second and third base. How far does the ball travel to first base when Brad throws it?

7. Work together.

   (a) Draw any circle and a diameter.

   (b) Draw a triangle with the diameter as one side and with all three vertices on the circle. What do you notice about the triangle?

   (c) Repeat (a) and (b) for other circles.

   (d) Suppose you are given a right triangle. How can you draw a circle that passes through its vertices?

383

You have learned that figures that have the same shape and the same size are called congruent figures. Figures that have the same shape but not the same size are called **similar** figures.

EXPLORATION ①   *Work with Others*

1. Pairs of similar triangles are shown on the dot paper below.
   (a) In △ABC and △DEF, one pair of corresponding sides is AC and DF. Measure the corresponding sides of each pair of triangles.
   (b) Find the ratios of the measures of the corresponding sides. In △ABC and △DEF, the ratios are $\frac{AC}{DF}$, $\frac{AB}{DE}$, and $\frac{BC}{EF}$.
   (c) What do you notice about the ratios of corresponding sides in similar triangles?

2. Draw pairs of triangles of your own on dot paper.
   (a) Have others in your class determine whether your triangles are similar.
   (b) Have them describe how they obtained their answers in (a).

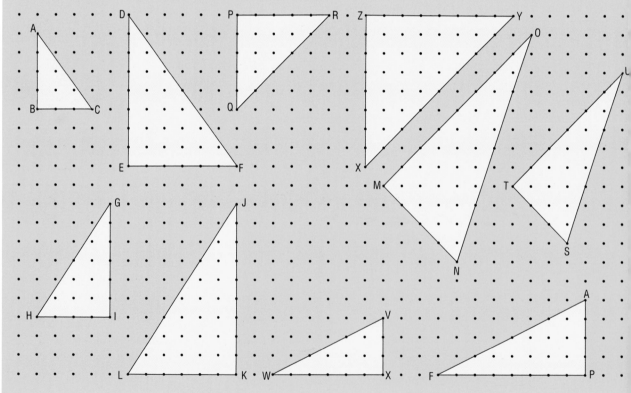

EXPLORATION ② *Work with Others*

3. Did you know that you can determine the approximate time of day by looking at your shadow? Follow these steps to find out how.

   Step 1 On a sunny day, hold a metre stick upright. Measure the length of the shadow of the stick each hour. Record the time of day.

Length of Shadow	Length of Shadow / Length of Metre Stick	Time of Day

   Step 2 Complete the chart using the lengths you have measured.

   Step 3 Stand upright and have a partner measure the length of your shadow.

   Step 4 How many times longer is your shadow than your height? About what time is it?

   Step 5 Use your chart during the week to tell time. Describe how you do it.

4. In your journal, explain why this method for telling time depends on which season it is.

12.13 USING SIMILAR TRIANGLES

To solve problems with similar triangles, use the same steps as you did with the Pythagorean Relation.

Step 1 You explore and summarize relationships in similar triangles.

In any pair of similar triangles,
- corresponding angles are congruent.
  $\angle A = \angle D; \angle B = \angle E; \angle C = \angle F$
- the ratios of the measures of corresponding sides are equal.

$$\frac{AB}{DE} = \frac{BC}{EF} = \frac{AC}{DF}$$

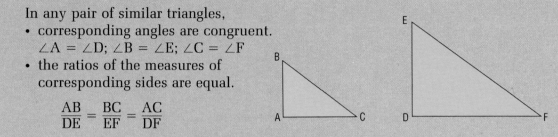

Step 2 You practise the concept learned. Practice is given in the exercise.

Step 3 You use the concept to solve problems like the following.

Jacqueline and Steve wanted to know the height of a flagpole. They measured Steve's shadow and the flagpole's shadow and drew the sketch shown below. Find the height of the flagpole.

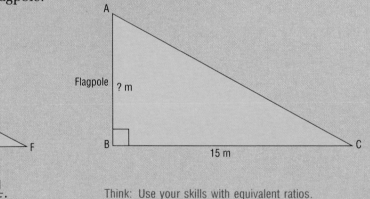

From the sketch, $\frac{2}{3} = \frac{\blacksquare}{15}$.

The ratio can be written as $\frac{2}{3} = \frac{10}{15}$.

Thus, AB = 10.

The flagpole is 10 m high.

Think: Use your skills with equivalent ratios.

$3 \times 5 = 15 \qquad 2 \times 5 = 10$

A Review your skills with ratios.

1. Find the missing measure in each pair of similar triangles.

(a)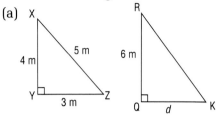

(b)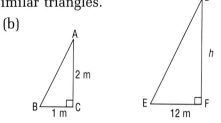

B Use your *Problem Solving Plan*.

2. The height, h, in metres is the altitude of a kite. Angles B and E are congruent. Find h.

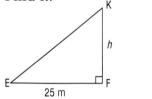

3. Sandra and Samfer worked together to find these measurements. Find the height, h, of the tree.

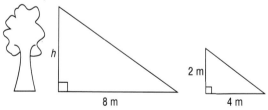

4. The triangles shown are similar, with $\angle A = \angle E$, $\angle DCE = \angle ACB$. Calculate the missing distance to find the width, w, of the river.

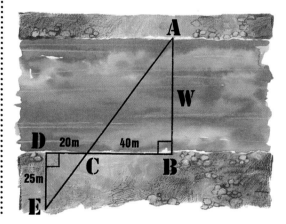

MAKING CONNECTIONS

Legend suggests that Thales once calculated the height of a pyramid without ever touching the pyramid. Use your library.

    (a) Describe how Thales measured the height of the pyramid.

    (b) Compare Thales' process to the one used by Jacqueline and Steven. How are they alike? How are they different?

12.14 PROBLEM SOLVING

Sometimes manipulatives that you find around your home can be used to help you solve problems. You need to use your imagination to see how it can be done. Try the problems in the exercise. Once you have finished, write in your journal about how you feel when solving problems with familiar manipulatives.

EXERCISE

B Review your estimating skills.

1. Triangles can be constructed using toothpicks and marshmallows.

   (a) Describe how you can construct such a triangle.

   (b) Construct the triangle. What kind of triangle is it?

2. You can use popsicle sticks and pipe cleaners to construct the instrument below.

   (a) Describe how the instrument can be used to construct parallel lines and perpendicular lines.

   (b) Make the instrument. Use it to verify your answer from (a).

   (c) How do you think a similar instrument can be used by an architect?

3. Use a strip of tape from an adding machine or a cash register.

   (a) Fold the strip of paper in half.

   (b) Open up the strip. Place it flat on your desk. Does the crease point up or down?

   (c) Close the strip and fold it in half again. Write a pattern to show whether creases are up or down.

   (d) Repeat part (c) until you see a pattern. Predict the pattern after ten such folds.

4. Work in a group. Label 15 ping pong balls from 1 to 15. Arrange 12 of them in an equilateral triangle and place 3 in the middle so that the sum in the middle and the sum along each side of the triangle is 39.

5. Vanita arranged 12 red checkers and one black checker. The red checkers were arranged in six rows and the black checker was placed to be the same distance from each row. Show the arrangement.

A computer is a machine that can store and manipulate data using a *list* of *instructions*. It needs both **hardware** and **software** to manipulate the data.

The hardware is the part of the computer that can be seen or touched while software is a general term for the computer's instructions.

To communicate with others about computers, you need to understand the vocabulary. Work with a partner to complete one of the activities below. Present your results to the rest of the class.

Activity 1
Have you played a video game recently? The cartridges that you use operate the **microprocessor** of a computer and let you play the game.

(a) What is a microprocessor?

(b) Briefly describe its function on a computer.

(c) Briefly describe how a video game operates on the microprocessor.

Activity 2
R2D2 and C3PO are robots that were created in the imagination of a writer. Today's robots are not quite as sophisticated, but they are widely used.

(a) What is a robot?

(b) Why are robots useful in certain situations? Provide examples.

(c) Briefly describe how a robot is 'taught' certain functions.

Activity 3
As more homes have computers, it is becoming more common to link them with the outside world. Computers are already able to draw on data banks stored anywhere around the world.

Briefly describe each of the following. What is the function of each?

(a) modem   (b) teletext   (c) videotext

1. Construct the following triangles.

   (a) $\triangle ABC$: $\angle A = 90°$, $\angle B = 45°$, $BC = 3.0$ cm

   (b) $\triangle PQR$: $PQ = 5.5$ cm, $PR = 12.2$ cm, $QR = 9.5$ cm

2. Are the triangles in each pair congruent? Explain.

   (a)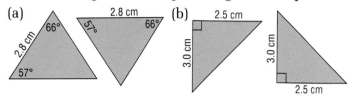

   (b)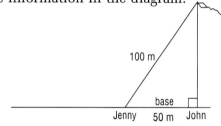

3. Jenny is flying a kite. John is standing vertically below the kite. Calculate the height of the kite using the information in the diagram.

   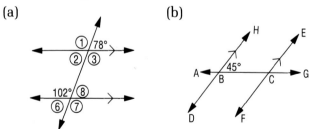

4. Find the missing measures of the angles in each of the following.

   (a)

   (b)

5. A baseball diamond is shaped like a square. The distance between each base is about 28 m.

   (a) Suppose the ball is thrown from home plate to third base and then to first base. How far does the ball travel in all?

   (b) Create and solve a similar problem.

THINKING ABOUT

What have you learned about triangles that you did not know before?

Are your solutions in your notebook becoming clearer as the year progresses? What can you do to make them even clearer?

How did you use patterns and relationships to help you learn geometry?

MAKING CONNECTIONS

Refer to the opening pages of the chapter.

(a) Create a problem of your own using the pictures. Solve your problem.

(b) Compare your problem with others in your class. Solve the other problems.

Do you prefer studying with a partner or on your own? Why?

How can you use manipulatives to help you study for a test?

Read the chapter again. Are the skills easier to understand? What can you do to make them even easier?

MATH JOURNAL

Geometric shapes occur often in architecture and design.

(a) List three geometric shapes that appear in the design of your home.

(b) Describe how your home might look different if the shapes in (a) were not used.

SELF EVALUATION

1. Find the length of the third side.

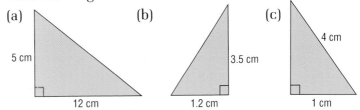

(a)   (b)   (c)

5 cm   12 cm   3.5 cm   1.2 cm   4 cm   1 cm

2. The size of a television is given by the length of the diagonal of its screen. Fred's TV screen has a width of 40 cm and a height of 32.5 cm. What is the size of Fred's TV?

3. Find the missing measures of the angles in the following.

(a)   (b)

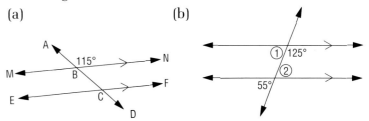

4. New Covenant Garden Flower Bed in London, England, is square and covers an area of $10\,000$ m^2.

(a) Find the measure of each side.

(b) Find the shortest distance to go from one corner of the flower bed to the opposite corner.

5. Which of the following triangles are congruent? How do you know?

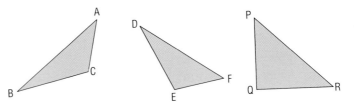

391

1. Use a pair of compasses and a protractor.

    (a) Construct a square, a parallelogram, and a trapezoid.

    (b) Draw a diagonal for each shape in (a).

    (c) In which shape(s) does the diagonal form two congruent triangles? Give reasons for your answer.

2. Write each number as a percent.

    (a) $\frac{3}{5}$ (b) 1.38   (c) 0.62   (d) $\frac{1}{8}$ (e) 0.05   (f) $\frac{1}{1000}$

3. Find the measures of all angles.

    (a)   (b)   (c)

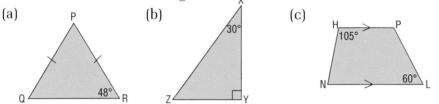

4. For each figure, find
    • the number of lines of symmetry.
    • the order of rotational symmetry.

    (a)   (b)   (c)

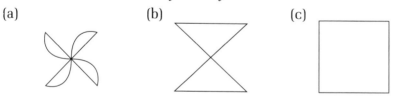

5. Rose and Gloria are constructing a circular swimming pool. A drain for the filter is to be placed in the centre of the pool.

    (a) Describe a process for finding the exact location of the drain.

    (b) Use dimensions of your own to test your process from (a). If it is not accurate, try again.

6. An elephant can reach a running speed of 40 km/h.

    (a) Calculate the minimum length of time for an elephant to run 96 km.

    (b) What assumptions have you made in (a)?

    (c) Are your assumptions in (b) reasonable? Why?

1. (a) Copy the diagram. Place the numbers 1, 2, 3, 4, 5, and 6 in the circles so that the sum along each side of the triangle is the same. Find a different solution to the problem.

   (b) Write and solve a similar problem of your own. Compare your problem with others in your class.

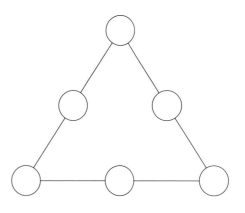

2. Mel bought speakers for his CD player for $195. He paid for the speakers in cash using six bills. What were the bills?

3. Trace the following triangles onto a piece of grid paper. Which regular polygon(s) can you construct using the triangles?

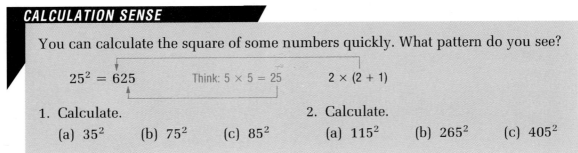

4. Pennies and dimes are arranged as shown to the right. A 'move' is made when one coin jumps over another coin into an empty space. Find the minimum number of moves needed so that all the pennies are to the right.

CALCULATION SENSE

You can calculate the square of some numbers quickly. What pattern do you see?

$$25^2 = 625 \qquad \text{Think: } 5 \times 5 = 25 \qquad 2 \times (2 + 1)$$

1. Calculate.

   (a) 35^2 (b) 75^2 (c) 85^2

2. Calculate.

   (a) 115^2 (b) 265^2 (c) 405^2

13 EXPLORING ALGEBRA

Did you know that Canada is rich in natural resources? Make a list of natural resources you think Canada has. How do you think these natural resources are obtained and sold to other parts of the world?

You have earlier worked with expressions with variables in them. To help you explore algebraic concepts, algebra tiles can be used. You can create your own algebra tiles like those shown below. The red and black square tiles are used to represent numbers. Each represents one unit and is called a **unit tile**. The red and black strips are used to represent variables. Each strip is called an **x-tile.**

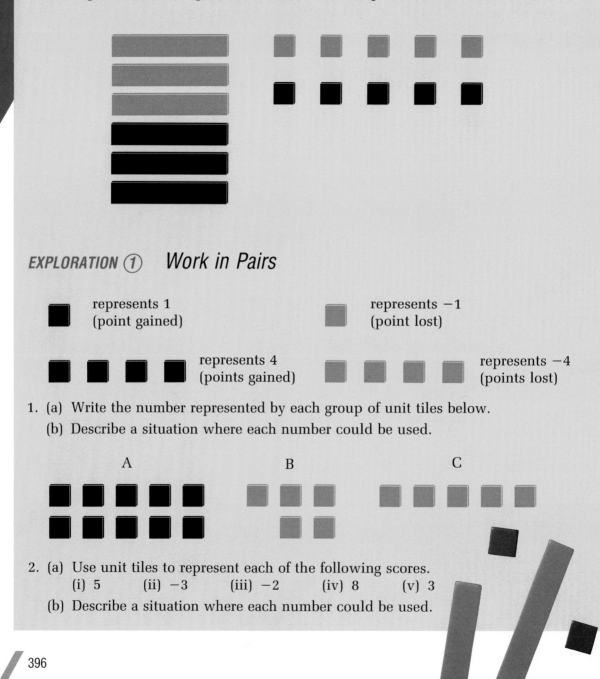

EXPLORATION ① *Work in Pairs*

represents 1
(point gained)

represents −1
(point lost)

represents 4
(points gained)

represents −4
(points lost)

1. (a) Write the number represented by each group of unit tiles below.
   (b) Describe a situation where each number could be used.

       A   B   C

2. (a) Use unit tiles to represent each of the following scores.
   (i) 5   (ii) −3   (iii) −2   (iv) 8   (v) 3
   (b) Describe a situation where each number could be used.

EXPLORATION ② *Work in Small Groups*

Your work with red and black unit tiles is similar to your work with integers. For example, a red tile together with a black tile gives a net result of zero. Thus, the net result of the tiles to the right is 2.

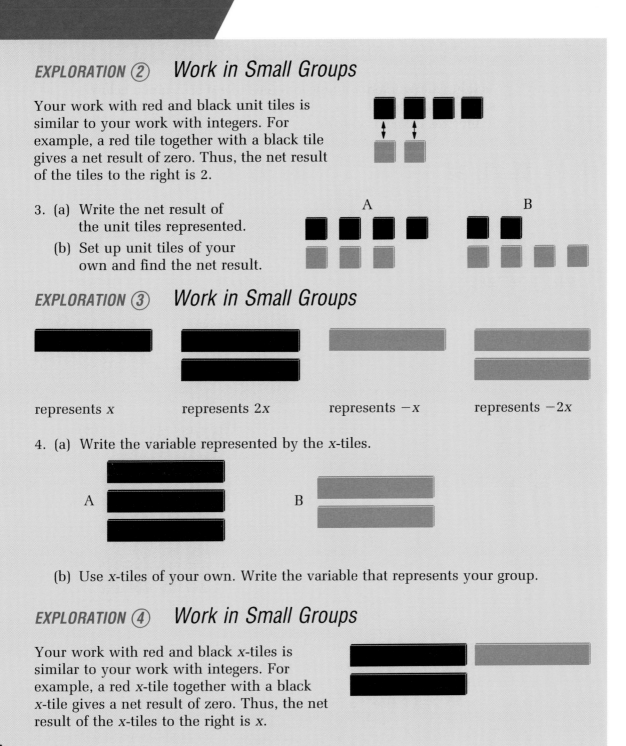

3. (a) Write the net result of the unit tiles represented.

   (b) Set up unit tiles of your own and find the net result.

EXPLORATION ③ *Work in Small Groups*

represents x represents $2x$ represents $-x$ represents $-2x$

4. (a) Write the variable represented by the x-tiles.

   A   B

   (b) Use x-tiles of your own. Write the variable that represents your group.

EXPLORATION ④ *Work in Small Groups*

Your work with red and black x-tiles is similar to your work with integers. For example, a red x-tile together with a black x-tile gives a net result of zero. Thus, the net result of the x-tiles to the right is x.

5. Set up x-tiles of your own and find the net result.

In the previous section, you worked with algebra tiles like those shown below. Each strip represented a variable and was called an *x*-tile while each square tile represented a unit and was called a unit tile.

represents 5   represents −5

represents 2*x*   represents −2*x*

ACTIVITY ① **Using the Tiles**

Use your materials to show the following.
A Write an expression to represent the pattern.
B Then, make algebra tile arrangements of your own. Write an expression for each arrangement.

(a)   (b)   (c)

Suppose the variable *x* in Activity 1 has a value of 5. Each variable expression is then evaluated as follows.

(a) Use $x = 5$.
$$2x - 3 = 2(5) - 3$$
$$= 7$$

(b) Use $x = 5$.
$$-x + 5 = -(5) + 5$$
$$= 0$$

(c) Use $x = 5$.
$$4x = 4(5)$$
$$= 20$$

Now, evaluate the expressions you created in part B of the activity.

A Use your tiles to help you.

1. Write an expression for the tiles shown.

(a) 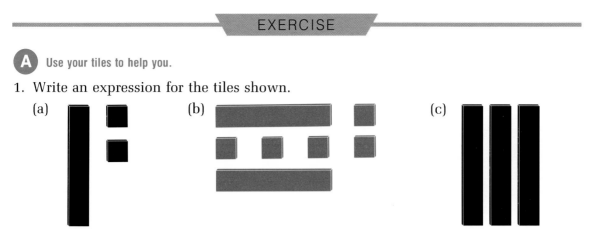 (b) (c)

2. Suppose $x = 5$. Evaluate each expression in Question 1.

B Any letter of the alphabet can be used as a variable.

3. Simplify each of the following.
   (a) $x + y + x$
   (b) $4p + q - 2p + 2q$
   (c) $3m + 5n - 3m$
   (d) $a - 2b - 3a + 4b$

4. Use $d = 4$. Evaluate each expression.
   (a) $8d$ (b) $7d - 3d$
   (c) $5d + d$ (d) $4d - 2d$

5. Mike is paid $25 for each prescription he fills at a pharmacy.
   (a) Write a variable expression for Mike's pay using p for the number of prescriptions filled.
   (b) How much will Mike be paid for filling 32 prescriptions?
   (c) Use your results from (a) and (b). Describe how you can solve the problem using tiles.

6. (a) Write an expression for the perimeter of the logging camp below.
   (b) Find the perimeter if x is 22 m and y is 34 m.

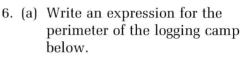

7. A piece of lumber has a length of $4p$. Three pieces of lengths $2x$, x, and p are cut from the lumber. Find the length of lumber remaining.

8. The cards □ , △ , and ○ represent three even digits. Use the expressions represented by the cards below to find the number to be written on each card.

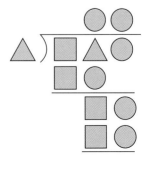

399

13.3 BRACKETS AND EXPRESSIONS

You can use your tiles from the previous section to help you write expressions like $3(x + 4)$ without brackets.

Step 1
Represent the expression inside the brackets using algebra tiles.

Step 2
Represent the expression from Step 1 three times. (Remember: $3(x + 4)$ means you have three expressions of $x + 4$.)

The total is $3x + 12$.

Step 3 Simplify.

Thus, $3(x + 4) = 3x + 12$.

Think: In your journal, write
• how these numbers are related.
• how these numbers are related.

The x-tiles can be used to represent any variable.
Thus, $3(y - 4)$ can be written without brackets as $3(y - 4) = 3y - 12$.

EXERCISE

A Use your tiles to help you.

1. Write an expression for each.

(a)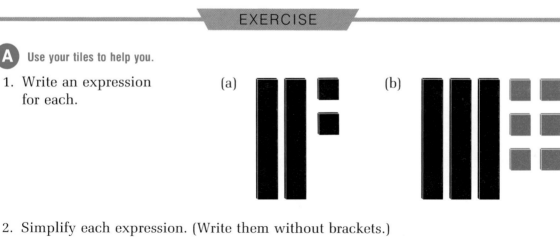

(b)

2. Simplify each expression. (Write them without brackets.)

   (a) $2(x + 4)$ (b) $3(x + 2)$ (c) $5(x + 4)$ (d) $2(x + 6)$

   (e) $4(x - 2)$ (f) $3(x - 5)$ (g) $2(x - 3)$ (h) $6(x - 3)$

3. Write each without brackets.

   (a) $4(y + 1)$ (b) $3(x - 4)$

   (c) $5(a + 6)$ (d) $7(m - 8)$

   (e) $3(k - 2)$ (f) $4(z - 5)$

4. Write each without brackets. Then evaluate for $x = 8$.

   (a) $3(x + 5)$ (b) $5(x - 2)$

   (c) $4(x - 6)$ (d) $3(x + 1)$

   (e) $5(x + 3)$ (f) $7(x - 3)$

5. Substitute $x = -2$ into each expression. Evaluate the expression.

   (a) $3(x + 5)$ (b) $5(x - 2)$

   (c) $4(x - 6)$ (d) $3(x + 1)$

   (e) $2(x - 1)$ (f) $6(x + 4)$

6. A garden is shaped as shown below.

   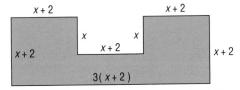

   The cost to fence x metres is $25.

   (a) Write an expression to find the total cost of the fence.

   (b) What is the total cost in (a) if $x = 5$?

7. Use $a = 2$ and $b = 3$ to evaluate each.

   (a) $3(a + b)$ (b) $2(a - b)$

   (c) $4(2a + b)$ (d) $3(3a - 2b)$

   (e) $2(5a - 3b)$ (f) $3(a - 2b)$

8. Use $x = -2$ and $y = -3$ to evaluate each.

   (a) $3(x + y)$ (b) $4(y - x)$

   (c) $5(2x - y)$ (d) $3(3x + 4y)$

   (e) $2(x - 2y)$ (f) $4(3y - 2x)$

9. (a) In your journal, describe how you might represent $-3(x + 3)$ using tiles.

   (b) Write $-3(x + 3)$ without brackets.

   (c) Write each of the following without brackets.

   (i) $-4(x - 2)$ (ii) $-2(x + 5)$

10. (a) Twelve toothpicks are used to form the shape below. How many squares are there in all?

    (b) Which two toothpicks will you remove to have two squares?

    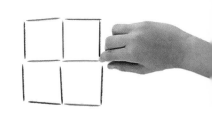

Part of a picture done by Albrecht Durer in the sixteenth century is shown to the left. The numbers form a magic square.

(a) What is a magic square?

(b) Find the magic square called IXOHOXI. What makes this magic square unique?

13.4 PROBLEM SOLVING: WORKING BACKWARDS

You can use manipulatives to write an expression with brackets using the steps below. Work with a partner and summarize any observations and relationships that can help you write $2x + 8$ with brackets.

Step 1 Show the expression.

Step 2 Separate the manipulatives into as many equal groups as possible.

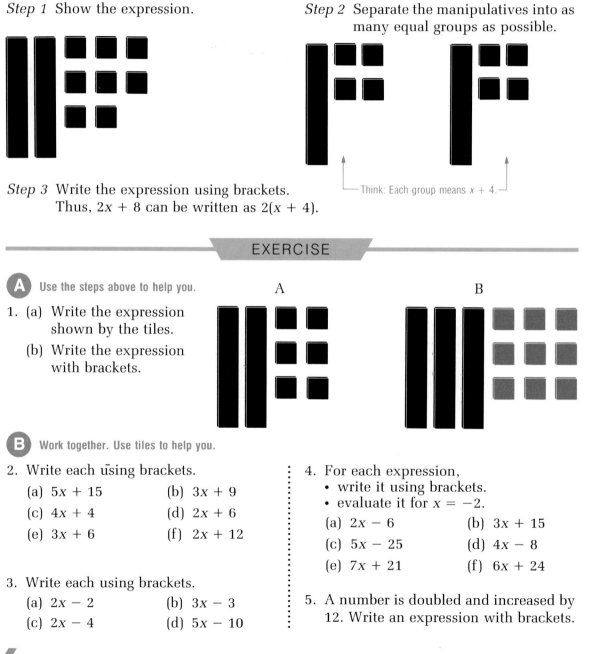

└ Think: Each group means $x + 4$. ┘

Step 3 Write the expression using brackets.
Thus, $2x + 8$ can be written as $2(x + 4)$.

EXERCISE

A Use the steps above to help you.

A   B

1. (a) Write the expression shown by the tiles.
   (b) Write the expression with brackets.

B Work together. Use tiles to help you.

2. Write each using brackets.
   (a) $5x + 15$ (b) $3x + 9$
   (c) $4x + 4$ (d) $2x + 6$
   (e) $3x + 6$ (f) $2x + 12$

3. Write each using brackets.
   (a) $2x - 2$ (b) $3x - 3$
   (c) $2x - 4$ (d) $5x - 10$

4. For each expression,
   • write it using brackets.
   • evaluate it for $x = -2$.
   (a) $2x - 6$ (b) $3x + 15$
   (c) $5x - 25$ (d) $4x - 8$
   (e) $7x + 21$ (f) $6x + 24$

5. A number is doubled and increased by 12. Write an expression with brackets.

13.5 PROBLEM SOLVING: SYSTEMATIC TRIAL

Sometimes, to solve a problem, you can try a solution and check your solution against known facts.

For example, the numbers 1, 5, 6, 10, 50, and 60 are to be arranged in a triangle so that each side has a product of 300. You can write the numbers on disks and experiment with the disks until you have found the answer.

Trial 1

Think: In trial 1, the bottom row has a product of 300. The others do not. Leave the bottom row and change the other rows.

Trial 2

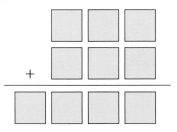

EXERCISE

B Use your *Problem Solving Plan*.

1. Arrange the numbers 3, 4, 6, 7, 50, and 53 in a triangle so that each side has a sum of 60.

2. (a) Use cards like those shown below. Write the numbers 0 to 9 on the cards so that the sum is true.

   (b) Use cards to create a problem of your own. Solve your problem.

3. Nine coins are used to pay a bill of $1.35. The coins are all quarters and dimes. How many quarters are there?

4. (a) Write the numbers 1 through 8 on cards and arrange them as shown below so that no two consecutive numbers share a common side.

   (b) Use cards to create a similar problem of your own. Solve your problem and compare it with others in your class.

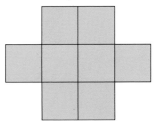

403

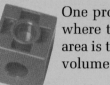

Manipulatives can often be used to create and solve problems. Suppose you are asked to create a problem that can be solved using the cubes on this page.

One problem you might create is "Form a solid where the number of units used for the surface area is three times the number of units used for the volume."

Is the arrangement shown a solution?

Volume = 18 cm³
Surface area = 42 cm²

Not a solution. Try again.

ACTIVITY

(a) Before trying the exercises, create another problem that can be solved using the cubes on this page.

(b) Record your problem in your journal and have a partner solve the problem.

(c) Find other manipulatives in the book. Create a problem that can be solved using those manipulatives. Have others in your class solve the problem.

The manipulatives shown suggest a solution to a problem.
- Create a problem whose solution is shown by the objects.
- Compare your problem with others in your class.

1.

4.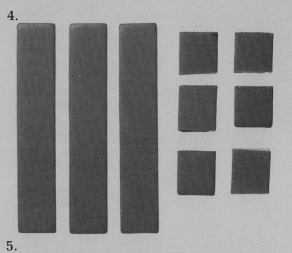

2.

5.

3.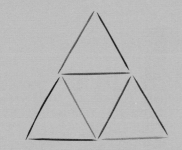

You have used algebra tiles to help you work with expressions. You can use algebra tiles to help you solve equations.

EXPLORATION ① *Work with a Partner*

1. (a) Write the equation represented by each of the following.
   (b) How can you use algebra tiles to help you find the value represented by the x-tile in each case?

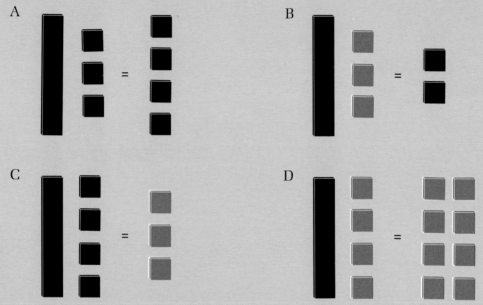

A   B

C   D

EXPLORATION ② *Work with a Partner*

2. (a) Use algebra tiles to represent each equation. (Hint: The x-tile can be used to represent the variable in each equation.)
   (i) $a + 5 = 3$ (ii) $p - 2 = 5$ (iii) $k + 3 = 12$ (iv) $m - 6 = 8$
   (b) Use tiles. Suggest what the value of the variable might be.

EXPLORATION ③ *Write Together*

3. (a) In your journal, describe how you found the value of the variable in each of the equations in Exploration 2.
   (b) Set up equations of your own using tiles. Find the value of the variable in each equation.

13.8 WORKING WITH EQUATIONS

In the previous explorations, you predicted the value of the variable in an equation represented by algebra tiles. Follow these steps to find the value of x in $x + 2 = 6$.

Step 1
Use algebra tiles to represent the equation.

Step 2
To isolate the x-tile, use an appropriate number of red unit tiles.

Step 3
Interpret your tiles. Write the value of x. In this case, $x = 4$.

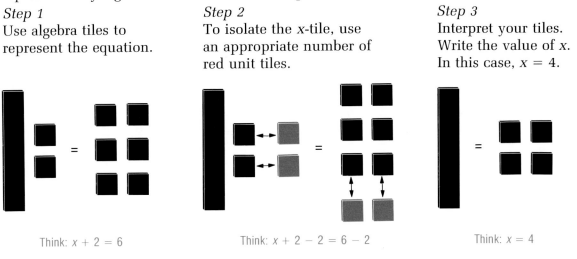

Think: $x + 2 = 6$ Think: $x + 2 - 2 = 6 - 2$ Think: $x = 4$

EXERCISE

B Remember: The x-tile can represent any variable.

1. Write the equation represented by these algebra tiles. Solve it.

(a)   (b)

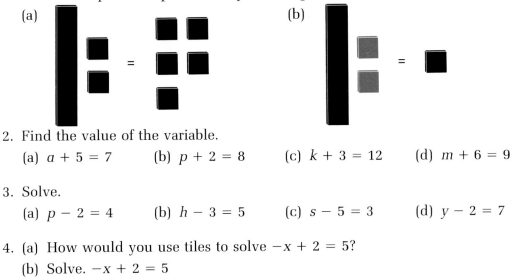

2. Find the value of the variable.
   (a) $a + 5 = 7$ (b) $p + 2 = 8$ (c) $k + 3 = 12$ (d) $m + 6 = 9$

3. Solve.
   (a) $p - 2 = 4$ (b) $h - 3 = 5$ (c) $s - 5 = 3$ (d) $y - 2 = 7$

4. (a) How would you use tiles to solve $-x + 2 = 5$?
   (b) Solve. $-x + 2 = 5$
   (c) Use tiles to solve each of the following.
       (i) $-x - 4 = 3$ (ii) $-x + 2 = 7$ (iii) $-x - 3 = -2$ (iv) $-x + 5 = -3$

13.9 MORE THAN ONE STEP

Manipulatives can help you solve problems. To develop strategies for solving equations, you need to understand how equations are built.

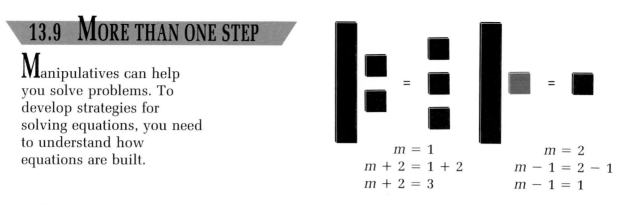

$$m = 1$$
$$m + 2 = 1 + 2$$
$$m + 2 = 3$$

$$m = 2$$
$$m - 1 = 2 - 1$$
$$m - 1 = 1$$

In the above examples, equations have been built. To solve the equations, you need to reverse the operations. For example, you use tiles to help you solve $2x + 3 = 1$ as follows:

Step 1
Use algebra tiles to represent the equation.

Step 2
To isolate the x-tiles, use an appropriate number of red unit tiles.

Step 3
Simplify.

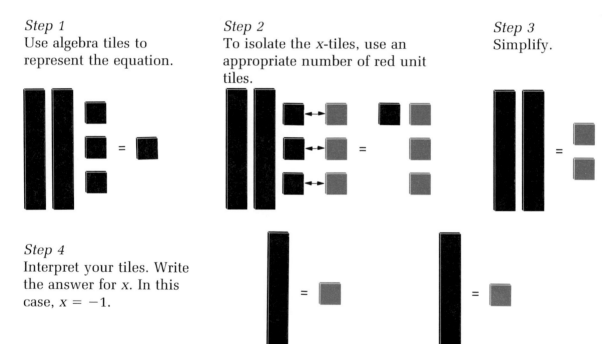

Step 4
Interpret your tiles. Write the answer for x. In this case, $x = -1$.

The above steps can be written in a compact form to show the solution to the equation $2x + 3 = 1$.

$$2x + 3 = 1$$
$$2x + 3 - 3 = 1 - 3$$
$$2x = -2$$
$$\frac{2x}{2} = \frac{-2}{2}$$
$$x = -1$$

Think: Check your solution.
LS $= 2x + 3$ RS $= 1$
   $= 2(-1) + 3$ The solution is correct.
   $= 1$

408

A Review your skills with integers and fractions.

1. Write the equation represented by the algebra tiles. Then solve.

   (a)   (b)

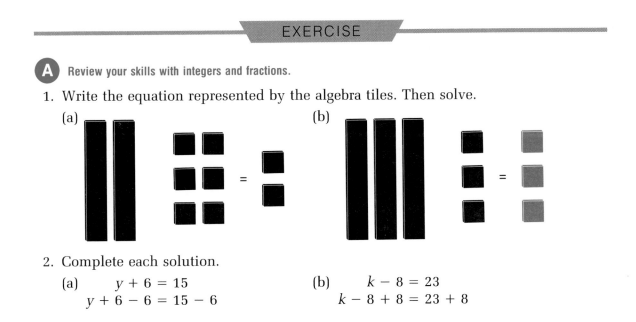

2. Complete each solution.

   (a) $y + 6 = 15$
          $y + 6 - 6 = 15 - 6$

   (b) $k - 8 = 23$
          $k - 8 + 8 = 23 + 8$

B Check your solution by substituting in the original equation.

3. For each equation, decide on the first step to solve the equation. Then solve.

   (a) $y + 8 = 16$ (b) $k - 3 = 9$
   (c) $m - 2 = 19$ (d) $k + 8 = 16$

4. Solve. Check your answers.

   (a) $y - 6 = 4$ (b) $k + 10 = 6$
   (c) $x + 15 = 13$ (d) $s + 3 = 11$
   (e) $k - 3 = -2$ (f) $m - 2 = -4$

5. Find each solution. Verify.

   (a) $k + 13 = 12$ (b) $a - 9 = 12$
   (c) $b - 6 = -2$ (d) $12 + t = 8$

6. Find the value of x.

   (a) $2x - 4 = 8$ (b) $3x + 6 = 3$
   (c) $5x - 8 = 7$ (d) $4x + 6 = 6$
   (e) $2x + 5 = 11$ (f) $4x - 7 = 21$

7. Solve.

   (a) $4x - 9 = -5$ (b) $3y + 2 = -7$
   (c) $5m + 12 = -18$ (d) $2k - 8 = -4$
   (e) $3c + 2 = -10$ (f) $4s + 5 = -11$

8. (a) What is the first step in solving $\frac{1}{2}x + 2 = 7$?

   (b) Solve the equation.

9. Solve.

   (a) $\frac{1}{2}x - 8 = 4$ (b) $\frac{1}{4}x + 2 = 3$

   (c) $\frac{1}{3}x + 2 = 4$ (d) $\frac{1}{2}x + 2 = -2$

10. (a) Suppose you have 24 tiles. Arrange the tiles so that you have 6 rows with 5 in each row.

    (b) Create a similar problem of your own. Solve it.

13.10 EQUATIONS WITH DECIMAL NUMBERS

The skills you learned for solving equations involving whole numbers can be used to solve equations involving decimal numbers. How are the solutions that follow like the solutions using whole numbers? How are they different?

Solve.

$$x + 4.5 = 7.3$$
$$x + 4.5 - 4.5 = 7.3 - 4.5$$
$$x = 2.8$$

Solve.

$$0.3x = 12$$
$$\frac{0.3x}{0.3} = \frac{12}{0.3}$$
$$x = 40$$

Think:

$\boxed{c}$ 12 $\boxed{\div}$ 0.3 $\boxed{=}$ 40

EXERCISE

 A Use a calculator to help you.

1. (a) To solve the equation $x - 2.3 = 4.6$, what is the first step?
   (b) Solve the equation.

2. (a) To solve the equation $0.5x = 25$, what is the first step?
   (b) Solve the equation.

3. (a) Solve. $x - 3.3 = 12.6$
   (b) Verify your solution.

B Review your skills for solving equations.

4. For each equation,
   • decide on the first step,
   • then solve.
   (a) $2p - 0.3 = 15.2$
   (b) $12x - 1.2 = 6.4$
   (c) $k - 2.1 = 14.2$
   (d) $15x - 8.9 = 11.8$

5. Solve. Check your answers.
   (a) $0.3x = 24$ (b) $1.6k = 12$
   (c) $2.5m = 15$ (d) $0.8y = 18$

6. Solve.
   (a) $0.5x - 12 = 22$ (b) $3.2y - 7 = 121$
   (c) $4.2m + 6 = 9$ (d) $5.2k - 8 = 17$

7. Solve. Verify your solutions.
   (a) $0.3p - 6.2 = 30.1$
   (b) $0.25k + 1.6 = 10.7$
   (c) $4.3m + 9.2 = 15.8$
   (d) $0.6y - 8.4 = 14.7$

8. For each,
   • write the fraction as an equivalent decimal number,
   • then solve the equation.
   (a) $\frac{1}{4}m + 4 = 13$
   (b) $\frac{1}{2}n - 9 = 15$
   (c) $\frac{1}{5}x - 0.5 = 0.8$
   (d) $\frac{1}{8}y - 4.5 = 114.6$
   (e) $\frac{2}{5}k + 16.4 = 12.9$

13.11 MATH AND LANGUAGE

To solve word problems, you need to develop skills for translating English into mathematics and mathematical symbols. For example, translate the following into mathematics. Then solve.

"A number when tripled and increased by 4 is equal to 19."

Let n represent the number.

a number is tripled — increased by 4

$3n + 4 = 19$ — equals 19

$3n + 4 - 4 = 19 - 4$

$3n = 15$

$\dfrac{3n}{3} = \dfrac{15}{3}$

$n = 5$

Think: Check your solution.
The number 5, when tripled, is 15.
The sum of 15 and 4 is 19. √ The solution is correct.

EXERCISE

 B Check your answer in the original problem.

1. Write an equation for each sentence. Then solve.

   (a) A number is multiplied by 6 and the result is 48. Find the number.

   (b) When a number is added to itself the result is 72. Find the number.

   (c) A number increased by 8 is equal to 108. Find the number.

   (d) One-half of a number decreased by 6 is equal to 3. Find the number.

   (e) Seven times a number, plus 4, is equal to 60. Find the number.

2. The sum of three consecutive whole numbers is 36. Find the numbers.

3. During a school election, 625 votes were cast. Rita received 75 more votes than Pierre. How many votes did each receive?

4. Twice the cost of an item plus $4 is equal to $75. Find the cost of the item.

5. Matthew is half as old as Alan. If the sum of their ages is 54, find their ages.

6. Next year, Victoria will be twice as old as Louis and the sum of their ages will be 42. Find their ages today.

7. Nina and Fatima have newspaper routes. Nina's weekly earnings are three times Fatima's. Together they earn $40.00. How much does each earn each week?

8. In a skating competition, Angela and Louise scored a total of 108 points. Angela scored one half of Louise's total plus 33. Who scored more points? By how many?

Have you ever looked up in the sky at night and wondered how many stars there are? Did you know that by looking through a pair of binoculars, you can see as many stars as are represented by k in $0.012k - 100 = 1000$?

In this section, you will use your skills for solving equations to discover facts about stars and the solar system. As you complete each exercise, write any facts you did not know in your journal.

ACTIVITY

(a) Solve the equation above. About how many stars can you see?

(b) Think about the number of space probes and satellites that are in orbit about the earth. What percent do you think are of no practical use?

(c) Write an equation whose solution is your percent in (b).

EXERCISE

 A Review your skills for solving equations. Use tiles to help you.

1. Hipparchus originally measured stars intensity on a scale of 1 to 6, with 1 being the brightest and 6 the faintest. Today, negative numbers describe stars whose brightness is greater than 1. The brightness of the sun is y in $y - 10 = -17$.

(a) Solve. $y - 10 = -17$

(b) What is the measure of brightness of the sun?

2. Look at the stars in the sky on a clear night. Find the North Star.

(a) Estimate the measure of intensity of the North Star using the scale in Question 1.

(b) Then solve $x + 3 = -2$ to find the measure of intensity of the North Star. How accurate was your estimate?

3. The earth has a diameter of about 13 500 km.

    (a) Write an equation to find the circumference of the earth.

    (b) Solve your equation in (a). What is the circumference of the earth?

4. Use your results from Question 3.

    (a) Light travels 7 times the circumference of the earth in 1 s. Write an equation to find the speed that light travels each second.

    (b) How far does light travel in one hour? one day? one year?

    (c) Interpret your answer from (b). How far is one light year?

5. Iridium is a rare element found in the earth's crust. More iridium is found in Italy than in the rest of the world. This can be expressed as z in $4z + 16 = 136$. How many times more iridium is found in Italy?

6. An eclipse of the sun occurs when the sun's rays are blocked by the moon. The number of days between successive eclipses is x in $0.5x - 77 = 105$.

    (a) Solve $0.5x - 77 = 105$.

    (b) How many days are there between successive eclipses?

    (c) In your journal, explain why it is possible to have a total eclipse and you not know it.

7. Canadian forest resources, one year, accounted for exports totalling $10 500 000 000.

    (a) Write an equation whose solution is $10 500 000 000.

    (b) Use your library to find the total exports for another of Canada's natural resources. Write an equation whose solution is the total you found.

    (c) Compare your equation with others in your class. Solve their equations.

Earlier, you solved problems using diagrams. When solving problems with equations, it is often helpful to record the information on a diagram.

The length of a rectangle is twice as long as its width. If the perimeter is 180 cm, find its dimensions.

Let w represent the width of the rectangle. Thus, the length of the rectangle is $2w$.

$$2w + w + 2w + w = 180$$
$$6w = 180$$
$$\frac{6w}{6} = \frac{180}{6}$$
$$w = 30$$

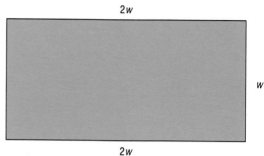

The rectangle has dimensions of 60 cm by 30 cm.

EXERCISE

B Use your *Problem Solving Plan.*

1. The perimeter of a square garden is 16 m.
   (a) Write an equation to find the length and width of the garden.
   (b) Solve your equation from (a). What are the dimensions?

2. For the diagram,
   • write an expression for the perimeter.
   • find the length and width if the perimeter is 72 cm.

3. The perimeter of the rectangle is 80 cm. Find its dimensions.

4. A patio is twice as long as it is wide. Its perimeter is 102 m.
   (a) Write an equation to find the length of the patio.
   (b) Solve your equation from (a). How long is the patio?

5. Use these equations.
   $$5^2 + 12^2 = 13^2$$
   $$9^2 + 40^2 = 41^2$$
   The numbers are Pythagorean Triples.

   (a) Find a Pythagorean Triple that uses the number 7.

   (b) Create a similar problem of your own. Solve it.

Music and computers have been linked since the 1950s. In fact, the first musicians to understand the power of the computer were composers Iannis Xenakis and Lejaren Hiller. They used the computer to program musical instruments.

Today, computers help musicians to compose and play music without the aid of instruments. In fact, in the Media Lab at Massachusetts Institute of Technology, computer scientists are designing computers that can play like veteran musicians!

You will find examples of the power of these *hyperinstruments* below. Work with a partner to answer the questions after each example.

1. Hyperinstruments are creating sounds that nobody has heard before.
   (a) Do you enjoy hearing new and innovative musical sounds?
   (b) How do you think new sounds will change the music industry?
   (c) Visit a music store. How many of the instruments involve computers that generate sounds?

2. It has been suggested that hyperinstruments will always produce the sound intended by the musician. This allows musicians to spend less time worrying about playing the correct notes.
   (a) What do you think musicians will spend most of their time doing?
   (b) Do you think that musicians who do not need to spend time playing the correct notes will become less creative?

3. Max Matthews, a *hypermusic designer*, predicts that by the year 2010, hyperinstruments will be able to simulate any musical instrument and any musical style.
   (a) Do you think this will take away the creativity of a musician?
   (b) Do you think that anybody will be able to become a musician?

1. Write the equation represented by the tiles. Solve the equation.

2. Use $m = 4$ to evaluate each expression.

    (a) $3m$ (b) $2m - m$ (c) $4m + 2m - 3m$

3. Solve.

    (a) $5a = 15$ (b) $4m - 2 = 8$ (c) $3b - 9 = -3$

4. Write and solve an equation to match each statement.

    (a) Nine times a number plus six equals 60.

    (b) Five times a number less seven equals 43.

5. Randi is one-third her father's age. Her father is 48 years old.

    (a) Write an equation to find Randi's age.

    (b) Solve the equation from (a). How old is Randi?

6. A ribbon is 72 cm long and is cut into two pieces. One piece is twice the length of the other plus 8 cm. Find the length of each piece of ribbon.

7. The length of a rectangle decreased by 1 cm equals the width of the rectangle. Its perimeter is 102 cm.

    (a) Draw the rectangle.

    (b) Write an equation to find the length of the rectangle.

    (c) Solve your equation from (b). What is the width of the rectangle?

THINKING ABOUT

What problem solving skills did you use in this chapter? What new problem solving skills did you learn?

Use Question 5 on this page. Explain another way to solve the problem. Compare your way with others in your class. Which do you prefer?

For which problems on this page can a diagram be useful in the solution? Give reasons for your choice.

MAKING CONNECTIONS

Refer to the opening pages of this chapter.

(a) Use the pictures to help you write a problem that can be solved using the skills in this chapter.

(b) Compare your problem with others in your class. Solve the other problems.

Pick any problem on this page. Explain to your partner how it can be solved.

How do you think a calculator can help you in this chapter?

When do you think working with a calculator takes longer than working with pencil and paper? Write examples to justify your answer.

MATH JOURNAL

In this chapter, you have learned to solve equations.
- Write and solve an equation using the skills in this chapter.
- Describe how you felt when you learned to solve a particular type of equation.

SELF EVALUATION

1. Write the equation represented by the tiles. Solve the equation.

2. Find the value of each expression when $a = 2$ and $b = 3$.

(a) $20a - 5a + 3a$ (b) $2(a + b)$

(c) $-9a + 2b - 6a + 4b$ (d) $3a - 5b + 2a$

3. Write and solve an equation to match each statement.

(a) The sum of a number and 5 is 23.

(b) Four times a number and 6 is 18.

4. Solve.

(a) $a - 31 = 10$ (b) $2x + 11 = 25$ (c) $3y - 15 = 6$

5. David earned $10 more than twice Sally's allowance. He earned $24.

(a) Write an equation to determine Sally's allowance.

(b) Solve the equation from (a). How much was Sally's allowance?

6. Jodi made a deposit into her bank account. If she had doubled the deposit and added $5, she would have deposited $75.

(a) Write an equation to find the amount she deposited.

(b) Solve your equation from (a). How much did she deposit?

7. The perimeter of this triangle is 62 cm. Find the length of each side.

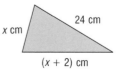

One of the world's newest domed stadiums, and one of the most modern, is SkyDome in Toronto. What makes the domed stadium unique is its retractable roof.

The roof has a mass of about 8500 t. It consists of about 7000 pieces of fabricated steel held together by almost 250 000 screws. It is covered by a layer of *Sarnafil* and has an area of about 122 000 m². There are four distinct panels, three of which move to close the roof. They each measure 205 m wide and are 87 m above the ground.

The roof closes in about 20 min. The three panels move simultaneously. The end panel, shaped like a semicircle, moves about 20 m each minute. The rectangular panels move about 15 m each minute.

When closed, the panels overlap. There are flexible seals between the panels, each about 0.5 m wide, which prevent leaks.

The computers that operate the roof will shut down when the winds that come off Lake Ontario exceed 60 km/h. It is interesting to note that only once in the last 100 years have the winds off Lake Ontario exceeded 60 km/h. However, engineers and architects have predicted that the roof will not work sometime in the next century.

B Use the information given about SkyDome to answer the following.

1. One storey in an apartment building has a height of about 3.1 m. How many storeys can an apartment building have and still fit into SkyDome?

2. (a) What is the mass, in kilograms, of one bag of sugar?

   (b) What is the mass, in kilograms, of the roof of SkyDome?

   (c) How many bags of sugar together will have the same mass as the roof of SkyDome?

3. How many screws per square metre are used on the roof?

4. SkyDome seats about 52 000 people for a baseball game. The first Blue Jays game was at about 93% of capacity. How many people attended the first ever baseball game at SkyDome?

5. Toronto played their first game in SkyDome in June 1989 against the Milwaukee Brewers. The Blue Jays scored only 3 runs on their way to a 5 to 3 loss. Of these runs, $\frac{2}{3}$ of them were scored by George Bell and $\frac{1}{3}$ of them were scored by Fred McGriff.

   (a) How many runs did Bell score?

   (b) How many runs did McGriff score?

6. Use a stadium in your area.

   (a) Find information about the stadium.

   (b) Write equations using variables to represent some information.

   (c) Compare your equations with others in your class. Solve the equations.

7. The south panel of SkyDome is a semi-circle that moves exactly 490 m when the stadium is being closed. What is the area covered by the south panel?

8. Use your library.

   (a) What was the first domed stadium ever built in Canada?

   (b) How did it differ from SkyDome?

419

14 Looking Ahead

Each of the technological advancements shown here can affect your daily life in important ways. For each example,

- decide how math was involved in its development.
- describe how your life might be different without the advancement shown.

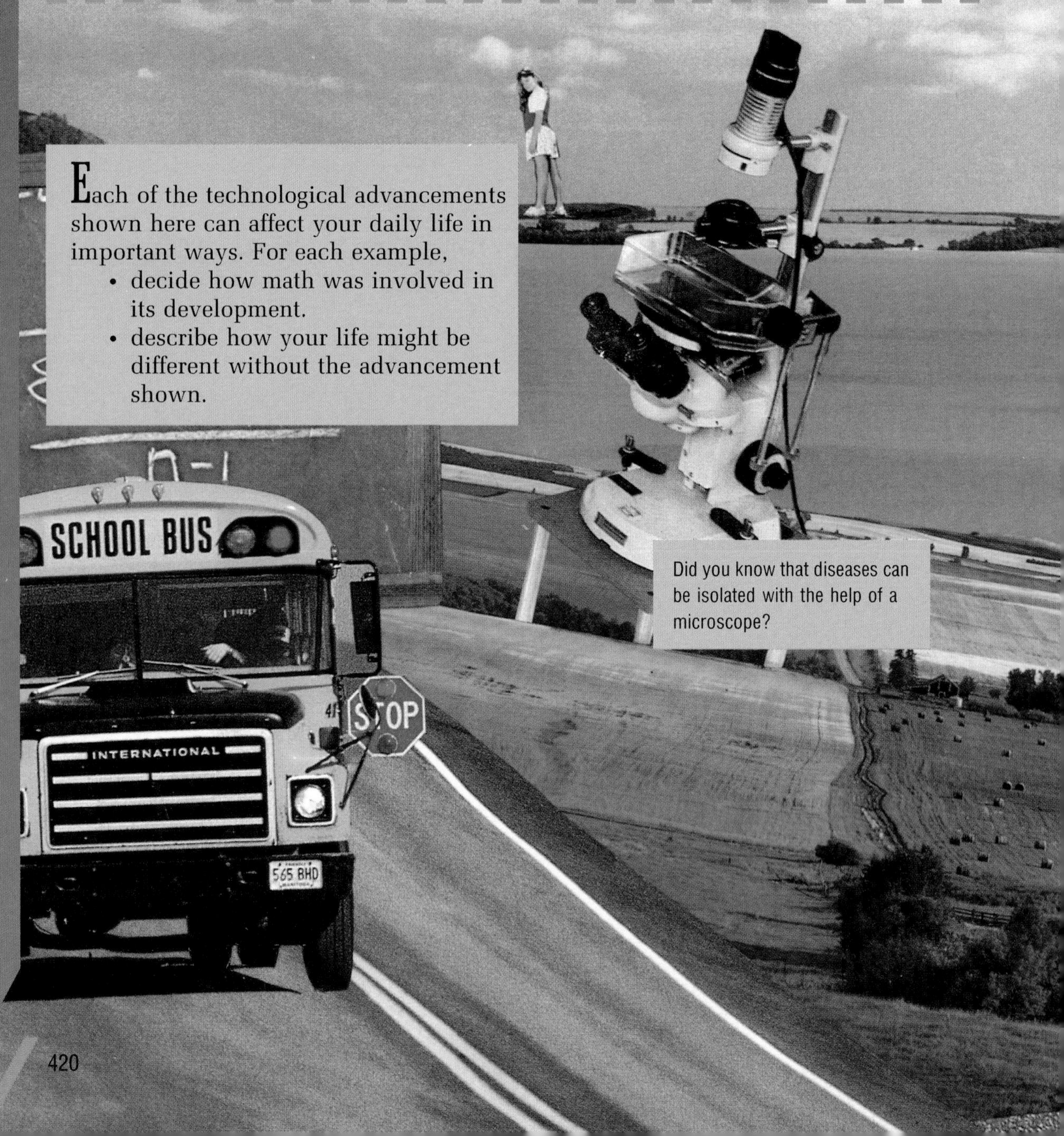

n-1
SCHOOL BUS
INTERNATIONAL
STOP
565 BHD

Did you know that diseases can be isolated with the help of a microscope?

Did you know that there are over 500 communication satellites orbiting the earth?

Did you know that less energy is used when you heat food using a microwave?

You have learned various relationships in geometry. Each of the following explores other relationships in geometry. Record your findings in your journal.

EXPLORATION ① *Work in a Group*

1. (a) Make a copy of the chart shown. Use the figures below to complete the chart.

   (b) Look at your chart. What patterns and relationships do you see?

2. (a) Use pipe cleaners and straws to create similar figures of your own.

   (b) Extend your chart. Do the patterns and relationships extend to your figures as well?

Figure	Number of Vertices	Number of Faces	Number of Edges
A			
B			
C			
D			
E			
F			
?			
?			

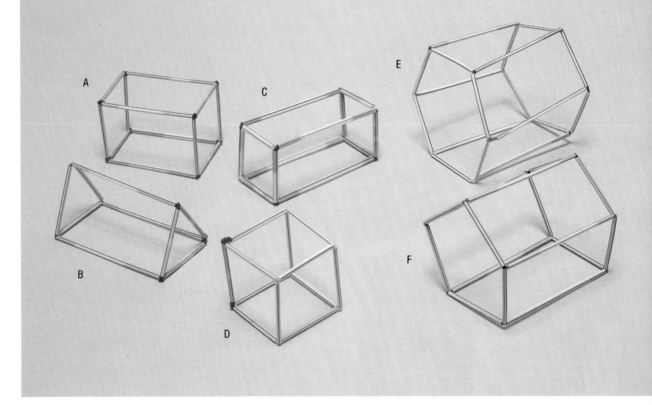

EXPLORATION ② *Work with a Partner*

3. (a) Use toothpicks and marshmallows to create four of each shape shown below.

   (b) Put one shape at each corner of a book to try to support the book. Which shapes cannot support the book?

   (c) Create figures of your own that you think can be used to support a book. Which ones were successful?

   (d) How are the figures that are able to support the books alike? How are they different?

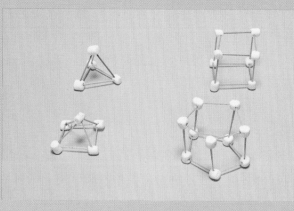

4. Place two stacks of books 20 cm apart on your desk.

   (a) Use toothpicks and marshmallows to construct a bridge between the two stacks of books. What shape(s) did you use?

   (b) What objects can your bridge support?

   (c) How can you modify your construction so that the bridge will support heavier objects?

Figures like regular hexagons have a common property. Try the following activity. What is the property?

Activity 1

(a) Try the steps shown below. What have you found?

Step 1
Trace the figure.

Step 2
Find a fold to show the hexagon as two equal parts.

Step 3
Unfold the paper. The crease shows a **line of symmetry**.

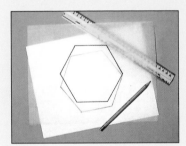
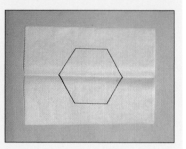

(b) Use the figures at the bottom of the page. Apply the steps above to the figures.

The hexagon has a **line of symmetry** in which one half of the hexagon is reflected onto the other half. The hexagon is said to have **reflectional symmetry**. How many other lines of symmetry does the regular hexagon have?

Activity 2

(a) Place a mirror or Mira on the hexagon. Move the mirror or Mira into a position so that the part of the hexagon seen and its reflection forms the complete hexagon. Hold the mirror or Mira in place and draw a line along its base.

(b) Use the figures below. Repeat part (a).

(c) Use figures of your own. Repeat part (a).

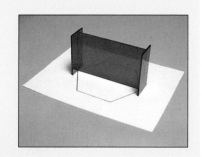

Activity 3

Step 1
Trace a figure. The centre of the figure is shown.

Step 2
Place the tracing on top of the original figure and hold it down at the centre. Rotate the tracing so that it matches the original figure.

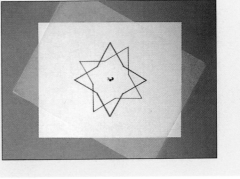

A figure is said to have **rotational symmetry** if it can be turned about its centre to match itself in less than one complete turn.

The number of times in one complete turn that the figure matches itself is called the **order of rotational symmetry**. Find the order of rotational symmetry for each figure to the right.

Activity 4

1. (a) Find logos and designs that have reflectional symmetry. How many lines of symmetry does each have?

   (b) Create logos and designs of your own that have at least two lines of symmetry. Show all lines of symmetry on your drawings.

2. (a) Find logos and designs that have rotational symmetry. What is the order in each?

   (b) Create logos and designs of your own that have an order of rotational symmetry of at least two. Have others find the order of rotational symmetry for them.

3. Find logos and designs from newspapers, the yellow pages, etc.

   (a) Which have only rotational symmetry? Which have only reflectional symmetry?

   (b) Which have reflectional and rotational symmetry?

   (c) In your journal, describe a business you might open in the future. Design a logo that has both rotational and reflectional symmetry for your business.

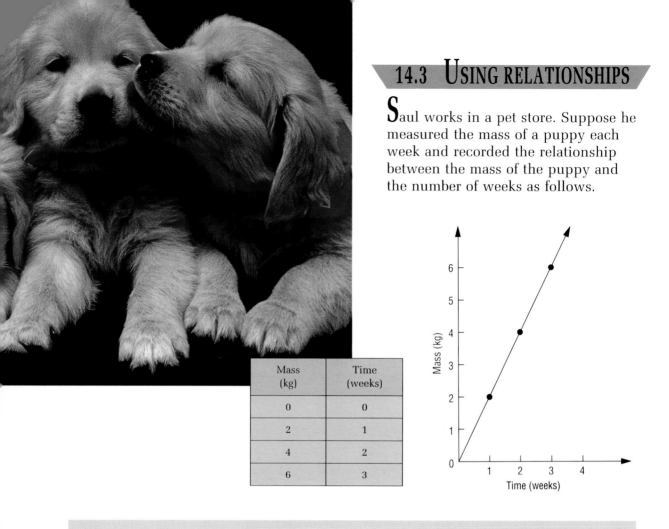

14.3 USING RELATIONSHIPS

Saul works in a pet store. Suppose he measured the mass of a puppy each week and recorded the relationship between the mass of the puppy and the number of weeks as follows.

Mass (kg)	Time (weeks)
0	0
2	1
4	2
6	3

Activity 1

From the graph, you can obtain information about points between the marked points. Finding information in this way is called **interpolation**.

(a) Estimate the mass of the puppy at 2.5 weeks.

(b) Estimate how many weeks it took the puppy to reach a mass of about 3 kg.

Activity 2

Copy the line graph above and extend the line. When the line is extended, you can predict further information. Finding information in this way is called **extrapolation**.

(a) Estimate the mass of the puppy at 5 and 6.5 weeks.

(b) Estimate how many weeks it will take the puppy to reach a mass of 12 kg.

B Remember: To obtain information, extend the graph.

1. The relation between the distance Roseanne ran on field day and the time taken is shown.

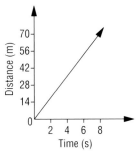

(a) How far did Roseanne run in 4 s?

(b) How far did she run in 12 s?

(c) How long did it take Roseanne to run 28 m?

(d) About how long do you think it took her to run 75 m? What assumptions have you made?

2. The relation between the number of pages of a book and the time Chrissy took to read is shown.

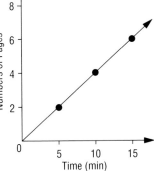

(a) How many pages did she read in 10 min?

(b) How many pages did she read in 18 min?

(c) How long did it take Chrissy to read 75 pages?

(d) About how long would it take Chrissy to read this book?

3. The graph shows the relation between the volume of water in a tank which is being drained and time.

(a) How much water is lost in 30 min?

(b) How long will it take to drain all the water?

(c) Create a problem of your own using the graph. Compare it with others in your class.

4. Work with a partner. Run a tap slowly into a container. The water from the tap must flow at a constant rate.

(a) As you fill the container, measure the water level each minute.

(b) Plot your data on a graph.

(c) Create a problem of your own using the graph. Compare it with others in your class.

(d) Repeat parts (a) to (c) using other containers.

14.4 NUMERICAL RELATIONSHIPS

Jasmine's class completed an experiment. They attached a dixie cup to an elastic, added pennies to the cup, and measured the stretch in length of the elastic. The results were recorded.

Number of Pennies	Stretch in Length of Elastic
5 pennies	1 cm
10 pennies	2 cm
15 pennies	3 cm

An arrow can be used to show a pairing rule for the data.

5 pennies → 1 cm
10 pennies → 2 cm
15 pennies → 3 cm

The pairing rule is read as "5 pennies stretches the elastic 1 cm", etc.

The pairing rule relates the number of pennies, n, to the stretch in length of the elastic.

$$n \text{ pennies} \rightarrow n \div 5 \text{ cm}$$

You can use a table of values to show data for the mapping $n \rightarrow n \div 5$. From the table of values, you can write ordered pairs. To see a picture of this relationship, you can draw a graph of the ordered pairs.

Table of Values

n	$n \div 5$
0	0
5	1
10	2
15	3
20	4

Ordered Pairs

(0, 0)
(5, 1)
(10, 2)
(15, 3)
(20, 4)

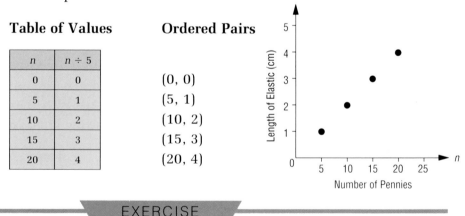

EXERCISE

A Review your skills with evaluating expressions.

1. Refer to the graph above.
   (a) Suppose Jasmine used 12 pennies, how far would the elastic stretch?
   (b) Suppose the elastic stretched 7 cm, how many pennies are in the cup?

2. Copy and complete the table of values. Write the mapping represented. Then, plot the ordered pairs on a graph.

(a)

n	$3n + 1$	Ordered Pair
0	1	(0, 1)
1		
2		
3		

(b)

x	$2x + 6$	Ordered Pair
0		
1		
2		
3		

(c)

k	$4k - 3$	Ordered Pair
0		
1		
2		
3		

3. (a) Make your own table of values and write the mapping represented. Then, plot the ordered pairs on a graph.

   (b) Interpolate and extrapolate values from your graph.

B Look for patterns.

4. Use whole numbers.

   (a) Construct a table of values for $n \rightarrow 0.2n + 4$.

   (b) Use the ordered pairs. Draw the graph of the relation.

5. Use a grid with each axis labelled from 0 to 15. Draw a graph of each relation.

   (a) $n \rightarrow 3n$, n is a whole number.

   (b) $n \rightarrow 3n - 1$, n is a whole number.

   (c) How are your graphs in (a) and (b) alike? How are they different?

6. (a) Draw the graph of each.
   $n \rightarrow n + 4$, n is a whole number.
   $n \rightarrow n - 4$, n is a whole number.

   (b) How are your graphs in (a) alike? How are they different?

7. A table was made of Gino's time in the 100 m race on a field day.

Time (s)	0	1	2	3
Distance (m)	0	5	10	15

   (a) Draw a graph of this information.

   (b) How far did Gino run in 1.5 s?

   (c) How long do you think Gino took to finish the race? Give reasons for your answer.

8. (a) Repeat the experiment on the previous page using different elastics.

   (b) Plot your results. How are your graphs alike? How are they different?

   (c) Write a pairing rule for each elastic.

429

14.5 PROBLEM SOLVING: CHOOSING A STRATEGY

Find the thickness of one sheet of paper.

1. Think About the Problem.

(a) Think about what you must find.
- The thickness of one sheet of paper.

(b) Think about what you are given.
- A sheet of paper and a ruler.

2. Think About a Strategy.

(a) Think of a strategy you could use.
- Find the thickness of 500 sheets of paper. Divide by 500.

(b) Think of a reason for the strategy.
- The thickness of 500 sheets of paper can be measured readily. Paper is sold in bundles of 500.

3. Work It Out.

A bundle of 500 sheets of paper is 5 cm thick.

Thus, 1 sheet of paper is $\frac{5 \text{ cm}}{500}$ or 0.01 cm thick.

4. Think About Your Solution.

Each sheet of paper is about 0.01 cm thick. Is your answer reasonable?
- Can you solve the problem another way?

Activity

(a) List other situations where the above strategy can be used to solve problems.

(b) Create and solve a problem using the above strategy.

(c) Compare your problem with others in your class.

Use your *Problem Solving Plan*.

For Questions 1 to 4, use the strategy of this section.

1. Find the thickness of one page in this book.

2. Find the thickness of one page in a newspaper or magazine.

3. A building is 73 m tall.
   (a) How can you find the number of layers of bricks in the building?
   (b) Use your strategy from (a) to find the number of layers of bricks.
   (c) Use your strategy to suggest a method to find the height of any building.

4. (a) How can you find the thickness of a penny? Find it.
   (b) Suppose pennies are stacked so that they are the height of your school. How many pennies are needed?

Use your previous strategies to help you solve the following problems.

5. The area of rectangle ABCD is 24 cm².
   (a) Find the area of the shaded part.
   (b) Solve the problem in a different way.

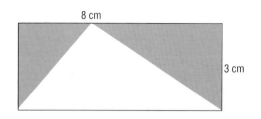

6. Tetrominoes are formed by connecting four congruent squares along at least one common side.
   (a) Use manipulatives to find how many tetrominoes there are.
   (b) Construct the tetrominoes. Create a problem using them and solve your problem.
   (c) Construct a similar problem of your own. Solve it.

MAKING CONNECTIONS

Rosalind Franklin is an X-ray crystallographer. She began her research by studying the crystal forms that hold coal together. She worked in dimensions that were so small that one unit of measurement was often one molecule of helium.

(a) What is an X-ray crystallographer?

(b) Research in your library to find examples of crystals (such as those shown below). What mathematics is suggested by the crystals? What relationships do you see in the crystals?

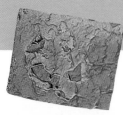

14.6 MATHEMATICS IN NATURE

Here is a chance to explore mathematics applied to natural phenomena. The activities involve objects in nature that have symmetry. Work with a partner and summarize your findings in your journal.

ACTIVITY ① Symmetry in the Ocean

1. Some ocean inhabitants are shown below.
   (a) Identify each ocean inhabitant.
   (b) What type of symmetry does each have?
   (c) Find out more about each ocean inhabitant.
   (d) What other ocean inhabitants could you add to the picture below? What symmetry do they have?

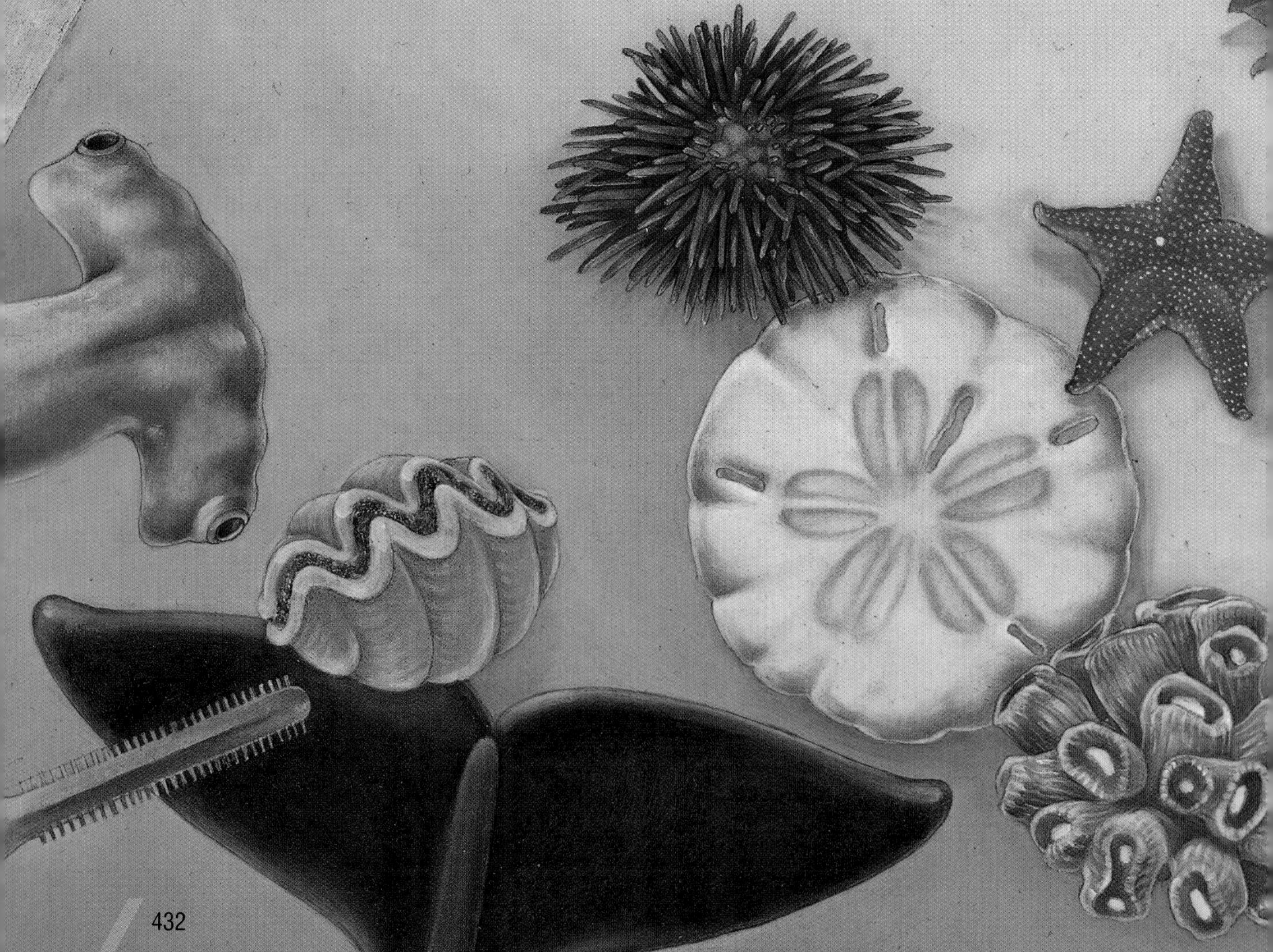

ACTIVITY ② *Symmetry in Flowers*

2. The provincial flowers are shown below.

   (a) Identify each flower.

   (b) What type of symmetry does each have?

   (c) Find out more about each flower. Why was each chosen as the provincial flower?

   (d) Find other flowers and determine the type of symmetry each has.

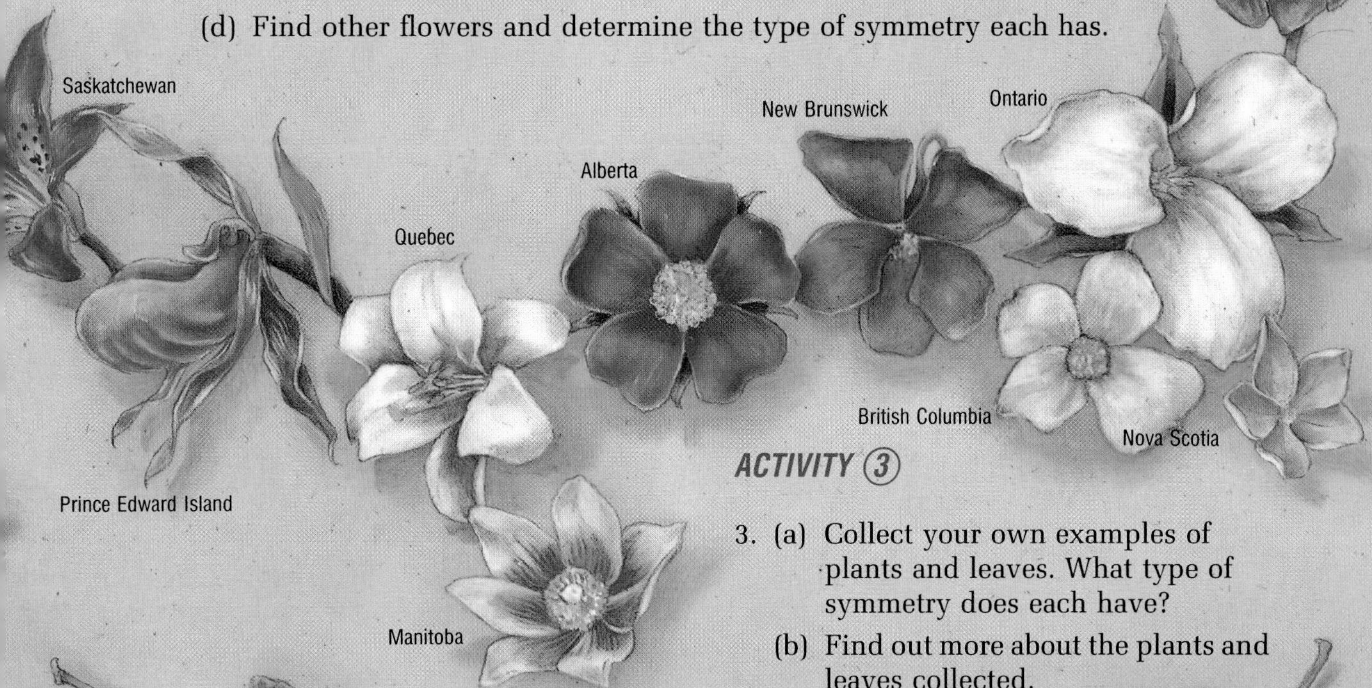

Newfoundland

Saskatchewan

Quebec

Alberta

New Brunswick

Ontario

British Columbia

Nova Scotia

Prince Edward Island

Manitoba

ACTIVITY ③

3. (a) Collect your own examples of plants and leaves. What type of symmetry does each have?

   (b) Find out more about the plants and leaves collected.

When people look ahead into the future, they often talk about the likelihood of something happening. For example, you might have heard people make statements like these:

- There is a 35% *chance* that it will snow tomorrow.
- The Jays will *probably* win.
- Tony will *likely* go to the game.

Probability is the branch of mathematics that deals with measuring the chance of an event occurring.

EXPLORATION ① *Work with a Partner*

1. (a) Flip the pages of a book. Stop randomly at a page and record the page number. Repeat 20 times.

    (b) Find the number of times the page number has a 4 in it. Write it as a fraction of 20.

    (c) Write the number of times the page number has a 6 in it as a fraction of 20.

    (d) Pick any number and write the number of times it appears in the page numbers as a fraction of 20.

    (e) Compare your results from (b), (c), and (d). How are they alike? How are they different?

EXPLORATION ② *Work with a Partner*

2. Copy the frequency table shown.

    (a) Complete the table by tossing ten coins ten times.

    (b) Write the number of heads and the number of tails occurring, each as a fraction of 100.

Experiment: Tossing Coins		
Event	Tally	Frequency
Heads	?	?
Tails	?	?
Total	100	100

3. (a) Obtain the results of four other groups. Add them to your frequency table.

    (b) Write the number of heads as a fraction of the total tosses.

4. Refer to your previous results.

    (a) How many heads might you expect in 1000 tosses?

    (b) How many tails might you expect in 1000 tosses?

EXPLORATION ③ *Work in a Group*

5. (a) Construct the pair of cubes shown to the right.

   (b) How many possible sums will there be when you toss both cubes together? Give reasons for your answer.

6. Copy the frequency table shown.

   (a) Toss your cubes 50 times. Record the number of times each sum occurs.

   (b) Write the number of times each sum occurs as a fraction of 50.

7. (a) Obtain the results of three other similar experiments. Add them to your frequency table.

   (b) Write the number of times each sum occurs as a fraction of the total tosses.

8. Refer to your results above. Suppose you toss the cubes 500 times.

   (a) About how many times will a sum of seven occur?

   (b) About how many times will a sum of eleven occur?

Experiment: Tossing Cubes		
Sum	Tally	Frequency
2	?	?
3	?	?
4	?	?
5	?	?
6	?	?
7	?	?
8	?	?
9	?	?
10	?	?
11	?	?
12	?	?

EXPLORATION ④ *Work in a Group*

9. Use the cubes above. Tape a penny to the side that shows the number 6 on each cube.

   (a) Repeat Questions 6 and 7 using your cubes.

   (b) What do you notice about the number that turns up on each cube?

   (c) What do you notice about each sum that turns up?

   (d) Repeat the parts above by also taping a paper clip to the side that shows 1 on each cube.

14.8 PROBABILITY

At a soccer game or a football game, the referee tosses a coin at the start of the game to decide which end a team will take.

Each team captain knows that the chances of winning the toss are equal. The coin, when tossed, will have an outcome of either heads up or tails up. Each possibility is called an **outcome**. Thus, each captain has a 1 out of 2 chance of winning.

How else could you decide which end a team takes? Write your answer in your journal.

You can write the probability of obtaining a head as follows:

$$\text{Probability of getting heads} = \frac{1}{2} \begin{array}{l} \leftarrow \text{number of favourable outcomes} \\ \leftarrow \text{number of possible outcomes} \end{array}$$

The probability of an event is usually written as a proper fraction. The number line to the right can help you interpret probability. Use it to help you interpret the following problem.

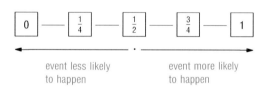

$0 \ —\ \boxed{\frac{1}{4}} \ —\ \boxed{\frac{1}{2}} \ —\ \boxed{\frac{3}{4}} \ —\ \boxed{1}$

event less likely   event more likely
to happen   to happen

Suppose you have a bag containing three dimes, six nickels, and a penny. You obtain a coin from the bag. What is the probability of obtaining a dime?

$$\text{Use probability} = \frac{\text{number of favourable outcomes}}{\text{number of possible outcomes}} \begin{array}{l} \text{— There are 3 dimes.} \\[6pt] \text{— There are 10 coins.} \end{array}$$

$$= \frac{3}{10} \qquad \begin{array}{l} \text{The event is less} \\ \text{likely to happen.} \end{array}$$

Thus, the probability of obtaining a dime is $\frac{3}{10}$.

B List all favourable outcomes and all possible outcomes.

1. A quarter is tossed. What is the probability that you toss

   (a) tails? (b) heads?

2. A marble is drawn from a box containing four black and six red marbles. Find the probability of drawing

   (a) a black marble.

   (b) a red marble.

   (c) What do you notice about the sum of the probabilities in (a) and (b)?

3. A spinner has different colours as shown. Find the probability of spinning red.

4. In response to a question, 12 people out of 20 asked said "yes". What is the probability of a person saying yes?

5. A coin is drawn from a box containing 10 pennies, 5 dimes, and 5 nickels.

   (a) List all possible outcomes.

   (b) What is the probability of drawing a nickel? a dime?

   (c) Create probability problems of your own using the coins. Compare your problems with others in your class.

6. A gum machine contains 40 white, 60 blue, 32 yellow, and 18 orange pieces of gum. Find the probability of getting a piece of gum that is

   (a) blue. (b) yellow.

   (c) orange. (d) white.

7. Flip a penny and a nickel.

   (a) List the possible outcomes.

   (b) What is the probability of each outcome?

8. Toss a penny, a nickel, and a dime.

   (a) List the possible outcomes.

   (b) What is the probability of each outcome?

9. Work together. Construct the cards shown below. Place all the cards in a hat.

   (a) Have each person draw a card from the hat. Determine and record the probability of each event occurring. Justify your probability.

   (b) Repeat part (a) by writing your own suggestions on cards and putting them in the hat.

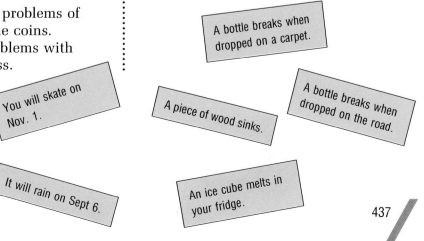

It will snow on Jan. 5.

You will skate on Nov. 1.

You will swim on Feb. 14.

It will rain on Sept 6.

A bottle breaks when dropped on a carpet.

A bottle breaks when dropped on the road.

A piece of wood sinks.

An ice cube melts in your fridge.

437

14.9 EXPERIMENTAL PROBABILITY

In the previous section, you calculated the **theoretical probability** by listing the possible outcomes and the favourable outcomes. Sometimes, you are not able to list all the outcomes. Thus, you need to collect data by doing an experiment.

Suppose a bottle factory wants to know the probability of a bottle being defective. To do so, it needs to collect data. A batch of 1000 bottles is tested and the result is shown.

Number of defective bottles 3   *Total number of bottles tested* 1000   *The probability is given by* $\dfrac{3}{1000}$

Since the probability is obtained from data in an experiment, you refer to it as **experimental probability**.

EXERCISE

B Work with a partner.

1. A light bulb factory tested 1000 bulbs. Of these, 11 were found to be defective. What is the probability of finding a defective light bulb?

2. Of 100 oranges examined, three were found to be bad. What is the probability of finding a bad orange?

3. A manufacturer tested 500 nails for strength. Of these, 22 failed the test. What is the probability of finding a weak nail?

4. Yannick tossed a spoon 25 times. It landed face up 16 times. What is the probability of the spoon landing face up?

5. A nickel and a dime are tossed.
   (a) List all possible outcomes.
   (b) What is the theoretical probability of tossing two heads? of tossing a head and a tail?
   (c) Toss two coins 100 times and record the results. Find the experimental probability of
      • tossing two heads.
      • tossing a tail and a head.

6. (a) List the possible outcomes of dropping a fork and a spoon together.
   (b) Drop a fork and a spoon together 50 times. Record the results.
   (c) Find the theoretical and experimental probability of each outcome.

14.10 WHAT ARE THE ODDS?

People often talk about the odds of something happening. Suppose you buy one of 2000 raffle tickets and there are seven prizes. The odds of your winning a prize are found as follows.

Odds (in favour) = number of favourable : number of unfavourable
$$\begin{aligned}
& \text{outcomes} && \text{outcomes} \\
=\ & 7 && : && (2000 - 7) \\
=\ & 7 && : && 1993
\end{aligned}$$

The ratio above suggests that the odds are *not* in favour of your winning a prize.

EXERCISE

B Review your skills with probability.

1. A single coin is tossed. What are the odds in favour of tossing heads?

2. Maxine has five quarters and six dimes in her pocket. She pulls out one coin.
   (a) What are the odds in favour of the coin being a quarter?
   (b) What are the odds in favour of the coin being a dime?

3. A pair of dice are tossed.
   (a) What are the odds in favour of tossing a sum of four?
   (b) What are the odds in favour of tossing an even sum?

4. A pair of dice are tossed.
   (a) What is the probability of rolling a sum of 6?
   (b) What are the odds in favour of rolling a sum of 6?
   (c) How are your answers in (a) and (b) alike? How are they different?

5. One card is drawn from a deck of playing cards.
   (a) What are the odds in favour of the card being a heart? a Jack?
   (b) What are the odds in favour of the card being the ace of spades?

6. What do you think are the odds that the following will happen?
   (a) It will rain tomorrow.
   (b) The leaves will turn colour before the end of September.
   (c) You will swim on October 30.

7. (a) List ways in which the word "odds" is used. Interpret what is meant by the word.
   (b) Compare your interpretations in (a) with those found in a dictionary. How are they alike? different?

Your journal is a place to record ideas and feelings about mathematics. By keeping notes, you will be able to see how your ideas change over time. Begin your journal for next year with these activities.

LOOKING AHEAD ACTIVITY 1

Some of the words you learned this year are the following:

area	right angle	hypotenuse	integer
similar	ratio	rate	factor
symmetry	congruent	simplify	equation

(a) Make sure you have a clear understanding of each word. Does your example illustrate the meaning clearly?

(b) Look through your text for other words you should know. Write them in your journal. Make sure you have a clear understanding of each word. Provide a clear example.

LOOKING AHEAD ACTIVITY 2

Look at the words in the index at the back of your book.

(a) Which words have you recorded in your journal?

(b) Which words do you think you should add to your journal?

(c) Make sure you have a clear understanding of all the words you added in part (b). Provide a clear example.

LOOKING AHEAD ACTIVITY 3

Some of the words you will learn next year are the following:

bearing	arc	average	data
monomial	binomial	axis	degree
image	incentre	circumference	interest

What do you think each word means? Record your meaning in your journal. Find out what each word means.

LOOKING AHEAD ACTIVITY 4

(a) How did you feel about mathematics at the beginning of the year?

(b) How have your feelings changed over the year?

LOOKING AHEAD ACTIVITY 5

In your journal, complete each of the following statements. Refer to them before you begin your classes next year.

(a) Some things I really do well in mathematics are ⬛⬛⬛ .

(b) Some things I don't do well are ⬛⬛⬛ .

(c) One thing I want to do better is ⬛⬛⬛ .

   I can start to do this better by ⬛⬛⬛ .

(d) I would like to spend more time studying by ⬛⬛⬛ .

LOOKING AHEAD ACTIVITY 6

(a) Make a list of ways that made working with others more helpful.

(b) Make a list of ways that you feel will help you contribute more to the success of a group in future years.

LOOKING AHEAD ACTIVITY 7

Have you ever thought about

- how many times a car wheel turns on a long trip?
- how long the strings on a tennis racquet are?
- how many spokes are in the wheel of a bicycle?
- how manufacturers decide on the size of a computer screen?

1. (a) A number of questions are suggested by the pictures below and the comments above. What question is suggested to you?

   (b) Research an answer. Who else might be interested in the answer?

2. (a) Choose a topic in which you are interested.

   (b) Find more information about the topic you chose. Who else might be interested in your information?

441

14.12 PROBLEM SOLVING: LOOKING AHEAD

To help you solve problems, you used a plan to help you organize your strategy. You used one similar to the *Problem Solving Plan* shown.

YOUR PROBLEM SOLVING PLAN

1. Think About the Problem
2. Think About a Strategy
3. Work it Out
4. Think About Your Solution

You have personalized your ideas and strategies so that your plan reflects them. Be sure to record your ideas in your plan for future years.

LOOKING AHEAD ACTIVITY 1

(a) Make sure you have a list of all problem solving strategies you used this year.

(b) Make sure you have illustrated each strategy in (a) with a problem.

(c) Make sure you have solved your problems in (b). You may need to review the strategy to solve further problems.

LOOKING AHEAD ACTIVITY 2

(a) Make a list of questions that you asked yourself when you were solving a problem.

(b) Compare your list with others in your class. Add to your list any questions that you think will be useful when you solve problems in the future.

LOOKING AHEAD ACTIVITY 3

Refer to the photograph above.

(a) List the types of problems the designers needed to solve.

(b) Choose a photograph of any structure. List the types of problems the designer needed to solve.

Do you think that you will ever speak to beings from other planets? Scientists have determined that the nearest planet that could have intelligent life is four light-years away.

Work with a partner on the following activities. Think about the future of space travel and the possibility of intelligent life on other planets.

Activity 1
Astronomers have sent coded messages into space.

(a) Use your library and find one of the coded messages. What does it say?

(b) If you were to send a coded message into space, what message would you send?

(c) Create a way to code your message so other intelligent life forms would be able to understand it.

Activity 2
(a) Draw a city that you think could exist on an imaginary planet. Give the planet a name.

(b) Describe a type of mathematics that can be used by the inhabitants of the planet.

(c) Describe the technology that would exist on this planet.

(d) Write a short story about life on this planet.

The fastest rocket travels about 50 000 km/h or $\frac{1}{22\,500}$ the speed of light. How long would it take to get to the nearest planet with intelligent life?

443

1. Christie walks to school at a steady rate of 1 m/s. A graph is shown.

   (a) How far does Christie walk in 1.5 s?

   (b) About how far do you think Christie will walk in 11 s?

2. (a) Draw the graph of each.
   $n \rightarrow 3n + 3$, n is a whole number.
   $n \rightarrow 3n - 3$, n is a whole number.

   (b) How are the graphs alike? How are they different?

3. (a) What type of symmetry does each have? Find the order of rotational symmetry.

   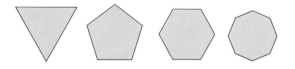

   (b) Use your results from (a). What relationship is there between the number of sides of the polygon and the order of rotational symmetry?

4. A nickel and a dime are tossed. List the possible outcomes. What is the probability of tossing

   (a) two heads?

   (b) two tails?

   (c) a head and a tail?

5. The graph shows the relation between the stretch in a spring and the mass attached. How much will the spring stretch if you attach a 30 g mass?

   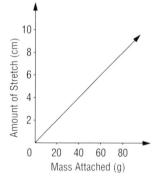

Amount of Stretch (cm) / Mass Attached (g)

MAKING CONNECTIONS

Refer to the opening pages of the chapter.

(a) Create a problem using the pictures. Solve your problem.

(b) Compare your problem with others in your class. Solve the other problems.

Are the solutions in your notebook presented clearly? Will you be able to follow them next year?

What have you learned this year to help you present your solutions more clearly?

MATH JOURNAL

Throughout the year, you have learned many skills and strategies for solving problems.

- Does your journal list all the strategies you know?
- Which skill or strategy do you think is most helpful?

SELF EVALUATION

1. A mapping is given by $n \rightarrow 2n + 1$.

   (a) Construct a table of values.

   (b) Use ordered pairs to draw the graph.

2. Squared paper is often used to create designs that have symmetry.

   (a) How many lines of symmetry does this design have?

   (b) Create a similar design. How many lines of symmetry does it have?

   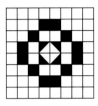

3. A coin can land either heads or tails when tossed.

   (a) What is the probability of tossing heads?

   (b) What is the probability of tossing tails?

   (c) For 100 tosses of a coin, how many times would you expect heads? tails?

4. Two coins are tossed.

   (a) What are the odds against both coins landing tails?

   (b) What are the odds in favour of one coin landing heads and one landing tails?

5. A record was made of Mario's time in the 200 m race.

Time Taken (seconds)	0	2	4	6	8
Distance Run (metres)	0	15	30	45	60

   (a) Draw a graph to show this information.

   (b) Use your graph to find how far Mario ran in 1.5 s and in 3.5 s.

   (c) Use your graph to find out how long it would take Mario to finish the race.

1. Find the volume and surface area.

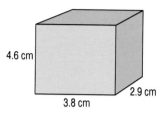

2. The greatest number of turns in skipping a rope without a break is 32 089 by J. Hughes. He took 3 h 10 min.

   (a) Find the average number of skips each minute.

   (b) Suppose J. Hughes was able to skip 18 times each second. How long would he take to pass his own record?

3. Dolores can type 49 words per minute. Every 10 min, she takes a 2 min break. How many words can she type in an eight-hour day?

4. Calculate those expressions whose values are greater than 5.

   (a) 3.2×4.8 (b) $4.6 + 3.8$

   (c) $4.45 \div 5$ (d) $6.8 - 3.9$

   (e) $9.83 + 3.62$ (f) $(4.8)^2$

   (g) 3.21×1.5 (h) $82.79 \div 17.0$

   (i) $14.26 - 3.98$ (j) $14.29 + 18.63$

5. Calculate.

   (a) $3(8 - 3) + 12 \div (8 - 4)$

   (b) $3.3(7 + 2.2) - 16.3 + 12.4$

6. Construct a triangle whose sides are congruent to the following.

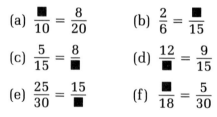

   (a) What measures do you need to calculate the area of the triangle?

   (b) Find the area of the triangle to the nearest square centimetre.

7. (a) In a right triangle, the measure of an angle is 38°. Find the measure of the remaining angle.

   (b) Construct a parallelogram whose largest angle is 120° and whose sides are all congruent. Classify the parallelogram.

8. Juan's father borrowed $1500 from the bank at an interest rate of $11\frac{3}{4}\%$ per annum. He repaid the loan with interest at the end of a year. How much did he pay?

9. Find the value of ■ in each.

   (a) $\dfrac{■}{10} = \dfrac{8}{20}$ (b) $\dfrac{2}{6} = \dfrac{■}{15}$

   (c) $\dfrac{5}{15} = \dfrac{8}{■}$ (d) $\dfrac{12}{■} = \dfrac{9}{15}$

   (e) $\dfrac{25}{30} = \dfrac{15}{■}$ (f) $\dfrac{■}{18} = \dfrac{5}{30}$

10. Write

   (a) $\dfrac{2}{5}$ as a percent.

   (b) 0.40 as a fraction.

   (c) $\dfrac{8}{20}$ as a percent.

   (d) 0.45 as a fraction.

446

11. Look at figure ABCD shown below.

   (a) Is the figure a square?

   (b) Use your construction skills to verify your answer.

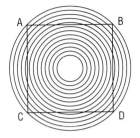

12. Cereal is shipped in a large rectangular box measuring 3.65 m × 2.95 m × 1.25 m.

   (a) How many boxes measuring 17 cm × 5 cm × 23 cm can be shipped in the box?

   (b) What assumptions have you made in part (a)?

13. (a) The area of a parallelogram is 65 cm². Find the length of the base if the height is 13 cm.

   (b) The base of a parallelogram measures 4.2 m. Find its height if the area is 23.1 cm².

14. Find each missing term.

   (a) $3:9:6 = 1:\blacksquare:2$

   (b) $1:\blacksquare:4 = 3:6:12$

   (c) $\blacksquare:18:9 = 4:6:3$

   (d) $12:8:\blacksquare = 3:2:5$

15. The measures of two angles of a triangle are 36° and 48°.

   (a) Calculate the measure of the third angle.

   (b) Sketch the triangle. What type of triangle is it?

16. A rectangular field requires 288.5 m of fence. The shortest side measures 46.3 m.

   (a) Find the area of the field.

   (b) How many times could your classroom fit on the field?

17. The points scored for a game are shown. The winner is the one with the lowest net score. Who won?

	Points Scored				Total
Jean	−3	−2	+5	−4	
Harry	−1	−3	−5	+6	
Steven	+6	−3	+2	−1	
Marcia	+4	−3	+1	−8	

18. Your pulse rate is the number of times your heart beats each minute.

   (a) Record the pulse rates for your entire class.

   (b) Find the mean, median, and mode of the pulse rates.

   (c) Display the data you have collected. What is the most appropriate graph?

   (d) Create two problems using the data. Solve them.

Use your journal to review all your problem solving skills and strategies. Use these skills to solve the following problems. Keep your journal for use next year as you will always be solving problems.

1. The perimeter of a rectangle is increased by 25% and the width of the rectangle is decreased by 30%. By what percent does the area of the rectangle change?

2. A square has an area of 144 cm². A regular octagon is drawn inside the square.

   (a) Draw the figure described.

   (b) Find the area of the octagon.

3. Construct the rectangle shown below.

   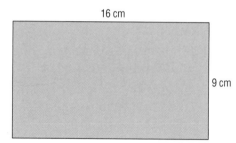
   16 cm

   9 cm

   (a) Find the least number of straight cuts needed so that the pieces of the rectangle will form a square.

   (b) What is the perimeter of the square?

4. Suppose a prime week is a week that begins with a date that is a prime number.

   (a) How many prime weeks are there this year?

   (b) What assumptions have you made in part (a)?

5. Twenty tiles are used to form the design below.

   (a) How many squares are suggested in the design?

   (b) Create and solve a similar problem. Compare your problem with others in your class.

   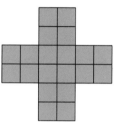

6. Sixty-four centicubes are joined to form a cube. A stripe is painted around the cube as shown.

   (a) How many of the cubes are not painted?

   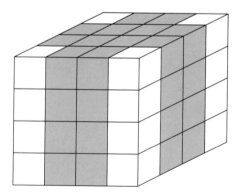

   (b) Create a similar problem. Compare your problem with others in your class.

EXTENDING SKILLS AND STRATEGIES

●●●●●●●●●●●●●●●●●●●

On the following pages you will find a selection of problems related to many of the sections within this book. (Solutions are provided at the end of the Answer section.)

You can use these pages in a variety of ways:
• by yourself, with a partner, or in a small group
• after each section, as confirmation that you have learned the skills in the section
• after each section, for extension and additional challenge
• after each chapter, for additional review or self evaluation
• after several chapters, as cumulative review, to help you see connections among math topics
• at the end of the year to review and extend your skills

CHAPTER 1

Section 1.2

1. Write the numbers in standard form.
   (a) The largest concrete dam in the world has a height of one hundred sixty–seven metres.
   (b) The longest street in the world has a length of one thousand eight hundred ninety–six kilometres.
   (c) A meteorite on exhibit weighs thirty thousand eight hundred eighty–three kilograms.

2. Write the numbers in expanded form.
   (a) The longest river in the world is the Nile in Africa, at 6690 km. The Amazon river in South America is 6280 km in length.
   (b) Newfoundland consists of Labrador, which is 180 521 km^2 in area, and an island which is 69 374 km^2 in area.
   (c) Skydome, in Toronto, has seating for 50 580 for baseball.

3. Find a number which requires the same number of digits to write in both standard and expanded form.

Section 1.3

1. Write these numbers in order from least to greatest. 44.99, 4.499, 449.9, 4499, 40.499

2. Write a number between the first and second number, and another number between the second and third.
   (a) 8.04, 8.40, 8.408
   (b) 4.004, 4.040, 4.400

3. How many numbers can be written between 5.1 and 5.3?

4. Dini bought 5 raffle tickets at $3 each and Rashid bought 4 raffle tickets at $4 each. Who paid more?

5. Estimate the dimensions of your classroom.

Section 1.4

1. Round as indicated.
   (a) 3.789 to the nearest hundredth
   (b) 78 294 to the nearest thousand
   (c) 10.989 to the nearest whole

2. Round as indicated.
   (a) 34.3 g to the nearest gram
   (b) 43.9 cm to the nearest centimetre

3. Round as indicated.
   (a) 1349 m to the nearest kilometre
   (b) 4965 mL to the nearest litre

4. John Olerud hit a home run 108.5 m. To the nearest metre, how far did the home run travel?

5. Explain why it is incorrect to round 6.49 to 7, even though the four in the tenths column position correctly rounds to 5.

Section 1.7

1. Divide. Round each answer to the nearest tenth.
   (a) 16.5 ÷ 1.3 (b) 27.45 ÷ 5.5 (c) 378 ÷ 8.8

2. It cost $147.50 to rent a bus for a field trip, and 27 students each paid $5.50.
   (a) Will the money collected cover the cost?
   (b) If not, how much more is needed? If so, how much extra is there?

3. Choose any number. Multiply it by 4. Divide the result by 2. Then multiply by 6. Finally, divide by 12.
   (a) What do you notice about the result?
   (b) Explain why the result in part (a) happens.

4. Femi drives her car at a speed of 95 km/h. Her parents live 445 km away. How long would it take her to make the trip to visit her parents? Round your answer to the nearest tenth of an hour.

Section 1.10

1. Replace ☐ with +, −, × or ÷ .
   (a) 10 ☐ 9 ☐ 50 = 40 (b) 18 ☐ 6 ☐ 3 = 1

2. Insert brackets and operation signs to make the equalities true.
   (a) 9 ☐ 6 ☐ 4 = 18 (b) 12 ☐ 3 ☐ 3 = 5

3. Write an original problem of your own similar to Question 2. Exchange with a partner and solve.

4. Fourteen jars were filled with honey from a pail. Each jar holds 275 mL of honey. If 148 mL of honey was left in the pail, what volume was in the pail originally?

CHAPTER 2

Section 2.2
1. Replace ☐ with either < or >.
   (a) +6 ☐ –7   (b) –18 ☐ –17   (c) –27 ☐ 17

2. Write an integer to show each of the following.
   (a) The lowest point on the earth's surface is 10 859 m below sea level.
   (b) Little Bear, a mountain peak in Colorado, is 4278 m above sea level.
   (c) The average depth of the Pacific Ocean is 4188 m.

3. List common words in English that suggest signs for integers. Find at least 5 words each for positive and negative.

4. High tide is 4 m above sea level. Low tide will be the exact opposite. Write the height as an integer for both tides.

Section 2.4
1. Find each sum. Then write the sums in order from least to greatest.
   (a) (+19) + (–11)   (b) (–7) + (+4)
   (c) (–8) + (–3)   (d) (+5) + (+5)

2. For 9 holes of golf, a player had these results. What is the final score?
   (a) –1, +1, par, +1, +1, –1, par, +1, +1
   (b) par, –1, –1, +1, –1, +1, par, +1, –1

3. The temperature at 02:00 was –5°C. Over the next two hours the temperature fell by 3°C.
   (a) Write a sum to represent this situation.
   (b) What is the final temperature?

4. Find each sum.
   (a) (+4) + (–2) + (–1)
   (b) (–9) + (–4) + (+7)
   (c) (+2) + (–3) + (–4) + (+5)

Section 2.5
1. Find the differences. Then write the differences in order from least to greatest.
   (a) (–6) – (+4)   (b) (+13) – (–6)
   (c) (–11) – (+7)   (d) (+8) – (+9)

2. Find the missing integer.
   (a) (+7) – ( ) = +2   (b) –4 – ( ) = +5
   (c) ( ) – (+2) = 14   (d) –9 – ( ) = 0

   (e) +12 – ( ) = –7   (f) 0 – ( ) = +3

3. At 15:30 the temperature was –11°C. Over the next four hours the temperature fell until, at 19:30, the temperature was –21°C. Write a subtraction statement that shows how the temperature changed. By how much did the temperature fall?

4. Calculate.
   (a) (+5) – (+2) – (–1)
   (b) (–3) – 0 – (+3)
   (c) (+6) – (–2) – (+5)

Section 2.8
1. Draw a coordinate grid. Follow these instructions.
   Join (–6, –2) to (–6, 4).
   Join (–3, 4) to (–3, –2).
   Join (–6, 1) to (–3, 1).
   What letter have you formed?

2. These ordered pairs represent a geometric figure.
   A(–5, –6) B(–5, +10) C(+8, +10) D(+8, –6)
   (a) Predict the shape of the figure.
   (b) Plot the ordered pairs and join the pairs in order.
   (c) What is the geometric figure?

3. The coordinates of parallelogram ABCD are:
   A(–6, –4) B(–4, +6) C(6, 6) D(,)
   (a) In which quadrant is vertex D?
   (b) Write the coordinates for vertex D.
   (c) What are the coordinates of the intersection of the diagonals AC and BD?

4. Draw an isosceles triangle on a grid following these directions.
   (a) The left side of the base is in quadrant 2.
   (b) The right side of the base is in quadrant 1.
   (c) The third vertex is in quadrant 4.

Section 2.15
1. Find the products. Which answers are the same?
   (a) (+2)(+8)   (b) (–3)(–6)   (c) (–4)(–4)
   (d) (–3)(+4)   (e) (–2)(–8)   (e) (–4)(+5)

2. Calculate. Write the products in order from least to greatest.
   (a) (+6)(+2)   (b) (–4)(–4)
   (c) (–5)(+4)   (d) (+7)(–3)

3. The temperature fell two degrees each hour for 5 straight hours. What was the total change in temperature over that time?

4. A weather balloon sank 15 m a minute for half an hour. What was the total change in altitude over that time?

Section 2.16
1. Divide. Which answers are the same?
   (a) $(+49) \div (-7)$ (b) $(-36) \div (-12)$
   (c) $(-12) \div (+2)$ (d) $0 \div (-3)$
   (e) $(+18) \div (-3)$ (f) $(+48) \div (-6)$

2. Calculate. Write the quotients in order from least to greatest.
   (a) $(-49) \div (+7)$ (b) $(-28) \div (-4)$
   (c) $(+35) \div (+7)$ (d) $(+40) \div (-8)$

3. Find the average of these numbers.
   $-8, +3, -25, +6, -1$

4. Shares in Diamonds Unlimited lost 42¢ in six days. Use an integer to indicate the average change in price per day.

Section 2.17
1. Calculate.
   (a) $(+24) + (-18) \div (-3)$ (b) $(-75) \div (+5) + (-10)$

2. Calculate.
   (a) $(+27) \div [(-9) - (-6)]$
   (b) $[(-27) - (+6)] \div [(-6) + (-5)]$

3. Tap water at 18°C was placed in an ice cube tray. If it took 3 h for the water to freeze, what was the average change in temperature per hour?

4. Calculate.
$$\frac{(+24) \div [(-8) - (-2)]}{(+64) \div (-32) \times [(-48) - (-46)]}$$

CHAPTER 3
Section 3.2
1. (a) Write all the factors for the numbers 14, 19, 41, and 93.
   (b) Which numbers in (a) are prime?

2. All the prime factors of a number are shown. What is the number?
   (a) 3, 5, 7   (b) 2, 2, 5   (c) 3, 11, 13

3. Write the prime factors of each.
   (a) 135   (b) 224   (c) 525   (d) 289

4. List all the factors of these numbers.
   (a) 128   (b) 284   (c) 300   (d) 525

5. What is the smallest number which has all of the first four prime numbers as its factors?

Section 3.3
1. Buses leave the Jane Street Station every 4 min. Subway trains leave every 3 min. How often does a train and bus leave at the same time?

2. A gear has 10 teeth. A connected, larger gear has 15 teeth. After how many turns will the teeth return to their original positions?

3. The greatest common factor of two numbers is 2. The least common multiple of the two numbers is 70. What are the numbers?

4. Find the greatest common factor.
   (a) 32, 48, 24   (b) +30, 45, 15   (c) +36, 54, 72

5. Find the least common multiple.
   (a) 2, 4, 8   (b) 6, 9, 12   (c) 3, 6, 4

Section 3.4
1. Use your calculator to find each square root.
   (a) $\sqrt{5.29}$ (b) $\sqrt{56.25}$
   (c) $\sqrt{22.09}$ (d) $\sqrt{70.56}$

2. Find the square root to the nearest hundredth.
   (a) $\sqrt{56}$ (b) $\sqrt{71}$ (c) $\sqrt{224}$ (d) $\sqrt{500}$

3. The area of a square field is 14 400 m². Find the length of fencing required to enclose the field.

4. The same number represents both the perimeter and the area of a square. What is the length of the side of the square?

5. A domino piece is in the shape of two squares. If the area of the domino piece is 882 mm², what are the dimensions of the domino?

Section 3.5
1. If the last two digits of a large digit number are divisible by 4, explain why the whole number is also always divisible by 4.

2. If the last two digits of a large digit number are divisible by 5, explain why the whole number is also divisible by 5.

3. If a number is divisible by both 2 and 5, explain why the number is also always divisible by 10.

4. If a number is divisible by both 3 and 5, explain why it is also always divisible by 15.

Section 3.9

1. Find the complement for each angle.
   (a) 37°   (b) 23°   (c) 81°   (d) 41°

2. Find the supplement for each angle.
   (a) 127°   (b) 77°   (c) 45°   (d) 118°

3. Find the missing measure.
   (a)   (b)   (c)

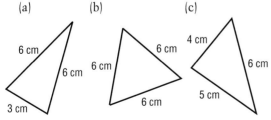

4. Find the missing measures.

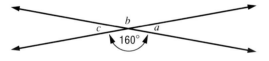

5. A straight line is made up of two angles. One angle is five times the measure of the second angle. What are the measures of the angles?

Section 3.11

1. Classify the triangles as equilateral, scalene, or isosceles.
   (a)   (b)   (c)

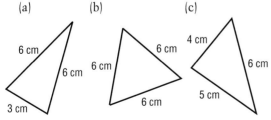

2. (a) Construct △ABC so that ∠A = 50°, ∠C = 50°, and AC = 6 cm.
   (b) Classify the triangle.
   (c) Find the missing angle measure.

3. The angles in a triangle are such that the second angle is 3 times the measure of the first; and the third angle is 6 times the measure of the first. What is the measure of each angle?

CHAPTER 4
Section 4.2
1. Write in exponent form. Then evaluate.
   (a) $7 \times 7 \times 7 \times 7 \times 7 \times 7$
   (b) $(-8) \times (-8) \times (-8) \times (-8)$

2. Write as repeated multiplication. Then evaluate.
   (a) $(-2)^4$ (b) 9^3 (c) 5^4 (d) $(-1)^7$

3. Each member of the telephone committee calls 3 other members. How many people are called in the fourth round of calls if the membership society calls 3 people in the first round?

4. Which value is greater: 2^8 or 8^2?

Section 4.3
1. Replace ☐ with < or >.
   (a) 3^2 ☐ 2^3 (b) 1^6 ☐ 2^3
   (c) 8^3 ☐ 6^3 (d) 6^4 ☐ 4^6

2. Calculate.
   (a) $3^3 - 3^2$ (b) $(3^2 + 7) - 2$ (c) $10^3 - (10^2 + 2)$

3. Calculate.
   (a) $3^4 \div 9 + (7 \times 3)$ (b) $2 \times (3^2 - 2^3)$
   (c) $(13^2 - 12^2) \div 5^2$

4. Every two hours, a starting number of 50 yeast cells squares in number. Every two hours, a starting number of 2 bacteria increases by an exponent of 3. After how many two hour intervals will there be more bacteria than yeast cells?

Section 4.4
1. Write each as a single power.
   (a) $7^5 \div 7^2$ (b) $4^6 \times 4^4$
   (c) $12^7 \div 12^2$ (d) $5^6 \times 5^5$

2. Evaluate.
   (a) $4^9 \div 4^5$ (b) $9^5 \div 9^3$ (c) $4^3 \times 4^2$ (d) $2^3 \times 2^5$

3. How many pennies are there in 10^3 dollars?

4. How many milligrams are there in 10^3 kg?

5. Evaluate $(4 + 3)^2 + 2^2 + 2$.

6. Use the same digits (4, 3, 2, 2, 2 and 2) to write another expression which has the same value as that in Question 5.

Section 4.7

1. Write each with a positive exponent.
    (a) 7^{-2} (b) 11^{-4} (c) $5^3 \div 5^5$ (d) $4^6 \div 4^{10}$

2. Evaluate. Write your answer as a positive integer.
    (a) 3^{-3} (b) 4^{-3} (c) $4^5 \div 4^7$ (d) $5^7 \div 5^{10}$

3. Calculate.
    (a) $4^5 \times 4^3 \div 4^6$ (b) $3^7 \div 3^9 \times 3^0$
    (c) $2^4 \div (4^2 \div 4^0)$

4. Rewrite each as a power with a negative exponent.
    (a) $\dfrac{1}{64}$ (b) $\dfrac{1}{125}$ (c) $\dfrac{1}{27}$ (d) $\dfrac{1}{216}$

5. What two digits can be used to write expressions equal to 8, 9, $\dfrac{1}{8}$, and $\dfrac{1}{9}$?

Section 4.10

1. Write each number in scientific notation.
    (a) 3 740 000   (b) 2 100 000 000 000
    (c) 9 348 000 000 000 000

2. Write each number in scientific notation.
    (a) 0.000 003 4   (b) 0.001 04
    (c) 0.000 000 000 46

3. Write each number in standard form.
    (a) 1.307×10^{-3} (b) 2.4×10^8 (c) 4.507×10^{-6}

4. The mass of a proton is 0.000 000 000 000 000 000 000 001 68 g. Find the mass of 2 000 000 000 000 000 000 000 protons.

5. The distance from Earth to the Sun is 152 000 000 km. If light travels 1000 km in 0.003 s, how long will it take light to travel from the Sun to Earth?

Section 4.12

1. Find the value if $y = 3$.
    (a) $3y$ (b) $y^2 - 4$ (c) $2y^3$ (d) $4y^2 - 3y$

2. Evaluate if $m = 2.5$ and $n = -1.5$.
    (a) $3m - n$ (b) $m^2 + 2n$
    (c) $4m^3 - n^2$ (d) $2m^3 - 2n^2 - n^0$

3. The distance travelled by a falling object is given by $d = 4.9t^2$, where t is the time in seconds and d is distance in metres. How far will a falling object travel in each of the following times?
    (a) 1 s (b) 2 s (c) 3 s (d) 4 s

4. In football, the score can be calculated using $s = 7t + 3f$, where t stands for touchdowns (and conversions), and f for field goals. Calculate the score if
    (a) $t = 4$ and $f = 3$. (b) $t = 5$ and $f = 2$.

5. The cost of printing textbooks is $4000 plus $1.30 a book.
    (a) Write an expression for calculating the total cost, T, of N textbooks.
    (b) Calculate the total cost for printing 1500 textbooks.

Section 4.13

1. Write each in mathematical symbols.
    (a) one fourth of a number
    (b) one half of a number plus three
    (c) twice a number minus seven
    (d) six minus one third of a number

2. The length of a metal wire is 15 cm plus 0.000 15 cm per degree greater than 30°C.
    (a) Write an expression for the length of the wire for temperatures above 30°C.
    (b) Calculate the length of the wire at a temperature of 40°C.

3. The height a ball will bounce on successive bounces is 48 cm minus 8 cm per bounce.
    (a) Write an expression for the height of a bouncing ball.
    (b) Calculate the height of the ball on the third bounce.

Section 4.14

1. Solve each equation.
    (a) $2x + 3 = 15$ (b) $4y - 6 = 18$ (c) $2z - 9 = 17$

2. Solve each equation.

   (a) $3x = 9$ (b) $\frac{1}{2}y = 9$ (c) $\frac{2}{3}z - 3 = 3$

3. The cost of taking a taxi is $C = 0.75 + 0.25k$ where C is the total cost in dollars and k is the distance in kilometres.
   (a) Find the distance travelled if the cost of the trip was $3.75.
   (b) Find the distance travelled if the cost was $7.00.
   (c) How far could you travel if you have $10.00?

CHAPTER 5

Section 5.2

1. Mr. Marwick asked Andrea to put a crepe paper border around the announcement board. The board is 2.5 m long and 1.5 m tall. If the crepe paper is 5 cm wide, how much paper will she need?

2. An aluminum edge is to be put around an octagonal table.
   (a) What length will the edge be if each side of the octagonal table is 0.45 m long?
   (b) What will the cost of the edging be if the price is $0.60/m?

3. Find the perimeter of this figure.

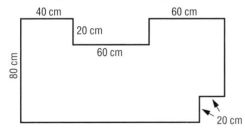

Section 5.3

1. Find the circumference of these circles.

   (a)   (b)

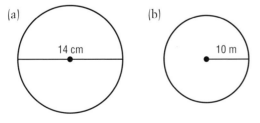

(c)

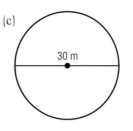

2. The front wheel of a bicycle is 60 cm in diameter.
   (a) How far will the bicycle travel if the front wheel turns 100 times?
   (b) How many times must the wheel turn to travel 1 km?

3. How much longer is the outer circumference of the donut than the inner circumference?

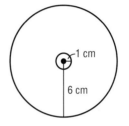

4. How many times will the small hoop have to roll to equal one roll of the larger hoop? Do your calculation mentally.

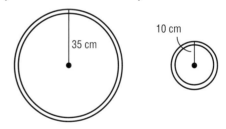

Section 5.7

1. Find the missing measure of the fourth angle.
   (a)

   (b)

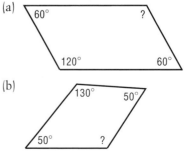

2. Find the missing measures.

(a)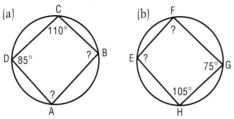

(b)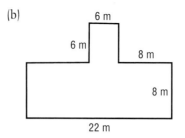

3. Construct a quadrilateral in which the diagonals are perpendicular bisectors.

4. Construct a quadrilateral in which the opposite sides are parallel and the diagonals bisect each other but do not form 90° angles.

Section 5.10

1. Calculate the area.

(a)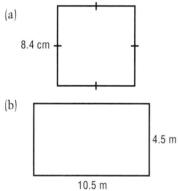

8.4 cm

(b)

4.5 m

10.5 m

2. How much sod is needed to cover a lawn 7.5 m by 15.0 m?

3. What will be the cost of the sod in Question 2 if sod costs $8.75/m²?

4. Calculate each area.

(a)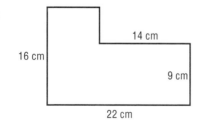

16 cm

14 cm

9 cm

22 cm

Section 5.12

1. Calculate each area.

(a)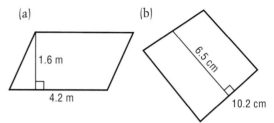

1.6 m

4.2 m

(b)

6.5 cm

10.2 cm

2. Draw a parallelogram in which the height is 8 cm and the base is 12 cm. Calculate the area of the parallelogram.

3. Find the dimensions of a parallelogram which has the same area of this rectangle.

120 cm

84 cm

4. Find the cost of seeding a corn field in the shape of a parallelogram if the base of the parallelogram is 180 m, its height is 120 m, and the cost of seeding is 12¢/m².

Section 5.13

1. Calculate the area of each triangle.

(a)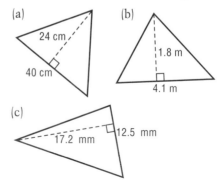

24 cm

40 cm

(b)

1.8 m

4.1 m

(c)

17.2 mm

12.5 mm

2. Draw a triangle in which the length of the base is 14 cm and the height is 8 cm. Calculate the area of the triangle.

3. Calculate the area.

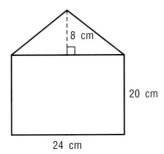

4. Calculate the shaded area.

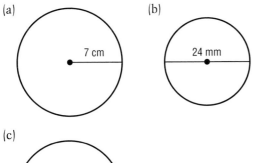

Section 5.14

1. Calculate the area of each circle.

(a)

(b)

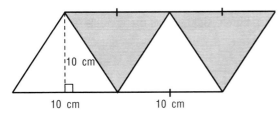

(c)

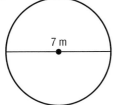

2. Find the radii of a dime, a nickel, and a quarter to the nearest millimetre. Calculate the area of each.

3. Which figure has a greater area, and by how much: a square with a perimeter of 40 cm or a circle with a circumference of 40 cm?

4. Calculate the shaded area of the figure.

Section 5.17

1. Calculate the shaded area of each figure.

(a)

(b)

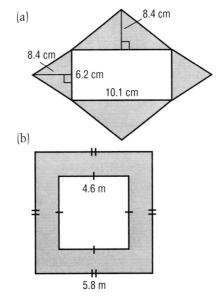

2. Calculate the total area.

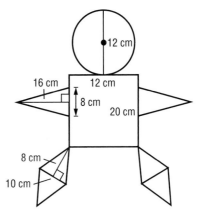

457

CHAPTER 6

Section 6.2

1. Draw a net for each package.

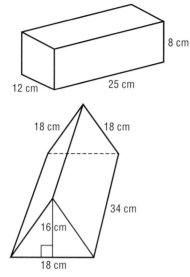

8 cm
12 cm
25 cm

18 cm   18 cm

34 cm

16 cm

18 cm

(a) Find the area of each face.
(b) Find the total surface area.

2. Mark the faces that have the same dimensions.

(a)   (b)

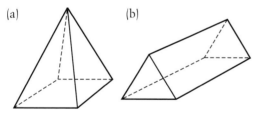

(c)

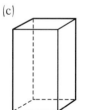

3. A triangular based prism is 18 cm tall. The triangular faces have sides of 10 cm and altitudes of 8 cm. What is the total surface area?

Section 6.3

1. Draw a net of the can.

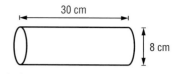

30 cm
8 cm

(a) Find the area of each circular face.
(b) Find the area of the rectangle.
(c) Find the total surface area.

2. The diameter of a can is 0.30 m. Its height is 0.45 m.
(a) Find the surface area of the can.
(b) If the cost of aluminum is $0.75/m², what is the total cost of the metal required?

3. Find the surface area of each package. Which package has the greatest surface area?

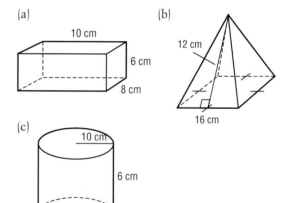

(a)

10 cm
6 cm
8 cm

(b)

12 cm
16 cm

(c)

10 cm
6 cm

Section 6.10

1. Find the volume of each.

(a)

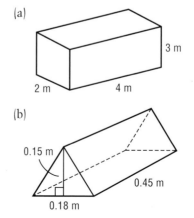

3 m
2 m   4 m

(b)

0.15 m
0.45 m
0.18 m

2. The dimensions of an aquarium are as follows: 45 cm long, 30 cm tall, and 20 cm wide.
   (a) Find the capacity in millilitres.
   (b) Find the capacity in litres.

3. The average volume of a popcorn kernel is 0.08 cm³. Calculate the number of kernels that can be packed in a box 5 cm wide, 10 cm long, and 20 cm tall.

Section 6.11

1. Find the volume of each.

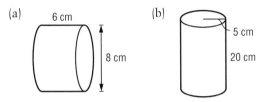

(a) 6 cm, 8 cm   (b) 5 cm, 20 cm

2. A car engine has 8 cylinders each with a diameter of 7.2 cm and a height of 8.4 cm. What is the total volume of the cylinders?

3. The diameter of a can of tomatoes is 9.4 cm and the height is 16.2 cm. Calculate the capacity in millilitres.

4. An oil drum is 94 cm high. The radius of the base is 35 cm. What is its capacity in litres?

Section 6.12

1. Find the volume of each.

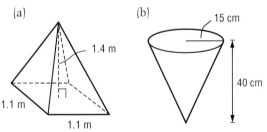

(a) 1.4 m, 1.1 m, 1.1 m   (b) 15 cm, 40 cm

2. A tent is in the shape of a pyramid. Find the volume of the tent.

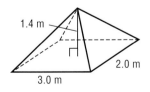

1.4 m, 3.0 m, 2.0 m

3. Road salt is stored in a conical pile. Calculate the volume of the pile if the height of the cone is 7.8 m and its radius is 16.2 m.

4. Calculate the volume of the unfilled space.

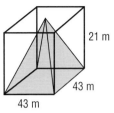

21 m, 43 m, 43 m

CHAPTER 7

Section 7.2

1. Write each as a mixed number.
   (a) $\frac{27}{4}$ (b) $\frac{19}{6}$ (c) $\frac{12}{5}$ (d) $\frac{22}{7}$

2. Write each as an improper fraction.
   (a) $3\frac{1}{4}$ (b) $4\frac{1}{3}$ (c) $3\frac{5}{7}$ (d) $2\frac{4}{9}$

3. What fraction of the letters of the alphabet are
   (a) vowels?
   (b) not vowels?

4. Write all the letters of the alphabet as capital letters. What fraction of the letters are made up of
   (a) straight lines only?
   (b) curved lines only?
   (c) both straight and curved lines?

Section 7.3

1. Write an equivalent fraction for each.
   (a) $\frac{3}{8}$ (b) $\frac{2}{5}$ (c) $\frac{5}{7}$ (d) $\frac{1}{6}$

2. Write each fraction in lowest terms.
   (a) $\frac{6}{8}$ (b) $\frac{9}{12}$ (c) $\frac{7}{28}$ (d) $\frac{24}{36}$

3. In Monday's game, the Tigers got 11 hits in 44 times at bat. On Tuesday, they hit 10 for 30. On which day did they get a greater fraction of hits?

4. Of the 24 student council members, 8 were absent from the last meeting. What fraction were present?

Section 7.5

1. Write each fraction as a decimal.

   (a) $\dfrac{3}{4}$ (b) $\dfrac{3}{25}$ (c) $\dfrac{7}{20}$ (d) $\dfrac{29}{50}$

2. Write each decimal as a fraction in lowest terms.
   (a) 0.60 (b) 0.20 (c) 0.48 (d) 0.76

3. Out of 95 points, Jean's score was 69. Opal got 65 points out of 90. Who had the better score?

4. In a football game, Lawson threw 23 passes and completed 12. Carter completed 10 out of 18. Whose passing performance was better?

Section 7.7

1. Add.

   (a) $\dfrac{2}{5}+\dfrac{1}{5}$ (b) $\dfrac{2}{7}+\dfrac{1}{7}$ (c) $\dfrac{1}{3}+\dfrac{1}{6}$ (d) $\dfrac{3}{8}+\dfrac{1}{4}$

2. Add.

   (a) $\dfrac{1}{3}+\dfrac{1}{4}$ (b) $\dfrac{1}{4}+\dfrac{1}{6}$ (c) $\dfrac{2}{3}+\dfrac{4}{5}$ (d) $\dfrac{4}{5}+\dfrac{1}{4}$

3. A machine gear is made from an alloy containing $\dfrac{3}{10}$ parts aluminum and $\dfrac{3}{100}$ parts copper. What fraction of the gear is made up of aluminum and copper?

4. A flower bed is $\dfrac{1}{4}$ roses and $\dfrac{5}{8}$ marigolds.

   What part of the flower bed is made up of roses and marigolds?

Section 7.8

1. Subtract.

   (a) $\dfrac{5}{8}-\dfrac{3}{8}$ (b) $\dfrac{11}{12}-\dfrac{5}{12}$ (c) $\dfrac{3}{4}-\dfrac{1}{8}$ (d) $\dfrac{5}{6}-\dfrac{1}{3}$

2. Subtract.

   (a) $\dfrac{3}{4}-\dfrac{1}{3}$ (b) $\dfrac{3}{5}-\dfrac{1}{3}$ (c) $\dfrac{7}{8}-\dfrac{1}{3}$ (d) $\dfrac{13}{14}-\dfrac{3}{7}$

3. Margaret has $2\dfrac{3}{4}$ h to complete her math and science homework. If she has spent $1\dfrac{1}{5}$ h on math, how much time does she have left for science?

4. Mike spent $\dfrac{1}{3}$ of the day sleeping, $\dfrac{1}{4}$ of the day at school, and $\dfrac{1}{8}$ watching TV. How much time does he have left for other activities?

Section 7.9

1. Multiply.

   (a) $\dfrac{3}{4}\times\dfrac{1}{5}$ (b) $\dfrac{4}{5}\times\dfrac{1}{3}$ (c) $\dfrac{2}{3}\times\dfrac{1}{4}$ (d) $\dfrac{5}{6}\times\dfrac{7}{8}$

2. Multiply.

   (a) $\dfrac{1}{2}\times\dfrac{1}{3}\times\dfrac{3}{4}$ (b) $\dfrac{3}{4}\times\dfrac{1}{4}\times\dfrac{6}{8}$ (c) $\dfrac{3}{5}\times\dfrac{1}{3}\times\dfrac{2}{9}$

3. Della spends $2\dfrac{1}{3}$ h studying each night from Sunday through Thursday. How many hours does she study each week?

4. Shawn's mother drove to work and back 20 times in the month of April. If each round trip took $\dfrac{1}{6}$ of a tank of gas, how many tanks of gas did she use getting to work in April?

Section 7.10

1. Multiply.

   (a) $\dfrac{3}{2}\times\dfrac{2}{3}$ (b) $\dfrac{4}{3}\times\dfrac{5}{3}$ (c) $\dfrac{5}{2}\times\dfrac{2}{3}$ (d) $\dfrac{3}{4}\times\dfrac{6}{5}$

2. Calculate.

   (a) $1\dfrac{1}{3}\times\dfrac{3}{4}$ (b) $\dfrac{4}{5}\times2\dfrac{1}{2}$

   (c) $1\dfrac{2}{3}\times2\dfrac{1}{3}$ (d) $2\dfrac{3}{4}\times1\dfrac{3}{5}$

3. Restyk can mow $2\dfrac{1}{4}$ hectares each morning as his part-time job. How many hectares can he mow in 6 mornings?

4. A snow making machine can deliver $3\frac{1}{2}$ cm/h. How much snow can be made in $4\frac{3}{4}$ h?

Section 7.12

1. Divide.

(a) $\frac{3}{4} \div \frac{1}{4}$ (b) $\frac{4}{5} \div \frac{2}{10}$ (c) $\frac{5}{8} \div \frac{1}{5}$ (d) $\frac{2}{3} \div \frac{1}{6}$

2. Calculate.

(a) $\frac{3}{5} \div \frac{1}{4}$ (b) $\frac{5}{9} \div \frac{1}{3}$ (c) $\frac{2}{3} \div \frac{3}{4}$ (d) $\frac{1}{4} \div \frac{2}{7}$

3. There are 8 large bags of pretzels for a party. If Kim uses bowls which hold $\frac{3}{4}$ of a bag, how many bowls will be needed?

4. It takes 14 h in all to seal a floor with varnish. If it takes $1\frac{3}{4}$ h for each coat of varnish to dry, how many coats can be applied?

Section 7.13

1. Divide.

(a) $1\frac{1}{2} \div \frac{3}{4}$ (b) $4\frac{1}{3} \div \frac{1}{6}$

(c) $2\frac{2}{3} \div \frac{1}{3}$ (d) $3\frac{1}{4} \div \frac{1}{3}$

2. Calculate.

(a) $2\frac{1}{2} \div 3\frac{1}{4}$ (b) $2\frac{3}{4} \div 1\frac{3}{8}$

(c) $3\frac{1}{5} \div 1\frac{1}{4}$ (d) $1\frac{4}{7} \div 2\frac{2}{3}$

3. How many guitar lessons $1\frac{1}{2}$ h long can be given in $7\frac{1}{2}$ h?

4. A race track is $2\frac{3}{4}$ km long. If a horse runs for 12 km, how many times will it circle the track?

Section 7.14

1. Calculate.

(a) $\frac{1}{2} + \frac{1}{3} \times \frac{1}{4}$ (b) $\frac{3}{4} + \frac{1}{2} \div \frac{1}{4}$

(c) $2\frac{1}{3} - 6\frac{1}{2} \div 3\frac{1}{4}$

2. Calculate.

(a) $\left(4\frac{2}{3} - 1\frac{1}{4}\right) - \left(1\frac{2}{3}\right)\left(1\frac{1}{8}\right)$

(b) $\left(\frac{4}{3}\right)\left(1\frac{4}{5}\right) - 2\frac{2}{3} \div 1\frac{1}{7}$

3. Follow these instructions.

(a) Increase the sum $\frac{1}{3} + \frac{1}{4}$ by the product $\left(\frac{9}{20}\right)\left(1\frac{2}{3}\right)$.

(b) Increase your answer in (a) by $\frac{1}{4} \div \frac{1}{8}$.

(c) Multiply your answer in (b) by itself.

(d) Decrease your answer in (c) by the result $3 \div \frac{1}{3}$.

(e) What is your final answer?

CHAPTER 8

Section 8.2

1. Write each rational number with a positive denominator.

(a) $\frac{1}{-3}$ (b) $\frac{-4}{-5}$ (c) $\frac{7}{-8}$ (d) $\frac{-11}{-12}$

2. Write another rational number equivalent to each.

(a) $\frac{-4}{3}$ (b) $\frac{-14}{-6}$ (c) $\frac{25}{-12}$ (d) $\frac{-66}{18}$

3. Write each rational number in lowest terms.

(a) $\frac{-6}{8}$ (b) $\frac{24}{-36}$ (c) $\frac{-28}{-7}$ (d) $\frac{-76}{38}$

4. Write each in lowest terms with a positive denominator.

(a) $\frac{5}{-25}$ (b) $\frac{-12}{-18}$ (c) $\frac{32}{-16}$ (d) $\frac{-16}{-12}$

Section 8.3

1. Write the decimal equivalent of each rational number.

   (a) $\dfrac{1}{4}$ (b) $\dfrac{-1}{40}$ (c) $\dfrac{4}{-9}$ (d) $\dfrac{7}{12}$

2. Which number in each pair is greater?

   (a) $+\dfrac{5}{11}, +\dfrac{6}{13}$ (b) $-\dfrac{7}{11}, -\dfrac{9}{14}$

   (c) $-\dfrac{12}{31}, -\dfrac{3}{8}$ (d) $+\dfrac{2}{7}, +\dfrac{7}{24}$

3. At the end of a game, the scores of three players were as follows.

   Player A: $4\dfrac{13}{15}$ Player B: $4\dfrac{15}{17}$ Player C: $4\dfrac{7}{8}$

   If the lowest score wins, who won the game?

4. Arrange the following numbers from least to greatest.

   $\dfrac{+6}{3}, \dfrac{-7}{4}, \dfrac{+4}{3}, \dfrac{-8}{3}, \dfrac{-25}{-5}, \dfrac{-24}{6}, \dfrac{6}{-8}$

Section 8.7

1. Find each sum.

   (a) $\left(+\dfrac{1}{3}\right) + \left(+\dfrac{2}{5}\right)$ (b) $\left(-\dfrac{1}{2}\right) + \left(+\dfrac{7}{8}\right)$

   (c) $\left(-\dfrac{4}{9}\right) + \left(-\dfrac{1}{3}\right)$ (d) $\left(+\dfrac{1}{4}\right) + \left(-\dfrac{5}{6}\right)$

2. Add.
   (a) $(+4.7) + (+1.3)$ (b) $(-6.8) + (-3.2)$
   (c) $(-2.5) + (+2.2)$ (d) $(+4.6) + (-2.1)$

3. A stock started the day trading at $\$+15\dfrac{1}{2}$.

   At the end of the day it showed a change of $\$-\dfrac{7}{8}$. At what trading price did the stock start at the next day?

4. The following are temperature changes recorded every hour for six hours.

   $+0.7°C, +1.5°C, +1.1°C, -0.6°C, -1.0°C, -2.4°C$

   If the initial temperature was 5.9°C, what is the temperature after six hours?

Section 8.8

1. Find each difference.

   (a) $\dfrac{3}{4} - \dfrac{7}{8}$ (b) $\dfrac{7}{10} - \dfrac{-3}{5}$

   (c) $-2\dfrac{9}{10} - 1\dfrac{3}{10}$ (d) $1\dfrac{1}{3} - \left(-1\dfrac{3}{4}\right)$

2. Subtract.
   (a) $(+11.8) - (+8.5)$ (b) $(-1.25) - (+0.75)$
   (c) $(-6.3) - (-3.9)$ (d) $(+7.75) - (-3.15)$

3. The world's highest point, Mount Everest, is +8848 m. The world's greatest depth, Mariana Trench, is –10 915 m. How much higher is Mount Everest than the Mariana Trench?

4. The sum of the scores of three players is $-4\dfrac{1}{8}$. If two players scored $-3\dfrac{3}{8}$ and $+\dfrac{1}{2}$, what did the third player score?

Section 8.9

1. Find each product.

   (a) $\left(-\dfrac{1}{5}\right) \times \left(\dfrac{3}{4}\right)$ (b) $\left(-\dfrac{3}{8}\right) \times \left(-\dfrac{4}{5}\right)$

   (c) $\left(-3\dfrac{3}{4}\right) \times \left(1\dfrac{3}{5}\right)$ (d) $\left(-1\dfrac{7}{10}\right) \times \left(-2\dfrac{2}{3}\right)$

2. Multiply.
   (a) $2.1 \times (-3.8)$ (b) $(-0.5) \times (-8.4)$
   (c) $(-6.8) \times (-1.5)$ (d) $(-0.375) \times 0.8$

3. The price of ATR stock changed $\$+\dfrac{3}{8}$ each day for three consecutive days and $\$-\dfrac{1}{4}$ each day for the next two days. What was the net change over the five day period?

4. Find the value of each expression if $t = \dfrac{1}{4}$ and $w = -1\dfrac{1}{2}$.

   (a) tw (b) $2t + w$ (c) $2w - t$ (d) $t + \dfrac{1}{2}w$

Section 8.10

1. Divide.

   (a) $\left(+\dfrac{2}{3}\right) \div \left(-\dfrac{1}{6}\right)$ (b) $\left(-\dfrac{3}{4}\right) \div \left(-\dfrac{3}{8}\right)$

   (c) $\left(+\dfrac{9}{16}\right) \div \left(-\dfrac{1}{4}\right)$

2. Divide.
   (a) $(-47.04) \div (+8.4)$ (b) $(+25.42) \div (-4.1)$
   (c) $(+8.91) \div (-3.3)$

3. Calculate.

   (a) $\left(-4\dfrac{3}{4}\right) \div \left(2\dfrac{3}{8}\right)$ (b) $\left(+5\dfrac{1}{3}\right) \div \left(-1\dfrac{1}{4}\right)$

   (c) $\left(-3\dfrac{2}{3}\right) \div \left(-2\dfrac{1}{2}\right)$

4. The temperature change was $-6\dfrac{1}{2}$ °C over 5 h. What was the average change in temperature per hour?

5. An airplane flying at 1750 m is coming in to land. After $3\dfrac{1}{2}$ min the plane lands. What is the average change in altitude?

CHAPTER 9

Section 9.2

1. These are the results of a fishing derby.

Fish	Tally	Frequency
Perch	ЖН II	
Bass	IIII	
Catfish	ЖН III	
Sunfish	ЖН	
Trout	II	

   (a) Complete the table.
   (b) Which fish was most common?
   (c) Which fish was least common?

2. Students were asked how many hours a week the did homework. These are the results.

   3 7 4 6 9 0 5 4 1 4 5 0 3 6 7
   8 8 6 0 5 4 3 2 6 9 4 7 8 0 4
   7 4 5 6 8 8 4 0 4 6 5 8 8 7 9

   (a) Construct a frequency table using this data.
   (b) How many students were surveyed?
   (c) How many students did homework for 3 h? 4 h? 1 h? 8 h?
   (d) What was the greatest amount of time spent on homework and how many students spent this amount of time?

3. Survey your class and construct a frequency table to determine:
   (a) the most popular colour worn by students in class today.
   (b) the most popular TV programme.
   (c) the most popular school subject.
   (d) the most popular movie released in the last year.

Section 9.3

1.

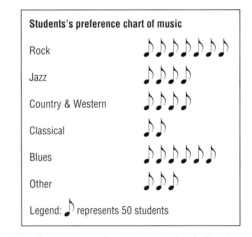

   Use the pictograph to answer the following.
   (a) Which type of music is most popular? least popular?
   (b) How many students like blues music?
   (c) How many students were surveyed?

2.

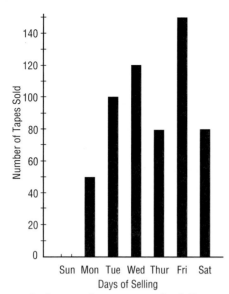

Days of Selling

Use the bar graph to answer the following.
(a) How many tapes were sold on Wed.? Fri.? Sat.?
(b) On which days were more than 85 tapes sold? more than 60 tapes sold?
(c) How many more tapes were sold on Friday than Monday?
(d) How many tapes were sold in all for Monday and Tuesday?

3. Survey your class and construct a pictograph or bar graph based on the results.
(a) Which is the most popular radio station?
(b) Which is the most popular musical group?
(c) Which is the most popular author?
(d) Which is the most popular after school activity?

Section 9.5

1.

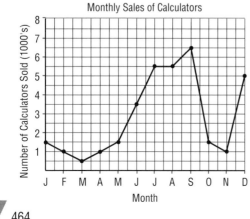

The graph shows the number of calculators sold during one year.
(a) During which month were sales the lowest?
(b) During which month were sales the highest?
(c) During which months were sales the same?
(d) How many calculators in all were sold during the year?
(e) If each calculator sold for $25.95, how much money did the company make during the year?

2. Draw a line graph to show the following data.
(a) Boy's Height/ Mass Chart

Height (cm)	140	145	150	155	160	165	170	175	180	185
Average mass(kg)	41	44	49	54	58	63	66	70	73	75

(b) Girl's Height/ Mass Chart

Height (cm)	140	145	150	155	160	165	170	175	180	185
Average mass(kg)	36	40	43	47	51	54	58	62	66	69

3. The cost to take a taxi is $0.75 plus $0.50 for each quarter of a kilometre travelled.
(a) Complete a table showing the cost for trips of 1 km, 2.25 km, 3.75 km, and 4.50 km.
(b) Use the data from the table to draw a line graph.
(c) What is the cost of travelling 2 km? 3 km? 4 km?

Section 9.6

1. The total sales for an appliance store in a month are shown in the circle graph.

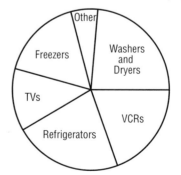

(a) What percent of the sales were for each type of appliance?
(b) Which item had the greatest sales?

2. Construct a circle for each of the following to show
   (a) 25% shaded.　　(b) 50% shaded.
   (c) 40% shaded.　　(d) 83% shaded.

3. This circle graph shows the content of white bread.

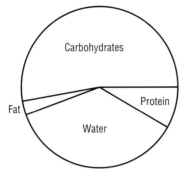

   (a) What percent of white bread is protein? water?
   (b) A loaf of bread costs $2.00. How much was paid for the water? for the fat? for the carbohydrates?

Section 9.7

1. Sales of cars in Canada during March, 1993, are given below for several major manufacturers. Use the data to construct a circle graph.
   GM 21 000　　　Ford 11 000　Toyota 5000
   Chrysler 14 000　Honda 6000　Mazda 3000

2. The medals won at the 1991 Pan Am Games are listed by country.
   　　U.S. 352　　　　Canada 127　　Mexico 75
   　　Columbia 46　Cuba 265　　　Brazil 79
   　　Argentina 55　Others 124
   (a) Find the percent of the total won by each country to the nearest percent.
   (b) Use the data to construct a circle graph.

3. Africa's leaders for money earned from tourism in 1990 are listed below. The values are given in millions of dollars.
   　　Morocco 1162　Kenya 483　　　Algeria 154
   　　Tunisia 1004　Mauritius 264　Others 264
   　　South Africa 815　Senegal 157
   (a) Find the percent of total money earned for each country to the nearest percent.
   (b) Use the data to construct a circle graph.

Section 9.11

1. Find the mean, median, and mode for each set of data.
   (a) 15　25　16　23　12　18　24　15　8　15　27
   (b) 7　13　14　8　9　12　8　10　14　8　7
   (c) 23　28　9　22　22　21　18　8　14　19　25

2. In August the newspaper reported that the median price of a home in Toronto was $189 500 and that the mean price was $209 100. Explain what this newspaper report is saying.

3. The prices of different brands of peanut butter were recorded for the same size of jar.
   $2.85　$2.79　$2.80　$2.77　$2.85　$2.93　$2.95
   $2.99　$2.88
   (a) Find the mean of the prices.
   (b) Find the median of the prices.
   (c) Find the mode of the prices.
   (d) Which of the mean, median or mode best describes the price of peanut butter?

CHAPTER 10

Section 10.2

1. Write a ratio to represent each situation.
   (a) ○ ○ ○ ○ ○　　(b) ✱ ✱ ✱ ✱
   　　◆ ◆　　　　　　　▲ ▲ ▲ ▲ ▲
   (c) AAAAA　　　(d) XX
   　　B　　　　　　　YYYY
   　　CCC　　　　　　ZZZ

2. Write 2 equivalent ratios for each.
   (a) 3 : 4　　(b) 7 : 5　　(c) 11 : 9　　(d) 4 : 5 : 7

3. Write each ratio in lowest terms.
   (a) 8 : 12　　(b) 9 : 3　　(c) 24 : 18　(d) 36 : 72

4. A bricklayer mixes mortar with three ingredients. She uses 5 parts cement, 14 parts sand, and 3 parts lime. What is the ratio of sand to cement to lime?

5. There are 98 coins in each register. The ratio of pennies to nickels to dimes to quarters is 6 : 1 : 3 : 4. What is the number of each type of coin?

Section 10.3

1. Replace the ☐ with a number to write an equivalent ratio.

(a) $\dfrac{4}{8} = \dfrac{\square}{16}$ (b) $\dfrac{\square}{6} = \dfrac{25}{30}$

(c) $\dfrac{4}{\square} = \dfrac{12}{15}$ (d) $\dfrac{2}{7} = \dfrac{16}{\square}$

2. Write an equivalent ratio.
   (a) $6 : 9 = \square : 3$ (b) $\square : 5 = 16 : 20$
   (c) $3 : \square = 1 : 2$ (d) $4 : 7 = 12 : \square$

3. Jason earns $5.50 for each hour he works at the convenience store. How much will he earn if he works 12 h this weekend?

4. A beef stew recipe calls for 500 g of potatoes and 200 g of beef. If Mark has 600 g of beef, how many grams of potatoes should he use?

5. The fuel for an outboard motor requires that 1.5 L of gasoline mixed with 150 mL of oil. How much gasoline should be mixed with 3 L of oil?

Section 10.8

1. Write a unit rate for each.
   (a) 330 cars assembled in 5 h
   (b) 240 pages read in 4 h
   (c) $67.50 earned in 9 h
   (d) 380 newspapers delivered in 4 days

2. If May can address 3 envelopes in 1.5 min, how many envelopes can she address in 18 min?

3. Marsha earns $50.00 if she works for 8 h. What is her hourly rate of pay?

4. A cat's heartbeat was recorded as 35 beats in 15 s.
   (a) How many beats per minute is this?
   (b) A dog has a heartbeat of 70 beats in 40 s. Which has the faster heartbeat, the cat or the dog?

5. A sprinter can run at a speed of 32.2 km/h. How long will it take the sprinter to run 200 m?

Section 10.10

1. Write each scale ratio in lowest terms. Interpret each scale.
   (a) 5 cm represents 50 km
   (b) 20 mm represents 1000 m

(c) 3 cm represents 750 m
(d) 10 cm represents 1.5 m

2. On a map, 1 cm represents 1.5 km. Find each actual length.
   (a) 3 cm   (b) 5 cm   (c) 7.5 cm   (d) 10 cm

3. The scale on a map is 1 cm represents 400 km. How far is Calgary from Ottawa if the distance on the map is 7.5 cm?

4. If you travel from the south of England to the northwest tip of Scotland, the distance would be approximately 1000 km. The scale on a map is 1 cm represents 50 km. How long is the distance on the map?

5. In a photograph Meegan is standing beside a pine tree. In the photograph Meegan is 3 cm tall. In reality, she is 1.5 m tall. How tall is the pine tree if it is 8 cm tall in the photo?

Section 10.11

1. The scale of the map is 1 : 1 000 000. Write the ratio in the form 1 cm represents $\square$ km.

2. Use the scale in Question 1. Measure the distance on the map and find the actual distance between each place.

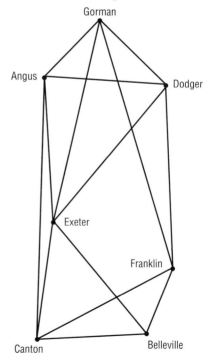

(a) Angus and Dodger
(b) Franklin and Canton
(c) Belleville and Exeter
(d) Gorman and Franklin

3. The actual distance from Angus to Exeter is 38 km. What should the distance on the map be?

4. What is the total distance of a trip from Angus to Dodger to Franklin to Canton, and back to Angus?

Section 10.12

1. The scale ratio on an enlarged photograph of a mosquito is 10 : 1. What are the actual lengths?
   (a) a leg 30 mm long
   (b) a wing 40 mm long
   (c) the body 60 mm long
   (d) the head 20 mm long

2. Write each as a scale ratio in lowest terms.
   (a) 10 cm represents 2 mm
   (b) 30 m represents 5 m
   (c) 75 cm represents 3.75 cm
   (d) 40 cm represents 4 mm

3. In order to make a drawing of a housefly, a scale of 50 : 1 is used. If the drawing of the housefly's wing is 30 cm long, how long is the actual wing?

4. A movie company makes a large model of a domino to a scale of 400 : 1. The actual length of a domino is 40 mm. How tall is the model?

CHAPTER 11

Section 11.2

1. John Olerud had 145 hits in 360 at bats.
   (a) Write his batting average as a decimal to the nearest thousandth.
   (b) Write his batting average as a percent to the nearest tenth of a percent.

2. Complete the table.

Fraction	Decimal	Percent
	0.83	
		41%
$\frac{5}{25}$		
$\frac{7}{20}$		
	0.27	
		33%
$\frac{17}{50}$		

3. A theatre is showing 2 movies. If 67 of the 100 people in line want to buy tickets for the adventure film, what percent wants to see the comedy?

4. Use trial and error to find a fraction that is equivalent to $0.\dot{2}$ (the dot means the 2 keeps on repeating).

Section 11.3

1. Write each as a percent.
   (a) 0.71   (b) 0.628   (c) 0.3   (d) 0.299

2. Write each as a fraction with a denominator of 100.
   (a) $\frac{3}{4}$ (b) $\frac{2}{5}$ (c) $\frac{3}{20}$ (d) $\frac{6}{50}$

3. On June 20, Devon White had hits in 27.5% of his 240 at bats. How many hits did he have?

4. The unemployment rate in New Brunswick was $8\frac{3}{4}$%. Out of 10 000 workers, how many would be unemployed?

5. Write each as a percent using a whole number and a fraction.
   (a) 0.1425   (b) 0.8675   (c) 0.534   (d) 1.666

Section 11.4

1. Calculate.
   (a) 45.5% of 200 (b) 87.6% of 150
   (c) 29.5% of 300 (d) 67.9% of 40

2. In a survey of the village of Holgrim, 32.5% of the homes were found to be in need of either major or minor repairs. How many homes need repair if there are 160 homes in the village?

3. Of the money collected by a charity, 13.5% is used to pay administrative expenses and the rest is used for providing shelter for homeless people. If $600 000 is collected, how much will be used for shelter?

4. Bank of Nova Scotia preferred shares are paying 8.45% per year. How much will be earned in 2 years if $8000 is invested?

Section 11.6

1. Complete the table.

Fraction	Decimal	Percent
		135%
$1\frac{3}{5}$		
	2.007	
$2\frac{3}{20}$		
	0.009	
		300%

2. This month Humber Valley Motors sold 70 cars. This represents 125% of last month's sales. How many cars were sold last month?

3. This month Humber Valley Motors expects their sales to be 107% of this year's sales. To the nearest whole number, how many cars will they sell if 615 cars are sold this year?

4. To make a profit, the Everlast Shoe Company must increase sales from last year by 105% and decrease expenses to 96% of last year.
   (a) If sales were $250 000 and expenses were $273 435 last year, find the amounts needed for this year to make a profit.
   (b) What will the profit be?

Section 11.9

1. The PST in Quebec is $6\frac{1}{2}$%. Calculate the provincal sales tax in Quebec on a greeting card costing $1.50.

2. The federal Goods and Services Tax (GST) is 7%. In New Brunswick, the PST is 11%. A pair of pants costs $35.00.
   (a) Find the GST on the pants.
   (b) Find the New Brunswick PST.
   (c) Find the total cost of the pants.

3. Using 7% PST for Manitoba and 7% GST, in one calculation find the total cost of a compact disc selling for $18.75.

4. In Ontario the PST is 8%. By mistake a clerk calculated the PST after adding in the 7% GST on a $15.00 pair of gloves. By how much did the clerk overcharge the customer?

Section 11.10

1. If 8% of a number is 32, what is the number?

2. The 7% PST on the purchase of a radio in Saskatchewan amounts to $11.55. What is the selling price of the radio?

3. This year attendance at the spring concert was 120% of last year's attendance. If 240 people attended this year, how many came last year?

4. GST is always 7% of the cost of an item. PST varies from province to province. Match the GST's with the correct PST's on the items and find the total selling price.

   GST Cost   Item's PST
   (a) $14.70   (i) $5.76 PST in Newfoundland at 12%
   (b) $1.12   (ii) $0.96 PST in British Columbia at 6%
   (c) $3.36   (iii) $8.80 PST in Ontario at 8%
   (d) $5.95   (iv) $21.00 PST in Nova Scotia at 10%
   (e) $7.70   (v) $8.50 PST in P.E.I. at 10%

Section 11.12

1. $1200 is deposited for one year at 6.5% per year simple interest.
   (a) Calculate the interest earned in one year.
   (b) Calculate the total amount in the account after one year.

2. Find the total amount if $900 is deposited for 9 months at a simple interest rate of 4% per year.

3. After one year $105 in interest was paid on an account earning 7% per year.
   (a) What was the original amount on deposit at the beginning of the year?
   (b) What was the total amount available at the end of the year?

4. Which account will earn the greater amount of interest over 18 months? How much more is earned by that account?
   (a) Account A in which $1800 earns simple interest at 9% per year.
   (b) Account B in which $1500 earns simple interest at 10.5% per year.

5. In three years, Dyal wants to have $2750 to buy a used car. If he deposits $2000 now in an account paying 10.75% simple interest per year,
   (a) will he have enough money?
   (b) how much more or less than $2750 will he have?

CHAPTER 12
Section 12.4
1. Follow these steps to construct a triangle.
   (a) Draw any angle using a ruler.
   (b) Construct a triangle using the angle you have drawn. Mark a length of 6 cm on one side of the angle and a length of 8 cm on the other side.
   (c) Construct the endpoints to form a triangle.

2. Use the triangle you drew in Question 1.
   (a) Construct the perpendicular bisector of each side of the triangle.
   (b) What do you notice about the three perpendicular bisectors?
   (c) Use the point where the perpendicular bisectors meet as the centre to draw the circle that intersects the vertices.

3. Use a copy of the triangle you drew in Question 1.
   (a) Construct the angle bisectors for each of the angles.
   (b) What do you notice about the three angle bisectors?

   (c) Use the point where the angle bisectors meet as the centre of a circle that touches the three sides of the triangle.

Section 12.9
1. Use cardboard strips 3 cm, 4 cm, and 6 cm long.
   (a) How many different triangles can you construct?
   (b) Measure the angles in the triangle. How many triangles can be constructed using these angles?

2. Use cardboard strips 3 cm and 4 cm long, and an angle of 45°.
   (a) Construct a triangle with the angle between the two sides.
   (b) Can you construct two triangles with the angle not between the 3 cm and 4 cm sides?

3. Use a cardboard strip 4 cm long and cardboard constructs of angles of 45° and 60°.
   (a) Construct a triangle with the 4 cm side between the angles.
   (b) Construct two triangles with the 4 cm side not between the two angles.
   (c) Are the two triangles congruent?

Section 12.11
1. Calculate the length of the hypotenuse to the nearest tenth.

   (a) 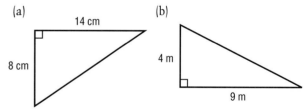 (b)

2. The Tripoli Square Garden is 300 m on a side. How much distance can be saved by walking across the park diagonally from A to C instead of walking from A to B to C?

   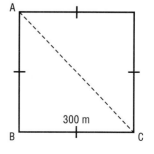

3. Fire regulations require that a ladder reach to the bottom of a second floor window when the bottom of the ladder is 3 m from the side of the building.

3 m

(a) How long must the ladder be to reach a window 5 m high?
(b) How long must the ladder be to reach a window 8 m high?

4. A ladder from Question 3 is 6 m long. How far up the wall will the ladder reach?

Section 12.13

1. Find the missing measure to the nearest tenth in each pair of similar triangles.

(a)

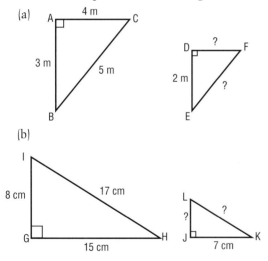

(b)

2. At the same time that Mira casts a shadow 1.4 m long, a house casts a shadow 15.4 m long. If Mira is 1.6 m tall, find the height of the house.

3. Each storey of a building is 3.5 m tall. The building is 6 storeys tall and it casts a shadow of 15 m. How tall is Ginny, to the nearest centimetre, if she casts a shadow of 1.1 m?

4. A rowboat starts out to cross the river from point A, and because of the current, the rowboat lands at point B. If the two triangles are similar, what is the distance the boat travelled?

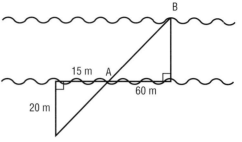

CHAPTER 13

Section 13.2

1. Simplify.
   (a) $2x + 3y - x + 4y + 2x$
   (b) $6p - 7q + 2q - 3p + 4p - 6q$
   (c) $x + 4z + 3y - 2x + 3z - 4y - 6x - 7z$

2. Simplify. Then evaluate if $e = 2$ and $f = 1$.
   (a) $3e - 4f + 2e - 6f$
   (b) $7f + 3e - 5e + 2f$
   (c) $4e - 5f + e + 3f - 7e + 2f + 8$

3. Rod is paid a base salary of $48 a day and a commission of $16 for each camera he sells.
   (a) Write a variable expression for Rod's pay (P) using the letter n for the number of cameras sold.
   (b) Calculate Rod's salary for the week if he has these daily camera sales.

Days	Mon	Tues	Wed	Thurs	Fri	Sat
Cameras sold	7	9	14	7	16	20

4. The perimeter of the figure is 84 cm. What is the length of each side?

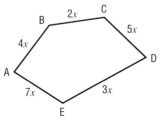

Section 13.3

1. Write each without brackets. Then evaluate if $p = 3$.
   (a) $2(p + 2)$ (b) $6(p - 6)$
   (c) $3(p - 3)$ (d) $5(p + 1)$

2. Substitute $m = -3$ into each expression. Evaluate the expression.
   (a) $2(m + 4)$ (b) $3(m - 3)$
   (c) $1(m + 3)$ (d) $4(m - 6)$

3. Evaluate if $x = 4$ and $y = -3$.
   (a) $2(x - y)$ (b) $3(2x + y)$
   (c) $2(2x - 2y)$ (d) $4(x + 4y)$

4. In this figure, $x = 3$ and $y = -1$.
   (a) Calculate the perimeter of the figure.
   (b) Write a description of the method you used to find the perimeter.

Section 13.8

1. Find the value of the variable.
   (a) $x - 4 = 6$ (b) $y - 7 = 10$
   (c) $p + 3 = 10$ (d) $q + 3 = 0$

2. Find the value of the variable.
   (a) $x + 2 = -4$ (b) $y - 4 = -6$
   (c) $p + 7 = -1$ (d) $q + 5 = 0$

3. Find the value of the variable.
   (a) $7 - x = -2$ (b) $8 + y = -3$
   (c) $11 - p = 4$ (d) $17 + q = 14$

4. Find the value of the variable.
   (a) $-x + 3 = 7$ (b) $-y - 9 = -11$
   (c) $-p + 6 = 0$ (d) $-q - 6 = -12$

Section 13.9

1. Solve. Check your answers.
   (a) $k - 2 = 6$ (b) $m + 6 = 2$
   (c) $6 - n = 1$ (d) $14 - p = 6$

2. Solve. Check your answers.
   (a) $4x = 16$ (b) $3y = 15$
   (c) $7p = -21$ (d) $4w = -32$

3. Solve. Check your answers.
   (a) $2x + 6 = 14$ (b) $3y - 9 = 6$
   (c) $7w - 4 = 24$ (d) $5q + 6 = 36$

4. Solve. Check your answers.
   (a) $\dfrac{1}{2}x - 4 = 8$ (b) $\dfrac{1}{4}y + 6 = 10$
   (c) $\dfrac{1}{3}c - 7 = 1$ (d) $\dfrac{1}{2}d - 12 = -6$

5. Tomas earns a base salary per week plus $4.00 for each lawn mower he assembles. Last week he assembled 83 lawn mowers and his total salary was $492.
   (a) Write an equation which can be used to calculate his weekly earnings.
   (b) Solve the equation to find the amount of his base salary.

Section 13.10

1. Solve. Check your answers.
   (a) $x + 4.5 = 9.5$ (b) $y - 2.35 = 4.05$
   (c) $q + 6.45 = 3.55$ (d) $p - 3.7 = -1.9$

2. Solve. Check your answers.
   (a) $17.2 + x = 40.3$ (b) $2.9 - y = -3.1$
   (c) $7.9 - c = 9.5$ (d) $1.3 + x = -5.5$

3. Solve. Check your answers.
   (a) $-f + 3.9 = 4.4$ (b) $-g + 5.9 = -17.1$
   (c) $-h + 2.6 = 0$ (d) $-k - 6.3 = 4.9$

4. Solve. Check your answers.
   (a) $3x - 1.65 = 15.90$ (b) $3p + 7.45 = 20.05$
   (c) $7p - 2.11 = -11.14$ (d) $2d - 8.3 = -25.84$

5. Paul's summer job is delivering grocery store advertising flyers. He is paid $32/d, plus $0.10 a flyer for each flyer over 400 he delivers in a day.
   (a) Write an equation that can be used to find Paul's daily earnings.
   (b) Calculate his day's earnings if he delivers 625 flyers.

Section 13.11

1. Write an equation for each sentence. Then solve.
   (a) A number decreased by 4 is 11. Find the number.
   (b) Twice a number increased by 6 is 16. Find the number.
   (c) One third of a number decreased by 4 is 6. Find the number.
   (d) Four times a number decreased by 3 is −11. Find the number.

(e) Half of a number plus 7.8 is 4.6. Find the number.

2. The sum of two consecutive odd whole numbers is 44. Find the numbers.

3. The sum of three consecutive even whole numbers is 60. Find the numbers.

4. Meegan's mother is three times as old as Meegan. Together their ages equal 60. How old are they?

5. Sonja has half as many compact discs as her brother. Together they have 75 CD's. How many do each have?

CHAPTER 14

Section 14.2

1. Find the order of rotational symmetry for each figure.

(a) (b)

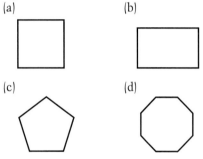

(c) (d)

2. Trace around a quarter. How many lines of symmetry are there?

3. Print all the letters of the alphabet in block, capital letters. For example, A B C D E F etc.
   (a) Which letters have lines of symmetry?
   (b) Which letters have rotational symmetry? What is the order of symmetry for each of the letters?

4. Find words which have horizontal lines of symmetry. For example, BOB has a horizontal line of symmetry.

Section 14.3

1. Ronika earns $7.00/h at her part time job as a cashier.
   (a) Construct a table showing earnings for these times: 4 h and 10 h.
   (b) Draw a graph of her earnings.

(c) Extend the graph line to show earnings for 0 h and 15 h.
(d) Use the graph to determine her earnings for these times: 1 h, 3 h, 7 h, 12 h, and 14 h.

2. A bath tub is 66 cm deep and it is filling with running water. For every minute the water runs, the water level rises 4 cm.
   (a) Draw a graph of the water level in the tub by graphing ordered pairs for 3 min and 10 min.
   (b) Use the graph to find the depth of water after: 5 min, 12 min, and 15 min.
   (c) How long can the water run before the tub begins to overflow?

Section 14.4

1. Use 2, 5, 8, and 10 as values for x.
   (a) Construct a table of values for the relation $x \rightarrow 3x + 2$.
   (b) Use the ordered pairs to construct a graph of the relation.

2. Sand is falling into the bottom half of a minute glass. Two cubic centimetres of sand fall each second.
   (a) Complete the table for the volume of sand that falls.

Time (s)	1	5	10	20	40	50
Volume (cm³)						

(b) Write the values from the table as ordered pairs.
(c) Draw a graph of the relation using the ordered pairs.
(d) How much sand is there in the glass?

3. Collect objects which can be stacked, such as pennies, checkers, or math textbooks.
   (a) Record the heights of the stacks for various numbers of objects in the stack.

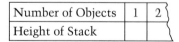

Number of Objects	1	2
Height of Stack		

(b) Write your data in the form of a relation: $n \rightarrow$?
(c) Write your data in the form of ordered pairs.
(d) Graph the relation.

(e) Use the graph to predict heights for twice and three times the highest number of objects you used.

Section 14.8

1. There are 3 quarters, 6 dimes, and 9 nickels in a purse. One coin is withdrawn at random.
   (a) How many possible outcomes are there?
   (b) What is the probability of drawing out a quarter? a dime? a nickel?

2. A claw machine game at the carnival has prizes of 10 toy tigers, 35 combs, 20 kazoos, 25 hair bows, 9 key chains, and 1 watch.
   (a) If the claw always grabs one prize, how many possible outcomes are there?
   (b) What is the probability of winning a comb? a hair bow? a watch?

3. Toss a penny, a nickel, a dime and a quarter.
   (a) How many possible outcomes are there?
   (b) What is the probability of tossing all heads? all tails?
   (c) What is the probability of tossing at least one head? at least one tail?
   (d) What is the probability of tossing 2 heads and 2 tails?
   (e) What is the probability of tossing 1 head and 3 tails? 1 tail and 3 heads?

4. There are 30 loose socks in a drawer. Half are white and the rest are black. The room is dark. How many socks must you take from the drawer to be sure to get a matching pair?

Section 14.9

1. Use a paper cup and drop it from a height of 1 m.
   (a) What are the three possible outcomes for how the paper cup will land?
   (b) Drop the cup 50 times (or ten students can drop 10 cups, five times each) and record how the cup lands.
   (c) What was the experimental probability for each of the three possible outcomes?

2. Breakfast Time Cereal includes one small NHL team logo in each of its cereal boxes.
   (a) Predict how many boxes of cereal you would have to buy to collect all 26 team logos.
   (b) Do this experiment to approximate the answer. Have each member of your class (26 students) choose one of the 26 teams and write that name on 10 slips of paper.
   (c) Put all the slips (260) in a box and mix them thoroughly.
   (d) Draw out slips, one at a time, and record the team names until all 26 teams have been drawn.
   (e) The number of slips approximates the number of cereal boxes required to get all the team logos.
   (f) If you performed the experiment again, would you get the same answers? Try it and find out.

302	068	416	505	346	808	242	349	956	892	265	546	092	488	336	201	057	728	343	640	895	202	076	619	431
809	229	534	531	633	874	682	353	794	607	039	713	764	623	563	527	794	604	069	799	480	655	454	224	163
186	408	090	103	644	774	892	279	486	409	124	305	294	429	903	019	884	456	332	049	041	294	453	190	852
806	288	827	206	422	754	358	536	443	239	557	307	438	468	847	699	863	930	558	362	302	114	600	193	879
561	451	088	502	255	677	218	380	672	059	585	703	955	914	203	172	855	871	751	277	363	227	400	302	089
296	316	999	001	673	088	446	143	823	127	813	138	477	779	987	249	241	394	580	874	690	595	366	060	061
221	135	036	015	710	844	616	339	385	911	155	745	130	754	364	167	217	550	050	439	443	283	754	354	725
430	842	575	965	692	648	655	436	558	359	446	124	353	779	993	137	282	748	196	546	096	829	270	129	882
503	267	339	408	077	922	397	456	309	538	363	219	371	222	088	567	664	162	373	300	066	188	585	699	847
690	599	249	213	883	471	946	899	126	718	609	101	208	604	067	056	378	576	968	645	745	125	508	483	546
078	998	022	103	730	287	923	410	168	418	591	504	309	563	533	573	862	948	933	626	641	878	595	382	790
711	796	541	265	500	140	801	419	617	350	978	444	204	287	951	998	038	981	383	818	013	289	767	711	802
411	225	172	869	786	814	095	987	251	378	566	619	428	951	992	157	907	064	933	622	526	816	046	626	637
999	007	478	742	047	998	025	258	954	941	793	637	992	160	607	025	588	592	470	924	432	766	677	204	298
149	041	487	362	290	698	826	199	210	812	144	745	128	920	433	065	536	458	418	560	413	323	549	014	078
941	803	385	926	480	667	090	042	646	721	540	313	826	200	106	767	700	872	736	123	213	480	516	795	588
615	285	952	978	427	986	278	465	689	568	692	653	499	104	882	503	277	364	189	704	996	071	799	476	805
321	695	739	031	609	100	017	494	079	630	787	765	654	490	242	316	977	462	560	408	088	397	449	001	566
632	824	147	265	515	749	243	219	357	583	790	693	680	304	186	414	392	711	800	450	046	541	252	511	600
200	126	688	537	408	095	966	671	046	805	328	287	934	643	824	144	697	781	919	316	984	306	322	609	097
646	731	247	079	565	585	704	983	331	089	341	511	595	362	281	674	118	584	737	092	281	670	003	723	473
954	929	546	095	971	570	767	720	560	424	874	676	176	634	903	025	314	868	829	268	269	193	821	078	936
691	612	211	948	938	737	091	201	067	018	430	848	725	407	033	263	665	129	825	160	592	464	676	193	894
229	532	601	165	011	926	466	746	161	487	368	029	354	723	485	471	969	612	194	779	977	450	051	700	872
718	606	002	809	224	094	775	906	046	650	615	288	889	348	919	321	687	505	369	072	601	167	295	407	033

During the eighteenth century, the *metric* system was adopted in France. In 1960, the International System of Units was introduced. Today, this system is used in almost all parts of the world. The following summarizes the conversions.

Prefix	Symbol	Length (metre)	Mass (gram)	Volume (litre)	Factor
kilo	k	km	kg	kL	$1000 = 10^3$
hecto	h	hm	hg	hL	$100 = 10^2$
deca	da	dam	dag	daL	$10 = 10^1$
		m	g	L	$1 = 10^0$
deci	d	dm	dg	dL	$0.1 = 10^{-1}$
centi	c	cm	cg	cL	$0.01 = 10^{-2}$
milli	m	mm	mg	mL	$0.001 = 10^{-3}$

Length
1 kilometre = 1000 m
1 hectometre = 100 m
1 decametre = 10 m
1 metre is the *basic unit*
1 decimetre = 0.1 m
1 centimetre = 0.01 m
1 millimetre = 0.001 m

Mass
1 kilogram = 1000 g
1 hectogram = 100 g
1 decagram = 10 g
1 gram is the *basic unit*
1 decigram = 0.1 g
1 centigram = 0.01 g
1 milligram = 0.001 g

Volume
1 kilolitre = 1000 L
1 hectolitre = 100 L
1 decalitre = 10 L
1 litre is the *basic unit*
1 decilitre = 0.1 L
1 centilitre = 0.01 L
1 millilitre = 0.001 L

Convert:

(a) 4.5 km to decametres.
    1 km = 100 dam
    4.5 km = 4.5 × 100 dam
           = 450 dam

(b) 162 dg to decagrams.
    1 dg = 0.01 dag
    162 dg = 162 × 0.01 dag
           = 1.62 dag

(c) 2.7 dL to kilolitres.
    1 dL = 0.0001 L
    2.7 dL = 2.7 × 0.0001 L
           = 0.000 27 L

Area
$1 \text{ cm}^2 = 0.0001 \text{ m}^2$
$1 \text{ hm}^2 = 10\ 000 \text{ m}^2$
$1 \text{ km}^2 = 1\ 000\ 000 \text{ m}^2$

Volume

1 cm
1 cm
1 cm
$1 \text{ cm}^3 = 1 \text{ mL}$

10 cm
10 cm
10 cm
1000 cm³ = 1 L

$1 \text{ cm}^3 = 0.000\ 001 \text{ m}^3$
$1 \text{ km}^3 = 1\ 000\ 000\ 000 \text{ m}^3$
$1 \text{ mL} = 1 \text{ cm}^3$
$1 \text{ L} = 1000 \text{ cm}^3 = 0.001 \text{ m}^3$
$1 \text{ kL} = 1 \text{ m}^3$

(a) Convert 1738 cm² to m².
    $1 \text{ cm}^2 = 0.0001 \text{ m}^2$
    $1738 \text{ cm}^2 = 1738 \times 0.0001 \text{ m}^2$
             $= 0.1738 \text{ m}^2$

(b) Convert 3 km² to square centimetres.
    $1 \text{ km}^2 = \dfrac{1\ 000\ 000}{0.0001} \text{ cm}^2$
    $3.2 \text{ km}^2 = 3.2 \times 10\ 000\ 000\ 000 \text{ cm}^2$
             $= 32\ 000\ 000\ 000 \text{ cm}^2$

(c) Convert 0.8 cm³ to millilitres.
    $1 \text{ cm}^3 = 1 \text{ mL}$
    $0.8 \text{ cm}^3 = 0.8 \times 1 \text{ mL}$
            $= 0.8 \text{ mL}$

(d) Convert 0.3 L to millilitres.
    $1 \text{ L} = 1000 \text{ cm}^3$
        $= 1000 \text{ mL}$
    $0.3 \text{ L} = 0.3 \times 1000 \text{ mL}$ or 300 mL

GLOSSARY

acute angle: an angle with a measure less than 90°

acute triangle: a triangle where each angle has a measure less than 90°

adjacent angles: two angles which share a common side and vertex, and whose interiors do not intersect

algebra: a generalization of arithmetic where symbols, usually letters, represent numbers and are related by operations

altitude: the perpendicular distance between a base and the opposite vertex

angle: the figure formed by two rays with a common end point. The measure of the angle is the number of degrees between the two rays.

approximate: almost exact. For example, an approximate number is a number obtained by rounding and is almost exact.

area: the number of square units needed to cover a surface

average: the sum of several numbers divided by the amount of numbers

axes: the intersecting number lines or scales on a graph

bar graph: a diagram that uses bars to display data or information

base (of a polygon): any side may be referred to as a base. In a triangle, the base is usually the side to which the altitude is drawn.

base (of a power): the number that is the repeated factor in a power. For instance, 2^3 has a base of 2.

bias: the deviation from true value or distortion of a statistic due to the neglect of a factor or factors

bisect: to divide in half

broken line graph: a graph made up of line segments joined end to end

capacity: the amount of substance a container can hold

centre (of a circle): the point that is an equal distance from any point on the circumference

circle: a closed curve such that all points on the curve are the same distance from its centre

circle graph: a diagram that uses a circle to display data or information

circumference: the distance around (perimeter of) a circle

commission: an amount earned from selling a product or service

common denominator: a number that is a common multiple of the denominators

common factor: a number that is the factor of each number. For example, 3 is a common factor of 6 and 9.

common multiple: a number that is the multiple of two or more numbers

complementary angles: two angles whose degree measures add to 90°

composite number: a number with 3 or more factors

computer: an electronic machine that can perform logical and mathematical operations at high speed

congruent: having the same size and shape

contained angle: in any polygon, the angle between any two sides

coordinate grid: a grid on which coordinates can be plotted. Also known as a Cartesian plane.

cube: a polyhedron with six congruent square faces

curve: any line that can be defined by an equation

data: facts or information

decimal number: a number written in the decimal system; the digits 0, 1, 2, 3, 4, 5, 6, 7, 8, 9 are used to record decimal numbers. Decimal numbers, including decimal fractions, are often called decimals.

deductive reasoning: reaching a conclusion using your reasoning skills

degree (measure of an angle): a unit for measuring angles; 45° means 45 degrees; 1° is the measure of $\frac{1}{360}$ of a complete turn.

denominator: in the fraction $\frac{2}{3}$, the number 3 is the denominator; the denominator tells the number of equal parts into which a whole has been divided; also used to refer to the second term of a ratio

diagonal: a line segment that joins two vertices in a polygon that are not adjacent

diameter: a line segment with end points on a circle and containing the centre of the circle

digit: a symbol used to record numbers; the symbols 0, 1, 2, 3, 4, 5, 6, 7, 8, 9 are used to record decimal numbers.

discount: the amount by which a price is reduced

distributive property: a property of numbers illustrated as follows;
$$3 \times (5 + 4) = 3 \times 5 + 3 \times 4$$
$$3 \times (5 - 4) = 3 \times 5 - 3 \times 4$$

divisor: 3 is the divisor in $12 \div 3$

edge: a line or line segment which is the intersection of two faces of a geometric figure

equation: a mathematical sentence that shows equality; the symbol = is used. For example, $4 + 5 = 9$.

equilateral triangle: a triangle with sides of equal length and size; a triangle with three lines of symmetry

equivalent fractions: fractions that can be reduced to the same lowest terms

even number: a number that has no remainder when divided by two

exponent: a number that shows how many times the base is used as a factor. For example, in 2^3, 3 is the exponent.

factor: any natural number that divides a number

factor tree: a diagram used for finding the prime factors of a sequence

Fibonacci Sequence: a sequence of numbers in the following form: 1, 1, 2, 3, 5, 8, 13, 21, 34, 55, 89, . . . Each number is the sum of the previous two numbers.

fraction: a number that represents a part of a whole. Common fractions are shown by numerals such as $\frac{2}{3}$ and $\frac{3}{4}$. Decimal fractions are shown by numerals like 1.3 and 0.9.

fraction form: a number written in the form $\frac{a}{b}$

geometry: the properties and relationships among lines, angles, points, surfaces, and solids

golden rectangle: a rectangle with a ratio of length to width of $1.6 : 1$

greatest common factor: the greatest factor common to two or more numbers

grid: a pattern of lines and dots; see also coordinate grid

inequality: a state where one quantity is greater than or less than another quantity

integer: one of the set of numbers . . . $-3, -2, -1,$ 0, 1, 2, 3, . . .

irrational number: a number that cannot be expressed as an integer or ratio of integers

irregular area: an area that's boundaries are not defined by straight lines

irrelevant information: information that is not necessary to solve the problem at hand

isosceles triangle: a triangle with two sides of equal length. It also has one line of symmetry.

kite: a quadrilateral in the shape of a kite with 2 pairs of adjacent sides equal in length

least common multiple: the lowest common multiple of two or more denominators

light year: the distance that light travels in one year. It is equivalent to 9 460 528 405 000 km.

line graph: a graph that uses a line to display data or information

line of symmetry (reflection): a line that divides a figure into two congruent parts

line segment: a part of a line with two end points

mass: the amount of substance or matter in an object

mean: the sum of several numbers divided by however many numbers there are

median: the middle number when a set of numbers has been arranged in ascending or descending order

mixed number: a number which has a whole and a fractional part. For example, $2\frac{3}{7}$.

mode: the number occurring most frequently in a set of numbers

multiple: A multiple of a number is the product of the number and another whole number.

natural number(s): one of the set of numbers 1, 2, 3, 4, 5 . . .

negative integer: one of the set of numbers $-1, -2, -3, -4, -5, . . .$

net: a pattern or arrangement of polygons to construct any polyhedron

number: a word or symbol used to denote an amount

numerator: the expression found above the line in a fraction. For example, in the fraction $\frac{2}{3}$, 2 is the numerator.

obtuse angle: an angle which measures more than $90°$ and less than $180°$

obtuse triangle: a triangle with one obtuse angle

octagon: a polygon with eight sides

odd number: a whole number which does not have 2 as a factor

opposite angle: two angles which are formed by two intersecting lines, and share a common vertex

opposite integer: The integers $+2$ and -2 are opposite integers.

order of operations: a set of rules which govern the evaluation of expressions

ordered pair: a pair of numbers in which the first number describes the horizontal displacement and the second number describes the vertical displacement

origin: the point at which the horizontal and vertical axes intersect

parallel lines: two lines in the same plane that will never have a point in common

parallelogram: a quadrilateral with opposite sides parallel

parsec: an astronomical measurement. A parsec is equal to approximately 3.2 light years.

pentagon: a polygon with five sides

percent: the number of parts per 100

perfect square: a perfect square is the value of any exponent to the power 2. For example 9 is a perfect square as it is the value of 3^2.

perimeter: the distance around any closed figure

perpendicular: two lines intersecting at $90°$

perpendicular bisector: a line that bisects a line segment and meets the line segment at $90°$

pi: a number, symbol π, which represents the ratio of the circumference to the diameter of a circle. It has an approximate value of 3.14.

pictograph: a diagram that displays data or information using pictures

place value: the value of the place of a digit in a numeral

point: an object having only one position in space

polygon: a closed figure made from line segments

polyhedron: a three-dimensional figure with faces that are polygons

population: the complete set of individuals or things from which statistical samples are drawn. For example, the population of students is the entire student body.

positive square: the positive value of the square root of a number

power: A power, such as 2^3, is expressed using a base, 2, and an exponent, 3.

prime factor: a factor of a number that is a prime number

prime number: a number with factors of only one and itself

principal square: see positive square

prism: a figure with two equal and parallel bases and whose other faces are parallelograms

probability: a number that gives the likelihood of an event occurring

product: the answer obtained from multiplication

property of one: When a number is multiplied by 1, the number is still the same.

proportion: an equation which shows the equality of two ratios

protractor: an instrument to measure angles

pyramid: a figure with a base that is a polygon and triangular faces that meet at a common vertex

Pythagorean Relation: theorem which relates the squares of the sides of a right angled triangle, whereby the square of the hypotenuse is equal to the sum of the squares of the other two sides

quadrilateral: a polygon with four sides

quotient: the answer obtained from division

radius: half of the diameter of a circle; a line segment that joins the centre of a circle to a point on the circle

rate: comparison of quantities expressed in different units

ratio: a comparison of two numbers

rational number: a number which can be written as an integer or a quotient of integers. For example, $-2, \frac{5}{8}, 6, \frac{-2}{3}$.

real number: any rational or irrational number

reciprocals: Two numbers are reciprocals of each other if their product is one. For example, $\frac{2}{3}$ and $\frac{3}{2}$ are reciprocals because $\frac{2}{3} \times \frac{3}{2} = 1$.

rectangle: a quadrilateral with opposite sides equal and angle measures of $90°$

repeating decimal: decimals that follow a pattern and that do not terminate

rhombus: a parallelogram with all sides equal

right angle: an angle which measures $90°$

rotation: any turn of a figure about a fixed point

sample: a random survey of a portion of a population

scale: the lengths on an enlargement or reduction of a figure are shown on the scale. The ratio of the distance on a scale to the actual scale.

scale factor: the number used to create an enlargement or reduction

scalene triangle: a triangle with all sides of unequal length

scientific notation: a form of writing numbers where the numbers are expressed as a decimal product of a power of 10. For example, 4200 would be written 4.2×10^3.

septagon: a seven-sided polygon

side: a line segment of a figure

signed numbers: positive and negative numbers

similar figures: figures that are the same shape but not always the same size

slide: moving an object without turning or flipping

square: a quadrilateral with four equal sides and all angle measures of 90°

square number: a number that can be expressed as a base to the power 2. For example, $6^2 = 36$.

square root: one of two equal factors of a given number

statistics: the collecting, organizing, presenting, and interpreting of data

stem and leaf plot: a diagram used to display information or data

supplementary angles: two angles that sum to 180°

surface area: the total area covered by all faces of a polyhedron

table: an organized listing of data or information

terminating decimal: decimals with a finite number of digits

terms of a ratio: the numbers used in a ratio

tetrahedron: a polyhedron with 4 faces

transformation: a translation, reflection, or rotation

trapezoid: a quadrilateral with one pair of opposite sides parallel

triangle: a polygon with three sides

variable: a symbol used to represent a number

vertex: the common end point of two rays; the point where two sides of a polygon meet; the point where three or more sides of a polyhedron meet

volume: the amount of space occupied by a three-dimensional object

whole numbers: the numbers 0, 1, 2, 3, 4, 5 . . .

zero property: the property whereby any number multiplied by 0 has a product of 0

ANSWERS

CHAPTER 1

Section 1.2

1. a) 100 000 **b)** 1000 **c)** 100 **d)** 1 000 000
e) 100 000 000   **2. a)** hundreds **b)** thousands **c)** ones
d) hundredths   **3. a)** $4 \times 10^2 + 8 \times 10 + 9 \times 1 + 3 \times \frac{1}{10} + 6 \times \frac{1}{10^2}$; four hundred eighty-nine point three six
b) $7 \times 10^3 + 8 \times 10^2 + 9 \times 1$; seven thousand eight hundred nine **c)** $1 \times 10^3 + 8 \times 1 + 2 \times \frac{1}{10} + \frac{5}{10^2} + \frac{6}{10^3}$; one thousand eight point two five six **d)** $3 \times 10^2 + 1 \times 1 + \frac{1}{10} + \frac{5}{10^3}$; three hundred one point one zero five

4. a) 5420.1 **b)** 9730.003   **5. a)** 34 981 orbits **b)** 613 km
c) 6015 km   **6. a)** $1 \times 10^6 + 3 \times 10^5 + 9 \times 10^4 + 2 \times 10^3$ **b)** $7 \times 10^8 + 7 \times 10^7 + 7 \times 10^6 + 9 \times 10^5 + 5 \times 10^4$ **c)** $2 \times 10^5 + 7 \times 10^4 + 3 \times 10^3 + 5 \times 10^2$

7. a) Answers will vary. **b)** Answers will vary.
8. a) 1268, 1286, 1628, 1682, 1826, 1862, 2168, 2186, 2618, 2681, 2816, 2861, 6128, 6182, 6218, 6281, 6812, 6821, 8126, 8162, 8216, 8261, 8612, 8621
b) $1 \times 10^3 + 2 \times 10^2 + 6 \times 10 + 8 \times 1$,
one thousand two hundred sixty-eight
$1 \times 10^3 + 2 \times 10^2 + 8 \times 10 + 6 \times 1$,
one thousand two hundred eighty-six
$1 \times 10^3 + 6 \times 10^2 + 2 \times 10 + 8 \times 1$,
one thousand six hundred twenty-eight
$1 \times 10^3 + 6 \times 10^2 + 8 \times 10 + 2 \times 1$,
one thousand six hundred eighty-two
$1 \times 10^3 + 8 \times 10^2 + 2 \times 10 + 6 \times 1$,
one thousand eight hundred twenty-six
$1 \times 10^3 + 8 \times 10^2 + 6 \times 10 + 2 \times 1$,
one thousand eight hundred sixty-two
$2 \times 10^3 + 1 \times 10^2 + 6 \times 10 + 8 \times 1$,
two thousand one hundred sixty-eight
$2 \times 10^3 + 1 \times 10^2 + 8 \times 10 + 6 \times 1$,
two thousand one hundred eighty-six
$2 \times 10^3 + 6 \times 10^2 + 1 \times 10 + 8 \times 1$,
two thousand six hundred eighteen
$2 \times 10^3 + 6 \times 10^2 + 8 \times 10 + 1 \times 1$,
two thousand six hundred eighty-one
$2 \times 10^3 + 8 \times 10^2 + 1 \times 10 + 6 \times 1$,
two thousand eight hundred sixteen
$2 \times 10^3 + 8 \times 10^2 + 6 \times 10 + 1 \times 1$,
two thousand eight hundred sixty-one
$6 \times 10^3 + 1 \times 10^2 + 2 \times 10 + 8 \times 1$,
six thousand one hundred twenty-eight
$6 \times 10^3 + 1 \times 10^2 + 8 \times 10 + 2 \times 1$,
six thousand one hundred eighty-two
$6 \times 10^3 + 2 \times 10^2 + 1 \times 10 + 8 \times 1$,
six thousand two hundred eighteen
$6 \times 10^3 + 2 \times 10^2 + 8 \times 10 + 1 \times 1$,
six thousand two hundred eighty-one
$6 \times 10^3 + 8 \times 10^2 + 1 \times 10 + 2 \times 1$,
six thousand eight hundred twelve
$6 \times 10^3 + 8 \times 10^2 + 2 \times 10 + 1 \times 1$,
six thousand eight hundred twenty-one
$8 \times 10^3 + 1 \times 10^2 + 2 \times 10 + 6 \times 1$,
eight thousand one hundred twenty-six
$8 \times 10^3 + 1 \times 10^2 + 6 \times 10 + 2 \times 1$,
eight thousand one hundred sixty-two
$8 \times 10^3 + 2 \times 10^2 + 1 \times 10 + 6 \times 1$,
eight thousand two hundred sixteen
$8 \times 10^3 + 2 \times 10^2 + 6 \times 10 + 1 \times 1$,
eight thousand two hundred sixty-one
$8 \times 10^3 + 6 \times 10^2 + 1 \times 10 + 2 \times 1$,
eight thousand six hundred twelve
$8 \times 10^3 + 6 \times 10^2 + 2 \times 10 + 1 \times 1$,
eight thousand six hundred twenty-one
9. a) 500 **b)** 5×10^2, five hundred

Section 1.3

1. a) 5.3 **b)** 7.4 **c)** 2.8 **d)** 3.9   **2. a)** < **b)** < **c)** < **d)** >
3. a) 0.3 **b)** 0.66 **c)** 1.5   **4. a)** 1.2, 2.2, 3.2, 4.2, 5.2; 6.2, 7.2, 8.2 **b)** 1.5, 3.0, 4.5, 6.0, 7.5; 9.0, 10.5, 12.0
5. a) 503.1, 504.9 **b)** 3635, 3640 **c)** 50.21, 50.3 **d)** 1.85, 1.88 **e)** 3.1601, 3.168 **f)** 2.258, 2.26   **6.** DBS Tower
7. Samir   **8.** Brown's; It's cheaper there.   **9.** Answers will vary.   **10. a)** 63; 1¢, 5¢, 6¢, 10¢ 11¢, 15¢, 16¢, 25¢, 26¢, 30¢, 31¢, 35¢, 36¢, 40¢, 41¢, 50¢, 51¢, 55¢, 56¢, 60¢, 61¢, 65¢, 66¢, 75¢, 76¢, 80¢, 81¢, 85¢, 86¢, 90¢, 91¢,$1.00, $1.01, $1.05, $1.06, $1.10, $1.11, $1.15, $1.16, $1.25, $1.26, $1.30, $1.31, $1.35, $1.36, $1.40, $1.41, $1.50, $1.51, $1.55, $1.56, $1.60, $1.61, $1.65, $1.66, $1.75, $1.76, $1.80, $1.81, $1.85, $1.86, $1.90, $1.91

Section 1.4

1. a) rounded up **b)** rounded down   **2. a)** tens
b) tenths   **3. a)** 5.8 **b)** 4.63   **4. a)** 80 g **b)** 5 g **c)** 496 mL
d) 35 m **e)** 5 kg   **5. a)** 88, 88.0 **b)** 225, 224.7 **c)** 687, 687.0 **d)** 10 759, 10 759.2 **e)** 365, 365.3   **6. a)** 10.9, 8.6, 5.1, 7.1 **b)** Arctic, Indian, Atlantic, Pacific
7. a) 54.9 m **b)** 18.5 m **c)** 17.4 m   **8. a)** 7024.4 km
b) 917.7 km **c)** 1524.7 km **d)** 17 792.1 km **e)** 5828.2 km
f) 1210.7 km **g)** 1107.7 km **h)** 10 843.4 km
i) 25 111.2 km **j)** 342.9 km   **9.** Yukon, Manitoba, P.E.I., Ontario, New Brunswick, Nova Scotia, B.C., Quebec, Newfoundland, Northwest Territories

Section 1.5

1. a) 30 **b)** 9.96 **c)** 8.9 **d)** 7.16   **2. a)** 854 **b)** 85.4 **c)** 8.54
d) 0.854   **3. a)** 3.6 **b)** 2.07 **c)** 0.95 **d)** 0.96   **4. a)** 577
b) 57.7 **c)** 5.77 **d)** 0.577   **5. a)** 30.46 **b)** 5157 **c)** 658.44
d) 2663 **e)** 0.46 **f)** 130   **6. a)** Chris, by 3.4 km
7. a) 1245.2 **b)** 8953.72 **c)** 123.37 **d)** 30.25

Section 1.6
2. a) 1, 1, 2, 3, 5, 8 **b)** The length of each square is the sum of the lengths of the two previous squares; length of tenth square; 55 units **c)** 1, 1, 2, 3, 5, 8, 13, 21, 34, 55, 89, 144, 233, 377, 610 **3. a)** Each number is the sum of the previous two numbers. **b)** 89, 144, 233, 377; A:33553, B:33552, C:1 **c)** The difference between the product of the outer pair and that of the inner pair is always 1. **5. c)** Most of the time, the answer is 4.2.

Section 1.7
1. a) 14.4 **b)** 175.75 **c)** 30.45 **2. a)** 0.35 **b)** 33.18 **c)** 2.1 **d)** 0.0861 **e)** 0.322 **f)** 48 **g)** 5.491 **h)** 183.372 **3. a)** 0.25 **b)** 10.752 **c)** 164.57 **4. a)** 90 **b)** 40 **c)** 111 **d)** 89 **e)** 0.9 **f)** 0.4 **g)** 0.7 **h)** 0.08 **5. a)** 0.52 m **6.** $3.20 **7.** $15.78 **8. a)** A **b)** A:2950 kg, B:2714.4 kg **9.** Answers will vary.

Section 1.8
1. a) 4680, 46 800, 468 000 **b)** 3710, 37 100, 371 000 **c)** 1.25, 12.5, 125 **d)** 15.7, 157, 1570 **2. a)** 46.8, 4.68, 0.468 **b)** 3.69, 0.369, 0.0369 **c)** 0.0129, 0.001 29, 0.000 129 **d)** 0.148, 0.0148, 0.001 48 **3.** Chart 1: 38.2, 382, 3820; 10.12, 101.2, 1012; 175.4, 1754, 17 540 Chart 2: 4.86, 0.486, 0.0486; 7.43, 0.743, 0.0743; 0.3892, 0.038 92, 0.003 892 **4. a)** 624.3, 624.3; 94.13, 94.13; 5.468, 5.468 **b)** The values are the same. **c)** Shift the decimal point one place to the left. **5. a)** 62.43, 62.43; 9.413, 9.413; 0.5468, 0.5468 **b)** They are the same. **c)** Shift the decimal point two places to the left. **6. a)** 6.243, 6.243; 0.9413, 0.9413; 0.054 68, 0.054 68 **b)** They are the same. **c)** Shift the decimal point three places to the left. **7.** Move the decimal point one, two, and three places to the right respectively for 0.1, 0.01, and 0.001. **8. a)** 680 **b)** 5 **c)** 35 000 **d)** 3.5 **e)** 95 000 **f)** 0.003 11 **g)** 0.0008 **h)** 23.5 **9. a)** 325 000 **b)** 0.12 **c)** 75 **d)** 0.42 **e)** 2100 **f)** 0.32 **g)** 0.003 11 **h)** 0.001 005

Section 1.9
1. a) 26¢ **b)** 31¢ **c)** 60¢ **d)** 4¢ **2. a)** $1.56 **b)** yes **3. a)** $11.67 **b)** yes **4.** Joe's market **5. a)** 67¢

Section 1.10
1. a) 2.9 **b)** 28.2 **c)** 0.7 **d)** 68.56 **e)** 4.62 **f)** 0.6 **2. a)** 3.46 **b)** 1 **c)** 5 **d)** 0.08 **e)** 13.92 **f)** 27.84 **3. a)** > **b)** > **c)** < **d)** < **4.** $64.80 **5.** 18°C

Section 1.11
1. a) 120 **b)** 120 **2. a)** 1770 **b)** 1770 **3.** 3680.25 km **4.** 16 250 000 **5.** Answers will vary. **6.** 7 **7. a)** 1860

Section 1.12
1. a) 9 **2.** Answers will vary: e.g., the 20th floor. She parked on level P above which is the ground level (the 1st floor). **3.** Answers will vary: e.g. 198 + 199 + 200 + 201 + 202 **4.** Answers will vary.

Chapter Review
1. a) tens **b)** hundredths **c)** tenths **d)** thousands **2. a)** 7911 **b)** 54.7 **c)** 3383 **d)** 42 688 **e)** 4736.5501 **f)** 4306 **3. a)** 750 **b)** 27.0 **c)** 1 658 000 **d)** 12.346 **e)** 12 900 **4. a)** 56 **b)** 28.3668 **c)** 2.75 **d)** 0 **e)** 360 **5.** 28 cm **6. a)** 470 250 **b)** 39 187.5 **c)** $77 591.25

Self Evaluation
1. a) > **b)** < **c)** < **d)** > **2. a)** 9708 **b)** 65.03 **c)** 36 524 **d)** 328 328 216 **e)** 422.46394 **f)** 43.2 **g)** 3.369 **3.** Answers may vary, e.g., 9000 (assuming 9 am − 3 pm). **4. a)** 4.1 **b)** 1266 **c)** 413.20 **d)** 5000 **e)** 220.23 **f)** 2.85 **5.** $124.50 **6.** Ostrich, 7.7 kg **7.** 72.4 mm **8.** 161.2 cm

CHAPTER 2
Section 2.1
2. a) +8; −8 **b)** −6; +6 **c)** −500; +500 **d)** +5; −5 **e)** +9; −9 **f)** +10; −10 **3. a)** +3 **b)** −7 **c)** −11 **d)** +13 **e)** +8 **f)** −1 **4. a)** +3, +6, −2 **5. a)** 0, 0, 0

Section 2.2
1. a) +8, +10, +11, −5, −11, −9 **b)** +7, +11, +90, 0, −3, −4 **c)** −2, −1, 0, −6, −7, −11 **d)** +4, +11, +13, −1, −2, −3 **2.** −4 < 0, −3 < −1, +2 < +4, +4 > −1, −1 < +2 **3. a)** +4 > −3 **b)** −1 > −3 **c)** +1 < +5 **4. a)** e.g. Dauphin > Cold Lake **b)** Brandon, Bonnyville **c)** +3, −2, −8, −10 **d)** Answers will vary. **5. a)** 80 km > 18 km **b)** −20 km < −0.5 km **6. a)** e.g., −5°C, 30°C, 15°C

Section 2.3
1. a) 6 black disks **b)** +6 **2. a)** 6 red disks **b)** −6 **3. a)** 2 red disks **b)** −2 **4. a)** 2 black disks **b)** +2 **5. a)** A: (+3) + (−1), B: (+2) + (−4); A: +2, B: −2 **6. a)** 2 black disks **b)** (+4) − (+2) = +2 **7. b)** (−4) − (−2) = −2 **8. a)** +3 **b)** −1 **c)** −3 **d)** +2 **9.** Answers will vary. **10. b)** +5 **11. b)** −5 **12. a)** A: −5, B: +9, C: +10

Section 2.4
1. a) A: −2, +3; B: −4, +6 **b)** (−2) + (+3); (−4) + (+6) **c)** +1; +2 **2. a)** +6 **b)** +2 **c)** −2 **d)** −6 **3. a)** +3, +4, +5, +6, +7, +8 **b)** −7, −6, −5, −4, −3, −2 **4. a)** up 2 steps, a drop of 4°C **5. a)** +2 **b)** −20 **c)** +6 **d)** −4 **e)** −20 **f)** −21 **g)** +4 **h)** +5 **6.** greatest: g); least: c) **7.** greatest: e) and f); least: b) **8. a)** −5, +9 **b)** +4 **c)** Al ran 4 m more than Ron. **9.** 4201 m **10.** 1485 m

Section 2.5
1. b) A: (−1) − (+2) = −3; B: (−1) − (−3) = +2; C: (−3) − (+1) = −4 **2. a)** +8 **b)** +1 **c)** −12 **d)** −4 **3. a)** +3, +4, +5, +6, +7, +8 **b)** −1, −2, −3, −4, −5, −6 **4. a)** +7 **b)** +16 **c)** −9 **d)** −20 **e)** +2 **f)** −10 **g)** +8 **h)** −2 **5. c)** **6. a)** **7. a)** +4, −2 **b)** +6 **c)** 6 m **8. a)** 2 m below the surface **b)** diving 6 m **9.** 1930°C **10.** 18°C **11.** 11°C

Section 2.6

1. a) $(+6) + (-8) = -2$ **b)** $(+9) + (-8) = +1$ **c)** $(+9) + (-9) = 0$ **d)** $(-7) + (-3) = -10$ **e)** $(-4) + (+3) = -1$ **f)** $(+6) + (+8) = +14$ **g)** $(+3) + (+2) = +5$ **h)** $(-4) + (+8) = +4$ **2. a)** $+8$ **b)** $+1$ **c)** -12 **d)** -9 **e)** -4 **f)** $+13$ **g)** -8 **h)** $+2$ **3. a)** -2 **b)** -10 **c)** $+7$ **d)** $+16$ **e)** -9 **f)** -20 **g)** $+2$ **h)** -10 **4. a)** -9 **b)** -7 **c)** -11 **d)** -12

Section 2.7

1. a) $+1$ **b)** $+7$ **c)** -5 **d)** -6 **2. a)** -1 **b)** $+8$ **c)** -7 **d)** $+3$ **3.** $+10$ **4.** $+8°C$ **5.** $+4$ m **6.** Schefferville, by 15°C **7.** 10 884 m

Section 2.8

1 a) E **b)** F **c)** G **d)** H **e)** I **2. a)** -3 or $+4$ **b)** $+2$ **c)** -3 or $+2$ **d)** -4 or $+4$ **e)** -2 or $+5$ **f)** -5 **g)** 0 **h)** $+7$ **i)** $+7$ **j)** -5, $+5$, or $+6$ **3. a)** III, IV **b)** IV **c)** IV, I **d)** II, I **e)** III, II **f)** III **g)** h. axis **h)** v. axis **i)** h. axis **j)** IV, I, I **4. c)** a right isosceles triangle **5. c)** an isosceles triangle **6. c)** a parallelogram **7. b)** 10 **8. a)** II **b)** $(-5, 3)$ **c)** e.g., $(7, 0)$ **d)** $(1, -1)$

Section 2.9

1. b) e.g., $(-3, \frac{4}{3})$, $(-4, -\frac{1}{3})$ **c)** e.g., $(-8, -7)$, $(1, 8)$

2. Answers will vary. **b)** $(2, 2)$, $(2, -2)$ **c)** $(0, 2)$, $(0, -2)$, $(-2, 0)$, $(2, 0)$ **d)** another square **3. a)** D(6, 3) **b)** A(1, 3), B(1, -7), C(11, -7), D(11, 3) **4. a)** M A T **5. a)** GO DOWN **6.** Answers will vary.

Section 2.10

1. a) 650 **b)** 250 500 **2. a)** 625 **b)** 250 000 **3. a)** 5 **b)** 2275 **4.** 1275 **5. a)** 27 **b)** -300 **6. a)** 105 **b)** The bus can hold all the passengers, and no one gets off. **7.** 24 **8.** e.g., $876 + 124$

Calculation Sense

1. a) $+2$ **b)** $+5$ **c)** -2 **2. a)** -9 **b)** -3 **c)** 0

Section 2.13

1. b) $+9$ **2. b)** -9 **3. a)** A: $(+3) \times (+3)$, B: $(+2) \times (-2)$, C: $(+5) \times (-6)$ or $(+6) \times (-5)$, D: $(+2) \times (+4)$ or $(+4) \times (+2)$, E: $(+3) \times (-2)$ or $(+2) \times (-3)$ **b)** A: $+9$, B: -4, C: -30, D: $+8$, E: -6 **4. b)** A: -15, B: -8, C: -12, D: -16 **5.** Answers will vary.

Section 2.14

1. a) -15 **b)** -15 **2. a)** $+2, 0, -2, -4, -6$ **b)** $0, -3, -6, -9, -12$ **c)** $-4, -2, 0, +2, +4, +6$ **3. a)** $+10$ **b)** -18 **4. a)** -18 **b)** -8 **c)** -18 **d)** -8 **e)** $+18$ **f)** -14 **5.** a, b **6.** They are all -36. **7. a)** positive **b)** negative

Section 2.15

1. a) $-3, 0, 3, 6$ **b)** $-5, 0, 5, 10$ **c)** $-8, -4, 0, 4$ **2. a)** 12 **b)** 30 **c)** 72 **d)** 10 **e)** 33 **f)** 60 **g)** 21 **h)** 16 **3. a)** 36 **b)** 40 **c)** 35 **d)** 18 **e)** 30 **f)** 24 **g)** 55 **h)** 108 **4. a)** 24 **b)** 0 **c)** 0 **d)** 132 **e)** 0 **f)** -56 **g)** 16 **h)** -20 **5. a)** 16 **b)** 18 **c)** -16 **d)** 132; $-16, 16, 18, 132$ **6. a)** negative **b)** positive **7. a)** 42 red, 8 black **b)** -34

Section 2.16

1. a) 6 **b)** -6 **c)** -6 **d)** 6 **2. a)** -5 **b)** -3 **c)** 6 **d)** 6 **3. a)** when both integers are the same sign **b)** when the integers are different signs **4. a)** -5 **b)** -3 **c)** 3 **d)** 5 **e)** 0 **f)** -7 **5. a)** -9 **b)** 0 **c)** -2 **d)** 11 **e)** 10 **f)** -12 **6. a)** -2 **b)** -6 **c)** -3 **d)** -5 **e)** 3 **f)** 4; $-6, -5, -3, -2, 3, 4$ **7.** Answers will vary. **8.** $-2°C$

Section 2.17

1. A: -10, B: -34 **2.** A: -36, B: -1 **3. a)** -8 **b)** -3 **c)** 77 **4. a)** 4 **b)** 4 **c)** -6 **d)** -2 **5. a)** -16 **b)** -8 **c)** 0 **d)** 2; $-16, -8, 0, 2$ **6. a)** -13 **b)** -31 **c)** 37 **7. a)** -233 m **b)** 233 m below ground **8.** $-1°C$

Section 2.18

2. a) 34 **b)** $+44$ in each square. **3. a)** 4 **b)** 10

Chapter Review

1. a) $+10$ **b)** -2 **c)** $+120$ **2. a)** $>$ **b)** $<$ **c)** $>$ **4. a)** $+3, +4, +5$ **b)** $+3, -4, +5$ **5. a)** 3 **b)** 9 **c)** -9 **6. a)** 28 **b)** 6 **c)** -9 **d)** -18 **e)** -1 **f)** -64 **7. a)** -1 **b)** -3 **c)** 4 **d)** -16 **8.** $+1, -2, +2, +2$

Self Evaluation

1. a) -4 **b)** $+2$ **2.** Answers will vary, e.g., **a)** 0, 1 **b)** $-5, -6$ **c)** 0, -1 **3. a)** $<$ **b)** $>$ **c)** $<$ **5. a)** $-6, -5, -3, 6, 9$ **b)** $-15, -11, -7, 8, 11$ **6. a)** 4 **b)** -7 **c)** -3 **d)** -1 **e)** -19 **f)** 21 **7. a)** -5 **b)** -28 **c)** 2 **d)** 0 **e)** 180 **f)** 4 **8.** Lori **9.** 6°C

Math in Calgary Olympics

1. 3 **2. a)** $55 + 34.5$ **b)** 89.5 m **3. a)** 1000 **b)** 1000 km **4. b)** 144 **5.** 5 **6. a)** 36.5 s **b)** 37.0 s, 48.6 km/h **7.** Karen Percy **8.** 4 km

CHAPTER 3
Section 3.1

1. a) A: 9 tiles, length: 3, width: 3; B: 16 tiles, length: 4, width: 4 **b)** number of tiles = length $\times$ width **2.** Answers will vary. **3. a)** A: 12 tiles, 3 by 4; B: 16 tiles, 8 by 2 **b)** number of tiles = length $\times$ width **4.** Answers will vary. **5. c)** Prime numbers; composite numbers **7. a)** A: 6, B: 15 **8.** Answers will vary.

Section 3.2

1. b) 3 and 11 are prime; 6, 15, and 21 are composite **2. b)**

4: factors $\{1, 2, 4\}$,	prime factors $\{2\}$
10: factors $\{1, 2, 5, 10\}$,	prime factors $\{2, 5\}$
20: factors $\{1, 2, 4, 5, 10, 20\}$	prime factors $\{2, 5\}$
25: factors $\{1, 5, 25\}$	prime factors $\{5\}$

3. a) 1, 2, 4, 5, 10, 20 **b)** 1, 2, 3, 4, 6, 7, 12, 14, 21, 28, 42, 84 **c)** 1, 3, 9, 11, 33, 99 **d)** 1, 2, 4, 5, 10, 20, 25, 50, 100 **e)** 1, 71 **f)** 1, 83 **g)** 2, 3, 5, 7, 11, 13, 17, 19, 23, 29, 31, 37, 41, 43, 47, 53, 59, 61, 67, 71, 73, 79, 83, 89, 97 **4. a)** 2, 3, 5 **b)** $30 = 2 \times 3 \times 5$ **5. a)** 30 **b)** 36 **c)** 105 **6. a)** 23, 83 **b)** 2, 3, 79 **c)** 2, 31 **7. a)** 1, 2, 3, 5, 6, 10, 15, 25, 30, 50, 75, 125, 150, 250, 375, 750 **b)** 25 m **8. a)** 210 **b)** 78

Section 3.3

1. b) 8: 1, 2, 4, 8; 12: 1, 2, 3, 4, 6, 12 **c)** 4   **2. b)** 15: 1, 3, 5, 15; 25: 1, 5, 25 **c)** 5   **3. a)** 3: 3, 6, 9, 12, 15, 18, . . . ; 5: 5, 10, 15, . . . **b)** 15   **4. a)** 4, 8, 3, 6 **b)** 36, 135, 200, 108   **5. a)** 4 **b)** 4   **6.** 111 m   **7.** 4 and 5   **8.** every 20 water stops

Section 3.4

1. a) 3 **b)** 4 **c)** 7 **d)** 9   **2. a)** 5 × 5, 7 × 7, 11 × 11, 13 × 13 **b)** The numbers are perfect squares. **c)** 5, 7, 11, 13   **3. a)** 11.18 **b)** 14.66 **c)** 2.1 **d)** 1.3   **4. a)** 5 m **b)** 4 m **c)** 1.2 m   **5.** 12 m × 12 m   **6.** 1.7 cm × 1 7 cm   **7.** 14 m × 14 m   **8.** 317 km   **9.** 1.8 m   **10.** 2

Section 3.5

1. a) 24, 38, 50, 16, 46 **b)** 24, 38, 50, 16, 46 **c)** if it is even   **2. a)** 10, 40, 15, 55, 70, 75, 25 **b)** 10, 40, 15, 55, 70, 75, 25 **c)** if it ends in 0 or 5   **3. a)** 3618, 4842, 2691, 2463 **b)** 18, 18, 26, 8, 18, 15; 3618, 4842, 2691, 2463 **c)** It's divisible by 3 if the sum of its digits is divisible by 3   **4. a)** 441, 48213 **b)** 9, 26, 18, 22; 441, 48213 **c)** A number is divisible by 9 if the sum of its digits is divisible by 9.   **5. a)** 6324, 9632, 38964 **b)** 24, 32, 64 **c)** A number is divisible by 4 if its last two digits are divisible by 4.   **6. a)** 8112 **b)** 112 **c)** A number is divisible by 8 if its last 3 digits are divisible by 8.   **7. a)** 42, 72, 66, 84 **b)** 42, 72, 66, 84 **c)** A number has 6 as a factor if both 2 and 3 are factors.   **8.** A number is divisible by 25 if its last two digits are 00, 25, 50, or 75.

Section 3.6

1. a) E.g., calculator, trial and error **b)** 8.66, 12, 27, 4.7, 3.6, 16.8   **4. a)** 2; 4 **c)** 56

Section 3.7

1. Parachutes; Volume P is in his hand.   **2.** No, the temperature is 5°C so the ice could be melting.
3. Since the shadows cast are very long, it could be early morning or late afternoon.   **4.** The building not entirely immersed in shadow.

Section 3.8

1. a) 30° + 60° = 90° **b)** 90° **c)** They are the same.
2. a) Their sum is 90°.   **3. a)** 120° + 60° = 180° **b)** 180° **c)** They are the same.   **4. a)** Their sum is 180°.
5. b) ∠AED and ∠BEC; ∠AEB and ∠DEC **c)** They are the same. **d)** They are the same.   **6. a)** Opposite angles have the same measure.   **7.** Answers will vary.

Section 3.9

2. c) Can be either depending on the cut.   **3. a)** 72° **b)** 27° **c)** 105° **d)** 38°   **4. a)** 70° **b)** 40° **c)** 75°   **5. a)** 157° **b)** 30° **c)** 65°   **6. a)** 40° **b)** 130°   **7. a)** 105° **b)** 120° **8. a)** 45°

Section 3.10

1. b) The angles are all the same.   **3. b)** ∠Q = ∠R **4.** The angles opposite the two equal sides are equal.   **5. a)** The three side lengths in each triangle are different. **b)** The angles are all different. **c)** A

scalene triangle has all sides different lengths, and all angles are different measures.   **6. a)** Corresponding sides and angles are equal. Orientation is different. **b)** Congruent scalene triangles.   **7. a)** 180° **b)** 180° **8. b)** a straight angle: 180° **c)** The sum of the angles in any triangle is 180°.

Section 3.11

1. a) Their sum is 180°. **b)** 75°   **2. a)** 91° **b)** 36° **3.** both isosceles   **4.** both scalene   **5. b)** 100° **6. b)** isosceles **c)** ∠A = ∠C = 76°, ∠B = 28° **7.** outside angles: 45°, angles in the middle: 90° **8. b)** 6, 2, 3

Section 3.12

1. b) The triangles have the same side lengths and angle measures, but different orientations.   **2. a)** The angles with the same names correspond and have equal measures. **b)** The line segments with the same names correspond and have equal lengths.
3. b) Same side lengths and measures, different orientation.   **4. a)** The angles with the same names correspond and have equal measures. **b)** The line segments with the same names correspond and have equal lengths.   **5.** The line segments and angles with the same names are equal.   **6. b)** Same side lengths and angle measures, different orientation.   **7. a)** ∠P = ∠P′, ∠Q = ∠Q′; ∠R = ∠R′ **b)** PQ = P′Q′, PR = P′ R′, QR = Q′ R′   **9. b)** A, D, E, G, H, J; B, C, I; F, K, L, M

Section 3.14

1. a) 1, 2, 5, 10, 13, 25, 26, 50, 65, 130, 325, 650 **b)** 25 m   **2.** 16¢   **3.** 8 m × 8 m   **5.** 10 560 km   **6.** 48

Chapter Review

1. 11   **2. a)** 2 **b)** 15 **c)** 6   **3. a)** 24 **b)** 34 **c)** 60   **4.** 9486, 4617   **5.** 7 km   **6.** from bottom left to bottom right: 50°, 130°, 80°, 50°, 130°   **7.** Answers will vary. e.g. **a)** 3152 **b)** 1836   **8.** 18 m × 18 m

Self Evaluation

1. 27, 49, 51   **2. a)** 12 **b)** 4 **c)** 4   **3. a)** 2 × 2 × 3 **b)** 5 × 7 **c)** 2 × 2 × 3 × 3 **d)** 2 × 3 × 3 × 3 **4. a)** every 36th person **b)** 800   **5. a)** no **b)** yes **6.** red: slide, green: turn, blue; flip

Practice: Cumulative Review

1. a) 0.125, 1.025, 1.25, 1.52 **b)** 3.039, 3.3339, 30.9, 33.09 **c)** 1.5, 33.1   **2. a)** 4.9 **b)** 389580 **c)** 1.34 **d)** 1.4 **3. a)** −3 **b)** −51 **c)** −252 **d)** 5 **e)** −16 **f)** −1 **4.** ten thousands   **5.** $24.73   **6.** 2 h 40 min **7. a)** Peter: 13, Bill: 18 **b)** 17

Calculation Sense

a) 552 + 653 = 1205 **b)** 378 + 219 = 597 **c)** 395 + 603 = 998

Problem Solving: Cumulative Review

1. Brian, by 2 m   **2. a)** 35 **b)** Answers will vary.   **3.** 44 **4.** Answers will vary.   **5. a)** Pour soda out of the glass until the surface of the soda in the glass runs from the lip of the container to the point where the opposite side meets the bottom. **6. a)** It divides evenly. **b)** It divides evenly. **c)** It divides evenly. **d)** The GCF of two numbers divides their difference evenly.

CHAPTER 4
Section 4.1
1. a) 1 **b)** 2   **2. a)** 2 **b)** 4   **3. b)** 8, 16   **4.** Answers will vary.   **5. b)** 4   **6. a)** 10, 11

Section 4.2
1. a) $3^2 = 9$ **b)** $(-4)^2 = 16$ **c)** $2^3 = 8$ **d)** $(-6)^3 = -216$ **2. a)** $3 \times 3 \times 3 \times 3 = 81$ **b)** $(-4) \times (-4) \times (-4) = -64$ **c)** $6 \times 6 = 36$ **d)** $8 \times 8 \times 8 = 512$ **e)** $10 \times 10 = 100$ **f)** $(-5) \times (-5) \times (-5) \times (-5) = 625$ **3. a)** 27 **b)** 256   **4.** $64, 8^2$ **5.** 1024

Section 4.3
1. a) 2 **b)** 3 **c)** 6 **d)** 3   **2. a)** 12 **b)** 3 **c)** 6 **d)** 27   **3. a)** 33 **b)** 13 **c)** 58 **d)** −399   **4. a)** 49 **b)** 17 **c)** 25 **d)** 7   **5. a)** 243 **b)** −2 **c)** $\frac{243}{17}$ **d)** 875   **6.** A   **7. a)** $3^2 + 2$ **b)** $4^2 \div 2^4$ **c)** $10^2 - 1^{100}$ **d)** $5^2 - 2$ **8.** 544   **9. a)** $8^2 + 7^2 + 6^2 + 5^2 + 4^2 + 3^2 + 2^2 + 1^2$ **b)** 204   **10.** from left to right, top to bottom: 4, 18, 8; 14, 10, 6; 12, 2, 16   **11.** 608

Section 4.4
1. a) $2^5 = 32$ **b)** $3^6 = 729$ **c)** $2^8 = 256$ **d)** $2^2 = 4$ **2. a)** 128 **b)** 243 **c)** 256 **d)** 729 **e)** 25 **f)** 100 **g)** 16 **h)** 5   **3. a)** 32 **b)** 440 **c)** −16 **d)** 148   **4.** 7   **5.** Answers may vary; e.g., **a)** 5 **b)** 200 times.   **6.** Kangaroo, 1.125   **7.** 9   **8. a)** 16

Section 4.5
1. a) 8 **b)** 2   **2. a)** 3, 9, 27, 81, 243, 729, 2187, 6561, 19 683, 59 049, 177 147, 531 441 **b)** 1   **3. a)** 1089, 110 889, 11 108 889 **b)** 111 111 110 888 888 889   **4. a)** 4 **b)** 9 **c)** 10 000   **5.** 4096   **6.** off   **7.** South

Section 4.6
1. a) 4, 5, 4, 7 **b)** 4, 5, 4, 7 **c)** 1   **2. a)** 1 **b)** e.g., $5^0 = 1$ **3. a)** 3, 4, 3, 2 **b)** $a^{-1} = \frac{1}{a}$ **4. a)** 1 **b)** 0.1 **c)** 0.01   **5. a)** $2^3, 2^2, 2^1, 2^0$ **b)** 4, 2, 1

Section 4.7
1. a) $\frac{1}{2^4}$ **b)** $\frac{1}{4^1}$ **c)** $\frac{1}{3^5}$ **d)** $\frac{1}{6^3}$ **e)** $\frac{1}{5^2}$ **f)** $\frac{1}{10^7}$ **2. a)** 3^{-3} **b)** 6^{-3} **c)** 4^{-2} **d)** 2^{-5} **e)** 10^{-4} **f)** 7^{-3} **3. a)** $\frac{1}{64}$ **b)** 126 **c)** $\frac{1}{3}$ **d)** $\frac{17}{16}$ **4. a)** $\frac{1}{9}$ **b)** 5 **c)** 244 **d)** 1   **5. c)** $\frac{1}{1000}, 10^{-3}$ **d)** $\frac{1}{10\,000}$, 0.0001, 10^{-4} **e)** $\frac{1}{100\,000}$, 0.000 01, 10^{-5} **f)** $\frac{1}{1\,000\,000}$, 0.000 001, 10^{-6} **6.** Answers will vary.   **7.** Answers will vary.

Section 4.8
1. a) 3^3 **b)** 2^8 **c)** 7^4 **d)** 3^7 **e)** 2^8 **f)** 3^0 **g)** 4^{-2} **h)** 2^1 **2. a)** $\frac{1}{125}$

b) 26 **c)** 90 **d)** 50 **e)** 10 **f)** 273 375 **g)** 24 **h)** 2893   **3.** dime; 2 000 000   **4.** Answers will vary; e.g., **a)** 4 cm **b)** 8 times

Section 4.10
1. a) 10 **b)** 100 **c)** 1000 **d)** 10 000 **e)** 100 000 **f)** 1 000 000 **g)** 0.1 **h)** 0.01 **i)** 0.001 **j)** 0.0001 **k)** 0.000 01 **l)** 0.000 001   **2. a)** 370 000 **b)** 48 000 000 **c)** 68 000 000 000 **d)** 0.000 000 028 **e)** 0.000 007 7   **3. a)** 1.25×10^5 **b)** 8.23×10^8 **c)** 9.27×10^8 **d)** 7.3×10^{-5} **e)** 1.48×10^{-7} **f)** 3.0×10^{-7} **4. a)** 152 000 000 **b)** 147 000 000 **c)** 0.000 000 003   **5. a)** 8.4×10^6 **b)** 5.0×10^{-6} **c)** 8.18×10^9 **8. a)** 3.89×10^{15} **b)** 1.26×10^{-11} **9. b)** 1.512×10^6, 7.031×10^{-5}, 1.472×10^{27} **10. a)** $1.837\,41 \times 10^{18}$ kg **b)** 5.56×10^6 m   **11.** Answers will vary.

Section 4.12
1. a) 17 **b)** 4 **c)** 17 **d)** 3   **2. a)** 18 **b)** 115   **3. a)** $\frac{5}{2}$ **b)** $\frac{3}{2}$ **c)** 1 **d)** 1 **e)** 6 **f)** 5   **4. a)** 13.2 **b)** 10 **c)** 6.6 **d)** 1.3   **5. a)** 9 **b)** 27 **c)** 125 **d)** 8 **e)** 12 **f)** 18   **6. a)** 7.8 **b)** −23.4 **c)** 15.3   **7. a)** $0.34m$ **b)** $44.88   **8. a)** $1.25f + 1.40r$ **b)** $73.25   **9.** 37.5 km   **10. a)** $2.32s + 3.15b$ **b)** $53.21   **11. a)** dime 1 mm; penny 1.3 mm **b)** $1.3p + 1.0d$; 23 mm **c)** 118 mm **d)** Answers will vary.

Section 4.13
1. a) $t + 3$ **b)** $t - 3$ **c)** $\frac{1}{2}t$ **d)** $3t$ **2. a)** $3n + 5$ **b)** $5(n + 3)$ **c)** $\frac{1}{3}n + 2n$ **3. b)** 13, 0, 10, 14, 32   **4. a)** $7w + 19$ **b)** 411 m   **5. a)** $3.65 + 1.5m$ **b)** $26.15   **7. a)** length = $3w + 22$ **b)** 514 m   **8. a)** 5 kg, 8 kg

Section 4.14
1. a) 5 **b)** 6 **c)** 0 **d)** 5   **2. a)** 4 **b)** 9 **c)** 4   **3. a)** 4 **b)** 4 **c)** 9 **d)** 10   **4. a)** $2n = 20$; $n = 10$ **b)** $n - 7 = 17$; $n = 24$ **c)** $7n + 4 = 60$; $n = 8$ **5.** 50 years   **6. a)** 406 **b)** 712   **7. a)** 11 **b)** It would take 11 magazines to make $49.   **8. a)** 82 **b)** It would take 82 bars to make $37.50.   **9.** Answers will vary.

Section 4.15
1. a) 5 **b)** 20 **c)** 8 **d)** 27   **2. a)** $2x = 10$ **b)** 5   **3. a)** 2 **b)** 8 **c)** 2 **d)** 10   **4. a)** 3 **b)** 5 **c)** 30 **d)** 20   **5. a)** $\frac{52}{7}$ **b)** 9 **c)** 21   **6.** 23 years old   **7. b)** 5 square units

Section 4.16
1. b) 116   **2. a)** $0.14d$ **b)** $52.50   **3. a)** 1.157×10^7 **b)** 8.6×10^4 **4. a)** 2 mm **b)** 0.002 mm

Section 4.17
1. Unreasonable, Harley hasn't been born yet.   **2.** No time left; it will take 1 min. to get to top at this speed.   **3. a)** 285 **b)** 1, 4, 9, 16, 25, 36, 49, 64, 81 square units   **4.** Impossible, 3 students not accounted for.   **5.** 1 Quarter, 1 Dime, 2 Nickels, 5 Pennies   **6.** 182   **7.** Impossible, number of students is always an odd number.   **8.** 8, 24, 24, 8

Chapter Review
1. a) 39 **b)** 41 **c)** 706 **d)** 53 **e)** 226 **f)** 24   **2. a)** 16 807
b) 4096 **c)** $\frac{1}{9}$ **d)** 23 **e)** 5 **f)** 27   **3. a)** $B + 2$ **b)** $R/3$
c) $B + 7$ **4. a)** 6 **b)** 10 **c)** 4 **d)** 8 **e)** 0 **f)** -3 **5. a)** \$19.75
b) 13   **6. a)** $65 + (h - 10)10.25$ **b)** \$85.50, \$121.38
7. 3 cm

Self Evaluation
1. a) $3^2 = 9$ **b)** $(-2)^5 = -32$ **c)** -121 **2. a)** 49 **b)** 17 **c)** 0
d) 1024 **e)** 4 **f)** 3888   **3. a)** 1 600 000
b) 0.000 000 004   **4. a)** 7.3×10^3 **b)** 4.75×10^{-5}
5. a) 6 **b)** 6 **c)** 14   **6. a)** 71 **b)** 7 **c)** 3 **d)** 7 **e)** 2 **f)** 4
7. a) $300p$ **b)** \$3000, \$4500   **8.** \$7

CHAPTER 5
Section 5.1
1. Answers will vary.   **2. a)** and **b)** are reasonable.
5. a) distance around = $\sim 3.14 \times$ distance across
6. A: 7, 1, 16, 7; B: 6, 3, 18, 18; C: 3, 3, 12, 9; D: 4, 3, 14,
12; E: 5, 3, 16, 15; F: 3, 2, 10, 6; H: 10, 2, 24, 20; I: 9, 2,
22, 18   **7. a)** distance around = $2 \times$ (length + width)
b) number of squares = length $\times$ width
Section 5.2
1. a) 1.94 m **b)** 60.2 m **c)** 4.8 m   **3. a)** 7.2 m **b)** \$5.76
4. \$14.95   **5.** \$75.60   **6. a)** 24.4 m **b)** 54
7. \$19 396.00

Section 5.3
2. a) 7.9 m **b)** 188 cm **c)** 236 cm   **3. a)** 10.68 m
b) 151 m **c)** 58.75 m **d)** 44.6 m   **4.** 78.5 cm   **5.** 28.3 m
6. a) 154.6 m **b)** 64.7   **7.** 4   **8.** 19.2   **9.** 343.6 m
10. Answers will vary.

Section 5.4
1. Answers will vary.   **2.** Answers will vary.
3. a) chords   **4.** Answers will vary.   **5.** Answers will
vary.

Section 5.6
1. a) rectangle: 2.2 cm $\times$ 4.2 cm, all angles 90°;
   square: all sides 2.5 cm, all angles 90°;
   rhombus: all sides 2.3 cm, 72°, 108°;
   parallelogram: 2.0 cm $\times$ 3.5 cm, 62°, 118°;
   kite: 1.4 cm $\times$ 2.4 cm, 60°, 95°, 110°, 95°;
   trapezoid: 1.7 cm, 2.4 cm, 4.0 cm, 2.4 cm, 120°,
   60°;
   b) Rectangle: opposite sides are equal
   Square: all sides are equal
   Rhombus: all sides are equal
   Parallelogram: opposite sides are equal
   Kite: 2 pairs of equal adjacent sides
   Trapezoid: 1 pair of opposite sides have equal
   length, the other pair are unequal
   c) The sum of the interior angles is always 360°.
   Rectangle, Square: all interior angles are 90°
   Rhombus, Parallelogram: opposite angles are

equal, angles on the same side sum to 180°
   Kite: 1 pair of equal angles
   Trapezoid. The pair of angles on each of the
   2 unequal sides are equal, and the pair of angles
   on each of the equal sides sum to 180°.
2. a) parallelogram: opposite sides equal and parallel.
   rectangle: parallelogram with interior angles
   equal to 90°.
   square: parallelogram with interior angles equal
   to 90° and all sides equal.
   rhombus: parallelogram with all sides equal.
   kite: two pairs of adjacent sides equal.
   trapezoid: one pair of parallel sides.
4. b) 360° **d)** 360° **e)** All quadrilateral interior angles
sum to 360°.   **5. a)** 180° **b)** 180° **c)** 180° **d)** For a
quadrilateral drawn within a circle, opposite angles
sum to 180°.

Section 5.7
2. a) square, trapezoid, rectangle **b)** square, rhombus,
kite   **3. a)** 140° **b)** 144° **c)** 82°   **4. a)** 70°, 70°
b) $\angle I = 115°$, $\angle J = 70°$ **c)** $\angle R = 72°$, $\angle Q = 106°$
5. a) square, rectangle, parallelogram, rhombus
b) square, rhombus **c)** square, rhombus   **6. a)** square,
rectangle, parallelogram, rhombus **b)** square,
rhombus, kite   **7. a)** square, rectangle, parallelogram,
rhombus **b)** square, rectangle, parallelogram, rhombus
c) square, rectangle, parallelogram, rhombus
8. $\angle R = 106°$, $\angle S = 77°$ **9.** $\angle C = 124°$, $\angle D = 64°$

Section 5.10
2. a) 3.22 cm² **b)** 18.56 m²   **3. b)** 254.25 cm²
4. 9841.26 m²   **5.** 176   **6. a)** 32495 km²   **7.** 403
8. Answers will vary.

Section 5.11
1. b) rectangle   **2.** area = base $\times$ height
4. area = $\frac{1}{2}$ base $\times$ height   **5. b)** parallelogram
6. area = $\frac{1}{2}$ (base + top) $\times$ height   **7. b)** 31.4 cm
d) parallelogram **e)** length = 31.4 cm, height = 10 cm
f) 314 cm²   **8. a)** area = πr^2

Section 5.12
2. a) 173.25 cm² **b)** 173.25 cm²   **3. b)** 336 cm²
4. 39 375 m²   **5.** 95.648 cm²   **6.** 21.76 cm²
7. a) 15 375 m² **b)** \$1619.95   **8.** Answers will vary.

Section 5.13
2. a) 6.51 cm² **b)** 5.265 cm² **c)** 62.92 cm²   **3. b)** 20 cm²
4. b) 171.71 cm²   **5. b)** 0.15 cm²   **6.** 4.16 km²
7. 69 s   **8.** Answers will vary.

Section 5.14
2. a) 12.6 cm² **b)** 38.5 cm² **c)** 5.3 cm²   **3. a)** 380 cm²
b) 6.2 m²   **4. a)** 870.9 mm² **c)** CD = 113.1 cm²; 13
5. a) 65.0 m²   **6.** Answers will vary.   **7. a)** 314.2 cm²
b) 42   **8. a)** 12 **b)** Answers will vary.

Section 5.15
1. 2 cm **2.** 7.5 cm **3.** 5 mm **4. a)** 2 m **b)** 12
5. 23.9 **6. c)** 48

Section 5.16
1. 2, 3 **2. a)** Answers will vary **3. a)** 1×16, 2×8, 4×4 **b)** 1 cm $\times$ 16 cm **4. b)** The width (or length) is always 1 for the greatest perimeter. **5.** Answers will vary.

Section 5.17
1. b) 2700 m^2 **2.** park: 5690.8 m^2; farm: 27 361.62 m^2; track: 34099.7 m^2

Technology Insight
1. 25.11 cm^2; 76.14 m^2 **2.** Change the 6 in line 40 to an 8; 61.92 cm^2; 339.36 m^2

Chapter Review
1. a) 11.6 cm, 6.51 cm^2 **b)** 16.7 m, 22.1 m^2
2. 26 848 m^2 **3.** 759 cm^2 **4. a)** 57.6 m **b)** 192
5. a) 254 m^2 **b)** 4.7 m **6.** 157.1 cm

Self Evaluation
1. a) 18.24 m^2 **b)** 8.58 m^2 **2. a)** 2.5 m, 0.5 m^2
b) 26.1 m, 54.1 m^2 **3.** 1 017 500 m^2 or 1.02 km^2
4. a) 216 m **b)** 216 **5.** 63.2 m, 48 m^2 **6.** rhombus

Mathematics in Castles
1. a) 27 cm $\times$ 27 cm **b)** 18.8 cm **c)** 24 cm
d) 7 cm along **2. a)** 18.8 cm $\times$ 10 cm **3. a)** 192 cm^2, 192 cm^2, 120 cm^2, 168 cm^2 **4. a)** 7 cm $\times$ 8 cm
b) 56 cm^2

CHAPTER 6
Section 6.2
1. a) A: 16 cm^2; B: 28 cm^2, 49 cm^2 **b)** A: 96 cm^2;
B: 161 cm^2 **c)** A: square prism; B: square pyramid
2. a) A: 120 cm^2, 96 cm^2, 80 cm^2; B: 25 cm^2, 47.5 cm^2
b) A: 592 cm^2; B: 215 cm^2 **3.** 1054 cm^2 **4.** 83.0 cm^2
5. 284.6 cm^2 **6. a)** 82 cm^2 **b)** 14.8¢ **7.** 12.1¢ **8. a)** 6
9. Answers will vary.

Section 6.3
1. a) 78.5 cm^2 **b)** 238.8 cm^2 **c)** 395.8 cm^2
2. a) 55.4 cm^2 **b)** 158.3 cm^2 **c)** 269.1 cm^2 **3. a)** 14.8 cm^2 **b)** 9.4 cm^2 **c)** 1.7 cm^2 **4.** Answers will vary.
5. a) 434.1 cm^2 **b)** 34.7¢ **6. a)** 9.7 m^2 **b)** 2 cans
7. a) most: rectangular prism, least: triangular prism
9. 540 cm^2

Section 6.4
1. a) 398 cm^2 **c)** 190 cm^2 **2. a)** 275 **b)** 6.2 m^2 **3.** 3
4. 8 **5. b)** 134.6 cm^2 **6.** cube **7.** Answers will vary.
8. a) 0, 1, 8, 27, 64

Section 6.5
1. a) 37 **b)** 22 **c)** 33 **d)** 31 **e)** 33

Section 6.6
1. a) 21 **b)** 18 **c)** 137 **2.** 83, 71; amoeba **3. a)** Quebec, P.E.I. **b)** Answers will vary.

Section 6.9
1. a) 3 cm, 3 cm, 8 cm **b)** 72 cm^3 **c)** $72 = 3 \times 3 \times 8$
2. a) $V = l \times w \times h$ **3. a)** 16 cm^3 **b)** 24 cm^3; Answers will vary, e.g., length is 4 cm, width is 5 cm, and height is 2 cm. **4.** Answers will vary. **5. b)** 3 times
6. b) 3 times

Section 6.10
1. a) 128 cm^3 **b)** 43.0 cm^3 **c)** 366.8 cm^3
2. a) 110.25 cm^3 **b)** 2375 cm^3 **3.** 38 255.3 cm^3
4. 2.6 m^3 **5.** 8.8 cm^3 **6. a)** 477.5 m^3 **b)** $48.94
7. 32 cm^3 **8. a)** It is a cube; $2 \times 2 \times 2$

Section 6.11
1. a) 312 cm^3 **b)** 114.2 cm^3 **c)** 65.8 m^3 **2. b)** A: 628 cm^3;
B: 2010 cm^3; C: 2290 cm^3 **3. b)** 1.4 m^3 **4.** Answers will vary. **5.** 679.6 cm^3 **6.** 30.1 m^3 **7.** 1570.8 cm^3
8. 994.0 cm^3 **9. b)** 515.8 cm^3 **c)** Answers will vary.
10. 21

Section 6.12
1. a) 0.64 m^2, 0.64 m^2 **b)** 2.4 m^3, 0.8 m^3
2. a) 37.0 cm^3 **b)** 29.4 m^3 **c)** 0.311 m^3
3. 980 907 m^3 **4.** pyramid **5.** 41.4 cm^3
6. 94.9 cm^3 **7.** 911.2 cm^3 **8.** no **9.** Answers will vary.

Section 6.13
1. 3190.7 cm^3 **2. a)** 7952.2 cm^3 **b)** the large intestine **3.** Answers will vary. **4.** about 1.0 kg
5. a) 195.2 m^2 **b)** 195 m^2 **6. a)** 30 m^3 **b)** 30 m^3

Section 6.14
1. a) e.g. 500 m $\times$ 250 m **b)** e.g. 300 m $\times$ 450 m
2. a) e.g. 3, 6 **b)** e.g. -9, -2 **3. a)** e.g. 50 m $\times$ 50 m
b) e.g. 25 m $\times$ 100 m **5. a)** e.g. $123 \times 012 = 1476$
b) e.g. $003 \times 979 = 2937$ **6. a)** e.g. $2 \times 2 \times 2 \times 2 = 16$, $2^2 \times 2^2 = 16$ **b)** e.g. $99 + 9 \div 9 = 100$, $99 \div 0.99 = 100$

Technology Insight
1. b) 1500 cm^3 **2. b)** 1500 cm^3 **3.** It will triple.
5. b) 12 560 cm^3 **6. b)** 25 120 cm^3 **7.** It will triple.

Chapter Review
1. b) 100.2 cm^2, 59.0 cm^3; 167.6 cm^2, 79.8 cm^3
2. b) 78.1¢ **3.** 5.5 m^3 **4.** 502.7 cm^2
5. a) 373 613.5 m^3 **6.** e.g. 60 cm $\times$ 60 cm $\times$ 20 cm

Self Evaluation
1. a) 11.4 cm^3; 37.6 cm^2; 2904 cm^3; 1298 cm^2
2. 128 m^3 **3.** 679.6 mL **4.** 110.8 m^3 **5. a)** 14.5¢
b) The box has only one flap on top and bottom.
6. 8612.9 m^3 **7.** 372.0 cm^2 **8.** Answers will vary, e.g. a 6 $\times$ 6 $\times$ 6 cube.

Practice: Cumulative Review

1. a) 5 **b)** 256 **c)** 42.875 **d)** 12 **e)** 4.74 **2.a)** 1, 3, 5, 15, 25, 75 **b)** 1, 3, 9, 27, 81 **c)** 1, 2, 3, 4, 5, 6, 8, 10, 12, 15, 20, 24, 30, 40, 60, 120 **d)** 1, 3, 7, 9, 21, 49, 63, 147, 441 **e)** 1, 2, 131, 262 **4. a)** 123, 567, 861, 61 500, 69 741 **b)** 76, 3114, 6330 **5. a)** -8 **b)** -60 **c)** 9 **d)** -3 **e)** 34 **f)** 14 **g)** 6 **h)** 9 **i)** 8 **6.** 5.3 **7.** \$1296.92

Problem Solving: Cumulative Review

1. a) D **2. a)** 11 **3.** \$3.65

Calculation Sense

1. a) 1331 **b)** 2530 **c)** 4642 **d)** 3454 **e)** 2233 **f)** 1551
2. a) 2123 **b)** 8965 **c)** 6655 **d)** 3344 **e)** 1738 **f)** 2970

CHAPTER 7

Section 7.1

1. b) half; half **c)** $\frac{1}{2}$ **2. b)** 4 **c)** $\frac{1}{4}$ **3. b)** 8 **c)** $\frac{1}{8}$ **4. c)** $\frac{1}{2} = \frac{2}{4}$
5. c) $\frac{2}{4} = \frac{4}{8}$ **d)** $\frac{1}{2} = \frac{4}{8}$ **6. c)** Yes **d)** $\frac{1}{2}$ **8. c)** 3 **d)** $\frac{1}{3}$

Section 7.2

1. a) $\frac{7}{3}$ **b)** $1\frac{3}{4}$ **2. a)** proper **b)** improper **c)** mixed number **d)** proper **e)** mixed number **3. b)** $\frac{5}{4}$ **4. a)** $1\frac{2}{3}$ **b)** $4\frac{1}{2}$ **c)** $2\frac{1}{5}$ **5. a)** $\frac{11}{4}$ **b)** $\frac{21}{5}$ **c)** $\frac{27}{8}$ **6. a)** $\frac{1}{2}$ **b)** $\frac{1}{4}$ **c)** $\frac{1}{6}$ **7.** $\frac{27}{52}$
8. $\frac{14}{22}$ or $\frac{7}{11}$ **9.** $\frac{7}{10}$ **10.** $2\frac{9}{12}$ or $2\frac{3}{4}$ **11.** Answers will vary.

Section 7.3

2. a) 6 **b)** 9 **c)** 1 **3. a)** 2, 2 **b)** 4, 4 **4.** Answers may vary, e.g., **a)** $\frac{6}{9}, \frac{4}{6}$ **b)** $\frac{8}{10}, \frac{12}{15}$ **c)** $\frac{4}{18}, \frac{8}{36}$ **5. a)** $\frac{3}{8}$ **b)** $\frac{1}{3}$ **c)** $\frac{5}{3}$
6. a) $\frac{2}{5}$ **b)** $\frac{1}{2}$ **c)** $\frac{1}{3}$ **7.** human **8.** Birchmount **9.** John
10. Answers will vary.

Section 7.4

1. a) $\frac{2}{5}$ **b)** $\frac{3}{5}$ **2.** $\frac{1}{6}$ **3.** $\frac{\pi}{4}$ or about $\frac{4}{5}$ **4.** $\frac{2}{3}$ **5.** Colin

Section 7.5

1. a) 0.5 **b)** 0.07 **c)** 0.257 **d)** 0.036 **e)** 1.26 **2. a)** 0.6 **b)** 0.875 **c)** 0.5 **d)** 0.6 **e)** 0.7 **3. a)** $\frac{3}{10}$ **b)** $\frac{3}{4}$ **c)** $\frac{11}{25}$ **d)** $\frac{41}{100}$ **e)** $\frac{3}{1000}$ **4.** 0.5 **5.** $\frac{1}{10}$ **6. a)** 183 000 000 **b)** $\frac{53}{183}$ **c)** 0.290 **7.** 0.2 **8.** Answers will vary. **9.** Answers will vary.

Section 7.6

1. b) 2 **d)** $\frac{3}{4}, \frac{3}{4}$ **e)** $\frac{3}{4}$ **2. b)** 6 **d)** $\frac{7}{8}, \frac{7}{8}$ **e)** $\frac{7}{8}$ **3. b)** 3 **d)** $\frac{5}{6}, \frac{5}{6}$ **e)** $\frac{5}{6}$ **4. b)** 2 **c)** $\frac{1}{4}$ **d)** $\frac{1}{4}, \frac{1}{4}$ **e)** $\frac{1}{4}$ **5. b)** 4 **c)** $\frac{1}{8}$ **d)** $\frac{3}{8}, \frac{3}{8}$ **e)** $\frac{3}{8}$
6. b) 3 **c)** $\frac{1}{6}$ **d)** $\frac{2}{6}$ or $\frac{1}{3}, \frac{2}{6}$ or $\frac{1}{3}$ **e)** $\frac{2}{6}$ or $\frac{1}{3}$

Section 7.7

1. a) $\frac{1}{2} + \frac{1}{4} = \frac{3}{4}$ **b)** $\frac{1}{2} + \frac{1}{8} = \frac{5}{8}$ **2. a)** $\frac{1}{5}$ **b)** 1 **c)** $\frac{4}{5}$ **d)** $1\frac{1}{2}$
3. b) $\frac{7}{12}$ **4. a)** $\frac{3}{4}$ **b)** $\frac{1}{2}$ **c)** $1\frac{1}{8}$ **d)** $\frac{13}{20}$ **5. a)** $1\frac{1}{4}$ **b)** $1\frac{1}{6}$ **c)** $\frac{1}{2}$ **d)** $\frac{23}{30}$ **e)** $\frac{19}{20}$ **f)** $1\frac{3}{8}$ **6. a)** $5\frac{4}{5}$ **b)** $4\frac{3}{4}$ **c)** $5\frac{1}{8}$ **d)** $13\frac{9}{10}$ **7.** $\frac{5}{8}$
8. $\frac{3}{4}$ **9.** $4\frac{3}{40}$ **10.** $3\frac{7}{8}$ **11.** $\frac{1}{8}$

Section 7.8

1. a) $\frac{1}{2} - \frac{1}{4} = \frac{1}{4}$ **b)** $\frac{2}{3} - \frac{1}{3} = \frac{1}{3}$ **2. a)** $\frac{1}{3}$ **b)** $\frac{1}{2}$ **c)** $\frac{2}{5}$ **d)** $\frac{2}{7}$
3. $\frac{1}{12}$ **4. a)** $\frac{1}{8}$ **b)** $\frac{1}{2}$ **c)** $\frac{1}{4}$ **d)** $\frac{13}{30}$ **5. a)** $\frac{3}{8}$ **b)** $\frac{1}{6}$ **c)** $\frac{1}{2}$ **d)** $\frac{2}{15}$ **e)** $\frac{3}{8}$ **f)** $\frac{5}{24}$ **6. a)** $1\frac{2}{5}$ **b)** $1\frac{1}{4}$ **c)** $1\frac{1}{4}$ **d)** $1\frac{7}{20}$ **7.** $\frac{3}{8}$ **8.** $\frac{4}{21}$ t
9. Saturday, $2\frac{3}{4}$ h **10.** $6\frac{3}{4}$ min **11. b)** 1

Section 7.9

1. a) $\frac{1}{2} \times \frac{1}{2} = \frac{1}{4}$ **b)** $\frac{1}{3} \times \frac{1}{2} = \frac{1}{6}$ **c)** $\frac{1}{2} \times \frac{1}{2} = \frac{1}{4}$ **2. b)** $\frac{1}{12}$
3. a) $\frac{1}{10}$ **b)** $\frac{1}{9}$ **c)** $\frac{8}{21}$ **d)** $\frac{1}{6}$ **4. a)** $\frac{6}{25}$ **b)** $\frac{12}{35}$ **c)** $\frac{15}{28}$ **d)** $\frac{15}{32}$ **e)** $\frac{5}{16}$ **f)** $\frac{21}{40}$ **5. a)** $\frac{1}{6}$ **b)** $\frac{6}{35}$ **c)** $\frac{3}{20}$ **d)** $\frac{40}{153}$ **e)** $\frac{21}{80}$ **f)** $\frac{13}{56}$ **6. a)** $\frac{3}{40}$ **b)** $\frac{25}{72}$ **c)** $\frac{7}{240}$ **d)** $\frac{3}{50}$ **7.** $\frac{3}{5}$ **8.** $\frac{1}{10}$ **9. a)** 27 **b)** $\frac{5}{27}$

Section 7.10

1. a) $\frac{1}{5}$ **b)** $\frac{1}{10}$ **c)** $\frac{1}{4}$ **d)** $\frac{2}{5}$ **e)** $\frac{2}{5}$ **f)** $\frac{3}{10}$ **2. a)** $\frac{1}{3}$ **b)** $\frac{2}{5}$ **c)** $\frac{1}{4}$ **d)** $\frac{3}{10}$ **e)** $\frac{1}{6}$ **f)** $\frac{2}{7}$ **3. a)** $4\frac{1}{6}$ **b)** $4\frac{11}{20}$ **c)** $4\frac{1}{8}$ **d)** $7\frac{7}{12}$ **4. a)** $19\frac{1}{8}$ **b)** $1\frac{11}{40}$ **c)** 7 **d)** $21\frac{7}{40}$ **e)** $33\frac{3}{4}$ **f)** $21\frac{41}{48}$ **5.** 3 h
6. 8 lengths

Section 7.11

1. a) 1, is **b)** $\frac{7}{64}$, is not **c)** 1, is **d)** 1, is **e)** $\frac{24}{25}$, is not **f)** 1, is **2. a)** 1 **b)** 1 **c)** 1 **d)** $\frac{2}{5}$ **e)** 3 **f)** 1 **3. a)** $1\frac{1}{2}$ **b)** $3\frac{1}{2}$ **c)** $2\frac{1}{3}$ **d)** $1\frac{3}{4}$ **e)** 3 **f)** $2\frac{1}{2}$ **4. a)** $2\frac{1}{2}$ **b)** $1\frac{9}{16}$ **c)** $2\frac{2}{7}$ **d)** $\frac{4}{9}$ **e)** 1 **f)** $\frac{5}{6}$

Section 7.12

1. a) $\frac{1}{2} \div 2 = \frac{1}{4}$ **b)** $\frac{1}{3} \div 2 = \frac{1}{6}$ **c)** $\frac{1}{2} \div 4 = \frac{1}{8}$ **2. a)** $\frac{1}{2}$ **b)** $1\frac{1}{2}$ **c)** $\frac{5}{6}$ **d)** 4 **3.** $\frac{1}{12}$ **4. a)** 4 **b)** 14 **c)** 21 **d)** $\frac{1}{3}$ **e)** $\frac{2}{7}$ **f)** $\frac{3}{25}$
5. a) 2 **b)** $\frac{5}{6}$ **c)** $\frac{11}{24}$ **d)** $\frac{8}{9}$ **e)** $\frac{4}{15}$ **f)** $\frac{9}{10}$ **6.** $\frac{1}{6}$ **7.** 15 **8.** 5

Section 7.13

1. a) $2\frac{2}{9}$ **b)** $5\frac{5}{6}$ **c)** $3\frac{3}{20}$ **d)** $2\frac{2}{5}$ **e)** $3\frac{3}{5}$ **f)** $2\frac{2}{5}$ **g)** $2\frac{22}{25}$ **h)** 14
2. a) $2\frac{1}{2}$ **b)** 8 **c)** 14 **d)** $\frac{4}{5}$ **e)** $1\frac{2}{5}$ **f)** $2\frac{10}{27}$ **g)** $3\frac{3}{5}$ **h)** $3\frac{13}{25}$ **i)** $2\frac{1}{2}$

j) $2\frac{8}{35}$ **3.** 12 pages/30 min **4.** $3\frac{8}{9}$ min/lap **5.** 30

6. a) $\frac{1}{2}$ **b)** $\frac{2}{3}$ **c)** $\frac{3}{4}$ **d)** $\frac{4}{5}$; Answers will vary,

e.g., $2\frac{1}{2} \times \frac{1}{3} = \frac{5}{6}$; $1\frac{3}{7} \div 1\frac{2}{3} = \frac{6}{7}$

Section 7.14

1. a) $\frac{1}{2}$, $\frac{23}{40}$ **b)** $1\frac{2}{3}$, $-\frac{1}{3}$ **c)** $\frac{11}{20}$, $\frac{3}{4}$ **2. a)** $\frac{3}{4}$ **b)** 1 **c)** $\frac{5}{6}$ **d)** $\frac{3}{4}$

e) $1\frac{3}{10}$ **f)** $\frac{2}{5}$ **3. a)** < **b)** > **c)** > **d)** < **4. a)** 31 ways.

Section 7.15

1. 219 150 hours **2.** 21 **3. a)** Tracy **b)** $\frac{1}{20}$

c) Tracy: 20 min, Jack: 15 min **4.** 17.5 min **5.** 36 L

6. $3\frac{1}{2}$ h

Chapter Review

1. a) $\frac{1}{2}$ **b)** $\frac{1}{3}$ **2. a)** $\frac{2}{5}$ **b)** $\frac{1}{12}$ **c)** $\frac{7}{20}$ **d)** $1\frac{8}{15}$ **3. a)** $1\frac{2}{15}$

b) $10\frac{5}{24}$ **c)** $3\frac{5}{12}$ **d)** $9\frac{31}{56}$ **4. a)** $1\frac{13}{15}$ **b)** $2\frac{2}{3}$ **c)** $5\frac{5}{21}$ **d)** $1\frac{7}{8}$

5. a) $\frac{3}{4}$ **b)** 1 **c)** $1\frac{3}{10}$ **d)** $\frac{2}{5}$ **6.** $\frac{1}{6}$ **7. a)** 9 **b)** 1

Self Evaluation

1. a) $\frac{3}{4}$ **b)** $\frac{7}{10}$ **c)** $\frac{5}{9}$ **d)** $\frac{1}{3}$ **2. a)** $\frac{1}{14}$, $\frac{2}{7}$, $\frac{5}{14}$, $\frac{4}{7}$ **b)** $\frac{2}{10}$, $\frac{3}{5}$, $\frac{2}{3}$, $\frac{4}{5}$, $1\frac{1}{2}$,

$2\frac{1}{2}$ **3. b)** 0.8 **c)** 0.625 **d)** 3.5 **4. a)** $\frac{7}{10}$ **b)** $\frac{1}{6}$ **c)** $\frac{3}{10}$ **d)** $1\frac{5}{6}$

e) $\frac{3}{7}$ **f)** $1\frac{2}{5}$ **g)** 2 **h)** $\frac{3}{10}$ **i)** $\frac{5}{12}$ **5. a)** $2\frac{8}{15}$ **b)** $\frac{5}{8}$ **c)** $2\frac{5}{12}$ **d)** $2\frac{11}{12}$

e) $6\frac{4}{15}$ **f)** $\frac{7}{9}$ **6. a)** 1 **b)** 1 **c)** 1 **d)** 1 **e)** 1 **f)** 1 **7.** $10\frac{1}{2}$

CHAPTER 8

Section 8.1

1. a) $3\frac{1}{2}$ **b)** $-3\frac{1}{2}$ **c)** $-1\frac{1}{2}$ **3.** Answers will vary.

4. 1 km **5. a)** A: 1, B: -2, C: 1, D: $\frac{1}{2}$

6. Answers will vary.

Section 8.2

1. a) $-\frac{5}{8}$ **b)** $\frac{3}{4}$ **c)** $-\frac{7}{3}$ **d)** $\frac{1}{10}$ **e)** $-\frac{4}{7}$ **2. a)** $-\frac{3}{2}$ **b)** $-\frac{7}{2}$ **c)** $\frac{7}{3}$ **d)** $\frac{9}{4}$

e) $\frac{5}{1}$ **3. a)** $-\frac{3}{4}$ **b)** $-\frac{1}{2}$ **c)** $\frac{2}{3}$ **d)** $-\frac{1}{3}$ **e)** $\frac{3}{4}$ **4. a)** $-\frac{1}{2}$ **b)** $-\frac{2}{3}$

c) $\frac{5}{3}$ **5. a)** -2 **b)** 2 **c)** 2 **d)** -5 **e)** 4 **f)** 5 **6.** Answers will

vary: e.g., **a)** $-\frac{8}{10}$, $-\frac{16}{20}$ **b)** $-\frac{4}{6}$, $-\frac{8}{12}$ **c)** $-\frac{2}{4}$, $-\frac{8}{16}$ **d)** $-\frac{26}{10}$,

$-\frac{260}{100}$ **e)** $\frac{2}{6}$, $\frac{3}{9}$ **f)** $\frac{14}{8}$, $\frac{-28}{-16}$ **7. a)** $-\frac{7}{5}$ **b)** $-\frac{1}{5}$ **c)** $-\frac{2}{3}$ **d)** $\frac{3}{10}$ **e)** $\frac{7}{2}$

f) $-\frac{6}{5}$ **8.** $\frac{1}{12}$, $-\frac{1}{2}$, $-\frac{1}{12}$, $-\frac{1}{8}$, $-\frac{1}{3}$, 0, $-\frac{1}{4}$, $\frac{1}{6}$, $-\frac{5}{12}$ **9. a)** 36

b) Answers will vary.

Section 8.3

1. a) 0.375 **b)** 0.4 **c)** 0.75 **d)** 0.125 **e)** 0.625 **f)** 0.5 **g)** 0.6

h) 0.875 **i)** $0.\dot{8}$ **j)** 0.75 **2. a)** $3.\dot{3}$ **b)** $3.\dot{7}$ **c)** $35.\dot{2}\dot{5}$

d) $21.\overline{312}$ **3. a)** 0.375 **b)** $-0.\dot{1}\dot{8}$ **c)** -0.875 **d)** $-0.\dot{6}\dot{3}$

e) $0.\dot{4}$ **f)** -0.429 **g)** $0.\dot{3}$ **h)** $0.41\dot{6}$ **i)** $-0.0\dot{6}$ **4. a)** 0.522,

0.483; $\frac{12}{23}$ **b)** -0.176, -0.192; $-\frac{3}{17}$ **c)** 0.071, 0.118; $\frac{2}{17}$

d) -0.16, -0.15; $-\frac{3}{20}$ **5.** Solution B **6.** Alain's

7. a) 0.5, 0.05, 0.005 **b)** 0.0005 **8. a)** $-0.\dot{16}$, $-0.0\dot{16}$,

$-0.00\dot{16}$ **b)** $-0.000\,016$, $-0.000\,0016$

Section 8.4

1. a) -26°C **b)** -37°C **c)** -40°C **2. a)** 2.5°C **b)** -2.5°C

c) -20°C **3. a)** -32°C **b)** 24 km/h **c)** -40°C

d) -42°C **4. a)** -33°C **b)** 16°C **5.** -59°C **6.** -30°C

7. b) -23°C **8.** -69°C **b)** No **9. a)** -77°C

b) Answers will vary.

Section 8.5

1. a) $6\frac{1}{4}$, $6\frac{1}{8}$ **b)** $20\frac{3}{8}$, $19\frac{7}{8}$ **c)** $16\frac{7}{8}$, $16\frac{7}{8}$ **d)** $8\frac{1}{4}$, $7\frac{1}{2}$

2. a) $-2\frac{1}{4}$ **b)** $-\frac{1}{2}$ **c)** $-\frac{1}{8}$ **d)** $+\frac{7}{8}$ **3. a)** Noranda Inc

b) Intl Cablecstng **4. a)** Taseko Mines **b)** Noranda Inc

5. a) Clearly Canadian, Cominco, MacMillan BF,

Noranda **b)** A & A Foods, Cam Net Comm, Intl

Cablecstng, Taseko Mines **6. a)** A & A Foods, Cam

Net Comm, Intl Cablecstng, Taseko Mines **b)** Cominco,

MacMillan bf, Noranda Inc **7. a)** A & A Foods

b) Clearly Canadian **8. a)** A & A Foods, Cam Net

Comm, Intl Cablecstng, Taseko Mines, Noranda

Inc, MacMillan bf, Cominco, Clearly Cdn. **b)** A & A

Foods, Cam Net Comm., Intl Cablecstng, Taseko

Mines, Noranda Inc., MacMillan bf, Cominco, Clearly

Cdn. **c)** Taseko Mines, Intl Cablecstng, MacMillan bf,

Cominco, Clearly Cdn, Cam Net Comm, A & A Foods,

Noranda Inc **9.** Noranda, Intl Cablecstng

Section 8.6

1. a) 5 **b)** 1 **c)** 6 **d)** Answers will vary. **2. a)** -6 **b)** -6

c) Answers will vary. **3. a)** 1 **b)** 0 **c)** 1 **d)** Answers will

vary. **4. a)** -1 **b)** -1 **c)** Answers will vary. **5. a)** 0

b) 0 **6. b)** 4 **c)** Answers will vary.

Section 8.7

1. a) 1 **b)** $-\frac{1}{2}$ **c)** $-\frac{1}{2}$ **d)** $-\frac{1}{3}$ **2. a)** 6 **b)** $1\frac{1}{2}$ **c)** -4

3. a) $-\frac{11}{8}$ **b)** $-\frac{3}{5}$ **c)** $-\frac{7}{10}$ **d)** $\frac{1}{4}$ **4. a)** $-\frac{4}{15}$ **b)** $-\frac{1}{6}$ **c)** $-\frac{27}{20}$

d) $\frac{23}{20}$ **e)** $-\frac{5}{6}$ **f)** $-2\frac{3}{10}$ **5. a)** 9.7 **b)** 1.1 **c)** -1.2 **d)** -5.3

e) Answers will vary. **6. a)** 9.6 **e)** 3.6 **g)** 0.3 **7.** 38.5°C

8. a) $\$7\frac{1}{4}$ **b)** Answers will vary. **9. a)** -5.5, -4.4,

-3.3, -2.2, -1.1, 0, 1.1, 2.2, 3.3, 4.4, 5.5 **b)** 0

Section 8.8

1. a) $\frac{1}{2}$ **b)** $-\frac{1}{3}$ **c)** $-\frac{1}{5}$ **d)** $-\frac{4}{5}$ **2. a)** $-\frac{3}{4}$ **b)** 1 **c)** $3\frac{3}{4}$ **3. a)** $\frac{1}{3}$
b) $\frac{1}{4}$ **c)** $1\frac{1}{6}$ **d)** $\frac{5}{8}$ **4. a)** 2.9 **b)** 8.3 **c)** -9.6 **d)** -18.3;
b is the greatest **5. a)** 0.4 **d)** 12.7 **6. a)** $-\frac{1}{2}$ **b)** $1\frac{1}{6}$ **c)** $\frac{11}{56}$
d) $\frac{3}{2}$ **e)** $-\frac{43}{35}$ **f)** $\frac{17}{12}$; d is the greatest **7. a)** $5\frac{1}{4}-3\frac{2}{4}$ **b)** $1\frac{3}{4}$
8. Answers will vary. **9.** 15.5°C **10.** 1.3, 0.3, 3.3, $-4.7, -2.7$

Section 8.9

1. a) $-\frac{1}{8}$ **b)** $-\frac{1}{4}$ **c)** $\frac{1}{8}$ **d)** $-\frac{1}{10}$ **e)** $\frac{2}{15}$ **f)** 1 **2. a)** 19.25
b) -16.25 **c)** -15.75 **d)** 8.4 **e)** -9.46 **f)** -16.92
3. a) $-\frac{1}{5}$ **b)** $\frac{2}{9}$ **c)** $-\frac{12}{35}$ **d)** $-\frac{1}{2}$ **4. a)** $-\frac{16}{25}$ **b)** $\frac{1}{2}$ **c)** 0 **d)** $-\frac{1}{4}$
5. a) $12\frac{3}{16}$ **b)** $-\frac{15}{32}$ **c)** $-1\frac{7}{10}$ **6. a)** $1\frac{2}{33}$ **b)** $19\frac{79}{84}$ **c)** $-7\frac{157}{182}$
d) $88\frac{1}{5}$ **7. a)** Answers will vary. **b)** Answers will vary.
8. $90.00 **9.** 19

Section 8.10

1. a) 2 **b)** -3 **c)** -3 **d)** -5 **e)** 3 **f)** 1 **2. a)** -2 **b)** $-\frac{2}{3}$ **c)** 2
d) $\frac{3}{2}$ **e)** $-\frac{8}{5}$ **f)** $\frac{8}{5}$ **3. a)** $-4.\dot{6}$ **b)** 3 **c)** -3 **d)** -2 **e)** 0
f) -7 **4. a)** $1\frac{1}{2}$ **b)** $1\frac{1}{8}$ **c)** $-2\frac{2}{3}$ **d)** $\frac{9}{2}$ **e)** $\frac{10}{27}$ **f)** $\frac{16}{27}$; $-2\frac{2}{3}, \frac{10}{27}$,
$\frac{16}{27}, 1\frac{1}{8}, 1\frac{1}{2}, \frac{9}{2}$ **5. a)** 1 **b)** 1 **c)** 1 **6. a)** $-\frac{3}{26}$ **b)** $-\frac{163}{40}$
7. 120 min **8.** -6.3°C **9.** $0.8\dot{3}$ **10.** 21

Chapter Review

1. a) $-\frac{1}{2}$ **b)** $\frac{3}{4}$ **c)** $\frac{1}{2}$ **d)** $-\frac{2}{3}$ **2. a)** > **b)** < **c)** > **3. a)** 0.571
b) -0.68 **c)** -0.65 **d)** $-0.\dot{3}$ **4. a)** 1.25 **b)** -0.75
c) -0.75 **d)** 7.0 **e)** -0.75 **f)** -7.875 **g)** -2 **h)** -3
5. a) -1 **b)** $-\frac{3}{4}$ **c)** $-1\frac{5}{28}$ **d)** $\frac{2}{5}$ **e)** $-1\frac{5}{16}$ **f)** $1\frac{1}{5}$ **6.** 87.5
7. Vito by 5 **8. a)** $-0.143, -0.286, -0.429$ **b)** -0.572, -0.715

Self Evaluation

1. a) $-\frac{3}{7}$ **b)** $\frac{5}{9}$ **c)** $-\frac{5}{2}$ **d)** $\frac{2}{7}$ **2. a)** $-\frac{3}{4}$ **b)** $-\frac{1}{2}$ **c)** $\frac{2}{3}$ **d)** $-\frac{1}{5}$
3. a) $-\frac{3}{4}$; $-\frac{1}{2}; \frac{2}{3}$; $-\frac{1}{5}$ **b)** -0.75; -0.5; 0.6; -0.2
4. a) $-\frac{5}{8}$ **b)** $\frac{17}{19}$ **c)** $-\frac{5}{7}$ **5. a)** -0.25 **b)** -0.25 **c)** -1.25
d) -4.1 **e)** 10.35 **f)** $-1.58\dot{3}$ **6. a)** -1 **b)** $-1\frac{1}{4}$ **c)** $-4\frac{3}{10}$
d) $\frac{1}{10}$ **e)** $\frac{5}{28}$ **f)** $-3\frac{17}{20}$ **7. a)** $\frac{1}{6}$ **b)** $\frac{11}{12}$ **c)** $-1\frac{1}{2}$ **d)** $2\frac{4}{9}$ **e)** 5 **f)** $\frac{3}{20}$
8. -9°C

CHAPTER 9
Section 9.2

1. b) Rock, Jazz **c)** C: 209, R: 507, J: 89, B: 447, Cl: 298

2. a) C: 21, T: 21 **b)** 1250 CDs, 1250 Tapes **3. a)** B: 9, D: 9, S: 12, H: 10 **b)** Soup: 750, Sandwich: 900, Daily Special: 675, Burger: 675 **4.** Answers will vary. **5. a)** Grape: 178, Strawberry: 342, Marmalade: 267, Honey: 312, Peanut Butter: 401

Section 9.3

1. a) 20, 100 **b)** Detective **2. a)** 90, 30 **3. a)** The number of points earned by each team **b)** New Jersey **c)** Yes. Answers will vary. **4. a)** The number of people in the most heavily populated countries. **5.** Answers will vary.

Section 9.4

1. a) 133, 742, 368, 877 **b)** This week: there were more viewers altogether. **2. b)** This month. There were more viewers. **c)** Answers will vary. **3. b)** Answers will vary. **4.** Answers will vary.

Section 9.5

1. a) Height of the plant. Time elapsed; cm, days **b)** 2.5 cm **c)** 12 cm **2. b)** 490 mL **c)** 4.3 L **3. b) i)** 18 m **ii)** 13 m **4. b)** No **c)** No **5.** Answers will vary. **6.** Answers will vary.

Section 9.6

1. a) 25% **b)** 33.3% **c)** 12.5% **2.** Apple: 40%, peach: 10%, orange: 30% **3. a)** 13% **b)** Answers will vary: e.g. percentage of time spent watching news. **4. a)** fat, protein **b)** water: 117 g, protein: 111 g, fat: 272 g **5. a)** O: 43%, B: 10%, AB: 5%, A: 42% **b)** type O **6. a)** 32% **b)** Answers will vary. e.g., the percentage of people who prefer to listen to CJME.

Section 9.7

1. a) BC: 42%, NS: 31%, Nfld: 19%, NB: 8% **b)** Answers will vary. **2.** Sponsors: 16.1%, Registrations: 67.1%, Dances: 9.4%, Ticket Sales: 7.4% **4.** Answers will vary.

Section 9.8

2. a) 1 **3. c)** trapezoid: 3 units², hexagon: 4 units², rhombus: 2 units², parallelogram: 2 or 4 units² **4.** A: 1, B: $\frac{1}{2}$ C: 2, D: 1, E: $\frac{1}{5}$

Section 9.11

1. a) mean: 4.3 median: 3 mode: 3 **b)** Answers will vary. **2. a)** No **b)** No **3. a)** mean: 5.6, median: 5.5, mode: 5.4 **b)** Answers will vary. **4. a)** mean: 5.8, median: 5.8, mode: 5.8 **b)** Answers will vary. **5.** The mode. It tells which size is bought most often. **6.** 6 doctors. This ensures that there will be enough doctors on staff even in the worst case. **7.** Answers will vary.

Section 9.12

1. a) 15 197 100 **b)** 17.9% **2. a)** 23 602 200 **b)** 27.8% **3. a)** 65 373 000 **b)** 77% **4.** Answers will vary. **5.** Answers will vary.

Section 9.13

1. a) Yes. The sizes of the pictures are not relative to the numbers.   **2. a)** Yes. The relative sizes of the picture don't agree with the values they represent. **3. a)** Yes. The shadows are misleading.   **4. a)** Yes. The relative numbers of pictures disagree with the actual values they represent.

Chapter Review

1. a) mean: 16, median: 13, mode: 12 **b)** mean: 10.0, median: 11.05, mode: 13.2 **2. b)** mean: 162.5, median: 161.5, mode: 159 **3. c)** most popular: Levis, Least popular: Designer **4. a)** Yes. 23°C is the mode. **b)** mean: 26.4°, median: 27° **c)** Answers will vary.

Self Evaluation

1. Answers will vary. **2. b)** Muscle **3. a)** The official rounded the mean attendance to the nearest 1000. **b)** Answers will vary. **4. b)** 5−10 min **c)** 180° **d)** 90°

CHAPTER 10
Section 10.1

1. a) 2:3 **b)** 4:6 **c)** 6:9 **5. a)** 9:12 **b)** 3:4 **c)** 18:24 **d)** They have the same proportion. They have different numbers.

Section 10.2

1. a) i) 2:1 ii) 4:2 iii) 1:3 **b)** i) 4:2 ii) 8:4 iii) 2:6 **2. b)** e.g. 6:3, 2:1, 4:2 **3. a)** 5:20; 3:12 **b)** 10:12; 20:24 **c)** 14:8; 21:12 **d)** 2:4:6; 4:8:12 **e)** 10:4:14; 15:6:21 **4. a)** 1:5 **b)** 5:3 **c)** 2:1 **d)** 1:2:3 **e)** 6:3:1 **5. a)** 2 cellos to 3 violas **b)** 3 violas to 2 cellos **c)** 11 violins to 2 cellos **d)** 11 violins to 3 violas **e)** 11 violins to 3 violas to 2 cellos **f)** 3 violas to 2 cellos to 11 violins **6. a)** 533:192 **b)** 533:192:160 **7.** 4:1 **8.** Answers will vary. **9.** 16 cucumber, 40 tomato, 8 bean

Section 10.3

1. a) 7 **b)** 8 **c)** 5 **d)** 5   **2. a)** $\frac{2}{1} = \frac{?}{2}$; 4 **b)** $\frac{3}{?} = \frac{6}{4}$; 2   **3. a)** 6 **b)** 4 **c)** 9 **4. a)** 10 **b)** 15 **c)** 6 **d)** 1 **5.** 8 **6.** 15 **7.** 28 **8. a)** $\frac{1}{2}$ is shaded; $\frac{1}{4}$ is shaded **b)** shaded: not shaded = 1:2, 1:4 **c)** Answers will vary. **9. b)** 24

Section 10.4

1. b) 2:3 **c)** 12 **d)** 240 **2. a)** 8:5 **b)** 200 **3.** 20 000 **4.** 40 h **5.** 306 **6.** about 2300 **7.** 4 **8.** Alex: 12 female, 16 male, Me: 8 female, 20 male **9.** Answers will vary.

Section 10.5

1. a) 1:2 **b)** 3:4 **c)** 1:10 **d)** 5:4 **2. a)** 87 **b)** 200 **c)** 70 **d)** 75 **3.** 250 **4.** 1030 **5. a)** 7:6 **b)** Answers will vary. **6. a)** 1287 **7.** 2 **8. a)** 1:1 **b)** 3:1 **9.** 20 g **10.** Answers will vary.

Section 10.6

1. 144 **2.** $60 **3. a)** A: 1, 3, 6, 10, B: 1, 5, 11, 19 **b)** A: 55, B: 109 **c)** Answers will vary.

Section 10.7

1. a) A: 4.1 cm, 2.6 cm, 1.58; B: 6.5 cm, 4.2 cm, 1.55; C: 13.9 cm, 8.8 cm, 1.58 **b)** They are all approx. 1.6. **2. a)** divide the length by the width, and see if the ratio is 1.6:1 or 1:1.6; i) and ii) are golden rectangles.

Section 10.8

1. a) 12 km/hour **b)** $9.50/album **c)** $1.67/hour **d)** 30 m/s **2.** Answers will vary. **3. a)** 80 km/h **b)** $133/week **c)** 40¢/bottle **d)** 33¢/can **4. a)** $7.22 **b)** $288.75 **5.** 14 **6.** Dartmouth **7.** 0.13 km

Section 10.9

1. a) $8.46 **b)** $67.68 **2. a)** $5.24 **b)** $52.44 **c)** $15.73 **d)** $34.09 **3. a)** 120 km **b)** 1200 km **c)** 360 km **d)** 780 km **4. a)** 80 km/h **b)** 360 km **c)** 6 h **5.** Answers will vary. **6. a)** 300 mm **b)** 2.25 m **c)** 7.875 m **d)** The rain continues to fall at the same rate. **7.** Supermarket **8. a)** Bear: 13.8, Cheetah: 31.3, Elephant: 11.1, Lion: 25.0, Rabbit: 15.2, Squirrel: 5.5, Zebra: 3.9 **b)** Bear, Cheetah, Lion, Rabbit **10. a)** 521 kg **b)** Answers will vary.

Section 10.10

1. a) 1 cm on the drawing represents 150 m on the actual object **b)** 1 cm on the drawing represents 3 km on the actual object **2. a)** 1:200; 1 cm represents 2 m **b)** 1:175; 1 cm represents 1.75 m **3. a)** 205 m **b)** 451 m **c)** 133.25 m **4. a)** 1 cm **b)** 2.3 m **c)** 0.87 m **5.** 1:320 **6.** 85.5 m **7.** Yes **8. a)** 1 cm represents 5 m **b)** Answers will vary.

Section 10.11

1. a) 10 km **b)** 50 km **c)** 35 km **d)** 112 km **e)** 67.6 km **2. a)** 10 cm **b)** 100 cm **c)** 125 cm **d)** 24.7 cm **e)** 3.25 cm **3.** none are the same **4.** 640 m **5.** Answers will vary. **6.** Answers will vary. **7.** 2.25 cm **8.** Answers will vary.

Section 10.12

1. a) 0.25 cm **b)** 0.27 mm **c)** 0.1323 cm **d)** 0.875 mm **2. a)** 50:1 **b)** 20:1 **c)** 50:1 **d)** 50:1 **3. a)** 3 mm **b)** 5 mm **c)** 10.1 mm **d)** 4.474 mm **4. a)** 5:1 **b)** L = 1 cm, W = 1 cm **5.** 2.8 mm **6.** 0.25 mm **7. a)** 0.7 mm **b)** 2.7 mm **8. a)** **10.** 2.6 mm

Section 10.13

1. a) 17.5 km **b)** 3.2 km/h **2.** Answers will vary.

Chapter Review

1. a) 1:3 **b)** 3:1 **c)** 4:1 **d)** 2:1 **2. a)** 4:1 **b)** 4:1 **c)** 10:1 **3. a)** $16/stick **b)** 3.8 ¢/m **c)** $9.29/m **4. a)** 6 **b)** 9 **c)** 15 **5. a)** 48 **b)** 144 **c)** 600 **6.** 24 **7.** Answers will vary.: e.g. **a)** 5:1 **b)** 1:9 500 000

Self Evaluation

1. a) 2:3 **b)** 10:1 **2. a)** 1.4 cm **b)** 0.7 cm **c)** 106 cm **3. a)** 2.25 **b)** 21 **c)** 5 **4. a)** 120 **b)** 16 **c)** 10.7 **5. a)** W 34:75, M 58:69, S 9:10 **b)** W 75:34, M 69:58, S 10:9 **c)** 75:69:80 **d)** 17:29:36 **6.** 3.5 h

Practice Cumulative Review

1. a) $\frac{7}{40}$ **b)** $\frac{8}{125}$ **c)** $\frac{1}{55}$ **d)** $8\frac{4}{45}$ **e)** $1\frac{235}{333}$ **2. a)** $2\frac{1}{12}$ **b)** $\frac{1}{3}$ **c)** $3\frac{1}{5}$

d) $\frac{1}{3}$ **3. a)** -3 **b)** -66 **c)** -1 **d)** -9 **e)** -3 **f)** 6 **g)** 15

h) -3 **4. a)** 1.52×10^8 km **b)** 1.1×10^{-1} m **5.** 18
6. 6 **7.** 319 cm^2

Calculation Sense

a) 180 **b)** 280 **c)** 240 **d)** 2800 **e)** 3600 **f)** 300

Problem Solving: Cummulative Review

2. 0, since 2 and 5 are among the first 16 prime numbers **3. a)** 50, -30 **b)** 80 m **4.** 75 **5. a) i)** $\times$, $-$ **ii)** $-$, $\div$ **iii)** x, $\div$ **6.** 4 h 50 min **7. a)** 44 km, 182 km **b)** Answers will vary.

CHAPTER 11
Section 11.2

1. 27%, $\frac{27}{100}$, 0.27 **2. a)** $\frac{73}{100}$, 73% **b)** $\frac{17}{25}$, 68% **c)** $\frac{3}{100}$,

3% **d)** $\frac{27}{50}$, 54% **e)** $\frac{8}{25}$, 32% **f)** $\frac{49}{50}$, 98% **3. a)** 17%,

0.17 **b)** 23%, 0.23 **c)** 11%, 0.11 **5. a)** 20% **b)** 45%
6. 90% **7. a)** about 23%

Section 11.3

1. a) 0.625 **b)** 0.128 **c)** 0.194 **d)** 0.753 **e)** 0.889
2. a) 73% **b)** 48% **c)** 60% **d)** 80% **e)** 66.7% **3. a)** 0.085,
$\frac{17}{200}$ **b)** 0.0925, $\frac{37}{400}$ **c)** 0.751, $\frac{751}{1000}$ **d)** $0.876\,25$, $\frac{701}{800}$

e) $0.046\,67$, $\frac{4667}{100\,000}$ **4. a)** 50 **b)** 10 **c)** 5 **d)** 96 **5.** 80%
6. 96% **7.** $\frac{1}{5}$ **8.** 66.7%

Section 11.4

1. a) 12 g **b)** 25 m **c)** 300 bikes **d)** 75 g **2. a)** 9
b) 78 **c)** $\$4.25$ **3. a)** 110 **b)** 47.4 **4.** 51 **5.** 110.07 g
6. 1605 **7.** 278 **8.** about 1300 km **9. a)** about 10%

Calculation Sense

1. a) 19.2 **b)** 13.1 **c)** 75.3 **d)** 98.6 **2. a)** 964.0 **b)** 958.2
c) 1437.1 **d)** 3072.2

Section 11.5

1. a) 71.4% **b)** 23.3% **c)** 36.7% **d)** 51.7% **2.** 25%, 75%,
50% **3.** 33.6% **4.** 16% **5.** 66.7% **6.** 9.3%
7. 22.3% **8. a)** June 29.1%, July 29.5%, Aug. 21.0%
b) July **9. a)** 84.4%

Section 11.6

1. a) 1.3 **b)** 2.5 **c)** 3.75 **d)** 0.0065 **e)** 0.0053 **f)** 0.0055
2. a) 150% **b)** 260% **c)** 0.8% **d)** 0.7% **e)** 525%
f) 437.5% **3. a)** 300 cm **b)** 175 mg **c)** 55 kg
4. a) 3.75 kg **b)** $\$1802$ **c)** 48.4 km **6.** 717 **7.** 91

Section 11.7

1. a) 8 **b)** 28% **2.** 20.5% **3.** 12 pecan, 18 blueberry
4. a) pool: 42% **b)** sidewalk: 58% **6.** 7825

Section 11.8

Investigation 3 **1. a)** A: about 92 m, B: about 51 m
b) A **c)** near the centre

Section 11.9

2. Que $\$26.78$, Ont $\$97.00$, Man $\$3.50$, Sask $\$9.72$,
Alta $\$0.00$, BC $\$5.58$, NB $\$15.90$, NS $\$15.62$, PEI
$\$35.30$, Nfld $\$103.44$ **3.** $\$2.22$, $\$36.14$ **4.** $\$3.69$,
$\$39.54$ **5. b)** $\$8.91$ **6. b)** $\$46.54$ **7.** $\$179.83$
8. a) Que $\$467.62$, Ont $\$1394.43$, Man $\$56.94$,
Sask $\$125.28$, Alta $\$427.99$, BC $\$90.91$, NB $\$170.52$,
NS $\$167.56$, PEI $\$413.00$, Nfld $\$1025.78$ **b)** Answers
will vary. **9.** Man, Ont, BC, Alta, Que **10. a)** PEI
b) NB, Nfld, NS **11.** Alta

Section 11.10

1. a) 300 **b)** $\$500$ **c)** 1720 **2. a)** 800 **b)** 1560 **c)** 120
3. b) 10, 40 cm **c)** 40 cm **4. a)** 400 cm **b)** $\$500$ **c)** 200 L
d) 200 kg **5.** 600 **6.** 500 **7.** 160 **8.** 525 **9.** 25 g
10. $\$75\,000$ **11.** 25 **12.** 600 **13.** $\$50$ **14.** 103 cm
15. a) 240 km **b)** Answers will vary.

Section 11.11

1. a) 17.6% **b)** 30 **c)** 440 **d)** $\$74$ **2. a)** $\$251.25$ **b)** 22.2%
c) 357.1 g **d)** $\$243.75$ **3.** $\$375$ **4.** $44\,118$
5. 29.2% **6.** 5.1 m^3 **7.** 350 **8.** 37.5% **9.** 264
10. 128 **11.** Answers will vary: e.g., 0%; 1 quarter,
1 dime, 13 nickels

Section 11.12

1. a) $\$15$ **b)** $\$22.10$ **c)** $\$131.25$ **2. a)** $\$230.40$
b) $\$243.60$ **c)** $\$25.88$ **3. a)** $\$4.50$ **b)** $\$7.50$
4. $\$160.5$ **5.** $\$552.50$ **6.** Answers will vary.
7. $\$3463.54$ **8.** $\$3048.16$ **9.** 4, 5, 6, 2, 1, 7, 3, 8, 11

Section 11.13

1. a) 25% **b)** 75% **2.** 4900% **3.** 346%

Technology Insight

1. a) $\$360$ **b)** $\$18$ **2.** $\$17.96$, $\$0.81$

Chapter Review

1. a) $\frac{3}{10}$, 0.3 **b)** $\frac{3}{4}$, 0.75 **c)** $\frac{4}{5}$, 0.8 **d)** $\frac{9}{20}$, 0.45 **2. a)** 80%
b) 90% **c)** 475% **d)** 65% **3. a)** 70% **b)** 50% **4.** 90
5. Amanda **6. a)** $\$31.25$ **b)** $\$1031.25$ **7.** 3.125 h
8. 35.5%

Self Evaluation

1. a) 0.15, $\frac{3}{20}$ **b)** 0.35, $\frac{7}{20}$ **c)** 1.05, $1\frac{1}{20}$ **d)** 2.45, $2\frac{9}{20}$
2. a) 16% **b)** 10% **c)** 60% **d)** 37.5% **3.** 12.5%
4. a) 4.4 cm **b)** 16 L **5. a)** $\$33.33$ **b)** 0.5 L **c)** 25%
6. 28 **8.** $\$153\,000$ **9.** $\$963.30$

CHAPTER 12
Section 12.1

4. a) The angles are the same. **b)** The side lengths are
equal.

Section 12.2
1. a) It means finding the midpoint of a line segment. **d)** It means drawing a line through the midpoint of a line segment which is at an angle of 90° to the line segment. **2. a)** It means dividing an angle into two equal angles.

Section 12.3
5. a) 3, 5, 7   **6. a)** 4, 6, 8

Section 12.5
1. a) $\angle A = \angle C$, $\angle B = \angle D$ **b)** AD = BC, AB = DC
2. b) AE = CE, DE = BE   **3. b)** opposite sides and angles are equal; the diagonals bisect each other.
4. b) all sides are equal **c)** all are 90° **d)** all are equal

Section 12.6
1. a) 204 cm² **2.** 8   **3. a)** 62

Section 12.8
1. b) 1, 3, 5, 15, 16 **c)** They are the same. **d)** 4, 8, 9, 10, 12, 14; They are the same.   **2. a)** 2, 11, 13, 18 **b)** The angles are the same. **c)** 6, 7, 17, 19; The angles are the same.   **3. b)** They are the same. **c)** no   **4. c)** no
5. b) They are the same. **c)** no   **6. c)** no   **7. b)** They are the same. **c)** no   **8. c)** no

Section 12.9
1. A: 1, 3, 5, 15, 16; B: 4, 8, 9, 10, 12, 14   **2.** 3
3. $\triangle$ABC, $\triangle$MNO; $\triangle$DEF, $\triangle$PQR; $\triangle$XYZ, $\triangle$KML; $\triangle$UVW, $\triangle$STU   **4. c)** $\angle I = 100°$, HI = 3.6 cm, IJ = 2.9 cm **d)** It is between $\angle H$ and $\angle J$.
5. c) JL = 7.8 cm, $\angle J = 50°$, $\angle L = 40°$ **d)** It is between JK and KL.

Section 12.10
1. c) 3, 4, 5; 8, 15, 17; 5, 12, 13   **2. b)** The area of the longest side is equal to the sum of the areas of the other two sides.   **3. a)** AC: 144 units², CB: 25 units² **b)** BA: 169 units² **c)** 169 = 144 + 25   **4. a)** 5 cm, 10 cm, 6.7 cm, 4.4 cm, 7.4 cm **c)** The area of the square on the hypotenuse is equal to the sum of the areas of the squares on the other two sides.

Section 12.11
1. a) 5 **b)** 13 **c)** 17   **2. a)** 13 cm **b)** 14.3 cm **c)** 17 cm
3. a) 10 cm **b)** 35.4 cm   **4.** 20 km   **5.** 2.5 m   **6. a)** 39.6 m **b)** 31.3 m   **7. b)** It is a right triangle. **d)** Use the hypotenuse as a diameter.

Section 12.12
1. c) The ratios of corresponding sides are equal in similar triangles.

Section 12.13
1. a) 4.5 m **b)** 24 m   **2.** 20 m   **3.** 4 m   **4.** 50 m

Section 12.14
4. Answers may vary, e.g. 13, 1, 6, 7, 12; 12, 9, 5, 2, 11; 11, 3, 4, 8, 13; 10, 14, 15

Chapter Review
2. a) Yes; two pairs of angles and their contained sides are equal. **b)** Yes; two pairs of sides and their contained angles are equal.   **3.** 86.6 m   **4. a)** 1, 3, 7:102°; 2, 6, 8:78° **b)** $\angle B$, $\angle C = 135°$ **5. a)** 67.6 m

Self Evaluation
1. a) 13 cm **b)** 3.7 cm **c)** 3.9 cm   **2.** 51.5 cm
3. a) $\angle B = 115°$, $\angle C = 115°$ **b)** 1 = 55° 2 = 55°
4. a) 100 m **b)** 141.4 m   **5.** none

Practice: Cumulative Review
1. c) Square, parallelogram   **2. a)** 60% **b)** 138% **c)** 62% **d)** 12.5% **e)** 5% **f)** 0.1%   **3. a)** $\angle P = 84°$, $\angle Q = 48°$ **b)** $\angle Z = 60°$ **c)** $\angle N = 75°$, $\angle P = 120°$ **4. a)** 0, 4 **b)** 2, 2 **c)** 4, 4   **5. a)** The centre is the intersection of the perpendicular bisectors of two chords of the circle **6. a)** 2 h 24 min **b)** The elephant can run for 2 h 24 min at 40 km/h **c)** No.

Problem Solving: Cumulative Review
1. a) 5, 2, 3; 3, 6, 1; 1, 4, 5 and 6, 1, 4; 4, 5, 2; 2, 3, 6
2. $100, $50, $20, $10, $10, $5   **3.** Square

Calculation Sense
1. a) 1225 **b)** 5625 **c)** 7225   **2. a)** 13 225 **b)** 70 225 **c)** 164 025

CHAPTER 13
Section 13.1
1. a) A: 10, B: -5, C: -5 **3. a)** A: 1, B: -2 **4. a)** $3x$, $-2x$

Section 13.2
1. a) $x + 2$ **b)** $-2x - 5$ **c)** $3x$ **2. a)** 7 **b)** -15 **c)** 15
3. a) $2x + y$ **b)** $2p + 3q$ **c)** $5n$ **d)** $-2a + 2b$ **4. a)** 32 **b)** 16 **c)** 24 **d)** 8   **5. a)** $25p$ **b)** $800   **6. a)** $4x + 2y$ **b)** 156 m   **7.** $3p - 3x$ **8.** circle: 4, triangle: 6, square: 2

Section 13.3
1. a) $2(x + 1)$ **b)** $3(x - 2)$ **2. a)** $2x + 8$ **b)** $3x + 6$ **c)** $5x + 20$ **d)** $2x + 12$ **e)** $4x - 8$ **f)** $3x - 15$ **g)** $2x - 6$ **h)** $6x - 18$ **3. a)** $4y + 4$ **b)** $3x - 12$ **c)** $5a + 30$ **d)** $7m - 56$ **e)** $3k - 6$ **f)** $4z - 20$ **4. a)** $3x + 15$; 39 **b)** $5x - 10$; 30 **c)** $4x - 24$; 8 **d)** $3x + 3$; 27 **e)** $5x + 15$; 55 **f)** $7x - 21$; 35   **5. a)** 9 **b)** -20 **c)** -32 **d)** -3 **e)** -6 **f)** 12
6. a) $(10x + 16)\dfrac{25}{x}$ **b)** $330   **7. a)** 15 **b)** -2 **c)** 28 **d)** 0 **e)** 2 **f)** -12 **8. a)** -15 **b)** -4 **c)** -5 **d)** -54 **e)** 8 **f)** -20 **9. b)** $-3x - 9$ **c)** i) $-4x + 8$ ii) $-2x - 10$
10. a) 5 **b)** The two from the middle that form a 90° angle.

Section 13.4

1. a) $2x + 6$, $3x - 9$ **b)** $2(x + 3)$, $3(x - 3)$
2. a) $5(x + 3)$ **b)** $3(x + 3)$ **c)** $4(x + 1)$ **d)** $2(x + 3)$
e) $3(x + 2)$ **f)** $2(x + 6)$ **3. a)** $2(x - 1)$ **b)** $3(x - 1)$
c) $2(x - 2)$ **d)** $5(x - 2)$ **4. a)** $2(x - 3) = -10$
b) $3(x + 5) = 9$ **c)** $5(x - 5) = -35$ **d)** $4(x - 2) = -16$
e) $7(x + 3) = 7$ **f)** $6(x + 4) = 12$ **5.** $2(x + 6)$

Section 13.5

1. a) 50, 7, 3, 53, 4, 6 **2. a)** Answers may vary, e.g.,
$849 + 753 = 1602$ **3.** 3 **4.** Answers will vary.

Section 13.7

1. a) A: $x + 3 = 4$, B: $x - 3 = 2$, C: $x + 4 = -3$,
D: $x - 4 = -8$ **2. b) i)** -2 **ii)** 7 **iii)** 9 **iv)** 14

Section 13.8

1. a) $x + 2 = 5$, $x = 3$ **b)** $x - 2 = 1$, $x = 3$ **2. a)** 2 **b)** 6
c) 9 **d)** 3 **3. a)** 6 **b)** 8 **c)** 8 **d)** 9 **4. b)** -3 **c) i)** -7 **ii)** -5
iii) -1 **iv)** 8

Section 13.9

1. a) $2x + 6 = 2$, $x = -2$ **b)** $3x + 3 = -3$, $x = -2$
2. a) $y = 9$ **b)** $k = 31$ **3. a)** 8 **b)** 12 **c)** 21 **d)** 8 **4. a)** 10
b) -4 **c)** -2 **d)** 8 **e)** 1 **f)** -2 **5. a)** -1 **b)** 21 **c)** 4
d) -4 **6. a)** 6 **b)** -1 **c)** 3 **d)** 0 **e)** 3 **f)** 7 **7. a)** 1 **b)** -3
c) -6 **d)** 2 **e)** -4 **f)** -4 **8. a)** isolate the x term **b)** 10
9. a) 24 **b)** 4 **c)** 6 **d)** -8

Section 13.10

1. a) add 2.3 to both sides **b)** 6.9 **2. a)** multiply
both sides by 2 **b)** 50 **3. a)** 15.9 **4. a)** 7.75 **b)** 0.63
c) 16.3 **d)** 1.38 **5. a)** 80 **b)** 7.5 **c)** 6.0 **d)** 22.5 **6. a)** 68
b) 40 **c)** 0.714 **d)** 4.81 **7. a)** 121 **b)** 36.4 **c)** 1.53 **d)** 38.5
8. a) 36 **b)** 48 **c)** 6.5 **d)** 952.8 **e)** -8.75

Section 13.11

1. a) $6n = 48$, 8 **b)** $2n = 72$, 36 **c)** $n + 8 = 108$, 100
d) $\frac{1}{2}n - 6 = 3$, 18 **e)** $7n + 4 = 60$, 8 **2.** 11, 12, 13
3. Pierre: 275, Rita: 350 **4.** \$35.50 **5.** Matthew: 18,
Alan: 36 **6.** Louise: 13, Victoria: 27 **7.** Nina: \$30,
Fatima: \$10 **8.** Angela, by 8

Section 13.12

1. a) -7 **b)** -7 **2. b)** -5 **3. a)** $C = 13\,500 \times \pi$
b) 42 412 km **4. a)** $s = 7 \times 42\,412$ km/s **b)** $1.1 \times$
10^9 km, 2.6×10^{10} km, 9.4×10^{12} km **c)** 9.4×10^{12} km
5. 30 **6. a)** 364 **b)** 364 **7.** Answers will vary.

Section 13.13

1. a) $4w = 16$ **b)** 4 m **2.** $6w + 2$, length: 24.4 cm,
width: 11.7 cm **3.** 13 cm $\times$ 27 cm **4. a)** $3l = 102$
b) 34 m **5. a)** $24^2 + 7^2 = 25^2$ **b)** Answers will vary.

Chapter Review

1. $3x + 3 = -2$, $-\frac{5}{3}$ **2. a)** 12 **b)** 4 **c)** 12 **3. a)** 3
b) $\frac{5}{2}$ or 2.5 **c)** 2 **4. a)** $9n + 6 = 60$; 6 **b)** $5n - 7 = 43$; 10
5. a) $R = \frac{1}{3}F$ **b)** 16 years old **6.** 21.3 cm, 50.7 cm
7. b) $4l - 2 = 102$ **c)** 26, 25 cm

Self Evaluation

1. $2x = -4$, -2 **2. a)** 36 **b)** 10 **c)** -12 **d)** -5
3. a) $n + 5 = 23$; 18 **b)** $4n + 6 = 18$; 3 **4. a)** 41 **b)** 7
c) 7 **5. a)** $2S + 10 = 24$ **b)** \$7 **6. a)** $2d + 5 = 75$
b) \$35 **7.** 18 cm, 20 cm

Mathematics in SkyDome

1. 28 **2.** Answers will vary. **3.** 2 **4.** 48 360 **5. a)** 2
b) 1 **6.** Answers will vary. **7.** about 13 400 m^2

CHAPTER 14

Section 14.3

Activity 1. a) 5 kg **b)** 1.5 weeks **Activity 2. a)** 10 kg at
5 weeks; 13 kg at 6.5 weeks **b)** 6 weeks **1. a)** 28 m
b) 84 m **c)** 4 s **d)** 11 s **2. a)** 4 **b)** $7\frac{1}{5}$ pages **c)** 187.5 min
d) 20 h **3. a)** 20 L **b)** 55 min **c)** Answers will vary.

Section 14.4

1. a) 2.4 cm **b)** 35 pennies **7. b)** 7.5 m **c)** 20 s

Section 14.5

1. 0.08 mm **2.** Answers will vary. **3. a)** Measure one
brick and calculate the number of bricks needed to
make up 73 m of height **b)** Answers will vary. **c)** By
measuring the height of one brick and counting the
layers of bricks, you could calculate the height of a
building. **4. a)** About 1.5 mm **b)** Answers will
vary. **5. a)** 12 cm^2 **b)** Answers will vary.

Section 14.7

5. b) 11

Section 14.8

1. a) $\frac{1}{2}$ **b)** $\frac{1}{2}$ **2. a)** $\frac{2}{5}$ **b)** $\frac{3}{5}$ **c)** They sum to 1 **3.** $\frac{1}{6}$ **4.** $\frac{3}{5}$
5. a) penny, dime, nickel **b)** $\frac{1}{4}$, $\frac{1}{4}$ **c)** Answers will vary.
6. a) $\frac{2}{5}$ **b)** $\frac{16}{75}$ **c)** $\frac{3}{25}$ **d)** $\frac{4}{15}$ **7. a)** P:H, N:H; P:H, N:T; P:T,
N:T; P:T, N:H **b)** $\frac{1}{4}$ **8. a)** P:H, N:H, D:H; P:H, N:H, D:T;
P:H, N:T, D:H; P:H, N:T, D:T; P:T, N:H, D:H; P:T, N:H,
D:T; P:T, N:T, D:H; P:T, N:T, D:T **b)** $\frac{1}{8}$

Section 14.9

1. $\frac{11}{1000}$ **2.** $\frac{3}{100}$ **3.** $\frac{11}{250}$ **4.** $\frac{15}{26}$ **5. a)** N:H, D:H; N:H,
D:T; N:T, D:H; N:T, D:T **b)** $\frac{1}{4}$, $\frac{1}{2}$ **c)** Answers will vary.
6. a) Fork up spoon down; Fork up spoon up; fork
down spoon down; fork down spoon up. **b)** Answers
will vary. **c)** Answers will vary.

Section 14.10

1. 1:1 **2. a)** 5:6 **b)** 6:5 **3. a)** 1:11 **b)** 1:1 **4. a)** $\frac{5}{36}$
b) 5:31 **5. a)** 1:3, 1:12 **b)** 1:51 **6.** Answers will vary.
7. Answers will vary.

Chapter Review

1. a) 1.5 m **b)** 11m **3. a)** reflectional and rotational; 3, 5, 6, 8 **b)** equal for regular polygons **4. a)** $\frac{1}{4}$ **b)** $\frac{1}{4}$ **c)** $\frac{1}{2}$

5. 3 cm

Self Evaluation

2. a) 4 **b)** Answers will vary. **3. a)** $\frac{1}{2}$ **b)** $\frac{1}{2}$ **c)** 50, 50
4. a) 3:1 **b)** 1:1 **5. b)** 11.25 m, 26.25 m **c)** 26.7 s

Year End Review

1. 50.692 cm^3, 83.68 cm^2 **2. a)** 169 **b)** 29 min, 43 s
3. 19 600 words **4. a)** 15.36 **b)** 8.4 **e)** 13.45 **f)** 23.04
i) 10.28 **j)** 32.92 **5. a)** 18 **b)** 26.46 **6. a)** base, height
b) 1 cm^2 **7. a)** 52° **b)** rhombus **8.** $1676.25 **9. a)** 4
b) 5 **c)** 24 **d)** 20 **e)** 18 **f)** 3 **10. a)** 40% **b)** $\frac{2}{5}$ **c)** 40%

d) $\frac{9}{20}$ **11. a)** yes **12. a)** Answers will vary, e. g.,

6375. **b)** You assume you were packing the large box
in the most efficient way **13. a)** 5 cm **b)** 0.55 mm
14. a) 3 **b)** 2 **c)** 12 **d)** 20 **15. a)** 96˚ **b)** scalene
16. a) 4535.085 m^2 **b)** Answers will vary **17.** Marcia
18. Answers will vary.

Math Journal

1. 9.4% **2. b)** 119 cm^2 **3. a)** 4 **b)** 48 cm
4. Answers will vary depending on the year. **5. a)** 29
b) Answers will vary. **6. a)** 24 **b)** Answers will vary.

ANSWERS FOR EXTENDING SKILLS & STRATEGIES

CHAPTER 1 page 450

Section 1.2 **1. (a)** 167 **(b)** 1896 **(c)** 30 883 **2. (a)** 6 ×
1000 + 6 × 100 + 9 × 10; 6 × 1000 + 2 × 100 + 8 × 10
(b) 1 × 100 000 + 8 × 10 000 + 5 × 100 + 2 × 10 + 1 × 1;
6 × 10 000 + 9 × 1000 + 3 × 100 + 7 × 10 + 4 × 1
(c) 5 × 10 000 + 5 × 100 + 8 × 10 **3.** For example, 1000
and 1 × 10^3

Section 1.3 **1.** 4.499, 40.499, 44.99, 449.9, 4499
2. Answers may vary. **3.** An indefinitely large
number. **4.** Rashid **5.** Answers will vary.

Section 1.4 **1. (a)** 3.79 **(b)** 78 000 **(c)** 11 **2. (a)** 34 g
(b) 44 cm **3. a)** 1 km **(b)** 5 L **4.** 109 m **5.** To the
nearest tenth 6.49 rounds to 6.5; but to the nearest
whole number 6.49 rounds to 6.

Section 1.7 **1. (a)** 12.7 **(b)** 5.0 **(c)** 43.0 **2. (a)** Yes
(b) $1.00 **3. (a)** You always get the number you
started with. **(b)** In effect you are multiplying and
dividing by the same amount (24). **4.** 4.7 h

Section 1.10 **1. (a)** ×,– **(b)** ÷,÷ **2. (a)** 9 × (6 – 4) = 18
(b) (12 + 3) ÷ 3 = 5 **3.** Answers will vary.

---

4. 3998 mL

CHAPTER 2 page 451

Section 2.2 **1. (a)** > **(b)** < **(c)** < **2. (a)** –10 859
(b) +4278 **(c)** –4188 **3.** Answers may vary. **4.** +4m,
–4 m

Section 2.4 **1. (a)** +8 **(b)** –3 **(c)** –11 **(d)** +10; –11,
–3, +8, +10 **2. (a)** +3 **(b)** –1 **3. (a)** (–5) + (–3)
(b) –8°C **4. (a)** +1 **(b)** –6 **(c)** 0

Section 2.5 **1. (a)** –10 **(b)** +19 **(c)** –18 **(d)** –1; –18, –10,
–1, +19 **2. (a)** +5 **(b)** –9 **(c)** +16 **(d)** –9 **(e)** +19 **(f)** –3
3. (–21) – (–11) = –10 The temperature fell 10°C.
4. (a) +4 **(b)** –6 **(c)** +3

Section 2.8 **1.** H **2. (a)** Answers may vary.
(c) rectangle **3. (a)** 4th **(b)** (+4, –4) **(c)** (0, +1)

Section 2.15 **1. (a)** +16 **(b)** +18 **(c)** +16 **(d)** –12 **(e)** +16
(f) –20; (a), (c), (e) **2. (a)** +12 **(b)** +16 **(c)** –20 **(d)** –21;
–21, –20, +12, +16 **3.** –10°C **4.** –450 m

Section 2.16 **1. (a)** –7 **(b)** +3 **(c)** –6 **(d)** 0 **(e)** –6 **(f)** –8;
(c), (e) **2. (a)** –7 **(b)** +7 **(c)** +5 **(d)** –5; –7, –5, +5, +7
3. The average is –5. **4.** –7¢/day

Section 2.17 **1. (a)** +30 **(b)** –25 **2. (a)** –9 **(b)** +3
3. –6°C/h **4.** –1

CHAPTER 3 page 452

Section 3.2 **1. (a)** 1, 2, 7, 14; 1, 19; 1, 41; 1, 3, 31, 93
(b) 19, 41 **2. (a)** 105 **(b)** 20 **(c)** 429 **3. (a)** 3, 3, 3, 5
(b) 2, 2, 2, 2, 7 **(c)** 3, 5, 5, 7 **(d)** 17, 17 **4. (a)** 1, 2, 4,
8, 16, 32, 64, 128 **(b)** 1, 2, 4, 71, 142, 284 **(c)** 1, 2, 3, 4,
5, 6, 10, 12, 15, 20, 25, 30, 50, 60, 75, 100, 150, 300
 (d) 1, 3, 5, 7, 15, 21, 25, 35, 75, 105, 175, 525 **5.** 210

Section 3.3 **1.** Every 12 min. **2.** 3 turns of smaller;
2 turns of larger **3.** 10 and 14 **4. (a)** 8 **(b)** 15 **(c)** 18
5. (a) 8 **(b)** 36 **(c)** 12

Section 3.4 **1. (a)** 2.3 **(b)** 7.5 **(c)** 4.7 **(d)** 8.4 **2. (a)** 7.48
(b) 8.43 **(c)** 14.97 **(d)** 22.36 **3.** The length is 480 m.
4. 4 units long **5.** 21 mm by 42 mm

Section 3.5 **1.** Multiples of 100 are always divisible
by 4. **2.** Multiples of 100 are always divisible by **5.**
3. 10 is the least common multiple of 2 and 5. **4.** 15
is the least common multiple of 3 and 5.

Section 3.9 **1. (a)** 53° **(b)** 67° **(c)** 9° **(d)** 49° **2. (a)** 53°
(b) 103° **(c)** 135° **(d)** 62° **3. (a)** 58° **(b)** 71° **(c)** 50°
4. $a = 20°$, $b = 160°$, $c = 20°$ **5.** 30° and 150°

Section 3.11 **1. (a)** isosceles **(b)** equilateral
(c) scalene **2. (b)** isosceles **(c)** 80° **3.** 18°, 54°, 108°

CHAPTER 4 page 453

Section 4.2 **1. (a)** $7^6 = 117649$ **(b)** $(–8)^4 = 4096$
2. (a) $(–2) × (–2) × (–2) × (–2) = 16$ **(b)** $9 × 9 × 9 = 729$

(c) $5 \times 5 \times 5 \times 5 = 625$ **(d)** $(-1) \times (-1) \times (-1) \times (-1) \times (-1) \times (-1) = -1$ **3.** 81 people **4.** 2^8 is greater

Section 4.3 **1. (a)** > **(b)** < **(c)** > **(d)** < **2. (a)** 18 **(b)** 14 **(c)** 898 **3. (a)** 30 **(b)** 2 **(c)** 1 **4.** 5 intervals

Section 4.4 **1. (a)** 7^3 **(b)** 4^{10} **(c)** 12^5 **(d)** 5^{11}
2. (a) $4^4 = 256$ **(b)** $9^2 = 81$ **(c)** $4^5 = 1024$ **(d)** $2^8 = 256$
3. $10^2 \times 10^3 = 10^5$; There are 100 000 pennies.
4. $10^3 \times 10^6 = 10^9$; There are 1 000 000 000 mg.
5. 55 **6.** $(4 + 2 + 2)^2 - 3^2 = 55$

Section 4.7 **1. (a)** $\frac{1}{7^2}$ **(b)** $\frac{1}{11^4}$ **(c)** $\frac{1}{5^2}$ **(d)** $\frac{1}{4^4}$
2. (a) $\frac{1}{27}$ **(b)** $\frac{1}{64}$ **(c)** $\frac{1}{16}$ **(d)** $\frac{1}{125}$ **3. (a)** 16 **(b)** $\frac{1}{9}$
(c) 1 **4. (a)** 8^{-2}, 4^{-3} or 2^{-6} **(b)** 5^{-3} **(c)** 3^{-3} **(d)** 6^{-3}
5. The digits are 2 and 3. $2^3 = 8$, $2^{-3} = \frac{1}{8}$, $3^2 = 9$,
$3^{-2} = \frac{1}{9}$

Section 4.10 **1. (a)** 3.74×10^6 **(b)** 2.1×10^{12} **(c)** 9.348×10^{15} **2. (a)** 3.4×10^{-6} **(b)** 1.04×10^{-3} **(c)** 4.6×10^{-10}
3. (a) 0.001 307 **(b)** 240 000 000 **(c)** 0.000 004 507
4. $1.68 \times 10^{-24} \times 2 \times 10^{21}$; The mass is 3.36×10^{-3} g
5. 4.56×10^2 s

Section 4.12 **1. (a)** 9 **(b)** 5 **(c)** 54 **(d)** 27 **2. (a)** 9.0 **b)** 3.25 **(c)** 60.25 **(d)** 25.75 **3. (a)** 4.9 m **(b)** 19.6 m **(c)** 44.1 m **(d)** 78.4 m **4. (a)** 37 **(b)** 41
5. (a) $T = \$4000 + \$1.30N$ **(b)** $5950

Section 4.13 **1. (a)** $\frac{1}{4}n$ **(b)** $\frac{1}{2}n + 3$ **(c)** $2n - 7$
(d) $6 - \frac{1}{4}n$ **2. (a)** $I = 15 + 0.000\ 15(T - 30)$
(b) 15.0015 cm **3. (a)** $h = 48 - 8b$ **(b)** 24 cm

Section 4.14 **1. (a)** $x = 6$ **(b)** $y = 6$ **(c)** $z = 13$
2. (a) $x = 3$ **(b)** $y = 18$ **(c)** $z = 9$ **3. (a)** 12 km **(b)** 25 km **(c)** 37 km

CHAPTER 5 page 455
Section 5.2 **1.** 8.2 m **2. (a)** 3.6 m **(b)** $2.16
3. 520 cm

Section 5.3 **1.** Using 3.14 for π **(a)** 44.0 cm **(b)** 62.8 m **(c)** 94.2 m **2. (a)** 18 840 cm or 188.40 m
(b) 530.8 times, rounded to nearest tenth
3. 31.4 cm **4.** 3.5 times

Section 5.7 **1. (a)** 120° **(b)** 130° **2. (a)** ∠A = 70°, ∠B = 95° **(b)** ∠E = 105°, ∠F = 75° **3.** Construct a square. **4.** Construct a rectangle.

Section 5.10 **1. (a)** 70.56 cm^2 **(b)** 47.25 m^2
2. 112.50 m^2 **3.** $984.38 **4. (a)** 254 cm^2 **(b)** 212 m^2

Section 5.12 **1. (a)** 6.72 m^2 **(b)** 66.30 cm^2
2. 96 cm^2 **3.** Answers will vary: one possibility is height 63 cm, base 160 cm, **4.** $2592 is the cost of seeding 21600 m^2.

Section 5.13 **1. (a)** 480 cm^2 **(b)** 3.69 m^2
(c) 107.5 mm^2 **2.** 56 cm^2 **3.** 576 cm^2 **4.** 100 cm^2

Section 5.14 **1.** Using π = 3.14 **(a)** 153.86 cm^2
(b) 452.16 mm^2 **(c)** 38.465 m^2 **2.** dime: 9 mm, 254 mm^2; nickel: 11 mm, 380 mm^2; quarter: 12 mm, 452 mm^2 **3.** Area of circle is about 127 cm^2; area of square is 100 cm^2. Circle has about 27 cm^2 greater area. **4.** The shaded area is 55.04 cm^2.

Section 5.17 **1. (a)** 136.92 cm^2 **(b)** 12.48 m^2
2. 641 cm^2

CHAPTER 6 page 458
Section 6.2 **1.** For rectangular prism **(a)** 96 cm^2 twice, 200 cm^2 twice, 300 cm^2 twice **(b)** 1192 cm^2 For triangular prism **(a)** 144 cm^2 for each triangle; 612 cm^2 for each of three sides **(b)** 2124 cm^2
3. triangular faces have 40 cm^2 each; rectangular sides 180 cm^2 each: total surface area 620 cm^2

Section 6.3 **1.** Using π = 3.14 **(a)** 50.24 cm^2
(b) 753.6 cm^2 **(c)** 854.08 cm^2 **2. (a)** 0.565 m^2 **(b)** 42¢ to nearest cent **3. (a)** 376 cm^2 **(b)** 640 cm^2
(c) 1004.8 cm^2; the cylinder has the greatest area

Section 6.10 **1. (a)** 24 m^3 **(b)** 0.006 m^3
2. (a) 27 000 mL **(b)** 27 L **3.** 12 500 kernels

Section 6.11 **1.** Using π = 3.14 **(a)** 301 cm^3
(b) 1570 cm^3 **2.** 2734.7 cm^3 to nearest tenth
3. 1123.7 mL **4.** 361.6 L

Section 6.12 **1. (a)** 0.56 m^3 **(b)** 9420 cm^3 **2.** 2.8 m^3
3. 2142.6 m^3 to the nearest tenth **4.** 25886 cm^3

CHAPTER 7 page 459
Section 7.2 **1. (a)** $6\frac{3}{4}$ **(b)** $3\frac{1}{6}$ **(c)** $2\frac{2}{5}$ **(d)** $3\frac{1}{7}$ **2. (a)** $\frac{13}{4}$
(b) $\frac{13}{3}$ **(c)** $\frac{26}{7}$ **(d)** $\frac{22}{9}$ **3. (a)** $\frac{5}{26}$ **(b)** $\frac{21}{26}$ **4. (a)** $\frac{15}{26}$
(b) $\frac{4}{26}$ **(c)** $\frac{7}{26}$

495

Section 7.3 **1.** Answers may vary. Some examples are **(a)** $\frac{6}{16}$ **(b)** $\frac{4}{10}$ **(c)** $\frac{10}{14}$ **(d)** $\frac{2}{12}$ **2. (a)** $\frac{3}{4}$ **(b)** $\frac{3}{4}$ **(c)** $\frac{1}{4}$ **(d)** $\frac{2}{3}$ **3.** Tuesday **4.** $\frac{2}{3}$ were present

Section 7.5 **1. (a)** 0.75 **(b)** 0.12 **(c)** 0.35 **(d)** 0.58 **2. (a)** $\frac{3}{5}$ **(b)** $\frac{1}{5}$ **(c)** $\frac{12}{25}$ **(d)** $\frac{19}{25}$ **3.** Jean had the better score. **4.** Carter's performance was better.

Section 7.7 **1. (a)** $\frac{3}{5}$ **(b)** $\frac{3}{7}$ **(c)** $\frac{3}{6}$ or $\frac{1}{2}$ **(d)** $\frac{5}{8}$ **2. (a)** $\frac{7}{12}$ **(b)** $\frac{5}{12}$ **(c)** $\frac{22}{15}$ or $1\frac{7}{15}$ **(d)** $\frac{21}{20}$ or $1\frac{1}{20}$ **3.** $\frac{33}{100}$ **4.** $\frac{7}{8}$

Section 7.8 **1. (a)** $\frac{2}{8}$ or $\frac{1}{4}$ **(b)** $\frac{6}{12}$ or $\frac{1}{2}$ **(c)** $\frac{5}{8}$ **(d)** $\frac{3}{6}$ or $\frac{1}{2}$ **2. (a)** $\frac{5}{12}$ **(b)** $\frac{4}{15}$ **(c)** $\frac{13}{24}$ **(d)** $\frac{7}{14}$ or $\frac{1}{2}$ **3.** $1\frac{11}{20}$ h **4.** $\frac{7}{24}$ d

Section 7.9 **1. (a)** $\frac{3}{20}$ **(b)** $\frac{4}{15}$ **(c)** $\frac{2}{12}$ or $\frac{1}{6}$ **(d)** $\frac{35}{48}$ **2. (a)** $\frac{3}{24}$ or $\frac{1}{8}$ **(b)** $\frac{18}{128}$ or $\frac{9}{64}$ **(c)** $\frac{6}{135}$ or $\frac{2}{45}$ **3.** $11\frac{2}{3}$ h **4.** $3\frac{1}{3}$ tanks of gasoline

Section 7.10 **1. (a)** 1 **(b)** $\frac{20}{9}$ or $2\frac{2}{9}$ **(c)** $\frac{10}{6}$ or $1\frac{2}{3}$ **(d)** $\frac{18}{20}$ or $\frac{9}{10}$ **2. (a)** 1 **(b)** 2 **(c)** $3\frac{8}{9}$ **(d)** $4\frac{2}{5}$ **3.** $13\frac{1}{2}$ h **4.** $16\frac{5}{8}$ cm

Section 7.12 **1. (a)** 3 **(b)** 4 **(c)** $3\frac{1}{8}$ **(d)** 4 **2. (a)** $2\frac{2}{5}$ **(b)** $1\frac{2}{3}$ **(c)** $\frac{8}{9}$ **(d)** $\frac{7}{8}$ **3.** 11 bowls **4.** 8 coats

Section 7.13 **1. (a)** 2 **(b)** 26 **(c)** 8 **(d)** $9\frac{3}{4}$ **2. (a)** $\frac{10}{13}$ **(b)** 2 **(c)** $2\frac{14}{25}$ **(d)** $\frac{33}{56}$ **3.** 5 lessons **4.** $4\frac{4}{11}$ times

Section 7.14 **1. (a)** $\frac{7}{12}$ **(b)** $2\frac{3}{4}$ **(c)** $\frac{1}{3}$ **2. (a)** $1\frac{13}{24}$ **(b)** $\frac{1}{15}$ **3. (a)** $1\frac{1}{3}$ **(b)** $3\frac{1}{3}$ **(c)** $11\frac{1}{9}$ **(d)** $2\frac{1}{9}$ **(e)** $2\frac{1}{9}$

CHAPTER 8 page 461

Section 8.2 **1. (a)** $-\frac{1}{3}$ **(b)** $\frac{4}{5}$ **(c)** $-\frac{7}{8}$ **(d)** $\frac{11}{12}$

2. Answers will vary. For example **(a)** $-\frac{8}{6}$ **(b)** $\frac{7}{3}$ **(c)** $-\frac{50}{24}$ **(d)** $-\frac{22}{6}$ **3. (a)** $-\frac{3}{4}$ **(b)** $\frac{2}{-3}$ **(c)** 4 **(d)** -2

4. (a) $-\frac{1}{5}$ **(b)** $\frac{2}{3}$ **(c)** $-\frac{2}{1}$ or -2 **(d)** $\frac{4}{3}$

Section 8.3 **1. a)** 0.25 **b)** -0.025 **c)** $-0.\overline{4}$ **d)** $0.58\overline{3}$

2. (a) $+\frac{6}{13}$ **b)** $-\frac{7}{11}$ **c)** $-\frac{3}{8}$ **d)** $+\frac{7}{24}$ **3.** Player A

4. $\frac{-24}{6}$, $\frac{-8}{3}$, $\frac{-7}{4}$, $\frac{6}{-8}$, $\frac{+4}{3}$, $\frac{+6}{3}$, $\frac{-25}{-5}$

Section 8.7 **1. a)** $+\frac{11}{15}$ **b)** $+\frac{3}{8}$ **c)** $-\frac{7}{9}$ **d)** $-\frac{7}{12}$

2. a) $+6.0$ **b)** -10.0 **c)** -0.3 **d)** $+2.5$ **3.** $\$+14\frac{5}{8}$ **4.** 5.2°C

Section 8.8 **1. a)** $-\frac{1}{8}$ **b)** $1\frac{3}{10}$ **c)** $-4\frac{1}{5}$ **d)** $3\frac{1}{12}$

2. a) $+3.3$ **b)** -2.0 **c)** -2.4 **d)** $+10.9$ **3.** 19 763 m

4. $-1\frac{1}{4}$

Section 8.9 **1. a)** $-\frac{3}{20}$ **b)** $\frac{3}{10}$ **c)** -6 **d)** $4\frac{8}{15}$

2. a) -7.98 **b)** 4.2 **c)** 10.2 **d)** -0.3 **3.** $\$+\frac{5}{8}$ **4. a)** $-\frac{3}{8}$

b) -1 **c)** $-3\frac{1}{4}$ **d)** $-\frac{1}{2}$

Section 8.10 **1. (a)** -4 **(b)** $+2$ **(c)** $-2\frac{1}{4}$ **2. (a)** -5.6

(b) -6.2 **(c)** -2.7 **3. (a)** -2 **(b)** $-4\frac{4}{15}$ **(c)** $+1\frac{7}{15}$

4. $-1\frac{3}{10}$°C/h **5.** -500 m/min

CHAPTER 9 page 463

Section 9.2 **1. (a)** frequency: perch 7; bass 4; catfish 8; sunfish 5; trout 2 **(b)** catfish **(c)** trout **2. (b)** 45 students **(c)** 3h - 3 students; 4h - 9 students; 1h - 1 student; 8h - 7 students **(d)** 9h - 3 students

Section 9.3 **1. (a)** rock; classical **(b)** 300 students **(c)** 1300 students **2. (a)** Wed. - 120 tapes; Fri. - 150 tapes; Sat. - 80 tapes **(b)** on Tues., Wed., and Fri. more than 85 tapes were sold; on Tues., Wed., Thurs., Fri., and Sat. more than 60 tapes were sold **(c)** 100 tapes **(d)** 150 tapes

Section 9.5 **1. (a)** March **(b)** September **(c)** July and August; January, May and October; February, April, and November **(d)** 34000 calculators **(e)** $882300 **3. (c)** 2 km - $4.75; 3 km - $6.75; 4 km - $8.75

Section 9.6 **1. (a)** To the nearest percent, Freezers - 17%, TVs - 13%, Refrigerators - 22%, VCRs - 19%, Washers and dryers - 24%, Others - 5% **(b)** Washers and dryers had the greatest sales. **3. (a)** protein 8.3%; water 36.1% **(b)** cost for water - 72¢; for fat - 6¢; for carbohydrates - $1.06

Section 9.7 **2. (a)** percents: U.S. - 31%, Cuba - 24%, Canada - 11%, Brazil - 7%, Mexico - 7%, Argentina - 5%, Columbia - 4%, Others - 11% **3. (a)** percents: Morocco - 27%, Tunisia - 23%, South Africa - 19%, Kenya - 11%, Mauritius - 6%, Senegal - 4%, Algeria - 4%, Others - 6%

Section 9.11 **1. (a)** Mean - 18, median - 16, mode - 15 **(b)** mean - 10, median - 9, mode - 8 **(c)** mean - 19, median - 21, mode - 22 **2.** The mean price is the average price, while the median price is the price at which half the homes sell for more and half for less. **3. (a)** mean - $2.87 **(b)** median - $2.85 **(c)** mode - $2.85 **(d)** Answers will vary.

CHAPTER 10 page 465
Section 10.2 **1. (a)** 5:2 **(b)** 4:5 **(c)** 5:1:3 **(d)** 2:4:3 **2.** Answers will vary. For example, **(a)** 6:8 and 9:12 **(b)** 14:10 and 21:15 **(c)** 22:18 and 33:27 **(d)** 8:10:14 and 12:15:21 **3. (a)** 2:3 **(b)** 3:1 **(c)** 4:3 **(d)** 1:2 **4.** 14:5:3 **5.** 42 pennies, 7 nickels, 21 dimes, 28 quarters

Section 10.3 **1. (a)** 8 **(b)** 5 **(c)** 5 **(d)** 56 **2. (a)** 2 **(b)** 4 **(c)** 6 **(d)** 21 **3.** $66.00 **4.** 1500 g or 1.5 kg **5.** 30 L of gasoline

Section 10.8 **1. (a)** 66 cars per hour **(b)** 60 pages per hour **(c)** $7.50/h **(d)** 95 newspapers per day **2.** 36 envelopes **3.** $6.25/h **4. (a)** 140 beats/min **(b)** The dog's heartbeat rate is 105 beats/min. The cat has the faster rate. **5.** About 22 s.

Section 10.10 **1. (a)** 1:1 000 000 **(b)** 1:50 000 **(c)** 1:25 000 **(d)** 1:15 **2. (a)** 4.5 km **(b)** 7.5 km **(c)** 11.25 km **(d)** 15.0 km **3.** 3000 km **4.** 20 cm **5.** 4 m tall

Section 10.11 **1.** 10 km **2. (a)** 33 km **(b)** 41 km **(c)** 39 km **(d)** 69 km **3.** 3.8 cm **4.** 192 km

Section 10.12 **1. (a)** 3 mm **(b)** 4 m **(c)** 6 mm **(d)** 2 mm **2. (a)** 50:1 **(b)** 6:1 **(c)** 20:1 **(d)** 100:1 **3.** 6 mm **4.** 16 m

CHAPTER 11 page 467
Section 11.2 **1.** Fractions: $\frac{83}{100}$, $\frac{41}{100}$, $\frac{27}{100}$, $\frac{33}{100}$ Decimals: 0.41, 0.2, 0.35, 0.33, 0.34 Percents: 83%, 20%, 35%, 27%, 34% **2. (a)** 0.403 **(b)** 40.3%

3. 33% **4.** $\frac{2}{9}$

Section 11.3 **1. (a)** 71% **(b)** 62.8% **(c)** 30% **(d)** 29.9%

2. (a) $\frac{75}{100}$ **(b)** $\frac{40}{100}$ **(c)** $\frac{15}{100}$ **(d)** $\frac{12}{100}$ **3.** 66 hits

4. 875 workers **5. (a)** $14\frac{1}{4}$ % **(b)** $86\frac{3}{4}$ % **(c)** $53\frac{2}{5}$ %
(d) $166\frac{3}{5}$ %

Section 11.4 **1. (a)** 91 **(b)** 131.4 **(c)** 88.5 **(d)** 27.16 **2.** 52 homes **3.** $519000 **4.** $676 per year for a total of $1352 over two years.

Section 11.6 **1.** Fractions: $1\frac{7}{20}$, $2\frac{7}{1000}$, $\frac{9}{1000}$, 3 Decimals: 1.35, 1.6, 2.15, 3 Percents: 160%, 200.7%, 215%, 0.9% **2.** 56 cars **3.** 658 cars **4. (a)** sales $262500, expenses $262497.60 **(b)** $2.40

Section 11.9 **1.** $0.10 **2. (a)** $2.45 **(b)** $3.85 **(c)** $41.30 **3.** 18.75 + (18.75 × 0.14) = 21.375 or $21.38 **4.** After rounding to the nearest cent, the overcharge was $0.08.

Section 11.10 **1.** 400 **2.** $165.00 **3.** 200 people **4. (a)** (iv), total cost is $245.70; **(b)** (ii), total cost is $18.08; **(c)** (i), total cost is $57.12; **(d)** (v), total cost is $99.45; **(e)** (iii), total cost is $126.50.

Section 11.12 **1. (a)** $78 **(b)** $1278 **2.** $927 **3. (a)** $1500 **(b)** $1605 **4.** Account A will earn $6.75 more **5. (a)** No **(b)** He will be short by $105.

CHAPTER 12 page 469
Section 12.4 **2. (b)** They intersect at one point. **3. (b)** They intersect at one point.

Section 12.9 **1. (a)** one **(b)** 26.4°, 36.3°, 117.3°; one **2. (b)** no, the lines won't intersect **3. (c)** No.

Section 12.11 **1. (a)** 16.1 cm **(b)** 9.8 m **2.** 175.7 m **3. (a)** 5.8 m **(b)** 8.5 m **4.** 5.2 m

Section 12.13 **1. (a)** DF = 2.7 m, EF = 3.3 m **(b)** LJ = 3.7 cm, LK = 7.9 cm **2.** 17.6 m **3.** 154 cm **4.** 100 m

CHAPTER 13 page 470
Section 13.2 **1. (a)** $3x + 7y$ **(b)** $7p - 11q$ **(c)** $-7x - y$ **2. (a)** $5e - 10f = 0$ **(b)** $-2e + 9f = 5$ **(c)** $-2e + 8 = 4$ **3. (a)** $P = 48 + 16n$ **(b)** $1456 **4.** AB = 16 cm, BC = 8 cm, CD = 20 cm, DE = 12 cm, EA = 28 cm

Section 13.3 **1. (a)** $2p + 4 = 10$ **(b)** $6p - 36 = -18$ **(c)** $3p - 9 = 0$ **(d)** $5p + 5 = 20$ **2. (a)** 2 **(b)** −18 **(c)** 0 **(d)** −36 **3. (a)** 14 **(b)** 15 **(c)** 28 **(d)** −32 **4. (a)** 48 **(b)** Expand each expression, add all like terms, substitute in values for x and y and evaluate.

Section 13.8 **1. (a)** $x = 10$ **(b)** $y = 17$ **(c)** $p = 7$ **(d)** $q = -3$ **2. (a)** $x = -6$ **(b)** $y = -2$ **(c)** $p = -8$ **(d)** $q = -5$ **3. (a)** $x = 9$ **(b)** $y = -11$ **(c)** $p = 7$ **(d)** $q = -3$ **4. (a)** $x = -4$ **(b)** $y = 2$ **(c)** $p = 6$ **(d)** $q = 6$

Section 13.9 **1. (a)** $k = 8$ **(b)** $m = -4$ **(c)** $n = 5$ **(d)** $p = 8$ **2. (a)** $x = 4$ **(b)** $y = 5$ **(c)** $p = -3$ **(d)** $w = -8$ **3. (a)** $x = 4$

(b) $y = 5$ (c) $w = 4$ (d) $p = 6$ **4.** (a) $x = 24$ (b) $y = 16$
(c) $c = 24$ (d) $d = 12$ **5.** (a) $S = B + 4L$ (b) $160

Section 13.10   **1.** (a) $x = 5$ (b) $y = 6.4$ (c) $q = -2.9$
(d) $p = 1.8$ **2.** (a) $x = 23.1$ (b) $y = 6$ (c) $c = -1.6$
(d) $x = -6.8$ **3.** (a) $f = -0.5$ (b) $q = 23$ (c) $h = 2.6$
(d) $k = -11.2$ **4.** (a) $x = 5.85$ (b) $p = 4.2$ (c) $p = -1.29$
(d) $d = -8.77$ **5.** (a) $E = 32 + 0.1(f - 400)$ (b) $54.50

Section 13.11   **1.** (a) $n - 4 = 11$, $n = 15$ (b) $2n + 6 = 16$,
$n = 5$ (c) $\frac{1}{3}n - 4 = 6$, $n = 30$ (d) $4n - 3 = -11$, $n = -2$

(e) $\frac{1}{2}n + 7.8 = 4.6$, $n = -6.4$ **2.** 21 and 23   **3.** 18, 20
and 22   **4.** 15 and 45 **5.** 25 and 50

CHAPTER 14 page 472
Section 14.2   **1.** (a) 4 (b) 2 (c) 5 (d) 8   **2.** There are an
infinite number of lines of symmetry for a circle.
3. (a) A, B, C, D, E, H, I, K, M, O, T, U, V, W, X, Y
(b) H(order 1), I(order 1), O(infinite), S(order 1),
X(order 3)   **4.** Examples, BED, BIKE, HIKE, etc.

Section 14.3   **1.** (a)

Time	4 h	10 h
Earnings	$28	$70

(c) Earnings for 0 h are $0; and earnings for 15 h are
$105. (d) 1h - $7, 3h - $21, 7h - $49, 12h - $84, 14h -
$98   **2.** (b) 5 min - 20 cm, 12 min - 48 cm, 15 min -
60 cm (c) 16.5 min

Section 14.4   **1.** (a)

x	2	5	8	10
$3x + 2$	8	17	26	32

2. (a)

Time (s)	1	5	10	20	40	50
Sand (cm³)	2	10	20	40	80	100

(b) (1,2), (5,10), (10,20), (20,40), (40,80), (50,100)
(d) 120 cm^3

Section 14.8   **1.** (a) 3 (b) The probability of drawing
a quarter is $\frac{1}{6}$; a dime $\frac{1}{3}$; a nickel $\frac{1}{2}$ **2.** (a) 6

(b) The probability of winning a comb is $\frac{7}{20}$; a hair

bow $\frac{1}{4}$; a watch $\frac{1}{100}$ **3.** (a) 16 (b) all heads $\frac{1}{16}$; all

tails $\frac{1}{16}$ (c) at least one head $\frac{15}{16}$; at least one tail $\frac{15}{16}$

(d) $\frac{3}{8}$ (e) 1 head and 3 tails $\frac{1}{4}$; 1 tail and 3 heads

$\frac{1}{4}$ **4.** 3 socks

Section 14.9 1. (a) Lands on   1. side   2. top
3. closed bottom.   **2.** (f) If tried a second time, the
results would likely not be the same.

INDEX OF THEMES AND CURRICULUM AREAS

Use this index to find additional activities that can help you extend your knowledge of a theme or subject area of particular interest to you. These may help you as you complete some of your projects. Where else could you look to find additional information about each theme? What additional themes would you add to this list?

Interesting Places (outside Canada)

Literature

Media

Nature

Part Time Jobs

People

Science

Sports

INDEX OF CREATIVE WRITING

Use this index to find creative writing activities of interest to you that you can complete throughout the year. The writing can be completed by working independently with a partner or within a group setting. Decide which ideas you would most like to write about.

INDEX OF WORLD RECORDS

Most world records are recorded in the *Guinness Book of World Records.*
Throughout the year, you will solve problems that reveal some of these records.
The following is a list of some of the records you can find. Add to the list as the
year progresses.

INDEX OF TECHNOLOGY

Technology and mathematics are closely connected. The following is a list of the technology discussed in this book. What other kinds of technology involve mathematics skills?

INDEX OF CAREERS

Did you know that almost all careers use mathematics? Shown below is an index of the careers presented in the book. List other careers that involve mathematics.

INDEX OF CANADIAN FACTS

Throughout the year, you have been solving problems that use Canadian facts and figures. Shown below is a list of pages where you can find information about each province.

I General Facts

II By Province

INDEX

ACKNOWLEDGMENTS

Photo Credits

Cover John Glos, **12** W. Hodges/First Light, **26 left** Larry J. MacDougall/Miller Comstock, **right** Phototake/First Light, **27** Gerard Champlong/Image Bank, **32 left** Pat Morrow/First Light, **right** Markham & East York Agricultural Society, **34** B.C. Parks, **38−39** James M. Carmichael Jr./Image Bank, **centre** Farrell Grehan/Photo Researchers, **42 top** Miller Comstock, **centre** Peter M. Miller/Image Bank, **bottom** Alvis Lipitis/Image Bank **49** Canapress, **52** W. Griebeling/Miller Comstock, **53** Dann Coffey/ Image Bank, **54 left** Tennis Canada Photo Library, **right** Steve Strickland/First Light, **66** Ripley's Believe It or Not, **88** Pelton & Associates Inc./First Light, **92** Poalo Koch/Photo Researchers, **103 bottom** Image Bank, **top right** Larry J. Pierce/Image Bank, **104** Antonio Rosario/Image Bank, **107** Graham Wiltshire/Canapress, **117** Topix, **122−3 left** Philip A. Harrington/Image Bank, **centre** Dr. Jeremy Burgess/Masterfile, **top right** Dr. Jeremy Burgess/ Masterfile, **bottom right** R. Forrester/Image Bank, **125** Biophoto Associates/Photo Researchers, **136 left** Il Klendler/Image Bank, **right** Dr. Jeremy Burgess/Masterfile, **139** René Lafontaine/First Light, **140** Al Harvey/Masterfile, **142 top** J.A. Kraulis/Masterfile, **centre** Foto: Comnet/First Light, **bottom** Warren Morgan/First Light, **144** J. Coolidge/Image Bank, **146 left** E.D. Gifford/ Masterfile, **right** NASA, **147 left** K. Nagai/Miller Comstock, **right** C. Quirk/Miller Comstock, **154 top** Miller Comstock, **bottom** George Hunter/Miller Comstock, **155 top** Netherlands Board of Tourism, **bottom** Mike Dobel/Masterfile, **157** CP Rail, **159** Ministry of Transportation Ontario, **160** Maple Leaf Village Amusement Park Ltd., Niagara Falls, Canada, **161** Canadian Tire Corporation Ltd., **166** Ontario Place Corporation, **186−7** Courtesy of British Tourist Authority, **188−9** Masterfile, **right** All Sport/ Masterfile, **202 left** First Light, **centre** Miller Comstock, **right** © R. Chambers/Miller Comstock, **213** Miller Comstock, **218** Miller Comstock, **219 top** Adolf Schmidecker/Masterfile, **bottom** E.R. Degginger, H. Armstrong Roberts/Miller Comstock, **227** Hans Vehrenberg/Hansen Planetarium, **228−9** W. Cody/First Light, **234** Jürgen Vogt/Image Bank, **237** Claus Andersen/Masterfile, **248−9 left** Fred Thornhill/Canada Wide, **centre** Bill Brooks/Masterfile, **right** Dick Luria/Photo Researchers, **258** Masterfile, **262** Ron Watts/First Light, **264** Gabe Palmer/Masterfile, **268** D. Roitner/ Canapress, **270** © 1955 M.C. Escher/Cordon Art−Baarn−Holland, **271** Ronnie Kautman/Masterfile, **274** Breck P. Kent/Earth Scenes, **275** Dave Gleiter/Masterfile, **278 left** Bob Chambers/Miller Comstock, **right** Greg Stott/Masterfile, **279 left** Dawn Goss/First Light, **right** E. Otto/Miller Comstock, **280** Wide World Photos Inc./ Canapress, **282 left** Photo used with permission from Playing With Time Inc., **right** CBC, **301** CBC, **304** Miller Comstock, **305** Francois Dardelet/Image Bank, **307** Larry J. MacDougall/Miller Comstock, **315** Henry Birks & Sons Limited, **317** Steve Proehl/ Image Bank, **321** Warren Faidley/First Light, **326** Royal Ontario Museum, **327 top** Canapress, **centre** Royal Ontario Museum, **338−9 top** Toronto Sun, **342** W. Griebeling/Miller Comstock, **343** Alan Becker/Image Bank, **347** Constance Reid, **352** YTG Photo, **354** Lawrence Migdale/Photo Researchers, **358** Zagon/Currency Museum Collection, **363** Art Resource **368** T. O'Lett/Athlete Information Bureau, **374 left** Uniphoto/Canapress, **right** Charles Moore/First Light, **378** E. Otto/Miller Comstock, **380** Miller Comstock, **394 left** Ken Straiton/First Light, **right** Eric Hayes/ Miller Comstock, **395** Gordon J. Fisher/First Light, **401** Mary Evans Picture Library, **412−3** California Institute of Technology, **415** Peter Menzel, **418−9** Ron Watts/First Light, **426** Uniphoto/ Canapress, **431 left** Dr Jeremy Burgess/Photo Researchers, **right** Éric Gravé/Photo Researchers, **436** Toronto Sun, **441 left** Bill Brooks/Masterfile, **centre** Jim Brown/Masterfile, **right** Ontario Hydro, **442** Al Harvey/Masterfile.

All other photographs are taken by Alexander Meyboom.

The publishers wish to express their thanks to Erin Mills Senior Public School, Mississauga, Ontario, for allowing photographs to be taken in its school area.

Other Credits

35 Advertisements courtesy of Miracle Food Mart.
44 KLEENEX and BOUTIQUE are registered trademarks of Kimberly-Clark Corporation. Advertisements are copyrighted by KCC. Used with permission. Colour Change Cars advertisements courtesy of Biway Store Ltd.
145 Advertisements courtesy of Miracle Food Mart.
159 Traffic signs courtesy of Ministry of Transportation Ontario.
162 Logo used with permission from Tennis Canada.
171 "SOCIABLES" ® is a trademark of Nabisco Brands Ltd, Toronto Canada, "© all rights reserved".
190 Catelli package used with permission of Borden Catelli Consumer Products. Allen's Apple Juice used with permission from Allen's Industries Inc. Jello used with permission from Kraft General Foods.
191−2, 205 KELLOGG'S BRAN FLAKES is a Registered Trademark of KELLOGG CANADA INC. © 1991.
193, 205 TOBLERONE ® is a registered trademark of Jacobs Suchard Ltd. Used with permission.
194−5 9 Lives Cat Food & Star-Kist Tuna used with permission from Star-Kist Foods Canada Inc.
195, 207 Campbell's Soup, * registered trademark of Campbell Soup Company Ltd., Toronto, Ontario, Canada. "DEL MONTE" ® is a trademark of Nabisco Brands Ltd, Toronto Canada, "© all rights reserved".
195 Paint can used with permission from Beaver Lumber Company Limited.
207 McCain Frozen Orange Juice, McCain Foods Ltd. Beans in Tomato Sauce, Miracle Food Mart.
215 Crackers, Miracle Food Mart.
255, 258 Smarties is a registered trademark used under license by Nestlé Enterprises Limited.
258 Chart used with permission from The Financial Post.
292 PEANUTS reprinted by permission of UFS, Inc.
317 VISA * registered trademark of Visa International Service Association.
356−7 Canada Savings Bonds, Bank of Canada.
427 Mr. Clean is a registered trademark of Procter & Gamble Inc.

*Every effort has been made to contact copyright holders of reprinted materials. Information that will enable the publishers to rectify any error or omission will be welcomed.